'*The Don* is a sterling biography . . . it gives a riveting account of many of Bradman's innings, and one can almost feel the excitement that gripped cricket fans when he strode out to bat.'
Herald Sun, Melbourne

'Perry keeps a compelling pace in the work . . . The Don always let his cricket do the talking and so does the author. Perry brings to life the various innings with colourful and detailed descriptions of the shots, bowling and fielding . . . a good read and a handy bench-mark for all the modern hysteria about Brian Lara and Steve Waugh, two fine players whose averages and performances are but a shadow of The Don's.'
The Daily Telegraph Mirror, Sydney

'A riveting and engrossing account of the life and times of cricket's mega hero . . . In a substantial book, Bradmanlike in research and presentation, Perry provides far more biographical and character detail on The Don and his life than previously published.'
Australian Cricket Magazine

'*The Don* is a major undertaking which will rank almost amongst the most important (biographies) of the year . . . It is thoroughly researched and well-written, nicely illustrated and with an outstanding statistical appendix . . . The Don's co-operation gives an important air of authenticity.'
Northampton Evening Telegraph

'Perry's momentous new book on Bradman will become an established classic.'
The Blackpool Evening Gazette

'Perry has provided an entertaining, breezily-written book that has drama and pace . . . (*The Don*) is a book which should be in every cricket library and has some superb photographs and many memorable quotes.'
The Birmingham Post

'*The Don* is a magnificent book. (Bradman's) story is wonderfully related by Perry – a monument both to his research and writing . . . Perry's joy in relating his greatest innings is infectious.'
Total Sport

Roland Perry's books include the international best-sellers *Programme for a Puppet* and *Hidden Power*, about the strategy behind the election and presidency of Ronald Reagan. He has written other biographies on people as diverse as the radical Australian journalist Wilfred Burchett (*The Exile*), the espionage agent Victor Rothschild (*The Fifth Man*), actor/director Mel Gibson (*Mel Gibson: Actor, Director, Producer*) and cricketer Shane Warne.

THE DON
The Definitive Biography of Sir Donald Bradman

ROLAND PERRY

Published in Great Britain in 2000 by
Virgin Publishing Ltd
Thames Wharf Studios
Rainville Road
London W6 9HA

Updated edition 2001

First published in 1995 by
Pan Macmillan Australia Pty Limited
St Martins Tower
31 Market Street
Sydney, Australia

A catalogue record for the book is available from the British Library.

ISBN 0 7535 0408 1

Printed and bound in Great Britain by CPD Wales

TO MY SON, ANTON

who on seeing his first one-day international game at the age of seven told me he would like to play for Australia – when he reached eleven. I told him this was a modest ambition. W G Grace had played first-class cricket at nine.

CONTENTS

ACKNOWLEDGEMENTS

My thanks go to Sir Donald Bradman for granting me the interviews which formed the basis of this book. I wish also to acknowledge his wife, Lady Jessie Bradman, whose insights helped give perspectives on her husband, and the events and issues of their exceptional lives. Not to interview her is to miss a vital part of the Bradman greatness and achievement. Their relationship began in 1919 – about the time the young Don first played in a cricket match, at the age of eleven.

Helpful views were also expressed by many who played at Test, Sheffield Shield, County and club level both with and against him. Comments also came from players and cricket administrators who were associated with Bradman in his days as a national selector.

The Bradman legend is so extensive and long that I collected innumerable stories and anecdotes from people who knew him or witnessed his exploits on and off the field. Sorting out (often with Bradman's help) what was apocryphal and what was true was part of the project. Forget Ned Kelly, Bob Menzies or Captain Cook. No-one in the nation's history has been more discussed or subject to more rumour and tale, tall and true.

One of the finest English cricket writers, Neville Cardus, who knew Bradman well, once said of an innings of his: 'He was never uninteresting; he merely abstained from vanity and rhetoric.'

This description applies to Bradman's responses in interviews. To carry the metaphor further, I imagine that bowling to Bradman was like interrogating him. Of the hundreds of questions put to him, he let only one go through to the keeper – was he for or against Australia becoming a republic? I give my own considered guess on his attitude in the last chapter, but I could be way off the mark.

Often when I thought a question might be difficult or awkward for him, he totally surprised me with his answer. It was equivalent to bowling a good away-swinger and being succinctly driven through extra-cover to the fence.

Detail is important to any cricket book and a major source for me was the efficient and helpful Melbourne Cricket Club library, where librarian Ross Peacock unlocked the glass book-cases for my perusal.

I have also had cooperation from Richard Mulvaney, the Director of Bradman Museum Trust at Bowral, which is set to be a fine cultural landmark in Australia. I am pleased to write that it will receive royalties for each sale of this book, in perpetuity.

Finally, thanks to John Miles, John Panteli, Robert Swan-Richards and Bruce Woodley for their advice on this project.

ROLAND PERRY
June 1995

PART ONE

PLAYER
1908–1928

1
THAT INNINGS

He was the original smiling assassin. Because he was small in stature, people underestimated his capacity to utterly destroy and demoralise an opposition. He enjoyed the challenge to tackle, beat and then obliterate every bowler he ever faced at every level of the game. From O'Reilly to Larwood, he delivered such fearful hidings that even those greats wished they had taken up other sports. He was the most gentlemanly, polite, ruthless and efficient sporting dominator who ever lived.
— TED A'BECKETT, AUSTRALIAN TEST PLAYER, FOOTBALLER AND DOMESTIC OPPONENT OF BRADMAN

CENTURION OF THE MORNING

All heads turned to the pavilion to see Don Bradman emerge into the thin, grey June light. The applause was respectful rather than rapturous. His previous knock of 254 at Lord's and his output of runs in the build-up to the Tests had earned him a sudden, awesome reputation, but he was still a largely unknown quantity for the knowledgeable, critical Yorkshire public. Bradman took his time on his now infamous funereal march out to bat after Archie Jackson had been caught by Larwood off Tate for one on the eleventh ball.

Bradman was never in a hurry, especially with Australia one for two on the first morning at Headingley in the Third Test of the 1930 Ashes. Many in the packed crowd, including a fourteen-year-old lad named Len Hutton, were aware that Bradman had scored four centuries against England in his last five Tests. Each one had been a bigger and better innings than the last — 112, 123, 131 and then that 'technically perfect' double century at the home of cricket.

Would the twenty-one-year-old go one better again? His Lord's effort had been hailed by many as the greatest Test innings ever. Yet still a few judges, such as the esteemed English journalist, Neville Cardus, were not convinced. They had stuck doggedly to assessments in the 1928–29 series in Australia, Bradman's first against England. He was cheeky, chancy and unorthodox — a fortunate run-machine rather than a great batsman in the Hobbs-Hammond league.

Yet that 254 at headquarters had launched him into the British public consciousness, and cautious Cardus had finally acknowledged Bradman was something special. But many fine players had scored doubles in Tests. It was an extraordinary feat, truly heroic, but not quite the stuff of English cricket legend, to which Australians had already elevated the Boy from Bowral. Besides, one critic pointed out, the England team at Leeds now included the express bowler Harold Larwood and the accurate George Geary. The England attack was stronger than at Lord's and would restrict him.

All the speculation and assessment were far from the batsman's mind as he took block — middle to leg — an alignment that he considered lessened the chance of being trapped LBW. Bradman was more interested in the position of his stumps than most players. He made more use of the crease than perhaps any player before him, sometimes ending with a foot some way *behind* the stumps at the finish of a shot.

He didn't just survey the field, he studied it. Bradman had what he called an 'X-ray picture' in his mind covering the position of every fieldsman before he played his first shot.

As he waited for Tate to deliver the first ball, he placed his bat between his feet — again something unusual. At the point of the bowler's delivery Bradman moved his back foot back and across. At the instant Tate let go the leather, the bottom of the blade was level with the top of the stumps. It was this preparation, coupled with his lightning feet, body movements and *fair* eyesight, that gave him technical and physical advantages over many other batsmen.

Even this was not the secret of his success. To those who played with and against him, it was the sheer determination that carried him further and faster than anyone in the history of the game. This grit and dynamic force could not be explained by a slow-motion camera, or a pointer on a blackboard. This was something intrinsic, like courage and the capacity for concentration, which a player either had or had not.

In typical fashion, Bradman clipped that first ball from Tate for two on the on-side. Two deliveries later Tate got an absolute pearler right through him and just missed his stumps. Undeterred, Bradman showed he was in an acquisitive mood, belting three fours in his first eighteen runs, which took him as many minutes. He batted from the first delivery as if he had a hundred behind him and stuck to his maxim — *if you don't lift the ball, you can't be caught.*

This kept the crowd enthralled as he strode to 30, 40 and 50. That first half-century was in the hurricane time of forty-nine minutes. The chart of his shots — the wagon-wheel — showed every stroke in the book and several that were not. Yet he mishit nothing. Larwood bowled at his fastest, but had no impact as Bradman picked the gaps with ease by sliding the ball both sides of the wicket with an unorthodox combination of foot and wrist-work. There was a little finesse but no flash. He demonstrated his outstanding skill of piercing a field in a way that frustrated captains and bowlers and threatened to run a fielding side ragged.

The canny packed Yorkshire crowd of 20,000 appreciated the science, brilliance and power of this little man from the former colony. They wondered if he could keep it up for the first session of a Test and secure a hundred, as only two audacious cricketers had done before. Their names were immortal — Australians Victor Trumper and Charlie Macartney. Trumper had done it with five minutes to spare, Macartney thirteen. Bradman thrilled the spectators and did it in just under thirteen and a half minutes before lunch, with a full-blooded drive through mid-on off Larwood for four. It was the fleetest pre-lunch ton ever.

Bradman was 105 not out as he marched triumphantly from the field. He had struck sixteen fours, and had left the fieldsmen floundering like schoolboys.

AFTERNOON LIGHTNING

At lunch, Bill Woodfull, the Australian captain, spoke to Bradman about 'going on with it'. After lunch he was subdued, for him. It was clear that he was settling in for something special, picking the loose ball and the gaps with monotony. Bradman embarrassed all the bowlers. No-one looked capable of penetrating his immaculate defence. Nor did any opponent manage to curb the amazing flow from his calibrated placement. At times he seemed to be toying with the bowlers, and he was severe on Larwood, the best fast bowler on either side.

On numerous occasions, the England captain, Percy Chapman, pulled a player from the off, say the covers, and placed him on the leg-side. The next ball, Bradman would step to leg and punch the ball through the spot where the cover had been, leaving Larwood standing mid-pitch, hands on hips and scowling. He would scratch his head, mumble under his breath and plod back to his mark, fuming.

At one point, Bradman repeated such a shot. Larwood consulted with his captain, and the much-travelled fieldsman was taken from mid-wicket and put back at cover. Bradman with flair and dare then carved the ball from the off through mid-wicket where the player had been.

Did he tip his baggy green cap at Larwood in acknowledgement of his opportunity to score? It was not the Australian's style. Yet Larwood, perhaps offended, steamed in with a short ball at Bradman's throat. The batsman moved to the off and hit the ball through mid-wicket again, this time to the boundary with such speed that not one fieldsman moved a foot before the ball was lobbed back from the crowd.

The spectators clapped the brilliance of this play. It wasn't a matter of majestic batting in the Hobbsian way. It was more the precision of the master surgeon. He made his slice and cuts with such unerring and unnerving exactitude that it went beyond judgement of the grace of strokeplay.

He was humiliating the opposition. The impact unbalanced bowlers and fieldsmen alike, for they sensed that his punctilious unpredictability was unstoppable. With all other batsmen in history, such a pace of accumulation led inevitably to a rush of blood, an injudicious cut, loft, or swipe, no matter how skilful. A good captain would make tactical moves and wait for the error. It would come sooner or later with the certainty of the law of averages, which kept the greatest batsmen in Test cricket history on batting averages between 45 and 60, mainly skewed — among the elite of all nations — to around 50.

But the mounting score from Bradman's bat defied all this. He was becoming a batting law unto himself. Yet he didn't just occupy the crease. He played to score the highest number of runs in the shortest possible time, and to stay in the middle until his team was in a winning position. In the process, the psychological effect on the opposition was devastating. Bradman's mastery focused on the mental aspect of cricket — *the* mind game of all ball games. His average of a century for every time he strode to the middle demonstrated not so much a statistical phenomenon, but a cerebral one. The public homage that was already being paid to this precocious youth was due to his capacity to win the game played inside his head as much as outside it.

The Bradman legend that marvellous day at Leeds was universally in place for the first time. His mentality and temperament were making sure of it.

Since lunch, Larwood had been straying down the leg-side and Bradman was punishing him to such an extent that the captain had to remove him from the bowling crease much earlier than planned, for the *second* time in the game. No observer could recall this happening to Larwood before. And Larwood, enjoying the outfielding not a jot, was fuming. For the first time in his career, he was not rolling his arms over to let his skipper know he wanted to have another go. He had scythed through the best batsmen in England and the world, yet he had never come across such an extraordinary destroyer. By mid-afternoon, one of the game's greatest competitors was beaten and reduced to chasing leather, for it was the boundary riders who did all the pursuing when Bradman was playing.

He mishit a slower ball from Tate at 140 but it lobbed to mid-on, wide of any fieldsmen. The crowd gasped. A buzz went round the ground. Bradman was fallible today after all. But he was still well in as he reached 150 after another seventy minutes. He was now accumulating rather than dominating. Then he accelerated with the fastest fifty so far, in forty minutes.

Bradman went to tea with a score of 220. He had hit another century in a session. His double came up in 214 minutes, the fastest 200 in Test history. There had been one more minor blemish — at 202 — with another miscue to mid-on. Once more, though, the ball was ten metres from a fieldsman. Bradman was not alone in the middle, although he could have been. Support had come from Woodfull (50), who had also been up the other end when Macartney scorched his way to a pre-lunch 100 on the same ground on the previous Australian tour in 1926. Woodfull was bowled by Hammond at 194. Then Kippax (77) joined Bradman for a 229-run stand, a second-wicket record.

At the short break, Bradman removed his boots, massaged his feet and then fixed himself one of his infamous 'cuppas' — an awful concoction consisting of a third of milk in the cup, to which was added half an inch of tea from the pot, and the rest hot water. He had been running hard, often breaking up the field with singles or by pushing ones into twos and twos into threes. He looked fit and relaxed, and even refreshed by his tea. There was nothing overly jut-jawed about his demeanour. Just quiet confidence, clear in his strong, settled face, which was a hint that he would go on all day and into the next.

After Lord's, Bradman was conscious of his 'failure' to beat R. E. Foster's 287, the highest Test score, without playing to pass it. His main aim was to put Australia into a winning position by stumps by building the biggest score possible.

AT THE OUTER LIMITS

Just after tea, Tate was carved away for successive fours in an over, from which Bradman took 12. Duckworth, the keeper, approached Tate.

'I thought you could get him out in this country when he plays cross-bat,' Duckworth said with a rueful grin. It was a telling remark. Players such as Tate and White, and observers including Cardus, Percy Fender and others had told Bradman during the 1928–29 season that he would have to remove his unorthodox shots: the cross-bat pull, his attempts to slide balls from off to on, and even his overuse of the cut. The batsman had taken note. He made his own assessment and ignored the advice.

In the last session Bradman hammered on. Larwood was called on for another stint and the batsman humbled him for the third time in a day. No bowler was spared as he picked out the weaker and older fieldsmen, such as Jack Hobbs and the rotund Dick Tyldesley, who was a trifle slow. The ball beat him to the boundary many times. Once when Tyldesley picked up a ball near the fence, a supporter called:

'He's damned good, isn't he?'

Without turning around, the sweating, tired bowler replied: 'He's no good to me.'

At just a little before 6 p.m. Bradman gave his first real chance of the innings, at 273. He flashed at a faster ball from Geary outside the off-stump and nicked one wide of Duckworth, who dived and got a glove to it, and spilled it. It was a hard catch. Duckworth was angry at himself. Geary stood where he finished his run and looked crestfallen. Bradman by contrast showed his cool as he approached Foster's record. He smiled then nodded consolingly to the keeper. The England players' despair was understandable. Not only had they failed to defend their fellow countryman's record. They had missed one of the main foe's rare offerings of his wicket. He had given just three chances in the entire series to that Third Test, which had seen him at the crease for fifteen hours. In other words, Bradman offered one opportunity for each day he batted. If the opposition missed it, they suffered.

He cruised past the record with a drive for three. Bradman removed his cap, waved his bat to the spectators' plaudits, and grinned, a boyish, ingenuous grin. It was the happy look of a youth unencumbered by the burden of greatness which would weigh upon him from now to eternity. The England team, led by Hobbs, shook his hand. He had created sporting history and they were part of it. Still, the Australian's rewriting of the record books was not finished. Twenty minutes later he pushed a single to mid-on to reach 300, the first cricketer ever to do it in a Test and inside a day.

As Bradman acknowledged the long applause, one East Yorkshire spectator was heard to ask another what he thought of him.

'With a bit of practice, he'll make a cricketer,' came the response.

The tyro hit a four to finish the day and reached 2,000 for the English season, the youngest player ever to touch that figure.

Bradman was footsore, but happy with his amazing feat (and dancing *feet*) as he strode off the field at 309 not out. He was mobbed by the appreciative crowd and had to be shepherded by police to the pavilion to avoid attempts to shoulder him. The generous Yorkshire fans who thronged in front of the pavilion could have been mistaken for Australians in their enthusiasm. They cheered and chanted his name. Bradman tried to ignore them as he removed his gear and put it with his now priceless red-dotted bat in his bag.

'They want you on the balcony,' vice-captain Vic Richardson told him.

Bradman was reticent. 'I don't want to go out,' he said, coyly.

'They really want you, Don,' another member of the team urged.

'All I want is a cup of tea.'

The shy new King of Cricket relaxed teacup in hand as a few well-wishers, important enough to be allowed into the dressing-room, paid homage. Among them was Charlie Macartney, now covering the tour for the *Daily Mirror*.

Bradman relaxed for half an hour and had another cuppa. When the spectators had dispersed, he and the team went to their hotel. Bradman did not celebrate, but shut his door on the world to listen to music, and write. It was his way of winding down. Instead of buying the rest of the team a drink (twelve of the fifteen didn't touch alcohol) or dinner and enjoying it with them, which was the usual Aussie thing to do, the introspective Bradman showed how he danced to a different tune.

Some took it as a snub, which was partly engendered by envy, for his feats were riveting attention on him, and not the team and other individuals. It was Bradman whom the King of England wanted to meet, Bradman who got the special individual attention, Bradman the young women sent notes to, Bradman the small boys swarmed around in the street seeking autographs. He could have assuaged the envious feelings by celebrating, and being photographed with them raising their cups and glasses. But this was not his style. Bradman was not 'one of the boys' or a drinker. Nor did he wish to make a fuss.

'Was I expected to parade the streets of Leeds?' he asked later. This was put up as 'uncharitable' by jealous detractors. Yet Bradman pointed out that he was contracted to write on the series for the London *Star* and the book publishers Hutchinson. He had disciplined himself to report in a thick diary every night. He was not afraid of his mild intellectual ambitions, which some fellow team members scorned. That particular evening in Leeds, he had a lot on which to report. Just as pertinently, he had the courage to recognise what suited his temperament in bringing the adrenalin down: thinking, writing, music and his own company. Some had to drink, lounge with the lads at the hotel bar, and be seen to be suitably modest. But Bradman wasn't about to say 'Aw shucks, I got lucky'. Everyone knew that the performance he had just delivered was not based on good fortune. Nor was it a one-off. It had been an expression of pure sporting genius.

His own opinion had a ring of integrity about it: 'I consider I was lucky to strike *my best form* on an ideal batsman's wicket.'

His *best form* was not dependent on the roll of the dice. When he struck it, he would dominate anything thrown at him, and for longer and with more skill than anyone else. No false modesty there — just thoughts honestly, directly put, always with a quiet message to his opponents. *Every so often he would strike his best form . . .*

The morning papers waxed lyrical about the Olympian feat of the previous day. The *Daily Express*'s Trevor Wignall summed up their collective thinking:

There are still those who question Bradman's right to be described as the most marvellous batsman of his time. He may not have the correctness of Hobbs or the perfect artistry of Woolley and Duleepsinhji, but what does that matter when he can get runs against the best bowling in England in the manner of shelling peas?

I can easily remember such stars as Spooner, Ranjitsinhji, Trumper and others of the truly great, but no one of them was better than this astonishing boy from a hamlet in Australia. If he has a fault at all it is that he makes cricket look too much like child's play . . .

Asked by a journalist about how many he would like to make in the innings, Bradman replied: 'If I thought about it at all it was that the morrow could look after itself.'

As it was, if Bradman were taken at his word, there was little incentive left on the morrow. His stated aim was to bat for the team and at three for 458 Australia was in a very strong position. Foster's record, made in 1903, was now Bradman's.

At 334 he nicked one to a grateful Duckworth off Tate. It had not been a cross-bat stroke. It was his fifth century in six Tests, and he had kept the sequence of scoring higher each time. Even Bradman, with his silent obsession of run accumulation and calculation, knew that he had reached the outer limits.

Where did he acquire his skills, confidence and cool character? For answers we must go back almost to Australia's beginning as a nation when this extraordinary sportsman was born.

2

THE BOY FROM BOWRAL

I would describe his batting as practically a freak. There is no other term that adequately describes it.
— GEORGE BRADMAN, FATHER

A VERY FAIR BAT

There is a billboard outside the little sheep and wheat country town of Cootamundra, 350 kilometres southwest of Sydney, which reads: 'Never Stumped in Cootamundra.' It's a discreet reference to the fact that Donald George Bradman, arguably the most famous and popular Australian ever, was born there on 27 August 1908. The Bradman family home, a humble cottage with a lawn and no garden, has been preserved as a museum in this quiet place, which seems to have no distinctive atmosphere, at least to those passing through. Travel writers have complained that there isn't even a decent pub to speak of. Cootamundra is a no-nonsense sort of town, caught in a rural time warp that prevailed when George and Emily Bradman added Donald George to their family of three daughters and a son.

Bradman's paternal grandfather, Charles, a farm labourer, emigrated from Cambridgeshire in England in 1852 to Australia with nearly 100,000 other free-settlers in that year, attracted by the news of gold discoveries in the colonies. They offered an incentive to escape agricultural depression in England and Charles, too, made the journey to the great south land halfway round the world.

The bold move was worthwhile for the Bradman lineage. Charles improved on his circumstance in the UK and became a respected small farmer in the Cootamundra district, marrying Elizabeth Biffen, whose family were sheep and dairy farmers. Their youngest surviving son of six children was George, who married Emily Whatman. Both her farmer parents were NSW-born, and like Bradman's grand-parents, were of British stock. George continued the Bradman/ Whatman farming tradition around Cootamundra, but also had a knack with machinery which proved helpful to his neighbours, who were often baffled by the new mechanical developments.

Early in 1911, Emily's prolonged ill-health caused the Bradmans to move closer to her family in Bowral, also southwest of Sydney but only 130 kilometres away in the southern highlands. Its 720-metre altitude made it a popular tourist and health resort. The transposition did the trick for Emily, whose condition soon improved.

George found work as a carpenter. The large family struggled, but got by. Both families had a great love of music and sport, dating back to their forebears' days in East Anglia, and in particular cricket. Just about all of them could play a musical instrument and most, the women included, liked nothing more than to get out with a bat and ball in the back-yard with varying degrees of skill. Such was the rhythm of leisure time for the young Don. In the summer it was the violin and the piano, cricket, tennis and athletics. In the winter the sport changed to rugby, but the music remained. The Bradman/Whatman families took their sport a step further and played for the town. It was inevitable that any child with a modicum of talent would slip into games. The easiest of all to commence and compete in was cricket.

BRANCHING OUT

Don Bradman first held a bat at the age of five — a piece of gum-tree branch fashioned like a baseball bat by his father. He showed nothing exceptional early, except two characteristics that he would never lose, and which went some way to lifting him above the average. The child would listen and concentrate. The instruction was limited early, for George, although he played for Bowral in the local competition, was not much interested in technique. The game was played for fun, not the drudgery of being taught orthodoxy.

At eight his father judged him 'a very fair bat', and that was it. He had a good eye, and had mastered the simple yet essential elements of footwork by watching. No-one instructed him that by the one movement of *back and across* he would have that extra fraction of a second to play a shorter ball, or that by moving his front foot forward towards the fuller-pitched ball he could master the delivery. The boy Don was an instinctive pragmatist. No matter that the back-foot movement led to an unorthodox whack to all points of the compass, or that the forward thrust would see the ball shoot off to leg or leg to off. No-one screamed 'straight bat'. No coach threw up his hands in horror at the ingenuity needed to avoid smashing a house window. That ingenuity would gradually, without anyone taking notice for years, become ingeniousness. Bradman's cleverness at contriving a way through any field-placing would be one of his trademarks. He worked out early that the way to win was to make the most number of runs in the shortest possible time, which at the age of eight was before Mum, who occasionally joined the games herself, called him in for the evening meal.

Ever since making a fifty in the back-yard, the prodigy would be transported to a singular world as a rhythm developed in his mind, which carried an easy mix of numbers and shot calculations as his score mounted. It was no coincidence that Bradman most liked mathematics as a school subject. Any natural inclination to the subject was intensified as he accumulated runs in what fast became his favourite sport. He liked tennis and was excellent at it. He was a tenacious rugby player, and a winner at every school race from 100 yards to the half-mile. But the challenge in cricket to Bradman was a combination of the ball skills needed for tennis, the tenacity required for rugby, the speed and endurance that were a must for athletics, and the mental acumen needed to play consistently well. Above all it was

a mind game, whether confronting, engaging with and finally dominating a bowler, or creating a strategy for victory. That excited him.
His will to win every competition he stepped into was apparent from
the beginning.

A TANK OF OPPORTUNITY

Bradman learned early to be at ease with his own company, because
there were few little mates close to his home. So like countless children before and since, he improvised, by devising ball games for one.
In the winter he picked imaginary football teams and played matches
in the back-yard with a footy. The garage door proved a useful
rebound surface for make-believe tennis games.

But it was cricket which drew out his real creativity. He put together
international teams in his head consisting of the stars from Trumper to
Hobbs, for whom he would act as a proxy bat or bowler depending on
their nationality. The unbounded arena of his dreams centred on an
800-gallon (3,600-litre) water tank at the back of his home, which
stood on a forty-five-centimetre-high circular brick stand.

'From the tank to the laundry door was a distance of eight feet
[2.5 metres],' Bradman noted with typical precision in his autobiography, *Farewell to Cricket*. 'The area under-foot was cemented and,
with all doors shut, this portion was enclosed on three sides and
roofed over.'

The boy's imaginary Tests in his modest stadium were at least not
stopped by rain, so the games went on for hours with just a stump
and a golf ball. With the door behind him as an outsize wicket, he
would throw the ball at varying speed and height at the brick stand
and hit it on the rebound for six and four, or a catch. The young
Bradman didn't realise it at the time, but the ball was often bouncing
at him as fast as anything he would ever face in his career.

Day in, day out, whatever the weather through endless summers,
he was learning to hook, pull, cut, late cut, drive, glance and off-drive
with a thin, round stump. The on-drive was curtailed because he
would play this into an open area, which necessitated a tiresome

chase. Bradman discovered he had to keep his eye on the unpredictable ball, so that a last split-second head or body movement would avoid being hit. If he looked away through fear, the fast-moving golf ball would strike him. He found that the faster he played, the quicker his reflexes reacted until he was soon, when 'settled' into an innings for, say, the famous Test player Jack Gregory, engrossed in a feverish concentration of shots and additions as the score mounted, mainly in fours. A modern equivalent would be a child captivated by video games, which need supreme concentration and can develop brain-eye coordination. But such games don't account for the *physical* involvement of scores of coordinated muscles.

If the little Bradman had had a playmate, it would probably have been with a bat, tennis or hard ball in a park, and he would have received one-tenth of the bowls at him over a much shorter period. The deliveries would have been much less challenging.

If there is one circumstance in Bradman's life that accentuated and elicited innate skills, which would lead him on to true greatness, it was having to face that bland and unprepossessing water tank. Necessity never led to greater invention in sporting history.

For variety, he would wander into a neighbouring paddock and throw a tennis ball, or an even more challenging golf ball, at a rounded rail on a fence from about thirteen metres away. The ball would fly back at various angles. He would catch it and hurl it back. If he missed the rail, it meant a trudge into the paddock. Bradman played a similar game on his walk home from school. Every telegraph pole and picket fence became a target for his best training mate, that fickle little golf ball, which sometimes deserted him when he missed the target and ended up in undergrowth, bush or drain. You could set a clock to the rattle of fence palings as the young Don bounced, leapt, caught and chased his way home. Again, over the years all this trained him to catch, and disciplined his accuracy. Bradman was not alone among kids around the world in devising techniques for solo catching practice. The factors which set him apart from 99.9 per cent of them were his capacity for prolonged concentration, his innate reflexes and his athleticism.

Unlike many cricketers who would go on to be outstanding, Bradman was a natural athlete. His average stature (he would grow to about 5ft 7 in — 172 cm) was irrelevant. The key was natural fitness and muscular agility. He was a near-perfect physical specimen, who could turn to sports from golf to squash with equal facility.

The local primary school (for ages five to ten) and then the intermediate high school allowed Bradman to interact with other kids in the daily summer scratch matches before class, at lunch-break and after school, but there were no facilities for organised games. Nor was there coaching. The headmaster was keen and joined in, but he distributed his limited thoughts on finer points among all the willing students. So while Bradman was *behind* in his experience at the age of nine compared with say England's W. G. Grace, who by that stage had actually played a county game, or Australia's Victor Trumper, who was performing in sub-district cricket when only a few years older, he was not getting orthodox instruction. There were advisers including his father, uncles and family friends, but no-one was telling him how to grip the bat, stand, place his feet, or play strokes. Cricket was played in the country for amusement, a summer pastime for everyone from workers and tradesmen to farmers and professionals.

If Bradman was taught anything, it was to enjoy himself while always trying to win. This partly explained his constant half-smile when on the field, which would later irritate his opponents at all levels when he destroyed bowling attacks. Until they knew him and his manner, some took that country boy grin as gloating.

HUCK FINN HEAVEN

At eleven, during the week, Bradman was a healthy mix of diligent student, practising choirboy for the local Anglican church, pianist and sporting all-rounder. (His parents were not particularly religious, but they instilled in him a strong sense of Christian principles.) Saturday night entertainment was self-generated in the Bradman home, the centrepiece being the piano, with recitals being given or the family and invited neighbours singing popular numbers. Bradman's father George played the violin, his sister Lillian the piano and the accordion. Lillian, a professional piano teacher, taught Don to play. She and the family regarded him as gifted, although Bradman did not regard himself this way. Yet his future wife Jessie, who had already observed him at close quarters at this time, later recalled: 'He could listen to a piece his sister was playing and immediately perform it by ear.'

On weekends he turned Huck Finn and loved walking for kilometres with his father, brother and uncles on rabbit-shooting expeditions or fishing in the local creek. Like many Aussie boys of the era, his early experiences gave him a maturity unheard of today. Given a gun and a rod, he could have survived in the outback alone. In many ways, he was already a young man when he played his first real cricket match.

Eleven was about the age most budding young Australians stepped off the street or out of the back-yard and started their 'official' under-age careers at school. This was their moment of truth. It was one thing to make a blinding fifty between the clothes line and the back fence or on the lawn in the street. It was another to see a *real* opposition team, with adult umpires, and play an organised school game with a real wicket and bails, all on a proper field. The pitch was the only concession to those endless scratch matches. It was simply a level bit of dirt.

So it was for the bright, young Don when he strode out on a recreational area called Glebe Park Oval (which would later become known as Bradman Oval). Bradman admitted to some nerves at that moment. It was his first game and he came to the wicket on a hat-trick. A swift left-hander had bowled an opener and dismissed the next boy. The score was two for none. The diminutive, 'none too confident' Don took block. At that moment, the quick-fire double centuries made as proxy for Macartney in front of that stolid water tank counted for nothing. He surveyed the field as if in a Test. In came that tall leftie from an exaggerated run. He bowled a fast straight one, which missed the bails by the proverbial coat of varnish, leaving the batsboy pushing forward. Bradman had expected to hear the worst sound for someone at the crease — the death rattle of the stumps and bails crashing behind him. But it didn't come. If he had made a duck, it would have been of little consequence to the future, except that the bowler would have gone down in history for getting Bradman for nought first ball in the first match he ever played in. As it was, that initial performance was the first sign that there just *might* be something special in the quiet little kid with the funny grip. Bradman proceeded to carve up the bowling while wickets fell about him. He ended with 55 not out, more than half the team's score.

I recall a player named Ken Jungwirth of that age in my team at Murrumbeena State School in Melbourne making exactly the same score in a primary school final. It was an exceptional effort. An astute observer would have judged that such a performance would separate the player from others in temperament and skill. Such a performer would *probably* play cricket at, say, district or club level — a level just below first-class in Australia — which was far higher than ordinary park or village green standard in England.

At eleven, that is where the young Don stood. He could be judged as *good*, nothing more or less . . . yet.

ENTER THE GREAT PARTNER

In 1920, aged eleven, Don Bradman first encountered an attractive blue-eyed daughter of a farmer from nearby Glenquarry, named Jessie Menzies. They met at the home of Don's parents soon after he had ridden his bike into a car backing out of a driveway. Don, nose bloodied and shaken, was introduced to the ten-year-old Jessie, who happened to be visiting his home at that time. They became good friends.

'I wanted to marry her in my late teens,' Bradman said of the attractive, vivacious, wavy-haired brunette, 'but I was too shy to ask.'

Jessie was equally in love with the young Don. During interviews for this book, in the Bradman home in Adelaide's leafy Kensington Park, the 86-year-old Jessie (since 1949, Lady Bradman) seemed fit and vibrant despite the effects of major heart surgery and chronic leukemia, which had been diagnosed five years earlier.

'Don's mother Emily Whatman and my father James Menzies lived next door to each other and they started school on the same day in 1877,' she recalled. 'That was nearly 120 years ago, and *their* parents were friends.'

James Menzies' father was a Scottish stonemason who had emigrated to New South Wales in the 1850s to work on the first building at Sydney University. He took up the government's offer of a grant of land near Glenquarry, eleven kilometres from Bowral, once the edifice was completed. The family subsequently moved to Glenquarry.

Jessie's father took her into Bowral to start at the local grammar school, but Don's mother persuaded him against it, saying it was a 'terrible' school.

Mrs Bradman suggested instead that Jessie enrol at the local high school and stay with the family. The offer was taken up. Jessie and Don developed a sibling-style friendship, affection and rivalry throughout 1920. They went to school together every day. It was the beginning of what Bradman would later call, 'the greatest partnership of my life'.

FIRST TON

At the end of that year, the first hint of his exceptional cricketing skills featured in an innings for Bowral High against the neighbouring Mittagong school. The pitch — common until the 1960s — was concrete covered with coir matting, which to Bradman was a step up in conditions from the dirt strip of his first game. This time he came in at the fall of the first wicket and notched 115 not out in a team score of 156. It was his first century.

The word 'exceptional' was now not adequate to describe this batting tyro. He had become a legend in his own lunch-break, so to speak. Bowral, in its short history of inter-school competition, had never had anyone to talk about like Bradman. But it wasn't just because he had scored eighty per cent of the team's total. Bradman was on edge with excitement as the headmaster began his address to school assembly in the playground next morning.

'I understood there is a certain boy among you who scored a century yesterday at Mittagong,' he began. Bradman's half-grin widened in anticipation of the words of praise to come. But moments later the smile disappeared as the headmaster added: 'Well, that is no reason or excuse why you should have left a bat behind.'

Young Bradman came crashing down to earth. But the headmaster soon found himself on Don's side when his opposite number at Mittagong High wrote to him formally requesting that 'the Bradman boy' be kept out of the Bowral team or there would be no future inter-school matches. He was just too good. Many administrators at higher levels and around the world would have similar sentiments for nearly thirty years to come.

Problems began to arise for Bowral in scheduling matches. The twelve-year-old Don was able to walk to the wicket for his school only once more with that formerly neglected bat. He notched 72 not out.

One spectator happened to be a sub-editor with the magazine *Smith's Weekly*. He couldn't justify reporting a junior school match, but remembered an incident which made a little news item under the heading 'Bounding Ball':

> *Saw a curious thing at a junior cricket match at Bowral (NSW) recently. Don Bradman (crack bat) sent a ball over the boundary fence. It struck half a brick, rebounded on to a fence post, poised there for an appreciable time and ran along the top of the palings the whole length of a panel of fencing before descending outside the boundary — 'John'.*

It was the first paragraph ever written about Bradman. He cut it out and pasted it into a scrapbook. 'Although many nice things have been written about me,' he noted in his two-volume published 'scrapbook' *The Bradman Albums*, 'that first paragraph still takes the bun.'

His school aggregate after that 72 not out stood at 242, a modest tally when compared with those of many boys who stayed longer at school and may have played for their first elevens for two or three seasons. Many top modern players such as Colin McDonald, Bob Cowper and Greg Chappell hit several centuries while at school and were easy to predict as future Test players. No-one could have quite foreseen the same destiny for Bradman based on his school career. But he was only fourteen when his formal education ended and no matter how impressive other schoolboy batsmen might have seemed, they often lost their wickets. Bradman was never dismissed. His average at school stood at *infinity.*

GLIMPSING THE GODS

In February 1921, the Fifth Test between England and Australia was scheduled to be played at the Sydney Cricket Ground. Bradman knew his father was going down to watch the first two days and begged for weeks beforehand to be allowed to come along until his father finally gave in. They travelled to the city by train and on Friday 25 February, still in short pants, Bradman saw the fabled arena for the first time.

It was a thrilling and inspiring experience.

The quaint English-style Members' Stand and other pavilions, the famed 'Hill', the crowd of more than 20,000 and the players themselves out on the ground were a sight to stay in Don's mind forever. Now instead of that unresponsive water tank stood the real thing — the very big time. The gods of the game bestrode the rich green surface. They were not just names in his head in those endless solo games, but on the field in fierce competition. On the English side were great names such as Hobbs, Rhodes, Hendren, Woolley and Parkin. The Australian side included Armstrong, Bardsley, Macartney, Taylor (Bradman's hero), Gregory, Ryder and McDonald. England was dismissed for 204, Frank Woolley top-scoring with 53 while Jack Hobbs, carrying a thigh injury, showed his class with 40. Jack Gregory, whom Bradman admired for his attacking play as bowler and batsman, took three for 42. Charlie Kelleway snared four for 27. 'Woolley's beautiful strokemaking, the smooth rhythm of Ted McDonald and the glorious catching of Parkin by Johnny Taylor still come back to me as though they happened yesterday,' Bradman remembered.

At stumps, Australia was two for 70, with Charlie Macartney in brilliant form with 32 not out. Next day, it was Macartney who showed the wide-eyed boy from Bowral at what level to pitch his dreams. Bradman and the 30,000 others packed into the SCG watched Macartney go on to 170 in one of his finest innings, with a range of shots from delicate leg glances and brutal pulls to slashing cuts and glorious cover drives. Don applauded as the crowd stood to cheer Macartney to the pavilion, and later Gregory, who contributed a fine 93.

Bradman also witnessed the 21-stone (138 kg) Australian captain, Warwick Armstrong, wade out to the wicket like a colossus only to be caught first ball by Woolley off Percy Fender. The big man had to trudge his way back to the dressing-room in utter silence, save for a few tart remarks about his girth from slim men on the Hill. The skipper's anger was assuaged by Australia's score of 392, which put them in a winning position.

Don was inspired enough to tell his father: 'I shall never be satisfied until I play on this ground.' George's response is not recorded. Was it amusement, pride, or did he hear a voice that told him his batting 'freak' of a son, as he called him, might just one day be sated? Probably all three reactions surfaced. He found it difficult to tear the boy away — after just two days of great Test match cricket which Australia later won by eight wickets — for the return to Bowral.

3
A BOY AMONG MEN

With a little [tennis] practice, Bradman would be a match for anyone in England or Australia outside the top ten.
— JACK CRAWFORD, AUSTRALIAN DAVIS CUP PLAYER

THE BREAK

After the thrill of that Sydney Test, the rest of 1921, Bradman's second year in high school, was mostly uneventful. He was an above-average student with a leaning towards maths and English. His numeracy skills were high and he had an exceptional early command of writing. The twelve-year-old may have learned his twelve times table by rote, but his mental creativity with numbers went beyond that kind of useful drudgery. When a teacher was doing an addition on the blackboard, Don would 'race him in his mind' and often have the answer before it was chalked up. This affection for numbers assisted his cricket, which in the summer months was restricted to a sports afternoon a week, as well as the usual scratch games at and after school. He acted as scorer for the Bowral town team — all adults — which played in the Berrima District Competition and other matches in the region. This needed sharp concentration, a head for figures and a good knowledge of the game, all of which Bradman developed. But he wasn't content with scoring off the field. He was determined to score on it.

In country cricket, there were always plenty of opportunities. It was never certain that a full eleven would turn up for a game. At the end of 1921, after Bradman turned thirteen, the day came when Bowral was one short. He asked his uncle and team captain, George Whatman, if he could play. Whatman had little choice. They were in Moss Vale and the nearest possible replacement was in Bowral, ten kilometres away. The diminutive teenager, still in white shorts, got the nod.

It was his biggest break yet. Uncle George put him second-last in the batting order. The coir matting wicket was still a luxury to him. At the fall of the eighth wicket and encouraged by a mentor in the team, Alf Stephens, he plodded out to the crease in comically large pads with a bat far too big and heavy for him, which restricted his shots to pushes, dabs and glances. Nonetheless, in his first hour of what he considered seriously competitive adult cricket, he scored 37 not out.

Bradman faced the fastest bowlers in the side, who soon became exasperated by this slip of a kid who handled everything they threw at him with ease. They quickly forgot his size and the fact that he had come in at number ten, traditionally a place for 'rabbits' who usually got gentle treatment from the pacemen. They did their best to remove him and wrap up the tail, but his defence was outstanding, especially in view of the difficulty he had handling his heavy bat. However, his eye was so good and his reflexes so fast that he overcame the handicap.

The bowlers were irritated by the boy in knickerbockers for another reason. He seemed not so much cheeky as serene in his pursuit of runs. Yet this was not youthful arrogance but the sheer joy of making the most of a chance. Even though he had seen a Test match, these stars of minor cricket at Bowral were his heroes, whom for years he had cheered against their country rivals. Now he was playing among them and doing well, not dominating as he had in those limited opportunities at school, but surviving with a surprisingly mature defensive technique while picking up runs from precisely placed pushes and deflections. At this point in his early development, that 37 not out felt as good to him as any double century he would ever score.

The following Saturday, when the game was all but over, Don was allowed to open. He scored 29 not out and batted with assurance.

His tally in five innings as a schoolboy and for Bowral was 308. Bradman had yet to be dismissed. His average still stood at infinity.

Sid Cupitt, a member of the Bowral team, became a footnote in sporting history when he rewarded Don by giving him his first real bat. It was one of big-hitting Sid's discarded weapons, with a crack at the base that had been taped, and its grip was disintegrating. But the recipient was so overwhelmed that he could only utter an effusive 'thank you'.

'That bat meant almost everything in the world to me,' Bradman said. He wondered at first how he would cope with it, but his father solved that difficulty by sawing some eight centimetres off the bottom, which also got rid of most of the crack. It had seen better days, but it would do. The only problem was that Bradman had nowhere to play. At thirteen, despite his distinguished beginning, he was too young to become a regular member of the local team. It meant that 1921–22 was a season of limited opportunities and he had to be content with his scorer's role.

The following season — 1922–23 — was no better as far as his cricket was concerned, for there was no junior team in Bowral. It was frustrating for such a budding talent not to have an outlet, yet he was not concerned. He was preoccupied with more important matters, such as looking for work, for he left school when he turned fourteen, the normal age at the time.

At the end of 1922, Bradman's headmaster wrote of him:

> Don Bradman has been a pupil of this school under my personal tuition for the past 18 months. He is truthful, honest and industrious, and an unusually bright lad. He is specially good at mathematics and French.
> P.S. He will, when the results appear, be found to have done very creditably at the recent Inter. Certif. [Intermediate Certificate] Examn.

This encouraging testimony, together with his sporting prowess, helped him find work. A local real estate agent, Percy Westbrook, was impressed with him as an individual and his exceptional skills as a cricketer and tennis player, and hired him. He began as a clerk and according to Westbrook kept his books 'clearly written, neatly ruled, and without a trace of a blot or smudge'. It was a clue to his mentality and character, as was his writing. All those who have received letters from him (including the author) have been struck by his clear, concise style and capacity to deal with the matter in hand, features which obviously spring from his exceptional ability to concentrate. It is no leap to extend these characteristics to his cricket.

His dedication to both work and sport impressed his employer. Westbrook, a prewar NSW champion bowls player, was generous in giving him time off for sport. Without a chance to extend his cricket, the fifteen-year-old Bradman spent 1923–24 competing in tennis. He played in no cricket match in that summer. Still, he enjoyed himself and proved nearly as adept at tennis, by winning a local under-sixteen championship.

The summer of 1924–25 was also almost entirely devoted to tennis, so that from the age of twelve to sixteen, crucial years in the development of any potential top-class sportsman, Bradman played practically no cricket. When he did, he could easily have been lost to the game permanently. At the end of the 1924–25 season he was given the chance to play for Bowral once more. He made a golden duck — out first ball. The only compensation was that for the first time in competitive cricket he had an average — 308. It was a critical moment. If he failed in his next dig, which was a semi-final against Wingello and possibly Bowral's last game for the season, he would consider devoting himself to tennis. His skill at the game may just have been enough to seduce him away from cricket for good.

He went to the wicket batting at number seven determined to redeem himself, yet feeling vulnerable for the first time in his short sporting life. He smelt the unfamiliar fear of failure and didn't like its odour. He began tentatively. Bowral lost a sixth wicket, then a seventh and Bradman had to hurry along. A few streaky shots intermingled with three lofted fours increased his confidence. He reached 50 in quick time and went on to 66, giving him a 'career' 374 runs at an average of 187, which was reduced to a more modest and realistic 66 outside his school games. Bowral lost the contest, but the game won Bradman. His performance convinced him to concentrate on cricket the following summer.

4

1925 — GENIUS ALIVE

I just could not assimilate the knowledge that a pocket-sized schoolboy could have given me such a complete lacing.
— BILL O'REILLY, AUSTRALIAN TEST PLAYER, AFTER HIS FIRST ENCOUNTER WITH BRADMAN

CLASH OF THE YOUNG TITANS

Tall, lanky William Joseph (Bill) O'Reilly was pulled off the train on his way home to his home town Wingello from Sydney and told he was wanted for an important game against Bowral. The Wingello captain told him about a 'kid' — Bradman — from Bowral who was 'bloody good'.

As they drove to Glebe Park, Bowral, O'Reilly wanted to know if he could play spin. The captain didn't know. Did this 'kid' play from the crease? Again his skipper was ignorant. Did he have a wide range of shots?

The captain paused, then suggested the player in question 'liked to hit them a bit'.

O'Reilly, a twenty-year-old student at Sydney Teachers' College, was already making a name for himself as a medium-pace leg-spinner, a young hopeful with a potential first-class future. He was the best bowler outside the Sydney club scene. Like Bradman, he mixed intelligence with skill in everything he did on the field. O'Reilly was fiercely proud of the fact that in three seasons of country cricket, no batsman had ever hammered him into submission. There would always be the odd big-hitter who would play as if there was no tomorrow, but the canny, aggressive Wingello lad of Irish stock would eventually snare the agricultural adventurer.

He had the staying power and intestinal fortitude to match attacks on his bowling with calculated belligerence. Even though just out of his teens, O'Reilly had everything in his armoury, including a slower, well-concealed wrong'un (googly). Like Bradman, he was unorthodox. He held the ball closer to the palm than the fingers. This curtailed his spin, but because of his strong wrists gained speed and accuracy. The unusual style also allowed for greater and more effective changes in pace. O'Reilly flighted the ball deceptively, and his height helped him extract lift from the pitch, especially with his faster ball.

If Bradman's presence stirred Wingello into action on that January Saturday in 1925, the sight of the rangy O'Reilly warming up caused as much comment among the Bowral boys, for he had a formidable reputation. Bowral batted first and Bradman opened. He was quickly into stride and scored 12 off the first fifteen balls he faced. The Wingello captain called O'Reilly to the bowling crease, for even in his early days he was regarded as a strike bowler, often an early first change. He took a long time setting his field and the Wingello captain, the safest catch in the side, placed himself at slip. Bradman did not become cautious with O'Reilly's appearance, although it took him a few balls to get used to the frenetic run to the wicket. The bowler's angular frame and long, loose limbs gave him the appearance of an over-heated electric fan.

Bradman seemed over-keen to master him early. In the first over he pulled him off the back foot through mid-wicket for four, then next ball lifted him first bounce over the mid-on boundary. In his second over, O'Reilly pitched up more and drew him forward. Bradman took three twos off him with superb placement. The spinner's third over was his best. Bradman nicked a fast-turning leg-break pitched on middle-stump. The ball travelled fast and low to the skipper's right hand. He spilled it.

O'Reilly gesticulated furiously, not at the captain, but at his ill-luck. Yet the bowler was encouraged. Pitching the ball up had worked. In the fifth over, he bowled a well-flighted top-spinner and Bradman edged it past the slip's outstretched hand. Apart from the dropped chance, that was the only opportunity Bradman would give for another two hours of the most remarkable batting anyone on either side had witnessed.

He proceeded to chop Wingello's bowlers to pieces. O'Reilly, riled by the dropped catch and being thrashed, responded, Bradman noted, 'like a disturbed hive of bees. He seemed to attack from all directions.'

On that hot January afternoon in Bowral, however, Bradman was the beekeeper. O'Reilly was obliterated with a rush of sixes and fours that left Bradman on 234 not out in 165 minutes. His last fifty included 48 in boundaries — four sixes and six fours.

'I could not assimilate that a pocket-sized schoolboy could have given me such a complete lacing,' O'Reilly remarked gratuitously.

At seventeen, Bradman was thin and about average height. Yet there was nothing schoolboyish about the power of his shots which crashed balls into the surrounding streets. O'Reilly's inability to 'assimilate' the hiding he had received was to be expected from such a competitive champion. Instead of accepting defeat he reacted with the champion's characteristic disbelief. It must have been an aberration. Bradman must be some sort of batting freak, but it seemed impossible that such unbelievable talent could have emerged from his neighbouring country town. The shock of the experience caused O'Reilly sleepless nights right up to the following Saturday when the match resumed and he would have to bowl at the prodigy again.

O'Reilly spent even more time than ever setting his field for the first ball of the day with Bradman on strike, this time at the Wingello Recreation Ground. O'Reilly had been through every type of ball he might deliver first-up, and could not decide on anything. Every type of delivery had been walloped over and to the fence during that . . .

aberration. In the end he calculated it simply. The batsman's eye would not be set. Why not give him a fast leg-break, pitched up and outside leg-stump? That was it, O'Reilly decided, a stock ball but not on line with leg or middle. In he whirled. He caught Bradman unprepared and in two minds. The fast ball hit the pitch close to the batting crease, spun sharply and collected his leg-stump. Bradman had been bowled round his legs, first ball . . . for 234.

THE GIFT

Just to confirm that this incredible performance was *not* a fluke Bradman clipped another two centuries, 105 and 120, before the 1925–26 season's final with Bowral's greatest rival Moss Vale on the latter's home ground. It was late because rain had interrupted earlier games, yet an enthusiastic crowd of several hundred turned out for the game played between 2 p.m. and 6 p.m.

Bradman's uncle George Whatman won the toss and decided to bat, and Don opened for Bowral. In a rain-reduced day, Bradman remained 80 not out from one for 140 at stumps. The following week uncle George and nephew Don took the score to one for 475. Bradman added 199 in another broken day to be 279 not out, with George on 119 not out. On day three, Bradman was out caught for 300. Uncle George went on to 227, his highest-ever score.

Naturally it was the younger man's effort that captured attention in the regional press after Bowral won the game by an innings and 338, with Bradman's leggies netting him four for 39. A local paper noted that his 300 was 'no fluke' and that his aggregate for the season was 1,318, at an average for twenty-three innings, including nine not outs, of 94.16. It also praised his bowling. He had taken thirty-five wickets at 8.5.

But the Sydney press ignored the feat. Those in the big smoke regarded mammoth country bumpkin scores with disdain. After all, they played on coir matting, not turf, editors sniffed dismissively. The only 'news' value the worldly *Sydney Sun* could see in it, in a cynical throwaway paragraph reinforcing the view that everything was slower in the bush, was the protracted nature of the game:

> *At last! Yes, it is really over. The final match in the Berrima District Cricket Competition has been brought to a conclusion. It was the easiest win in the history of the Berrima District Cricket, but it took Bowral five weeks to vanquish their persevering rivals.*

There was no mention of the 323-run partnership between two relatives or that one of them, aged seventeen, had hit a triple century after scoring a double century a few weeks earlier. Still, the 300 did earn him a reward and trip to Sydney with his father to buy a cricket bat — a gift from his mother who had promised him one if he scored a century in the final. Don tongue-in-cheekily suggested he had earned three.

The young man went about choosing the reward as if he were to be given three by inspecting a dozen pieces of willow at a big Sydney sports store. His father stood by patiently while the salesman handed him bat after bat from the store's extensive range. Bradman carefully tested each one, examining the splice, the grip and the grain of the wood, frowning and criticising as he did, then shaped up before a mirror playing shots as if he was back facing O'Reilly.

After three-quarters of an hour, he settled on a 'Roy Kilner' bat, made by the Yorkshire company of William Sykes. It was Don's first *new* piece of crafted willow and, like the gift from Sid Cupitt, he would never forget his mother's generosity. Nor would time erase the memory of the combined gifts from his father and uncles of new cricket shirt, boots and a blazer, which Don chose with alacrity.

It was clear that if the Sydney press were not impressed by the bush boy's run bonanza, the extended Bradman family was. None would have predicted even a first-class career just yet, but they were prepared to help him along the way, and make him at least look the part. With his new cricket uniform and that unblemished bat he was already aching for the next season, which because of the late end to that of 1925–26 was only a matter of four or five months away.

5
NET PROFIT

Bradman possesses an excellent defence, and should make runs when he masters the turf wickets.
— PRESS REPORT, 12 OCTOBER 1926, THE DAY AFTER BRADMAN'S FIRST 'NET' IN SYDNEY

CANNY CRANNEY

Harold ('Mudgee') Cranney moved around behind the nets at the Sydney Cricket Ground No. 2 among the small cluster of spectators watching twenty young hopefuls bowl and bat. These junior players had been invited by the NSW Cricket Association to show their *bowling* skills to the State selection committee and a small group of former Test players. Cranney, very much the 'junior' selector — it was his first season in the job — had for the moment forgotten the business of watching the bowlers from in front of the nets, which gave the best view of their actions. He had been drawn to look closer at one of the select group, a leg-spinner from Bowral who was having a bat. His footwork was more impressive the closer Cranney got to him.

From a distance he looked a bit awkward, or at least typical of country kids who had been brought up on matting and concrete and were not used to wearing spikes. But up close his footwork seemed swift and decisive. The first thing that struck Cranney was his perfect defence. Whether forward or back, the elbow was high, the balance perfect, the head over the ball. There was no lifting of the head like

34

the other bowlers having a hit. Cranney then noticed that when he attacked with cut or hook, the ball crashed low into the net, never uppishly, or with a nick. That drew the observer to the teenager's unusual grip.

Cranney had never seen anything like it. Both hands held the bat in an unorthodox fashion. The right or lower hand was turned over so far that the handle *pressed* against the base of the thumb, instead of *resting* against it. The left or upper hand was turned so that the wrist was behind the handle. This produced three unique outcomes whether in attack or defence. First, the bat sloped at about forty-five degrees to the ground, ensuring the ball was kept down. Second, when the player hooked or cut, the wrists rolled the bat over the ball so that with normal contact, the ball was kept down. Third, with a clean drive straight, or to off or on, Cranney noted, the player didn't loft the ball, because the top or left-hand grip acted as a brake. He only lofted the ball when he wanted to.

Cranney moved back to his position and sidled up to a big lad having a rest after strutting his stuff. He had been bowling short balls that lifted into the ribcage, and bumpers, much to the consternation of the batsmen, most of whom reacted by backing away to the leg. While the wickets were turf, they had a few cracks, which added to their worries. Cranney asked him to have another bowl at the eighteen-year-old he had been watching and to give it 'everything'. Cranney rearranged the bowlers and then wandered over to an official who had a list of the players.

Cranney asked the name of the batsman.

'Bradman', came the reply. 'J. Bradman, from Bowral.'

'J for what?'

The official shook his head.

Cranney then joined the other selectors, A. G. 'Johnnie' Moyes and R. L. ('Dick') Jones. Standing nearby were former Test players C. T. B. Turner, Harry Donnan and Dr H. V. Hordern. The fast lad lumbered in and delivered a short ball, which Bradman ducked under. The next was similar and Bradman ducked again. The third delivery was marginally off-line and the batsman moved inside it and hooked, rolling his wrists so that the ball collected the net low-down. Another bowler steamed in. Bradman late-cut him. An off-spinner lobbed one up and the batsman danced down the wicket and hit the ball straight out of the nets over the heads of the watching selectors. The next delivery from the big quick was pulled from outside the off-stump over mid-on. Both hits were clean and long.

Someone growled that the ball should be kept *down*. Bradman obliged.

Cranney asked what the others thought of him. Dick Jones was impressed and thought he was raw, but determined with quick reflexes. Cranney went over to the former Test players and asked their opinion. One responded that he didn't like his footwork much, but qualified it with a remark about his 'good eye'. It was noticed that if Bradman got in a minor tangle with his feet to a spinner as he waltzed down the wicket, he still managed to reach and drive the ball even when it was pitched wide.

Cranney, himself a hard-hitting, Sydney first-grade player and an occasional State opener, liked Bradman even more when he hit the ball hard, causing it to bullet out of the nets along the ground. Even if the others were not quite as struck with the Bowral tyro as Cranney, he knew talent when he saw it. After the net he asked the teenager if he would be interested in playing for Cranney's club, Cumberland. It was the only invitation from anyone, but only one was needed and it appeared an important break.

Bradman was delighted. He was in Sydney, enjoying the challenge, but was ready to play for any district club which wanted him. He said he would be pleased to join Cumberland, then went back to Bowral with his father. Negotiations fell through. Cumberland couldn't meet the costs of his weekly trips to Sydney. The main bill would have been eight shillings and sixpence for the train fare. In other words, in late 1926 Don Bradman wasn't worth ten bob a week — perhaps $50 in today's values — to Cumberland, which no-one could have predicted would be the sporting under-valuation of the century.

He was disappointed. No Sydney club was so far interested in him and he was eighteen. The prospect of going back to games in the bush didn't exactly fill him with enthusiasm after that promising net and the prospect of playing club cricket in Sydney. That was only one step short of first-class, Sheffield Shield level. The national selectors chose the Test team from the latter competition. Yet now he was back at a level he had conquered.

Bradman buried his feelings with a chanceless 170 not out for Bowral against Exeter. Cranney, Jones and Moyes heard of the score. Bradman's name again crept rather than stormed into their discussions about the hopefuls they had observed. Yet his run-getting and raw talent were difficult to ignore. They picked him in a euphemistically named 'Possibles' team to play against the 'Probable' State side before the State team was selected to tackle Queensland at Brisbane.

Bradman received an urgent telegram:

You are selected to play trial match Sydney Cricket Ground Wednesday tenth commencing ten o'clock fares will be paid wire stating whether available.

This was a surprise after the breakdown of negotiations with Cumberland. What's more, it was not just a net, but a real chance under match conditions. Twenty-seven players were selected, and they all were given a chance. It was Bradman's primary opportunity on a first-class ground and his initial try-out on turf. On top of that, the opposition was composed of fine cricketers, some of them established Test players. It was heady stuff for a teenager who had last seen such talent in 1921 during an Ashes Test, and who was used to playing bush cricket on matting. Yet Bradman was excited rather than apprehensive, nervous yet determined. His dream of playing Test cricket seemed much more real.

The 'Possibles' batted first, with Bradman going in down at number seven. When he got to the wicket the side was reeling, having lost two quick wickets to Gordon club leg-spinner J. N. Campbell, and R. L. A. McNamee, a medium-pacer from Randwick. Bradman decided to take it easy in the tight circumstances. He didn't want to

37

be out for a bright boundary or two and so blow his chances through impetuosity.

He started slowly, and seemed confused when running between the wickets, as if it was all a bit different from what he was used to in the country. Yet his score grew. He played the pace cautiously and looked comfortable early against the faster deliveries from Mosman's Hal Hooker. Spin on the unfamiliar turf was more appetising, for he could use his fast-moving feet to kill anything the different surface might present, which he did often against Campbell.

His tally mounted and his confidence with it. In ninety-seven impressive minutes he scored a respectable 37 not out, the same score as his first innings at the age of thirteen for Bowral. It was the second-highest score, with D. Mullarkey topping with 64 retired. Campbell, whom Bradman had more than contained, took five for 79.

On reflection, Bradman was content. He had taken on the best NSW could offer and had passed the examination. He hadn't set the field alight, but he had grasped his chance and not failed.

The 'Possibles' tally was ten for 237, both sides batting more than the standard eleven men. The 'Probables' responded with nine for 302, and Bradman enjoyed fielding in his usual outstanding manner to Test player and State captain Alan Kippax (58), and a brilliant youngster, Archie Jackson (53 retired), who was a year younger yet a year ahead of Bradman in his development. Jackson was scoring well for Balmain. His name was on everyone's lips, whereas the name 'Bradman' had not travelled nearly so far. The Bowral youngster was still more in the thoughts of selectors and knowledgeable observers than the general public.

Jackson was dashing and aggressive — a Test prospect in everyone's mind, while the impressive Bradman was just a *prospect*. His rural unorthodoxy worried the purists, although more astute observers like Kippax, Johnnie Moyes and Cranney were beginning to appreciate his skills. They all liked him and his temperament. But he had not shown enough. The day after the trial the NSW State side to play Queensland was announced. Bradman was not among the names. Yet again, there was an encouraging consolation for him.

State selector Dick Jones, who had seen Cranney rush to sign Bradman at Cumberland, was now interested enough to invite him to join St George. The club was willing to pay for his round trip and gave him one pound in spending money, which had to cover the 8/6 return train trip and all meals. Don was now worth a quid — just — to a club.

GOODBYE TO TENNIS

Bradman sensed that even though he had been overlooked for the State side there was still a keen interest in him. This prompted him to make the most important decision of his sporting life. The multi-talented athlete, who by now was showing outstanding ability in both cricket and tennis, was forced to choose between them. After his successful net and one-day trial, he was selected to play for the Goulburn District team against South Coast at Goulburn on 13 November 1926. This was a trial match for the forthcoming Country Week carnival in Sydney. He top-scored with 62 retired, and was chosen for the Southern Districts team to play in Sydney. So far he had seized every chance and succeeded.

However, he had kept playing tennis and was also chosen for that week's Country Week tournament, which was to follow the cricket. Bradman relished the idea of performing in both. But his employer, Percy Westbrook, would not allow him time off work for both weeks. One would have to go. Bradman reluctantly gave up the tennis, for cricket was now indisputably his top sporting priority. Besides, he knew that he would be observed by the State selectors during that vital Sydney week. It was another chance to make them take notice of his unique unorthodox talent.

For people brought up on the necessity of the straight bat for almost everything, Bradman would have to be an acquired taste. At first sight for the not so far-sighted, he was a surprise. He seemed always on the move. The bat was not always angled close to his body and he seemed to take risks while attacking. A second view in those early days was less unsettling for the open-minded, as one impression became apparent. Not very much, if anything *at all*, slipped through to the keeper. He hit everything. In short, he had incomparably fast reflexes, which allowed him to manoeuvre with alacrity in order to strike the incoming missile. He could also become the outgoing missile to meet the ball on his terms.

With a range of people who could influence his career looking on each day of Country Week from 22 to 26 November, Bradman — on turf wickets — ran up consistent scores of 43, 24, 41, 27 and 25, and took one bag of four for 44 with his leg-spinners against Newcastle. While not displaying fireworks, he showed his temperament and concentration by not failing in any knock.

Bradman's captain in all five games, Alan Sieler, found him a 'silent worker, a deep thinker . . . the game was treated by him as a business . . .' Bradman disagreed. 'I was a kid, enjoying myself,' he said with a grin. 'I was just doing my best.'

His efforts were certainly enough to be picked for Combined Country against a City team, which was the culmination and highlight of the week.

In the meantime, Bradman had taken up Jones' offer to play club cricket with St George. Its selectors chose him immediately in their first-grade side. His initial game was on Saturday 27 November, straight after his run of Country Week matches. For many players, a sixth game in so many days would have been too much, but Bradman's ambition was matched by his fitness and determination. His confidence was high.

The club game was against Petersham on its home ground. The opposition had perhaps the strongest bowling line-up in the competition and this first chance at Sydney club level promised to be exacting. District cricket had and has always been fiercely competitive in Australia. It provided the pools of talent around the country from which State and ultimately Test players were mainly selected. In many ways, there was more at stake than in the State trial game, where twenty-seven players had taken part and some retired when they had made 'enough' — not quite an atmosphere of life or death.

Bradman batted at the fall of the third wicket and the atmosphere drew more out of him than in the Country Week games. It was the moment to take calculated risks against Petersham's international bowlers, such as Sam Everett and Tommy Andrews. Already more comfortable on turf, Bradman bolted out of the blocks with a variety of cuts, hooks and pulls. He survived a near run-out and a few other anxious moments, which was only to be expected when a player was scoring at a run-a-minute.

His first fifty took an hour, and he reached 98 in 97 minutes. On that score he broke his bat, the one his mother had given him. He brought up his century with his next shot and was finally run out for 110, in 110 minutes. Dick Jones, who was playing with St George himself, was nearly as pleased as Bradman. His judgement had been vindicated and made up for the countless disappointments State selectors faced in a largely thankless task.

There had probably never been a more auspicious debut in Australian club cricket, considering the rapid rate of scoring and the strength of the opposition. Jones, an achiever in his own right, would be remembered for eternity as 'the man who gave Don Bradman his chance'.

The Bowral boy's name was now on the selectors' lips along with that of Archie Jackson, who had been promoted to the State side. Bradman's century and the way in which he made it earned him an immediate reputation. He had done such deeds in the bush, and now he was repeating them in the city. If there were any doubts about his being selected for the Combined Country team to play the City XI, they were now dispelled. He was picked to play in the game for the following Monday, November 29.

After six successive innings in as many days, he had a break on the Sunday before the big game against the City XI. It was another huge challenge — a step up from the earlier trial match, and even more important than his extraordinary start in club cricket. Sieler moved up to captain the Country team.

Bradman was both thrilled and overawed by the choice of the City captain — the great Charlie Macartney. He was now forty and retired from Test cricket, but he was still equipped for the big time. It was

Macartney with his great 170 in 1921 who had inspired a twelve-year-old boy to announce that he would only be satisfied if he played on the SCG. A child's back-yard daydreams had suddenly become reality.

However, Bradman had no time to reflect on his rapid rise. Two days after he had taken off the pads at Petersham they were on again at the Sydney Cricket Ground No. 1, but not before he had fielded to the City team. Macartney, batting at number three, gave a fine display with a selection of copybook leg glances and drives. Bradman fielded many of them as the City piled up eight for 301 declared.

When the Country lads batted, they were soon in trouble. Bradman again had no time to dwell on the big occasion before he was in, also at first drop. His innings was a continuation of the last week, especially Saturday. As two of his partners went cheaply, Bradman marched into the twenties with panache. At the fall of the third wicket, a Hunter River batsman with real promise, Frank Cummins, came in and stayed.

Bradman slipped through thirty, forty and fifty before stepping up his rate. They managed a strong 82-run partnership, of which Bradman notched 60 and Cummins 19. Two more wickets fell as Bradman went into the nineties. Macartney extended the game by one over to give Bradman a chance to reach his century, but he was out caught in slip going for his tenth four.

He had scored 98 out of seven for 171. If there had been a 'man of the match' award, he would have received it, despite Macartney's artistry. Yet the most important outcome of all was Bradman's belief in himself, which now had validity beyond the bush. He could not just match it with anyone. He could rise above all rivals. If this was not appreciated beyond Sydney on 29 November 1926, it mattered not a jot. Bradman himself knew that he could do it.

IN THE CLUB

A few weeks later, in December, he was made aware of the State selectors' opinion of him when he was selected to play for the NSW second XI against Victoria's seconds, which would start the New Year.

At the end of 1926, the judges placed him behind only a dozen men in NSW, but ahead of about 150 others playing first-grade cricket in Sydney, not to mention many talented country players.

Some journalists criticised the selectors for not taking a chance with him in the first XI, but Bradman himself felt he was doing well enough. 'I was happy to get the chance,' he noted. 'It's so easy to criticise selectors, but they didn't have all that much to go on [in December 1926].' He celebrated his new upgrade by belting an unbeaten 103 for Bowral against a visiting Sydney team and taking eight for 36 with his leg-spinners.

A sprinkling of spectators at the SCG watched the interstate second-eleven game on New Year's Day, 1927, which began badly for the home side. It was three for 47 when Bradman strode out to join Dudley Seddon — a future NSW selector. They put on 58 before Seddon was dismissed and Don went on to 43 before pulling a ball from Hans Ebeling, a future Test bowler, into his stumps. He had top-scored, which was satisfying but not sufficient to make the selectors do any more than say they were pleased with his performance. It had not been enough for a passport to the seniors. Aware of this, Bradman went out in the second innings determined to push for advancement. At 8, he pulled one hard to the square-leg fence, but slipped as he watched the ball bouncing into the pickets. His left foot touched the leg-stump, dislodging a bail. The keeper appealed belatedly, unsure if it had happened in the actual process of playing the shot. But the square-leg umpire, George Borwick, had seen it all and delivered his verdict — out, hit wicket. Bradman trudged from the field disappointed. It seemed an unfair way to go, especially as the bowler had been despatched so decisively for four. Yet such were the rules of cricket, which throughout the Don's long career would work for and against him like all other mortals.

His top-score of 43, however, more or less summed up the rest of 1926–27, which saw him mainly playing for St George on Saturdays. 'I had to get up at 5 a.m., and catch a train at six, which got me into Sydney by 9 a.m.,' he remembered. 'After play I would catch the return train back to Bowral by midnight.'

It was arduous, even for the super-fit youth. He began to realise then that if he were ever going to make it in senior company, he would have to be Sydney-based. Nevertheless, he made 289 at 48.1 in six completed innings for St George by the end of the season, which was more than adequate considering it was his first on turf wickets. Only one other player in the club — Scanes — did better with 547 at 49.72. Such an average of around fifty in district cricket was a fair indicator that a player had a future at first-class level. The competition was fierce and not always on ideal wickets, which would more often be encountered in State games.

Bradman ended the season on a note which would be writ large in local folklore when he batted for Bowral against Moss Vale in the final. Moss Vale, at home on Lackey Oval, crumbled for just 73. Bradman opened with Alf Stephens, and they quickly passed the opposition score. At stumps Bradman was 58 not out. The next Saturday, Stephens fell for 30, and Don's brother Vic joined him briefly before being bowled for 13. Then Sid Cupitt, the donor of that first Bradman bat, joined him for a staggering 200-plus partnership. Cupitt made 60, his best for the season, but the afternoon was left to his partner. A local paper reported on the following Monday:

> *Don Bradman excelled himself, and the few spectators were given a rare treat. Getting his eye in quickly Don commenced to pepper the bowling and was not long in reaching his century (87 minutes), after which he gave a remarkable exhibition of batting activity.*
>
> *Never before had the Moss Vale bowlers received such an unmerciful flogging; good and bad were treated alike, the balls whizzing to every part of the field, and only those who attempted to stop them know how much ginger was behind them.*

Bradman hit six sixes, one five and forty-three fours. Two-thirds of his score came from boundaries, allowing him to bat through day two for his 320 — out of Bowral's total of 480 for nine. One Bowral player was absent, but he was hardly needed as Bradman slaughtered the opposition. Such was the annihilation of Moss Vale that 'first-grade' or Sydney club cricketers were henceforth banned from the competition. Bradman himself, and other observers, felt his performance had easily eclipsed his 300 a year earlier. His development through his experience in Sydney club cricket was evident.

'I obviously gained a lot in the company of players such as Kippax, Jackson and Kelleway,' Bradman explained. 'I worked hard and watched them closely.'

He noticed that none of these stars had a grip like his. 'It [the grip of the bat] had been developed on concrete wickets,' he observed. 'It helped me pull a ball, and was good and safe for on-side shots. I felt handicapped, however, in striking the ball between mid-off and point.'

Bradman experimented in the nets for much of the season with various other grips until, he said, 'I found I could loft the ball when I wanted to, and play those off-side strokes when I set my mind.'

His power and timing meant he could play any shot he wished. The ball would travel with speed and accuracy wherever he wanted. In the end he decided not to change the way he held a bat. He was criticised for it, but retorted with his high scoring, maintaining that if it worked and led to no obvious error, there was no need to change.

'A player is not necessarily wrong just because he is different,' Bradman noted in his autobiography. The grip was good enough to allow him to amass 1,577 runs in all games in 1926–27, with five centuries at an average of 78.85.

This was exceptional, and although he was a name in Sydney, he had not yet made his first-class debut. He was still just a one-day player, who was yet to even practise regularly on turf wickets. Other junior champions had similarly outstanding records as they approached their nineteenth birthdays, and like a legion of others before and after him, Don wondered if he was really destined for the big time.

6

TRAVELLING FIRST-CLASS

When nearing the century he did not potter about for singles in order to claim the coveted honour of making a century in his first Sheffield Shield match, but smacked boundaries with a delightful abandon . . .

— PRESS REPORT ON BRADMAN'S FIRST FIRST-CLASS HUNDRED, 16 DECEMBER 1927

THE BREAK

The first ten weeks of the 1927–28 season were marked by Bradman's omission rather than his selection. He was still making the arduous round trip from Bowral and he made a meagre fist of his first opportunity for St George with a 4 and 7 versus Petersham, against whom a year earlier he had scored that initial grade century. His failure in the cut-throat, competitive atmosphere meant he was overlooked for Alan Kippax's side in its warm-up country tour. Nor was he selected for Arthur Mailey's Sydney team, which visited Singleton.

However, Bradman was undeterred. He felt confident that if he progressed as much in the new season as he had in 1926–27 he would have a chance of representing the State before it was over. His next grade match was against Randwick, but he progressed no further, again scoring just 7. Consequently he was not included in the State practice squad of twenty-nine for the early games against New Zealand and the other States.

In October, Charlie Macartney decided to end his first-class career, leaving a massive gap in the NSW batting line-up, but still Bradman was not ranked in the first thirty in the selectors' collective mind. In effect, Bradman would have been fortunate to make a third XI. He was now nineteen — an age when most Aussie youngsters regard themselves at the crossroads of their careers. Either he would go on to play State cricket or end up in the park back in Bowral.

Still, Macartney's retirement meant that a batsman with drive could ride a slipstream into the Shield team with a couple of resounding big hundreds. Traditionally selectors liked to replace a type of player with one of the same persuasion. And Bradman, like the electric young Archie Jackson, was one of the few youthful fast-scorers with the necessary potential in the grade competition.

Mindful of the hole left by Macartney, Bradman appeared for his third chance on an overcast Sydney day in late October at Hampden Oval when St George played Paddington, whose side included Test all-rounder Jack Gregory. Bradman launched himself at the spinners, showing that, despite his lack of practice on turf, his footwork was nimble as he drove to perfection in the arc between cover and mid-wicket.

State selector Dick Jones watched in admiration from the other end and then from the pavilion as his protégé plundered his way to a century before lifting the tempo a notch with some outlandish lofted cuts and hooks on his way to an undefeated 130. It was the highest score and best batting of the grade round that week, and possibly the season. The next night at the selectors' table, Jones pressed hard for Bradman's inclusion in the State team. However, he was outvoted by the others, who agreed the newcomer had a touch of magic about him, but felt he should be nurtured more.

Bradman battled on in the next four club games with scores of 2, 40 not out, and 47. The latter two knocks were solid and confirmed Jones' feeling that he was ready for the step up. However, his cause for the season looked a lost one when NSW piled up 578 in 278 minutes — a rate of 123 an hour — against New Zealand. Bradman's main rival for Macartney's spot, the mercurial Archie Jackson, smashed 104 in 72 minutes. His young 'enemy' Bill O'Reilly also made his debut, two years after Bradman had despatched him into the surrounding streets at Bowral Oval en route to 234. With peers like this making it, Bradman was encouraged to battle on.

He played for St George in a return game against Randwick, and this time made a forceful 87, while those same NSW peers crashed for 167 in the Queensland State game. It was Country Week time again, and Bradman, remembering his modest but consistent successes of a year ago, opened for a combined St George-University side against Riverina at Hurstville. In a losing side, he belted 125 not out and once more prodded the minds of the State selectors. They met soon afterwards in late November, but once more could not find a place for him in the NSW twelve, which was due to tour the southern States. Jones was overruled a second time.

The thought of those slow-moving trains on warm nights, with fans that didn't work, warm beer, noise and little sleep deterred Jack Gregory and H. S. Love, who pulled out of the trip. A hurriedly reconvened selection meeting saw Jones triumph with a vengeance. He got two fellow St George players, the experienced Albert Scanes and Bradman, into the team. Don was named as twelfth man. He had slipped in by default, but at least he was in.

NO FOOL ON THE HILL

The Bowral paper waxed loud about its home-town boy, noting that 'judging by city reports, Donald has not contracted swollen head, the most deadly disease that waylays a youngster in any branch of sport, and his steady devotion to the game is bound to take him far . . .'

This was literally true for Don, who had never been out of NSW before. Moreover, he was the only team member not to have had first-class experience. He was the callow youth of the side, who would have to go through the usual juvenile tribal initiations to show he was 'one of the boys', and that he could 'take it'.

The older members of the team, with Kippax the leader in place of Macartney, were relieved to be away from everyday worries. This two-week break in December 1927 was as good as a vacation for them. The team dined together on board, and the players then retired to their carriages in an attempt to sleep as the train wound through the Blue Mountains on its way to Adelaide via Broken Hill.

Within hours Bradman realised one of the possible reasons why Gregory and Love decided to give the tour a miss. He tossed and turned in the stifling compartment, angling the fan so that it blew on his face, but still could not get to sleep. When the train reached Broken Hill, he had a weeping eye, which the team manager Dr F. V. McAdam diagnosed as the result of a cold. Don was confined to bed on the first day while the others went off down the silver mines and sightseeing. The other minor casualty was Jackson, who had a boil on his knee. This was to be a stroke of luck for Don. He slept tight the following night in a stationary hotel and sweated out the cold. Next day, McAdam declared the hobbling Jackson unfit, but passed the sniffling Don, which meant the might of NSW could field an eleven.

A crowd of several thousand turned up at the primitive Jubilee Oval to watch the State side take on the Barrier District in a one-day game on a concrete pitch, which even had concrete bowlers' run-ups. Lack of rain in the last two years had reduced the ground to hard-baked red earth. Whenever the ball hit the ground it sent up a puff of red dust. To make matters worse, a strong wind stirred up the oval during the morning's play, but it did not deter the spectators, many of whom endured far worse down the mines earning a living.

As he couldn't wear his sprigged cricket boots on the concrete strip, Bradman walked out to bat in his street shoes. But he more than made up for his inappropriate footwear with his experience on concrete. At the fall of the second wicket he joined Kippax, the man the crowd had come to see. The more astute among the onlookers were just as impressed with the slight, shy boy who wore that permanent half-grin as he proceeded to carve up the second-rank opposition as if he were back with Bowral.

In a stand of 97, Bradman matched it shot-for-shot with Kippax before attempting one dance too many down the pitch to a local leg-spinner. He was out stumped for 46 and later managed to souvenir the bigger old-style ball, which was going out of fashion. At about 4 p.m. a severe dust-storm swept over the area and the game had to be abandoned. 'I had to switch on the light back at the hotel because the thick dust had made the place so dark,' Bradman recalled.

His first outing for the State was only marred by a badly bruised finger. McAdam would have to choose between Don's injury and Jackson's 'suppurating tumour', as the official medical report described it. On the morning of the first day of the match against South Australia, Jackson's boil was harder and more inflamed. McAdam diagnosed him less fit to play than Bradman, who was thus an automatic selection for his initial first-class game.

GRIMMETT v THE GRINNER

Such a long tour brought out the jokers in the NSW squad, who put the young Don to the test soon after the team arrived at their hotel in Adelaide. He was asked what else he did besides cricket. Bradman spoke modestly about his tennis and mentioned his piano-playing. That raised mock eyebrows and it was explained by one player that the reason for Bradman's skills would be revealed if he would play at the hotel piano. Don, the innocent, obliged.

'No wonder you're good at cricket,' the player remarked. The others pretended to look for an explanation: 'Piano-playing tunes up the wrists and back muscles.'

This caused a spoof argument and bets were made. Bradman had to remove his shirt and play as the leg-pullers hummed the tune. Fingers were run over his lean, sinewy back. All agreed. It gave new meaning to the concept of 'piano tuning'.

The leg-pulling dispensed with, discussion turned to the talk of Adelaide, Clarrie Grimmett, the slow leg-break bowler, who had come to South Australia some years before from New Zealand via Victoria, which had rejected him. Grimmett was not the best turner of the ball, nor did he have a great wrong'un like Arthur Mailey, but he was unerringly accurate. If he bowled a bad ball in a day's play it was remembered. The local cricket world anticipated a grand clash between him and the strong NSW batting line-up of Phillips, Morgan, Andrews, Kippax, Scanes and Oldfield. There was a modicum of interest in the Bowral Boy batting at number seven, who most thought would be easy prey for the wily Grimmett, who was not called 'the Fox' for nothing.

NSW won the toss, and the advantage, for the Adelaide wicket was hard and fast — perfect for batting. The temperature was forecast to top 96°F (36°C), which would make it tougher for the fielding side. NSW began well with Phillips and the first drop, Andrews, carving a steady second-wicket stand of 122 before the latter fell attacking Grimmett. Kippax came to the wicket in the afternoon session with the score at two for 137 and the temperature gauge trying to match the score. Kippax seemed affected from the start, but managed to fight his way through to 50 before retiring with heat exhaustion.

That brought Bradman's St George team-mate Scanes to the wicket. Next to go was Phillips for 112. Bradman felt a mild flutter of butterflies. But he was calm enough to realise that he was making his debut in the best possible circumstances. NSW was three for plenty and Kippax was recovering from dehydration and preparing to bat again.

At 250, Bert Oldfield, the NSW keeper, was out for a bright but short-lived 12. Kippax nodded to Bradman that it was his turn and out he strode onto the lush green Adelaide Oval with the spire of St Peter's Cathedral rising in the background, in the confident manner that always suggested something special was about to happen. If there was a trace of nerves in his half-grin and firm-set jaw, it did not show as he squinted into the sky, adjusting to the bright, harsh sunlight that had wilted Kippax, fielders and spectators alike.

Grimmett was on, having just dismissed Oldfield. He had six balls left of a standard eight-ball over, which was then the rule in Australia. Bradman took block. Grimmett did not move one fieldsman. The batsman held up the bowler like a veteran as he noted every field placement. In looped the spinner. Bradman played him from the

51

crease, blocking. He danced out to the second ball and slammed it hard to cover. No run. Grimmett varied his line to just outside leg-stump to test the new man and was astonished to see him move his back foot swiftly into position as the ball spun across him and heave it against the spin through mid-wicket with a fearsome roll of that thin but power-packed right wrist. The ball went straight to the deck and crashed into the pickets.

Grimmett took note. For every bowler from the outback to the city, the first sight of Bradman early in an innings was misleading. Everyone was encouraged by such audacious aggression and unortho-doxy. This adventurer would be an easy notch on the belt, Grimmett thought like O'Reilly before him, given the right ball.

Grimmett's step was sharper, the fielders clapped encouragement. If they could get this swashbuckler out quickly NSW might collapse. The cool concrete of the dressing-room and a well-earned drink beckoned. Grimmett gave him another ball just outside leg, but this time with more loop and bounce. Bradman used his feet and drove to mid-on. He blocked the next ball. Grimmett tossed another one up on the leg and the batsman moved swiftly forward. The ball sped along the ground again between mid-on and mid-wicket. Four more. In the first over he had faced in the big time, he had despatched the best slow bowler of the era for two boundaries.

Scanes held up one end as the tyro collected 50 — with a tea-break in between — in just sixty-five minutes. He then went into his shell, but was there at the close on 65 not out and with NSW seven for 400.

News reached Adelaide from the MCG that the Test opener Bill Ponsford was 234 not out in Victoria's score of two for 400 against Queensland. Ponsford was the Australian pioneer of the mammoth score, having already posted a staggering Shield innings of 429. The sporting world wondered if he would beat that. He was certainly set up for it with great weather, a good MCG wicket and plenty of partners in hand.

The next morning, Saturday, in Adelaide, Kippax, who had recov-ered overnight, came in to join Bradman and they mounted a strong partnership, which saw the nineteen-year-old sail towards three figures in the continuing heat before a big crowd.

On 97, the off-spinner Perker Lee bowled him a short ball on middle stump. Bradman threw his right leg across and back and pulled the ball hard to the fine-leg boundary. He didn't have to run as his score registered 101. There had been no finer debut by an Australian at first-class level. Kippax shook his hand and Bradman acknowledged the applause with a modest wave of the bat. As in his first club cricket start of 110 against Petersham a year earlier, Bradman had risen to the moment. If ever the cliché 'first impression lasting impression' applied accurately, it did with this teenager over an innings.

Kippax fell at 511 for 143, leaving Bradman with a couple of bunnies. He was out caught cutting to third-slip Williams for 118 just before lunch, having batted for 180 minutes. He had won the first important round with Grimmett, as he had with O'Reilly on a concrete track at Bowral two years earlier. The South Australian's figures were his worst for some time at three for 160 off thirty-one overs. Like O'Reilly, he went to lunch that afternoon pondering if he'd just had a bad day, or if the opposition had been *that* good. Kippax was a superb striker of the ball, but this compact young fellow from the bush had the more proficient footwork. More pertinently, he had the confidence to use those dazzling feet on that one-two-one glide down the wicket to the pitch of the ball. Even if beaten by the flight, Bradman would hit the ball as if his feet *were* in the right place. His light frame facilitated speed, and at times he seemed to *know* what was coming before it left the bowler's hand. Was it Grimmett's action that was giving him away?

The bowler didn't know. Grimmett, again like O'Reilly, admitted on reflection that he had never encountered a batsman like Bradman. He was the most complex yet exhilarating puzzle with a blade Grimmett had ever encountered. Yet he accepted the new talent as a challenge. Bradman was now his special target.

Over lunch on day two, word reached the teams that Ponsford had climbed to 300 at the break in Melbourne. Bets at Adelaide and

Melbourne were being placed that he would make an assault on his 429 and win. At stumps that day, the news came through. *Ponsford, 437, a new world record.* He was the first player in first-class cricket in Australia to score 400 and now he had done it twice. The conventional wisdom among cricket players and aficionados was that he would be the biggest scorer the game had seen. No-one could ever match such an awesome feat, and there were still plenty of years left in battling Bill, who had started his career as a cautious, stodgy opener, long on defence and short on sparkle.

Observers said there was not a soul like the amiable but lugubrious Bill, the accumulator. There might be spirited men like Trumper and even this new kid from Sydney, Archie Jackson. But they would never be stayers with the powers of concentration of the often ponderous Ponsford. Fortunately, the game could cope with both kinds, but never would the twin capacities of fast, brilliant scoring and run-aggrandisement be found in the one individual. That was not possible, everyone agreed at the end of 1927.

The papers next morning concentrated on Ponsford, while the efforts of Kippax and Bradman gained a few pars downpage. While praising the new star, journalists were wary of labelling him a future champion. He was the sixteenth Australian player to score a first-class century on debut and none of the other fifteen had ever played Test cricket. England's Patsy Hendren, who was coaching in Adelaide, saw the game and was not moved to make any special note of the newcomer's effort. However, an umpire in the game, George Hele, bracketed him with other NSW greats — Charles Bannerman, William Murdoch, Victor Trumper, Charlie Macartney, Reggie Duff and Alan Kippax. Hele was impressed with his confidence in the high-class company. Bradman seemed at ease with them and himself. Hele was especially taken with the new player's athletic outfielding. 'He could throw a ball as fast as any big opening bowler,' he commented. 'And I had never seen anything as accurate.'

A *Sydney Morning Herald* writer thought his cut stroke was vulnerable, but added: '. . . the rapidity of his advance from the matting wicket standard he was accustomed to only a season ago leaves no room for doubt that he will acquire an all-round mastery at no distant date.'

In two seasons Bradman had come from second-grade cricket and third-rate conditions to mix it with the best in the game, and he was unfazed. Yet he was aware he was still learning. After stumps one night, Grimmett mesmerised him with his ability to spin a soft rubber ball on a table. 'He was a magician with the ball,' Bradman said. 'No-one else could perform such tricks.'

Grimmett used his magic in the second innings and had Bradman bowled off his pads for 33 in a sixty-four-minute innings, making his first-game tally 151 in a little over four hours. The match itself was a thriller. NSW scored 519 and 150, and South Australia 481. The locals had to make 189 to win, but crumbled to 185 for nine. McNamee, who had taken five for 53, bowled a 'shooter' or 'grubber', which hardly rose above the pitch and just missed the stumps. The ball beat the keeper and ran towards the boundary as Perker Lee and Williams scampered four byes, giving South Australia victory by one wicket.

WATCHING WOODFULL, PONDERING PONSFORD

The disappointed NSW lads took the Overland Express for Melbourne with some apprehension about facing their main Shield rivals, Victoria, who featured Test players such as the formidable Ponsford, the redoubtable Woodfull, and the two wily old bowlers, Don Blackie and Bert Ironmonger. The visitors' fears were justified. Ponsford compiled a faultless, patient 202, making his tally in two innings 639. His second-innings lapse of 38 was understandable. Not to be outdone by his heavy-scoring opening partner, Woodfull hit 99 and 191 not out and it was Bradman's turn to be more than impressed.

The young newcomer didn't mind the leather-chasing. It was like being in class to the best teachers in the world. Bradman came out to bat to a surprisingly supportive reception from the Melbourne crowd scattered around the ground, which was the biggest in the country. Victorians had always been as parochial as anyone else, but like most cricket followers they respected and encouraged a 'goer', someone who went out of his way to entertain. Victoria was the home of Australian Rules football, the fastest ball game of all, and the State's sports fans were not always patient when it came to the summer game. In addition, some of the spectators had seen Bradman's spectacular fielding. They knew an athlete when they saw one, and this slip of a lad was as fit and as brilliant as anyone ever to grace the MCG's hallowed turf.

Furthermore, Bradman's opening hundred had thrown him into the spotlight. The locals were keen to see if he was really good, or just another battler who had been lucky first-up. While the more astute spectators had nothing more than a few cautious press reports to go on, it was clear from the moment he took block that Woodfull, the Victorian captain, had been doing some extra homework on him. Woodfull placed himself close to the batsman at silly point. Bradman glanced at him several times as if questioning the wisdom of the move. Woodfull was engaging in some legitimate gamesmanship. Bradman had to be in awe of Woodfull, because of his reputation and what he had seen of him from having run the boundary fielding to him.

Blackie was bowling. His first ball was well up and Bradman stepped into it, hitting it through mid-off to the fence. The crowd loved it. Here was a kid, first ball, treating a tried and trusted performer as if he were a park bowler. But Woodfull kept the pressure on. He had been told that Bradman was a weak cutter, so he planned to use Blackie to probe him as much as possible outside the off-stump, hoping to induce a false stroke by placing himself so close. At the same time he tried to keep NSW's first drop, Tommy Andrews, bottled up by medium-pacer F. L. Morton at one end, while Blackie pegged away at Bradman at the other. However, the ploy failed as Bradman moved steadily along to 31. Woodfull then brought on Hartkopf, who trapped him LBW. According to Arthur Mailey, Bradman had batted in a 'natural manner' for less than an hour, and had shown an 'excellent style'.

However, there was no room for superlatives when Blackie yorked him for five in the second innings and ensured a Victorian victory. Bradman remembered the ball and the bowler well. 'Blackie was then about forty,' he said. 'He was a very slow, very flighty off-spinner. He threw the ball higher than most off-spinners. His tantalising flight would deceive the batsmen. He was a very good bowler indeed.'

Bradman had similar respect for 'Dainty' Ironmonger, also a vintage player in his forties.

'He was a slow-medium, left-hand, first-finger spinner,' he noted. 'Like Hedley Verity, Underwood and Tufnell. He was unusual because he had lost the top joint of the first finger of his left hand. The result was he couldn't grip the ball with his first finger like a normal person. He had to push the ball into the hand. He *fired* it out rather than spun it out. He spun the ball hard and was very accurate — another very, very good bowler.'

The always difficult southern tour had been a failure for the competent NSW team, but Bradman came back to Sydney fairly pleased with his efforts. He had only failed once in four innings and was averaging just under 47. This by no means would make him a permanent fixture in the State team, but it was going to be tough to dislodge him.

PARTNERSHIP RESUMED

Bradman was still juggling his life between Bowral, where he still lived and worked in real estate, and Sydney. One compensation for this unsatisfactory set-up was a chance to see more of Jessie Menzies, with whom he formed a closer relationship. They had never lost contact since meeting in 1920 when they were both about eleven. While Jessie's family had moved to Burwood in Sydney, they still owned the cattle and dairy farm at Glenquarry and would go back there for holidays. Don and Jessie never lost their affection for each other, which had grown as they matured.

Jessie had left school at sixteen to do a three-year business college course before entering the Commonwealth Bank of which her uncle,

James Kell, had been the second governor. She was the first woman it employed as a ledger-keeper. Her father liked cricket and she too enjoyed the game and appreciated its finer points. Jessie used to watch Don play on Saturday afternoon for St George. The first big game she ever saw was his premier appearance in Sydney at the SCG for NSW against Queensland, in the last Shield match for 1927.

NSW showed its great batting strength on the first day with Kippax in full flight. Bradman remembered his performance as 'a most graceful batting effort'.

He had a lot of time to observe Kippax's knock. The NSW captain was into the 200s when Bradman joined him on the second morning with the score on 427 for six. He was mentally prepared to do well, but Kippax was making it look too easy. He had thrashed the Queensland attack into submission, and by the time Bradman came to the wicket a part-time off-spinner named Gough was on, the main strike bowlers having been forced out of the firing line.

The last man had been dismissed on the final ball of the previous over. Bradman looked on from the non-striker's end as Gough served up a slow off-break to Kippax, who pushed it to mid-on for a single. Bradman faced up, thinking that a similar shot would be a nice way to get off the mark. Not for the first time in his short career, he had made up his mind which stroke he would make *before* the ball was bowled.

Gough bowled a faster, straight ball. Anticipating something slower and turning, Bradman pushed towards mid-on, but the ball came straight through and took his middle peg. The apprentice walked away feeling cheated — by himself. With a resolve that would revolutionise the meaning of the word in sport over the next two decades, Bradman vowed that he would never again decide on a shot beforehand in a serious innings.

He sat back in the pavilion watching Kippax carve out a little piece of history with a scintillating 315. Despite this Herculean effort, NSW looked likely to lose the match on the final day when it collapsed to be six for 60 in its second innings, with seventy-five minutes to the close and no chance of winning outright.

Bradman came to the wicket to join wicket-keeper Hughie Love. Queensland's fast-medium bowlers Hurwood and Nothling had skittled the batsmen and looked certain to clean up the tail until Bradman showed them a broad defensive blade, and a hitherto unrevealed side to his game. Although he was making a name for himself as a fast scorer, he also had an immaculate defence, which was rarely demonstrated by the game's dashers.

On that late December day in 1927, Bradman first gave notice of his fighting qualities in adversity. The wicket was deteriorating, a thunder storm threatened, the light was failing and the bowling was hostile as he displayed his faultless defensive skills for sixty-nine minutes.

On thirteen, with six minutes to play, Bradman received a 'kicker' which caught the shoulder of his bat and flew to Queensland keeper O'Connor. Bradman had taken most of the strike, and NSW was able to play out the remaining over and a half to draw the game.

At a casual glance, Bradman's 0 and 13 for the game did not look exactly impressive, on top of his 31 and 5 in Melbourne, and the promise of that 118 start against Grimmett and Co was urgently needed again to show the selectors that he was not going the way of those fifteen other first-up first-class centurions, who were but a footnote to cricket history for their failure to make it to the very top.

SYMMETRY OF PROMISE

The much-needed second big knock did not come in his next innings at the SCG, in the return match against South Australia. He had scored just 2 when he was caught and bowled by Dr Douglas McKay trying to glide a swinging full toss to the on-side. His scores since that fine debut innings were now 33, 31, 5, 0, 13 and 2. However, he grabbed his chance in the second innings with a forceful 73, which saw him fearlessly leaving his crease to take on Grimmett again. The great bowler finally beat him with flight and had him caught. In that first Shield season encounter with Grimmett honours were about even, Bradman having won the first battle, Grimmett the second and the pair about even when the youngster made 73.

The opening day of the final game against the reigning champions, Victoria, at the SCG, attracted a record Shield crowd of 30,386, the biggest Bradman had played in front of. He failed in the first innings with 7 (out stumped), but became one of the eight to score a ton in the match with a superb 134 not out in 225 minutes in the second innings. In that dig, he mastered Blackie and Ironmonger and lived up to expectations.

The century gave a promising symmetry — a hundred on debut and another to close the season — to 1927–28. It also brought him in second in the NSW Shield averages with 46.22, but it was a long way short of Kippax's 80.70 and not yet enough to suggest he should be elevated to the next level.

He was consistent in the Sydney grade matches, averaging 58.71. Even though he was still bowling respectably, taking four for 55 in a game against Manly, he had become aware that only his batting was likely to take him higher.

Bradman had a light end to the season on country tours with Sydney and NSW sides. The first was home to Bowral to open the new turf wicket at Loseby Park, which had been upgraded by the council. In April 1928 and over Easter, he joined Arthur Mailey's so-called 'Bohemians', half of whom were State players, for a tour through southwest NSW. With the pressure off, he batted only ordinarily and scored just 77 in seven innings — including a run-out for 1 at his birthplace, Cootamundra — giving him an un-Bradmanlike average of 11.

Despite these ups and downs, Bradman's rise was unprecedented in cricketing history. No-one had ever gone from playing competitive cricket for the first time in a country town at the age of seventeen to being a Test prospect just two years later. Bradman had moved steadily up the ranks in just three seasons from his huge scoring efforts for Bowral in 1925–26, then his impressive Sydney grade debut in 1926–27, and finally his initial effort for the State in 1927–28. It had been a gradual but strong preparation for the coming season's visit of the touring MCC team, but still he was ranked only fourteenth in all Shield averages. In statistical terms, that put him behind a complete team of batsmen with a couple of reserves. No matter who saw his potential at Test level, it would be hard after just five Shield games to justify promoting him into the national team. Bradman would need to lift his performance a fourth notch in four seasons to do that.

Practical notice of this position was given at the end of 1927–28 when he failed to make the side to tour New Zealand led by Victor Richardson, though he was named as one of three stand-bys should someone drop out. Richardson, the South Australian captain, had fielded to Bradman when he scored his 118 and then again in Sydney for that 73. He was aware that the young player was already a match for bowlers of the calibre of Grimmett. Bradman's reserve position left him either dangling, or poised for entry to the Australian XI in 1928–29.

But that final promotion had always proved the hardest to make.

PART TWO

DOMINATOR
1928–1932

7

MCC'S FINEST

He was a shortish boy with a grim nervous face. He looked about nineteen and not very formidable.
— WALTER HAMMOND ON FIRST SIGHT OF BRADMAN IN THE FIELD IN 1928

GONE TO THE TEST

The MCC team arrived at Fremantle in October 1928, stayed several days in Perth and then began the thirstiest temperance train trip of their lives 3,000 kilometres across barren desert to Adelaide, before going on to Melbourne and then Sydney. Some of the towns they passed through or noticed on maps caused amusement with their mix of English and Aboriginal names: Cook, Hughes, Deakin, Loongana, Nurina, Haig, Rawlinna, Naretha, Kitchener, Zanthus, Coonana. The touring party, from the upper-class amateurs such as Douglas Jardine to the professional ex-coalminer Harold Larwood, were astonished at the parched sprawling plains, so different from England's green and pleasant land. More than once they glimpsed groups of ragged Aborigines beside the line as they passed.

The vastness awed the visitors. Australia, they were informed by a train attendant, was about as big as China, and the US minus Alaska. After a couple of hours' travel, no-one doubted the exaggerated claim. In 1928, Australia's population of about five million was clustered mainly on the eastern seaboard in and around Sydney and Melbourne. This, too, became apparent with the long intervals between homesteads and other signs of habitation along the way. The bush telegraph alerted the outback that England's finest were passing through. People came out to wave and watch wistfully as the train slowly disappeared into a mirage of sand and scrub.

Percy Fender, the cricketer and journalist, was travelling with the team, but as an observer, not a player. He was enjoying his more sedentary role, despite being disappointed to miss selection after making 1,376 runs at an average of 37.18 and taking 110 wickets at 28.17 in a fine all-round performance in the County season just finished. Fender noted one incident that illustrated both the impact of Australia's awesome size and its thirst for the game. He had run out of toothpaste between Kalgoorlie and Port Augusta, but was told there would be a stop in twenty minutes where he could buy some. A fellow passenger took him to a shop in the small town. It was closed. There was a notice on the window which said:

'Closed. Gone to the Test.'

The town was over 3,000 kilometres and four days' train journey from Brisbane, venue of the First Test.

The great interest the tour was arousing in Australia reflected the fact that England had arrived with a strong team hoping to capitalise on its Ashes victory in the UK in 1926 when it won one-nil with four drawn games. The English selectors were, however, mindful of the fact that Australia had won nine of the last ten Tests in Australia (1920–21 and 1924–25). Their selections were more tough-minded than on previous tours, but they seemed to have made an error in not selecting more all-rounders. Apart from Fender, eight other players — Jupp, Tate, Newman, Townsend, Barratt, Kennedy, Astill and Root — had all completed the double of 100 wickets and 1,000 runs in the 1928 English County season, but only one — Maurice Tate — was chosen.

Even so, the line-up led by Percy Chapman from Kent and vice-captain Jack White from Surrey was well-balanced, with the young Walter Hammond — a future England captain and outstanding batsman — providing useful support to Tate as an all-rounder with his medium pace. Hobbs and Sutcliffe, the great openers, were set to take up where they left off in the last series in England. Jardine was expected to show again that he was a fine, solid player, and perhaps the best player of speed in the team. Patsy Hendren, of Middlesex, who had toured Australia twice before, was regarded as the most likely consistent run-getter, and big hopes were also pinned on Lancashire's mercurial Ernest Tyldesley and the brilliant yet unpredictable young Maurice Leyland from Yorkshire. The unflappable Phil Mead would, it was expected, be the team's anchor — a foil for the dashers.

Then there was Larwood, the fastest bowler England had ever produced, his speed combining with his equally formidable control to make him a true match-winner. George Geary and Sam Staples were to provide good support with line and length, while the orthodox slow left-hander White would offer variety with the right-arm leg-spinner A. P. 'Tich' Freeman. George Duckworth was the keeper, with Leslie Ames his strong-batting understudy.

Hobbs, Sutcliffe, Freeman, Mead, Hendren, Chapman and Tate formed a powerful nucleus of seasoned campaigners who had visited Australia before and were expected to help the other ten newcomers not only to adjust to the different playing conditions but to cope with the demanding travel and general living arrangements of the tour.

If they needed proof of the grip the game had in Australia, it came one evening when the train stopped to take in water halfway between Perth and Adelaide. Beside the line was a 'pitch' made out of railway sleepers where three boys — two white and one Aboriginal — were playing with an old ball torn and tattered from years of use and a bat shaved down from a builder's plank. Some of the Englishmen joined in. One of the kids, not realising who they were, told them: 'We'll be Australia, you be England.'

The scene reminded Larwood of his own rugged beginnings in the tiny Nottinghamshire mining village of Nuncargate where youngsters would similarly use anything at their disposal to play the game. Lack of means had also caused many in the Australian outback to try out to see if they could make it to the big time. Most would fail. Even if they managed to claw themselves up through country, club or district ranks to challenge for State selection, they had no economic security in lean economic times.

One such country hopeful whom only a couple of the tourists had heard of was contemplating his chances as the MCC party continued their epic journey.

THE BIG MOVE

Bradman, just twenty, decided on a major move in his life. If he were to make it at the top level he would have to relocate to Sydney to give himself the best opportunity. As there were only six Sheffield Shield matches a season — for which players received a pittance of twenty shillings a day at home and twenty-five shillings interstate in 'expenses' — he would obviously have to get a job once he got there. Fortuitously, his Bowral employer, Percy Westbrook, decided to open a real estate office in Sydney under the name of Deer and Westbrook Ltd. Bradman was offered the job of company secretary. Apart from that, he carried out much the same duties as those he had done in Bowral of collecting rents and showing clients properties.

Bradman found accommodation with the family of a country traveller for a Sydney insurance company, G. H. Pearce, who had visited Westbrook's office in Bowral many times and become friendly with the young cricketing clerk. The move from Bowral to Sydney's Concord West was a wrench for Bradman from his close family ties and Bowral friends. His parents were reluctant to let their youngest child leave home, but unless he based himself in Sydney, he knew he could forget his aspirations to play for his country. His strong belief in himself had been confirmed by his short but productive career so far and he wanted more than anything else to fulfil his dreams of excelling for Australia. As he later commented:

Clem Hill, a great left-hander, was only a teenager when he made the Test team. I was already twenty and really prepared, deep-down, to move. I was showing enough to give it [big cricket] a real crack. The first advantage was the chance to practise on turf wickets. That gave me the opportunity to improve my cricket.

Despite his success in such a short time, Bradman was prepared and disciplined enough to learn more. He would not be content with making the next step. In his mind, he wanted to do it to the best of his ability. And he knew he was still nowhere near the peak of his powers.

THE OPENING

Bradman opened the season with an electric innings for St George of 107 in 130 minutes against Gordon at Chatswood Oval. Soon after he was selected to play in a trial game in Melbourne between Australia and The Rest, which would influence Test selection. He was in The Rest led by Vic Richardson, against the Australian XI under Bill Woodfull. Bradman made only 14 and 5 against Grimmett and Ron Oxenham. Ponsford remarked that The Rest's batsmen had taken the game too seriously, which was a strange observation because its players were on trial for Test positions. Perhaps Ponsford resented the pressure the opposition attempted to apply, albeit without much success. He more likely objected to the fact that the Melbourne crowd had typically barracked for the underdogs.

They encouraged Bradman in the outfield and applauded his lightning sweeps along the boundary and fast, accurate, flat throwing. Young players like him were speeding up the game, whether fielding or batting. Crowds were growing as a result.

'I felt I had done badly,' Bradman said of his performance for The Rest. But it wasn't so much that Grimmett and Oxenham had removed him cheaply. He was peeved because they had bowled well and he had not risen to the challenge. Yet he was not alone. The top score for The Rest was just 31. Bradman had not enhanced his chances of Test selection. Nor, by comparison, had he harmed them. Still, he was in need of a spectacular showing at his next outing. Despite his failure in Melbourne, he felt in good mental and physical shape and considered his naturally good footwork was improving. His range of shots was widening and in particular he had honed his late cut, of which he was already one of the country's leading exponents. He was also disciplining himself not to loft the ball.

A week after the Melbourne debacle he turned out for NSW in his first Shield match for the season — against Queensland at the Exhibition Ground in Brisbane where the first Test would be played. Queensland batted first and an even effort saw it compile 324, with NSW paceman Halford Hooker taking six for 46. Kippax sent Loder and Archie Jackson in to open and asked Bradman to go in at number three. He had batted at number six in the Melbourne trial match and never higher than four for St George. Kippax, however, liked the number four spot himself in State games. He had batted with Bradman enough now to know his ability and potential. It was time to give him his chance in the prime batting position.

Loder left with the score on 7 and this brought Bradman to the wicket for the first time in Queensland to partner his main rival for a Test spot. Bradman outscored Jackson 67 to 44 in an exciting partnership of 113 before Jackson was dismissed for 50. Then followed another good run-for-run connection of 93 with Kippax before the skipper was bowled by Thurlow for 47.

Bradman reached his hundred during the partnership in 164 minutes, in an innings characterised by brilliant timing and some wonderful on-side play. But he delighted the spectators with all the shots in the book and more. His late or back cuts were becoming unique. Bradman tried to keep the innings together, but the last eight wickets fell for only 35. He was dismissed going for runs at 131 in 212 minutes with fourteen fours, as NSW scrambled to 248. Queensland batted a second time and managed 322, thanks to a forceful 158 not out by F. C. Thompson.

NSW had to make 399 in its second innings to win. It began well with Loder (49) and Jackson (71) in an opening stand of 121, when they were both dismissed soon after lunch on the fourth day. This immediately brought Bradman and Kippax together and they embarked on another productive partnership, this time of 185, matching each other run-for-run until Kippax was out caught for 96 trying to reach his century before stumps. Bradman was on 88 not out at the close, with NSW three for 317, still eighty-two runs short.

Shield games then were played over four days of five and a half hours each, with an extra two and a half hours on a fifth day, if required for an outright result. Next morning Bradman wisely took his time as he neared the milestone of a century in each innings, pushing for singles for thirty-four minutes until he reached the coveted double. He went on to be 133 not out and hit the winning shot for NSW to finish on four for 401. He had batted for 211 minutes in a remarkably even effort, scoring at exactly the same rate in each knock. It was only the tenth time in Sheffield Shield history that a player had scored two centuries in the same match.

More often than not, a three-figure score in the first innings of a game is often followed by failure in the second, and to be able to repeat the performance indicates an unusually determined temperament — not to mention physical fitness — as well as considerable talent. It's doubtful that more than one of the people about to make judgement on Bradman's selection had themselves scored the double. It was an exhibition to be remembered when the selectors conferred to pick the side for the First Test. They could not have failed to notice that in both innings Bradman had outscored Jackson, his main rival, and Kippax, his champion State captain.

The Boy from Bowral had slipped out of the pack and was about to sprint for the line. His timing had been immaculate. However, it was still Jackson who was seen as the great new potential champion. People, including the leading cricket authority, J. C. Davis, were comparing him to Trumper because of his 'grace and timing'. However, Bradman's double had placed him close behind in expert analysis. The British magazine, *The Cricketer*, compared him with Australian Harry Graham, known as 'The Little Dasher', and considered Bradman was 'in the running' for a Test place:

> *Bradman of NSW shapes as if he has the brains to know what to do with the bowling, physical ability to do it, and the courage to carry it out. He is a product of a rural district, but, though aggressive, is not agrestic* [wild or uncouth]. *Fearless footwork is the foundation of his batting, which is eminently sound.*

On 2 November, the day after his triumph in Brisbane, the couth and tame country lad was chosen for NSW in its clash with the MCC to commence a week later. It would be the first time he had played against an international side.

FIRST ENCOUNTER

The MCC team arrived in Sydney well-tuned and confident after having been on top in all three drawn encounters with State sides in Perth, Adelaide and Melbourne. Jardine, with the bat, and Larwood, who had devastated the strong Victorian batting line-up with the ball, were leading the English assault.

A huge crowd of 43,000 virtually packed the Sydney Cricket Ground for the first day of the game on 9 November. Among them were the eagle-eyed selectors, Warren Bardsley (NSW), Dr C. E. Dolling (SA), J. S. Hutcheon (Qld), and E. E. Bean (Vic). Top of their viewing list were Jackson and Bradman. The better performer in these near-Test conditions would probably take the last remaining batting spot, number six, for the First Test. If they did more or less equally well, the decision would be a matter of debate and opinion, which most selectors did not revel in, for it sometimes created ill-feeling or promoted interstate hostility.

Within hours of the start, the selectors had headaches of another kind as the MCC got off to a strong start of 148 before Sutcliffe was dismissed. Jardine opened in place of Hobbs, who was resting after reaching 50,000 runs for his career at Adelaide. He and Hammond shared the next big partnership before Jardine was bowled by Hooker for 140.

It was Bradman's first look at Jardine. I asked for his opinion of him as a man and a batsman at that stage.

'Remember I was not a senior player at the time,' he replied. 'We just didn't fraternise with the opposition as they have in recent years. There was no post-stumps contact. So I had no way of judging his character. I could only assess his batting. Jardine was a very good bat indeed.'

Jardine's dismissal brought Hammond and Hendren together for a sustained stand. Midway through the second day, when they had added well over 200, Kippax threw the ball to Bradman. Gregory, Kelleway, Hooker, Campbell, Nichols and Morgan had all been treated with scant respect. Why not try a part-timer, who was a useful net-bowler of leg-spin?

Hammond wandered down the wicket to Hendren, but didn't even bother asking who it was. Hendren knew. He had seen Bradman's 118 in his debut for NSW against South Australia. Hammond strolled back to his crease and observed the youngster as Kippax and he discussed his field placings.

'[He was] a slim, shortish boy with a nervous face whom I had never seen before and whose name was unfamiliar to me,' Hammond later recalled. 'He looked about nineteen and not very formidable.'

Hammond was about right from a bowling perspective. He and Hendren — both professionals in approach — would assess him and then take appropriate action.

'The bowling appeared mediocre, but since Australian colts sometimes carry a hidden kick, I took no liberties for three overs, and nor did Patsy,' Hammond noted in his autobiography, *Cricket My Destiny*. 'Then Patsy grimaced at me, and I knew the novice was "for it".'

With Hendren on 151 and with 580 on the board, Bradman came on for another over. Hendren straight-drove him for four off the first ball, chopped another for four, then slammed two sixes into the Ladies' Stand. A little daunted by now, Bradman nonetheless still kept the ball up and Hendren got under one. He was caught by Campbell in front of the Members' Stand. He had made 167 out of 596. The partnership had collected a colossal 333 for the fourth wicket, but the two men were disappointed that their run-spree had ended. 'We both thought we were set for the rest of the tour,' Hammond recalled.

Left-hander Maurice Leyland joined Hammond for the run feast and pushed a two in the next over, which left Hammond on strike for Bradman. The batsman wanted to 'revenge Patsy' and bury this bowling pretender. He belted 6, 2, 4, 4, 4, 4 from six of the eight balls, and Bradman was 'rested' with figures of one for 55 from five overs. He sauntered to his fielding position at mid-off smarting under the humiliation that only such a hiding of twenty-four off an over can bring.

Hammond and Leyland held a mid-pitch conference, where the expressionless Hammond smiled for the first time in the game. He was on 225 and travelling well enough to go for 300 in quick time. Leyland was happy to give the strike to his white-hot partner.

On the second ball of the next over from Kelleway, he stroked the ball wide of mid-off and called for the run. Hammond glanced towards the fieldsman, judged that it was going past him and set off. He was halfway down the wicket when a lightning throw came in over the stumps and keeper Bert Oldfield whipped off the bails, with Hammond out by metres. The batsman threw his head back and set off for the pavilion to a prolonged ovation for his fine knock.

He was still annoyed at himself in the dressing-room as he removed his pads. The chance of a triple hundred had gone begging. He asked Patsy Hendren how it happened.

'He always throws like that,' Hendren said. 'There's no better fielder in this country.'

'Who was it?' Hammond asked.

'Don Bradman.'

'The one who got you?'

'Yes,' Hendren smiled. 'He got us both.'

Hammond made a mental note of the name and reflected later: 'Because I could see that there was no doubt about him as a fieldsman, I wanted to mark him down for the next time.'

Hammond decided then he would never try his luck against Bradman's arm again. The departure of the two best batsmen on the day didn't bring the innings to an end. The tourists were enjoying the fast Australian wickets, which allowed free and attacking strokes, and kept NSW out in the field until finally declaring at seven for 734, scored well within two days. The massive innings was designed to run their top players into best form and demoralise the Australians.

The twenty-five-year-old reserved but polished Hammond of Gloucestershire was the most impressive of the England bats. He had none of the crowd-pleasing flamboyance of Hobbs and Hendren, but his cool and confident demeanour sent a chilling message to the Australian camp. He would be the most difficult to remove and would grind England to a winning position at every opportunity.

Jardine, a twenty-eight-year-old lawyer, was different again. Educated into the élite via Winchester and Oxford, he was an intensely private 'junior' member of the party. If Hammond was indifferent to the public, Jardine was positively frosty. His patrician bearing and dress — notably the silk neck 'choker' and the Harlequin cap — brought ridicule from the Sydney Hill and Melbourne outer, for nothing offended the locals as much as 'pommies' presenting an image of superiority in egalitarian Australia, still sensitive to its largely convict origins. Without conscious effort, Jardine did everything to stir old passions. Feelings ran high against him when he was batting or chasing a ball.

Yet the barracking, which could be barbed, amusing or abusive, only exacerbated his attitude. Jardine, of Scottish descent, was the Bombay-born son of a cricketer/barrister and regarded 'colonials' with disdain. But he also harboured a particular resentment towards Australians. In 1921, he made 96 not out for Oxford against Warwick Armstrong's all-conquering team, but the Australian captain refused to extend the match an over or two to let him notch the coveted three figures. Big Warwick, who couldn't have cared if a prince or a pauper was a shot away from glory, thought the tour too long anyway. He was not about to bend the rules to let some capable undergraduate, or anyone else, score a century.

Armstrong had already insulted many at the ancient university by insisting that the scheduled three-day game be cut back to two because it was too close to the First Test. It was a blunt Aussie-style snub, and caused some of the visitors' down-under toughness to rub off on the equally ruthless Englishman. Left without the boast that he had been one of the few to score a century against this mighty team, adjudged at that time to be the best to ever tour England, Jardine swore to be as uncompromising as his opponents in future encounters.

Yet Jardine could be disarmingly charming at formal functions and an engaging after-dinner speaker. In 1928, he was a top-class if not potentially great batsman. While his deportment might antagonise the masses, his outstanding but sometimes stolid batting did nothing to check that attitude. He was determined and resistant, not spirited. As with Hammond, Australia would be hard put to break his strong will at the crease. It was a quality they had both demonstrated in Sydney in building that 734.

EMERGENCE

New South Wales batted for an hour until stumps, and both openers, Jackson (4) and Morgan (1), were back in the pavilion with the score at 7. Tate had bowled Jackson before the young dasher had a chance to get into stride. It was a blow. He had failed the crucial test at the top of the innings, which was perhaps unfair considering he would not displace Ponsford or Woodfull in the Australian side. His hope lay in the number six spot, but he had been examined in another role which demanded a different style. Jackson was the type to carve up an attack, not brunt it.

Andrews joined Kippax, fiddled with the medium pace for forty minutes and was out bowled by Tate for 14. NSW was three for 38. Kippax thought about a nightwatchman but decided against it. In came Bradman to a hopeful roar from the crowd. Could he last out the few remaining minutes? To the tourists he was just another eager young hopeful who would be easy pickings for their bowling line-up.

Bradman asked the umpire for 'middle to leg'. This raised eyebrows in the field. He was exposing his wicket just that little bit more to offer encouragement to the pacemen with a well-directed away-swinger aiming to uproot the off-stump or take an outside edge. Chapman shrewdly brought on Larwood, who had been held back. England were loath to give any potential Test opponents a sight of their champion strike bowler. But with a few minutes to stumps, the moment was propitious and the temptation too great. Unfortunately Larwood was uncharacteristically wayward and Bradman (6 not out) and Kippax (22 not out) looked assured as stumps were drawn.

The third morning saw the pair — for they now were a near-perfect combination — move at crowd-thrilling pace. They shared the strike and the runs as was their habit. Moments after Bradman reached his first fifty against an England team in eighty-five minutes, Hammond deceived Kippax with a slower one and he was on his way, LBW for 64. Three for 128 and out of a rut, but still 606 short.

Kelleway joined Bradman for a stand of 68, and just when Bradman looked set for his first hundred against the number one enemy he was bowled by an 'unplayable' ball from 'Tich' Freeman for 87. He batted 131 minutes and hit eight fours, which in both time and boundaries had already in 1928–29 become his standard rate.

Kelleway hung on in his usual determined manner for 93 not out as NSW struggled to 349. England's key bowlers, except for Larwood, had had a useful work-out. With only a day of the four-day encounter to go and a lead of 385, Chapman enforced the follow-on.

In came NSW and a thankful Jackson, until he was run out for 40, hesitating on an easy single. He was disappointed, but that short innings had given the national selectors something to go on. It lifted Jackson's chances of slipping into the Test side, if not from the start, then during the series. He attacked the bowling in a way which would have given the opposition concern.

At three for 115 soon after lunch Bradman again joined Kippax. The partnership began watchfully against Larwood, who earlier had Morgan caught behind by Ames for 18. He was accurate and fast. The pair saw him off, then slipped up a gear and wore down Tate, Hammond, Freeman and Leyland. England's hopes of a strong psychological victory faded as the two batsmen took control.

For the first time, Bradman dominated the partnership. He reached 50 in 65 minutes and took only 128 minutes to pass his century. This superb innings made the selectors sigh with relief. At last one of their prospects had given them a solid reason for picking him. He was driving with certainty and aggression on both sides of the wicket and he was attacking the slower bowlers with confidence. But above all it was his temperament they loved. The more discerning among the MCC tourists agreed.

'Most of us realised that here was a batsman,' Hammond noted.

'Young Bradman looked as if he could stay for ever. None of our bowlers could do any more than feed him runs that day.'

Here was a batsman who could have put up the shutters and played for 60 or 70 not out to give himself a more than respectable double for the match. Instead he had gone after the bowling until he had all but obliterated it. Bradman's name was pencilled in to the list of fourteen from whom the Test side would be chosen.

Kippax also passed a hundred and with less than an hour to go the game was dead. Chapman put his bowlers out to pasture and brought on Jardine, Hendren and Sutcliffe to roll their arms over. Bradman and Kippax duly played out time, with NSW finishing at three for 364 — still 21 short of the England first innings total. The unbroken partnership produced 249 of which Bradman scored 132 and Kippax 136. Bradman hit 14 fours and batted 156 minutes. His tally for the match was 229 and only once out, marginally more than Hammond's 225.

The apprentice had become the master. The England team kept their appreciation of what they had seen among themselves. There was no point in letting the Australian selectors know their fears or in giving this confident lad any more to smile about. But they must have realised that Bradman was on the threshold of a brilliant international career.

ENCOUNTER OF A SECOND KIND

Bradman was selected for an Australian XI to play the MCC on 16 November, which was expected to sort out problems for the Australian selectors, who were yet to decide on the final twelve for the First Test. The touring team rested both Chapman and Hammond and Jack White captained the side, which included the medium-pacer George Geary.

The Australian XI batted first and lost Richardson (24) and his fellow South Australian Gordon Harris (19) to the unusual combination of White's slow guile and Larwood's class speed. Jackson came in for his third attempt to prove himself, only to be unsettled by

Larwood who soon dismissed him for 14. Three efforts for no really strong impression were marked down against the dasher. Andrews batted well for 39 before White deceived him with a quicker one.

This brought Bradman in at four for 101. Larwood was on for a second spell and bowling fast — while not quite 'slipping himself'. He held no terrors for the new man, who played him with ease. But White bottled him up for an hour with a display of the spinner's art such as Bradman had never experienced.

'It was a real education,' Bradman said. 'He was a very, very good slow bowler of a type I'd not encountered before. He always tantalised and teased. White would toss it up and make it dip in. I watched him very carefully indeed.'

The opposition also had more time to assess Bradman again, especially now that he was a fair chance to make the Test XI. He gave them plenty to look at, but apart from taking to Larwood, he was unable to repeat his dominating performance for NSW. This time they saw Bradman the fighter, the defender, the watcher. On a difficult wicket and against White, a world-class slow left-armer, he took a painful — for him — seventy-seven minutes to reach 20 and went on to a top score of 58 not out while wickets fell cheaply around him. His fifty — in 165 minutes — was the slowest he had ever made, and harvested at about one-third the rate of his forceful last innings for NSW. His copybook defence was matched by a steely concentration lasting 200 minutes in all. The only player he attacked was Larwood, of whom he had had the better now in two games.

The tourists had now fielded to him when in both attacking and defensive mood for eight hours for 277 runs and one dismissal, and that to a ball that probably no-one on either side could have played. It was clear Bradman would not surrender his wicket to another country in an international match without a real fight for supremacy. Hammond's judgement that he looked a nervous 'boy' may have been accurate. But appearance belied a cool interior that would not be challenged in any situation.

Seasoned observers began to speak out in support of Bradman for a Test spot. Charlie Macartney watched the 58 not out and handed him a Test locker. English writer Sydney Southerton looked far into his crystal ball. He called Bradman 'Australia's brightest new star', and predicted he would 'make his mark on English wickets in future tours'. It was the first time anyone had placed him in front of Archie Jackson, who until the last two weeks had been everyone's first new twinkle in the firmament.

The Australian XI scored 231. Tate's three for 38 off 16.7 overs, and White's three for 47 off twenty-eight showed that the host side was nowhere near mastering these skilful practitioners. Larwood's figures of three for 80 off eighteen overs were blemished by Bradman's controlled assault on him. The bowler had let himself go for a few overs but was yet to 'slip himself' for a really savage spell.

Hobbs came in to open for the MCC and Bradman saw him for the first time. He made 58 and gave onlookers time to assess the player who was judged by many to be the greatest cricketer ever after W. G. Grace. 'He was past his best when I saw him first,' Bradman remarked. 'Yet he could still deliver the range of strokes, the skills and the timing.'

England batted evenly for 357 with Mead (58) and Tyldesley (69) making bids for a Test berth. Nothling put his hand up for a place in Australia's Test side with three for 61 off nineteen overs. The Australian XI's bats again performed ordinarily, collecting 243 in the second innings. Harris hit a solid 56, and Jackson, more subdued than normal, finally managed to pass fifty against the tourists, eventually being caught behind off Tate for 61. Bradman also fell victim — LBW — to a slower one from Tate for just 18. England, with Hobbs (67 not out) leading the way, then wrapped up the match by scoring two for 118.

At the end of the game the Australian selectors scratched their heads. Jackson or Bradman? Bradman was in front for two reasons. First, he had now performed better against the tourists so far with 295 at an average of 147.5 in four innings, whereas Jackson had only 119 at 29.7. Bradman had also scored close to 600 first-class runs at 85 for the season. He could not have done any more in his bid for selection, and he rested easy knowing it. Second, his defence was better than Jackson's.

The positive aspect for the selectors was that they had two more than promising youngsters who sooner or later could clearly both make it to the top.

Bradman was aware that his youth and inexperience were against him. The selectors were not keen on the young, but if they did take the plunge on them they did not want to see them devoured either. A premature chance against such a strong English side could set a player back years, or see him banished from the Test scene forever. Some on the panel would push for a player of the vintage and experience of Kelleway (39), Jack Ryder (39), Grimmett (36), Blackie (46) and Ironmonger (45). These aging stars were not pretty to watch in the field, but they knew their stuff bowling and batting in the Test arena. On the other hand, there was a clear chance to be daring and throw in a Jackson, or a Bradman, or even a young all-rounder like Victoria's Ted a'Beckett.

The dilemma about youth and experience dominated the selectors' deliberations on the evening of Monday 19 November after the third day's play in the Australian XI v MCC game. They couldn't make up their minds. Sydney radio station 2FC said it would announce the team at 9 p.m. Bradman sat by the radio with the Pearces, at whose home he was living, at the appointed hour. But then an announcer said the selectors were still 'deadlocked'. Bradman had more cricket the next day in the MCC match so he prepared for bed. He thought he would have to wait until the next day to hear or read the news. The radio was still on in the living room when Bradman went to bed. He was just settling down to sleep when he heard an announcer come on and say:

'At last we can tell you the composition of the Australian Test side to play the MCC at Brisbane on 30 November. The players, in alphabetical order, are: D. G. Bradman; J. M. Gregory; C. V. Grimmett . . .'

Bradman didn't get out of bed to accept congratulations from the Pearces, who were more excited than he was. He simply shut his eyes and went to sleep. To him, it was not a dream. It was the fulfilment of an ambitious goal, nevertheless one he believed he could achieve.

8

GROUNDING IN DISASTER

There is something special about a batsman's first ever
appearance in a Test. It's the hope, the naivety in us all, which
wishes and prays that the newcomer, in his own naivety, will
ignore his lack of experience at the top level and bat, carefree,
as if against children. That is the way it began with The Don.
— SUMNER REED, WRITER

FOR GLORY, NOT MONEY

A telegram next morning from W. H. Jeanes, secretary of the
Australian Board of Control, gave substance to the report
Bradman had heard over the air the previous night: 'Confirm your
selection in 12 from whom first Test team will be chosen . . . necessary arrive Brisbane twentyseventh letter following.'

The letter informed Bradman that he would receive a match fee
of £30, his rail fares and thirty shillings a day expenses. He had to
apply for his travel expenses, and make his own arrangements for
accommodation. Though he did not dwell on it at the time, it also
underlined the fact that he could never rely on cricket or any sport
for a living. He competed for enjoyment and achievement, not
money. That, in his mind, would have to come from a regular job.
Bradman was conscious of the fact that he was not qualified as a

82

lawyer or accountant. He would be on the lookout for a future other than cricket. But for the moment, the thrill of reaching the pinnacle of his chosen sport dominated his thoughts.

On arriving in Brisbane, Bradman came under the media circus spotlight for the first time at the national level. As the designated team 'baby', especially in a group of players some of whom were nudging forty or more, reporters and photographers wanted him. Newspaper artists had a field day capturing his calm, determined manner and cheeky grin in sharp but sympathetic caricature, framed by his fashionably upturned shirt collar.

Bradman took it all in his stride, handling the interviews and answering questions clearly and concisely. As with his cricket, there was no flamboyance or bombast about him, but just an air of natural confidence with a hint of underlying humour in his quick, straightforward responses.

A DEBUT TO REMEMBER

England won the toss at the Exhibition Ground on Friday 30 November and batted in typically humid Brisbane weather. Hobbs and Sutcliffe started well, as was their habit. Bradman got over any first-game nerves early in the piece with his brilliant fielding. He saved plenty at mid-off, and his throwing had the crowd hailing him as a champion long before they saw him bat, as he made many of his older colleagues look like dodderers in the field.

At 85, Sutcliffe fell to a change of pace from Gregory and was caught by Ponsford at cover for 38. Ten minutes later, Hobbs, who had missed seeing Hammond run out against NSW, tried for a third run as Bradman gave chase through the covers and picked up. Hobbs' aging legs pumped hard as the long, flat throw flew in over the stumps and beat the batsman. The whole touring party scribbled mental notes: Don't run on this man's arm, even if he's on the fence.

The crowd was ecstatic. Gregory's maturity had taken the first wicket, but youth had brought the second. The wily Grimmett lifted their hopes by sweetly trapping Mead LBW for 8. England was three for 103, and the crowd delirious. Hammond and Jardine, however, steadied the situation until Gregory had Hammond caught by Woodfull for 44 at 161. Jardine was in a defensive mood, which riled the spectators until Ironmonger caused him to misjudge the flight and had him caught by Woodfull for a laborious 35 at 217. Hendren, in good touch, was joined by captain Chapman and they lifted the tempo considerably and took England to five for 272 at the close. Chapman was 39 not out and Hendren 52 not out.

At 291 on the next day — Saturday 1 December — Chapman (50) became Gregory's third and Australia's sixth victim. But England moved steadily on with everyone contributing to a big tally. At lunch they were seven for 366, with Hendren on 80 and Larwood, the surprise, on 27. Australia had tried to keep the latter on strike, but he played everyone with ease and polish. It was Larwood (70 off 132 balls), more than the patient Hendren, who engineered England's big score. However, Hendren, who eventually fell to Ironmonger for 169, faced 314 balls, which showed he certainly had not plodded. But he was made to look slow because each of his partners outscored him by facing more deliveries than he did.

Near the end of England's long innings towards the end of the second day, Gregory fell heavily attempting a catch, damaging an already worn knee cartilage. He finished with three for 142 from forty-one overs. Grimmett's figures were even less flattering at three for 167 from forty. Only Ironmonger with two for 79 off 44.3 overs had a respectable return out of England's prolonged 521.

Larwood was in devastating form when he bowled at the Australians in the last hour, ripping through their top order to snare Woodfull for a duck, Ponsford for 2, and the solemn Kelleway for 8 — all three clean-bowled. Tate chimed in and caught and bowled Kippax for 16. Australia was in disarray at four for 44 at the close. Gregory added to its woes by limping into the dressing room after treatment on his injured knee to announce with tears in his eyes: 'Boys, I'm through, I've played my last game.'

Bradman was saddened. He regarded the New South Welshman as a 'magnetic personality' whether fielding (thirty Test catches), bowling (seventy wickets at 33.77) or in his hard-hitting batting (941 runs at 34.85). Yet the show had to go on.

When play resumed on Monday after the Sabbath rest-day, Bradman sat in the pavilion watching the skipper Jack Ryder and lanky all-rounder 'Stork' Hendry face the terror of Larwood and the guile of Tate and Hammond. Even so, he would admit only to slight apprehension. It was, after all, essentially a matter of bat versus ball. The opposition could only bowl at him when he reached the centre of the oval. No matter how much speed Larwood was generating, or spin and flight White was imparting, they could only deliver one ball at a time.

'It was the waiting for the start that was hard to take,' he said, 'but not the actual playing. Once the game got under way, I was fine. I couldn't wait to bat. I never suffered from stage-fright. The bigger the occasion, the tenser the atmosphere, the more I liked the game. It just happened to be part of my make-up.'

Hendry was trapped LBW by Larwood for 30. With the score at 71 for five and Australia 450 behind, Don Bradman strode out, with a marginal tingle in his spine. The hopes of people following the game across the nation went with him. He was the untried novice of the national team. He also represented youth in a side of aging sportsmen, even by cricket's standards at the time.

The Brisbane crowd gave him a hopeful rather than inspirational reception. Even after his impressive recent performances, with half the side out and such a massive deficit, the best that could be expected from this newcomer to the Test arena would be a respectable fifty. A hundred was too much to ask of him.

England was ready for him. A team meeting before the game decided that Bradman was a chancer who could be dismissed with careful planning. Tate noted that he 'played across the line a lot' in the MCC v Australian XI match when he had got him LBW cheaply in the second innings. He would keep it up and on the stumps. Larwood thought his stance left him vulnerable to a fast yorker on off-stump. He would force him back with a few short ones, and then rip one in under his guard. Captain Chapman suggested his tendency to play the odd cross-bat stroke would induce catches behind the wicket. Hammond was instructed to cramp him outside the off with out-swingers aiming for an edge into the slips. White planned to entice him down the wicket, where he was apt to come at any opportunity, seeking to beat him with flight for a stumping or return catch from a mistimed stroke.

Larwood had one ball to bowl in his fifth over when Bradman arrived at the wicket. The new boy pushed carefully forward and played it safely away. Chapman then surprised by taking Larwood off, but he had seen how the 'colt', as the English referred to him, played even express pace without any fear in the two Sydney games when Bradman had taken to the champion speedster with such relish.

It appeared the English skipper had studied him well, for not much got through Chapman's well-set field. Tate pinned Bradman down with line and length and sent down twenty-four deliveries for one scoring shot. Bradman, mindful of that LBW dismissal in the previous encounter with Tate, drove at him once for a streaky leg-side boundary. Ryder was playing tentatively at the other end, but not penetrating the field either.

Hammond was brought on. Bradman remembered the belting he had received from him in the NSW game. That score had more or less been settled by Bradman's batting in that game. But this was another, higher contest. Earlier, Hammond had tied up one end for an economical 1.5 runs an over while Larwood did his damage at the other.

Bradman played the first three balls watchfully. Then he cut, drove and pulled three successive balls to the boundary. The crowd were alight for the first time in the match. Hammond, irked by such irreverent behaviour, finished the over with a bouncer. It was a long time since he had been slammed for three fours in a row at first-class level.

However, Bradman's bravado was short-lived. Tate beat him with a slower ball and trapped him LBW again, and once more at 18. Bradman had lasted just thirty-three minutes. He had looked more at ease and aggressive than any other Australian, but this was small compensation for himself and his team. He had not delivered the big innings he was hoping for just when it was needed.

As Bradman walked off the field, the news was flashed across the nation over the radio. In Melbourne, scores were posted outside the offices of *The Herald* in Flinders Street. In Sydney, miniature cricket-fields had been built outside *The Sun*'s offices in Martin Place, and on a board hanging from a building in Elizabeth Street facing Hyde Park. Fielders, bowlers, ball and batsmen were represented by white markers. Reporters at the ground kept phone lines open so the markers could be moved in response to each stroke, and scores changed. Thousands gathered each day to watch the ball-by-ball diagram as moves were made as if on a chess board.

When Bradman's marker was removed there was a loud groan from the onlookers. According to writer Philip Lindsay, they then fell into a 'terrible silence of despair'.

And so did Australia. Apart from stubborn resistance from Ryder (33), the tail was docked, leaving a paltry score of 122. Larwood was at his blistering best with six for 38 off 14.4 overs, supported by Tate with three for 50. Australia expected to follow on 399 behind, but Chapman ultra-cautiously decided to bat again. The crowd was furious, but press observers were split in their opinions. Some said he was 'killing' the game; others thought him justified, given Australia's strong batting line-up, the problem England had with just four front-line bowlers, the fact that the Test had no time limit and the uncertainty of the Brisbane weather. There was also the debatable argument that if Australia managed to score 500 and it rained, England might be caught on a wet wicket, drying into a 'sticky'. That would mean a score of 100 would be tough.

Australia trudged onto the field, one front-line bowler in Gregory short and demoralised by the state of the game. Some overnight rain on the uncovered wicket had created a difficult strip so Ryder opted for spin early. Soon Grimmett and Ironmonger were bowling in tandem and causing concern.

Grimmett struck first, trapping Hobbs (11) with one that straightened. Mead joined Sutcliffe and played with more flair than in the first innings. Ironmonger had Sutcliffe caught for 32 at 69, but there was little cheer in the Aussie camp. England were 468 ahead and eight in hand. The slim chance of a sensational breakthrough by the spinners subsided with the improved weather. Even the spirit of youth faded as Bradman missed two catches he would normally have held.

At the close on day three, England was two for 103. On the fourth day, after a little rain overnight, they handled the damp pitch skilfully until it dried out again in the afternoon, with everyone making a contribution. Hammond (28) was useful, Mead (72) effective, Jardine (65 not out) stolid, Hendren (45) commanding, Chapman (28) superfluous, and Tate (20) vigorous. Larwood (37) again showed he could wield the willow well, taking his tally for the match to 107 to give him a fine double.

England closed, for the first time ever in a Test in Australia, at eight for 342 at 5 p.m. Grimmett was the pick of the bowlers with six for 131 off 44.1 overs, while Ironmonger was helpful though not as penetrating with two for 85 off fifty overs.

When Australia batted again, Larwood beat Ponsford with sheer pace and had him caught behind for 6. It drove home the harsh reality of Ashes Tests. A year earlier the Victorian champion had been the toast of the cricketing world with his record-breaking 437 in a State game, and had been in prolific form ever since. But in a big contest against England he would have settled for a humble hundred in exchange for that record and his previous 429 thrown in.

Heavy rain fell during the fourth night and a hot sun in the morning turned it into the worst possible 'sticky', which in essence was a pitch predictable only in its unpredictability — slow, but turning considerably with the ball 'popping' disconcertingly at irregular heights. Orthodox techniques went out the window and experience became paramount. The best idea was to push forward and try to 'read' every ball off the deck, killing it before it bounced. Pads were important, and the bat became an instrument for possible deflections rather than a weapon against the ball, which took on demon qualities, particularly in the hands of finger-spinners.

Australia resumed on the fifth-day death-trap at one for 25, with a target of 742 to win and now two batsmen short. Kelleway added to the home side's woes by developing ptomaine poisoning and joined Gregory as a spectator for the rest of the game.

Chapman was tempted to open with White and Tate, but after his brilliance in the first innings, Larwood could hardly be denied first use of the ball. Kippax joined Woodfull, who was in his element defending. But his partner was uncomfortable against Larwood's speed. At 33 the bowler struck again towards the end of a spell, when he got one to sit up on the dangerous wicket and Kippax (15) punched a catch back to him. Larwood's two for 30 off seven overs gave him match figures of eight for 62.

Tate was bowling steadily at the other end without success until White came on to replace Larwood and had Hendry caught for 6. One run later Tate struck and removed Ryder for 1. Australia was now four for 47 and in reality six for 47 without Gregory and Kelleway.

Bradman came in for his first experience on a gluepot. He had made 13 eleven months earlier on a mild sticky in a Shield game against Queensland, but this was far worse. His naivety and self-confidence, however, caused him to look on the positive side. He had faced White in a rear-guard action two weeks earlier and had won the contest. Coupled with that, Woodfull was somehow lasting with his grit and improvised defensive methods.

Bradman took his customary middle and leg and examined the pitch, then settled over the bat. White pushed the first one up to him. Bradman nudged it to the on and scampered through for one. The crowd cheered. Woodfull the watchful jerked, pushed, and padded his way through the rest of the over. This gave Bradman the strike next over to Tate, who was hungry for wickets on a pitch considered perfect for spinners. He particularly wanted Bradman's again. Bradman saw the over out, but then found himself down the other end to face White.

The wily spinner crowded more fieldsmen around the bat and bowled two balls with a low, fast trajectory, and then slowed one up through the air with a clever change of pace. Bradman was deceived as he pushed forward and gave an easy catch to silly mid-off. The crowd gasped. The Englishmen moved leisurely towards each other as Bradman departed for one, the game as good as over. 'I wanted him,' Tate jokingly said to White. 'He was my rabbit.' Bradman did not hear the remark, but it was reported to him later.

Australia collapsed for 66, with Woodfull carrying his bat for a courageous 30 not out, leaving it 675 runs short — the biggest losing margin in history. White finished with the rare figures of four for 7 off 6.3 overs, well supported by Tate, who took three for 26 off eleven.

In Martin Place, the crowd dispersed in disappointment, some even in disgust. The post mortem soon began on Bradman. Team-mate Kelleway, perhaps concerned with his own position, declared imprudently after the game that Bradman was 'not up to Test standard'. Former supporters such as A. G. Moyes expressed second thoughts in press articles that the four wise selectors were sure to read. It was a moment when only the individual himself could judge his worth, when many around him were devaluing it, despite the circumstances.

9

MANSERVANT EXTRAORDINAIRE

Bradman as a young man had the magic to bring crowds pouring back to the game — probably more so than any other cricketer in the history of the game.
— RICHIE BENAUD, FORMER AUSTRALIAN CAPTAIN

DRINK-WAITER

Jack Ryder met Bradman in the dressing room on the first morning of the Second Test in Sydney on 14 December 1928 and told him he would be twelfth man. In effect, he had been made the scapegoat for a team which had featured seven other failures. Only Grimmett with match figures of nine for 198, Ironmonger and Woodfull could point to a good or passable effort. Bradman had not performed worse than anyone else with the bat overall, but the selectors were loath to let the experienced players go. They selected thirteen for Sydney. The average age of the other twelve was thirty-five with the next 'youngest' after Bradman being Nothling and Ponsford, both twenty-eight.

The consensus around the selectors' table was that despite the unprecedented defeat, there was no need to panic. The older players might still come good. It was too early to jettison experience and thereby admit they'd been wrong before. But the panel was not unanimous. They became deadlocked over whether or not Bradman would play. New South Wales's Warren Bardsley wanted to give him a second chance. So did South Australia's Dr Dolling. However, Bean from Victoria and Hutcheon from Queensland wanted him out. They cited his two dropped catches as the reason. Dolling finally relented and left Bardsley one-out in support of Bradman.

So acrimonious and divided was the discussion that Aubrey Oxlade, chairman of the Board of Control, the governing body of cricket in Australia at the time, publicly called for an odd number of selectors so that a majority decision could be reached. The eventual relegation of Bradman defied public opinion, a problem that Australian selectors had never before faced to the same degree.

He was already something of a national idol. His support was not confined to Sydney or New South Wales. People everywhere sensed something in his nerveless demeanour and the way he went about destroying the bowling — here was a champion in the making at a time when the country was desperate for heroes. Bradman, they felt, should be given 'a go'. Needless to say, they would have to wait before he got it.

Australia's changes for the thirteen-man squad were Andrews, Richardson and Blackie for Oxenham (twelfth man in the First Test), Kelleway, who was still ill, and Gregory. Andrews missed out on the final twelve. On paper the bowlers looked weak, and the batting suspect.

Ryder won the toss and batted. Woodfull played superbly against Larwood again at his best and fastest, but Richardson, who had scored a double century for South Australia against England earlier on the tour, was always under pressure. They were partners until Larwood clean-bowled Richardson's off-stump for twenty-seven with the score at fifty-one. It started a rot. Kippax (9) was unluckily bowled off his legs, then Larwood broke Ponsford's wrist — and Australia's resolve — forcing him off the field and out of the game for 5. Geary chipped in to get rid of Ryder (25) and the stubborn Hendry (37). Plucky Oldfield (41 not out) played well and enabled the innings to struggle to 253 early on the second morning, Saturday, in front of 58,456 people — the biggest crowd ever to watch a cricket match anywhere. On the Hill people were stacked together like upright proverbial sardines.

Geary took the bowling honours with five for 35 off eighteen overs, ably supported by Larwood with three for 77 off 26.2.

Australia's paucity in the bowling department was shown by the fact that Grimmett opened with his slow leg-breaks, to be supported by Ironmonger and Blackie. Only Nothling delivered speed and was unable to make a breakthrough. When Ironmonger removed Sutcliffe, Hammond came to the wicket feeling that he had never had a better opportunity in his Test career. The bowling was relatively weak. The wicket was playing true. He knew that if he were watchful against the abundant slow stuff, which was not extracting much spin, the odds were that he could get something like his 225 at Sydney a few weeks earlier. He proceeded to stroke the ball forcefully, with the timing of a master batsman at the top of his form.

Poor light forced the players off in the afternoon and offered an opportunity to honour Jack Hobbs, who was to turn forty-six the next day, Sunday, when there would be no play. A Sydney paper had organised a public 'shilling appeal' for a suitable gift for the great player, which former Australian captain M. A. (Monty) Noble presented to him in front of the Members' Stand. The crowd joined in singing 'For He's a Jolly Good Fellow' and gave him a hearty three cheers. Hobbs was touched by the tribute, and added only six runs after the break before being stumped by Oldfield off Grimmett.

Hammond now seemed more determined than ever on a big innings. With his new partner, Jardine, content to hold an end up, when play resumed on the Monday he continued on his stately way. But with the score at 148, he pushed Blackie for what seemed an easy single in the covers, only to have the bowler, showing an agility which belied his age, pick up on his follow-through and throw the wicket down at the batsman's end. It just beat Jardine (28), who strode off without a flicker on his patrician visage despite the rousing farewell from the mob on the Hill. Australian crowds resented his stiff-backed air and barracked him unmercifully throughout the tour. In turn, Jardine made no secret of his disdain for these impolite, irreverent larrikins.

Next man in was Hendren, a real crowd-pleaser who continued where he had left off in Brisbane with a forceful 74 before Blackie had him caught. England was 293 for four and looked like repeating its performance in the previous Test, except that this effort promised even more with Hammond in such command. He gave a difficult caught-and-bowled chance to Ryder at 148 and survived a near-stumping at 183, but otherwise moved on relentlessly, with some glorious cover drives.

Bradman was on as a substitute for the stricken Ponsford and revelling in the chance to show that he was worth his spot for his fielding despite catching blemishes in the First Test.

'I enjoyed it,' he recalled, 'I was never a great catch, but had ability in the field. I had confidence in my outcricket and that allowed me to have fun out there . . . I have heard of other players being often concerned when the ball came their way. I can't say I felt that way. On the contrary. I loved it.'

Other players disputed his self-deprecating assessment of his catching, and all said he was a great all-round fieldsman who held some screaming chances.

Having now fielded to big innings by Ponsford, Woodfull and Hammond (twice), Bradman was encouraged to do the same, for in his short career he had himself demonstrated a penchant for the knock that went on. Mammoth performances were in vogue in the late 1920s. They needed concentration and the capacity to wear the opposition down until they became demoralised. Bradman had shown those characteristics in the bush, and he was hungry for the chance to display them in the big time, but would have to wait until his next Shield innings or a return to the Test side. For now, he was learning the responsibilities of being manservant for the team. Bradman passed messages, carried drinks, and fetched gloves, forgotten protectors, pullovers, bandages and caps with dignity and good humour.

At the close of the fourth day, England was five for 420 with Hammond 201 not out, his first Test double century and his second of the tour, which made him without doubt the pre-eminent player of the season so far, starting with his 145 against Western Australia in Perth in late October. Now he was conscious of his compatriot Reg Foster's record of 287 on the same ground in 1903. He reached 251 and looked set for 300 when Ironmonger tied him up for two overs until he played a ball onto his stumps. It was a sad end to one of the finest innings in Test cricket, which enabled England to amass 636. Only Blackie with four for 148 from fifty-nine overs had respectable bowling figures.

Australia went in again late in the day, losing Richardson for a duck — caught by Hendren off Tate. Hendry joined Woodfull for the best Australian partnership so far, totalling 215. In response, Tate, Geary and Larwood resorted to 'leg theory', pitching on or outside leg stump with two short legs, a long leg and a mid-on, and only one slip. It was negative and ugly to watch, and also ineffectual against these two batsmen, who thrived on leg-side shots.

Two former respected Australian captains were compelled to comment. Warwick Armstrong didn't like what he saw, especially from Larwood. If England persisted with leg theory, he wrote, it would run the 'risk of unpopularity in Australia'. He singled Larwood out for special mention in a piece for a London paper:

> *He appeared to be bowling deliberately at the batsmen. He has great pace and could afford not to bowl at the man. If he continued these tactics the spectators here might think there are more sporting ways of getting results, and it would be a pity if a player like Larwood ran the risk of unpopularity when he has the talent to send the ball up differently.*

Monty Noble was even more to the point:

> *Despite his direct method of attack on the wicket, at times he is not over-particular where the ball goes, delivering it well outside the off-stump, outside the leg-stump, or direct to the body or head. The working of this trap is easily discernible from the pavilion, for a man is always placed in a position to bring about the batsman's*

95

downfall in the case of a mishit. It may be that this method is adopted to impress the faint-hearted with the possibility of injury, and so cause them to draw away or nibble at the ball instead of boldly facing it with the bat well in front of the body or allowing the bumpy ones to pass harmlessly over the wicket.

Noble, however, also thought Larwood's tactics would prove 'too expensive to be persevered with'. This was accurate then, because Larwood and Co only resorted to it when the batsmen were on top. It was seen as just another strategy for breaking a partnership. It was not used at the start of an innings to intimidate openers or crash through a number three. In other words, leg theory was only used in reaction to circumstances. It seemed to have little effect on Hendry and Woodfull.

Just before tea, Tate got Hendry LBW for 112. After tea, Woodfull ran himself out and put Australia in jeopardy at three for 234. Kippax (10) also went LBW to Tate twelve runs later. Ryder resisted the only way he knew by going after the bowling and spreadeagling the field. England looked rattled and Australia reached four for 329 at stumps.

Next morning, Larwood began by loosening up with the first five balls of military medium. Then he let one rip short. Ryder, always ready for the challenge, attempted to hook and only succeeded in lobbing an easy catch to Chapman at square leg. Tate then dismissed Oldfield LBW, and Australia crumbled to be all out for 397, with only Nothling showing any resistance until he was run out for 44.

Chapman sent in his tail-enders to polish off the 16 needed, which they duly did with the loss of Geary for 8 and Tate for 4, the latter caught by Bradman at mid-off. England's win by eight wickets widened the gap created by the First Test. The selectors came under heavy fire. The press and public demanded that they stop rearranging the old deck chairs on the *Titanic*. It was time to give youth a serious chance.

10

REDEMPTION

Don Bradman's reception was the greatest I have heard on any cricket field. The crowd cheered for five minutes. We just couldn't go on with the game.
— HAROLD LARWOOD ON THE CROWD RESPONSE TO BRADMAN'S INITIAL TEST CENTURY AT MELBOURNE, JANUARY 1929

THE RETURN

Bradman had two chances to regain his place in the Test XI in a big State game against Victoria on the MCG on 22–27 December, finishing just two days before the Third Test. 'Stork' Hendry dismissed him for 1 in the first innings, leaving Bradman with a run of failures — 18, 18, 1 and 1. On his form to date that summer of 1928–29, he was due for a recovery and it came at the death — when he notched a brilliant 71 not out in 103 minutes on the last day of the game.

The selectors could not ignore his claims for another break, in a vital match which could decide the Ashes. Victorian selector E. E. Bean was at the game and that innings swung him in support of Bradman. He reported to the panel that his form was convincing and recommended that he be picked because of the confidence he displayed on the hard, bouncing Melbourne wicket.

In effect, Bradman slipped in because of Ponsford's injury. Two young all-rounders, Queensland's Ron Oxenham and Ted a'Beckett of Victoria, were brought in to strengthen the bowling, which had looked so weak in the first two Tests, and to bolster the batting as well. Nothling (also from Queensland) and Victoria's Ironmonger were dispensed with, but Vic Richardson was retained.

By chance more than design, the Australian team now had a healthier blend of youth and experience and the fielding began to challenge England's, which had so far been much superior. The twenty-one-year-old a'Beckett, an Australian Rules footballer during the winter, brought his superb all-round athletic skills to the Australian side, and effectively boosted Australia's previously lamentable fielding by two men, for the discarded 'Dainty' Ironmonger was useless except when bowling.

The chosen team evoked much press comment. Former Test captain Warwick Armstrong showed that he was not afraid to criticise the popular inclusion of Bradman when he remarked on the day before the Test: 'For his batting I would have preferred [Gordon] Harris to Bradman, who will probably be a good player later but, I think, is not a Test player at present.'

Bradman was aware of the comment, but it had little impact on him and only spurred him to do well. 'At that point no-one was to know what was to come,' he commented. 'I was just a youth with an aim to do my best. I had confidence in myself. That's what really mattered.'

On the opening day, Saturday 29 December, Australia won the toss and batted, but had trouble with the fast, unpredictable wicket, a traditional problem on the first morning of a Melbourne Test. Larwood and Tate took advantage of it and removed Richardson (3) and Woodfull (7) by the time the imposing MCG scoreboard had registered 15.

This brought Hendry and Kippax together, the latter virtually on trial for his position after four successive failures — 16, 15, 9 and 10. They steadied the innings until Hendry paid the penalty for backing away from Larwood and was caught by Jardine in the gully, the same fate which had befallen Woodfull. Australia was three for 57, and watching the Ashes fade. However, Ryder came to the wicket and just managed to survive with the chancy Kippax to lunch, taking the score to 63.

The next session was one of the few that belonged to the home team so far in the series and the partnership looked sound with a tea score of three for 158. In Sydney, Ryder had shown that the English bowling could be hit and, encouraged by his vociferous Melbourne fans, he went about the task with similar intent and even better effect.

Kippax, who had also attacked, got his three figures, and salvation, off Larwood, who waited until the appreciative crowd settled down and, sensing Kippax's relief, tore in and bowled him a bouncer. Kippax obliged by hooking it straight into the waiting hands of Hendren on the long-leg fence. Australia was four for 218, the partnership having yielded 161.

The big MCG crowd cheered Kippax all the way to the pavilion. Then the stadium went dead calm.

'I was in the dressing room with Don,' Ted a'Beckett told a Melbourne reporter after the game. 'There was this eerie drop in the volume, as if someone had shut a window suddenly. I wished him luck and he walked out. Then there was a colossal roar which hit us like a tornado in a wind-tunnel as Bradman became visible to the spectators. I had heard mighty roars in [football] games, but nothing like that spontaneous blast. It was absolutely uplifting to every member of our team.'

Bradman was watchful for two overs from Larwood, and got off the mark with a push to the on-side. Then he cracked the paceman for two fours in three balls and took ten from the over. Bradman saw Larwood off and stayed with Ryder for the last hour when the Victorian reached his hundred. He and Bradman (26 not out) were together at stumps with Australia's score four for 276.

The day's break did Ryder no good and he fell to Tate early on Monday for 112, followed quickly by Oldfield, making Australia six for 287. a'Beckett, the local new boy, joined Bradman and the pair batted doggedly, with Bradman finally reaching his first Test fifty after just on an hour's play, to enthusiastic applause from the crowd. The two novices struggled on until lunch — aided by a smile from Lady Luck for a'Beckett, who was dropped — and swung the game back in Australia's favour.

Although they had only added fifty to the break, six for 337 looked healthy and 400 or more seemed a real possibility. Bradman was 60 not out, a'Beckett 20.

A decent tally appeared even more likely until Hammond came on, with the score at 373. Bradman, remembering his dominance of the all-rounder in their three encounters so far, launched into him and took 12 off ten balls. Three deliveries later, however, he played over a yorker and was bowled for 79. He had batted for 194 minutes and hit nine fours, facing 223 balls. His rate was just twenty-four runs an hour, but statistics added up to just one measurable point. Bradman had arrived at Test level. He had laid the foundations of an illustrious career.

HAMMOND'S HAMMERING

Ted a'Beckett's fighting knock of 42 was over soon after when he became adventurous against White and edged one to keeper Duckworth. With the back of the batting broken, England wrapped up the innings at 397 — the same score as Australia had made in the last innings of the previous match. Geary had the best figures with three for 83 off 31.5 overs. Larwood took three for 127 off thirty-seven and Tate demonstrated his great accuracy with two for 87 off forty-six overs, including seventeen maidens.

It seemed that midway through the series the home team had steadied, at least in the batting department. With a little more resolve from the bowlers and fieldsmen Australia could yet challenge the visitors.

England began well in the last hour of day two, and none of the attack looked like penetrating Hobbs and Sutcliffe. Then the medium-paced a'Beckett bent his back with a short, wide ball which Hobbs (20) slashed at and nicked to Oldfield. Hammond came in to join Sutcliffe instead of Jardine and England were one for 47 at stumps.

New Year's Day, 1929, began strongly for England, and Hammond looked ominous against the substandard opposition, Grimmett excepted. In Sydney Hammond had played the cover drive to perfection mainly off the front foot. Here he adapted to the slower but more pronounced bounce on the Melbourne wicket by concentrating on back-foot drives, making use of his powerful wrists and forearms to force the ball through both sides of the field in a wide arc from point to mid-wicket, a difficult shot for all but the best batsmen to master. Hammond also signalled to the opposition and spectators that another grand total was in the offing. The hook was out, and so was any shot that put the ball in the air. Bradman was fielding to many of these skimming strokes, and it reinforced a point he already appreciated: the really big innings needed total concentration and discipline.

At 161, in the middle of the afternoon session, Sutcliffe, who had laboured long, was bowled by Blackie for 58. Hendren looked menacing until he hooked a ball face-high and very hard at a'Beckett, who held a beauty. But England was still travelling well with three for 201 and clearly heading for another big one. Chapman still kept the defensive Jardine back and came in next himself, obviously intent on forcing the pace, but in one rush of blood too many was also bowled by Blackie for 24 at 241.

Jardine finally arrived at the crease for another tedious display, taking most of the strike as he could see that Hammond was tiring as he moved through 150. The pair were still there at the close, with England on four for 312 and set to take the lead around lunch-time on day four.

Early that morning Hammond stroked a ball through the covers for two and another superb 200, with England now thirty-five short and still only four down. But next ball from Blackie, he forgot his golden rule of nothing up, and marginally lifted a powerful on-drive, only to see the athletic a'Beckett fling himself horizontal at full stretch for the catch of the season. It took such a feat to tilt the game and perhaps the series. Hammond had now hit two successive Test double centuries, and three more in first-class games for the season. His dominance of the memorable Australian summer was almost complete.

Only Jardine stood between the home side and a chance to hold sway as England's wickets tumbled. Gradually, however, they managed to edge past 397. Jardine then lashed out for four fours in two overs off Blackie, but the veteran spinner struck back to claim him caught and bowled for 62, followed by Larwood (0) the same way. Grimmett chimed in for the quick wickets of Geary and Tate, Blackie bowled Duckworth and England was all out for 417, just 20 ahead. Blackie took the bowling honours with six for 94 off forty-four overs with thirteen maidens, supported by Grimmett with two for 114 from fifty-five overs with fourteen maidens.

Australia was now in with more than a chance if it could just bat as well in its second dig as it had in the first. Richardson demonstrated his weakness against Larwood's speed again and was bowled for 5. Then Hendry held up any possible Larwood onslaught, while Woodfull got into gear until the score was 60, when White wove one past Hendry and had him stumped for 12. Australia was just 40 ahead with two down.

Kippax the cautious and Woodfull the watchful eased the home team to 118 at stumps without further loss. The lead was nearly a hundred and with eight wickets in hand, the game was finely balanced but favouring Australia.

BRADMAN, FIRST BLOOD

The fifth day, 3 January, was a scorcher that only Melbourne could provide with a hot northerly wind adding to the humidity. It was better to be batting than fielding. Kippax and Woodfull moved on, intent on saving their energy and sapping that of the English. At 138, Tate got one to shoot under Kippax's bat and take his off-stump for 41. Ryder came in and dabbed 5 in two balls before being bowled by Geary. At 143 for four the game had swung back to the tourists.

In came Bradman to another reception several decibels higher than for any other player. However, the little man with the big pads seemed oblivious to the noise, and perhaps the expectations. The crowd was conferring hero status upon him before he'd really earned it. Bradman has little recollection of that event of nearly seventy years ago, but explained his apparent calm and lack of tension by 'the confidence I had in myself'.

Bradman seemed already to have the right qualities to take advantage of the level playing field of Australian life and his chosen sport, compared with the privilege and class-background which so often interfered with attitudes and even selection with the game in Britain. But even if he was another Clem Hill, Victor Trumper or Charlie Macartney, the British remained sceptical about Bradman at this stage of the series. Percy Fender hardly mentioned him in his despatches, except to carp about his perceived flaws and unorthodoxy. The criticism may have been justified, but it was also meant to create psychological doubts in the player himself. If Bradman could be persuaded he was flawed and fallible, if he cut out the audacious shot, or changed his grip or stopped hooking and cutting, then he would be quickly reduced to the field of might-have-beens.

The situation at which he arrived in that second innings of the Third Test was a tough one. He had to bat patiently against accurate professional bowling. Many a player with a competent 70 or 80 to his name in the first knock would relax in the second, content that he had 'done enough' for both his team and further selection. Furthermore, Australia was in front — not by much, but nonetheless ahead.

However, according to Ryder a lead of 118 was not enough. The skipper wanted something around 300 to feel comfortable. He instructed the new man to stay with Woodfull as long as he could, without resorting to fireworks. It was a time to consolidate. Bradman, always the team player, carried out the directive to the letter. Down went the head in copybook back defence.

It came up briefly after just two overs, when Larwood came back on. The speedster was restricted by a pulled tendon in his heel, and Bradman took full advantage of it to punch him through the field and force him out of the attack and off the field. Larwood was limping noticeably as he retired to the pavilion for repairs. It was another minor victory for the beginner in their fifth serious encounter to date.

Bradman and Woodfull had edged the score forward by 30 to 168 for four at the break. Australia was just 148 ahead. After lunch with the crowd swelling to more than 40,000, Bradman put his head down again and stayed with Woodfull who was playing a classic, memorable innings. The opener was essentially a stayer who did everything to minimise his chances of getting out while nudging the score along. He kept his backlift as low as possible, his bottom hand unusually far down the handle, which gave him a rocklike defence but restricted his attacking shots. His cuts, too, were dainty dabs rather than a swordsman's slash. Legside singles predominated on his wagon-wheel. His game this day was just right, for as the Australian score mounted the English wilted under that other enemy, the blistering sun, which some had never experienced.

The partnership began to gather momentum as the heat took its toll. Woodfull reached a century and Australia approached 200. With Larwood injured, Tate and White took the new ball forty-five minutes before tea, and Tate removed Woodfull (105) caught behind. Australia was five for 201, Bradman just 24 not out and the game finely balanced again.

White then swung it back to England with two deceptively gentle balls to Oldfield and a'Beckett, who tried to glide them away but were beaten and bowled. Bradman reached his fifty in 143 minutes. At tea, Australia was 250 for seven, 230 ahead with Oxenham now at the crease.

Tate opened after tea full of fire, but Bradman, taking all the strike to the dangerous stuff, saw him off. With the crowd still growing, he now went on the attack, demonstrating his killer instinct for the first time at this level. The bowlers had put in, and with Larwood missing, they were flagging. Bradman brought out his full array of strokes to pierce the field again and again. Then he and Oxenham began to take audacious singles, and England began to make the odd mistake in the field. Even skipper Chapman, a model all day, let one through his legs, as Bradman moved inexorably towards his hundred. England did everything to stem the run-rate, Geary meandering through one over in eight minutes — a minute a ball.

On 96, at 5.30 p.m. Bradman on-drove a well-flighted dipper from White past Chapman. Jardine had a long run round the boundary as the huge crowd roared and stood as one to watch the race. The batsmen sprinted three as Jardine reached the ball centimetres inside the fence. Bradman looked up and hesitated. Oxenham shouted to him but could not be heard. Jardine heaved his return high as Oxenham waved Bradman through and ran to the bowler's end. He made it with a stretch, with Bradman looking back over his shoulder.

Four all run, and Bradman 100. His second fifty had taken eighty-three minutes.

He was the youngest player ever — at twenty years and four months — to score a Test century and the only other Australian (apart from Ponsford) under twenty-five to do so since the World War. The great Australian gamble — for it was a gamble of judgement after just eleven first-class games — had paid off on a youth who had played his first full season of cricket in the bush only three years earlier.

The tumult that followed could be heard in Collins Street, to be matched in Sydney by several thousand more in Martin Place outside *The Sun*'s office. Hats and umbrellas were hurled in the air, as people clapped and cheered as if they were actually at the ground. Sydney's *Evening News* said the demonstration outside its offices was unprecedented. 'Some pictures on life's canvas are quickly obliterated,' the paper noted extravagantly. 'Others, like this one, are unforgettable.'

Meanwhile, at the MCG, play was held up for minutes as the crowd went wild. 'There was such a demonstration,' Jack Hobbs noted in his diary, 'that we all sat down on the field.'

Oxenham wandered down the wicket to Bradman, who by this time was leaning on his bat after acknowledging the prolonged ovation, and shook his hand. At last, the noise subsided. White got up and walked back to his mark. He was about to turn and bowl when he saw the umpire's arm up, halting his run. Bradman was taking block again. A terrific roar went up as the crowd appreciated this nuance of cricket combat. It was an impudent signal to the opposition that he had no intention of throwing his wicket away. If he could, he would settle in for another hundred in the heat.

Nonetheless, he did not last long. After straight-driving White for four, he cut and hooked Geary to the boundary, breaking his bat on the second shot. There was a delay while a new one was brought out from the dressing-room, and either the interruption or the unfamiliar bat seemed to unsettle him. Almost immediately he was out, edging a ball to Duckworth which he would normally have put away for 4.

Bradman was done at 112, and so to all intents and purposes was England. He had stopped a possible rot in both innings, and in the second had hauled the game around his team's way. Australia was eight for 347 at stumps — a lead of 327, with Oxenham on 39 not out. White had five for 107 off 56.5 overs, with twenty maidens, and was the pick of the England bowlers.

It rained that night and Percy Fender, tucked up in bed at the Windsor Hotel in the city, heard the staccato sound on the roof. 'It was like listening to nails being driven into England's coffin,' he remarked. 'I had seen and played on Australia's wet wickets.'

SUTCLIFFE'S STICKY

The MCG wicket presented a sticky as the rain continued and the next morning bets were hurriedly placed on Australia to win. Some commentators expected Ryder to declare and 'get stuck into' the opposition. But he blundered and batted on when play finally got under way at 12.30 pm. His counterpart, Chapman, fared no better in the tactical stakes by failing to instruct his bowlers to avoid taking wickets. England needed to keep Australia batting for as long as possible to let the wicket dry out and improve. Instead, White bowled Oxenham third ball with no runs added and a few overs later similarly removed Blackie. Australia was all out for 351, leaving England 332 to make. Everyone, including many in the tourists' camp, shook their heads and said 'impossible'. A team score of a hundred would be a brave feat on that sticky dog.

Hobbs and Sutcliffe saw out two overs until lunch, then resumed with the wicket drier but still behaving unpredictably. Hendry dropped a sitter from Hobbs in the slips, in the first over after lunch. But nobody seemed to mind. A chance like that was expected at least every other over. The ball did demon tricks. Most deliveries stopped when they hit the pitch. A few each over popped up head and shoulder high, but the experienced openers took them on the body from pads to shoulder rather than use their bats and give chances.

If the Australians bowled too short, the batsmen had their revenge, for there was the odd occasion when they had time to get into position and hook. Some short balls lobbed even over the keeper's head, but usually didn't reach the boundary as twenty-one extras were logged between lunch and tea.

Ryder crowded the bat to each bowler, but Hobbs and Sutcliffe avoided playing what they didn't have to. If they did play, it was with 'soft hands' and a dead bat. Often they played down the line and missed, dropping the wrists at the last moment as the ball fizzed, spun or popped past. Rarely have two such masterly players put together a finer partnership under such difficult conditions. They lasted until tea, then posted the century partnership in 133 minutes, oddly their first for the tour. Their timing in more ways than one was immaculate.

At 105, Hobbs was given out to a tough LBW decision off Blackie, with the ball hitting the pad questionably high after popping off the deck. Everyone expected to see Hammond stride through the gate, but instead in came the imperious figure of Jardine. Chapman had made up for his early mistake in wrapping up the Aussie tail by heeding Hobbs' advice to send in the best defender in the team. Jardine looked uncomfortable but played with guts as the wicket improved in the afternoon. He managed to stay with Sutcliffe until stumps, with England on one for 171 and 162 runs behind. It had been a phenomenal fighting recovery. The game was once more in the balance. The local illegal bookies had odds favouring the visitors.

The wicket was better on the final morning but there were divots on a good length, which had to be somehow negotiated. Sutcliffe, a professor of such wickets, and Jardine the battler struggled to 199 before Jardine unluckily played on. Then Hammond was in and on the improving strip batted as if England should win easily. At two for 222 at lunch it seemed more likely than not.

When the score was 257, and England had just 75 to win, Hammond jumped down the wicket to Grimmett and jammed down on the ball. It cork-screwed back behind him on the off. Old-field grabbed it half a metre from the stumps and removed the bails. Hammond was run out, not stumped, for 32.

Hendren came in and played his natural game to hit 45 out of a partnership of 61 with the patient yet magnificent Sutcliffe. The Australians were dispirited now in the field, for they knew they had somehow bungled a chance for victory. A game which should have been theirs had slipped through their fingers as embarrassingly as Hendry's dropped dolly in slips off Hobbs.

Sutcliffe finally lost patience after his marathon knock with a wild swing at Grimmett and was trapped LBW for 135. As England was certain to win now, this Test would go down in history as Sutcliffe's triumph as much as marking the commencement of the Bradman era.

Just before tea, Hendren was bowled by Oxenham for 45, at five for 236. After the break, Chapman fell for 5 and Tate was run out before the visitors got the last six runs with three wickets in hand, to go three-up in the series. The Ashes were theirs, but Australia had at least salvaged some hope and pride. They would go into the next encounter a bit more confident, but still unsure whether they could ever beat this powerful and determined England team.

The locals had also unearthed a true champion in Bradman. Experts were now seriously bracketing him with Trumper and marvelling at the maturity of his temperament, for one who was still only twenty. Bradman's coolness in a crisis was evident in the Third Test, not once but twice. He added courage and assurance to a soft middle-order. If there was one member of the team who deep-down believed it could beat this formidable opposition it was he.

11

THE ACCUMULATOR'S WARNING

While he despatched deliveries to the fine leg, straight drive, square, and back-cut boundary, he wore a cheerful grin.
— NEWSPAPER REPORT ON BRADMAN'S FIRST TRIPLE CENTURY IN FIRST-CLASS CRICKET

A BAT FOR THE BIG ONE

There was a four-week break in January 1929 between the Third and Fourth Tests. The tourists continued on their winning way against various country and State sides. For the Australians, it was a time for reassessment and experimentation. With Ponsford out and Richardson unsuited to opening, the selectors were trying out all available prospects for the job, including Bradman. He was sent in to start the NSW innings in Adelaide against South Australia on 11 January, but only managed to stay at the crease ten minutes before being caught at square leg for just 5, and then in the second innings was bowled for 2 in the first over. It was only the second time in any match in his career that he had been dismissed twice in a match for under ten runs.

Bradman didn't necessarily think that opening was tougher than any other position, particularly first-wicket down, which soon became his regular spot. 'I virtually had to come in very early anyway,' he commented. 'Also if a batsman comes in after a few overs, bowlers usually have their line and length right. That's a more dangerous time to face them.'

Shortly after this, Bradman was approached by the bat-makers Wm Sykes Ltd. They wanted to use his name on their bats, and he agreed, not the least reason being the fact that he was already familiar with their product. He had chosen a Sykes bat when his mother had rewarded him for his triple century for Bowral. The company gave him a new blade for the next Shield game, against Victoria at the SCG commencing 24 January — the biggest State game of the season.

Kippax won the toss and batted, with Bradman coming in just before lunch, this time at number three, with the score at 76. His first 50 took eighty-five minutes after which he slowed down somewhat to reach his hundred in 189 minutes. Everyone who had seen him bat before sensed he was pacing himself for a big one. At stumps he was 129 not out in 241 minutes — fast enough compared with most of his peers, but a trifle slow for him.

Next morning, with the addition of four more, he had reached a thousand in a season for the first time. No NSW batsman had achieved the milestone before the end of January, and he was the youngest Australian — at twenty years and 151 days — ever to do so. At lunch he was 196 not out. It had taken him 357 minutes. Soon after the break he passed 200 for the first time at State level and then with a series of powerful square-cuts raced through his next fifty in only thirty-four minutes. At 250, he had the Victorian attack at his mercy, but instead of throwing his wicket away he dropped his rate a mere fraction and methodically flayed the attack with shots all round the wicket. His 300 came up just before tea in 453 minutes.

Kippax declared at a colossal six for 713, leaving Bradman on 340 not out after 488 minutes and accelerating. He had hit thirty-eight fours in his longest innings and the longest ever played by a NSW player in a Shield game. The cricket world was astounded and even those in Australia who had little comprehension of the game could not help wonder at the feat, which was highlighted in front-page stories around the country.

It was an innings for statistical buffs. Records, full of cricket idiosyncrasies, tumbled. His 340 was the highest score ever on the SCG. It was a record for a match between the country's two main rivals — NSW and Victoria. It was the highest score ever made by a NSW player, and the highest by any player who had not yet attained his majority.

Young Don had been in the realm of the 300s twice before for Bowral. It was territory he did not covet but nevertheless enjoyed. The MCC tourists playing in Adelaide heard the news and reacted phlegmatically. They offered congratulations, but when pressed noted that Australia's four-day first-class games were tailor-made for monster scores, and remarked that over a dozen players in county games had reached 300-plus before. Besides the tourists had Hammond, who was still the dominant player of that extraordinary summer with three double centuries so far.

Yet they could not discount the significance of the feat. It was not just a matter of Bradman's immense powers of concentration but the manner in which he went about the task. He had notched his runs at the astonishing rate of 70 per hundred minutes and 73 per 100 balls (a rate that would place him only behind Viv Richards in modern one-day cricket).

Observers predicted that Don Bradman could possibly join Ponsford as the nation's biggest run accumulator, but what excited everyone was that with his exhilarating attacking approach to the game he was a great natural crowd-pleaser. Spectators watching Bradman were likely to get more runs for their money than for any cricketer before him. He had become cricket administration's greatest dream. This player would make the turnstiles click five times higher than normal every time he competed. A game which had developed in the last century as an aristocratic recreation in England where spectators were barely tolerated was now becoming mass entertainment in England and Australia alike. Bradman promised to be its prime inspiration.

JACKSON FULFILLED

Despite Australia's thrashing so far, interest in the Adelaide Test was high. The home side's effort in Melbourne meant that the two sides were evening up, and there was anticipation of an Australian victory. The local crowd also would be rooting for its spinning hero Grimmett, and there was much interest in Bradman and new-boy Archie Jackson, in for his first Test, even if he had replaced Vic Richardson, a South Australian.

There was more than residual feeling about the latter's demotion. Commentators pointed out that he was such a good fieldsman that Australia would suffer without him. Furthermore, he was a number four or five, not an opener (yet), and it was a tough demand to expect him to take on the England attack from the beginning. Richardson, however, was sacrificed for Jackson.

England won the toss on Friday 1 February and batted, and its openers continued with the devastating form that had demoralised their opponents in Melbourne. They did better on the scoreboard too, with an opening stand of 143, which was only broken at 3.30 p.m. when Hobbs was caught by Ryder off Hendry for 74. In the next over, Sutcliffe moved adventurously down the wicket to Grimmett and was stumped by Oldfield for 64. England was two for 143, and the game had changed.

Jardine came in to join Hammond. Soon after tea, he was LBW to Grimmett for 1 and England was three for 149. At 179, Blackie bowled Hendry for 13 with a quicker one, and Australia was on top. Chapman then settled down with Hammond, who was looking ominously comfortable with those back-foot drives. Near stumps, Ryder bowled several shrewd deliveries to his opposite number and enticed him to flash. He nicked one to the brilliant a'Beckett who snaffled it in his right hand. England was five for 246 at the close and the honours were about even.

Next day, England battled on to nine for 312, when last-man White joined Hammond, who was on 97. The England star farmed the strike, reached his century for the third time in four Tests and with White's passive assistance managed to drag England up to 334. He remained unbeaten on 119. His scores in the Tests had been 44, 28, 251, 200, 32 and now 119 not out, which meant that he had not really failed in any innings. His tally so far in six knocks was 675 at an average of 135. No series in history had seen a greater dominance by one batsman, and he still had up to three innings left.

Grimmett challenged him for innings honours with five for 102 off 52.1 overs, including thirteen maidens, demonstrating what his home-town pitch meant to him. It was his best performance of the series.

Australia started disastrously, losing Woodfull for 1 brilliantly caught by Duckworth down the leg-side off Tate, Hendry (2) again caught by the agile keeper, this time off Larwood, and Kippax (3) bowled by White at 19.

Emerging from the debris, Jackson, the Boy from Balmain, began firing like a veteran. He, like Bradman, had the measure of Larwood, who was bowling at his quickest early. Jackson played every shot with style and refinement. There was an elegance about his batting that was a decade beyond his nineteen years. Comparisons with Bradman were inevitable. Jackson was regarded as more 'shot perfect', an artist with every stroke. Bradman, however, had the temperament and skill for every occasion — the sticky wicket perhaps excepted at this stage in his development.

Both youths had tremendous natural ability, with Bradman marginally the more freakish. He could at times play the impossible shot — the one not in the book, which depended on amazing reflexes — and inevitably score runs from it. Both also scored rapidly, and with the prospect of these two being in the side in the next decade, Australia and its supporters anticipated great achievements.

They witnessed one that hot Saturday as Jackson unveiled stylish cuts and drives to both sides of the wicket. Ryder was with him driving with his usual power. They had a storming partnership of 126 —

running over into the third day, Monday — of which Ryder scored exactly half before White trapped him LBW on Monday morning. Australia's score of four for 145 was a recovery but it was still 179 behind.

The Boy from Bowral joined the Balmain Boy, so that Australian commentators could go into alliterative overdrive. Jackson, no doubt thinking too much about the possibility of a hundred before lunch, mistimed several shots and was lucky not to get himself out with uppish shots just wide of fieldsmen. Bradman, too, seemed to have a dose of Mondayitis mishits, although with him observers wondered. Had he deliberately placed the ball where by rights it shouldn't have gone, or had he simply misjudged it? Those who had seen a lot of him were starting to believe in his game of unorthodox chance. Others were less convinced. Percy Fender, a strong Bradman critic, was perplexed.

'This batsman [Bradman] made at least six bad mishits,' he noted about that pre-lunch session, 'any one of which might have cost him his wicket, but each time the catch just going wide of the fielder.'

Nevertheless, the two carried on to the break, Bradman (34 not out in a partnership of 56) outscoring Jackson (97 not out), who had gone into his shell as the magic three-figures loomed. Australia was four for 201.

The two lads, whose combined age of thirty-nine was less than that of several players on either side, walked out again to face Larwood with the new ball. Bradman, sensing Jackson's insecurity after his retreat in the first session, wandered down the wicket as Larwood rolled his arm over.

'Being so much older [one year],' Bradman recalled, 'I had the temerity to give him some advice. I told him: "Take your time and the century will come."'

Jackson relaxed, but he didn't take his time. First ball he square-drove Larwood for four, with a shot Bradman reckoned could not be bettered, to bring up his ton. He had now supplanted his partner as the youngest player ever to score a Test hundred. Bradman shook his hand, patted him on the back and proceeded to take a back-seat as the new centurion resumed the free-scoring approach that had been the feature of his first 50. Jackson scored 20 of the next 26 and was 117 when Bradman was caught by Larwood at second slip off Tate for 40. Australia was now five for 227. a'Beckett then joined Jackson in a free-wheeling attack which yielded 60 runs. At 287, a'Beckett became England's sixth victim when he was bowled by White for 36. Then Jackson fell LBW to the same bowler for 164 at 323.

The England team joined in the applause as Jackson departed, for it had been a classic display, if not the finest first-up Test knock ever seen. Oldfield (32) and Oxenham (15) then took Australia into a first-innings lead for the first time in the series. The score of 369 meant a lead of only 35, but it was a big psychological boost for the underdogs. For England, White with five for 130 off sixty overs and Tate with four for 77 off forty-two overs were outstanding. Larwood had been subdued by the two Australian youngsters and took one for 92 from thirty-seven overs in his least effective effort in the series.

England began badly on the fourth day, losing Hobbs (1) caught behind at the same score. Sutcliffe (17) started with promise, but a'Beckett got him with a just playable away-swinger, which he nicked to Oldfield. England was two for 21 and had not yet wiped out the 35-run deficit.

This brought Hammond and Jardine together. The latter always seemed to find himself in a situation which demanded all his fighting abilities, and this was no exception. They batted prudently, with Hammond on the lookout for runs but restricted by tight field-placings and Jardine, though less aggressive, keeping pace with him, until England was out of trouble and into a strong position by stumps at two for 206, a lead of 166 with eight wickets in hand. Jardine was on 73 and Hammond 105, thus becoming only the third man, after Bardsley and Sutcliffe, ever to score a century in both innings of a Test match.

The fifth day began with a crawl in the ninety-minute morning session, Jardine scoring just 17 and Hammond 37 as England added another 55. Hammond was 142 not out at the break and feeling the heat. He had been on the field for all but a few hours of the match and the strain was telling.

Twenty-five minutes into the afternoon session Jardine was caught at silly point for 98, driving at Oxenham's slower ball. He left the field to the usual mixture of jeers and polite applause, for he had batted at a snail's pace at times. Jardine had been desperate for that century against Australia ever since being denied it by Armstrong at Oxford eight years earlier, but he could be well-pleased with the position in which he had placed his country. The partnership had yielded 262 for the third wicket, leaving England three for 283 and again on top.

Hendren moved to 11 when he lofted Blackie over mid-on where Bradman, who had dropped Tate in the first innings, leapt high for the ball, running back to bring off a spectacular one-handed catch. Relieved and elated, Bradman kissed the ball. It was a rare show of emotion and the crowd loved it.

Chapman fell for a duck to Blackie in the same over, caught by Woodfull in the covers, and Larwood followed soon after for 5, leg-before to Oxenham. A fatigued Hammond reached 177, well in sight of a record that would surely last — three double centuries in a series — but played a tired shot at Ryder and returned an easy catch to the bowler. He had been painfully slow at times, but his effect had been crushing.

Tate came in with the score eight for 327 and the lead 288, still not quite enough to be safe. He came in with every intention of making sure and launched into Blackie and Grimmett, helping himself to 47 in fifty balls before Oxenham came on and trapped him LBW. England's score had been lifted to 383 giving it a lead of 348. The deceptive Oxenham had the outstanding figures of four for 67 off 47.4 overs, including twenty-one maidens, with his clever variation of pace and flight, having hardly bowled one bad ball in the 380 he sent down. Blackie, despite the pasting at the finish, still returned an economical two for 70 from thirty-nine overs (eleven maidens).

Australia was in a real fight. Woodfull and Jackson came to the wicket at 5.30 p.m. to face Larwood, who was fired up for a short stint. Woodfull kept Jackson away from him and the two were there at stumps with 24 on the board.

On the sixth day, 7 February, they began well again, but Jackson was lucky to survive when he jumped down the wicket to White and spooned the ball into the covers, only to see it land safely between Jardine and Larwood. Otherwise, he looked in control until, on 36, he tried an audacious cut at a short ball from Geary and edged it to Duckworth, with the score at 63. He could reflect with some satisfaction on his 200 for the match, and it would feel even sweeter if his team were to win.

Soon afterwards, Woodfull (30) went to play one from White on the on, but it jumped nastily and he edged it to Geary at slip. Australia went to lunch two for 71. Straight after the break, Hendry made a half-hearted drive at White and was easily caught by Tate at mid-on. Australia was three for 74 and in trouble.

Ryder joined Kippax and immediately went on the attack, but Chapman set an astute field and limited his penetration. The partnership mounted well into the final session until Kippax, who had uncharacteristically contained himself, went for a rare off-drive off White and was caught by Geary at second slip. Australia was four for 211.

DESTINY DIRECTOR

With the game now on a knife's edge, all eyes turned to the pavilion to watch Bradman coming out. He seemed determined, alert and ready. In the First Test, the game was lost on a sticky when he came in during the second innings. At Melbourne, he had met the challenge of building what appeared a winning score, but it was not quite the pressure he was under now. For the first time, Bradman felt the weight of the destiny of a Test on his shoulders.

He started with a gentle push for a single to the on. The crowd roared as if he had hit it into the surrounding park. Everything now depended on him and his hard-hitting captain. However, a big match-winning partnership between them was not to be. On 87 Ryder smashed one back over White's head, but the bowler put up a paw and it stuck. Australia was tottering at five for 224.

Out strode a'Beckett, who had been so effective in Melbourne with his raw aggression, despite his unpolished if not crude technique which did not inspire great confidence in such a tight situation as this. Just before stumps, after reaching 21, he got a ball from White which kicked and took the edge of his bat for Hammond to make a match-winning reflex catch at second slip. Australia at the end of the day was six for 260, with Bradman just 16 not out in a cautious sixty-eight minutes and Oxenham 2 not out. Australia was still 88 short and with four wickets left. England was favoured. It only had to get Bradman and it would probably take the game.

The match now entered a second week. Day seven was blustery and hot. It began with Larwood building up terrific pace from his first over, in which he resorted to leg theory, with three players close in on the leg-side and three more out deep. This, in effect, was what would come to be known as bodyline, for Larwood was aiming for the batsman's body as much as for the stumps. His intention was to bounce and bruise Bradman out. The batsman met him with scintillating shots and one fearsome hook off his eyebrows straight to the square-leg boundary. Twenty-two runs sizzled off Bradman's bat from two Larwood overs. His audacity paid off.

'Bradman seemed to find [Larwood] so much to his liking,' Fender observed from the press-box, 'that he was too expensive to be kept on in that critical stage of proceedings.'

Round one for the day had gone to Australia, as a dejected Larwood was banished to the covers, his fearsome leg theory just a failed premise. Bradman moved brilliantly on to fifty, his 36 in the morning taking only forty-three minutes. Every scoring stroke in this cameo performance brought applause in the electric atmosphere as Australia moved steadily past 300.

At 308, with only 41 wanted and victory in sight, Oxenham drove White low to Chapman at mid-off and was out for 12. Given Bradman's great form and presence, it was a tragic loss. The tension grew and the incoming Oldfield was clearly on edge, looking for runs too quickly as the score moved on to 320. Oldfield then hit White hard and straight to Hobbs at cover and called Bradman through. An older Don might have yelled 'no' to his partner, but it was the senior man's call. Hobbs hurled the ball in low to Duckworth's feet. He scooped it at the stumps but it fell free before his glove crashed into the stumps. Bradman ran through late but relieved. The England players appealed, more in hope than expectation, and the square-leg umpire, who had been unsighted by Duckworth, promptly raised his finger. Bradman was given out for 58. Spectators in a position to see, especially those with binoculars, were stunned. Bradman, however, bush-trained in good sportsmanship, marched off without even glancing back. He had been at the wicket for 128 minutes in an innings of calm authority, which with Ryder's punishing performance should have manoeuvred the home team into a position to grab victory.

In came Grimmett. The crowd now reacted feverishly to every ball, as he and Oldfield struggled through to eight for 226 at lunch, leaving them 23 to get with two wickets in hand, under a sweltering sun and in a swirl of hot north wind.

They batted sensibly after lunch until on 336, with only thirteen to make, Grimmett hooked White to Tate, who got a hand to it, knocked it up and took the catch on the second attempt. Australia's hopes now rested on Oldfield and last man Blackie, who managed to survive the remaining four balls of White's over. Oldfield took a two in the next from Tate but could not get up the other end on the last ball, leaving Blackie exposed to White for up to eight deliveries.

White sent down four on a good length, which Blackie fended off well enough. Then came the inevitable short one. Blackie laid back and heaved it high to deep mid-wicket for Larwood to come around and take a good running catch. Australia had failed by eleven runs. Oldfield, not out for a painstaking 15, could only agonise over his early jitters, when he ran out Bradman and so almost certainly lost Australia the match. White finished with the great figures of eight for 126 from 64.5 overs, twenty-one of them maidens, giving him match returns of thirteen wickets for 256 off 124.5 overs. He joined a select few in Test cricket who had snared five or more in both innings and more than twelve in a game.

Warwick Armstrong now proved he was a big man in more ways than one by admitting he had not judged Bradman correctly when he said before his selection in Melbourne that the twenty-year-old was not yet up to Test standard. Armstrong now appreciated Bradman's special skills, but more than this, his temperament. As captain, Armstrong had always had vision and foresight. He recognised a player with the mental capacities for the big time, for he had been one himself. Temperament kept a player calm under pressure. It meant concentration, the ability to stay at the wicket for a long period yet keep scoring in a crisis. 'He [Bradman] is a fine player, and will be a still finer one,' Armstrong now conceded. 'Today he never allowed the crisis to worry him.'

Despite its disappointment at having let two games in a row slip from its grasp, Australia salvaged something more than hope out of a creditable performance. It had shown it was more than competitive, and unlucky not to win. History would record a four-nil lead to England at that point, but the underlying truth was a far more even struggle in the Third and Fourth Tests. Australia had one more chance to show that it could rise above the psychological blow of the series on paper so far, and come through with a strong win at Melbourne in the Fifth.

THE BITE

While Bradman was consolidating his cricket career, his working life was becoming increasingly insecure. Economic conditions in the nation following the long postwar boom were deteriorating, causing businesses to cut back or go under. Among them was Deer Westbrook's Sydney real-estate office. It had been set up to sell housing estates, but this type of operation went flat in the early stages of the Depression. Deer Westbrook closed its doors. Bradman was out of work, although he could have gone back to Percy Westbrook's Bowral business which was still operating successfully. That would not have helped his cricket career, so for a few days he contemplated what sort of work he might get in a tight Sydney market.

For the first time in his life Bradman was very briefly a statistic off the cricket field as well, as unemployment in the first quarter of 1929 rose from 9.3 to 12.1 per cent. Every day in Sydney and all around the country tens of thousands of what the *Labour Daily* called 'ill-dressed, sad-eyed and gaunt-faced men' gathered outside government Labour Bureaus to collect their meagre food coupons, which could be exchanged for meat, groceries and other items and then redeemed from the government in cash by the shopkeeper.

Bradman never joined the dole queues, but he and everyone else were aware of them and the difficulty of finding work. His plight was news in Sydney sporting circles. During the Fourth Test, the advertising and public relations representative for the sporting goods company Mick Simmons Ltd, Oscar Lawson, offered Bradman a job at its store and offices in the Haymarket. A major part of the firm's business consisted of selling everything from tennis racquets and fishing tackle to boxing gloves and golf clubs to retail outlets throughout NSW, which it had been doing successfully since 1870.

The company allowed Bradman time off to play cricket as much as he wished. The rest of the time, his main responsibility as part of its PR operations was to coach schoolboys in Sydney and the country. Sensibly, the sporting and cricket community were looking after him with employment and accommodation. Bradman had moved from the Pearces' home in Concord West to that of Frank Cush, a St George official, in Rockdale, close to Hurstville Oval. This way, Bradman would be living in the club's territory and therefore qualified to play for it.

Bradman was grateful for the help and the job. But it reinforced to the young man how vital it was in these increasingly tough times that he secure for himself a trade or profession that would bring him not only a stable income but financial independence. He was confident about his cricket, but having just made the national team, he had no grand vision of a never-ending future at the top. Even if he had, Bradman knew he would still have to find useful employment, if he were to marry his sweetheart Jessie and support a family. Cricket would not afford that, no matter how he performed. He would always be dependent on the largesse of others.

Bradman realised that his new occupation was tenuous and offered no prospects for a long-term career. He was never keen on being a 'personality'. By nature, he was well-mannered, polite and modest, but not an overt charmer of all who met him. Bradman was more suited perhaps to, say, accounting or even the law, where behind-the-scenes calculations and tactical skills were the most important factors. He had a brain for planning, with the patience for administrative detail.

However, in February 1929 he had little choice but to work for Mick Simmons. The knowledge that he had employment gave him the security he needed at a critical time in his early career. Without any major concerns going into the Fifth Test, he was very keen to repeat his successes in Melbourne and help Australia to a much-needed win.

12

MATCH-WINNER

It is quite possible that Bradman will prove to be the finest run-getting machine ever known, and as a stylist he improves at each appearance.

— DAILY PICTORIAL, SYDNEY, EDITORIALISING ON BRADMAN IN 1928–29

YOUTH v MATURITY

Australia continued its policy of youthful transfusion for the final encounter of the series and included Bradman (20), Jackson (19), a'Beckett (21), Alan Fairfax, an all-rounder from Bradman's St George Club (23), South Australian paceman Tim Wall (25), and left-arm orthodox spinner Percy Hornibrook (30). It dropped Blackie and Hendry. a'Beckett was made twelfth man and could consider himself unlucky after acquitting himself well in his two Test appearances. England was forced to leave out Sutcliffe, who was injured, and captain Chapman, who had the flu. The latter was no loss after his poor showing in the series.

White captained the team while Leyland and Tyldesley came in, giving England its best side of the rubber. Only the inclusion of Sutcliffe would have made it better. The tourists made it clear that they desperately wanted to make it a five-nil whitewash. There would be no slackening off, so Australia would have to fight hard to break through.

The game began on Friday 8 March, when the autumn weather in Melbourne could be unsettled, providing sun, wind and rain in the one day, and wildly fluctuating temperatures. This opening day it was sunny but cold. White celebrated his captaincy by winning the toss and sending in Hobbs and Jardine.

These two crawled to 51 at lunch, but could not be totally blamed. There was no point in throwing the willow about on the first morning in a timeless Test, especially in Melbourne, which invariably saw wickets tumble in the initial session. To have all wickets intact at lunch was always any side's aim, if only occasionally achieved.

After the break, Wall dismissed Jardine (19) with a short ball which the batsman skied to Oldfield. Hobbs should have been out with the score at 77 when Hornibrook took a ball in slips but in his excitement threw it up before he had really ensnared it and failed to catch it on the way down. Hammond (38) was snaffled more surely in the gully by Fairfax, again off Wall, with the score at 146. It could hardly be called a failure, but it was low for one of the world's most prolific batsmen. The Australians were relieved, but Hobbs was looking secure and enjoying the cool weather. It was more like home. At tea he was there with Tyldesley and the score was two for 159. After tea, he reached his twelfth century against Australia, a record. It was also his fifth ton on the MCG, an unprecedented Test exhibition.

Then near stumps, Ryder came on and trapped him LBW for 142 at 235. Hobbs had been unlucky. A shadow from the stands had lengthened right over the wicket and he lost sight of Ryder's first ball to him as it passed from sun into shade. Tyldesley (31) was out probing for one from Ryder in the same conditions at 240. England had lost four wickets in the process, which made the day roughly even, with the provisional thought in the back of everyone's mind being that the side batting first would hold the advantage.

Next morning, nightwatchman Duckworth (12) did his job for half an hour before Fairfax caught him off Hornibrook, making England five for 260. Hendren and Leyland then began at a good rate. Grimmett had taken a blow on the knee from Hobbs, which left him unable to bowl. Ryder thus felt compelled to reduce the scoring pace by introducing 'off theory' — stacking the off-side field and bowling outside the off-stump. It was as tedious to watch as leg theory although less perilous.

Despite this check of their aggression, Hendren and Leyland put on 141 and showed great understanding in taking cheeky singles. They were not separated until England was 401, and on top. Hornibrook repaid Fairfax by taking a catch off the youngster's bowling to get rid of Hendren for 95. Leyland continued on with an innings full of powerful drives. He reached a hundred but lost Larwood and Geary quickly. Tate stayed for twenty-five minutes and made a handy 15, leaving England nine for 485 by stumps.

On Monday morning, White (9 not out) and Leyland (137) added 34 before the latter was taken in the slips by Fairfax, who was having a good day in the field in his first Test with three catches. It was Oxenham's only wicket. Bowling credits were shared by Wall with three for 123 and Hornibrook, three for 142. Ryder chipped in for two for 29 off 18 overs.

Australia's Woodfull and Jackson added 19 before lunch. They batted on slowly afterwards until Jackson slipped when going for an easy run and was run out for 30 with the score at 54. Woodfull was in sound if stodgy form. In the recent match between Victoria and England 'The Rock', as he was known, had notched a great 275 and was fine-tuned for a big effort in the Test, especially in front of his home-town crowd. He and Kippax took the score to 79 at tea, adding only 60 in the session. At 142, Kippax (38) edged one to Duckworth off White. His runs had taken two hours, a far cry from some of his brilliant displays during the season against lesser bowling and not in the Tests. Australia crawled to two for 152 at stumps and seemed to be intent on matching England's worst display of tardiness on the first day, except that the tourists had had a few bright spots.

Ryder had caught plod's disease and he accompanied Woodfull on a slow march to 200. At 203 a double disaster struck for Australia. Geary caught Woodfull off Larwood for 102. Then in the final over before lunch, Ryder, sick of the defensive game which had yielded just twenty-two singles in the past hour, lashed out at Hammond and handed Tate an easy catch in the gully.

This put Bradman and Fairfax together for the second session under a blazing sun. The weather had reverted to full summer heat, which took its toll on the Englishmen who had preferred the comforting coolness of the first two days.

Bradman came out of the members' enclosure to rapturous applause from an impatient crowd, which had seen enough pushing and prodding to last them a decade. If recent form was anything to go on, he was as well-prepared as Woodfull, having scored 175 not out against South Australia in Sydney two weeks earlier. It was an innings in keeping with his 340 against Victoria — full of command, concentration and flowing shots, which allowed him to maintain an outstanding run-rate of about 80 per 100 balls faced.

His presence in the middle had by now made him the biggest drawcard the game had seen anywhere. Real fans would go to three days of a Shield match rather than two if he was likely to bat. Even those ignorant of the finer points would rush out to a ground if they heard that Bradman was in, or about to go in. The writer Sumner Reed noted in his diary:

> I had heard that Ryder and Kippax were well settled, so I was in no particular hurry, although I knew that [Bradman] was next man in. I was walking down from the Richmond station when I saw scores of people running towards the MCG. Some were moving rapidly across the rail yards oblivious of obvious dangers. Then I heard a roar that was truly awe-inspiring. The noise continued unabated. I knew instantly the reason for the haste of those ahead of and around me. No one needed to say anything. I realised I was late.
>
> Bradman was in.
>
> I could have kicked myself. I wouldn't see him take block! I had been at big boxing contests here and in the home country. I had seen my beloved Chelsea and Collingwood run out to do battle in finals. But to me there was nothing more emotive, nerve-tingling or anticipatory than watching Bradman hold the bat straight and lift his chin to the umpire at the bowler's end. No thumbs up from a Roman Emperor, no touching of gloves by two boxers, no holding the ball aloft by an umpire — nothing equalled the feeling on

seeing that enigmatic character under the baggy green prepare for battle. If I were ever confused about whether I was English or Australian, my doubts evaporated in those precious seconds before Bradman received a ball. And every time he faced the England side, I had my patriotism reaffirmed. That is why, on considered reflection, I hated missing the very start of that innings . . .

Thankfully, Bradman was blissfully unaware of this capacity to settle people's nationality. Yet he was aware that the crowd was with him and there was a big task ahead. If starts counted for anything, the crowd was in for a treat. Bradman changed the tempo of the entire game by going after his shots from the first ball and encouraged Fairfax to stay with him. Word swept through Melbourne like a bushfire that the nation's newest hero was in. City office workers suddenly arranged extended lunch-breaks with phantom clients. Within half an hour after the break the crowd swelled to an estimated 20,000, almost double the number at the start of play.

When he reached 5, a cheer went up from a section of the crowd in the outer. Someone had noted that Bradman had passed the highest aggregate for an Australian first-class season of 1,534 runs, made by South African tourist Aubrey Faulkner in 1910–11. It took Faulkner twenty-seven innings. Bradman made his runs in just twenty-three visits to the crease.

Larwood was on. Before he could get his rhythm going, Bradman went after him with cuts, hooks and drives, and after three overs White took him off. No batsman had ever treated Larwood with such disdain. Bradman had beaten or humiliated him in seven successive innings encounters.

White, as leader, felt compelled to tackle Bradman and put himself on. This slowed him marginally, but he refused to be pinned to his crease and went down the pitch to him, driving him into the covers or straight. The field was difficult to penetrate. Unperturbed, Bradman went on to the back foot and dragged him around to the leg against the spin for impudent singles. This way he would not be bogged down, but his method upset the purists. It appeared risky.

Percy Fender continued to be perplexed by Bradman's batting. Writing for the London *Star* and *Daily News*, he said:

> *Bradman is such a curious mix of brilliant and very mediocre batting. He will make a number of glorious shots, and then, in attempting another, he will fluke the ball in some totally different direction from the one he intended, and practically always just out of a fielder's reach.*

Fender, an astute commentator, was having difficulty coming to terms with Bradman's style. He had never seen anything like it. Fender formed his opinions from years of practical experience as a fine international player. Yet he had never come up against anyone like Bradman, and he became frustrated in the press-box watching him beat the field. It would take a personal encounter for him to reach a final conclusion one way or the other concerning his capacities. Was Bradman a phenomenon or a fluke, pretender or prophet? It was impossible for Fender to make up his mind. He couldn't wait for the chance to captain a side against such a batsman and bowl to him. Only then, he felt, would he fully comprehend this most intriguing individual. Fender was, like many of his countrymen outside the fence, partly reacting to the hero worship with which Australians were already treating the new star.

On the field it was different. Bradman had something special. Opposition players could not articulate it yet. They were too busy chasing leather.

HAPPY SOULS AND PARASOLS

White kept on at one end and replaced Larwood with Tate. Bradman started playing him to fine leg and mid-wicket. Tate changed his line, and Bradman followed it like a predator, driving. Beaten for the moment, White took himself off and put Geary on. His fast-medium deliveries fared no better. On 46, Bradman stepped into a cracking drive to mid-on. Geary flung out a right hand, but failed to hold the hot catch. Instead, he was left examining a red and stinging thumb.

Bradman's power was deceptive because of his light frame. But when he hit a ball he put tremendous effort and perfect timing into it. Pictures, still and moving, of his body and bat after making contact for an off-drive show an uncommon force, which finished with his bat well back over his left shoulder. A similar still or moving frame of the bigger Hammond playing exactly the same stroke showed the Englishman's bat stopping a metre further forward. Players from Hobbs to Hassett who fielded to both attest that each hit the ball about as hard as the other.

This compact power was another distinguishing factor in Bradman's unique game. His eye was so exceptional that he had the luxury of time, measured in just milliseconds, but vital as a measure of his superiority. Bradman saw the ball so well he felt on occasions as if he could do anything with it. If players with lesser physical gifts tried to emulate him, half the time they would be out mishitting a catch. Ninety-nine per cent of the time Bradman would make the right contact. This led to another of his outstanding features: the capacity to pierce the field.

Hammond demonstrated time after time in that 1928–29 series his masterly back-foot drive in the wide arc from the covers to mid-wicket. But he was not great at puncturing the field. His patience and concentration kept him at the wicket long enough to make those big double hundreds, but he was not exciting to watch. Bradman's skill by comparison, even in that first series, was uncanny. It wasn't that he bisected the field every time. Playing, for example, White's bowling to a packed off-side field would have made that difficult. More to the point was Bradman's capacity to place the ball with such dexterity that he would often glide or smash it just wide enough to perforate the most meticulously placed outfield defenders. This left baffled observers in 1928–29 such as Fender thinking he was 'lucky'. Only time would show that Bradman's game was the least fortunate by comparison with others at Test level in his era. His performances were the result of imaginative management, not good fortune.

Bradman's fifty took just seventy-one minutes, the fastest of the series, and he was 62 not out with Fairfax on 23 at tea. Bradman slowed the rate, but still scored respectably into the last session. White was frowning. How could he break this youthful spirit? So far Larwood, Hammond, himself, Tate and Geary had tried and failed. Even Leyland had been brought on to try his hand.

White tossed the ball to Larwood. He gave no instructions. Larwood had to get the Australian any way he could. This time he was to bowl from the Members' end. The speedster tore in, but the Melbourne wicket was giving him no assistance. Bradman cut his first ball for four. Larwood asked White for a deep-backward point and got one. Bradman cut again, this time for two. Six in two balls, and Larwood was steaming.

He bent his back for a short one straight at Bradman's throat. Bradman slid his back foot back and across, and pulled it hard for three. It was not perfectly timed, but that now-familiar roll of the wrists crushed any chance of it flying. Nine runs off three balls. Larwood glanced at Bradman. There was no leer or gesture, just that permanent, settled grin of delight in his craft.

Larwood remarked later: 'He seemed not to notice us [the bowlers]. But he really seemed to enjoy his batting.'

The bowler was pleased to be firing at Fairfax, who treated him with much more caution and respect. Bradman was quiet again against Geary, but launched into Larwood for a straight-driven four. The bowler responded with two very quick, straight bouncers. Bradman ducked one and positioned himself to hook the other, but left it alone. Larwood tried a yorker, but Bradman made it a full-toss and kept it out. The last ball was another bouncer, which Bradman ignored. The fast bowler repeated the dose with the first ball of his next over, but it didn't get up and Bradman hooked it so fast to the boundary that Jardine at square leg could only watch it skim past and rattle the pickets in front of the scoreboard. Larwood bowled out the over, took his sweater and retired to the covers.

Bradman moved commandingly towards his century, with the crowd yelling itself hoarse. Then as he reached 98, a silence filled the stadium. Bradman broke it by on-driving Larwood for two, to reach his second century of the series. It had taken 172 minutes and was the fiftieth century scored against England on Australian soil. Bradman received a standing ovation from the members, something usually reserved for a Victorian such as Ryder in full flight. They were claiming him with as much propriety as anyone on the SCG Hill. Even a dejected Larwood managed to bring his hands together in the semblance of applause. Hobbs trotted over and shook the batsman's hand.

In the last session the light deteriorated. The batsmen appealed against it twice and finally stumps were drawn at 5.42 p.m. — forty-eight minutes early. Bradman was on 109 with Fairfax 50 in an unbroken stand of 164 which left Australia on four for 367 overnight. A journalist for the *Daily Pictorial* described the crowd's reaction as the two players made their way from the field:

'At stumps 20,000 pressed madly to greet the two colts as they left the wickets, cheering round after round rolling away in great waves of sound, while hats waved in the air with parasols and handkerchiefs.'

RE-EVALUATION

At the end of the day, Australian scribes were less concerned with 'unsound' strokes, and more impressed with the sheer brilliance of Bradman's batting and the consistency of his Test performances under all conditions and against all bowlers. After his start of 18 and 1, he had notched 79, 112, 40, 58 and now another century. Added to that were his other first-class efforts against the tourists of 87, 132 not out, 58 not out and 18. Only Hammond had fared better on either side. Bradman had continued his inexorable climb to the top of world cricket. His efforts from that first runaway start with Bowral in 1925–26 had never stopped improving. In the minds of public and selectors alike, he could only go one step further — win a match for Australia at last.

However, rain intervened at night to turn the wicket into a sticky once again and make it far tougher to play on day five. Geary dismissed Bradman for 123 caught by Tate at short leg with the tally at 386. He had hit eight fours. The partnership had been worth 183, a record for the fifth wicket in any Test. Fairfax contributed 55. It had taken 217 minutes.

Almost predictably, Fairfax was out soon afterwards for 65, LBW to Geary with the score at 399. It was then a steady procession as Geary hit his straps and removed Oxenham (7) caught behind, Oldfield (6) caught and bowled, and Wall (9) caught behind. Geary's sustained spell had taken out half the side. His figures had gone from nought for 60 to five for 82 — five for 22 in twelve overs of sustained pace bowling.

Australia was rocking on nine for 432, still 89 behind. Grimmett and Hornibrook, however, put in more effort than expected from tailenders in a series not noted for excessive wagging by either side. They scraped together a morale-boosting last-wicket stand of 59 runs so that Australia's tally of 491 was just 28 short. Geary had the figures at five for 105 off a marathon eighty-one overs — or 648 deliveries. His steadiness was implied in the thirty-six maidens he sent down. White battled for two for 136 off an almost equally expansive seventy-five overs including twenty-two maidens.

England batted again late in the day, and ran into a Wall who relished the tricky conditions. His first ball to Jardine kicked into the batsman's ribcage. He tried to fend it off and was caught by Oldfield on the leg-side. A roar went up from the Melbourne crowd who had stayed late in the hope of seeing English blood, or at the least, a wicket. It couldn't have pleased them more that it was Jardine.

He disappeared into the pavilion to be replaced by Larwood, a popular identity who had earned the respect of crowds across Australia because of his aggressive brilliance with the ball and his corresponding attitude with the bat. They also appreciated that unlike Jardine he had come from an under-privileged background. His batting as nightwatchman that torrid evening was sheer grit, testimony to his tough upbringing in the Nottinghamshire mines. He faced up to Wall and was immediately hit. He hardly flinched, demonstrating he could take it as well as dish it out, which only endeared him further to the crowd.

He and Hobbs scraped through to stumps, the score at one for 15. Rain fell during the night and it drizzled enough in the morning to liven up the pitch for Wall. He displaced Larwood's middle stump with a superb yorker of which the departing bowler himself would have been proud.

England was two for 19 and Hammond, the scourge of the locals, reached the wicket. The Australians, however, felt Wall had a chance to unsettle him early. The paceman was making the ball kick alarmingly off a good length. Hobbs showed his respect for the tricky wicket and belied his forty-six years by batting as the master he had been in a faultless display of his craft. Hammond, two decades younger and more troubled by all the bowlers, let Hobbs have the strike and played apprentice. Wall could have dismissed Hammond twice, but Ryder dropped two straightforward catches in slips. It set the shaky batsman up for Fairfax, who made one hold up outside off stump. Hammond (16) pushed without his usual conviction and the Australian captain redeemed himself a little in slips and held one. Hammond had scored 885 runs at an average of 110.63, but his dismissal had left England three for 75, its lead at 103 and its grip on the match faltering.

Tyldesley joined Hobbs, who was next to go for 65, caught by Fairfax at short third man, while attempting a delicate late cut for a single off Grimmett, who had suffered most from the veteran opener during his haul of 207 in both innings.

Grimmett's revenge was even sweeter when he bowled Hendren (1) before he had settled in. The scoreboard said four for 123. The crowd, swelling again in the afternoon, now wondered aloud about Australia's chances of victory. Eight runs later Wall moved one away from Tyldesley on 21, and it grazed an edge on its way through to Oldfield. England was five for 131. The scales were now tipping in Australia's favour.

Leyland, who had looked sound, was joined by Tate, who proceeded to hit at everything. It was his way, and perhaps the only way out for England now. He succeeded in hammering Grimmett, who bowled too many balls outside leg-stump to an unprotected boundary.

Tate found it often and agriculturally wafted his way towards fifty. Leyland moved from sound to safe and the partnership mounted.

Ryder belatedly replaced Grimmett with Hornibrook, who got a short one to lift more than expected. Tate moved inside to pull, top-edged the ball to Fairfax in the slips and was on his way for 54. England were six for 212 — 230 ahead and now with a fair chance of notching that desired five-nil series score-line.

Leyland battled to keep the strike, but Wall caused the fall of Geary (3), clean-bowled, and White (4), caught by Oxenham. Duckworth hung on in a last-wicket stand of 26 before Oxenham had him LBW. Leyland remained unconquered on 53, giving him 190 for the match and grand promise for the next Ashes series. Wall had the impressive first-up figures of five for 66 off twenty-six overs with five maidens. Despite his pasting from Tate, Grimmett returned a fair two for 66.

England had crawled and clawed its way to 257, leaving Australia 286 to make for that elusive victory.

Ryder deliberately kept his top-order men back and opened late on the sixth day with Hornibrook and Oldfield, who could both bat more than a bit. They were instructed to stay there if possible and appeal against the light often. It was soon upheld and the risk had been worth it. Australia was none for 7 at the close, with 279 to get and all hands on deck.

GAMBLING WITH RABBITS

The pre-lunch session on day seven was a tough, slow scrap full of reprieves and opportunities lost. Hornibrook, who had been rewarded for his last-ditch first-innings fight, was now living up to Ryder's faith in him. He was prepared often to use his pads — anything in fact — to keep the ball out. Oldfield was simply lucky. He was dropped twice and should have been run out when the ball was returned to the wrong end. Oldfield had been responsible for the mix-up, as he had in Adelaide with Bradman. However, in this contest he got away with it. Relieved, he put his head down and kept on fighting.

Miraculously, the two stand-ins looked as if they would make it until lunch. But Hammond came on and bowled Hornibrook (18) and Australia went to the break at one for 51. Just 44 had been added in the session, yet it had been a determined effort which gave the other nine in the dressing room more than hope.

Woodfull joined Oldfield and they motored smoothly into the afternoon. Woodfull was in full defence mode and garnered the strike once he was set. He did not care how long his innings took. It was a timeless competition and in theory could carry on until April when the football season started. The Rock's plan was to wear down the England bowlers in the stifling heat made worse by Melbourne's swirling north wind.

At 80, Hammond struck again and bowled Oldfield for 35. Inspired, he launched himself at new man Jackson, and got one to cannon into his chest. It hurt. Jackson doubled up at the wicket. The next ball reared past the batsman's head and collected Duckworth in the neck.

After this, Woodfull put the shutters up, at least until tea. The batsmen did the great Australian crawl to 109 for two, with only Jackson ticking the tally up. There were still 177 to collect.

Just before tea, Larwood summoned up that extra bit of pace and unsettled both players. This set Woodfull up for Hammond, who bowled him for 35 at 129. The Melbourne crowd was stunned. Woodfull had been known as The Rock by most, but also as The Unbowlable by many, simply because he was, almost — at least on his home turf.

Hammond, with Larwood's connivance, had once again dented Australia's morale. Kippax came in next and enlivened proceedings. But with the score at 158, White put Geary on at the pavilion end for the first time and he bowled Jackson (46) with his third ball. Ryder emerged grimly from the pavilion to stem the tide. He dug in and saw him off. But still there was Larwood, who bent his back in a final three-over burst before stumps. Tate came on, then White, who had held himself back for a tilt at his opposite number, whom he had measured well before. However, the batsmen's perseverance and

Ryder's ultimately successful appeals against the light prevented another wicket falling on the day, which had seen a grinding advance of just 166 runs.

Australia was four for 173, needing only 113 more with six wickets intact. The game was evenly poised for day eight in one of the longest-running clashes on record. And Bradman was next man in. This prospect and the closeness of the contest had spectators queuing long before the gates were open.

England was clearly on edge, and up for far more appeals than normal. It was unlucky when Tate seemed to trap Kippax LBW. Larwood looked spent, and was soon replaced by Hammond. At 201, Kippax forced a ball towards the square-leg boundary, and the batsmen completed three as Leyland reached the ball. There was an easy four in it, and Kippax set off from the bowler's end. But the aging Ryder said no, although Kippax kept coming. Ryder stayed put and Kippax (28) was beaten by Leyland's return to Tate at the bowler's end. It was a needless, wasted fifth wicket lost by Australia, with the score at 204 — still 82 short.

TIME FOR TEMPERAMENT

The crowd was too shocked to give Bradman his usual welcome as he stepped through the gate. He had been conscious of his own poor running up until this season. Yet with so many big innings in 1928–29, he was confident he had now mastered the art and that he understood the idiosyncrasies of all his team-mates between the wickets, including those with whom he did not play regularly in State games. Nevertheless, there was always the little problem with the captain, which was often a difficulty — especially with autocratic types like Ryder. You ran when the leader wanted one, not when you did.

There was drama straightaway. Bradman had only been in an over or two when he jumped out to White and missed, but Duckworth failed to gather the ball. If he had, Bradman would have been in trouble. Then next ball he took a single. Ryder, still unsettled by Kippax's unnecessary dismissal, stepped into White and belted the ball back to the bowler. White got a hand to it, but it ricocheted towards mid-on. Ryder called Bradman through as Leyland picked up and threw. He hit the stumps with Ryder a stretch of his bat out. But in the confusion of bowler, fielders and batsman the umpire was unsighted and he shook his head at England's appeal.

The crowd was stunned by this sudden turn in Australia's luck after it had eluded them so much in the two previous Tests. Ryder settled down and Bradman settled in. The runs came steadily, without alarm, both men content to play within themselves. White rang the bowling changes: himself, Hammond, Geary and Tate. Larwood was tried again, but he seemed exhausted after eight days of this game and the long season before it. Bradman was severe with him again and brought up Australia's 250 with a slashing cover drive.

At 260, the two batsmen were untroubled. The crowd relaxed. Excited cheering for everything became more measured. They began savouring a rare moment against this mighty England side, which through the whole glorious summer had been superior in every department — batting, bowling, fielding, strategy and tactics. It had the batsman of the series, Hammond, and the bowler, Larwood. Its keeping was superior, as was its catching close to the wicket or in the outfield.

For that small moment in Melbourne however, Australia was on top, the crowd was in a joyous mood, and as the score edged closer to that decisive 286 Bradman was thinking how he might engineer the strike for Ryder.

'We had the game won,' Bradman recalled. 'I wanted him to hit the winning run. He hit one towards the boundary and it looked like four. Maurice Tate was sure of it. He grabbed a couple of stumps as souvenirs. But the ball was fielded short of the boundary and thrown in. Maurice was left laughing as he restored the stumps. We still had a couple to make. Unfortunately the runs which gave Australia her one victory in the series were from byes.'

Byes or not, they were still runs. Ryder (57 not out) uprooted his own stumps as souvenirs, thus beating Tate to a couple. Many of the elated crowd jumped the fence and invaded the arena. Bradman (37 not out) made a dash for the pavilion, while Ryder was hoisted on shoulders and led back through a wild, cheering throng. Delirious supporters tried to storm the pavilion.

Inside, several of the team were still lounging about in their playing gear and celebrating. Bradman, Jackson, Fairfax and Kippax, however, scrambled to shower and change. They had a train to catch for Sydney.

They had to struggle through the mob outside. Bradman had his bag snatched by an admirer who insisted on carrying it for him and finding the Sydney lads a hansom cab. The four players clambered aboard and just made the train.

On the sleepless trip home, they had the chance to reflect on their personal achievements, as well as all that might have been. Bradman was satisfied he had cemented himself a place in the Test side with an aggregate of 468 at 66.85, which was the best-ever effort by any player under twenty-one years of age. His overall performance during the season added to his pleasure. His final tally of runs for 1928–29 was 1,690, which was 156 ahead of the previous record. Bradman's first-class average came out at 93.88, which surprised the statistically-minded, for he had just pipped Hammond at 92.06. Despite the Englishman's dominance in the Tests, Bradman had a better season.

His Shield average was 148.83 and NSW had moved from bottom of the competition to top. Even at club level he topped the averages with 65.25.

Yet Bradman's insatiable appetite for runs did not stop. After the Tests he joined a State side touring the country and notched 34, 128 not out and 117. At Tamworth on April 1 he was out for 0 after an outrageous LBW decision, given by an umpire who locals reported was overwhelmed by the moment. His finger was elevated before an appeal from the lucky trundler, one G. Bell.

In all cricket in 1928–29 he stepped out to bat forty-two times and scored 2,616 runs — including fifteen centuries — at 76.94. On average he reached a century every third time he went to the wicket. His record was unprecedented, and yet because his rise had been so sudden there were some who doubted, and others who wondered, if such a sustained performance could ever be achieved again.

Bradman now had silenced all his critics at home. Even the most pedantic were unable to find anything to carp about in either his make-up or his cricket. Naturally, English commentators and opponents were more reserved. They were not about to indulge in hero worship of the enemy. Advice was given freely and without malice, especially on how Bradman might play under English wickets. There was talk of his grip, his strokes — especially his adventurous cutting and penchant for the hook. He might find it tougher against spin too. It would be better if he curbed his waltz down-wicket and used his pads more.

Percy Fender, who had been the least generous of the England observers, wrote in a book about the series that Bradman was 'one of the most curious mixtures of good and bad batting I have ever seen'. He thought the new star had a long way to go yet before he proved himself, and predicted:

> *If practice, experience and hard work enable him to eradicate the faults and still retain the rest of his ability, he may become a very great player; and if he does this, he will always be in the category of the brilliant if unsound ones.*
>
> *Promise there is in Bradman in plenty, though watching him does not inspire one with any confidence that he desires to take the only course which will lead him to fulfilment of that promise. He makes a mistake, then makes it again and again; he does not correct it, or look as if he were trying to do so . . .*
>
> *He seems to live for the exuberance of the moment.*

In all the torrent of words about the new champion these got closest to the way Bradman felt himself. He had simply enjoyed the chance to represent his country and to do his best at the sport he loved. He did not gloat about his efforts or demean them with false modesty. Bradman was not dropping a cliché when he looked back at his cricket of 1928–29 and remarked, 'It was still just a game.'

Australia was drifting into a brutal Depression, which would make a third of the work-force unemployed.

'I had no profession,' he noted, 'I wasn't a lawyer or an accountant. There wasn't professional cricket, and even if there had been I would not have been one.'

Uppermost in his mind was his future in tough times.

13

SONATA FOR A BAT

*. . . Perhaps the most outstanding feature of his amazing
psychology is his relentlessness. He may relax physically, but
never mentally, and he certainly has no mercy.*
— ERIC BALFOUR ON BRADMAN'S BIG-SCORING CAPACITY

SEAL OF APPROVAL

Bradman had little respite from cricket after the end of the
1928–29 season. In April he was in a near-Shield strength team
sent by the NSW Cricket Association to country centres to enthuse
young players. The NSWCA wanted to encourage junior talent and
persuade their clubs to upgrade their wickets from concrete to turf to
improve the standard of the game and the conditions under which it
was played. Bradman was a big drawcard, and the classic example of
a country colt made good.

The team's tour was designed for learning more than competition.
Coaching sessions were conducted during breaks in the game or
afterwards to help the local players develop their technique. Big
crowds turned up at these exhibition matches to catch a glimpse of
the sensational new star in the cricketing firmament, the twenty-
year-old Don Bradman.

At Singleton in 42°C heat, he smote a century in an hour. At
Maitland, he was out for a second-ball duck to a ludicrous LBW
decision. One septuagenarian complained to Bradman he had
travelled far to see him. The star apologised, but explained that he

could not be expected to perform well on every occasion, especially in the face of bad luck and even worse umpiring. In fact, Bradman found performing far less appetising than competing in serious matches. He was not by nature a showman and only really came alive when he had a challenge. He wasn't stimulated by a crowd who had come to see him hit balls around a field or in a net.

From May to October he was a full-time performer for Mick Simmons, visiting country towns where there was a sporting goods outlet. The local retailers were excited at his appearance at their stores, and delighted to chat with him about his Test centuries, his 340 against Victoria, the speed of Larwood, the batting of Hammond, the captaincy of Ryder and so on. When not on tour, he was at the Simmons store in George Street, which saw a steady stream of admirers come in to pretend to look at a cricket bat or football, in the hope of seeing or maybe even shaking hands with him and having a quick chat. The compliments from his adoring fans multiplied.

Bradman hated excessive publicity and never sought it. He began to withdraw to a private world, in which he felt totally at ease, centring on his romance with the beautiful Jessie. Bradman particularly liked going to her family home in Burwood for musical evenings. There, among close friends, he enjoyed performing jazz and classics on the piano with Jessie and her sisters and brothers. It reminded him of his own family's Saturday night entertainment in Bowral.

Apart from that and visits with Jessie to the 'talkies', as the first movies with sound were called, Bradman relaxed in the winter months of 1929 by taking up golf. This was an entirely different ball game and like any new player, Bradman struggled initially with putting and driving accuracy. But every now and again his extraordinary eye, timing and coordination came to the fore. Will Corry, a golf pro attached to Simmons, played with Bradman and soon realised that with practice and experience he would be very good. Bradman liked the new challenge. Golf was not a team game but another kind of battle — the individual against the elements and that little white ball.

BRING ON THOSE FLANNELLED FOOLS

Bradman was refreshed and ready for the new challenges of the 1929–30 season. Observers were marking him down for the tour of England in May, but not Bradman himself. He felt he would have to repeat his performances of the previous year in order to make sure of his place in the team. It was the pinnacle of every international player's ambitions and he badly wanted to go. He also wanted to hit form right from the opening game.

A big crowd was on hand for his first club game for St George against Glebe on Saturday 28 September, including all Sydney's leading cricket writers. He started like a hurricane, was dropped early and reached fifty in forty-one minutes. At the close of the innings he was 180 not out. Scribes were ecstatic and as one in their appraisal: Bradman was set to do at least as well as in 1928–29.

He had two good warm-up opportunities starting with a strong NSWCA team led by Macartney, which played five matches in various western country centres. They started at Orange where he scored only 5. On 22 October, while Bradman was belting 88 off the finest of Dubbo, stocks were taking a similar hiding on the floor of the New York Stock Exchange, which triggered the Great Depression. Australia, already feeling the pinch more than the US and nations of Europe, braced itself for further deprivation and economic misery. The Wall Street crash was a talking point across the country, but life went on. The Scullin Labor Government was sworn in after winning the Federal election on 12 October. Macartney's marauders moved on to Parkes on 24 October and Bradman hammered 76 as an opener. Against Far West he managed 50 and in Bathurst 84. Then he went north with a similar team for a round of matches in Taree, Wauchope and Moree.

In the first State game, against Queensland in Brisbane in early November, Bradman started well with 48 in sixty-six minutes before being run out. But in the second knock he went unaccountably quiet and scored just 66 in 209 minutes, one of the slowest fifties of his career. Some scribes even wondered if he were ill. NSW won a tight game, in which none of its other star bats performed well. On the way home, the team played Newcastle and Bradman began his innings as he had left off in the State game. He was slow, watchful and indecisive for the first 20 or so in forty-odd minutes, then he went up a gear and crashed the next 91 in an hour.

A local medico, Dr James Clarke, then twenty-four, who had watched cricket in Newcastle since he was a child, saw the innings and never forgot it:

> *That performance was the greatest innings I ever saw. He played himself in and then without warning took the bowling apart with an array of shots I didn't think were possible coming from one player. Some bats, even at Test level, have their favourite strokes, but every one seemed to be The Don's that day. He hooked and cut ferociously. Fielders on the fence seemed to freeze as the ball shot past them. His cover and on-drives were fluent and in another class altogether . . . I don't think I'd ever really seen a late cut until I saw his. It was so late that it seemed to defy physics. How could a speedily travelling ball be past a bat, and yet not? Somehow Bradman managed to nudge the leather on its way. A slow motion camera might have explained it to me, but I doubt it . . . That innings changed the way I watched cricket — forever.*

That innings at Newcastle was a prelude to NSW's match against an MCC team en route to New Zealand. It became a high-class contest — somewhere between County, State and Test standard because of the personnel involved. The MCC featured experienced captain Harold Gilligan, the renowned Frank Woolley, the rising star Kumar Duleepsinhji, Eddie Dawson, Fred Barrett and Maurice Allom. NSW played Fairfax, Kippax, Jackson, Oldfield and Bradman.

On the first day at the SCG on 22 November, Bradman came to the wicket at 26 to join Jackson. The sight of English players opposing him seemed to lift his competitive spirit like nothing else and he dominated the first-wicket partnership of 117. Bradman's form was an extension of his effort at Newcastle, without the warm-up. He sprinted to 50 in forty-five minutes, leaving Jackson to play second fiddle, and was 71 not out at lunch. After the break and with the score on 143, he lost Jackson, whom he had outscored 74 to 39.

He kept up his pace and moved through a hundred in 103 minutes, then hit 86 in the afternoon session before Worthington bowled him on the last ball before tea for a chanceless 157, in 175 minutes. Maurice Turnbull, one of the MCC side, noted that the Bradman they had read and heard about in England was some way from the batsman they fielded to. There was none of the flaws attributed to him that had been mentioned in despatches from the 1928–29 Ashes series, he said:

> *Bradman's innings eclipsed anything we had seen before in Australia. The others were always giving us a chance of getting them out . . . Don Bradman played some glorious back-foot shots reminiscent of Charlie Macartney, and hardly missed a ball at which he struck.*

This assessment was on its way to England before the match was out and endorsed by reports from others. It whetted the appetite of fans for a feast in the coming England summer, but in the minds of the British public Bradman was still just one of several exciting players with a chance of making the touring squad. They also heard about a newcomer named Arthur Allsop in this game, who hit a strong 117, and another brilliant new country lad, Stan McCabe, who scored 90.

NSW declared at eight for 629. England replied with 469, an innings dominated by Woolley, who hit 219. Bradman was impressed and could still recall the Englishman's majesty:

> *Woolley was then in his early forties, so he was past his best. But still his strokes were full of fluency. It was a classic innings. His*

*timing and ease of stroke-play were remarkable. I appreciated then
why he was ranked amongst the great stylists the game had seen.*

Turnbull also scored a hundred. NSW declared its second innings
closed at three for 305, and Jackson came good with his favourite
score against England, 164. This caused journalists to comment that
he and Bradman could 'pack their bags for the UK tour'. But neither
batsman was about to start reaching for his socks and underwear just
yet.

More important was the trial match between Ryder's XI and
Woodfull's XI at the SCG, beginning on Thursday 6 December. The
fifteen bound for England would most surely come out of this match.
Bradman was reminded of his double failure in the equivalent match
a year earlier.

Ryder's side batted first. Jackson and Ponsford opened with a partnership of 278 before Blackie removed Ponsford for 131. Jackson hit
a powerful, stylish 182 and was told by many more now that he
should start folding his shirts. Ryder's side amassed 663. Even Bradman had a bowl. He took one for 56 off twelve overs, which was fair
considering the brutality to which the others — Blackie, Burrows,
Wall, Hornibrook and Fairfax — were subjected.

Bradman was confident and ready to go one better than his friend
Archie Jackson. He arrived at the wicket late on the second day, Friday, and careered to 54 in the hour before stumps. He brought up his
century in 122 minutes and was last man out for 124 in 166 minutes, hitting sixteen fours. Only Keith Rigg from Victoria gave him
sound support in a 171 partnership for the fifth wicket. Woodfull's
team scrabbled together 309, with Oxenham the star with the ball,
taking five for 42, including the prize wicket of Bradman, while
Grimmett took three for 68.

Ryder enforced the follow-on, which may have been an error.
Bradman was hot and Woodfull sensibly sent him in to open, so that
he had just the ten-minute break between innings before going in
again in oppressive 40°C heat.

He attacked the tired bowlers from the first ball and drove his way to 50 in eighty chanceless minutes, losing opening partner Woodfull — caught and bowled Grimmett — for 43 at 94. Grimmett struck again, this time having Fairfax stumped for 26, but not before Bradman had slipped into overdrive. His second fifty took just forty-eight minutes, giving him the ton in 128 minutes, a swashbuckling piece of theatre considering Woodfull's team was well-down. Bradman now became the only player to hit back-to-back centuries in the one game twice.

Kippax knuckled down with Bradman, and once more spectators saw how the new star could turn near-certain defeat into a possible victory. Bradman raced on to 150 in 158 minutes. With Grimmett, Oxenham, Alexander, Whitfield, Ryder, McCabe and Marks conquered and down, Bradman demonstrated his killer-instinct more graphically than ever as he went on an uncharacteristic, uncontrolled slog. Perhaps the sweltering heat had got to him, or the dust storm which hit the SCG. But he lifted balls as if he was determined to make up for those rigidly disciplined days when he had never given his shots air.

He took fifteen off an over from Marks, then a further fifteen off one from Grimmett, and was dropped in the outfield at 203. At stumps he had taken his tally to 205 not out in 210 minutes, out of a score of two for 341. His last 55 had taken just twenty-eight minutes. In the complete day's play he had compiled 275 in 323 minutes. It was his best one-day accumulation so far.

For the first time also Bradman was adjudged a 'run-scoring machine'. It was an epithet that might stick, but it did not adequately explain his brilliance. Bradman was far from a robot. His shots were innovative, daring and aggressive. He was monotonous only by way of hitting fours — twenty-eight of them, and one five — in this latest innings. The only computer-like quality about him was his methodical destruction of bowlers. Even the great Clarrie Grimmett, perhaps the most successful of the trade against him to that point, capitulated humbly at the finish.

On the Monday, Grimmett managed minor revenge by trapping him LBW for 225, which meant Bradman had scored 506 runs in his last three innings at the astonishing rate of 51 per hour. Grimmett returned the fine figures under the circumstances of seven for 173 off thirty-three overs, giving him ten for 241 for the game.

Kippax finished with 170, which certainly enhanced his chances of joining Woodfull, Ponsford, Jackson and Bradman for the UK. The doubts now centred around the selection of two from Fairfax, Ryder and McCabe, to complete the seven-man batting squad in the touring party.

Bradman and Kippax lifted the Woodfull XI's second innings tally to 541, giving Ryder's boys a target of 188 for victory. They did it with just one wicket to spare. Only McCabe batted serviceably with 46. Hornibrook and Blackie took three wickets apiece and began thinking about their luggage for England.

The post mortem on the game centred on Bradman's feat. Sports writers agreed. Bradman was an even more rounded and accomplished player than in 1928–29. His timing was better, he seemed more balanced in his stroke play and his shots were more accurate.

Soon after his trial match triumph, Bradman joined NSW, captained by Kippax, for the arduous thirty-two-hour train trek to Adelaide, where he had mixed success with scores of 2 run out and 84. The latter was a titanic struggle with Grimmett.

'He completely bamboozled me [during that innings],' Bradman recalled. 'Clarrie had me in a tangle . . . made me look like a schoolboy. He should have had my wicket long before he got me LBW.'

In Melbourne a few days later, Bradman ended 1929 with 89 and 26 not out. It had been a good year. He was a national champion sportsman, he had a job and he was in love. Bradman, at twenty-one, however, was still restless for more security, and ambitious for bigger achievements.

14

GENESIS OF GENIUS

. . . I definitely and deliberately set out to establish a record.
The highest individual score in first-class cricket was
the one record I wanted to hold, and the opportunity came
my way in this match.
— DON BRADMAN, ON HIS WORLD-RECORD SCORE OF 452 NOT OUT IN 1930

IN THE MOOD

Bradman and his NSW team-mates had to return to Sydney from the southern tour on a New Year's Eve overnight train, which was a gruelling way to celebrate the advent of the 1930s. The team had little time to freshen up and prepare for a match at SCG against Queensland, commencing on 3 January.

Bradman was keen to hit the New Year running, but instead began it opening unsuccessfully. Hurwood had him caught behind for 3 and a lethargic NSW team was dismissed for 235. Only Andrews (56) scored a half-century. Hurwood took four for 57. Queensland replied with an uninspired 227, its batsmen apparently also in less than new year cheer. Bensted batted belligerently for 51, while tail-ender Goodwin smashed 67. Stan McCabe, a better than change bowler, took advantage of the opposition's lack of ebullience by taking five for 36 with his troublesome medium-pacers.

'Stan was a bit like Greg Blewett today,' Bradman remarked. 'He opened the bowling for Australia once, although he wasn't really good enough for that job.'

During the morning's play, with Queensland's tail wagging, the Sydney crowd built on the Hill and in the stands. For many people, Saturday morning was work time and from noon onwards waves of spectators arrived at the SCG in bright sunshine. There was one man in particular they had come to see.

In the second innings, Kippax tried Fairfax as opener and put Bradman back to number three, which was fast becoming his true spot. NSW struggled through to lunch at none for 15. A band played cheerful tunes from *The Gondoliers* and other pieces during the break. Andrews and Fairfax resumed. At 22, Fairfax was caught off Hurwood. Now came the moment the crowd was waiting for.

A roar went up as Bradman appeared and made his way to the wicket. He took his time looking around the field to adjust to the bright light before facing up. He began with his hallmark push to the on, not for a single this time but a quick two. The crowd cheered. Bradman was obviously in a hurry today. This is what they had come to see. The stock market had collapsed, the economy was in a tail-spin, the dole queues were lengthening and Communists were trying to take over the Miners' Federation, but for a few hours 25,000 fans could forget their woes and the nation's problems as their hero held sway.

At 33 Andrews, the mainstay of the first innings, was also sent on his way by medium-pacer Alec Hurwood for 16, and NSW was in trouble. Kippax came to the wicket. Three seasons earlier against Queensland, on the same ground, Kippax had scored 315 while Bradman looked on in awe. Now their roles were reversed.

Bradman's first fifty took 51 minutes. He slid his way through a century as if shelling peas. His third fifty in the post-tea session was on the board in 146 minutes. He was accelerating, and the score-board was having trouble keeping up with him as he despatched balls to all points of the compass. Whereas in the first innings just four bowlers were used, now Queensland tried everyone except the keeper. But nothing could stem the tidal wave of runs. At 176, a scoreboard operator scrawled a chalk sign that Bradman had passed 1,000 for the season for the second time in his career. Only Ponsford and Kippax had previously reached the mark twice.

Bradman was 205 not out at stumps in a score of three for 368, having lost Kippax (115) in the final session at 303. In just 145 minutes they had put on 272 for the third wicket — a record in matches between the two States and in any game Queensland had played in its three seasons in the Sheffield Shield. The NSW skipper was bitterly disappointed at his dismissal. He had desperately wanted to out-stay Bradman. It was well-known in cricketing circles that Kippax was no great fan of the younger star. He was eating up too many records and was stealing the spotlight from Kippax and his ilk who otherwise would have been the big names of the era.

Bradman had come after them and was already out-performing them in astounding ways. The blaze of publicity around him was hard to take. In the press, Bradman attracted far more headlines and longer stories than anyone else. At the matches, Bradman was the crowd-puller, the player with the charisma. Women liked him, small boys clustered around him for his autograph and wanted to emulate him. Mature spectators respected his skill and were warming to his methods. Even the older purists, though they might shake their heads about his style, had to agree he got more runs quicker than the rest, and that he had all the shots. Human nature being what it was meant that some of those playing with and against him in early 1930 would be envious, even spiteful and jealous. Once acquired, fame did strange things to egos. Once reduced or removed, it did even stranger things. Bradman's performances were rapidly placing him on a pedestal above the rest. Naturally, it was resented, even if he did not encourage the media and public-driven elevation.

On top of that, Bradman had made Mick Simmons the main sports store in Sydney, taking business away from Kippax's own shop in Martin Place, which the NSW skipper resented even more.

McCabe, another emerging talent, had replaced Kippax and was playing the support role. Bradman was ten ahead of the clock, having taken just 195 minutes to reach his unbeaten 205. One scribe noted that he was scoring 200s as frequently as the best first-class players were scoring centuries. Another wrote:

Some of Bradman's drives were immense, revealing perfect timing. The wicket was such that the ball came through truly and soon lost all vestige of nip . . . One of Bradman's most furious and fruitful strokes was a square drive. Repeatedly he stepped back and crashed the ball back past Brew, who was impotent to prevent a four.

Bradman made his way back to the dressing-room to standing applause from supporters, few of whom had left the ground during that exalted afternoon. The Queensland team trailed in tall behind him and McCabe, having given of their best. Stumps had stopped the slaughter. They had Sunday to lick their wounds and prepare to capture Bradman early on Monday.

That Saturday night he spent with Jessie and other friends. On Sunday, listening to music alone, he thought about his position. It was an ideal opportunity to attempt to break a record. He decided to begin again on Monday as if it were the start of a new innings. If he reached 300, then he would set his sights clinically on passing Ponsford's highest score of 437.

'I felt everything was just right,' Bradman mused, 'the state of the wicket, the state of the game, the state of my health. Also I was in the mood for runs.'

On Sunday afternoon he rested and prepared himself.

'I'm in the mood for a lot more', he informed Jessie, whom he would often tell he was in the right frame of mind for 'a hundred'.

'When he said he would do it,' she said, 'he usually did.'

FOUR HUNDRED AND BEYOND

On Monday 6 January, about 5,000 fans turned up in hope of seeing a run-glut. They were not disappointed. Bradman continued in exactly the same manner as that in which he had finished on Saturday. He scored 59 in less than an hour before he reached 264, when he mistimed a drive off Rowe. Thurlow at short mid-on was slow to move and the ball lobbed a metre or so away from him. Bradman reached his triple century in 288 minutes — the fastest ever in Shield cricket. He was now set for a serious assault on Ponsford's 437. Bradman went on to another pre-lunch century. He was 310 in 301 minutes at lunch with the score of five for 551, having lost McCabe for 60 (after a 156 fifth-wicket stand in eighty-one minutes), and Marks for 5. Both had fallen to Hurwood, who had taken four for 130. The bowler would not give up and his determination was being noted by the selectors for the coming England tour.

Bradman had a light lunch and his usual horrid tea concoction, and was his calm, quiet and normal self. The 300 was not such a big thing for him. In five seasons since 1925–26 he had now reached it four times, twice with Bowral and once in the State match against Victoria a year ago. But as he sipped away, he contemplated the realm of 400, where only seven other first-class players had been. It was now a tangible challenge, given the way he was travelling. He could smell that 437 beyond it. It was sweet and alluring.

Meanwhile, Ponsford had reached 110 in a State game, 800 kilometres to the south in Melbourne. He was aware of Bradman's effort and thought that he would have a fair chance of beating his record, depending on whether he ran out of partners, or Kippax declared. In just two years their roles also had been reversed. Bradman was then scoring a Shield ton — his first — in Adelaide against Grimmett, while Ponsford was pushing towards his own record of 429, which he broke and then went on to 437.

Kippax gave Bradman no instructions during lunch, and the batsmen thought the innings would go on until the fall of the last wicket, or at least until stumps. NSW would then have the fourth day, Tuesday, and two and a half hours on Wednesday to dismiss Queensland, easily enough time on a wearing wicket, which was already playing indifferently.

After the break, the crowd doubled as Bradman began his climb into another historic sporting achievement. He took just five minutes to pass Kippax's 315 of two seasons earlier (also against Queensland) and twenty-seven minutes to reach another milestone, his own 340 not out of a year earlier. Even the umpire, George Borwick, shook his hand. So did Allsop (66), who added 180 for the sixth wicket with him in ninety-three minutes. NSW, as a team, was now powering along at just under two runs a minute.

At 384, he had passed C. W. Gregory's 383 in 1906–7 as the highest-ever score for NSW. At 391, he drove a ball between mid-on and mid-wicket and set off for four all-run. It was his forty-fourth four, and showed that he had the stamina to go on, and on.

After 377 minutes he became one of only eight batsmen ever at any level to reach 400 in first-class cricket. However, his innings was faster than any of the other seven's by at least two hours. Bradman waved his bat, grinned as he had at 100, 200 and 300, and took block for the fourth time.

Despite the pressure and the time at the wicket, Bradman had not slogged a single shot. There was no rush of blood to his head as there had been in the second innings of the Test trial match. He now had a mission and moved on remorselessly, stepping up his pace as the bowling wilted. The Queensland captain, O'Connor, rang ineffectual changes as players who rarely even rolled their arms over in the nets were thrown the ball.

At 3.40 p.m. Bradman late-cut a ball for one to reach 430, and erased Ponsford's second-highest score. In the next over, Thurlow bowled an attempted yorker, which Bradman straight-drove for four. The following delivery was thumped by the bowler hard but short into the pitch on middle stump. Bradman, on 434, swivelled and hooked with vicious power. The ball shot through square leg and hammered into the fence. He did not need to move as the scoreboard registered his new world record.

Bradman held his bat high, then raised his cap to the cheering spectators, who included the seventy-eight-year-old Charles Bannerman, the man who scored the first century in Test cricket, way back in 1877.

As the applause continued Bradman's partner, Davidson, congratulated him. Spontaneously, the entire Queensland team lined up to shake The Don's hand. O'Connor called for three cheers, an honour reserved for retiring greats. Bradman was possibly two decades from quitting the game. He grinned, wiped his brow, wandered back to his crease and looked over towards the dressing-room. There was no signal from Kippax that he was declaring.

Bradman could savour the moment and go on. He scored another 14 to reach 452 not out before Davidson was caught and bowled by Goodwin for 22 after an eighth-wicket partnership of 91, which neither batsman would ever forget. It was tea. NSW was eight for 761, and if the last two wickets could stay with him, Bradman had the strength and spirit to continue. At his current tempo, he would have been looking at another eighty or more in the first hour after tea, which might see him up around 550.

One of Mick Simmons' staff jumped the fence and tried to hoist Bradman onto his shoulders. 'We both finished in a heap with me on his chest,' Bradman recalled in his autobiography. 'The Queensland players, tired as they must have been, very generously picked me up and carried me off.'

Once in the dressing room, the batsman himself did not seem drained as he made himself that milk, tea and water potion, and sat back with his boots off and feet up. Other team members and former players came up and offered congratulations.

'You should go on and get 600,' someone said. 'You've just got your eye in!' Bradman grinned.

Kippax finally came over to him. 'I'm declaring,' he said. Bradman, Stan McCabe and two others players were surprised, but said nothing.

'Do I have time for a shower?' Bradman asked.

'No,' Kippax snapped. 'Just because you've broken a world record doesn't mean you don't have to come out on time with the rest of us.'

Bradman's thoughts about going on were erased. His record would stand at 452. He had hit forty-nine fours, the most in any match at any level in recorded cricket history. The innings had taken 415 minutes. His other scoring shots comprised thirteen threes, forty-six twos and 125 singles. He had mastered all bowlers. Hurwood, however, had his respect. He had taken six for 179 off thirty-four overs with a solitary maiden, the only one of the entire innings, thanks to Bradman's rapacious display. It meant Hurwood could start to think about the boat trip to England.

Was Bradman overwhelmed by his world record? Had he felt anything special?

'No,' he replied, 'there was no let-down either. I was completely satisfied. I had achieved what I had set out to do.'

Queensland batted a second time, and not surprisingly crumbled for 84, Sam Everett taking six for 23, with just under eight hours of play left in the game, leading to speculation about what Bradman might have scored had Kippax allowed him to bat on. Theoretically, if Davidson and the remaining two NSW batsmen had been able to stay with him, in another seven hours at the same rate of scoring he could have topped 900. Given the full 470 minutes available and the increasing rate at which he was scoring towards the end of the 452, it's statistically conceivable he would have reached 1,000 not out — assuming, of course, that his remarkable stamina and normal quota of good luck held up.

He scored 142 between lunch and tea on the second day of his innings, and his fifties went like this:

- 50 in 54 minutes;
- 100 in 103;
- 150 in 140;
- 200 in 185;
- 250 in 230;
- 300 in 288;
- 350 in 333;
- 400 in 377;
- 450 in 414;
- 452 in 415.

Ponsford, who had scored his 437 in a more than creditable 621 minutes, wasted no time in sending Bradman a telegram: 'Congratulations great feat player of your ability deserves the honour.'

Bradman knew Ponsford's gesture was sincere. Rather than resenting the younger man's success he encouraged it. Ponsford, who according to journalist Geoffrey Tebbutt, suffered 'from an excess of modesty which amounts almost to an inferiority complex', was looking ahead to England and especially further encounters with Larwood. The English quick had broken his arm and fractured his confidence in Brisbane in the 1928–29 Ashes series. After that humiliation, the accomplished opener wanted players like Bradman with guts, skill and ruthless dedication alongside him in the next battle.

Naturally those with a vested interest also sent felicitations. Sykes wanted their bat expressed to them so they could use it for 'advertising propaganda purposes'. Mick Simmons Ltd placed advertisements about the achievement and invited people to 'come along and meet this unassuming young man. His charming personality, his happy smile and expert advice are at your service.'

While Bradman would rather not have basked in the glory like this, such promotions reminded him that he was fast becoming public property. He met his obligations, but they accentuated his desire for a profession away from sport and the spotlight.

'I hated publicity and having to do that,' Bradman recalled. 'But I had no choice. I was under contract. It was part of my job.'

Bradman spoke on radio station 2FC, and retained his composure like an old politician, but with humour. He thanked everyone who had sent him a message and especially the 'Taralga Girl Admirers': 'The thought strikes me that perhaps my luck is out that I am not up at Taralga instead of speaking by wireless.'

He handled the pressures easily, mainly because of his solid family and country roots to which he drew closer as the adulation mounted. His parents were never far from his thoughts. Once, when selecting a gift to be presented to him during a dinner for the NSW cricketers, he was shown an array of glassware and pottery. Instead of choosing an expected set of crystal glasses, he chose a rose bowl, not for himself but for his mother.

There was also the vibrant Jessie, whom he loved more than anyone else. They shared the same background, values and aspirations.

157

They both had a no-nonsense, unpretentious yet still caring outlook on life. Even then, Bradman put his relationship with her above cricket. Jessie was his bedrock, his strength. But the more the young man showed that he was genuinely untouched by fame and glory the more the papers, responding to public demand, sought him out.

Bradman was now a national hero. Journalists and others groped for words to describe him and his feats. The one that emerged for the first time early in 1930 was 'genius'.

15

DONALD THE CONQUEROR

In the summer of 1930 a cricketing machine, by name of Donald Bradman, played havoc around county grounds of England, pulverising the finest bowlers in the land, shattering records right, left and centre, and making a tour debut the like of which will surely never be seen again.
— W. H. FERGUSON, SCORER FOR THE AUSTRALIANS

THE ULTIMATE COMPETITOR

There were good things and bad about the long boat trip to Europe. Most players enjoyed the break and the places they saw. After a long season at home they needed to relax and enthusiastically joined in the swirl of shipboard social activities. Deck tennis and quoits and even just splashing around in the tiny swimming pool helped them maintain some level of fitness. Some lost a little weight on board. Bradman, a trim 10 st 5 lb (68 kg), dropped under ten stone (65 kg). He was competitive to the point of obsession in all the deck games, noting in his diary the details of the events he took part in, and usually won. Not much appeared about the meals or books he was reading or people he met, most of the entries consisting of succinct summaries such as this:

159

Monday, 31 March
  Game of tennis and swim before breakfast.
  Beat Mr. Gay 6–1 in ball tennis singles then beat Kippax 6–0
in semi-final.
  Final played at 3 o'clock before a large gallery and I beat Alec
Hurword 6–1, 7–5.

The point that a professional analyst would have noted was his determination to win every event in which he competed. If he lost a game of deck quoits one day, he would bob up with a win at tennis the next. The same mentality applied on the cricket field. He might be dismissed under forty in one innings. But one could bet he would come up with an eighty or a big hundred in the next. He was never down. Bradman thrived on challenge and competition. Endless debate over his alleged cross-bat shots meant nothing. The ability and passion to conquer his opponents was the vital factor. Bradman's extraordinary mental application made sure of it. Cricket was his major sport. He had found the way to force victory at it: score the most runs in the quickest possible time.

'It was the way I always approached the game,' Bradman emphasised. 'If we were to win, we had to build up the biggest tally possible as quickly as possible so that our bowlers had time to get the twenty wickets required.'

If a team stuck to that and succeeded, the odds would always be in its favour. This was his basic philosophy of the game. It was simple enough. But many in cricket history had lost sight of that strategy. Not only had this lost chances for victory — it had diminished, even ruined cricket as a spectacle. Bradman, even at twenty-one, wanted to restore it and win for Australia.

There were incentives to perform on the trip and bring back the Ashes, although the general opinion, even from Australian observers such as Charlie Macartney, was that the team was not up to it. Each player earned £600 for the tour (not a bad sum considering a weekly wage of £5 was adequate in 1930), made up of £50 for equipment, £400 during the tour, and £150 on return to Australia, provided manager W. L. Kelly reported they had been 'satisfactory'. This pertained more to a player's performance off the field than on. But if Kelly thought an individual had not tried to give his best, he reserved the right to recommend the last payment be withheld.

Penalties applied for such transgressions as engaging in journalism. Clause 11 of each player's contract with the Board of Control forbade him to 'accept employment as a newspaper correspondent or to do any work for or in connection with any newspaper or any broadcasting'.

The Australians took four weeks before reaching Naples on 20 April, travelling on the SS *Orford* via Colombo, Aden and Suez. They then took a train to Paris via Rigi, Switzerland, and on their first night in the French capital went to the Folies Bergere theatre. On 22 April, they crammed in a day of the usual sightseeing up the Eiffel Tower, along the Seine and under the Arc de Triomphe, where the team watched manager Kelly and captain Billy Woodfull place a wreath on the tomb of France's Unknown Warrior. The Australians spared a thought for the number of ANZACs — more than French soldiers themselves — who had died defending France in the Great War.

At night Bradman and McCabe went dancing in the Latin Quarter and Bradman noted in his diary of the trip that the French had 'strange customs' such as 'shows that ran all night'. Bradman had kept his elegant feet moving on the boat with dancing, and could not wait to exercise them again on a cricket field.

The team took a cross-Channel steamer to Dover on 23 April, then a train to Victoria Station in London. They were met by Lord Plumer and Lord Decies, and began a round of formal lunches and dinners in the capital of a nation feeling not the bite but the ravages of a deepening Depression — the worst economic conditions since the war.

Unemployment was soaring over two million and inspiring George Orwell to write his *Down and Out in Paris and London*. Labour had been voted in by a people fed up with the iniquities resulting from the extreme divisions of class and wealth. The Moscow-controlled Comintern was infiltrating Oxford and Cambridge and recruiting brilliant agents from the British intellectual élite in the hope of achieving the class revolution the British had never had. Beggars were on the streets. Above them a sign of 'progress' in the form of the airship, the R101, sailed for those with the income to fly, it was claimed, without the dangers of the propeller plane.

The team were lodged at the old, spacious, ugly Gothic Midland Hotel, above St Pancreas Station. 'When they awoke on that first morning [24 April] there must have been disappointment,' wrote Australian journalist Geoffrey Tebbutt.

> *True, the red buses of London — those blurs of scarlet that had been familiar pictures since boyhood — thundered past, but this world of gigantic posters, dingy and crowded shops, shabby women, and oppressed looking men in an estuary of dull grey streets — was it London? . . . The cricketers gradually realised that the London they had heard about lay only a few minutes south and a few minutes west . . .*

Bradman, for one, was pleased by at least the location of the hotel, for it meant that he was free of playing Pied Piper to a continual throng of small boys armed with pens and autograph books, who would have plagued him in London if the team had been stationed at the defunct Hotel Cecil between the Strand and the Embankment, which had been the base for previous tour parties. Fleet Street reporters were now some way from the temperate, publicity-shy members of the team too. Led by Woodfull, the most sober member of the party, whom Bradman always admired, this group enjoyed the moments of anonymity squeezed in between their busy social engagements.

But they were there to play cricket and no sooner had they settled in on 24 April, a bitterly cold, grey London day, than Bradman had his first net at the game's headquarters, Lord's, in St Johns Wood. Several hundred overcoated fans turned up for the first sight of the Australians, who practised eagerly. Prompted by the experts in the press, the public's troubled mind was temporarily turned to the squad from down-under for entertainment in the national sport. Just how good were they?

SUBSTANCE OVER STYLE

Discussion was now renewed about Bradman's style by many more English observers. They looked in vain for his infamous cross-bat, and several journalists came to the conclusion that though Bradman's backlift did drift out towards slips, when he brought it forward to meet the ball it was dead perpendicular. Still, his unorthodox pull shot from off to on raised the purists' eyebrows.

'I liked this stroke,' Bradman remarked. 'It scored me many runs in Australia and I saw no reason to eliminate it in England. The fact is, to place the wider ball on the off onto the on-side you are compelled to play cross-bat. There is no other way to achieve it.'

His powerful cutting and hooking also had the critics chit-chatting. It was fine to play so aggressively in the nets, they murmured, but it could be his undoing in matches. Kippax and McCabe impressed with their greater flourish and fluency. Grimmett created a great impression with his spin. All agreed this team would draw big crowds, especially if it got off to a strong start in a week or so.

The Australians practised at Lord's again on 26 April, lunched at Wembley as guests of the Football Association, and then joined the biggest crowd they had ever seen — 92,000 — to watch Arsenal beat Huddersfield Town 2:0 in the Cup Final. During the match, they looked up to see the German version of the airship, *Graf Zeppelin* — like a long, silver cigar and, it later proved, even more inflammable — hovering above, then gasped as the pilot let the huge craft suddenly and dangerously drop a hundred metres or so. Men inside could be seen waving their handkerchiefs and women their jewellery.

The exciting atmosphere buoyed Bradman and put him in combative mood for the first game of the tour, at Worcester, commencing on 30 April. The night before the game, *The Times* writer Beau Vincent caught a glimpse of him in the Worcester Hotel:

163

He was sitting in front of the fire-place in the public writing-room — alone and thinking. And I feel that all through his illustrious cricket career he has always been thinking, concentrating on what has to be done. Master of himself, just as he has unquestionably been master of bowlers.

Next morning, on the beautiful ground ringed by great elms and set under the majestic cathedral, the game began before a hardy crowd in freezing wind and rain. Fortunately for the tourists, Worcestershire batted first in the awful conditions. None of the home bats looked comfortable and they were dismissed for 131. Grimmett may not have warmed up, but his form was hot with four for 38. Fairfax, who would not have worn a sweater all year in Sydney, took four for 36.

Archie Jackson and Woodfull walked out to open while Bradman padded up, put on a sweater, blazer and overcoat and sat in front of a dressing-room fire, waiting his turn to bat. Jackson became the first Australian victim for the season for 24 at 67. Just after the tea-break, Bradman peeled off his overcoat and blazer and strode out to the middle to join his skipper. A fine sheet of rain drifted across the oval as he began and immediately prospered. As the cathedral chimes pealed 'Home Sweet Home' at 5 p.m. he was 18 in twenty-three minutes. In that short time he had produced a fearful cut, a withering cover drive, a stylish late cut, drives to mid-wicket and mid-on and a strong pull.

After an hour he was 51, and had made a few thousand converts. Despite the bleak weather the crowd was not about to leave until Bradman was dismissed or stumps were drawn. At close of play after ninety minutes he was 75 not out. Woodfull, 95 not out, was batting purposefully and was not overshadowed.

After play, the Australians attended a reception at the Guildhall. Bradman listened to the speeches, finished his meal and excused himself early at 9 p.m. He had a job to do next day.

The papers that morning concentrated more on Australia's bowling, which was labelled 'average', 'uninspiring', and 'steady'. The comments on Australia's batting were limited to a few pars. Woodfull was a known quantity in England. Bradman was new, and he received a sentence or two more.

When play resumed, he brought out his full range of shots as he added 25 to reach his first century on English soil in 120 minutes. The partnership drove on until Woodfull tried to smash a straight one and was bowled for 133. Bradman was in no mood to donate his wicket so easily. He had much more to prove than his skipper and was 173 not out, having missed a century before lunch by just two runs. In all, he had batted 210 minutes and had hit eighteen fours. McCabe (24) gave only a glimpse of his skills, Richardson ran himself out for just 15 and Fairfax was caught for a duck, while a'Beckett managed in his unpretty way to stick around for fifty minutes.

Meanwhile, Bradman powered on to 200 in 250 minutes and made history as the youngest player — Trumper was three weeks older — ever to run up a double ton in England.

Woodfull called a halt with the score at eight for 492 and Bradman on 236 not out in 276 minutes. The small crowd gave him a generous reception. It was the highest first-up score by a tourist in England, eclipsing Hugh Massie's 206 in 1882, but it was also one of the most significant innings of Bradman's career, for it served warning that he would be as heavy a scorer in England as he had been in Australia, dispelling all the speculation about the inadequacy of his technique on English wickets.

However, the critics were reserved and still batting for the home team. H. J. Henley in the *Daily Mail* conceded that Bradman 'had not been overrated . . . but from an English point of view there is one consolation — Worcestershire bowling isn't England bowling.' But Yorkshire's great all-rounder, Wilfred Rhodes, saw the game at Worcester and privately told a friend that he had just watched 'the greatest batsman the world has ever seen'.

Half-forgotten in the torrent of appraisal was Grimmett's fine match. He took five for 46 in Worcester's second dig of 196, giving him nine for 84 in all, which ranked close to Bradman's effort with the bat. Australia's decisive first-up victory of an innings and 165 runs was an early boost to morale.

On they went to Leicester by train for a game which began the next day in depressing conditions again. Grimmett continued his outstanding form with the ball, taking seven for 46 as the home side crumbled for just 148. Wall took three for 37 and Oldfield's understudy Walker brilliantly stumped three off Grimmett. Australia batted and lost Jackson for 4. Bradman was 9 not out at the close with Ponsford on 19.

The next morning the Aussies looked in trouble as Bradman defended and they lost Ponsford (25), Kippax (22) and McCabe (2). Richardson came in and acted as a foil, allowing Bradman to step up a gear. He reached his fifty after lunch in 175 minutes, and then accelerated, his second fifty coming in 71 minutes. With a century behind him and Richardson batting strongly, Bradman, as one paper put it, 'commenced to hit out at tremendous pace.' His next fifty took just thirty-six minutes as he stepped into Test bowler George Geary. The bowler had pinned him down early, but Bradman had his revenge and scored a moral victory before the First Test, hitting him for most of 33 in a twenty-minute spell.

Rain drove the players from the field at 5.25 p.m. with Bradman on 185 (315 minutes, sixteen fours), Fairfax on 21 and Australia five for 365. The next morning play was abandoned due to the continuing foul weather, thus robbing Bradman of his second double century in successive innings. He had now scored 421 runs without being dismissed in his first 600 minutes of batting in England.

This effort brought the papers out trumpeting for the first time. 'It is joyous to see Australia's second Trumper in his varying phases,' the *Morning Post* said. The new man was still being labelled and compared. Yet the word 'potential' had been dropped from reviews and previews.

GRIMMETT THE DECIMATOR

The team selectors rested Bradman for the third game against Essex, on 7–9 May. Kippax got 57 out of Australia's dismal 156. But the damp wicket proved too much for the home team, which collapsed for 67 — Hornibrook taking six for 11. Australia's second effort was better at six declared for 264. Woodfull continued his good form with 54, while Fairfax hit an encouraging 53 not out.

Essex improved marginally on the weather-advanced better wicket and reached 146. Hornibrook took four for 29, giving him ten for 40 for the game, which Australia won by 207. No-one was able to say, 'no Bradman, no Australia', although none of the other bats took control and dominated as he had in the first two games.

He returned to the team on 10 May for the fourth match at Bramall Lane, in the heart of Leeds' grimy heavy industry. Yorkshire batted first and were rolled by Clarrie Grimmett, who put in the best performance by any bowler in an innings in 1930. The South Australian leggie took all ten wickets for 37. Sutcliffe managed 69, but the other big names in the side — Percy Holmes, Leyland and Rhodes — were all dismissed cheaply.

Bradman came to the wicket late in the afternoon once again in conditions better suited for winter football. The light was poor, due partly to cloud but mostly factory smog. Woodfull did not appeal against the pollution, wanting his squad to get as much cricket as possible. George Macaulay, a local spinner, fancied himself against Bradman because of his penchant for coming down the pitch and had boasted to Test bowler Bill Bowes that he would get the Australian caught and bowled. Macaulay varied his flight and tried to lure his prey into a drive. It didn't work.

At stumps Bradman was 24 not out in thirty-eight minutes, and Woodfull 12. The wicket was damp on Monday morning and playing tricks, but Bradman adapted, dominating the morning partnership with a brisk 50 in seventy minutes. 'I found the English wet wickets less fearsome than the Australian variety,' he commented.

But Macaulay had the last laugh. His plan for a catch off his own bowling had a better show in the slippery conditions, and he finally tempted Bradman into a drive, which he hadn't quite reached. He was indeed out caught and bowled for 78.

It was Bradman's first dismissal in England after 499 runs, which was his average at that point. It had taken fifteen bowlers nearly twelve hours to achieve it, in all conditions, but mainly adverse for the batsmen. He had shown a controlled attack, a sound defence and skill on wet wickets, which were said to be his downfall. He had come a long way since that first Test sticky in Brisbane eighteen months earlier, although he had still not played on more than a handful of pitches like it.

Bradman quickly realised that English wickets changed in character far more than Australian during the course of a game. 'The heavier atmosphere is more conducive to swing,' he said in his autobiography, *Farewell to Cricket*, 'and the more grassy wickets enable bowlers to get some assistance from the pitch. Nevertheless, the ball usually comes off the ground at a slower speed.'

Bradman considered his lack of height and his preference for shots off the back foot advantageous. He began to enjoy batting on slower wickets.

His partnership with Woodfull against Yorkshire was 107, and the skipper went on to a laborious but important 121. His form in this vital early part of the tour was second only to Bradman's and they were the mainstays of a batting line-up that otherwise so far looked brittle. The other nine batsmen against Yorkshire, for instance, could only scramble 120 between them. The game was washed out on day three.

The team travelled on to play Lancashire at Liverpool. On the morning of the match they were waiting in their hotel to speak by phone for the first time to Australia. Bradman was tinkering at a piano and chatting to Fairfax, Kippax and Arthur Mailey, who was covering the tour for Australian papers.

Mailey reported that at one point Kippax said to Fairfax: 'What are you going to say to your mother, Alan?'

'I'll tell her that I've seen the changing of the guard at Buckingham Palace,' Fairfax replied.

'What on earth is the use of telling her about that?' Kippax asked. 'She can see the changing of the guards at the Waverley tram depot any day.'

According to Mailey, Bradman collapsed over the keyboard.

They then headed down to Liverpool's Aigburth ground, where the county side went down meekly for 176, with only Eckersley (54) showing resistance to Grimmett, now the grim reaper of English wickets, harvesting six for 57. However, the tour design finished there. The Australians ran into the Victorian former Test speedster Ted McDonald. He had joined Lancashire in 1924 to play professionally.

As a twelve-year-old schoolboy, Bradman had seen him nearly a decade earlier in that Test against England at the SCG in January 1921. Then McDonald had formed a fierce opening combination with Jack Gregory. He still had plenty of pace, which he turned on against the Australians.

'It was hard to visualise a more beautiful action,' Bradman commented. 'Coupled with splendid control and pace, he was the most feared bowler in England, as he had been before in the Australian team.'

Bradman came in at one for 4. He seemed in no trouble, although he watched McDonald closely. The paceman tested him with short balls, which were not a worry. Then he bent his back and delivered a fast in-swinger. Bradman moved across to the off and audaciously attempted to hit it to the square-leg boundary. He missed it and looked back to see his middle-stump uprooted. He had scored 9 in nineteen minutes.

The extent to which the team had been relying on Bradman's dominance now became obvious. Australia collapsed for a pathetic 115. McDonald took three for 51, Hopwood four for 13 and Test player Tyldesley three for 17. Lancashire batted again and were dismissed for 165. This time Hornibrook's left-arm spinners took five for 38.

Australia began its second innings on the last day, 16 May, with 227 to make in 160 minutes. It lost a couple of early wickets and decided not to go after the runs. Bradman was not about to do anything rash after his cheap dismissal in the first innings. He played straight to McDonald, who worked up even more pace than in the first innings. Bradman weathered the onslaught and remained 48 not out in Australia's two for 137.

The press attacked the team for not chasing the runs. 'For all the purpose they served the players might as well have spent three days in the nets,' *The Times* cricket writer complained. The Australians were accused of being 'precious' about the 'remote prospect of losing'. Woodfull was the target, although criticism of Bradman was also implied.

He had now made 554 at an average of 277. There was some talk about him reaching 1,000 runs before the end of May, a feat never before achieved by a tourist. Bradman had perhaps five or six innings left to do it, and the odds were against him because of the weather. However, bets were being laid in London and the punters turned their eyes to Lord's and Bradman's first appearance there, against an MCC team.

The Marylebone Cricket Club, which administered English cricket from Lord's, chose a powerful bowling combination comprising three pacemen, G. O. ('Gubby') Allen, Allom and Kennedy, and two leg-spinners, Ian Peebles and Greville Stevens, in the hope of gaining a psychological advantage against the rain-sodden Australians, who had scored only two victories so far, thanks to the weather.

Woodfull won the toss and batted in bright sunshine in front of 30,000 people, only to lose Jackson for 0. Bradman joined his skipper and they proceeded cautiously, in a quasi-Test match atmosphere. Bradman gradually unveiled his strokes, but carefully watched all the bowlers, none of whom he had faced before. He reached a measured fifty in the good time of eighty-five minutes. Just before lunch he attempted to cover-drive Allom but edged the ball onto his stumps. He had scored 66 in 110 minutes. Woodfull made 52, and Ponsford found some welcome touch with 82 not out. But again, the tourists looked scratchy in compiling 285.

The MCC fared no better in putting together 258. Duleepsinhji (92) came closest to scoring the first ton in six matches against the Australians. He batted with grace and style and looked to have booked himself a First Test place. Fairfax enhanced his chances with six for 54.

Australia batted a second time and lost Woodfull at 14, bringing Bradman to the wicket for a torrid twenty minutes in which he looked out of sorts before falling LBW for four to a delivery that straightened from Stevens, whose googlies were turning. Bradman's season tally had reached 624, and his average — now down to 156 — was looking more human with every match. The chance of scoring that coveted 1,000 in the first month of the cricket season appeared remote. He seemed off the boil. The consensus of opinion based on this showing was that he would hold few terrors for England in the Tests.

Jackson finally found some useful form with 64 as Australia struggled to 213, with 'Gubby' Allen, the future Test fast bowler, managing four for 28. The MCC did not have time to bat a second time and the game was drawn.

On 20 May, the Australians took the train for Chesterfield for the match against Derbyshire and read the unfavourable press. It was the coldest day of the tour so far and Derbyshire could not counter Hornibrook, who took six for 61. He complained that he should have taken all ten wickets, and would have had the icy conditions not stiffened up his spinning fingers. Derby cobbled 215 and Australia began its reply. The bright spot with the First Test in mind was the form of Ponsford and Jackson. They put on 127 for the first wicket, before Jackson was dismissed for 63.

Bradman again peeled off layers of clothing and shivered his way out to the wicket. He received three short balls early, which he fended off with his forearm, rather than give a catch. No amount of rubbing in the freezing conditions relieved the numbness, which made even holding the bat difficult. The blows unsettled Bradman and his performance was scratchy. After eight-five minutes he was caught at the wicket for 48. Ponsford went on to 131 and Australia tallied 348.

It was enough for victory. Derbyshire scored 181 in the second dig, and Hornibrook skittled six more for 82, giving him the best match figures for the season so far of twelve for 143. Australia got the 52 required and won by ten wickets. It was another morale booster, similar to the first-up win against Worcester, but the press were unimpressed and continued to disparage the team's efforts.

16
FENDER BENDER

I suppose no man has ever been more of a master of his job than Bradman is master of his job. He is as good a batsman as Bach was a composer.

— SIR NEVILLE CARDUS, CRICKET WRITER AND MUSIC CRITIC

PERCY'S PROBLEM

The tourists returned to London and their hideaway hotel above St Pancreas station and prepared for their game against Surrey, captained by Percy Fender, at The Oval starting on Saturday 24 May. The team included Mr M. J. C. Allom, who had dismissed Bradman at Lord's, and Fender's great friend, Douglas Jardine, who needed a big score to impress the selectors.

Bradman had noted and underlined the criticisms by Fender, especially his comment in the 1928–29 series that the Australian was 'brilliant but unsound'. Fender had addressed luncheons and dinners before and during the tour, but was still unrepentant in his remarks about Bradman. His only concession was to avoid his earlier criticism of Bradman's alleged lack of style and substance. But he still contended that Bradman was a batsman who 'did not correct mistakes or look as if he were trying to'.

Fender's approach was only to be expected. He was one of the best tacticians and most knowledgeable cricketers of the era. Many people thought him uncharitable and perhaps even jealous in his attitude to Bradman, but like his pal Jardine, he was not about to give this formidable opponent any advantage. While Bradman was the talk of the country like no other visitor since Trumper, Fender refused to pronounce him a great player. To do so would be to give the Australians' morale an unnecessary boost.

Cricket was as much a mind game as a physical one. Bradman had proved successful so far with 672 runs at 112 per innings, but he had yet to face the might of England in the pressure of a Test on English wickets. If his opponents could gain the psychological upper hand now, when his rush of early form had faltered, they could push him into a trough of failure. It had happened before with visiting teams and would again. While some careers had been made on such a tour, others had been broken, or at least held back.

Woodfull won the toss and batted under gloomy London skies in cold, damp conditions with the constant threat of rain. The experiment of opening with Jackson seemed to be failing as he waved his bat at a rising ball from Allom and was caught behind for the third time in three matches. Doubts about his soundness at the top of the order were now being voiced.

Bradman strolled out with a real challenge in mind. He wanted a big one against Fender, Jardine and Surrey. 'I was determined not to make any mistakes that day,' he recalled.

Fender moved two men close in on the leg-side to exert extra pressure. The Surrey captain too was out to prove a point as he conferred with Jardine and Allom before it was set.

Bradman was cautious against Allom, who forced him to play and miss several times, but survived a shaky start and settled down in the hour before lunch, scoring 28 not out. After the break, he added 22 in a half-hour to reach 50. It had taken 90 minutes. Fender brought himself on and had Woodfull caught for 50. The two batsmen had once more put on a century (116) stand for the first wicket.

In came Richardson, ready to attack. Fender bowled his first full over to Bradman, who late-cut him for two, then pushed him to mid-wicket for two more. The Surrey skipper pitched one wide outside off-stump, but Bradman dragged him round to the mid-wicket fence and next ball hooked him square for another two. Fender took his sweater. Ten had come off the over, the best for the tourists in the innings so far. Bradman was into the seventies and looking set. He bruised Fender with another eight off his next over, and the unhappy captain took himself off. Bradman cruised into the eighties.

Desperate to stop Bradman's century, Fender made a double bowling change, bringing Allom back on with the economical Shepherd. Bradman cut with polish, taking singles and the occasional two as he coasted through the nineties. He brought up his century with a push to mid-wicket off Allom. It had taken him 145 minutes, the last fifty in just fifty-five minutes. Fender did not clap. Nor did Jardine. As Allom turned to run in, the umpire's arm went out. Bradman was taking block again. He was letting Fender know who was in charge on the field, without a word being spoken.

In the hour before tea, Allom had Richardson caught for 32. He and Bradman had put on 113 for the second wicket, the latter scoring 80 of them. Ponsford came in and Fender immediately brought himself back on. He trapped the Victorian LBW for 1, in what may have been a preconceived plan.

Stan McCabe came in, looked uncomfortable from ball one, and was soon caught by Fender off Allom. Australia was five for 197 and struggling. Bradman took over the strike and shielded Fairfax, who looked uncertain early against both Fender and Allom, but Bradman literally drove the Surrey captain out of the attack again with successive boundaries either side of the wicket. At tea, he was on 142 not out, having scored 114 in the session between lunch and tea — his first century in a session for the tour. Australia was five for 240 and back in the saddle.

Bradman had won the day and settled the argument about his ability. But he had decided that this would be the day of atonement for Percy Fender. After tea, Bradman moved in for the kill, cutting like a master surgeon in a hurry, but always with a clinical control, as the Surrey bowlers kept feeding him outside off-stump in the hope that he would mistime one and give a catch. Fender rang the changes wildly, but not a single delivery went through to the keeper as Bradman proceeded to shred the attack.

According to many witnesses that day, Bradman seemed to be deliberately sliding balls past Fender himself, making the tired skipper chase and chase. It was most likely an optical illusion, brought on by the fact that the confrontation between these two had been publicised and anticipated. Nonetheless, Fender had to do more than his share of sprints. Bradman himself denied the charge that he had set out to humiliate Fender:

> *It's simply not true. I was concentrating on making runs as fast as possible without concern for any particular fielder. No. I'd never even spoken to Fender, full stop. I was just a junior member of the team. Fender was a senior English player and captain of Surrey. Only the captains spoke to each other in those days. There was no fraternising after the game as there is now.*

Nor, he added, had he ever spoken to Jardine up to that point in 1930.

Bradman now went on to crack his second hundred in a breathtaking eighty minutes. His 200 was posted in 225 minutes. At one point he scored 51 to Fairfax's 1. The party didn't end there, as he stepped into the bowling and even began to loft balls. At 207, he swivelled into a hard hook off Allom, and mishit one to Bert Lock at short square leg. The fieldsman was so shocked that he spilled it.

Bradman plundered another 50 in forty-five minutes until his score was 252 not out from Australia's five for 379, with Fairfax 28 not out in an unfinished partnership of 129, when the rain came down half an hour before stumps and ended Fender's embarrassment. Bradman had hit twenty-nine fours, and at a rate of fifty-two an hour and rising.

Fender hurried from the field, making no effort to congratulate Bradman. The crowd surged onto the ground as the batsman ran to avoid both well-wishers and rain. The police formed a small corridor and ushered him through before the mob swamped them. 'Fender didn't tell us what he thought of the innings,' the Surrey bowler Bert Lock recalled, 'but it can only be described as magnificent.'

175

The Surrey skipper didn't need to say anything. He had been forced to eat humble pie in silence. Fender had captained the county since 1920 and this 252 not out was easily the highest score ever made against him. The time of 290 minutes would have driven home the import of this knock, which cricket writers and other experts agreed was the finest innings of the season to that stage. As *The Observer* commented:

> *Bradman's innings was a marvellous display of clever, stylish, and almost faultless batting. The most ardent Surrey partisan could not grudge any of his runs. Recollection of the innings will always be happy to those privileged to witness it.*

After the innings, Bradman had some tea and watched the bleak vision of the rain teeming down. At least the wicket was being covered for Saturday night. Woodfull had not declared, so Bradman could expect to bat on Monday. When the umpires abandoned play for the day, he showered and changed. There was no car waiting for him, and he was forced to take the Underground train at The Oval stop, which was a short walk from the pavilion exit.

The moment he stepped out of the ground, he was mobbed. Half the throng was made up of small boys. People clawed, pawed and asked for autographs. Bradman obliged, edging his way to the tube. But the fans, especially the boys, would not leave him. A swarm followed him onto the platform and the train. Bradman would have preferred to be just another commuter. He was looking forward to a meal, a pot of tea and some music in his room at the Midland before going to the theatre with the team. The mob stayed with him until he got off at Kings Cross.

TOWARDS A MAY THOUSAND

Bradman awoke early Sunday to drizzling rain and was pleased about those covered wickets at The Oval as he set out to meet a golfing appointment at the Shirley Park Golf Club. The papers were waxing lyrical about him and he accepted for the first time that he had a real chance of scoring a thousand runs in May. His 252 had landed him on 922, and he thought that with luck he might knock them off next day.

The papers also listed the records his big double century had broken, including the highest score by an Australian against Surrey, and the highest tally by any tourist from any country at The Oval.

He was keen to improve on all these but awoke Monday at 6 a.m. to more depressing rain. However, his spirits were lifted by an international call from Australia — a novelty still just three weeks old. His record score was forgotten as his diary in *The Bradman Albums* shows:

> *Monday, 26 May*
> *Awakened early. Phone call from Australia came through.*
> *I spoke to mum, dad, May, Mr. and Mrs. Cush, Mr. and Mrs. Jones. Uncanny feeling. Voices clear but very suggestive of power and distance. The radio phone has only been open for three weeks.*
> *Rain. No Play today.*
> *Into Imperial Advertising Co. Received camera, film, safety razor, pocket knife, wristlet watch.*
> *To the Coliseum Theatre in the afternoon with Stan. Round London afterwards.*
> *Surrey County C.C. dinner in Skinner's Hall at night. H.D. Leveson-Gower, 'Plum' Warner, Lord Chelmsford and others spoke. Beautiful old hall built in 1300 odd.*

The weather may have held back his record-breaking, but his enthusiasm for these experiences was undiminished. The Surrey game had to be abandoned and Bradman missed out on a triple century and the 1,000 in one hit. However, there were still a couple of matches before May closed. The first was at Oxford against a weak University side. Bradman looked certain to clock up the 78 needed until the openers for the match, McCabe and Ponsford, got going.

McCabe made 91 and brought the long-waiting Bradman to the wicket in the afternoon session. He set out to stroke the required runs by tea, but was bowled for 32. His tally would sit at 954. Ponsford went on to some useful batting practice against the second-rate attack, scoring 220 not out. Kippax managed a quick 56 not out and Australia declared late in the day at two for 406.

Oxford kept things symmetrical and scored 124 in both innings. Grimmett took five for 48 in the first innings and Wall four for 29 in the second. Australia won by an innings and 158. Woodfull, charitably and sensibly, included Bradman in the side for the following game against Hampshire at Southampton. The game began on the last day in May — a Saturday. It was imperative that the Aussie skipper won the toss. He didn't. Hampshire's skipper, the languid, flamboyant Lord Tennyson, just off the boat from the US, put his own side in.

Bradman, ever the realist, looked up at the skies and thought the odds were heavily against him creating history in this merry month. Hampshire's openers started well, with Brown dominating, and his partner, Hosie, dropping anchor. Brown, taking a lot of cheeky singles, advanced well to fifty while Hosie propped. At 66, Brown (56), who evidently had not consulted Hammond, Hobbs or indeed any of the 1928–29 MCC touring team about certain Aussie fieldsmen, stroked a ball seemingly wide of Bradman's hand at mid-on and set off. Bradman moved fast, gathered the ball, turned and threw down the stumps at the bowler's end. One down, nine to go and storm clouds gathering.

Then Grimmett, the other hero of the tour, rolled the team out with his immaculate length and variation, taking seven for 39 as Hampshire were tumbled for 151. Woodfull the generous put Bradman in to open with Jackson. He had just 48 to get. He collected 28 by tea, but as the players hurried off the field it began pouring. Bradman worried his nails and watched the clock.

The hands were 'rushing round to stumps [6.30 p.m.]', he recalled. It was torrenting down. Bradman was convinced the weather had beaten him. Then at 5.37 p.m. a little ray of providence appeared. The rain abated. The umpires squelched out and play started again. Bradman hoisted his score to 39, or 993, but it began to bucket again.

The umpires looked over at Tennyson. His lugubrious features gave away nothing as he tossed the ball to Jack Newman, indicating he wanted one more over. The good Lord then trotted over to the bowler for a quick consultation. What instructions he issued are open to conjecture.

Newman began with a full-toss on the leg stump, which Bradman crashed to the boundary for 997. In loped Newman again and delivered a fast, short ball. Bradman pivoted into history once more with a sizzling pull and another crashing four, to bring up 1,001.

The runs had taken him exactly twenty-four hours at a rate of 41.70 runs an hour and often against top-quality opponents. In the course of that complete day of batting in nine matches he had faced twelve bowlers who would go on to take 100 first-class wickets for the 1930 season.

The players raced for the dressing-room as the rain came pouring down. At the gate Tennyson caught up with Bradman, smiled and shook his hand. Staying on the field had been a generous act of sportsmanship, one which could have been chosen by Warwick Armstrong in 1921 with Jardine so close to a century. Tennyson's attitude made a lasting impression on Bradman. He himself would always be ready with an appropriate sporting gesture in similar circumstances.

Even the way Tennyson handled questions from journalists after the game showed a certain style. He was asked whether he had instructed Newman to bowl easy ones. Tennyson shook his head, smiled enigmatically and replied: 'Perhaps the wet ball slipped out of his hand.'

Bradman's batting on the Monday, 2 June, was freer. The wicket had dried out in a way impossible in Australia — damp and tough to bat on, but not as bad as a sticky. Bradman plundered on. He reached a century in 135 minutes and scored 109 before lunch, making him 156 at the break. Only McCabe (65), now in excellent form, was able to stay with him in the trying conditions.

Bradman went on to 191 before being caught. Australia folded for 334. His first ten innings' performance ranked him far above Victor Trumper in 1902, whose aggregate was 723 from fifteen knocks at an average of 48.2, and also Charlie Macartney in 1912 (804 in twelve innings at 67). Bradman already had 1,145 from eleven innings at 143.12. These comparative figures were astonishing to most observers, who had been loath to put Bradman in the same bracket as the other two. However, gradually — with analysis of such statistics — the reality about his dominance began to sink in.

Grimmett ran through Hampshire a second time, taking seven for 56 in the county's total of 175. He had taken fourteen for 95, the new best effort for the season. Despite Bradman's achievement and near-double century, Grimmett would have taken any man-of-the-match award. Australia's chances of winning the Ashes now seemed to rest primarily with these two. Bradman would have to score the runs, and Grimmett would have to make sure England was dismissed twice.

Middlesex was the next game. The scenario was the usual one, and the county was dismissed for 103. This time Hornibrook got in first and took seven for 42. Grimmett backed him up with three for 36. Australia replied with 270. Kippax finally got a century (102), just in time to justify his Test selection, while Bradman 'failed' with 35. The news was better for England with Gubby Allen taking six for 77. Another Test player at Middlesex, Patsy Hendren, struck form with 138 in the second innings out of 287 — the first century and best batting performance against the tourists so far. Hornibrook kept up his touch with four for 60.

Australia replied with five for 121, thus winning the match by five wickets. Bradman dropped his average with a second low score of 18.

In the final pre-Test county game, against Cambridge, he definitely relaxed and did much of the bowling (three for 35) with McCabe (four for 25) as the University team folded for 145. Australia replied with eight for 504 declared. Woodfull was in wonderful touch and boosted his average with a powerful 216, while McCabe edged closer to a ton, this time making 96. Bradman hit 32 in quick time, which was marginally better than a good net. Cambridge improved in the second dig and reached 225, McCabe getting another four for 60 and Bradman three for 68. These were Bradman's best first-class bowling figures. His leggies and wrong'uns were working serviceably and he collected a good bat, E. T. Killick, in both innings to give him nine first-class wickets for the tour so far. It was a nice, easy work-out, with the tourists winning by an innings and 134.

During the Sunday break, most of the tourists were invited to lunch at Hillinton Hall, King's Lynn, which bordered the royal estate at Sandringham. After lunch, their host, Lord Downe, decided to take them in to meet his neighbour, the King of England. George V, in his country tweeds, wandered around and mixed informally — if that would ever apply to meeting royalty — with the players. He surprised them with his 'common touch' by calling Lord Downe 'Jack' and chatting with Woodfull like an old acquaintance. 'George' singled out Bradman to congratulate him.

'I hope to see you play,' he told them, 'probably at Lord's.'

The tall, austere figure of Queen Mary approached.

'Here comes the Queen', the King said. 'Must introduce you boys to her,' and he did. 'The boys' were allowed the freedom of the grounds. They inspected gardens, stables, dairy, the new museum, stud farms, and the church. It was an afternoon to savour for later dining out in Australia. The team members asked the royals if they could take photographs.

'Fire away,' the King said, 'take as many as you like'.

For once, the players were just like those irksome press people and eager fans, as they manoeuvred around the royals and snapped them. The Queen winced a royal smile or two. 'Would love to have copies,' she said, convincingly enough.

Later the team put the best shots, signed by 'the boys', in a gold-decorated, leather-bound album and presented it to their majesties, who were no doubt enchanted by the amateur efforts. At least the King said so, in a 'charmingly-worded' acknowledgement. The album shots were placed not on the wall in the royals' favourite loo, but in the photographic collection among the archives at Windsor Castle. Diplomacy and good relations with the Realm's biggest, most far-flung Dominion were alive and well. There wasn't a republican in sight.

Geoffrey Tebbutt, in his book *With the Australians in 1930*, summed up the mood and the fragility of the monarchy:

> *The fine impression his Majesty's reception of the team created in Australia was evident from the repeated references to it in letters to cricketers from relatives at home. And, like the Rugby Union from NSW — the Waratahs — who walked out shooting with the King at Sandringham two years before, the heightened regard for the Throne, and the more real understanding of the hold its occupant has upon his people, cannot fail to act as a binding element.*

Meanwhile, back on the cricket field, the team was preparing for the nearest thing to war between the friendly, monarch-linked nations. The green fields of England were where the two different cultures could forget the niceties of diplomacy and tact, and attack each other with bat and ball. For it was on the field that the raw differences in character and culture emerged. If tough Larwood, who originated from a mining village nearby, could leave the Aussie bats bruised and intimidated, he would — for England. If Bradman, from an outback 'hamlet', could humiliate every bowler by smashing them to every point of the field in front of their loyal countrymen and women, he would not hesitate to do so — for Australia.

As his country's main gladiator, much was expected of him now that he had compiled 1,230 runs in fourteen innings, at 111.92, the best-ever aggregate for a tourist before a Test. He may have been off the boil, but it was difficult to tell, for he seemed to relax in the weak games and lift himself when challenged in the bigger events. With the First Test at Nottingham a few days away, the moment to produce a big one was now, if the tourists were to begin the Ashes series with a victory.

17
ENGLAND TAKES THE BRIDGE

Don Bradman is a monopoly. Drama is afield the moment this jaunty dignity and purposeful poise emerge from the pavilion.

— C. B. FRY, CRICKETER AND WRITER

CLARRIE'S CLARION

Woodfull hid his team away from the growing legion of English pressmen in secret quarters at Bath for a few days before the First Test. *The Times* accused him of being over-cautious 'like his batting' and of 'coddling' the players. But The Rock had toured before and knew the pressures, and the tricks journalists got up to just before big games. Late-night calls and doorknocking were common, and Woodfull wanted his players to get their sleep. 'Do not disturb' signs were hung outside all doors.

Bradman's friend and mentor from Bowral, Alf Stephens, visited him during that critical build-up and helped him to relax. Stephens had always said he would be there for Bradman's first Test in England and he was true to his word.

The team came out of seclusion and went to the Black Boy Hotel in Long Row, in the centre of Nottingham. Woodfull, a light sleeper, had been kept awake before by hourly 'Little John' clock chimes in the Council House opposite the hotel. He had the bells stopped for the duration of the Test.

Early on Friday morning, 13 June, Long Row began to fill with fans hoping to catch a glimpse of Bradman. By 9 a.m. it was jammed with people. Bradman was tense as he always was prior to a big match. Over breakfast, players became aware of the crowd in the street outside. Bradman found the waiting excruciating. His good friend 'tea' helped sooth his adrenalin, just a little. He wanted to get out to the ground, go through the rituals of changing into combat gear, touch turf and do battle.

Trent Bridge — even the name conjures conflict — originated in 1837 when local bricklayer/cricketer William Clarke married Mary Chapman, owner of an inn with a pavilion on flat land next to the River Trent. To celebrate the bond, William, the best layer in Nottingham, erected more structures on her pavilion and began organising matches there. The inn disappeared but the cricket endured. It had always been a batsman's paradise, which prompted Neville Cardus to write, 'it was always afternoon and 360 for 2.'

England would have settled for less than that in the grey gloom after Chapman won the toss and batted. The formidable order comprised Sutcliffe, Hobbs, Hammond, Woolley, Hendren, Chapman, Larwood, Robins, Tate, Tyldesley and Duckworth. To oppose them Australia left out Jackson, who was ill, and played Woodfull, Ponsford, Bradman, Kippax, Fairfax, McCabe, Richardson, Oldfield, Grimmett, Hornibrook and Wall. a'Beckett could consider himself unlucky not to be in the XI, although his form had not been top-class.

The old England opening firm began well until Fairfax had Sutcliffe caught for 28 at 53. Woodfull brought Grimmett on first-change and at 63 the spinner trapped the dangerous Hammond for 8. On the same score he lured Woolley from his crease for Oldfield to stump him for 0. At 71 he bowled Hendren for 5. England had lost four for 18 runs.

Hobbs and skipper Chapman, batting with his usual hurry, settled the ship until Hornibrook had the latter caught for 52. Hobbs finally succumbed to McCabe for 78 and England was six for 188. The tail of Larwood (18), Tate (13) and Robins (50 not out) wagged hard and the home team went from eight for 241 on the rain-interrupted Friday to a similarly broken Saturday when it finished on 270, in 255 minutes of frenetic and indifferent batting. Grimmett, maintaining his great form, took five for 107 off thirty-two overs.

Australia faced delays before it could shape up on the wet, greasy wicket, which was a delight to Tyldesley and Tate. The latter had Ponsford (3) and Woodfull (2) back in the pavilion with the score at 6. Ponsford, who looked most uncomfortable, had been set up by Larwood and lasted six overs. The 23,000 crowd reacted with hard applause when Bradman moved out in the thin Saturday afternoon light. This was what they had come from all over England for. This was what many had missed in Long Row, when the team had been bundled into cars and whisked to the ground — Bradman on public display.

They were quickly disappointed. He had trouble from the first ball. His timing was out. Deliveries were 'standing up' or skidding on the uncertain surface. Bowlers couldn't wait to get at the gladiator, who seemed stricken by the conditions. 'Tyldesley bothered him,' Cardus wrote with undisguised glee. 'Tate tormented him until mercifully bowling him with a backbreak to which Bradman held out a bat as limp as it was crooked.'

He wandered back to the pavilion looking not so much crestfallen as serious. Australia was three for 16. Kippax rose to the occasion and looked like turning the game around until Robins got Fairfax for 14. Four for 57. McCabe couldn't cope and was caught by Hammond for four off Robins. Australia was a low five for 61. Kippax took control at one end, and found a partner in Richardson who was willing to hit out. He collected 37 of a 44-run partnership before his adventurous effort was finished by Tyldesley, who bowled him.

Kippax played excellently on the sticky but at 64 not out ran out of partners early on the third day. Australia had scraped up 144. Tate (three for 20), Robins (four for 51), Tyldesley (two for 53) and Larwood (one for 12) combined to banish the opposition.

185

HOBBS, HENDREN AND HOPE

Hobbs and Sutcliffe got on top of the Australian attack in their second effort and stayed there. Only a fierce bouncer from Wall, which collected Sutcliffe's hand as he protected his face, could break the stand at 125. Sutcliffe whipped off his glove and everyone gathered to examine a very red and sore thumb. He tried to flex it. Instead of movement he got pain and was forced to retire wounded at 58.

Openers are like Siamese twins. Once one feels agony and goes, the other follows. At 137, the cagey Grimmett enticed old Jack (forty-eight years and seventy-one runs) out of his crease and Oldfield removed the bails. He had hit 149 for the game at a good rate, and with more than glimpses of his glorious past. He always found that little bit extra against the young enemy.

Hammond faced Grimmett, whose length was now centimetre-perfect. The Fox had trapped him with a top-spinner in the first innings. Hammond was looking for it, watching the bowler's hand for a clue. Grimmett noted his uncustomary uncertainty and bowled leg-breaks, edging the ball straighter. Then he bowled a fuller, faster leg-break. Hammond missed it, dead in front. He was on his way, LBW for 4.

Any bowler who could twice in a match dismiss Hammond — one of the two best batsmen in the world in the 1930s — by beating him each time, and not by buying his wicket or sensational catching, deserved to be called truly great. England was two for 137. Grimmett the Great had given his team the slimmest of hope. The lead was now 263. Wall increased that thin expectation by bowling Woolley (5), with a stunning in-swinger.

The next partnership between Hendren and Chapman was telling. It produced 64 quick runs before Wall delivered a swinging yorker and bowled the captain for 29. England was now four for 211 and Sutcliffe, his thumb broken, unlikely to bat again.

Hendren had little faith in England's long tail and sensibly decided to keep hitting and stealing the strike from Larwood, who was not insulted. Better Hendren than him. However, Harold could run but not hide. Grimmett pursued him like a farmer would a rabbit, and shot him with a big-breaking leggie that wheeled past the startled batsman and bowled him. Grimmett now had also picked Larwood up twice in the match. Harold, like Bradman, was big on retribution. He would search for Grimmett later.

In the meantime, he and Hendren had lifted the England score to 250, giving it a lead of 376. It was 386 when Hendren (72) was caught off Wall. With Bradman in the opposition, this was not considered enough. England somehow dragged itself to 302. Grimmett took five for 91 off thirty overs, giving him ten wickets for 198 for the game. No bowler on either side so far had been as dangerous or penetrating. Wall, in form, took three for 67 in a creditable effort.

England's lead was 428. No team had got anywhere near that sort of score during the last innings of a Test — but then again, no other team had ever had a Bradman in it.

FIGHT-BACK

The Australians went in at the end of the third day with fifty-three minutes to see out. Larwood generated pace from his first over. With the score at 12, he beat Woodfull for sheer speed and had him caught by Chapman at slip for 4. Bradman walked out to a big ovation, and even bigger expectations. Both teams knew it, as did the crowd: Bradman was the only player capable of winning the match from here. Batsmen such as Hammond and Ponsford were capable of the gritty double hundred on their very best days. But neither of them could reach that sort of score rapidly. That was the difference. Only this slight figure, looking jauntily out from underneath his baggy green cap, had the mind and the body to achieve a scoring rate that would challenge England. This did not mean thrashing everything, but adapting defence here and attack there.

Yet there was a psychological hurdle to get over. While Bradman had scored double, triple and quadruple centuries at first-class level, he had not yet reached 200 in nine Test innings. Then again, however, Bradman thrived on challenges.

He started with a characteristic push to the on for a single. He was a totally different performer to the first innings, and from his first few shots appeared like a man with a century behind and not perhaps in front of him. He late-cut to third man with his typical aplomb, drove through the on with swift footwork, and while hooking and pulling moved that back foot around the crease like a Spanish tap-dancer.

At stumps after thirty-five minutes, people looked at the score-board and were surprised to see Bradman on 31. He seemed to have stolen his way there with insolent ease, whereas Ponsford was still playing without conviction against his nemesis, Larwood. Memories of pain in the last series were strong.

Neville Cardus, performing a bit of gamesmanship for the England team as Australia prepared for the vital last day, began the next morning where the cudgelled and silent Percy Fender had left off. Great critic he may have been, but he would never have to bowl and set a field to, or be humiliated by, the batsmen he deprecated.

'Neither Bradman nor Ponsford exactly looked to be great batsmen,' he wrote, 'yet both of them are beaters of MacLaren's highest score. From this morning I concluded their superiority with MacLaren is strictly statistical.'

This slight, with which the writer had slipped from commentator to propagandist, was a pompous dig at both the batsmen and the standard of Shield cricket. It had the desired effect by riling the thirty-year-old Ponsford, but not Bradman, the junior partner. The latter never let such trivial matters as comparisons go to his heart. They were, instead, stored in his head for later accounting, the best way he knew — on the cricket field.

Before play Ponsford told journalists that he would be informing next man in Kippax 'not to bother changing' into his cricket clothes. In other words, he and Bradman would be knocking off the rest of the 429 required for victory.

The two started well enough with Bradman continuing to resist England's finest, not with attack as in the previous evening, but impenetrable defence. Ponsford looked solid but not as threatening as in the dressing-room.

At 93, Tate bowled him for 39, and Cardus was smiling, perhaps having won a little tactical ploy on behalf of his country.

Kippax, dressed appropriately for the occasion after all, joined Bradman and the latter changed gear again after scoring 50 in 100 minutes. He was in a stand of 59 before Robins had Kippax caught by Hammond for 23. Australia was three for 192 at lunch, with Bradman on 88 not out and Fairfax on a patient 4.

During the break, Chapman approached Woodfull and told him that Larwood could not continue. He had gastritis. England's twelfth man, Duleepsinhji, was already on the field for the injured Sutcliffe. Chapman explained that he did not have a thirteenth man, or emergency.

'Would you let me use one of the [Notts] ground staff?' Chapman asked innocently.

Woodfull nodded his agreement without checking on the player, Copley, whom the shrewd England skipper had in mind. Copley was regarded by the locals as the best fieldsman the county had ever had.

After lunch, Bradman took charge again. He brought up his century in his first Test in England with a flick to the on at 2.45 p.m. It had taken 215 minutes and was crafted perfectly for Test match conditions. He was calculating his attack and defence as the bowling and fielding tightened. However, Fairfax was never comfortable as he struggled up to 14 and then was caught by Robins off Tate. Australia was four for 229.

There were now 200 to go for victory with 225 minutes to get them. The situation demanded that someone stay with Bradman for a really solid partnership. McCabe looked the colt most likely, although he was playing with perhaps a bit too much adventure. He dashed to 49 in a partnership of 67. With the score at 296 he smashed a ball from Tate which would have passed most fieldsmen, but Copley at mid-on, showing fine anticipation, snaffled it.

If that was the catch to change a match, then Robins, the leg-break bowler, came up with a ball to win one. Bradman was on 131 and the score 316, when Robins produced a googly (wrong'un). Bradman, realising that the ball's spin through the air was different, went onto the back foot. In that fraction of a moment when a decision is made, Bradman was caught in two minds as the ball pitched outside off and broke sharply the wrong way. It took off-stump. It was a delivery in a million for a batsman in a billion.

189

'I got my feet and laces in a tangle,' Bradman recalled. He was stunned as he looked over his shoulder at the broken wicket. He had batted 267 minutes with ten fours.

He left the field annoyed at himself for having made a misjudgement, but in reality the ball was unplayable. His superb display of sound defence and efficient attack always threatened to bring Australia victory, but now the game was lost.

Australia was 316 for six and still 123 short. The next four wickets fell cheaply and the visitors were all out for 335 — a record score for the fourth innings of a Test — but 93 runs behind. Tyldesley did his part in collecting three of the last four. But Tate and Robins with three apiece had done the damage.

The post mortems on the game centred largely on Bradman's second-innings knock, which was one for connoisseurs. Trevor Wignall wrote:

> [It] will have to be remembered with the great classics of the past. He will not be 22 until next August, but here he is with only Jack Hobbs, who is old enough to be his father, competing with him for the distinction of being described as the world's greatest batsman.

The *Daily Mail* summed up public opinion in an editorial:

> It should be remembered that the Australians, in an uphill battle made a record score in the fourth innings of a Test in England. The youthful Bradman showed nerves of iron and the poise of a veteran. Cricketers will be proud of and still prouder to think that it was accomplished against foemen such as these.

Cardus however, mindful of his priggish outburst in the previous morning's paper, avoided anything but faint praise for Bradman's effort and concentrated on England's fine win, which he may have felt he assisted. There was nothing like Ashes cricket for eliciting chauvinism from even the seemingly most erudite and unbiased commentators.

After Trent Bridge Australia was one-down and in need of about as much improvement as the weather.

18

TECHNICALLY
THE BEST

I think it was the best innings, in a technical sense, I ever played.
— BRADMAN ON HIS FIRST INNINGS IN A TEST AT LORD'S, 1930

THE COME-BACK

The players were flat after the Test loss and Woodfull had a job enthusing them for the next round of county games before the Second Test. In the first, against Surrey again at The Oval, the home team were rolled for 162, mainly thanks to the bowling star at Trent Bridge, Grimmett, who took six for 24. Woodfull led the way in the reply with 141 and a'Beckett did his chances of Test selection some good with 67 not out in five for 388 declared. Bradman only managed 5 and was out, caught by Shepherd, off Allom. Surrey replied with two for 249, and Hobbs took advantage of a listless Aussie effort in the field with a fine 146 not out.

The second game against Lancashire (minus the fierce McDonald this time) at Manchester was simply batting practice, with Kippax (120), Fairfax (63), Jackson (52) and Bradman (38) taking their time in building 427. Lancashire were dismissed for 259. Wall was in touch in a long spell taking four for 92, while Fairfax had the figures with four for 29. Australia sauntered to one for 79 (Bradman 23 not out) in the second innings. Both matches were drawn, and while some journalists said the tourists would have been better off sight-seeing, the players themselves were able to get good practice in the middle, which was far better than in the nets. It also gave the tour selectors a chance to assess form for the Second Test.

England was forced to leave out the injured Sutcliffe, who was replaced by the brilliant young Indian Duleepsinhji. Jack White replaced Tyldesley, and Gubby Allen took the place of the still-ill Larwood, who would be missed.

For Australia, Bradman (1,435 runs for the season in fifteen matches at an average of 95.66), Woodfull (836 at 59.71), Kippax (671 at 55.91) and Ponsford (668 at 51.38) picked themselves, while Fairfax, McCabe and Richardson had done enough in the First Test to earn another game. There was similarly no question of replacing any of the bowlers, although most observers thought they could have done with more back-up than just the serviceable, but not penetrating, McCabe. Jackson was unlucky to be twelfth man again. His improved form should have given him a place.

The team assembled at the ground on a sunny first morning at Lord's on Friday 27 June to be introduced to the Duke of York (later King George VI). The players were jokingly warned not to call him 'Mr York', in view of the 1926 *faux pas* by a player who called his wife (later Queen Elizabeth, the present Queen Mother) 'Mrs York'.

Two British papers later carried a story that Bradman had 'over-slept' and was late for the game, but he was emphatic that it wasn't true. 'We had the choice of going to the ground by tube or taxi, in groups,' he said, 'and there was no way any of us would be late for a Test.' Apart from anything else, Kelly and Woodfull met the troops in the hotel lobby before each day. The mischievous reports were meant to suggest that there was an irresponsible streak in Bradman's make-up.

Chapman won the toss and decided to bat. Fairfax's start gave Australia a good beginning when he had Hobbs caught behind for one at 13. Hammond joined Woolley and they proceeded to play the bowling with ease. Woodfull brought Grimmett in to see if he could trap Hammond for a third successive time. The two became locked in a tight duel. In the meantime, Woolley was caught off Fairfax for 41. England was two for 53.

Duleepsinhji came to the wicket with his famous uncle, Ranjitsinhji, looking on. He settled in well with Hammond, who continued to cross swords with Grimmett. But at 105, the Australian spinner broke through and bowled Hammond (38) with a wrong'un. Hendren and Duleepsinhji then put on a fast century stand before Fairfax struck again. He had the dangerous Hendren (48) caught and England were four for 209. Chapman (11) came and went flashing and snicking Wall to Oldfield. Gubby Allen (3) was quickly Fairfax's fourth victim, and honours were even with the score at six for 239.

The dashing Duleepsinhji reached his century in 130 minutes. His graceful, classic innings was one of the best first-up hundreds in history, ranking with Jackson's 164 in 1928–29. The Indian found a staying partner in Tate and they slammed the flagging attack for a brisk 98, before Wall belatedly broke through to remove Tate for 54. This partnership turned the busy day England's way, but at seven for 337 there were more surprises after Hornibrook dismissed Robins for 5.

White stayed with Duleepsinhji, who was stroking the ball magnificently to all parts of the field. One of the highlights for Australia was the dash in the field of Bradman and McCabe, who saved perhaps 50 or 60 with their chasing and throwing. No England bat now was running on Bradman's arm. He was one of the nimblest fielders ever seen, and young McCabe was not far behind.

At 387, Bradman took a running catch on the boundary to dismiss Dupleepsinhji for 173 off Grimmett, who deserved the wicket. He was having a lean day, but still performing at his top. Duleepsinhji had played him better than anyone else had ever done, except perhaps for Bradman.

England was nine for 405 in an outstanding day's Test cricket. It had gone to the home side, but the visitors had never given up in the field. The next morning the last two in — White and Duckworth — continued on until their valuable stand of 37 ended at 425, when Wall took the new ball and had the English keeper caught behind for 18.

Fairfax had the figures at four for 101. Wall was expensive with three for 118 from 29.4 overs. Grimmett took two for 105 while Hornibrook (one for 62) was steady without causing the batsmen much concern.

LORD OF LORD'S

Ponsford and Woodfull strode out to commence Australia's reply knowing that failure would probably mean forfeiture of the series. England's 425 was formidable and they knew they had to dig deep for something extra. On a personal level, though Woodfull had failed twice his place was not in jeopardy. Ponsford, however, could not afford another poor performance. At least the weather was like Melbourne's on a cool summer's day.

Woodfull took twenty-five minutes to score his first single, amid jeers from the crowd. Undeterred, Woodfull laboured on, picking up his rate as the morning progressed. After lunch, with Ponsford playing his most important innings of the tour, the two openers lifted the tempo and took control.

All the while Bradman waited and watched, for he was a great learner. When other cricketers played cards, read the papers, or chatted to dressing-room visitors, Bradman observed every move and counter-move by the opposition. Where was Hammond today? What was Duleepsinhji like in the field? Was Tate getting much movement with the ball? And how was Allen's throw under pressure with the batsmen chancing a third run? He was, he recalled, 'definitely anxious' before his initial entrance onto the stage of cricket's finest theatre — 'very anxious to do well.'

With the score at 160 play was halted so that the two teams could be introduced to the King, whom they had already seen at Wembley and had met at Sandringham. But protocol was protocol — or was it an ingenious British trick to break the mighty opening stand?

The players lined up and Woodfull introduced them one by one to His noble Majesty. Bradman, padded up ready to go in, took it all in his stride, but the royal interruption seemed to have a different effect on Ponsford. After the King's few polite words, Ponsford hit out and was caught by Hammond. The wicket belonged to George VI. Tate was credited with it for technical reasons.

It was 3.30 on a Saturday afternoon. The ground was full with 31,000 spectators, the sun was out, the wicket was true, the King was sitting, not on his throne, but in a balcony box, and Australia was one for 162, chasing a big score. The stage was set for Bradman to give a brilliant performance. The crowd roared in anticipation as he appeared.

He took block and settled in over his bat to face White. The bowler sent down a ball short of a length. Bradman pounced and crashed it to long-off for a single. It was a brash stroke so early against White, and it had more impact than if he had planted one foot down the wicket and hit it for six. Never, never had Jack White been chased out in such an intrepid manner by anyone in England. It was accepted up and down the country that you took no liberties like this with him.

It was the shot of a player who had scored not 100, but 200. He went after every bowler — White, Allen, Tate, Robins and Hammond — and took fours off all of them in his first fifty, which took just forty-five minutes. The crowd, including the more sedate yet appreciative Lord's Members, stood and applauded as if he had reached a century instead of 54 not out, with the patient Woodfull sitting on 90 and looking as solid as the Rock of Gibraltar.

After tea, Bradman cut daringly, leaving one journalist description-less, except for a few vivid observations:

Hammond was put at the pavilion end to bowl defensively and was doing his job quite well. Naturally he had a defensive field, with only one man in the slips. He sent down a fast good length ball which broke viciously towards the middle and off stumps. Bradman met it with an orthodox-looking back-stroke, which had the effect of a late cut. The ball flew, and clearly was meant to fly, wide of the solitary slip and fine enough to beat the deep third-man ... The crowd twice paid him unusual but well-deserved compliments. They gave Tate one of the loudest rounds of applause heard during the afternoon when he succeeded in bowling a maiden over to him. And once when he shaped to cut at a dangerous ball from that bowler some 2,000 people appealed for the expected catch at the wicket, and were badly scored off when he checked his stroke.

Woodfull moved to a century and then 155, while Bradman reached 150 after having given him 77 start. They had put on 231, taking the score to 393 at ninety runs an hour, when Woodfull got carried away down the wicket to Robins. He missed a drive and was stumped by Duckworth.

Kippax joined Bradman and was there with him at the close on Saturday night with the score on two for 404. Bradman had moved from 54 to 155 — 101 in the session. He was just ahead of the clock, having batted 150 minutes.

Neville Cardus now forgot Trent Bridge and waxed extravagant about the afternoon's play:

Young Bradman knocked solemnity to smithereens and attacked with a bat which might well have appeared excessively care-free even on the smooth lawn of a country house cricket match . . . The advent of Bradman was like combustible stuff thrown on fires of batsmanship that had been slumbering potentially. The bat sent out cracking noises: they were noises quite contemptuous. Nearly every ball was scored from; maiden overs seemed beyond the reach of possibility . . . When he batted eleven men were not enough. Lord's was too big to cover; holes were to be seen in the English field everywhere. Chapman tried his best to fill them up but in vain . . . Bradman today established himself amongst the authentic batsmen of England and Australia of all time. Quality does not need to argue itself; we feel it intuitively the moment we see it. Until today I had looked at Bradman's batting as a thing of promise; I have now seen signs of a glorious fulfilment.

Despite this unacknowledged eating of his words about him in the First Test, England's most celebrated cricket observer was still struggling, however eloquently, to come to terms with Bradman's unique talent. First he was a pyromaniac. Then there were 'signs' of promise fulfilled.

The actual participants in the game were less grudging. The words of Frank Chester, one of the umpires in the game, seemed to come right from the heart. 'I left the Lord's Test in 1930, after watching Bradman,' he said, 'firmly convinced that he was the greatest batsman of all time.' Wilfred Rhodes, who had been the first to say this after Bradman's 236 at Worcester, now had his view confirmed by another highly qualified observer.

On Monday 30 June, the third day of the Test, the house-full sign went up again. This time 32,000 were sardined in. The Sunday break had given the populace a chance to absorb the reports on Bradman's Saturday-afternoon entertainment. He continued on a fraction more defensively until he reached 191. Until that point he had not made a single false shot or error. Hammond was bowling. Bradman tried one of his favourite shots — a pull to the on, off Hammond. The ball bounced marginally higher than expected. Bradman changed his mind in mid-shot, and the ball took the outside edge of the bat and went through slips, along the ground. It was not even the semblance of a chance. But such was his continued dominance and perfection of stroke play that the crowd reacted. Bradman had erred.

At 198, he cut a ball for four to reach his first Test double century. An Australian spectator retrieved the ball and kissed it. There was speculation all around Lord's now and further afield as to whether Bradman would go for Englishman R. E. Foster's 287, the record set in 1903 in Sydney. Bradman was conscious of it, but not anxious. He was already used to setting records, and this would be just another one. Bradman could count on being able to bat until at least tea that day, which gave him plenty of time to go beyond it.

At lunch, he was 231, having scored 76 in the session. Kippax was travelling well on 50 and Australia were more than a hundred ahead with eight wickets still in hand. After lunch the two motored on until the score was at 585, when Bradman launched into a beautiful drive through extra-cover off White. It shot low, hard and fast, but incredibly Chapman threw himself full stretch to his left and caught it. The crowd roared and Bradman was on his way for 254 after 325 minutes. He hit twenty-five fours — a century in itself — and the innings was the highest ever at Lord's or in a Test anywhere in England.

'The innings was the best of my life in a technical sense,' Bradman commented. 'Every ball went where it was intended, even the one that got me out.' He emphasised that though it was the best technically, it was not necessarily the best innings he had ever played. He left that judgement to others.

Now even his strongest critics were acknowledging his pre-eminence. Percy Fender, who had been noticeably quiet on Bradman since his 252 not out destruction of Surrey in mid-May, became fulsome in his praise. 'It was as perfect an example of real batting, in its best sense, as anyone could wish to see', he remarked, without engaging in comparisons with other great figures in the game. Fender could be generous, but he wasn't going to extend his praise further, certainly while England was engaged in a tight series.

Former England captain Plum Warner could afford to be more magnanimous: 'Don Bradman is now the champion batsman of the world,' he wrote. 'He stands on the threshold of what, given good health, must surely be a career which will equal and surely surpass that of any other batsman.'

The rest of Australia's innings at Lord's was now academic as Kippax was soon after bowled by White for 83 at 588. McCabe (44), Richardson (30), Oldfield (43 not out) and Fairfax (20 not out) continued on to the massive score of six for 729 before Woodfull called a halt to give his side time to dismiss England again.

The home team started its rear-guard action with more aggression than guard and Grimmett was able to snatch three prize wickets — Hobbs, whom he bowled for 19, Woolley who was out hit wicket for 28 and his old scourge Hammond, whom he also bowled for 38, for the fourth time in all four innings and more cheaply than in the last series. The bowler's hold on England's best bat was a key to Australia's fighting back in the series.

Duleepsinhji looked like emulating his first-innings effort until Hornibrook had him caught behind for 48, giving him 221 for his first Test. Grimmett's removal of Hendren for 9 left England five for 147. But then Chapman and Allen rescued the situation with an attacking, fighting partnership. Chapman had a let-off when Ponsford and Richardson failed to go for a simple catch. Feeling that luck was going his way the England captain leapt into the bowling, particularly Grimmett, to hit two sixes and seven fours in a stand of 125 with Allen. At 272, Allen (57) became Grimmett's fifth victim, trapped LBW by what looked like a variation of a flipper — where the ball is released with the hand below the level of the wrist and carries straight on without turning.

Chapman gunned on to a captain's century, showing why the selectors had had faith in his batting and leadership qualities for so long. He smashed another two sixes and five fours, taking England into the lead. Eventually he ran out of partners and was last out still going for the bowling — caught behind for 121. England had mustered a good 375, making 800 in two innings, just 71 ahead. Grimmett took six for 157 from a marathon fifty-three overs, and was well supported by Fairfax who took two for 37.

Australia polished off the runs after an early scare when it lost three for 22 — Ponsford for 16, Bradman for 1 (caught by Chapman a second time, this time off Tate third ball), and Fairfax for 3. Woodfull (26 not out) fittingly stuck there for the winning run with McCabe who was unbeaten on 25.

Australia won comfortably in the end by seven wickets and the series was all-square after two matches with three to go. With Bradman and Grimmett in spectacular touch, Australia had surprised the cricket world and was now an even-money bet in the battle for the Ashes.

19

SIMPLY THE BEST

The opening day of the Third Test at Leeds must rank as the greatest of my cricketing life.
— Bradman on scoring 309 not out on the first day of 1930 Test at Leeds

IN DEMAND

Bradman's performance at Lord's rocketed him to super-stardom. Now it was not just Australian companies who were interested in using his name. Bradman was approached by a London literary agent, David Cromb, who had an introduction to him through a contact in Sydney.

Cromb had heard reports of the past Australian season and the form of each of the fifteen tourists. He had seen Woodfull and Ponsford on previous visits. He was aware that Kippax and McCabe were regarded as great stylists, but they were not viewed as match- or series-winners. Yet Bradman was categorised this way even before he reached England and he had proved himself in the first two Tests. He had also captured the nation's imagination like no other tourist in the history of the game. The name Bradman was suddenly marketable internationally.

Cromb was watching the cricket for himself and reading the rave reviews and predictions about the new champion. Bradman was no flash in the pan. It was time to move quickly to sign him up. Several publishers were interested in a book by him, even if he was responsible for crushing England. Such was his appeal that not only English cricket followers but the public generally would be eager to read what he had to say.

Cromb offered him a publishing deal. The young cricketer owed it to himself and his possible future marriage to do as well as he could for himself. He didn't want a career as a store dummy or circus freak at Mick Simmons. He had no choice but to take up any decent proposition that did not compromise his cricket or his contract with the Board of Control.

Bradman told Cromb about Clause 11 of that contract, which prevented him being employed as 'a newspaper correspondent or to do any work in connection with any newspaper or any broadcasting'. But it made no mention of books. 'I informed him I couldn't write anything about the tour while it was in progress,' Bradman said. 'I agreed to start a book as long as it was published not earlier than September, when we would be on the homeward-bound boat.'

Cromb was satisfied and there didn't seem to be a problem, although Bradman was aware that the book would be serialised in a London paper and that the rights would be sold in Australia. 'Serials' were important for publishers. They could recoup any advance money paid to an author, and excerpts in a high-circulation paper meant excellent promotion for a book.

This pecuniary step forward, in addition to the exciting atmosphere in England, buoyed Bradman and put him in combative mood for the Third Test at Leeds after two county games against Yorkshire and Nottinghamshire.

Australia batted against Yorkshire at Bradford first and Ponsford dominated the innings, making 143 out of 302. Jackson (46) and McCabe (40) had useful practice while Woodfull (3), Bradman (1) and Richardson (3) failed. Grimmett then tied up the Yorkshire bats as he had two months earlier and took six for 75, with a'Beckett (three for 42) giving support, in the first-innings score of 146. The Yorkshiremen were forced to follow on and managed only 161. Grimmett took five for 58, supported by Hurwood with four for 35, giving him eleven for 133 for the match to complement his ten for 37 previously. Australia won by ten wickets.

Then it was on to Notts and a refreshed Larwood keen to resume combat with the tourists. Bradman was left out of the match and the batting line-up struggled against the best county pace attack in the country of Larwood and fast left-hander Bill Voce to post 296. Larwood renewed his grip on Ponsford by uprooting his off-stump for 6. Kippax (96) continued his strong season, while Richardson (55) and McCabe (58) looked capable against the speed. Larwood showed form and pace with three for 59, while Voce took four for 89.

Notts replied with 433 of which Whysall scored 120 — a rare hundred against the tourists for the season. Australia replied with more batting practice against the strong pace combination, scoring four for 360. Jackson and McCabe each made 79, while Kippax helped his average with 89 not out. Richardson scored a useful 69 in light of the pressure being put on several batting spots by Jackson.

Bradman took advantage of the respite from media attention and cricket and went sightseeing in London. 'I loved the place,' he said, 'but of course I was on tour and only saw the bright side.' He visited the Tower, wandered around the business hub of the City, and went for a boat ride along the Thames to Richmond. Later in the week he watched the Wimbledon tennis finals, delighted at the chance of seeing his second sporting love played at the highest level.

He was in a good frame of mind again when he motored north in a baby Singer on 9 July to Leeds, the venue of the Third Test, which was to begin two days later at Headingly. Both teams were booked into the Queen's Hotel and Bradman found the city in chaos in preparation for the game as thousands of visitors arrived.

DAY OF THE TRIPLE

Archie Jackson was selected to replace Ponsford, who was ill with gastritis, and Fairfax was dropped for Ted a'Beckett. England replaced practically half its side — Woolley, Robins, Hendren, Allen and White — with Sutcliffe, Leyland, Larwood, Geary and Tyldesley. Larwood and Geary would strengthen England's attack. Sutcliffe's automatic return and Leyland's good form ensured the batting was even better.

Woodfull won the toss and batted in front of 20,000 at Headingly on 11 July. Bradman had held a bat just twice since the Second Test — at Bradford for a few balls and in the nets the day before the game — and the rest was just what the doctor ordered midway through the series. He was mentally ready when Jackson was caught by Larwood on the eleventh ball of the match — the fifth of Tate's first over. Bradman was virtually opening now as he walked sweaterless past photographers to the wicket on this cool mid-summer day.

He always considered that going in at number three was tougher than opening because, he said, 'the bowlers were not often completely on-line when they started bowling. Wicket preservation was often easier, and runs could be scored from loose balls.' The number three spot could also mean long, anxious waits, which were never Bradman's fondest pastime.

Though he had failed opening for his State, as he pointed out he had also failed at times in other places in the order. In other words, he could cope with opening if that position had fallen to him. His innings of 191 against Hampshire when he topped 1,000 in late May supported this view.

The Headingly crowd were waiting to see for themselves if he was as good as the papers said he was after Lord's. They were among the most critical spectators in the land. By the time they reached for their thermos flasks and sandwiches at lunch, they would be convinced that Bradman was even better than the dizzying descriptions of him. After the break he continued at even greater tempo. Geoffrey Tebbutt summed up his impressions by describing just one single in Bradman's day-long innings:

[The shot] *was a remarkable illustration of his speed of foot, the activity of his mind, and the resource that is repeatedly getting him out of trouble.*

He had jumped out, confidently and rather a long way, to drive Dick Tyldesley, to whom, like every other bowler in that outstanding innings, he had 'helped himself' and suddenly found that the flight and length of the ball had beaten him with his stroke only half played. The ball was travelling past him, the spin from the leg carrying it across towards his off-stump, and for a fraction of a second he hesitated. Then those little feet of his twinkled. Down he went on his right knee, and, stretched out like an acrobat, he deliberately tapped it back through the slips, and was off like a hare for the run!

His fifty took forty-nine minutes and the team total was just 61. Woodfull (50) partnered him in a 192-run stand which took only 159 minutes. Was this a tight Test or a festival game? His first 100 in 99 minutes was as fast as it was skilful. On 138, Bradman had reached 1,000 in Tests — all against England — in just seven matches and thirteen innings. It was the quickest trip to four figures in Test history. Bradman reached 200 at 4 p.m. out of two for 268, after just 214 minutes. After tea he on-drove Tate for four to reach Foster's record of 287, and next ball hit a single to leg to make the record his. It had taken him 314 minutes. Foster had batted 419 minutes. Shortly afterwards he lost Kippax, who had helped him to add 229 for the third wicket in 163 minutes, Bradman's share being 151. He reached 300 after 336 minutes at the crease. With one ball for the day to go, he was on 305 not out. He produced one of the finest shots of the innings for a crashing off-drive for four, which left him on 309 not out in 344 minutes at the crease. The tourists were three for 458 at stumps. That last shot saw him reach 2,000 for the season. This made him the youngest cricketer in history (at twenty-one years and 318 days) to reach that milestone in an English season.

The 309 in a single day's play broke several records. It was the most runs ever made in the single day of a Test ever, anywhere.

THE MORNING AFTER

Bradman was about to go out to bat on the second morning in front of 33,000 when he received a telegram: 'Your house is on fire and your girl wants you back — go home.'

He laughed at the joke and went on to 334 (he was out at 508, the sixth wicket to fall). He was supported by Woodfull (50), Kippax (77), McCabe (30), a'Beckett (29), and Grimmett (24). Australia was all out well before lunch on the second day for 566. Such was his dominance that the other ten batsmen between them had mustered only 232 — 112 fewer than Bradman's score. He scored 257 more than the next highest score by Kippax (77), which was a Test match record. He was now creating records that no-one, except cricket statisticians, had heard of, or could think of.

Bradman was most brutal towards Larwood, who had the crushing figures of none for 103 at the end of the first day and just one (he bowled McCabe) for 139 off thirty-three overs at the end of the Australian innings. It was a most impolite way to welcome the Notts speed merchant back to Test cricket, especially after illness. Larwood was desperate to settle just one of many scores against Bradman now in lopsided battles which stretched over several games in two seasons. Larwood had never captured his wicket and never looked like getting it. He made a spurious claim about having him 'caught' early in the big Leeds innings. But none of the England team, the umpires or spectators recalled it. He never actually appealed once for Bradman's wicket. It was purely wishful thinking on the speedster's part.

Tate had done very well considering the massacre, taking five for 124 off 39 overs, including Bradman's prize wicket. The others — Hammond, Geary, Tyldesley and Leyland — were but fodder for his voracious blade. He had become the first Australian to score two Test double centuries and now had four for the first-class season. He had scored 589 in three Test knocks, and had reached three figures in four successive Tests, setting further records along the way.

Back together once more, England's grand old firm of Hobbs and Sutcliffe came out determined to deliver an opening stand to match Bradman's monster effort. They saw off Wall, a'Beckett, McCabe and Hornibrook, but could not get past the magnificent Grimmett. a'Beckett took a 'blinder' of a catch in the gully off him to dismiss Hobbs (29) and Hornibrook caught Sutcliffe (32).

Hobbs, unfortunately, was unsure if he had been caught. He went to the Australian dressing room to explain his hesitation at the wicket and met a barrage of unnecessary abuse from Richardson, who told the Englishman to check the scoreboard. Next morning the papers carried several photos, which showed a'Beckett's great catch had been legitimate.

England was two for 64, but with Hammond in and looking sound, except of course against Grimmett's mesmerising leg-spin. Hammond was due for a big score, having failed to reach fifty in four innings. He was supported by Duleepsinhji (35) until the elegant Indian fell to Grimmett. As he walked off to be replaced by Leyland, a telegram was sent out to the Australian skipper, who passed it on to Bradman. He opened it on the field. It said:

> *Kindly convey my congratulations to Bradman. Tell him I wish him to accept 1000 pounds as a token of my admiration of his wonderful performance. Arthur Whitelaw, Australia House.*

Bradman laughed, thinking it was another hoax. But Woodfull assured him it was genuine. Whitelaw, from Auburn in Victoria, had settled in England. He was a clean-living man with a soap-manufacturing business and a motto of a 'cake for every bath-tub', and had amassed a fortune. Whitelaw, a cricket lover, expert bridge player and former Melbourne wallpaper maker, had parted with a very small portion of his fairly gotten gains, he said, because 'Bradman's performance merited such recognition . . . this is not so much a gift as a mark of appreciation on behalf of all Australians.' The gift would be worth about £30,000 or $A66,000 today.

Bradman went on fielding with extra spirit. First there had been Cromb's book deal, now this gratuity. He felt it would all help if Jessie would say 'yes' to marrying him.

Meanwhile England battled on, losing Leyland for a well-compiled 44 at 206. Geary was sent in as nightwatchman but was run out to make England five for 206. Duckworth was sent in next and struggled with Hammond until the score was 289 on the Monday morning when the latter was caught behind off McCabe for 113. Hammond's knock showed glimpses of his 1928–29 form in

Australia. Chapman again held up proceedings with some big-hitting, losing Duckworth for 33, caught behind off a'Beckett at 319.

Then Grimmett came back to strike three times, bowling Chapman (45) and having Tate (22) and Tyldesley (6) caught. England were all out for 391, 175 short. Grimmett was yet again the destroyer with five for 135 off 56.2 overs. After him, the Australian bowling looked ordinary, with a'Beckett perhaps the best and steadiest of the rest with one for 47 off twenty-eight overs.

England batted again in deteriorating weather. At 23, Sutcliffe played a ball to Bradman at deepish mid-on for a single. The batsmen made it easily. Bradman stayed in the place he had fielded the ball without returning to where he had been five metres back. Hobbs pushed the ball for a single to mid-on, unaware that Bradman was closer. He set off for the run and called Sutcliffe through. Bradman swooped to his left and threw the wicket down from side-on leaving Hobbs halfway down the pitch. Instead of continuing on, he turned and started for the pavilion, head-down and wondering how he could have fallen to Bradman's brilliant fielding again.

England lost Hammond once again to Grimmett, caught behind for 35, and then Duleepsinhji for 10, but the weather closed in and eventually ended play with England on three for 95, still 80 short and doing everything possible not to play. With the last day a wash-out, the game was drawn with Australia well on top.

Bradman found time to cable Jessie and wish her a happy twenty-first birthday. With his recent gift from Whitelaw, he bought her a stunning diamond watch, which would be part of her engagement present. The trip to England and his amazing success had not lessened his feelings for her. He would marry her on his return.

WRONGED AGAIN

The tourists left dreary Leeds and headed further north across the border to Scotland to discover how bad cricket conditions could be. A game against Scotland at mist-shrouded Edinburgh was washed out with the home side on three for 129. Bradman had time for some sightseeing before the team moved on to Glasgow for a second fixture. Rain reduced the game, but the Scots scored six for 140 and declared to give the crowd a look at Bradman. Australia replied with nine for 337. Bradman made 140 in a little over an hour, smashing nineteen fours and one towering six, something which he had restrained himself from doing in the Tests and first-class matches.

Later he grabbed the chance to play golf at Gleneagles. Arthur Mailey, travelling with the team, said about his prowess:

He has the uncanny faculty of adapting himself to golf, just as he has with other games. He can drive a ball 260 yards without any trouble and play approach shots like an expert . . . I would not be surprised if the Bowral lad made a name for himself at golf.

The one other game scheduled before the Fourth Test at Manchester was washed out before a ball was bowled, so that the team had no first-class play in the ten-day break between Tests. Bradman's caning of Larwood left the selectors no choice but to dump him. He was not alone in the humiliation, with Tyldesley and Geary also being dropped. The three were replaced by speedster Morris Nichols, off-spinner Tom Goddard, and Middlesex's Scottish leggie Ian Peebles. Australia swapped a'Beckett for Fairfax again, and brought back Ponsford for Jackson.

A crowd of 20,000 turned up in surprisingly good weather for the opening day on 25 July. Woodfull won the toss and batted, but then had to wait half an hour for the damp turf to dry out. He and Ponsford began with a partnership of 106 which took them into the afternoon before Tate had Woodfull caught behind for 54.

Bradman came in to face Tate and Peebles, whom he had played twice before without any trouble against Oxford and MCC. The leggie bowled well, turning the ball prodigiously enough to have Bradman groping. He stayed for thirty uncomfortable minutes, scoring 14, before Peebles held back a wrong'un to him. Bradman was beaten through the air and presented an easy catch to Duleepsinhji. It was the second time in the series that a leggie had trapped him with the wrong'un, and it annoyed Bradman because he was a second-string leg-spinner himself. The crowd, however, was thrilled. His dismissal seemed to make a contest of the match. Every Englishman present thought the national team now had a chance.

But while English hopes rose and Bradman contemplated working on his wrong'un problem in the nets, Australia put in an even performance. Ponsford collected his second Test eighty in succession before Hammond bowled him. Kippax (51) kept up his steady form until Nichols had him caught. Australia suffered a mid-innings mini-collapse when they lost McCabe (4) LBW to Peebles' straighter one, and Richardson (1) bowled by Hammond. Fairfax (49) justified his reinclusion until he was trapped LBW by Goddard, while Grimmett showed he could bat a bit with a fighting 50 before Peebles had him caught.

Australia totalled 345, a respectable score on the difficult wicket and against an in-form attack. Peebles looked most impressive with three for 150 off fifty-five overs. Nichols returned two for 33 from twenty-one overs and generated pace, but many observers thought he was lucky to be playing. The consensus was that Larwood had been dealt with too harshly. Goddard proved a fair balance for Peebles with two for 49, and Hammond bobbed up with two for 24 from twenty-one overs, proving he was the most effective all-rounder in the series.

With bad weather threatening, England's opening combination matched Australia's with a stand of 108 before Wall broke through and had Hobbs caught behind for 31. The fast man then bowled Hammond for 3. Soon afterwards Sutcliffe went for a big hit off Wall, and connected well. The ball looked to be going for six, but Bradman, looking into the sun, positioned himself at deep mid-wicket centimetres from the boundary rope at the feet of spectators. He held the tough catch, signalling that he had not stepped over the line. Sutcliffe was on his way for 74.

Rain intervened, allowing only intermittent play on Saturday and Monday in which Australia moved slowly through the England batting. McCabe dismissed the stubborn Duleepsinhji caught by Hornibrook for 54 and bowled Leyland for 35. Hornibrook then had

Chapman caught for 1 and England's resistance crumbled until rain stopped play at eight for 251. McCabe claimed the figures on the damp pitch with four for 41 off 17 overs, whereas Wall ended with three for 70 off thirty-three overs after his initial burst.

The pitch was flooded so badly that the game was abandoned. For the second successive Test, Australia had the upper hand. It gave the tourists confidence for the Fifth Test, which would now decide the series, providing the weather held up.

CENTURIES AND SERIAL RIGHTS

Australia began its show-down Test tune-up of four scheduled first-class games by motoring south to Somerset for a match at Taunton. The tourists took a different attitude to the game. No batsman was going to throw his hand away in the interests of spectator enjoyment. Jackson, for instance, was fighting for a Test spot. Bradman, on the other hand, wanted to maintain his sensational form. His occasional lapses against second-rate bowling and in the absence of a challenge would be put behind him in the build-up to the final encounter at The Oval.

Australia managed 360. Jackson (118) and Bradman (117) had a solid, unadventurous partnership of 231 in 215 minutes — a very good rate — which somehow upset the crowd. They had read and heard the appraisals of Bradman's 254 and 334 and were expecting a gung-ho show. Instead they saw technically correct batting of the highest order. Every shot was measured, and in Bradman's case, down. There would be no lashing out for a lusty six as at Glasgow. Showing exemplary discipline, he chalked up his ninth century of the tour. The rest of the tourists had scored only two more.

The hype and hero-worship after Leeds never affected him, as he demonstrated a fully professional approach, almost as if his personal livelihood depended on it. But remuneration was not on Bradman's mind. He wanted to be part of a winning Ashes team. Underlying the superficial press criticism of his display was a clear message to the opposition: Bradman was putting his recent devastating performances in the background in his preparation for the series decider.

Somerset was rolled for 121 and then just 81, thanks to Grimmett who again returned school house-cricket figures with seven for 33, which allowed the tourists to walk away with the game by an innings and 158 runs.

Bradman's self-discipline carried over into his leisure time, much of which he spent writing his book. He also went off sightseeing alone and was not always to be easily found by the press, so that the only saleable line they could get on him was that he was a mysterious 'loner'.

The product of his literary labours was passed by his agent to his publisher in July. The publisher had sold the newspaper serial rights to *The Star*, and Bradman had been assured that the excerpt would not be published while the tourists were involved in the 1930 season. *The Star* had given the publisher a vague undertaking that it would not publish 'too early' and this had been passed on to Bradman by his agent. However, Bradman was hot news now. His thoughts, no matter how fascinating or otherwise, would sell far more papers than when the series was over and he was on the boat home. The editors took into account the material. There was no comment on the current series. Nor was there even one paragraph of controversy. The extract centred on his early life at Bowral and how he started in cricket, which would be absorbing to the British public hungry for an account of his roots and explanation of his genius. But it would not be topical. *The Star* decided to publish the extract on 4 August, about a month earlier than Bradman thought prudent in view of the controversial clause in his contract with the Board of Control.

Bradman was annoyed by the decision, but quickly put it behind him. He had a job to do as Australia played Glamorgan at Swansea in South Wales in front of 28,000, the biggest county crowd of the season. The surprise publication didn't affect his performance, although he played more circumspectly than normal, collecting the innings top-score of 58 in 100 minutes. Ponsford and McCabe each made 53 out of Australia's ordinary tally of 245. Glamorgan was all out for 99 and like every other county had no answer to Grimmett, who spun out four for 34. Acting-captain Richardson then allowed his players to sprint to one for 73 (Bradman 19 not out) before he declared, giving the home side a sporting chance of scoring 218 in 225 minutes.

It was almost too generous as Glamorgan courageously gathered seven for 197 to draw the match just twenty-one runs short. Grimmett removed another four for 69. The crowds of 28,000 on Saturday and 25,000 on the Monday of the Bank Holiday long weekend rescued Glamorgan from a financial deficit for the first time in four years, thanks to Bradman's top-billing and Richardson's decision to make a game of it.

The team moved on to Birmingham for a match against Warwickshire, but it was rained out after only three hours' play, in which the home team hit three for 102. The counties were complaining. The season, one of the wettest on record, was causing them to miss huge gates, especially with Bradman and the Australians as the biggest drawcard ever.

The sun shocked the tourists by appearing at Northampton on Saturday 9 August, only to disappear again during Northamptonshire's innings of 249. It rained all Sunday and into Monday, leaving Australia on a rotten sticky, which off-breaker Vallence Jupp relished. He took six for 32, including top-scorer Bradman (22), and Australia folded for 93 in front of 10,000 astonished spectators. The tourists were forced to follow on and made eight for 405 on an improved wicket.

Woodfull (116), Richardson (116), Jackson (52) and Bradman (35) were allowed useful batting practice in the last chance before the Fifth Test, much to the chagrin of the British press. But Woodfull was not Richardson. The Aussie skipper saw no value, apart from dubious public relations, in declaring early to give Northants a chance to please their supporters. The Rock was already in Test mode with the biggest match of the tour just three days away.

20

THE 1930 ASHES DECIDER

Think of it — a brilliant batsman with no edge to his bat and who doesn't take a risk.
— Neville Cardus

CAPTAIN CASUALTY

The biggest casualty of Bradman's batting dominance by the end of the series was not Larwood, who came back into the side for the last Test, but Percy Chapman. He was omitted by the selectors, who demanded a win in the final game to secure the Ashes. Chapman's do-or-die style was not right, the thinking went, for this Test, which was to be timeless, whereas the dour approach of the replacement skipper, R. E. S. (Bob) Wyatt, was the right temperament for not losing in a game, which, given Bradman's predilections and the weather, could go on until Christmas.

Goddard and Nichols were dropped for Larwood and Whysall, the latter being rewarded for scoring 120 against the Australians.

The tourists gave Jackson a second chance. He replaced Richardson, the vice-captain, in a tough decision. The Australians were in a confident mood by the time they reached The Oval, and someone leaked to the press that Bradman was preparing to 'break his own Test record' in this game. This was bluff, and not all that astute, for players like Larwood were pushed that fraction harder to dismiss him. The speedster, for one, would be desperate to get rid of him early, for another pummelling such as at Leeds would do his future at Test level no good. But the ploy did at least make the England team focus on one player, and there was no doubt it had Bradman-itis before the game even commenced.

The first day, Saturday 16 August, saw Wyatt win the toss and bat. England started solidly. But while Sutcliffe dug in for the long haul, Hobbs holed out for a short push of 47 and was caught by Kippax attempting to hook Wall for six. Whysall found the step up too much and was out for 13, LBW, to Wall again. All England was wishing for a Hendren or better still under the conditions, a Jardine. Nevertheless, there was great batting to come. Duleepsinhji breezed his way to 50 and looked like taking over the day, when Grimmett had him caught by Fairfax, also attempting a big hit.

England was three for 162, not a bad score for its best bat to grace the crease. Hammond had been dropped down the list by Wyatt to give him a better chance of a big innings. The tactic failed and he was bowled for 13. Meanwhile Sutcliffe was plodding on and England was maintaining a fair rate — not far below a run a minute — in its four for 190. Minutes later, the game swung Australia's way when Grimmett struck an important blow by bowling Leyland (3) with a big-breaking leggie. The score at tea was five for 197. After the break, England fought back through a 119-run partnership between the immovable Sutcliffe and the redoubtable Wyatt. In this session only Wall looked in form with the ball and only Bradman shone in the field, leaving the home side on five for 316 at stumps (Sutcliffe the slow hero on 138 not out) and in a sound position. The two batsmen were mobbed by the enthusiastic crowd as they walked off. Yet not even the most optimistic scribe would say it was a winning break when in theory Bradman could bat into the New Year in a possible two innings.

That fear multiplied on Monday morning, when England lost its remaining five wickets for 89. Fairfax claimed the stubborn Wyatt for 64 and Sutcliffe for 161, both caught behind by Oldfield. Then

Grimmett stepped in to help Fairfax wrap up the tail so that England was dismissed for 405. Grimmett managed four for 135 off 66.2 overs and was never mastered, while Fairfax, three for 52 off thirty-one, and Wall, two for 96 from thirty-seven, contributed big-hearted efforts.

Woodfull and Ponsford moved out to face a tricky twenty-five minutes before lunch. Larwood had so far mastered Ponsford, but the Victorian was a determined type. He decided to go on the attack against England's striker, in much the way Bradman had, and it worked. The openers survived until lunch and went on with it afterwards. Ponsford continued to take the attack up to Larwood, until he was removed from the bowling crease.

Peebles finally broke the stand with enough drift and turn to beat Ponsford and bowl him for 110 at 159. His aggressive innings set the stage perfectly for Bradman. But it was tea. Then the rain came, and the expectant crowd had to lift umbrellas and wait another hour before play resumed and Woodfull walked out with Bradman. It was just the sort of atmosphere the latter revelled in. An Ashes series was at stake, the biggest reward in cricket at the highest level. Now records were incidental. Winning was everything.

Which way would the cricket gods throw the dice tonight in a failing light? Could Peebles enfeeble The Don with another wrong'un or perhaps a top-spinner this time? Could Woodfull hang on?

The gamblers looked at Bradman's scores so far in the Tests: 8, 131, 254, 334, 1, 14. They might have figured he was on a low roll, and put their money on 10. But a statistician would say he was due for a big one — a double hundred.

There was more tension at The Oval and outside than at any previous match in the series as Bradman faced Peebles, who had not completed his over after dismissing Ponsford. England and its supporters wanted Bradman out. If he went early, the Test, the series and the Ashes would be in the home team's grasp.

The light was indifferent, the wicket slightly damp, but playing well. Peebles had two men close — at short-forward square leg — hoping to force Bradman into a false stroke from a wrong'un as he had at Manchester. The batsman surveyed the field, making a mental note of where the nine men were placed before settling over his bat. The crowd went silent. The umpire withdrew his arm and the close fielders went down. Peebles turned from his short run, and was in . . .

BEGIN, THE DON

Bradman cut the first ball for one, when any other batsman under the tight circumstances would have let the delivery go. Then he faced Tate at the other end. The first ball was turned to leg, in typical fashion early, for two. The crowd sensed ominous intent. Bradman looked at ease. Then Tate beat him outside the off-stump twice. The batsman seemed baffled, yet not out of tune. He played the rest of Tate's over carefully and watched Peebles bowl to Woodfull.

At 5.25 p.m. the Aussie skipper appealed against the light twice and was successful second time around. Off they trooped. Five minutes later, they were on again as the light improved.

This on-off play, the bad light, the slippery conditions and damp pitch were not ideal for batting. They called for more nerve than verve, concentration not dissipation. Woodfull cut Tate for four. Bradman kept pushing singles and twos, and would not be bogged down. He was conscious of Peebles' leg-trap, but played shots through it to make a point. Once he made a rare swipe over their heads for three. The crowd reacted, for by now almost everyone watching knew Bradman's self-imposed rule of nothing airborne. He had even been writing about it.

At 190, Woodfull on 54 pushed at a good leg-break from Peebles and edged it to a grateful Duckworth. Rain stopped play with Bradman on 27 not out, Kippax on 8 and the total one for 215.

The weather was not promising on Tuesday, although play began on time and in sunshine. Bradman settled in again — his third start in the innings. He saw off Peebles after a long duel, which put paid to any argument about the batsman's extra-susceptibility to leg-spin. Wyatt tried Larwood.

The Notts star started with a good bouncer. Bradman swayed under it, eyes on the ball. Larwood threw everything at the batsmen, but they both coped well. He wasn't able to get the kick he wanted. Wyatt kept him on, almost as a stock bowler in an attempt to seal one end. He brought back Peebles from the other to relieve the marathon-running Tate.

Kippax (28) appeared sound until he tried to flick-drive Peebles through the leg-trap. It seemed through, but Wyatt threw out a hand and took a brilliant reflex catch. Australia was three for 263, still 138 in arrears, with Bradman on 68 not out.

In walked a nervous Jackson, the main promise unfulfilled on the tour. Many had backed him to do better than Bradman under English conditions, but his perpetual, undefined ill-health had not allowed him the freedom to produce his best. So far in the Tests he had scored one run from his single chance, which was not enough opportunity for one so gifted.

The sight and sound of his NSW team-mate and good mate at the other end eased the nerves just enough. Despite innuendo to the contrary, most of the Australian bats — Woodfull, Ponsford, McCabe and Jackson — liked Bradman, but all, regardless of other feelings, respected him. They knew that while he was alive at the crease there was a chance for glory.

Jackson started tentatively, as anyone would with just one run on the board in the games he had made the long boat trip for. The laconic Woodfull had turned strict schoolmaster. Jackson had a plan to work to. He had to stay at the wicket, just plonk there. This was never Jackson's style. He was an artist. The captain was asking him to make only dabs of one kind. A series depended on it. The batsman had to curb his creativity for the team good. 'Let Don take control,' were the final instructions.

Bradman began to do just that. Wyatt tried Hammond now as the 'plugger' at one end and Peebles at the other. Bradman took full-blooded pulls for four from off to leg from both. Tate was brought on, then Wyatt himself. It was Larwood's turn again when Bradman was 99. The batsman drove him for four to record his fourth century in the series in five Tests, and his sixth in eight Tests against England. Bradman removed the baggy green, raised his bat, not as a weapon, but in salute, and smiled. It was not the look of a craftsman who had endured, but a young man who had enjoyed his effort.

Yet he knew that the job was not even half-done. With the tourists just over 300, they were still a hundred behind. He had to go on and smother England's chances, for unlike the other four there was no way out of this Test with a draw. There had to be a winner. Bradman's aim now was to climb well beyond England's score, so that when it went in again, its batsmen would be faced with a demoralising no-retreat position.

Jackson felt lifted. Bradman was on top, relaxed and encouraging. He moved on into the second century with ease, letting the right ball go by when he had to. He was now picking Peebles' wrong'un, and scoring off it. At lunch Australia was three for 371 — just 34 short and closing on England. Bradman was on 112 not out, having scored 85 before lunch in a tenacious display.

The batsmen were looking forward to a well-earned respite. There was a heavy shower and the interval was prolonged. While waiting to resume, the MCC produced the royal card, this time the debonair Edward, Prince of Wales, and future King, in hat, bow-tie and double-breasted suit. Would the splendour of his delivery trap Bradman as the King had Ponsford at Lord's?

The Prince met the Australians and engaged Bradman for the usual small talk. Bradman grinned. The Prince smiled, chatted jovially, and wished him luck. Edward, like most of the royals, had no deep passion for cricket. But he knew that the photo opportunity of the summer was not at colourful Ascot mixing in the Members' enclosure with the upper class, or green Wimbledon jawing with other royals and dignitaries. The snap was at the grey Oval in front of all classes near that ugly gasometer, and preferably shaking hands with a twenty-one-year-old country lad from a one-time British penal colony. But it was too wet outside and no photographer was in the dressing-room.

The post-lunch session could not get under way because of rain until 3 p.m. Fifty minutes' play saw thirty-one runs scored in the drizzle, then rain stopped the war of attrition with Bradman on 129 out of Australia's three for 402. The patient Edward had had enough. He left and was snapped getting into his car outside the ground. Meanwhile, real fans stayed in the hope of seeing Bradman make his sixth start to the innings.

Wyatt and Woodfull disagreed on a resumption. Woodfull said it was too grim to go on. Wyatt wanted to confront the Australians in conditions that would give the bowlers an edge.

Five minutes before stumps were to be drawn, when many thousands had straggled away from the ground long after their future monarch, the batsmen were invited out to play a few balls. Despite the abuse and booing from supporters at Douglas Jardine's home ground, they negotiated the mini-crisis to be three for 403 — just two runs short of England's score — as stumps were drawn with Bradman 130 not out.

Even England's staunch ultra-conservative supporter, the *Daily Mail*, was in a mood of churlish capitulation. It editorialised: 'There is nothing to say about this match except that Bradman is a definite menace to English cricket.'

Jardine, who was at the game for some days, couldn't agree more. He had seen Bradman in four matches now in the summer and from his point of view it was depressing. He was indeed a menace to England's image and superiority in the country's national game.

LARWOOD'S LAST LASH

Day four, Wednesday 20 August, was the most critical for England. If it couldn't claim a wicket, preferably Bradman's, early in the first session, it would face defeat. The wicket was hard, fast, uncertain and dangerous. Larwood and Hammond were now in a position to do the menacing in an attempt to break through. It was a last, legitimate resort, for all else had failed.

The two young Australians faced their toughest assignment. Hammond at first collected both of them on the body. Then Larwood retrieved his best rhythm and hit top speed and accuracy.

He got one to lift from a good length. The ball cannoned into Bradman's sternum and doubled him up. He took a few seconds to recover and shaped up again. Two balls later, Larwood found that spot on the strip again and the ball crashed into the batsman's fingers. They were poorly protected by the flimsy glove. Bradman moved off the pitch, put down his bat and examined the damage. The fieldsmen looked on as umpire Parry did some repairs.

Larwood stood nearby, hands on hips and interested. This was the first time he had ever had the Australian on the defensive. He could sense a chance to claim a wicket. It was now or never. Play resumed and he steamed in. Bradman stepped inside another fast lifter and crashed it through mid-wicket for four. Larwood slipped him an away-swinger. The batsman cut him to the fence. Bradman had decided to do what he had done with Larwood on every previous occasion: hit him out of the firing-line.

In his next over, Larwood tried the same tactics against Jackson, who took a bruiser on the hip-bone. Then the bowler launched one which bounced into the ribs. Hammond got the idea, but Bradman hooked him into the fence, and cut him for three to reach 182. Jackson faced the all-rounder, who pitched one short. It didn't rise as expected and Jackson fended it off with his elbow. It hurt. Bradman wandered down to console and encourage him. Jackson was ill. His partner may have reminded him of the team's position. Australia was more than fifty ahead. Jackson, eyes watering, took some deep breaths and faced up.

The Test had come alive in the fourth morning as England developed some needed spite. Yet not even Larwood's thunderbolts could stop Bradman now, for he was developing his own cadence — the steady beat of wood on leather. He delivered his *coup de grâce* for the morning and possibly the match with a straight drive past bowler Tate to reach 200.

It was 12.55 p.m. on Wednesday and Bradman, literally, had been in all week. His stay at the wicket, between the rain and other breaks, was then just under six and a half hours — 383 minutes. He acknowledged the prolonged applause with the same unlined grin as at 100. Jackson walked up and shook his right hand a fraction too enthusiastically. Bradman winced. Those bruised fingers hurt.

After Bradman had reached his third double hundred for the series, Wyatt took Larwood off. He had delivered bruises, but Bradman had left a huge black and blue weal on Larwood's ego, after defeating him in yet another encounter. This time the 'loss' hurt more than even the belting at Leeds and the dumping from the England line-up. Australia was tightening its grip on the Ashes.

The batsmen had seen off the pacemen with attack. Wyatt brought himself on. Jackson relaxed just a fraction, having won the vicious battle against bounce and bump. He struck out at the England skipper and was easily caught by Sutcliffe in the covers for 73. Australia was four for 506 — 101 ahead. The most critical partnership of the summer had produced 243 runs. Jackson had proceeded at just half Bradman's rate, yet he had stayed in the middle with grit. His selection for the tour and the match had been justified by that one fighting and most timely knock.

McCabe was in now and also lifted by his good friend's performance as Bradman's unstoppable tempo saw him pound towards a century before lunch. He fell two short, and was 228 not out at lunch. Australia was 150 ahead and still with six wickets in hand. Woodfull and Bradman, however, were still not satisfied. Seven hundred, they agreed, would be a satisfactory team total, which would give Australia a lead of around 300.

After lunch, McCabe had most of the strike in the first twenty minutes. Larwood was on, and Bradman advanced slowly to 232. The bowler produced a fast, lifting ball, which swung away late. Bradman noticed the swing and turned his bat at the last second and the ball flew harmlessly through to Duckworth. Larwood, reacting to having nearly beaten Bradman's bat for the first time in three days, swung around and appealed. The keeper always threw the ball in the air and yelled if he thought a batsman was out. Yet a picture of the incident shows no reaction at all from Duckworth or Hammond at slip.

Much to Bradman's chagrin, the umpire upheld Larwood's solitary appeal, and the batsman was on his way. His 254 at Lord's had been his technically best innings, and his 334 at Leeds had been his most thrilling. But this 232 was the most important performance of his career. It was also the most mentally and physically courageous. It had put Australia in a strong position to take the Ashes.

Bradman's 'dismissal' left Australia on five for 570. McCabe (54), Fairfax (53 not out) and Oldfield (34) helped take Australia on another 125, so that it reached 695 — just five short of Woodfull's target. Bradman thought Fairfax and Oldfield had put in their best-ever batting performances in a Test. So had Ponsford. Bradman's effort would rank with his greatest innings given the circumstances, and Jackson's was his most determined at the highest level, so that five of the batsmen had excelled and shown spine at precisely the right moment. Normally a team could count on one or two players coming good, but this was extraordinary and a credit to Woodfull's leadership and Bradman's influence.

Peebles took six for 204 off a long-distance seventy-one overs. Hammond with one for 70 off forty-two was the most economical, while Larwood was the most expensive pro rata with one for 132 from forty-eight. In his last two bowling stints against Australia in Tests he had now legitimately taken one (if Bradman's removal is discounted) for 271 runs off eighty-one overs. His series record, Bradman's dubious scalp included, was four for 292 from 101 overs at an average of 73 per wicket. Most of those runs had come from Bradman's bat. Larwood had delivered 147 balls to him during the series and Bradman had taken 137 runs off them, which was a rate of 93.21 runs per 100, a higher rate than any one-day player in the modern era.

Bradman had made 974 runs at an average of 139.14.

Cardus was eating the words by which he had lived:

We have now seen Bradman the brilliant and Bradman the shrewd, playing four day cricket and cricket that takes no heed of the clock. In these different circumstances he has shown command over the appropriate methods; his versatility is astonishing and he indeed is a great batsman.

He added: '. . . though I still doubt whether he is yet equal to the challenge of a great spin bowler on a bad wicket.'

Without specifying who and where, this caveat was as inane as it was meaningless — a little 'out' clause for his earlier pronouncements. Perhaps Cardus was thinking of Grimmett bowling on a moon-crater.

HORNIBROOK'S HURRAH

After fielding so long, Hobbs and Sutcliffe had to come in for a dangerous last fifty-five minutes. Woodfull called for three cheers for the forty-eight-year-old Hobbs, who was making his final Test appearance. He seemed unaffected and commenced well. But on 9 with the score on 17 he pulled a short-pitched ball from Fairfax onto his stumps and marched out of Test cricket forever with a fine record — seventy-one innings for 3,636 runs at an average of 54.26, and a highest score of 187.

Whysall came and went for 10, caught by Hornibrook off the irrepressible Grimmett. England was two for 37. The final day was fine enough to predict no interruptions and Hornibrook broke through at 118 and 137 before lunch, dismissing Sutcliffe (54) and Duleepsinhji (46), both caught by Fairfax. Hammond was in form, but it was Hornibrook's day. He broke through again at 207 and 208, bowling both Leyland (20) and Wyatt (21).

Hammond began a post-tea rearguard action with three wickets to defend, but in the rush to keep the strike ran out Tate for a duck. Then Hornibrook had Larwood (5) caught and bowled Duckworth (15). Peebles, a true rabbit, joined Hammond who struck out and was dropped by Bradman in the deep. Thinking the Aussies needed more catching practice he leapt into Hornibrook and was this time swallowed by Fairfax for 60.

England was all out for 251 in the last session of the fifth day, thanks to Hornibrook who took seven for 92 and had a hand in another. Australia had finished with a hard-fought, crushing victory by an innings and 39 runs.

It also took the series two-one, and the Ashes, thanks mainly to Bradman with the bat and Grimmett with the ball. These two were the decisive difference.

BEYOND 3,000

The jubilant Australians took the train to Bristol to play Gloucestershire on 23 August, and started by ripping through the home side, which scored just 72. Hornibrook was in the mood to make up for lean times earlier in the tour and took four for 20, whereas Grimmett managed his usual minimum quota of three for 28. Australia replied with a poor 157, Ponsford making 57 and Bradman 42. Gloucester scored 202 in the second dig, with Hammond hitting 89, his best innings of the season against the tourists. Hornibrook continued his late form with five for 49.

Australia then had a delayed reaction to their success and collapsed. Ponsford (0), Kippax (0), Richardson (3) and Bradman (14) had post-series blues. Australia scrambled an ignoble 117 and not a draw but a tie. The excitement nearly buried the fact that after thirty-two innings in an England season Bradman had passed Trumper's 2,570 in fifty-three innings in 1902 for an England season. On 27 August, the sun was hot for Bradman's twenty-second birthday, as the tourists batted first against Kent at Canterbury. Everywhere now, crowds were turning up to see Bradman score or be dismissed, and he was being presented with challenges, records to break and bowlers who wanted his scalp so they could one day tell their grandchildren, I got Bradman . . .

It wasn't so unusual considering Bradman would normally be removed by one or two bowlers every match he played, yet it would forever be the boast of a player and his descendants down the generations. At Kent's St Lawrence ground, it was the worthy leggie, 'Tich' Freeman, who got him LBW for 18. Bradman was one of his 252 wickets for the season, and he headed the wicket-taking in England in 1930 by exactly a hundred dismissals. (Grimmett was Australia's best with 144 wickets at 16.85.) Freeman ended with five for 78 from Australia's 181 and Kent replied with 227. In Australia's second attempt, Bradman threw off lethargy and concentrated on the Freeman challenge. In a 343-minute display that could have formed a film and book entitled *The Art of Playing Spin Bowling,* Bradman's 205 not out was a demonstration of footwork which witnesses claimed was the best ever seen in Kent, if not England. It was his sixth double century for the tour. Australia declared at three for 320 with Jackson scoring 50 not out. The game dwindled away to a draw when Frank Woolley hit 60 not out of Kent's reply of two for 83.

Bradman didn't play in the next game against Sussex at Hove, which was drawn. Kippax, without the dominant shadow up the other end, hit 158 and 102 not out. The tired team could have done with a week lying on Hove's rocky beach in the welcome sun, but they were needed for more action at Folkestone, this time against a South of England XI. The southerners hit eight for 403 declared — there was a ring of familiarity in that score — with the rising young wicket-keeper-batsman Leslie Ames (121), Hammond (54), Wyatt (51) and Tate (50) getting a little pride back, but the weary Australians found a bit extra. After all, the opposition team did have England in its title. Jackson (78) looked as if he was ready for another series, while Ponsford (76), at top form, and Bradman (63), rarely away from his, took the tally to 432. a'Beckett hit a strong 53, making him more than a footnote in what was a disappointing tour for the Melbourne lawyer. The game fizzled to another exhibition draw, with only a statistic to distinguish it in a thousand years' time. Bradman's 63 brought his tour tally in all games to 3,000 runs.

The penultimate tour game was at Lord's against a Club Cricket Conference XI. Australia scored 278. Bradman managed to raise his bat in anger again with 70, and the opposition fell apart for 133 and 104 (a'Beckett three for 1). Australia won by an innings and 41. The tourists then moved on to the 'Festival' match at Scarborough against H. D. G. Leveson-Gower's XI. Fittingly, the weather reverted to showers and the game was more feisty than festive. The strong opposition included Larwood, Tate, Parker and Test veterans Wilfred Rhodes, Jack Hobbs and Maurice Leyland. They hit nine for 218 declared. Australia replied and the final confrontation between Larwood and Bradman for 1930 was staged. The speedster was unconcerned that visitors had come to the fair and the cricket for some fun. He had a job to do, and he did not wish to be bludgeoned by Bradman yet again in a sorry season of one-sided contests. He bent his back for one last attempt to take the Australian's wicket legitimately. Bradman hit him out of the attack on the evening of the second day scoring 73 not out in 108 minutes, in one last reminder of who was boss in 1930. Rhodes, a youthful fifty-two-year-old, took five for 95. He nearly dismissed Bradman first ball by deceiving him with flight, the batsman's drive dropping just short of Wyatt at mid-off. In the opposition's second innings, Hobbs beat his age with a fine 59. Rhodes repeated his mature assessment of Bradman after his opening tour game against Worcester, without the qualifications insisted on by Cardus and the strategic judgements by Fender:

'He is the greatest batsman the world has ever seen.'

Bradman's final score of 96 in the Scarborough match brought his 1930 first-class tally to 2,960 and was a fitting end to the tour, for it was just short of his season average of 98.66. The few thousand spectators saw him on a medium day. His total tour aggregate, taking in his 140 against a Scottish XI and the Club Cricket Conference 70, was 3,170 at 99.06.

Woodfull's team in all played thirty-three tour matches, won twelve, lost one (the First Test at Trent Bridge), tied one and drew nineteen. It had restored Australia to dominance in world cricket, a situation that several Englishmen saw as unacceptable. They included Fender and Jardine of Surrey and England, who would have two seasons to contemplate how to restore their country to the top. The problem was focused yet not simple. They had to create a plan to combat Bradman, who in the final analysis had been the main difference between winning and losing the Ashes.

21

COMET WITH A
LONG TAIL

*Let there be no fear that this dynamic personality is likely to
become no more than a lofty crag in a range of spent volcanoes.
He is a national figure and is likely to remain such.*
— BILL O'REILLY

HOMECOMING KING

Bradman was still employed by Mick Simmons Ltd and it wanted
to take full advantage of its great publicity asset. The sports store
group combined with the Australian branch of the US General
Motors Corporation to bring Bradman home ahead of the rest of the
team, which prompted one newspaper to remark that the team
would become 'a comet with a long tail — Bradman being the head
and the rest of the team the tail'.

This remark naturally was not appreciated by the tail, who did not
need reminding that Bradman had been the star of the tour. It was
true that without him they would never have won the Ashes, but still
it was a team game and each player had played his part in Australia's
glory. Grimmett in particular would have been disappointed. He had
been the best bowler of either side and had played a big part in the
series victory.

'There was nothing I could do about it,' Bradman commented. 'I was still employed by Mick Simmons. When they organised my return, I had no choice. I was pleased at the reception and it was good to see family and friends, but I certainly didn't revel in all that.'

As General Motors chauffeured him home to Bowral and finally presented him with a car, Bradman repeatedly stated:

> *If credit is due to any player more than another it should go to our captain, Billy Woodfull. His opening partnerships with Ponsford made things much easier for those who followed him . . . and we must not forget that wonderful bowler, Clarrie Grimmett, whose work throughout was phenomenal.*

But his modesty fell on deaf ears as he attended reception after reception, organised and disorganised at aerodromes and town halls as tens of thousands flocked to get a glimpse of him. Bradman's dislike for publicity turned to little less than loathing and he wished for the chance of some peace and quiet with his family and Jessie. Yet he wasn't about to get it. Team manager Kelly, reflecting his and perhaps a couple of the players' irritation at Bradman's stealing of the limelight, recommended that the Board of Control cut his £150 'good conduct' money for having his memoirs published in the London *Star*. Bradman was thus fined £50, whereas Grimmett, who had also written in the press during the series, was let off because 'journalism was his profession'.

Bradman had to suffer this petty victimisation, his first experience of the price of fame. However, the loss was soon made up when *The Referee* magazine offered him a deal to write for it, which he took up. The controversy surrounding his return reinforced his concern that he would have to find a 'profession', which would at least give him independence from employers interested only in feeding off his fame.

The day before Bradman arrived back in Sydney, a big-hearted racehorse, Phar Lap, won the Melbourne Cup, part of a winning sequence in 1930–31 of thirty-one wins and two seconds in thirty-three starts. He was a dream horse and a bookie's nightmare who arrived on the racing scene at a time when punters, like the rest of the population, were down on their luck because of the Depression. This mighty beast of the course was now coupled with Bradman as the most popular living creatures in the land. They were both winners, and the greatest performers the country had ever seen in their respective fields. They were also stayers, who were rarely beaten, and if they were, they came up trumps the next time. Phar Lap and Bradman had become the nation's icons, and typified the spirit of a country, or at least the spirit to which people aspired.

Bradman was beginning to comprehend his fame and stature, which did not always sit easily with him. He fought for his right to privacy, but it was a losing battle. He appreciated public acclamation for his performances as a sportsman, but grew to hate what he called 'the lionising with which people are afflicted only because they are temporarily in the headlines'.

WINDIES' WOES, 1930–31

After England in 1930, others had wanted him to cut records as a pianist, write articles, make speeches, and do sales pitches for sports goods and cars. The only way he could restore not so much normality as some degree of order to his hectic life was to concentrate on the new cricket season in Australia.

'I found the bounce here difficult at first,' he recalled, after the slower wickets in England where he had found a rhythm for those 3,000 runs. 'It took some time to accustom myself. However, there was an incentive. The West Indies were coming on an inaugural tour and there were Tests to be played.'

Bradman began his adjustment in front of bumper club crowds for St George. His initial first-class game was for NSW against South Australia, which began on 7 November at Sydney. In the first innings his timing was out and he applied himself to sound defence. His 61 took a respectable 108 minutes and he was glad to be back on track. In the second innings he batted with vintage Bradman touch, scoring 121 in 142 minutes.

In a warm-up game for NSW against the West Indies, he hit 73 and 22. The form of the Australians in the build-up to the Tests was ordinary against a below-standard West Indies team. This side was nothing like the mighty teams led by Worrell and Sobers in the 1960s and the world-beaters of the 70s, 80s and 90s. The 1930–31 team was weak in batting, with only the diminutive George Headley classed as top-drawer. Their fielding varied from brilliant to erratic, but they did have three good quicks — H. C. Griffith, G. Francis and Learie Constantine.

The following week in Melbourne, Bradman played for 'Australia' in a game against 'The Rest of Australia', in a three-day testimonial match for Jack Ryder. 'The Rest' batted first and made 293. Grimmett, in early season form, took five for 89. The national side replied with 367, and Bradman had a battle with top veterans Blackie, Ironmonger and Mailey in reaching 73 in 128 minutes. Mailey tied him up with his leg-breaks. He played back to one and was bowled. Kippax was in form with 70, and the ever-steady Woodfull got 53.

Ryder made 65 not out and Keith Rigg 74 in The Rest's second innings of three declared for 191. The declaration in the rain-restricted game left 'Australia' with 118 to win in eighty-five minutes. Woodfull sent Bradman in to open, but he was restricted by fine bowling to 29 in an hour. He was again trapped by Mailey — this time caught and bowled — for 29 out of Australia's mini-collapse of five for 96, which was 14 short.

Four first-class innings were poor preparation for a Test series, but with the restricted Shield competition Bradman and the other Australians had to focus quickly on the main contest.

In the First Test at Adelaide commencing 12 December, the West Indies batted first and scored 296, a fair effort, but their players — except for G. C. Grant with 53 not out — had no answer to Grimmett, who took seven for 87, including Headley, LBW for a duck, and top-scorer Bartlett, LBW for 84. Australia began before lunch on the second day and lost Ponsford for 24 just after the break at 56. Bradman came, fiddled around unconvincingly for fifteen minutes and was out caught in slips for four off Griffith. Jackson was caught soon after for 31 and Australia was three for 64. Kippax (146) and McCabe (90) then restored order with a 182-run partnership. Fairfax (41 not out) showed his usual consistency and Australia managed 376 — not a great effort considering the opposition. The slow off-spin bowler Scott struck at the end of Australia's innings with a spell of four for 0, and finished with four for 83.

The visitors could cobble only 249 in the second dig, Grimmett again doing the job with four for 86. Grant once more remained unconquered, this time on 71, completing a fine double. Bradman snared his first Test wicket, Barrow LBW for 27, to finish with one for 8. Australia easily polished off the 172 required with Jackson hitting 70 not out and Ponsford 90 not out. The ten-wicket win reflected the gulf between the two sides.

Half the national team — Bradman, Kippax, Fairfax, Jackson and McCabe — stayed on in Adelaide for what was a more challenging event than the Test — NSW against Grimmett and the South Australians. Kippax won the toss and batted. Grimmett came on early and had Fingleton stumped for 6 at 24. Bradman joined Jackson and they went on the rampage in a sensational record 334-run partnership for the second wicket in just 223 minutes. They ganged up on Grimmett and this day proved his master on a good wicket. Bradman hit his first fifty in seventy-nine minutes and reached a century in 128 minutes, which was about his normal rate. Thereafter, in keeping pace with Jackson, he even lifted his tempo, although he did not get tempted into six-hunting.

It took second-stringer White to pick up Jackson for 166 in 229 minutes. Bradman went on, as usual untroubled by losing a partner, and careered from 150 to 200 in thirty-eight minutes of controlled, power hitting. Just before stumps when he was on 258, another net bowler in the form of Vic Richardson bowled him after 269 minutes. He hit thirty-seven fours in reaching his tenth double century in the first-class arena, which put him in front of all Australians. Despite the savage attack on him, Grimmett was not disgraced with five for 180 off 48 overs. He even squeezed in five maidens during the onslaught. South Australia followed on but was all out for 304, giving NSW the match by an innings and 134 runs. The surprise of the match was that Bradman ended with creditable best bowling figures of three for 54 off twelve overs.

Rain ruined the traditional end-of-the-year game at the MCG between NSW and Victoria, but not before Ponsford played a superb innings on a difficult wicket to carry his bat for 109 not out in Victoria's 185. NSW replied with six for 97, a'Beckett having Bradman caught in slips by Hendry for 2. It was not the ideal tune-up for the Second Test, which began on New Year's Day 1931 in Sydney.

Woodfull won the toss and batted. It was Ponsford's turn to maul the opposition, but Bradman failed again, this time collecting 25 in forty minutes before Francis had him caught. Only Woodfull, dropping down to number six to allow Jackson to open, gave his former opening partner solid support. They put on 183 before Constantine had the skipper caught for 58. Ponsford was eventually bowled by Scott — the ball coming off his bat as he charged the spinner — on day two for 183 in 348 minutes. Australia tallied 369. This again was a mediocre effort and it seemed that the team was off the boil after their long, triumphant tour of the UK.

However, the bowlers mopped up the West Indians twice for 107 and 90 to win easily by an innings and 172 runs. Grimmett (four for 54) in the first and Hurwood (four for 22) in the second took bowling honours. Ironmonger made a return to the Test arena with one for 20, and three for 13. Headley still failed with just 14 and 2. The attendance peaked at 18,025 on the second of the two-and-a-bit-day match. The public was not ignoring the Tests. They were curious to see the development of the Aussie batsmen since England, but the uneven contest would see interest dwindle as the series progressed.

The Third Test began at the Brisbane Exhibition Ground eleven days later. Australia batted first in extremely hot conditions and, as was the custom in the series so far, Bradman didn't have to wait long to bat. Jackson fell LBW to Francis at 1.

Before this game, Bradman's reputation had been under scrutiny off the field because of the £50 Board of Control fine and his lacklustre performances in the series so far. He looked to be continuing his low-scoring pattern when he was dropped in slips on four. But it was the prod he needed. His fifty took 80 minutes and Ponsford went with him in the heat, scoring at about the same rate to reach his century in the afternoon session. A minute or so later, it was Bradman's turn to take a bow, just as Australia passed the 200 in 138 minutes. Bradman knuckled down with another hundred on his mind. Then, after a partnership of 229 (a record for the second wicket in Australia), Ponsford was caught for 109. It had taken them just 162 minutes.

Kippax started overcautiously, then settled in for another big stand. Bradman was 129 not out at lunch. The visitors felt the pinch in the post-tea session, but responded with steady bowling and some brilliant fielding as Bradman showed them why he was now regarded as the finest batsman of the era. He reached 200 in just 251 minutes and charged to 223 not out at the close, scoring 94 in the session and hitting twenty-four boundaries. The team's 300 was up in 221 minutes and 400 in 267 minutes, but Kippax was bowled for 84 by Birkett just before stumps with the score on 423. The pair had added 193 in the equal highest partnership for the third wicket in Australia.

The home side was two for 428 at stumps in 294 minutes. Bradman was back doing what he did best — breaking records. The 223 was the most runs made in one day in a Test in Australia, and it was the second time a player had reached a double century in a day in a Test. He had joined other double-century makers in Australia — S. E. Gregory (201 in 1894 against England at Sydney), Trumper (214 against South Africa in 1902 at Adelaide) and Ryder (201 not out against England at Adelaide in 1924–25).

Another big crowd turned up next day to see if Bradman could make an assault on Foster's 287 in 1903–4 (the highest Test score in Australia), but he was caught hooking a skier to square leg without adding to his overnight score. Australia then lost McCabe (8) and Woodfull (17) cheaply and looked like being dismissed for under 500 until Oxenham (48) and Oldfield (38) stayed proceedings for an eventual total of 558.

Headley then showed his determination and skill in scoring 102 out of 193, but the rest of his colleagues failed to stay with him.

Grimmett, as ever, provided the backbone of the attack with four for 93 off 41.3 overs, though Oxenham (four for 39) took the figures and a nice double for the game. Ironmonger earned his place with two for 43 from twenty-six overs. The West Indies followed on and again capitulated. Only Headley (28) reached 20 and the visitors were rolled for 148. Grimmett proved too much again with five for 49.

Four days later, NSW played Victoria at Sydney in a big Shield clash and Bradman hit 33 in forty-seven minutes and 220 in 308 minutes against a top-class attack which included Ironmonger, Blackie, a'Beckett and Ryder. During the innings he became the first player ever to pass 1,000 in a season three times. Clem Hill and Bill Ponsford had done it twice.

In the Fourth Test at Melbourne, the West Indies won the toss, batted, and were dismissed in less than two sessions for 99. Ironmonger, on his home turf, took seven for 23 off twenty overs, and Grimmett two for 46 off nineteen. Australia reverted to the old firm of openers Ponsford and Woodfull, and they did better with an opening stand of 50 before Ponsford was stumped off Constantine just after tea.

Bradman, with two double centuries behind him already in 1931, was in a frame of mind to continue his run of big innings on a ground that had been happy hunting turf for him twice in the 1928–29 Ashes series. He opened like a young man in a hurry and scored his fastest test fifty — in forty-five minutes. He was 92 not out in seventy-eight minutes at stumps. His progress looked to be stymied by overnight rain, but the resultant sticky held no terrors for him, although he was missed at silly point before he had added to his score. He took advantage of the lapse and recorded another Test century, in 102 minutes — his fastest since Leeds in 1930 and the quickest ever in Australia.

The sticky provided problems, but the West Indies didn't have a Grimmett to take advantage of them, which allowed Bradman to master the conditions. He powered on, losing Woodfull (run out for 83), Jackson (15), and McCabe (run out for 2) along the way. The visitors' speed in the field caused some indecision between wickets.

Woodfull called for what seemed an easy single, but Bradman failed to respond. Later, McCabe and Bradman found themselves at the same end in a running mix-up. The bails were removed by Constantine at the other end, and Bradman immediately headed off although he was the 'safe' player of the two. The umpire called him back and ruled McCabe the man out. Bradman resumed his quick scoring, reaching 150 in just 147 minutes, the fastest of his Test career.

He had forsaken his rule of not lifting shots during the series and it again proved his downfall. He was caught in the deep for 152 in 154 minutes, leaving Australia five for 286. Bradman's morning batting yielded 60 runs in seventy-six minutes in his best display yet on a sticky.

Woodfull declared at eight for 328, and the West Indies again collapsed for just 107. Fairfax (four for 31), Ironmonger (four for 56, making a record eleven for 79) and Grimmett (two for 10) shared the wickets and Australia won with ease again by an innings and 122 runs.

The West Indies gained some respectability in the Fifth Test at Sydney when they batted first and declared at six for 350 to put Australia in on a sticky. Martin scored 123 and Headley lived up to his reputation with 105. Grimmett took three for 100 off thirty-three overs, and Ironmonger two for 95 off forty-two. Australia struggled and was rolled for 224. Bradman virtually opened again, as he had many times in the season in Tests and Shield games, and made 43 in fifty-one minutes before being caught in slips off a viciously kicking ball. Only Fairfax with a stubborn 54 made more. The tourists declared again at the fall of the fifth wicket at 124, giving them a lead of 252, and a chance for victory on a still problematic pitch, which had received more rain and was a gluepot once more.

Ponsford and Woodfull gave chase with a partnership of 49. Bradman came in, made an uncharacteristic swing at a good-length yorker and was bowled for a duck, his first in a Test. McCabe (44) showed some fight and Fairfax again could not be removed easily. However, he ran out of partners and was left on 60 not out thinking of what might have been if someone had managed to stay with him. Australia was dismissed for 220, giving the tourists victory by just 32 runs in a series which ended four-one in the home side's favour.

Bradman finished the season on a tour of country Queensland as a member of Kippax's XI. He welcomed the chance to travel once more, this time by boat from Sydney to Townsville. He was impressed by the vastness of the 'fertile land', and in his autobiography lamented the fact that more 'settlers' were 'not immigrating North to enlarge the population, which could be safely carried in that rich area'.

The conditions and the enthusiastic supporters inspired Bradman. He found touch with four centuries, an 80 and a 90, to end a season that seemed to be now standard. In all first-class games he scored 1,422 runs at 79 and was the dominant batsman in the country for the third successive season. Unfortunately, he badly sprained his ankle at Rockhampton, which put him in hospital for eighteen days. But it gave him time to think.

'The enforced convalescence may have been a blessing,' Bradman noted. 'It certainly gave me a rest . . . and provided a tonic for a constitution somewhat jaded by concentrated cricket and publicity.'

THE TEMPTATION

This perpetual pressure caused Bradman to contemplate his future. He felt he had none with Mick Simmons, where his contract would expire in February 1932. He was twenty-two and eager to get married, yet he could not provide the security he would like for a family. The problem, which was pushed aside temporarily in early 1929 when he began at Simmons, was now haunting Bradman again. The Depression in Australia had reached its depth and work was very difficult to find. The money he had saved from the tour gave him some resources, but it was not a propitious moment for investment in business. Besides, Bradman had no background in business and was more concerned with finding solid, suitable employment which would form the basis for a career.

He had no wish to continue in his promotional job which was on offer for extension, so the winter months in Australia in 1931 were spent considering limited options. Bradman discussed his dilemma with close friends. If necessary, he was even prepared to give up cricket for the sake of a secure future. Instead, however, he investigated another avenue.

Learie Constantine, whom Bradman had got to know during the West Indies' visit, was sounded out by a mutual friend, Claude Spencer. Constantine was a professional with the Nelson Club in the Lancashire League in England. The Accrington Club came up with an offer to Bradman of £500 a season for three years. While secret discussions were going on, the press got wind of what he had in mind.

Bradman negotiated his salary up to £600 and for just two seasons, but still hesitated over signing a contract. It was possible that he could squeeze in playing in England during the Australian winter and come back for the Shield competition in the summer. But his Test career would be finished because of his contract with the Board of Control, which prevented a 1930 tourist playing in Britain for the next two years. In effect, Bradman would become an English pro and would be unlikely to make the boat trip every six months to play cricket in Australia as well. He could develop other interests and end up staying most of the time in the UK.

Bradman was troubled by turning his sport into a profession. It was something he disdained. If he played as a pro in England, the enjoyment would go out of the game for him. It would also restrict his chances of taking up other work. On the other hand, his reputation after the 1930 tour could open up new business opportunities. He loved London and England, but he was realistic enough to perceive that he had seen the country through distinctly rose-coloured glasses. Mixing with royalty and being feted by the high and the mighty were not the norm. His fame had carried him so far, but as a pro he would lose his appeal, as several other Aussies had once they made the move.

Jessie was leaving the decision to him, but she preferred the idea of staying in Australia, with family, friends and connections. With the matter public, Bradman would not be forced into a hurried decision. Editorials in the press began to pronounce on the matter, and the nation reacted with disappointment that it might be losing its greatest sporting son. Yet Bradman did not regard himself as public property. Sentiment didn't pay the bills in a depression or provide the necessities for a young family.

However, Frank Packer, a Sydney newspaper proprietor who loved his sports — namely cricket, yachting and Rugby — decided along with F. J. Palmer's department store and the broadcaster 2UE to make young Bradman an alternative proposition to keep him in Australia. They offered him a three-pronged deal, which was close to the amount offered in the Accrington contract, whereby he would write for Packer's Associated Newspapers Ltd, which published the Sydney *Sun*, broadcast on 2UE, and work for Palmer's in promotions and coaching of juniors, in a similar way to his duties at Mick Simmons.

Bradman liked the Australian deal better. He enjoyed writing and was willing to take on the challenge of radio, in which he would join 'Uncle Lionel and the Listerine Serenaders' in making nightly cricket reports.

It settled the matter and he stayed in Australia. By then, it was October 1931, and South Africa was about to tour Australia. Bradman could once more turn his mind to the game without worrying about his work career. It also meant he and Jessie could at last get married. They announced their engagement early in November and set a date for the end of the 1931–32 season so that a honeymoon would not interfere with the first-class matches. Bradman's long-held ambitions beyond his sporting achievements were coming to fruition.

22

THE SOUTH AFRICAN BEAT

It is not necessary to be a cricketer to realise as the Don takes his place at the wicket that he is a man who knows his job. You have the same feeling when Toscanini walks onto the platform.
— G. F. McCleary

DOUBLE-MINDED

Prodding at a sharply lifting delivery, O. Wendell Bill was out caught behind from the first ball of the 1931–32 season for NSW batsmen. The game was against Queensland at Brisbane on 6 November. Bradman, now twenty-three years old, strolled out to start his fifth season with his State looking fit and ready. The fact that he was in second ball, and virtually opening did not worry him. He had been used to this for three seasons since becoming a regular number three for NSW and Australia.

The Queensland bowler, a slight Aborigine of medium height named Eddie Gilbert, held some terrors. He didn't run but shuffled in from only four or five paces, and let the ball go at an alarming pace. Bradman fenced at the first ball, which lifted chest-high on the leg-side. The second dipped in at Bradman's midriff and knocked the bat out of his hand. The third was outside the off-stump. Bradman played and missed. Gilbert's 'chest-on' rather than side-on approach

239

was accompanied by a whipping arm that created suspicion that he was a thrower, or 'chucker'. Only close scrutiny of a slow-motion camera could detect for certain whether or not he might have been bending his elbow as well as the rules. However, it certainly looked bent to the naked eye of observers close to the wicket, especially when he hurled in a faster one.

His next ball, his fourth to Bradman, was quick and lifting. He tried to get his bat out of the way, but snicked it to the keeper. 'The keeper took the ball over his head,' Bradman recalled, 'and I reckon he was halfway to the boundary.'

The score-sheet read: Bradman, caught Waterman, bowled Gilbert, 0, NSW was two for 0. Half a century later, Bradman remembered the occasion vividly:

> *That day he was faster than even Larwood at his peak. From the pavilion his bowling looked fair. But in the middle his action was suspect. He jerked the ball and only delivered it from a very short approach. It's very hard that way to generate such speed with a legitimate delivery. He was only about nine stone (57 kg), but had very long arms.*

Four other NSW players went further and said bluntly that he threw his fastest ball. There was no doubt that he had developed his speediest delivery for Bradman, and the NSW manager A. L. Rose told the press this at the end of the match and accused him of throwing. The world's number one batsman was creating complexes for opposition teams and bowlers, who were resorting to any means to counter his batting dominance.

At one point in those sensational first few overs, Gilbert had three for 12, and the targets reckoned he was chucking two-thirds of his deliveries. However, his excellent throwing arm tired and his speed on the Brisbane green top was not maintained. This allowed McCabe to get on top and give a sizzling display of power batting to notch 229 not out from NSW's 432 in reply to Queensland's 109. The locals managed just 85 in their second dig.

Bradman didn't have time to dwell on this inauspicious opening to the season. Nor was he concerned. He had been in scintillating form in the opening weeks on another profitable Kippax-organised tour of country NSW with three centuries. In club games for St George he belted two double centuries. The first — 246 — was against Randwick and took 205 minutes, and the second — 201 — was against Gordon in 171 minutes.

These games gauged Bradman's attitude in his fifth season crusade. He was now not content with centuries even in club games. He was in the mood to go on, and he was lifting the ball and even going for sixes. In the game against Gordon, his last 100 came in just forty-five minutes and he hit five sixes. They were deliberate, calculated hits. One was a clout over point from a half-volley.

'You were lucky,' a fieldsman called to Bradman.

'What?' Bradman asked.

'That was a mishit.'

'You think so?'

'You couldn't do it again.'

Bradman smiled wryly. He waited for a similar ball, which came a few overs later, and clipped it over the short boundary at point once more. The fieldsman who had challenged him shook his head in amazement.

On 3 November, he was invited to play in an exhibition match at Blackheath for a combined Blue Mountains team against the Lithgow Pottery Cricket Club. Blackheath Council was opening a new ground and testing a new malthoid wicket, a rubberised tar surface which didn't need matting.

Bradman came in when the score was one for 16 and moved to 54 in about twenty-five minutes against the second-rate bowling. The fielding captain 'rested' one of his opening 'quicks' and brought on Bill Black, an off-spinner.

'What does this fellow bowl?' Bradman asked the keeper, Leo Waters, as Black placed his field.

'Don't you remember this bloke?' Waters replied. 'He bowled you in that Lithgow match [on the Kippax tour] a few weeks ago. He's been boasting about it ever since.'

Bradman didn't react. He glanced round at Black's ambitious attacking field and faced up. The first ball was walloped for six over mid-on and the tall Monterey pines on one side of the ground. The second ball went straighter for six more. A boy retrieved the ball which ended up well down a nearby street as Black asked his captain if he could have two more men in the deep. His third ball was straight-driven for four. The fourth was driven through mid-wicket for two. More consultation between bowler and captain saw changes, but Bradman hammered 4, 4, 6 and 1 to take 33 off the over in four minutes, which was twice as long as normal because of the ball fetching.

He had retained the strike and had the taste for blood. The next bowler was hit by Bradman for 40 — 6, 4, 4, 6, 6, 4, 6, 4 — in another four minutes, to the great joy of the crowd watching the ball sailing high out of the ground. His batting partner, Wendell Bill, took a single off the first ball of Black's next over to bring Bradman on strike. Black had six men in the deep. Bradman sent his second and third balls sailing over mid-wicket and the pines. He had hit 86 off nineteen balls and needed 14 for a century in three overs. Bradman got a single off the fourth ball. Wendell Bill took a single off the fifth, giving Bradman the strike. Black had three balls to complete his over. Bradman lofted two fours and one more smash for six over the pines to reach 100 in twenty-two balls. He had moved from 54 to 154 in just twelve minutes, the fastest 100 runs ever recorded in a game of cricket. Black's two overs cost him 62 runs, and now he had a far bigger boast than capturing Bradman's wicket, which had been achieved by hundreds of bowlers over his career. For the record, Bradman went on to 256 before being caught just short of those now-famous Monterey pines.

This big hitting and huge scoring demonstrated his advance in 1931–32, and there was little doubt he was in for a prolific year. However, he was perhaps over-zealous, three days later, when facing the 1931–32 tourists from South Africa, who were making only their second visit, the first having been in 1910–11. The visitors had a stronger reputation than the West Indies of a year earlier, with many highly competent players in all departments of the game, who had performed exceptionally well against England in a recent series. The skipper, H. B. Cameron, was a top-class keeper, and the two outstanding batsmen were Jim Christy and Herb Taylor. The better bowlers were Neville Quinn, a medium-pace left-hander, and fast bowler Sandy Bell. Q. McMillan was a high-standard slow bowler, but not in the same class as Grimmett, who by 1931–32 was the finest spinner in the world.

South Africa batted first against NSW and made 425, with Taylor making 124. Bradman as good as opened again, coming in with the score at one just before lunch. His timing was out and he struggled to 30 in eighty-seven minutes before giving a simple return catch to McMillan. NSW didn't recover and were all out for 168.

South Africa's skipper Cameron sportingly declared at three for 190, at the end of the third day, giving NSW a day (300 minutes) to make 448 to win at an average of ninety an hour. This would not have worried an in-form Bradman with partners to stay with him. But his season's start of 0 and 30 didn't augur well. However, it was a challenge and Bradman responded in a partnership with opener Jack Fingleton. C. L. Vincent was bowling on a good length, which tied down Fingleton, but not Bradman, who either played right back and whipped the ball wide of mid-on, or straight past the bowler. One newspaper report noted the 'sheer power of his wrists combined with delicate placing'.

Bradman also quickly conquered McMillan. When he pitched up, Bradman used his feet to make the ball a full-toss, often placing it between mid-on and square leg. A chess game developed between the touring captain and Bradman. A player would be moved from mid-on to mid-wicket. Bradman would strike the ball straight through mid-on. The moment a gap was plugged, the batsman would find another.

The result was a Bradman century in 100 minutes. He went on to 135 in 128 minutes before being dismissed caught after a low cut to backward point. He hit fifteen fours in a 216-run partnership with Fingleton who went on to 117. An additional 79 not out by McCabe left NSW on three for 430 — just 18 short in one of the best last-day chases in Australian first-class history.

In a busy November, Bradman appeared again in Brisbane, this time for Australia against South Africa in the First Test, which would give a true indication of his frame of mind for the season. He didn't have long to wait. Woodfull won the toss from Cameron, batted and lost Ponsford for 19 at 32. The wicket was similar to the green top which had seen Gilbert rip through NSW's early bats in the State game. Bradman's lofting mentality got the better of him and an attempted hook turned out to be a skyer, which lobbed luckily clear of fielders. On 10, he unintentionally bisected first and second slip with a streaky shot off medium-pace left-hander Quinn, who was 'puzzling' Bradman. On 15, he gave a tough chance off the same bowler and was dropped. No side in big cricket had ever made such a run of lapses against Bradman without suffering.

News that Bradman was in and flashing swept Brisbane and the crowd packed into the ground, causing such a crush that the fence was broken at several places. With a full-house watching, Bradman's approach changed as he summoned himself for a grand performance. He settled down, picked the pace of the pitch and moved to 30 at lunch. He reached his fifty soon after in 62 minutes, then measured his scoring rate once more and trotted along for 50 more in 82 minutes. Bradman went to tea on 108, having hit a steady 78 in the session. After his mishook early, he kept everything down with typically disciplined Bradmanesque method.

Woodfull was with him until the score was 195 after tea, when Vincent trapped the skipper LBW for 76. Kippax had recovered from a shattered nose on the country tour earlier, but he was now cautious about hooking, which had been a big asset for him. His confidence had gone and Vincent had him caught for 1.

Bradman then took charge and lifted his output a notch with late and square cuts and drives, scoring 92 in the final session to be 200 not out at stumps in 253 minutes.

He reverted to big hitting the next morning as if he were playing for St George and passed Victor Trumper's record in Australia–South

Africa Tests of 214 not out. At 226, Vincent trapped him LBW and only Oldfield (53 not out) held up the rest of the innings, which finally reached 450.

It was too much for South Africa and its bats collapsed twice for 170 (Ironmonger five for 42), and 117 (Wall five for 14, Ironmonger four for 44). The tourists were poorly served except by Mitchell, who was run out for 58 in the first innings, and H. W. Taylor, who scored a useful 41 and 47. Australia's victory by an innings and 163 runs was a surprising disparity, but with Bradman's score out of it the game would have been a closer affair. His batting and Ironmonger's consistent bowling were the difference.

THE PEAK

Bradman seemed to be at the peak of his powers. He was physically hardened and fit, and his mind was at ease outside cricket with his two-year work contract. He could concentrate on his cricket and extend himself, if that were possible. He also had the taste for big scores, having hit four double centuries at three levels of the game already with the season just into December.

A week into the month he was representing NSW in another chance to destroy South Africa, whose players now understood how he had gained his reputation. Its bowlers, Bell, Morkel, Quinn, Vincent, McMillan, Brown and Mitchell, were all capable, but there didn't seem to be a strong team plan to counter Bradman. Like all teams who had fielded to him so far, they had no answer to his relentless displays once he was set.

When he took block for NSW, it became a psychological block to the opposition. They were partly defeated before he played his first push to the on to get off the mark. He was in at one for 8, and both openers — Bill and Fingleton — were out at 14. In sixty-six minutes he had 50, and after 127 minutes he had reached a hundred. Despite his dominance, NSW was struggling at five for 159. However, Bradman was in full stride in a 99-run partnership with Oldfield (29), and another of 90 with Hird (45). He reached 200 in 214 minutes at a

245

pace reminiscent of his 334 at Leeds in 1930. But his mind was not in Test mode, for at 219 he hit wildly at McMillan and was caught in the deep. Bradman batted 234 minutes and hit fourteen fours in launching NSW to 500. The tourists were one for 185 when rain stopped play and the game, which it had reduced to two days.

This second first-class double century in succession brought him next to only Ponsford and Hammond for performances in Australia. Much interest in the Second Test in Sydney, commencing on 18 December, centred on whether Bradman could make it three in a row.

South Africa won the toss, batted and collapsed to be all out for 153, thanks mainly to Grimmett, who took four for 28. Australia lost Ponsford just before stumps on the first day. Victoria's Keith Rigg, who had replaced the injured Kippax, came in and joined Woodfull in a 137-run partnership which took them to just before lunch on the second day. The skipper was dismissed for 58 at 143, and the ground began to fill up as word spread that Bradman was 11 not out at lunch.

Every time he was at the wicket now, it was assumed he would perform some new feat. Today was no exception, as he glided to a half-century in eighty-five minutes. 'When Bradman batted,' a sports writer on the *Sydney Morning Herald* noted, 'he would be there seemingly no time at all, and he would be into his 30s. You would look up at the scoreboard to see why the crowd was cheering. He would be 50.'

By his usual combination of style, stealth and aggression, he went on to top 100 in 127 minutes, which was a quite common rate for him now. Throughout Test and first-class history, a century or near it in a two-hour session has been a sensational effort. Bradman had done it several times, but he was now often reaching the 90s in two-hour stretches, and it was natural that his batting was consistently attracting big crowds. Thousands would drift into a ground when he was first at the crease, and then thousands more would drift away when he was out.

Bradman, who was limping from a strained ankle, became bogged down after reaching his ton. On 112 he had a rare lapse in concentration and lofted the ball high into the deep for a simple catch to Viljoen off Morkel. He had batted 155 minutes, and his 1931–32 tendency to get up and under the ball and go six-hunting had claimed him again, for it was not the bowlers who were doing it.

Nevertheless, the statisticians reached for their *Wisdens* once more to search for new, obscure records broken or equalled. Four successive centuries? Bradman was the fourteenth player to do it but the first to do it in Australia. Four against a touring team's bowling? Bradman stood alone.

Meanwhile out on the ground, Rigg — eventually bowled by Bell for 127 in his first Test knock — stayed with him to net 111 in ninety-three minutes for the third wicket, while McCabe, later caught off Vincent for 79, had linked with him for 93 in an hour for the fourth wicket.

Bradman's scoring wagon-wheel was instructive, for the South Africans were playing to his strengths rather than avoiding them. Seventy per cent of his runs came from the on-side. He only scored six runs behind the wicket on the off-side, so while the bowlers kept their attack on leg-stump, he was still striding along at his usual hot rate.

Australia's tally of 469 was enough. Grimmett tied up South Africa again and took four for 44, backed up by Ironmonger who managed three for 22. The tourists were dismissed for 161, giving the home side their second successive runaway win by an innings and 155. All general interest in the series was waning, except for how much Bradman would score. Although the purists were happy to watch Test cricket no matter what the gulf between the sides, even they were yearning for the visit by England next year, for people such as its former Test captain Plum Warner were already predicting an England victory.

WISDEN WISDOM

Bradman commenced his fifth successive game against the tourists on New Year's Eve 1931 on the MCG in front of a packed house. Woodfull won the toss again, batted and soon found himself back in the pavilion, caught off Bell for 7. Bradman was in, and the Melbourne crowd gave him a booming reception as he walked out to bat. However, they sensed something was amiss as he took ten minutes to open his account. Four minutes later, he was caught at the wicket for 2. The crowd was stunned for several moments before they clapped him off the ground. His amazing sequence against the tourists — 30, 135, 226, 219, and 112 — had been broken.

Australia floundered without its power hitter at the wicket, but Kippax (52) and Rigg (68) helped the score up to 198. Bell with five for 69 and Quinn (four for 42) were the destroyers. South Africa replied with their best effort yet — 358 — and were making a contest of the series at last. In a steady effort, only Viljoen (111) managed a half-century against honest bowling from Wall (three for 98), Ironmonger (three for 72), McCabe (two for 21), and Grimmett, who sent down sixty-two overs and took two for 100.

Australia batted again midway through the post-lunch session on the third day, and Ponsford (34) made way for Bradman with the score on 54, shortly after tea. He seemed to have a different attitude this time and put the pull shot and several drives on display from the first over he faced. He slammed 50 in just over an hour and reached 97 not out at stumps. Thanks to him and Woodfull, Australia ended the day ahead on the run ledger, and after starting its innings 160 behind.

Bradman had the strike first-up next morning. Cameron placed his field meticulously in the hope of bottling the batsman in the nervous 90s. The crowd fell silent as Bell ran in. The ball was on a good length on middle stump and Bradman drove it straight down the ground. He and Woodfull charged and ran three to thunderous applause. Bradman had his fourth century of the series and his fifth against the tourists. Scribes in the press-box reached for their *Wisdens* again. It was his fastest Test 100 ever — in ninety-eight minutes, just a minute quicker than his morning effort in the Third Test at Leeds in 1930.

Bradman then settled down for a relatively sedate morning with Woodfull. Then at 328, just before lunch, Vincent trapped him LBW for 167. The 274 partnership was the highest for the second wicket in all Tests, beating another partnership by Woodfull with Macartney of 235 against England in 1926.

Woodfull went on to 161 when McMillan had him caught. Kippax (67) completed a useful double, while McCabe (71) added good support, so that Australia lifted its second innings to 554. This left South Africa a tough challenge and it wasn't up to it, especially facing Grimmett (six for 92) on a turning last-day wicket. Ironmonger, too, was dangerous and took four for 54. South Africa's 225 left it 169 short and meant Australia had won the series, leading three-nil with two Tests to go.

After an unprecedented run of scoring for nearly four months, even Bradman's most demanding critics could have forgiven him a slackening off by late January. But he was still keen to go on and murder every attack on offer. Challenges too were still coming, and the rivalry between Victoria and NSW was high when the two teams met each other for the return State game in Sydney beginning January 22.

The Victorians had a powerful bowling line-up of Ironmonger, Lisle Nagel, Ted McCormick, Len Darling and a'Beckett. They all strained to remove Bradman, particularly a'Beckett, who had toured England with him in 1930 and knew most about his strengths and possible foibles. Ironmonger claimed his scalp in the first innings for 23, which was a notable feat considering he had failed only once during the season to hit a century in a game. McCabe made up for it by scoring 106 out of NSW's 348, which eclipsed Victoria's moderate 204.

In the second innings, Bradman came in at one for 28, two minutes into the third morning, and was unusually subdued. Such a start meant either one of two outcomes. Either he would fiddle on and be out going for a big hit through frustration, a trait common to most batsmen, or he would lift his tempo and take control, often after a 'life'.

Bradman took thirty-seven minutes reaching double figures, his slowest beginning since 1928, due to Ironmonger's skill and a'Beckett's pinpoint accuracy on his off-stump. At 44, he lunged at Ironmonger and was dropped at slip. Victorian heads went down.

'It was so frustrating,' Ironmonger told a Melbourne *Sun* journalist. 'You had to get him early or face a massacre that would make Custer's last stand look like a tea party.'

His fifty took ninety minutes, which demonstrated his respect for the bowling. Then after lunch he got on top. He cut a four to reach 86 and 1,000 runs for the season in just ten innings, which was one fewer than his previous record set up in 1928–29. Bradman went to 100 in 166 minutes, which was about forty minutes slower than his norm. He was 140 at the beginning of the last over before lunch to be bowled by Darling. With NSW on top and nothing to lose, Bradman smashed 20 off six balls to go to the break on 160. He was bowled going for another big hit at 167 after batting 224 minutes. McCabe, completing a fine double with 103 not out, went with him in a 110-run partnership and NSW carried on to win easily by 239 runs.

Bradman had scored his sixth century in successive first-class matches. The public now expected a big innings from him in the Fourth Test, beginning on 29 January at Adelaide, where he had yet to score a century in a Test. South Africa won the toss, batted and collected 308, with Taylor (78), Mitchell (75), Cameron (52) and Vincent (48) all playing strongly. Grimmett ran through the visitors taking seven for 116 off forty-seven overs, and was well-supported by Bill O'Reilly with two for 74 off 39.4 overs in his first appearance for his country.

Australia started its response twenty minutes before lunch and Ponsford was soon out, bowled by Quinn for 5. Bradman went in for an awkward ten minutes, but seemed untroubled on 2 not out at the break. He stepped straight into the bowling after lunch and reached 50 in little over an hour. Good defensive bowling by Quinn particularly held back his rate marginally and Bradman went to tea on 84 not out. He slipped into the 90s without any sign of nerves. Woodfull was caught off Bell for 82 in a second-wicket stand of 176 in 126 minutes. Kippax came in to join Bradman on 99. Mindful that he was creating history if he scored another century, Bradman called the nervous Kippax through for a tight run and the new man was run out without facing a ball.

It was a piece of careless, unnecessary cricket. Yet the offender took it out on the tourists, as if it had been their fault and not his. His fourth century of the series, and seventh in seven first-class matches, came in 133 minutes. He had completed Test hundreds in Adelaide, Sydney, Melbourne and Brisbane. Twenty minutes later he was 109, which gave him 1,000 runs, including six centuries, against the South African bowling alone. Bradman hooked, cut and drove his way to 170 not out at stumps.

On Monday morning, following the Sunday break, 15,000 spectators turned up to see Bradman go for the double hundred. But they were disappointed not to get fireworks as he showed the South African bowlers as much respect as he had Ironmonger at Sydney and cautiously played himself in. He wanted that 200 milestone again and more. At 185 he gave a tough chance in the slips off Bell and looked indecisive for the next half-hour as he crawled into the 190s. After eighty minutes of play, some of the crowd grew restless, but most were content to let The Don do it his way, no matter if it took a week.

He reached the double with a late cut for four all run. He had been at the wicket for 284 minutes, and went to lunch on 219 not out, having scored just 49 in the morning session. Australia was five for 389 and consolidating its lead.

Keith Rigg (35) was painstaking but had a useful 114-run partnership with Bradman, who took over the strike when linked with Oldfield (23) and Grimmett (21). Bill O'Reilly came to the wicket at the fall of the eighth wicket. The spinner had a long memory of Bradman's relentless batting going back five years to 1925–26 when he was hit all over the park at Bowral by the unknown prodigy. O'Reilly was pleased to be on Bradman's side now as he tore into the bowling, knowing that he was running out of partners. The spinner managed to stay with him in a 78-run stand until the score was 493, making 23 himself.

Bradman was on 280, and anxious now to top Foster's record Test score in Australia of 287 and then the 300. Thurlow, a definite rabbit, strode in. A tactical battle developed with the tourists, who were

251

determined to stop Bradman getting his triple hundred. The batsmen were running for dangerous singles. Spectators were on their feet with every stroke as Bradman fought to farm the strike.

At 286, he cut a ball for two to break Foster's record. Now he moved rapidly towards the 300. On 298, he placed the ball to mid-wicket and tore down the pitch. He reached the bowler's end, turned, called for the second and then saw the ball in a fieldsman's hand. Bradman stopped and sent the faithful H. M. Thurlow back. But it was too late and he was run out, leaving Bradman on 299 not out and Australia on 513.

The tourists batted again and at three for 224 looked like crawling out of their invidious position, but then O'Reilly struck twice with vicious, fast leg-breaks and bowled Taylor for 84 and Cameron for 4. Once through the top order, Australia then had Grimmett to bamboozle the tail. Only Mitchell (95) and Christy faced him with any confidence, but he trapped them both on his way to another great haul of seven for 83.

As in England, Grimmett with the ball and Bradman with the bat were the chief difference between the two sides, with Ironmonger serving to accentuate the gap. Australia had a lead of four-nil and were looking to the Fifth Test at Melbourne on 12 February for a clean sweep.

Australia dumped W. Hunt and H. M. Thurlow, who between them did not take a wicket or make a run in the Fourth Test, and replaced them with Ironmonger, who had been injured, and Laurie Nash, a burly, aggressive speedster from Victoria. All interest now centred on whether Bradman would overtake Hammond's 905 in 1928–29 — the best aggregate in Australia — and become the first player ever to reach 1,000 in a series. His 226, 112, 2, 167, and 299 gave him 806 at an average of 201.50. He would have a possible two visits to the crease to score a century to beat Hammond, and 194 to reach four figures. The press focused almost exclusively on the Bradman assault and fans around the country waited in anticipation.

Cameron won the toss and decided to bat, despite a wet wicket. As Woodfull called his team out of the dressing-room, Bradman jumped down from a form, caught his boot sprigs in coir matting and twisted his weak ankle. The resultant sprain meant he was unable to field or bat at any stage in the game, leaving his Test figures as they had been.

By the time word reached the big MCG crowd that he was unlikely to bat in the game, its disappointment was tempered by the joy of watching two Victorians, Nash and Ironmonger. Nash, a local Australian Rules football star, brought his fire into the summer game in a dangerous opening spell on a wet wicket in which he captured three of the first four wickets. Then Ironmonger proceeded to wrap up the South African innings for just 36 runs. Only Cameron (11) reached double figures. Nash took four for 18 in twelve overs. Ironmonger bowled 7.2 overs, including five maidens, for an amazing five for 6. Grimmett did not get to roll his arm over.

By the afternoon when Australia replied, the wicket had become a gluepot. Fingleton (40), Rigg (23) and Kippax (42) batted commendably under the conditions as Australia was dismissed for 153. Bell, Quinn and McMillan each took three wickets.

South Africa batted again on the second day, with the wicket ruined by more rain. Nash caught and bowled Christy in his first over for a duck and started the rot once more. Woodfull put Ironmonger on to open the bowling at the other end and he bowled right through the innings, taking six for 18 off 15.3 overs. O'Reilly, who had not been used in the first innings, took three for 19. South Africa were shattered for 45, giving Australia a win by an innings and 72 runs in just two days. The series went to the home team, five-nil.

The game ended without Grimmett, arguably the best bowler in the world, bowling a ball, and without Bradman, the world's premier batsman, batting. Ironmonger had the figures for the series with thirty-one wickets at the outstanding average of just 9.67 runs per wicket. Grimmett took thirty-three wickets at 16.87. After Bradman's freak average of 201.50, Woodfull averaged 70.16 from an aggregate of 421. Rigg was third with 50.60 from 253. McCabe, Kippax and Ponsford had poor series, which was a worry for the Australians with England due in 1932–33. For South Africa only Bell turned in a decent performance for the series with twenty-three wickets at 27.26.

Meanwhile in England, the press were carrying daily reports of Bradman's performances, just as the MCC was beginning to prepare for the 1932 home season. The leaders and bowlers for the tour of Australia to follow would be chosen with a sole aim in mind: to contain and defeat Don Bradman.

London's *News Chronicle* amusingly reflected this obsession in an editorial on how to restrict him:

> *As long as Australia has him she is apparently invincible, for he always seems able to score the number of runs required at any given time. In order to keep alive the competitive spirit of the game the cricket authorities might take a hint from billiards. As soon as a player invents a shot that can produce an unlimited number of points they put a legal limitation on its use.* [This was done with Walter Lindrum.] *It is almost time to request a legal limitation on the number of runs Bradman should be permitted to make.*

START OF THE BIG PARTNERSHIP

Bradman ended the season the way he began it: with a duck. In the final Shield game, against South Australia at Sydney, he made 23 in the first innings and was bowled by Tim Wall in the second after five balls without scoring. His limited Shield opportunities had seen him score 0, 23, 167, 23 and 0. It wasn't the kind of return he would prefer, but in the context of his formidable run of performances against the South Africans, Bradman was satisfied with his most consistently brilliant run of big scores yet.

Two weeks later, on 6 April, he was the country's only popular living legend, when his rival for top status departed for greener pastures.

In his *History of Australia*, Australian historian Manning Clark noted:

> *The [politically] divided nation was united by the death of a horse. The mighty Phar Lap, winner of the Melbourne Cup, the performer*

*of miracles on the race track comparable with Don Bradman's per-
formances with the cricket bat and Nellie Melba's with the human
voice, died in a stable in California.*

With his triumphant season behind him, Bradman now prepared for
his long-awaited marriage to Jessie on 30 April. They were joined
together in holy matrimony at St Paul's in Burwood, Sydney, by
Canon E. S. Hughes of St Paul's Cathedral, Melbourne. A cartoon
depicting the event in a Sydney paper had a gentleman representing
the sporting public handing the couple a bouquet and saying, 'Just
hoping this is a record partnership, Don.' The public got its wish. At
the time of writing in 1995, the marriage had lasted sixty-three years.
They had known each other for seventy-six years.

They drove on a short honeymoon to Melbourne and then on an
extended vacation of Canada and the USA during the winter
months, thanks to the organising ability of former Test player and
friend Arthur Mailey. With the backing of Canadian Pacific Railway,
he arranged for a team to play a series of exhibition cricket matches
across baseball-loving North America.

The trip was dependent on Bradman going and he would not tour
without Jessie. They saw it as a once-in-a-lifetime opportunity to see
the United States. One of the many highlights of the trip was a
meeting with the American baseball star Babe Ruth, who had been
compared with Bradman by the *New York Times* for his 'ball hitting
and scoring skills'. Their rendezvous was a baseball game at Yankee
Stadium in New York between the Yankees and the White Sox. A
photograph of the meeting shows a lean, fit Bradman in a smart,
three-piece suit shaking hands with a chubby-faced, unathletic-
looking Ruth.

'Ruth was injured that day and that's how I got to meet him,'
Bradman recalled. 'I tried to explain cricket to him as we watched the
game, but it wasn't easy, never is. Ruth couldn't believe we didn't have
to run when we hit the ball.'

Ruth didn't have to explain baseball to Bradman. He took a 'keen
interest' in it in Australia. The American asked him what impressed

255

the Australian about the game. Was it the catching of the outfielders? No, Bradman replied, he expected good catching, especially from professionals who wore gloves and 'did nothing else'. It was the 'quick decisions', the 'businesslike' way in which the game was conducted that impressed him.

'In two hours or so the match is finished,' Bradman said. 'Each batter comes up four or five times. Each afternoon's play stands on its own.' With his incomparable appreciation of cricket and his long view of the game, Bradman appreciated even then that there was merit in an alternative to the slower, drawn-out competition of first-class cricket.

The *New York Telegram* noted that 'the Babe sat resplendent in brown sports coat, white-striped trousers, buckskin shoes and a white cap — the true nabob. [He] was surprised by Bradman's lack of size and weight. The greatest batsman cricket yet has boasted is not bigger than Joey Sewell. Don weighs 145 pounds, is 24 years of age, and according to the cricket experts . . . is a scientist rather than a powerhouse.'

In an attempt to portray them as clean-cut, equivalent 'national symbols', the journalist failed to report that Ruth lived in a whorehouse and was a chain-smoking alcoholic, rather than the All-American hero. Nor did he remind readers that Ruth loved the sleazy nightlife, or that during one game he punched one umpire, threw dirt on another and came to blows with several hecklers in the stands. The reality of this spicy contrast, of course, would have spoiled a great photo opportunity that was flashed across the Atlantic to the London press. It reminded the MCC of Bradman's status as it was selecting a team to tour Australia with a mission to win back the Ashes, at any cost, within the laws of the game.

PART THREE

BODYLINE AND BEYOND
1932–33 — 1934

23

LEG, CHEST AND HEAD THEORY

Mr Jardine asked me if I thought I could bowl on the leg stump making the ball come up into the body all the time so that Bradman had to play his shots to leg.
— HAROLD LARWOOD ON HIS MEETING WITH JARDINE AT THE PICCADILLY HOTEL, LONDON IN AUGUST 1932

A LITTLE PRACTICE MAKES PERFECT

The ball crashed into Victor Rothschild's ribcage as he tried to take evasive action against Larwood. The lean, handsome, eighteen-year-old scion of the banking dynasty walked a few paces away from the wicket and took some deep breaths in order to regain his composure. He was on 30 in less than an hour's batting in the county game of 28–30 August 1929 for Northamptonshire against Nottinghamshire. Rothschild, still a schoolboy at exclusive Harrow, had come in on a 'fiery pitch' for Northampton with the score at five for 39. He had attacked the bowling of Larwood and Bill Voce, collecting seven fours mainly by positioning himself to leg and angling square-cuts past cover-point's left hand. There was a price for this dashing display. The future third Lord Rothschild and later espionage agent had been hit 'at least a dozen times' according to his sister (the Honourable) Miriam, who was present at the game. At the end of his innings he had had enough of the terror bowling, euphemistically known as 'leg theory'. He was a victim of something that Larwood and Voce had toyed with in the late 1920s under the direction of Notts skipper, Arthur Carr, but which they perfected during the summers of 1931 and 1932 in occasional bursts against several county sides.

'Victor was a batsman of graceful aggression,' Miriam Rothschild recalled, 'and he had not avoided blows this day [in 1929], but after so many I think he decided enough was enough.'

After Larwood (match figures eight for 84) and Voce (match figures seven for 44) had softened him up, Rothschild was out caught Staples bowled Barratt for 36 after an hour at the wicket. In the second innings he was again attacked, then bowled by Voce for 5.

Rothschild later showed his sister a 'mass of bruises'. A fellow player asked him what he thought of Larwood's so-called 'leg theory' tactics.

'You mean, leg, chest and head theory,' Rothschild replied. He later became the first voice of protest against this aggressive, dangerous but then still legitimate form of bowling. Rothschild retired from first-class cricket to make his point. But Larwood and Voce did not attempt this style of bowling consistently enough for the MCC then to consider action to ban it.

Larwood in particular worked on his accuracy after the debacle of the 1930 Ashes series. Coupled with his pinpointing of length, he had the great ability to make a ball rear off a good length, which went some way towards explaining his claim that he had the capacity to 'hit any batsman at will'.

Larwood had the most flowing and rhythmic of actions in a smooth, unfolding run of fourteen paces, which allowed him to propel a ball at more than 90 mph (144 kph). Accuracy, pace and lift made him the best and most lethal fast man in the world in 1932 and possibly of all time. He had been arguably the best in 1930, but now he had picked up a 'yard' and calibrated his line and length far better.

While practitioners such as Larwood and Voce, who also started his working life as a miner, were perfecting 'leg theory', England's newly anointed captain in 1932, Douglas Jardine, was having second thoughts about touring and tackling Bradman. He told the team manager, Plum Warner, he would be turning down the appointment. Warner saw his father, M. R. Jardine, the former Advocate-General of Bombay, and told him it was 'important for England's chances' if Douglas led the side.

'I'll have a word with the boy,' Jardine senior said. At the subsequent father-and-son chat Douglas complained about the Australian crowds, the heat and the flies, but this was brushed aside by the former subcontinent administrator, who knew much about crowds, heat and flies. He told his son it was a great honour to lead his country. It was his duty to tour and win back the Ashes for England.

Jardine's deeper fear and loathing centred on Bradman. It was obvious from almost every word he wrote about him in several books and nearly every comment ever attributed to him about the Australian. He despised Bradman for humiliating the home side in 1930 and the way even English supporters applauded him. Most of all he hated the man because he was a colonial who was just too good. From the moment he decided to take on the job of touring skipper, he became obsessed with stopping Bradman, which would mean winning the Ashes. Hate, like love, is a great motivator, and Jardine was a driven man with a challenging mission by August 1932.

'That little bugger', as Jardine referred to him, had to be stopped any way within the law. It would have been impossible for a legally-trained mind like Jardine's to think otherwise. But the quaint thing about cricket was that its rules were flexible. No law in 1932 said you could not pack the leg-side close to the wicket. Nor was there a clause that said that you could not hit the batsman with the ball as many times as you wished. Umpires could only adjudicate under the laws of 'fair and unfair play' of which the umpires were 'the sole judges'.

Once committed to the 1932–33 tour down-under, Jardine got busy meeting practitioners of leg theory, such as Frank Foster of Warwickshire, the fine pre-World War left-hand 'quick', and theorists such as Percy Fender, who was a great advocate of it. Fender, Jardine's friend and mentor at Surrey, had encouraged him to go to Australia if invited, and to have a committed plan to use leg theory. Jardine sought details on field-placings from exponents and experts in order to know how to restrict scoring. For instance, he dined with Foster, the left-arm pace man who bowled 'normal' leg theory — that is, deliveries on a good length on the leg-side — during the 1911–12 tour of Australia, when he headed the Test averages with thirty-two wickets at 21.6 runs apiece.

Foster did not know what was on Jardine's mind. The new England captain was secretly concentrating on how to remove Bradman. The fieldsmen had to be in a close ring of five on-side catchers waiting for the ball, which would be popped up by a batsman fending off a delivery directed at hip, midriff, chest, arms or head. There would be two back on the leg-fence fine and square ready for a catch from a desperate hook.

But there was one vital proviso. This 'fast leg theory', as Jardine preferred to call it, was futile against great bats if not delivered by super-fast and accurate bowlers. The catch was that there were only two or three bowlers in the country who could deliver it effectively. Two of them were Larwood and Voce. The latter, a left-armer, was not express like Larwood, but he was fast with a good in-swinger. He bowled a good bouncer and didn't use it sparingly. Larwood was right-arm with an out-swinger, and this made them an effective, at times brilliant and brutal, combination with the new ball. Jardine's main concern was not swing, or getting an edge. He was more interested in what his charges could do with a slightly worn ball, bowled short. Could they effectively threaten and if necessary make direct hits on the batsman himself? They had to be sure of themselves, otherwise players such as McCabe, Ponsford, Richardson and Kippax would pick them off. As for Bradman, he would just grin what Jardine saw as that smug little grin and slaughter them.

Jardine had a chance to talk with Larwood and Voce at the end of the traditional Surrey versus Notts Bank Holiday fixture at The Oval early in August 1932. He arranged a meeting at the grill room of the Piccadilly Hotel with them and their captain, Arthur Carr, by now a strong advocate of using leg theory to intimidate and restrict batsmen. He had captained England once in 1926, and was remembered for having erred by sending Australia in first and losing. Carr had a similar outlook to Jardine. They were both amateurs who played the game as vigorously as professionals, and they shared a distinct distaste for Australians.

The dinner discussion was dominated by comment about Bradman and how to combat him.

'Jardine asked me,' Larwood recalled in *The Larwood Story*, written in collaboration with Australian journalist Kevin Perkins thirty-three years after the event, 'if I thought I could bowl on the leg-stump making the ball come up into the body all the time so that Bradman had to play his shots to leg.'

Larwood also created the myth that Bradman had been frightened at The Oval in 1930, and that is why he and Jardine had decided to use intimidatory tactics. In that Oval innings, as described earlier, Bradman made 232 in a courageous stay at the wicket of more than seven hours, which won the game, the series and the Ashes. Larwood tried bumping him out and did hit Bradman and Jackson on several occasions. But it made no difference to Bradman's batting in that innings. He dominated Larwood more than any other bowler, especially in the pre-lunch session on the second-last day when he made 98 on a rain-affected wicket, which gave the bowlers great assistance. Every observer at the game and the statistical analysis of their one-on-one Larwood-Bradman battle verifies the batsman's superiority in that whole innings.

It was, of course, misleading for the Notts speedster to suggest his decision to use intimidatory fast leg theory was based on that performance. Jardine had not made his judgements on that game either and he contradicted Larwood later in his own book when he pointed to a match in Australia in 1932, in which he claimed to have discovered a weakness in Bradman and other Australian bats on the leg stump. It was a clumsy and transparent attempt to counter allegations that their subsequent actions were the result of a conspiracy with the connivance of the MCC Committee in mid-1932 — before the tour down-under.

The important point about the Piccadilly meeting was not the myths about it or anything alleged to have been said. The vital factor was that Jardine, who did most of the talking, walked away from it knowing that the two exceptionally able prospective accomplices in the plan to defeat Bradman were willing and eager to carry it through. Dissent or reservations would have seen the plan abandoned. But neither bowler hesitated in his support. They were buoyed by the knowledge that their tough new national team skipper would allow them to use the bruising methods uncompromisingly. The three of them understood that there would be objections to the way it was used, even within the touring team itself. Jardine told them he wanted all discussions on the matter kept secret, and left them pleased that he would have something effective to work with in Australia.

In conjunction with the MCC he selected his touring squad: himself, Bob Wyatt (vice-captain), Hammond, Sutcliffe, Larwood, H. Verity, Voce, Bill Bowes, Eddie Paynter, Les Ames (keeper), F. R. Brown, T. B. Mitchell, the Nawab of Pataudi, Leyland, Tate, Duckworth (keeper) and Gubby Allen. It was a strong side with the three top bowlers, Larwood, Voce and Bowes, a 6 ft 4 in (193 cm) rangy Yorkshireman, all primed for fast leg theory. Only the fourth quick, Allen, was not consulted about it, for Jardine knew that he would be against the tactic. He would consider it unfair, unsportsmanlike and unBritish. But then, Allen was Australian by birth and rather fond of the place. He might not understand fully what was at stake. Yet it mattered little to Jardine what Allen thought, for he was the skipper and there would be no overt dissent concerning his methods.

MORE BOARD SQUABBLES

While Jardine was plotting Bradman's downfall, the Australian Board of Control was unwittingly helping England's cause by reaffirming its ban on player-writers. It made this plain as Bradman sailed into Sydney on the steamer *Monowai* at the completion of his grand three-month tour of North America.

He came back fatigued after bowling a lot and batting in fifty-one innings for 3,792 runs at an average of 102.1, which was the equivalent to about four Shield seasons. As the star attraction he had to play every game, which on top of the socialising and sightseeing took its toll. Consequently, a tired Bradman was not in a combative mood when he arrived home. He wasn't prepared for controversy and the constant pestering by the press and public, which he had blissfully done without across Canada and the USA, where he was a minor media novelty, someone viewed as quaint and 'British'. The return to Australia and the prospect of clashes with the Board changed all that. He was forced to obtain a silent telephone number, and occasionally disappear from his house.

Bradman's response to the Board's ultimatum was to deliver one of his own. He would honour his job contract, even if this meant not playing in the Ashes series. The pressure of the confrontation affected his health, which began to deteriorate. Nevertheless, he started his sixth successive pre-season with 108 not out for St George against Gordon in less than seventy minutes, 105 not out in 120 minutes against Mosman, and 145 in a State trial game.

Bradman came to a temporary agreement with the Board that he 'would not write anything' during the First Test and would not do so until a Board meeting just before the Second Test. If agreement could be reached then, he would be available the rest of the Ashes series. If some accord was not made, then he would not play.

He was selected in a 'Combined Australian XI' to play the MCC in Perth and he made the long trip by train across the continent for the match. The first day attracted 20,000 people, which was a huge turn-out considering the population of the city, but the spectators were disappointed when Jardine won the toss and batted. The England skipper had deliberately left his front-line bowlers — Larwood, Voce and Bowes — out of the side.

England went on for two days and compiled seven for 583 declared. Sutcliffe (169), Pataudi (129) and Hammond (77) got some early form against the weak Combined XI attack. Even Bradman was thrown the ball for the longest spell of his career — nineteen eight-ball overs — in which he took two for 106. Much to Jardine's chagrin, Bradman got him out caught on 98. Gubby Allen was his other victim.

It rained overnight and developed a useful sticky for Verity on the third day. The Combined side lost their first wicket at 61. Bradman scored 3 in seven minutes. Verity bowled him a good-length ball, which lifted sharply and got an edge. Hammond, at second slip, threw out his right hand and took a superb catch. Thereafter, Verity ran through the Australians, taking seven for 37, and they were dismissed for 159.

Jardine enforced the follow-on that afternoon and Bradman found himself at the crease with the fall of the first wicket at 0. He struggled for twenty-two minutes. On 10, Allen had him caught at short leg, and Bradman for the first time felt the ignominy of being rolled twice in the one day. The Combined XI hung on to be four for 139 at the end of the match, with Fingleton a solid 53 not out.

Bradman had only a few days' break before he faced another challenge in the NSW-Victoria game in Sydney, and there was no time to dwell on the double failure in Perth. Victoria batted first and extremely well with Woodfull (74) and Ponsford opening with a 138-run partnership. From then on, Ponsford took control and in a fine innings reached 200, his ninth double century, which drew him level with Bradman. Victoria were all out after lunch on day two, Saturday, for 404.

A big crowd of nearly 27,000 were at the SCG to see Bradman come to the wicket with one down for 16. He soon engaged with the left-arm googly bowler 'Chuck' Fleetwood-Smith, playing his first game for his State, and others he had faced before — Darling, Alexander, Ironmonger and Blackie. But he was in murderous mood against the spin, as he took just thirty minutes to reach 50, and only 73 to reach his century. He kept up the rate all afternoon to reach 200 and go ahead of Ponsford once more, and finally threw his wicket away to Fleetwood-Smith, deliberately lofting catches into the outfield until one was taken. He had scored 238 in just 210 minutes, which was his (and the) fastest double hundred to that point.

According to all accounts of the performance, his footwork, timing and stroke play were unsurpassed. It was better than Trumper at his best according to observers who had seen them both. In the second innings, he scored 52 not out in bringing NSW a nine-wicket victory.

TACTIC EXPOSED

Two good, cathartic innings and a heavy win cleared his head for the next encounter with the tourists in Melbourne on 18 November, once again playing for 'An Australian XI'. Jardine selected Larwood, Voce, Bowes and Allen in an all-pace attack, but did not play himself. Instead, he went trout fishing on the Kiewa river in country Victoria and let Bob Wyatt lead the side. He won the toss and batted and the MCC made 282, with Sutcliffe keeping up his form hitting 87. Oxenham took five for 53.

Bradman came in on the second afternoon with the score of one for 51. For the first time on tour, Larwood had his leg-trap of five in place close on the leg, and another two on the fence square and fine. Leo O'Brien, a solid Victorian batsman who batted with Bradman that day, remembers the occasion vividly:

> *The atmosphere was electric as Bradman strode in. Here was the man the England players most feared. They were prepared to get stuck into him. There was a lot of action. They all seemed to be up on their toes, and getting ready. They attacked him remorselessly. The wicket was a little on the green side and Larwood and Allen had him in a bit of trouble.*

Bradman ducked and weaved, determined not to get hit as Larwood charged in bumping balls at him. Yet he was still playing his strokes in between the head-hunting, mainly against Larwood and Allen, who refused to set leg theory fields. After forty-five minutes Bradman had collected 36. He seemed to observers to be getting on top, but then he received a bad LBW verdict with Larwood bowling.

'It was a rough decision,' O'Brien recalled. 'It didn't look out from where I was [at the bowler's end].'

Yet it wasn't so much that the decision was poor — that happens for and against any batsman in every season. It was just the timing of the umpire's judgement. If Bradman had been able to bat on and combat the leg theory first-up, it may have put the season in a different perspective. As it was, his 36 was second top score to O'Brien, who made 46 of the Australian XI's 218.

This important encounter brought various reactions. Larwood was delighted that he had Bradman 'jumping out of the way' and 'clumsily waving his bat in the air like a wood-chopper'. After his humiliating belting in 1930, it was highly gratifying to the Notts miner's son to gain some revenge. His hard work in sharpening his bowling and employing the leg theory, or 'bodyline' as it was now being called, seemed to have paid off.

Retired Australian Test player Hunter Hendry noted the now obvious. The 'shock tactics' were put on for Bradman:

> It was the Englishman's policy to break Don's morale at any price
> . . . they adopted the tactics of 'if you can't bowl 'em out, well,
> knock 'em out'. Larwood placed his field in a manner that left no
> doubts about his intention to 'bowl at the man'.

Jack Hobbs, who was covering the tour as a writer for the London *Star*, saw more personal light and shade in the dramatic events:

> It gives a certain satisfaction to know that Don is human after all,
> having the same dislike for lightning bumpers as all other batsmen
> . . . I felt a lot safer in the press box, for the bowling looked very
> dangerous stuff. I found it amusing, your feelings are different
> when just watching. The newspapers will have very unpleasant
> things to say about these undoubted shock tactics and attacking
> methods England evidently intends to adopt.

When England batted a second time it managed only 60 on a rain-affected wicket, with the 6 ft 6 in (198 cm) medium-pacer Lisle Nagel taking eight for 32.

Bradman was concerned with how to counteract the bowling:

They had seven men on the leg-side and with the bowler and keeper it made nine, leaving just two on the off. The only place you could score any runs with any certainty at all was on the off. This was very, very difficult to do when the ball was coming straight at your body and around about chest high. I tried to combat it that day, by sometimes pulling away to the leg to play strokes on the off.

At the start of the last day, the Australian XI had only 125 to make, but rain again intervened, and the wicket was 'vicious' according to commentators. Larwood and Allen found an extra notch in pace and worked up to extra-fast spells. Both got the ball to fly dangerously from a length. Woodfull was removed for a duck, bringing Bradman to the wicket for a nasty period of seventeen minutes. He began playing streaky shots at Larwood's deliveries, trying again to score by pulling away to leg and driving into the off in a manner now common in one-day cricket, when players become unorthodox in order to score quickly.

On 13, he tried to cut with the same tactic and was bowled by Larwood. This wicket gave the paceman more excitement than anything he had ever achieved in cricket. At The Oval in 1930, he knew he had not got Bradman caught behind for 232. In the first innings in this game, he had read the newspaper comments, which confirmed everyone else's opinion that he had been lucky with the LBW decision. But there could be no doubt that this time he had snared him legitimately, clean bowled. Wait until Mr Jardine hears about this!

Australia were two for 19 when the weather intervened, and Jardine was indeed pleased about the morale victory scored against the main enemy. It was a psychological blow, but only one in the war.

Bradman thought the bodyline strategy was dangerous. 'It turned a game into a battle,' he said.

This was exactly how Jardine viewed the Ashes. Regaining them in front of hostile Australian crowds would be the nearest thing to a battle that one could reach in sport. Bradman, as ever, viewed events in context. He foresaw 'serious trouble unless the matter was dealt with'. At the risk of being seen as a 'squealer', he 'privately reported' this to 'certain' cricket administrators. His advice fell on deaf ears. At that moment, the only people concerned were the Australian bats, who would have to face the rough stuff out in the middle.

Bradman had no time to assess his position, for three days later in Sydney, he was playing for NSW against the tourists and batting on the first morning, 25 November. He was in with the score at 43, and batted defensively, trying to find a way of dealing with Voce, who was sending down an abnormal number of short, rearing balls. Larwood had been rested, and it was Bradman's friendly old rival, Maurice Tate, who benefited from the batsman's discomfiture. He was on 18, and looking unusually negative after forty-one minutes, when Tate trapped him LBW. Fingleton did his Test chances some good with a fighting 119 not out, and McCabe, hooking gamely if not wantonly, notched a carefree 67 as NSW compiled 273. Allen, in form with the ball, took five for 69.

England then batted for two days in amassing 530, with Sutcliffe sending out more warnings about his capacity to sit long and score big. His 182 was the highest MCC score so far. Duckworth's ostensible understudy as keeper, Les Ames, improved his Test chances with a chanceless 90, and Wyatt found some form with 72. Hird took six for 135 for NSW.

Bradman contracted flu on the second day and was confined to bed. Nevertheless, he got up to bat on the last day. He was soon in and appeared his most at ease in six innings against the visitors, until Voce's overuse of the short ball caused him to make an error. Bradman saw one pitched short, and eased his body to the off to let it fly past. Instead, the ball hit the stumps. Bradman, arms shouldered, was on his way back to bed after making 23 in fifty-one minutes.

There was rejoicing in the England camp. Verity, Allen, Larwood, Tate and Voce had all dismissed him in six innings in which he had compiled 103 runs. With the First Test just three days away, the momentum was with the tourists. Then the ACB doctor examined Bradman and ruled him unfit to play, which made England super-confident about victory. His flu and a throat infection had compounded his generally run-down condition, and he had to sit out the match. Rumours abounded about his condition, but a gaunt-looking Don was at the game some days fulfilling his obligations to radio station 2UE.

LARWOOD, FIRST BLOOD

Bradman left a massive hole in the Australian Test line-up of Woodfull, Ponsford, Fingleton, Kippax, McCabe, Richardson, Oldfield, Grimmett, Nagel, O'Reilly and Wall. England selected a strong, form team without any surprises: Sutcliffe, Wyatt, Hammond, Pataudi, Leyland, Jardine, Verity, Allen, Ames, Larwood and Voce. On paper, England looked stronger in both batting, with depth to number nine, and bowling.

Woodfull won the toss at Sydney on 2 December and went in with Ponsford to face Larwood and Voce on a fast track. The tactics were now clear. The two started with a red cherry bowling their high-quality swingers. When the ball had lost its shine and swing after three overs, they switched to bodyline. Larwood clapped his hands and with military precision the field would set itself. Three to five men in short-leg positions and two, sometimes three in the deep fine and square.

The new style of attack was not used all the time, but in bursts, and for full psychological shock against the batsmen. First Woodfull fell caught by Ames at the wicket off Voce for 7 when the score was 22. Then Larwood collected Ponsford on the arm. An over later it was the shoulder as the great opener did his best to avoid contact with the ball. It was unsettling and wearing. At 65, a softened-up Ponsford was hit in the arm and shoulder. The batsman had over-come his *bête noire* at The Oval in 1930 with that dashing 110, but now the beast was back, more fierce than ever. Ponsford played all over one from Larwood and was bowled.

Fingleton looked lead-footed and was hit twice before Larwood had him caught in the leg-trap for 26. Australia was three for 82. Kippax ducked, weaved and sparred, but was soon trapped for 8 and Australia was tottering on four for 87. McCabe stood his ground and started hooking and pulling. He was hit, but managed to cause some consternation in the leg-trap. Richardson stayed with him and they put on 129 for the fifth wicket until Hammond caught him off Voce for a brave 49.

During this stanza, the crowd became vocal. Amongst the less than genteel offerings proffered to the England fieldsmen, came an admonition to Jardine, who had learned the 'Australian salute' to rid himself of ever-present irritating flies. 'Leave our flies alone, Jardine,' came the cry from the Hill.

A bruised McCabe was having a charmed life as he raced to a great century under the circumstances. He was dropped twice in the deep and several times skied the ball with mistimed hooks, which fell unsafely to earth close to a fieldsman. Yet he survived playing conventional shots, his feet well-planted in orthodox positions.

McCabe had come to the conclusion that playing a normal defensive innings to such terror bowling had no future. It was a case of hit out or get out. He stood and delivered 187 not out in one of the two great innings of his life, and arguably one of the finest of all time, while the other bats struggled and eventually crumbled around him, leaving Australia on 360.

If only the rest could play like McCabe, spectators, commentators and journalists thought aloud. But against this fierce attack it was a tall order. Larwood took five for 96 in thirty-one overs, and bowled with fire, menace and brilliance. Voce was not quite as dangerous, but nevertheless effective with four for 110 from twenty-nine overs. Bodyline had taken all but one wicket — that of Wall, a rabbit, who was snapped up by Hammond. Jardine could not have wished for a better start. All his diligence, stealth and planning were paying off.

England replied with a 112-run opening stand before Wyatt (38) was trapped by Grimmett. Sutcliffe dug in for a long stay and let Hammond take the bowling. They rode on to 300, when Hammond (112) was caught off Nagel for yet another Test century — his fifth in Australia. Pataudi and Sutcliffe took them on past Australia's score with eight wickets still standing.

These two took the score to 423, before Sutcliffe fell LBW to Wall with a new ball on 194. He had held his form and seemed immovable as he had in his last Test appearance against Australia at The Oval in 1930, with 161 and 54. Wall then had Leyland caught behind for 0, and England was four for 423 — 63 runs on with six wickets in hand. Jardine (27) was caught behind off McCabe, but not before he helped increase his team's commanding lead in a solid 57-run partnership with Pataudi. The Indian reached 102, in his first Test innings against Australia, before he was bowled by Nagel. O'Reilly, who had had 100 hit off him without taking a wicket, saved his position by wrapping up the tail to end with three for 117 off sixty-seven overs. Wall took three for 104, and Nagel two for 110.

England's 524 gave it a lead of 164, which was daunting, especially as Australia's battered batsmen would have to weather a rested Larwood. The old opening firm didn't last long. Woodfull was sensationally bowled by Larwood in his first over, and Voce soon after uprooted Ponsford's leg stump. Australia was two for 10, 154 behind and no sign of Bradman strolling to the wicket. Still there was McCabe, but he was nowhere near the player of the first innings, the strain and stress of which had sapped him. He hung on and saw off Larwood and Voce with Fingleton, only to relax against Hammond just enough to fall LBW to an optimistic lunge for 32. Hammond soon after had Richardson caught for 0, and Australia at four for 61 was finished. The scorecard looked rather strange without Bradman as the side crumbled under a third-spell bodyline onslaught by Larwood. He had been held back for short bursts by Jardine, who didn't wish to overbowl him or bodyline.

Larwood was his one-man shock battalion and the key to the Ashes. He removed Kippax, Oldfield and Grimmett in quick succession, leaving Australia seven for 105. A rearguard effort by Nagel and Wall held up England, who did not use bodyline against the tail. Australia's total of 164 meant the tourists only had to make one to win, which they did in fifteen seconds for an overwhelming ten-wicket victory.

Long before the game was over, the press and public were talking about Bradman and clamouring for his return.

273

24

RETURN OF
THE UNPRODIGAL

*There were amazing scenes and a wonderful demonstration
when Bradman reached his century with the last man,
Ironmonger, his partner.*
— Press report on Bradman's Ashes century at Melbourne,
2 January 1933

PLAN OF COUNTER-ATTACK

Bradman returned refreshed from a two-week break with Jessie at a cottage owned by a masseur friend on the coast south of Sydney. He had not been inactive, having been involved in fighting a bushfire while he was there. But it gave him time away from the public spotlight and moments to think. He decided on a set strategy to counteract Larwood. There was no future in normal batting methods against bodyline. First, it meant that run-scoring would be difficult, and to Bradman that was the only way of winning a game. He refused to countenance pure defence and staying at the wicket for the sake of a draw or wearing down the opposition.

England had three fast men to bowl bouncers and at the body. Unless all the tourists broke down, Australian batsmen would have the short deliveries pitched at them for the remaining four Tests.

Bradman also considered the 'McCabe' option of playing the two

274

orthodox attacking shots left to the batsman, the hook and the pull. But this brave stand-and-deliver response had fatal drawbacks. First, the odds were that a batsman would get caught. Bodyline was designed to encompass the foolhardy and brave hitter with two, even three men on the fence fine and square, and players in the close leg field for the skied mishit. Second, no matter how tough and brave, the human body was not designed even with padding for a constant battering. The batsman might have extraordinary physical courage, but it would amount to nought with a broken limb, bruised chest and dented skull. Eventually, the sufferer would be rendered useless either by immobilisation or demoralisation.

Bradman had noted McCabe's incredible guts and skill in Sydney. But he had been very lucky in the first innings and ineffective in the second. McCabe was also sore from the hits he had taken and might find it hard to come up mentally and physically again.

Bradman's logical approach left him with one option, and he was the only cricketer in the world who had the equipment to consider it. He would use his fast feet to scamper across to the off-side for shots through and over the trap or to leg for shots on the off. Both, he was aware, would create risks. He would find himself wide of the leg-stump or wide of the off-peg, thus leaving himself vulnerable to being bowled. It was one thing to have a terrific eye when keeping the head steady as a ball came down at speed. It was another to be moving across the line of flight to play a shot in the middle of the bat. In effect, he would introduce a bit of tennis in playing his shots, by moving across the wicket. He also knew he would be labelled 'frightened' if it failed often.

I asked him about this accusation. 'I had no desire to get hit,' he replied with a wry smile.

I saw no advantage to me or the team whatsoever in standing still and being struck. If you view film of Larwood bowling to me [in an ABC TV documentary], you'll notice where the ball passes when I move away. If I had remained where I was I would be struck in the chest or head. The only sensible way was to move into position to avoid the fast-rising delivery or in order to play scoring strokes.

Bradman remarked that his counteraction would in fact increase the chance of his being hit.

The orthodox manner of playing the fast lifting ball is to move across to the off and out of the line of flight. The ball on middle and leg will go by and you're unlikely to get hit. The danger of being hit is if you stand precisely where you are, or if you back away a bit to the leg-side to try to play it on the off, because the ball is then following you. What I planned put me in much graver danger of being hit than if I had adopted an orthodox method. But there was no way I was going to get runs playing orthodox cricket.

Bradman's high-risk approach would be based on attacking the bodyline using orthodox shots in order to blast the theory from the bowler's armoury. He would make it too expensive to bowl, at least against him. This led to another problem that Bradman would not bother to dwell on. For no matter how successful he was, the rest of Australia's top bats were likely to be rendered impotent against this new and effective bowling weapon. If bodyline could not be obliterated or perhaps made illegal, then the Australian batsmen would be less and less effective as the series progressed.

The problem with the Board of Control over his contract lingered, and the press lambasted its short-sightedness. His newspaper outlet — Associated Newspapers — was also criticised for holding Bradman to his contract. Mid-December, R. C. Packer, the Editorial Director of the newspaper group, became concerned that he would be blamed for Bradman not playing against England. Rather than face the opprobrium involved, Packer released him from his obligations to write for the Sydney *Sun*, which was the issue upsetting the Board of Control. In its wisdom, or lack thereof, it was prepared to let him speak over the airwaves, but not to put his thoughts on paper for public consumption. Perhaps the Board was swayed by the belief that ideas were lost in the ether when expressed on radio, but if they appeared in print, they could be circulated widely and often.

The upshot of Packer's problem-solving meant Bradman could return to the Australian team for the Second Test clash at the MCG beginning on 30 December. In the meanwhile, he could have a timely dress rehearsal at the Melbourne ground in the return Shield game between Victoria and NSW. He looked tanned and fit, a far cry from his unhealthy lean days in November, but had to wait for Melbourne's fickle weather, which washed out the first two days' play.

A big holiday crowd of 21,000 turned up when it finally began on Boxing Day, in a no-lose situation. If Victoria batted, its supporters would see their favourites Woodfull and Ponsford, and cheer for Leo O'Brien, who was being touted as a possible Test selection, primarily because he was an exceptionally gutsy batsman. If NSW batted, then they would be watching, judging and encouraging Bradman, the most popular player from elsewhere, in Victoria's parochial history. He transcended State boundaries because of his talent and desire to score big and quickly. Melburnians were the most avid sports lovers in the country, and it was long said of them that they would turn up to the opening of an envelope. Give them Bradman and they would be there in bulk.

Woodfull won the toss and sent NSW in. Fingleton and Bill Brown batted slowly until lunch, testing the crowd's patience. In the last over before the break, Alexander hit Brown, 35, on the body. He retired hurt. Word swept through the crowd that Bradman would be batting after lunch. When he stepped out with Fingleton he was given a tremendous reception.

His batting was more controlled than normal. Rather than complaining, the crowd encouraged him, knowing that this tune-up was vital for the forthcoming Test. He took ninety minutes to accumulate 50, and moved to a century in 157 minutes. The crowd were over-demonstrative in response, but there was much behind it. Australia's loss at Sydney and England's tactics had raised the level of interest in cricket to new heights. Nationalist passions were beginning to rise.

The press, while trying to appear neutral, were leaning to the home side at a time of expected crisis, and this was stimulating public opinion and feeling.

Bradman gave them something to cheer about as he went into overdrive to reach 130 and complete 10,000 runs in all first-class cricket. It had taken him 126 innings. Ponsford, the former record-holder, had made another thirty-five visits to the crease to get there. The more observant in the crowd noticed Bradman's footwork as he swept to 157, scoring his last 57 in forty-two minutes before he was caught in the deep off Ironmonger. He was moving into unorthodox positions to play audacious strokes in preparation for his battle against Larwood and Voce.

Fingleton (85) looked sound. McCabe, however, was tentative for him. His pummelling in the Sydney Test had taken its toll and he scored 48 in the slow time, again for him, of eighty-one minutes. He was always troubled by Alexander's pace until that bowler trapped him LBW. Kippax, too, seemed unsure against speed and scratched about for just 17. His injury on that Queensland country tour a year earlier and now Larwood were reducing his effectiveness against real pace.

NSW were all out early on day four. When Victoria batted, Woodfull and Ponsford were also ordinary and out early for 19 and 12 respectively. O'Brien enhanced his chances of Test selection with a forceful 53 and Victoria reached 258. The game, reduced to practice for the Test aspirants, fizzled to a draw.

Bradman always hated the days before a Test, which put him on edge. He was never nervous or motivated by fear of failure in the traditional way of players before a big contest. Nevertheless, this game was testing his calm and stretching his nerves like no other. He was raring to go more than in any other contest.

BOWES-TIED

The build-up to the Second Test was so big that a world-record crowd of 63,993 packed the MCG under a hot sun on 30 December

1932. My father, aged thirteen and no cricket lover, was among the many present who had never seen a big match before. Such was the pull of Bradman, the hero, against Larwood & Co, being billed as the villains, that people who had scant regard for the game were attracted to the drama at the MCG colosseum.

Woodfull won the toss. He came into the dressing-room and told the Australian players they were batting. The batsmen looked up at the scoreboard to see that England had reinforced the point about pace by picking four speedsters. Verity and spin were sacrificed for bumpers and Bowes. '"It's on again," we thought,' O'Brien recalled. He had gained selection with Bradman, replacing Ponsford and Kippax, who were dropped. Ironmonger took Nagel's place.

O'Brien went over to the wall where Woodfull had posted a sheet of paper with the batting order:

> *I thought I would be five or six, but I was number three. I began to pad up. Don was padding up beside me. He looked at me and said: 'You don't seem to have much faith in me, Leo.' I replied 'I wouldn't say that, Don, not by any chalk. But I just had a look at Woody's batting order.' He dropped his other pad and went over and had a look. With that, he removed the one pad he had on, and sauntered off to have a look at the game.*

Woodfull had placed Bradman at number four. Bradman didn't complain or concern himself. 'If that was where the captain placed you,' he remarked, 'that's where you batted.'

But what was Woodfull's reasoning?

'Billy never told the reason or discussed it with you. In this case O'Brien sometimes opened for Victoria, and he was a stodgy sort of bat. The idea was probably to put him up the front to face Larwood, and leave the more aggressive bats until later.'

Australia began slowly and lost Woodfull for 10 at 29, bowled by Allen, who once more refused to bowl bodyline. This and orthodox bowling tied up Fingleton and O'Brien to such an extent that they had barely reached 50 by lunch. The huge crowd would never have stayed so long had not Bradman been next man in. O'Brien was run out for 10 and Australia was two for 67. It was precisely 2.57 p.m.

The biggest single roar ever heard at the Melbourne stadium went up the moment Bradman came through the gate. A few metres onto the field he passed Herbert Sutcliffe, who remarked: 'Wonderful reception, Don.'

'Yes, Herbert,' Bradman replied, 'but will it be so good when I'm coming back?'

The tension surrounding Bradman's return had made him think about the first delivery he would receive. He had a premonition that it would be a short ball. He was determined to hook it to the fence.

Bradman took his time walking to the middle, then took guard from umpire Hill. Tall bespectacled Bowes was bowling. He had a six-three field — four clustered round the bat close in on the leg, two in the deep on the leg and three on the off-side. Bradman surveyed the placings, then settled in over his bat. Bowes took a few steps forward, then stopped. He motioned to Jardine that he wanted Hammond to go from mid-off to the leg-trap. Hammond jogged across to his position to make up the classic bodyline field.

Bradman noted the change and settled down again. Bowes stopped at the top of his run once more. He waved to Larwood at fine leg, pushing him finer. The crowd barracked this second delay. Bradman again looked hard at the change. It confirmed to him that he would receive that expected short ball. He leaned over his bat again and waited. Bowes ran in and thumped the ball in short. It rose chest high. Bradman moved his back foot across and back to the off and took a tremendous swing at the ball. It hit the bottom edge of the bat and crashed down into the base of the leg-stump.

He was out for a first-ball duck. Bowes was elated at his luck. He noticed 'Jardine the sphinx'. He had forgotten himself for the first time in his cricketing life. The England skipper had clasped his hands above his head and was 'jigging around like an Indian doing a war-dance'.

'I could have tried for fifty years to hit the ball where it went,' Bradman remarked, 'and couldn't do it. I walked back past Herbert again in complete silence.'

One woman alone began clapping and the gigantic crowd, not yet over the shock, broke out in excited chatter. Back in the dressing-room, O'Brien came out of the shower.

'What the devil happened to you?' he asked Bradman.

'I got bowled first ball,' Bradman replied, not bothering to mention he had played it on to his wicket.

Thereafter, Australia went slowly downhill to be dismissed for 228. Fingleton (83) resisted most, but it was grim, laborious going against this fierce top-quality attack. Allen had done his bit by bowling both the openers and taking two for 41. Voce perhaps bowled best, picking up McCabe (32), Richardson (34) and Grimmett (2) in the close leg-trap. Larwood only got two tailenders, but his presence and pace unsettled every Australian.

England fared worse and were dismissed for 169. Only Sutcliffe (52) could hold out the great fast turn of O'Reilly, who took five for 63 off 34.3 overs — half of them maidens. Wall lifted his rating enough to take four for 52. When he clean-bowled Hammond for 8 and had Jardine caught behind for 1, he generated the biggest roars of the second day, New Year's Eve.

An even bigger crowd than for the first day of the match greeted the cricketers for the first day's play in 1933.

Australia started badly again. Allen had Fingleton caught behind for 1 at 1, and O'Brien was bowled by Larwood for 11. Australia was two for 27 at 12.54 p.m. and the atmosphere was again charged with tension. Bradman strode out to face big Bill Bowes as in the first innings. Jardine clapped hands and the leg-trap moved into position. Bradman scrutinised it carefully. There was a gap between short-forward square leg and mid-on. Apart from that, there were eager waiting hands for any stroke, defensive or attacking, to leg.

He settled down over his bat. Bowes ran in, brought his big front foot down hard and thumped the ball short in almost the identical position as the fatal first innings ball. Bradman moved that back foot across and back in an action replay. He again played a vigorous hook shot, rolling the wrists in his characteristic manner. The ball bisected forward short leg and mid-on and raced to the boundary.

The gallery let out a deafening roar, more in relief than immediate appreciation of this great, aggressive opening stroke. Bradman was four, but with a long way to go. Now he was intent on staying he would have to face Larwood and Voce. That was what the crowd had paid their money to see.

Jardine wasted no time in giving them value. He removed Bowes from the attack, bringing Larwood on to join Voce. Shrewdly, the skipper started them both with orthodox, predominantly off-side fields. Bradman and Woodfull played them with appropriate orthodoxy. Then Jardine made his double clap. Time for bodyline.

Larwood steamed in at Bradman on 8. The first ball reared over his leg-stump as Bradman ducked. The second ball was fuller. Bradman brought gasps as he backed away and lashed it through the vacant cover field for three. From then on, whenever Larwood and Voce delivered balls for the leg-trap, Bradman either stepped away to leg or off to play strokes, or he ducked away. The tactic brought much comment from the crowd and frustration for Larwood and Voce, but it worked.

Woodfull, less gifted and fleet-footed, had to stand, accept or weave under the 'scone' balls, as some in the home team called them. Bradman's scoring rate was steady until he was 20 just on lunch. Twenty minutes afterwards, Woodfull, who had led from the front, was out caught in the leg-trap by Allen for 26 with the score at 78. Australia's lead was 147 with seven wickets left.

Voce then shook up McCabe, and Allen soon bowled him for a duck. The home team was four for 81 and wobbling. Richardson came in and showed fighting spirit in a 54-run stand with Bradman: big partnerships were a distant memory. They withstood everything thrown at them by Larwood and Voce. Neither could make a direct hit on Bradman, whose footwork and body movements were too quick. However, Hammond, now reduced to a change-bowler, had Richardson LBW for 32. Australia had half its side out but were 197 ahead.

In the meantime, Bradman had reached 50 in ninety-three minutes of riveting batting. Even when retreating to leg to play his shots, he had the crowd yelling with delight. He was taking most of the bodyline, which was directed in shrewd bursts by Jardine, who was keeping the more vulnerable Bowes out of the attack.

Voce beat Oldfield with an extra quick one and soon after did the same to Grimmett. Australia was seven for 156 and in danger of effectively squandering that 59 lead on the first innings. Bradman went to tea on 77 and running out of partners. His 50 in the session was slow for him, but defence more than attack was the important factor in survival, in an innings the huge audience was appreciating as much, if not more than one of his fast double-hundreds.

After tea, Wall hung around pluckily for half an hour to score three before Hammond broke through again and dismissed him LBW. Bradman was now in charge. He took nine off one Larwood over of bodyline and Jardine took him off, to be banished once more by Bradman's blade, this time with shots not found in the manual. O'Reilly stayed for three overs while Bradman skilfully found his way to 98. Australia was nine for 186.

Ironmonger, not even a rabbit but a ferret, came to the wicket. One story about him was that once his wife rang the pavilion to speak with him as he walked out to bat. When she was told this, she said she would stay on the line. The story had some merit in view of Ironmonger's last five Shield innings. He had made five runs.

Bradman walked over to give him a few words of encouragement. Ironmonger, old enough to be Bradman's father, said to him as he approached: 'Don't worry son, I won't let you down.'

He had two balls to face from Hammond. His method was basic. He put the bat in the block-hole and when Hammond bowled, he simply bent the handle forward. Both balls just missed the off-stump. Bradman had the strike to Voce, who was bowling to an orthodox field. The batsman played the first five balls cautiously. The sixth was down the leg-side. Bradman turned it behind square leg and darted off for three, bringing himself to 101 in 185 minutes of gladiatorial combat. The crowd cheered and clapped him on their feet for fully three minutes. Moments later, Ironmonger was run out, leaving Bradman on 103 not out with Australia on 191. It was his seventh century against England in his past ten Tests. He had hit just seven fours, but it ranked with his greatest innings so far. In this chanceless exhibition, Bradman faced 146 balls, eighty-three of them from Larwood and Voce, from which he scored 52 runs.

The lead was 250. The onus was now on the tourists to lift their batting. But the spin combination of O'Reilly (five for 58) and Ironmonger (four for 26) ruined their chances. O'Reilly bowled top-scorer Sutcliffe for 33 and had the dangerous Hammond caught for 23. Much to the fourth day crowd's delight, Ironmonger had Jardine caught for a duck, leaving him with a solitary run for the match. England was all out for 139, giving Australia a win by 111 runs.

Bradman made a point of speaking with his contacts on the Board of Control and complained about bodyline. He had many objections to it. He personally had avoided hits on the body, but not one of his fellow batsmen had been so skilful, for avoiding the bruising was not a matter of luck but ability.

'Sooner or later, someone would receive serious injury,' Bradman told them, 'not necessarily from an erratic ball but from the very nature of the bowling.'

The Board representatives noted that he and McCabe had scored great centuries, and no-one had been badly hurt. 'If they hadn't faced it,' Bradman reflected, 'they didn't appreciate the problem. Even the opposition players were indifferent until they later had to face it.'

However, the Board was deaf to any argument, with record crowds filling the grounds to see the combat. The England tourists were helping to bring in record revenues and money talked.

Bradman further argued that with the restriction of scoring shots the game would deteriorate for the spectator. Run-making opportunities would dry up to a trickle. Bodyline, with its emphasis on leg-side bowling to a set field, was totally negative. He also told the Board that the methods would be copied around the country, from children to grade and country cricket, with dangerous consequences.

Bradman urged them to protest to the MCC now, while Australia was on top, so that the arguments would have more weight. But the Board simply noted his remarks. It had been unhappy with his public rebuking of them in recent weeks over his contract and was not now going to jump when he whistled, even if it had the inclination, and it did not.

Did he think he could handle the English attack, the Board asked? Bradman replied that he thought so, but that this was not the point. Did he think Australia could retain the Ashes in the next three games? Yes, but again, the point had been missed.

The Board of Control did nothing. It was confident that bodyline would be overcome and Australia would win the series. In England, the MCC had no way of comprehending the change, conflict and bitterness in the game that bodyline had brought. The tyranny of distance was keeping the MCC ignorant of events and the ramifications of bodyline.

25

THE EMPIRE STRIKES BACK

There are two teams out there. One is trying to play cricket and one is not.
— AUSTRALIAN CAPTAIN, BILL WOODFULL, TO ENGLAND'S MANAGER, PLUM WARNER, DURING THE ADELAIDE TEST, JANUARY 1933

WOODFULL'S WOUNDS

The ten days before the Third Test at Adelaide saw chauvinism dragged into the sporting arena, where it had no place. The game was in danger of being used for national and extreme political purposes. Adelaide, an attractive, quiet, church-oriented town, seemed most unlikely as a place of violence and political disturbance. Yet just a year earlier, on 9 January 1931, there had been a fight between unemployed men and police in a protest against cuts in dole rations. A year on, the left-wing labour press was articulating these economic grievances and putting them in recent historical perspective. Workers and the nation were reminded that it was Sir Otto Niemeyer, a director of the Bank of England, who had advised Australia in July 1930 to 'balance its budgets', stop raising loans and cut back on expenditure on public works. Australia was forced to repay its 1920 loans to British banks. Such debatable advice had led directly to cuts in the dole and other social services.

The labour press claimed Australia's Depression was largely engendered by this advice. It had been taken in a 'supine' way by the establishment, which included the ruling Federal Labor government of James Scullin. The British were billed as the enemy. The workers and the general public did not catch sight of Niemeyer in the middle of 1930 when he came to Australia to give his gratuitous advice. He was busy lunching at establishment strongholds such as the Melbourne Club. But they had an opportunity to see the embodiment of British 'imperialism' at the Adelaide Oval. It took the form of the grim, hard-backed Douglas Jardine in his harlequin cap and his ever-present silk neck-choker.

Unmoved by press comment, Jardine won the toss on Saturday 13 January and batted, making himself opener. His thinking was that he could both improve England's start and boost his own poor form. He dropped Bowes for Verity, and Pataudi for Paynter. Australia brought back Ponsford at O'Brien's expense.

The South Australian police, or at least their political masters, had been reading the press. They turned up in numbers, but were subtle enough to keep their mounted troopers and squads of foot police mainly out of sight in the No. 2 ground. Yet with England batting they were not needed. No-one was going to riot when an English wicket fell or if Wall could get a bouncer into an imperial ribcage.

As it turned out, the paceman did get a couple to lift, and while Jardine was expecting another, Wall pitched one up and bowled him for 3, making his tally 31 in four knocks. It sent the crowd delirious. They hurled abuse at him as he left the field. Then Wall struck a more important blow by having Hammond caught behind for 2. England was two for 16. Woodfull brought on O'Reilly early. First the deadly spinner troubled, then bowled Sutcliffe. England was three for 16. At 30, Ironmonger got into the act and bowled Ames for 3. The tourists were tottering, but they were not done yet, such was their depth. Leyland and Wyatt settled in for a strong partnership of 156, taking the score to 186, when Grimmett broke through in front of his home crowd and had Wyatt caught for 78.

Ten runs later O'Reilly bowled Leyland for a well-made 83 and

England was six for 196. The left-handed Paynter came in, held up one end and helped lead his country back to a strong position before Wall had him caught for 77. The tail, with Verity (45) featuring, stayed with him to lift the final total to 341. Wall bowled with fire and consistency to collect five for 72. Grimmett (two for 94) and O'Reilly (two for 82) gave support.

Australia batted at 3.15 p.m. on the second day and promptly lost Fingleton for 0, bringing Bradman to the wicket with the score at 1 just as police began to file into positions around the ground. The Adelaide spectators greeted him with gusto all the way to the wicket. He defended out the rest of Allen's over and then Larwood came down-wind, his speed picking up. Woodfull defended grimly. Bradman got off the mark with a gentle push to the on off Allen and the crowd greeted it as if it were a six. Woodfull faced Larwood again, still with an orthodox field. The speedster managed to get a very fast ball to rear up hard into the Aussie skipper's chest.

Woodfull dropped his bat and staggered away from the wicket clutching his chest. Shocked silence followed, then an eruption from the crowd as players and umpires gathered around the stricken batsman. Abuse was hurled at Larwood. Bradman thought the crowd was so incensed that it might invade the ground. Jardine sidled up to Larwood.

'Well bowled, Harold,' Jardine said to both bolster his pace weapon and upset the Australian skipper further. Woodfull, pale and unsteady, resumed his place at the crease. This calmed spectators. Larwood went back to his mark, keen to get in at his softened opponent. Then he stopped as Jardine clapped his hands above his head. The skipper did his double clap for bodyline. Six players automatically took up positions. When the move dawned on the crowd it roared in fury again.

Larwood uncoiled himself with his graceful run to deliver a sharp lifter, which knocked the bat out of Woodfull's hands. The crowd turned mob and counted Larwood out — one to ten — as he delivered the next ball and another.

The spectators were so vociferous that Allen, in the leg-trap, asked umpire George Hele to leave him a stump if the crowd came over the fence.

'Not on your life,' Hele replied, 'I'll need all three myself.'

By luck more than design, Jardine had Allen on instead of Voce at the other end. Allen was still refusing to set the bodyline field, so this lowered the mob's collective temperature again. But with each ball Larwood bowled there was baying for his blood.

In the next over from Allen at Woodfull a flock of seagulls flew over the ground. During a lull, one of the few true wits at the match pointed to Jardine and yelled: 'There he is at mid-off.'

The next over, from Larwood to Bradman on 8, was no laughing matter. The bowler had the leg-trap in place and bowled a set of short balls to it, causing Bradman to cut into the off. Larwood bowled a good-length ball for variety and Bradman played an orthodox leg glance — straight into Allen's hands at short leg. Larwood leapt in the air and waved his fists. The Englishmen moved to him to offer congratulations. Jardine was grinning with delight. It was the first time Larwood had legitimately taken Bradman's wicket in fifteen Test innings of bowling at him. It had not been obtained directly by bodyline, but the wicket was certainly a legacy of it. The little victory was sweet for the bowler, but not nearly enough. Larwood had vivid memories of pastings from him in 1928–29 and 1930. He would not be satisfied until he had him again and again . . .

In his collaborative book with Perkins in 1965, Larwood demonstrated he would have liked to have made a few body strikes as well in retribution for all those fours smashed off him, particularly at Leeds and The Oval in 1930, in front of English crowds, an experience which hurt and humiliated the most.

'Bowling to Australia's batsmen was rather like potting pheasants on the wing,' he wrote. 'But with Bradman it was like trying to trap a wild duck, his movements were so swift.'

Bradman had faced just seventeen balls in eighteen minutes. Australia was two for 18 and McCabe was at the wicket. He looked concerned as Larwood lifted deliveries into his side and ribs. One too many of these dangerous balls saw him edge one to Jardine at short-forward square leg for a catch. Australia was three for 34 and rocking as England was early in its innings.

Ponsford joined the suffering Woodfull, who, battered and groggy, was hanging on with sheer guts until tea. The cool-down in the break exacerbated Woodfull's pain and caused him to lose a little concentration. At 51, Allen bowled him for 22. Richardson came to the crease in front of his home crowd and continued the fight with Ponsford, who was on the attack.

Back in the dressing-room, Woodfull had showered when Plum Warner entered. Also present was Australian twelfth man Leo O'Brien. Warner, a polite diplomat, who secretly had no time for bodyline, extended his sympathies for the injuries received. Woodfull, also a sportsman of the old school, as good as told Warner to leave.

'I don't want to see you, Mr Warner,' the bruised Australian skipper responded. 'There are two teams out there. One is trying to play cricket and one is not. It is too great a game for spoiling by the tactics your team is adopting. I don't approve of them. It might be better if I do not play the game.'

This final remark indicated Woodfull was considering not letting his team play on. Warner left distressed by this breakdown in the normally polite harmony between the two teams. O'Brien spoke to other members of the team about the incident. One was Jack Fingleton, who passed Woodfull's words on to two journalists.

Warner was approached by one of the journalists, Claude Corbett. Warner was upset that the remark had leaked to the media.

'Who told you that?' Warner demanded to know.

'Jack Fingleton,' Corbett told him.

Warner was incensed. He went straight to Larwood. 'I'll give you a pound if you can get Fingleton out quickly in the second innings,' he told him.

(Fingleton, himself a journalist, just before he died decades later made up a story saying it was Bradman who had told Corbett about Woodfull's snub of Warner in a 'clandestine night time meeting'. Corbett was by then dead and could not deny Fingleton's fabrication.

Fingleton had a long-running vendetta against Bradman, whom he blamed for his non-selection for the 1934 England tour. Fingleton thought — correctly — that Bradman favoured Bill Brown as an opener on English wickets. Fingleton's grudge showed consistently in acts on and off the field and in decades of writing.)

The story of Woodfull's reaction was run in the press on Monday and caused a furore. The English press responded by saying the Australians were squealers and the verbal war began in earnest, with journalists lining up firmly for or against bodyline, and not always along national lines.

On the field on Monday, Richardson battled on for a valuable partnership of 80 with Ponsford, who was in good form. Again Allen broke through, this time bowling Richardson for 28. Australia was five for 131 and struggling 210 behind. Oldfield came in and gave Ponsford determined support in a stand that threatened England's supremacy when they made it through to lunch at 185.

After the break, Ponsford was bowled by Voce for 85 with the score at 194. It had been a good knock, full of cuts and drives, especially off Larwood, in another fascinating round of their long-running battle. At 200, Larwood took the new ball with Allen and the latter dismissed Grimmett for 10. Australia was seven for 212 and folding. Oldfield decided to go for the runs and, on 41, received a bouncer pitched on middle and off stump from Larwood. Oldfield hooked at it, missed and was collected on the front of the head. He went down. Woodfull came onto the arena and escorted his semi-concussed keeper from the field amidst angry booing of Larwood. Oldfield was found to have a linear fracture of the right frontal lobe. He was out of the match, but he defused some of the tension by saying publicly that he blamed himself for playing the hook, and not Larwood for hitting him.

But the incident had occurred with a bodyline field in operation and the crowd was hostile again. They had read about Woodfull's remarks to Warner, which were not meant to be public. They could now see Australians going down from heavy blows. What made matters worse was the scoreboard. The home team were all out for 222

— 121 behind. Allen, with four for 71, had bowled best. Larwood took three for 55 and did the damage in more ways than one.

Jardine started England's second innings as if he were batting for a draw, and lost Sutcliffe for 7 to Wall at the same score. Wyatt joined his skipper in the slow grind through to stumps.

The Board of Control now decided to act on bodyline by holding a press conference and sending a cable to the MCC:

> *Bodyline bowling has assumed such proportions as to menace the best interests of the game, making protection of the body by the batsman the main consideration. This is causing intensely bitter feelings between the players, as well as injury. In our opinion it is unsportsmanlike. Unless stopped at once it is likely to upset friendly relations between Britain and Australia.*

The timing was out and the wording amounted to what appeared to be an ill-considered over-reaction. Comments that links with the UK were at risk would not have sounded credible halfway round the world at Lord's.

Back on the field of play the next morning, day four, Jardine was struggling on, determined now that England would not lose. He and Wyatt reached lunch, which seemed to come and go with the same intensity as the play. It was clear that Jardine was aiming to preserve wickets and add gradually to England's lead.

At 91, O'Reilly removed Wyatt (49). Jardine was adjudged LBW to Ironmonger for 56 at 132, giving England a strong 254-run lead with seven wickets in hand. The England captain, in one respect, had done his job very well, but at the game's expense as a spectacle. Yet everything had to be viewed in the perspective of his main commission of winning back the Ashes.

Allen was LBW for 15 at 154, and this left Leyland in attacking mood with Hammond, until after tea he swung wildly at Ironmonger and was caught for 42. He was on his way at 245. England was now secure with half its side remaining and Hammond in spasmodically good form.

All seemed lost for Australia, when Woodfull put Bradman on just before 6 p.m. His first ball was a full-toss. Hammond played, missed and was bowled for 85. It was Bradman's first English Test wicket. As his over was incomplete, he opened the bowling next day. Ames and Verity resisted in a valuable stand of 98 and made England impregnable at 412 in all and with a lead of 532. No team had managed 400 let alone 500 in the last innings of a Test.

Larwood began bowling at the Australians with an off-side attack, for it was believed that this was Fingleton's weakness. The crowd cheered this field. In any case, he bowled Fingleton for a duck and later collected his pound from a satisfied Plum Warner. In came Ponsford, almost opening as usual for another confrontation with his main rival in world cricket. Larwood enticed him outside the off-stump and he back-cut a ball straight to Jardine. Another round to the bowler. Australia was two for 3 and the bowler was pleased to hear genuine applause for his efforts. He felt counted 'in' with the spectators now, after their unfriendly behaviour on Monday.

Every spectator and every player in the game knew that only Bradman could conceivably even threaten to turn this game around. As he took block, many eyes turned to Jardine. Would he change to a body-line field?

He decided against it. The shine was not yet off the ball and the bowler was doing brilliantly with an orthodox set-up. Larwood steamed in. Bradman let the first one go outside the off-stump. In again. It was short and head-high. Bradman hooked it off his chin to the square-leg fence. Next ball, he late-cut for four. The crowd went wild. Bradman's counter-plan today was to hit back. Voce bowled to a stubborn Woodfull. In Larwood's next over Bradman cover-drove him for four. At the end of the over, the bowler left the field.

A spectator in the Members' stand yelled: 'Hey, Larwood, gone to see if the MCC has replied?'

In fact, he had boot trouble. On his return, Bradman cover-drove him for four more. Jardine had a word to him. The bowler sent down two balls on the leg-stump and Bradman pushed him into the vacant leg-side field for twos. The following over, Jardine and Larwood had to make a move to stop Bradman, who seemed ready to go rampant. They added three men to the leg-side, making a near-bodyline field. The crowd reacted. Bradman hit out wildly at two balls on the leg-side but failed to connect.

In the next few overs, Bradman reverted to his unorthodoxy, stepping back to hit Larwood and Voce into the off-side when anything was up. The unconventional strokes brought gasps, but Bradman kept scoring. Larwood ran out of puff and Jardine removed him. Honours went to Bradman again, although the bowler's initial burst in taking two wickets had been top-class. Allen and Hammond were tried, but were not penetrating against Woodfull's sound rearguard play and Bradman's attack.

When Jardine brought left-hander Verity on, Bradman moved down the wicket to him with relish and moved past 50 in sixty-four minutes, a whirlwind yield in any Test, especially this one. He swept to 60 with two terrific pulls for four and then launched into Verity with a mighty six over mid-on and into spectators sitting in front of the grandstand. It was a disarming experience for a woman who was struck near the elbow, but she was not badly injured. The crowd was alight, while commentators were stunned. It was Bradman's first six in an Ashes Test.

Verity bowled a fraction shorter. Bradman, adrenalin pumping, jumped at the next ball and smashed it straight back to the bowler, who accepted the chance.

He was on his way for 66 in seventy-three minutes, leaving Woodfull disappointed at the other end. The Australian skipper had been grimly holding up one end, waiting for a player to stay with him. While that contrasting 88-run stand was in progress there was hope, but Bradman's flash of genius had been expunged about two hundred short of requirements. Australia was three for 100, some 432 behind. Without Oldfield to bat it had just six wickets left.

McCabe (7) tried to take up the attack and hit Allen beautifully down Leyland's throat at fine leg. Richardson joined Woodfull, who was 36 not out, and a light appeal was upheld at 5.30 p.m.

On the sixth and final day, Larwood eventually broke through and had Richardson caught in the leg-trap for 21 at 171. Woodfull stayed but the remainder of the Australians were ineffective against steady bowling from Larwood and Allen in tandem. Australia was dismissed for 193. Woodfull, who had taken a lot in both innings, showed great courage in carrying his bat to be 73 not out. Allen was the pick of the bowlers with four for 50. Larwood, who was in fair form, finished with four for 71, while Verity took one for 26 off twenty overs with twelve maidens. If Bradman had not been so audacious both would have had even more economical figures.

England's win by 338 runs was overwhelming and the tourists were now two-one ahead with two to play.

Two days after this big win, the MCC replied with indignation to the Board of Control's cable:

> *We, Marylebone Cricket Club, deplore your cable. We deprecate your opinion that there has been unsportsmanlike play. We have fullest confidence in captain, team and managers and are convinced that they would do nothing to infringe either the Laws of Cricket or the spirit of the game. We have no evidence that our confidence has been misplaced. Much as we regret accidents to Woodfull and Oldfield, we understand that in neither case was the bowler to blame. If the Australian Board of Control wish to propose a new rule or law, it shall receive our full consideration in due course.*
>
> *We hope the situation is not now as serious as your cable would seem to indicate, but if it is such as to jeopardize the good relations between English and Australian cricketers and you consider it desirable to cancel remainder of programme we would consent, but with great reluctance.*

The tourists then said that unless the Board of Control's cable was 'withdrawn', they would refuse to play in the Fourth Test. The Board had no choice but to back down and to let the tour go on. Bodyline was alive and well.

LARWOOD TIPS
THE SCALES

And why shouldn't I copy the master?
— Ray Lindwall in 1948, when accused by a spectator of copying
Larwood's style

THE DECIDER

The MCC kept up its high morale with a four-wicket win over
NSW at the end of January. Bradman was contained in the first
innings, being beaten by a top-spinner from Derbyshire googly
bowler Tom Mitchell and bowled for 1. But in the second, he played
another gem, scoring 71 on a sticky out of NSW's 128. Hammond
showed his versatility by bowling off-breaks to a leg-trap and taking
six for 43, including Bradman, caught behind. Less than a week later,
on a fast but true Sydney wicket, he again played a lone hand, scoring more than half the team's total (extras excluded) in a State game
against South Australia. Wall ran through NSW and took all ten
wickets for 36 out of a total of 113. Bradman was ninth man out for
56 in a remarkable collapse. He came to the wicket at 12 and put on
75 in a second-wicket stand with Fingleton, who was out at 87. Then
eight fell for 26. In the second innings, Bradman led the way with a
forceful top score of 97 and was out trying to force the pace. NSW
recovered and won by 98 runs.

Bradman's scores for the season read: 3, 10, 238, 52 not out, 36, 13, 18, 23, 157, 0, 103 not out, 8, 66, 1, 71, 56 and 97. This was not the spectacular scoring of other years, but he had still been remarkably consistent by scoring fifty in half his innings, totalling 952 at an average of 63.5. He may have been struggling with bodyline, but it had not dented his confidence or reduced him to abject failure. If this was a slump, then he was still in better form than any player in the country, the tourists included, considering the opposition and demanding situations in which he batted.

A few days later, on 10 February, he was in Brisbane for the Fourth Test. Jardine dropped Voce and brought in Mitchell, another former coalminer, after giving the spinner a work-out on a worn wicket in the middle of the morning of the match. Woodfull and the Australian selectors had been under great pressure to fight fire with fire. Vic Richardson had urged that the rough and aggressive Laurie Nash should be brought in to 'give the Poms back some of their own medicine'. Nash, a sort of Merv Hughes of his day, was quick. But the Board of Control, having protested so strongly to the MCC about bodyline, could hardly turn around now and employ tit-for-tat tactics. In any case, Woodfull was against such a move because he genuinely felt it was unsportsmanlike. Bradman had protested, as explained, on several other grounds, which were based on what was right and fair for the game as a spectacle, and for its future.

'I didn't agree with Vic on this,' he said, 'but I had no say officially. I was not then a senior member of the team.'

Even if Richardson had held sway, Nash would probably have been ineffective. He was not as accurate or astute as Larwood, and he would have needed two seasons' preparation — as Larwood did — to employ bodyline half as effectively.

In the end Australia's response at the selection table was much tamer and more sane. It brought in Love for the injured Oldfield, and dropped Fingleton and Grimmett to make way for two left-handed batsmen, Ernie Bromley and Len Darling. They were included to provide greater depth and to upset the line of England's fast men, who would have to keep adjusting their leg-side fields and direction for both right- and left-handers. On paper, this had merit. But then again, so did body-padding, but it wasn't deterring bodyline.

Woodfull won the toss, batted and continued to show grit and form with Richardson in an opening stand of 133. The heat seemed to take the sting out of Larwood when he bowled bodyline and Richardson was severe on him, forcing him out of the attack. It took Ames, standing up to Hammond, to stump Richardson for a splendid 83. Bradman came in and Allen gave him an uncomfortable couple of overs, but he made it through to the tea-break on 14 not out.

After tea, Larwood came back for a tremendous burst in an attempt to break the Woodfull-Bradman link. Somehow they saw him off. Just after 5 p.m., with the score on 200, Woodfull played a tired shot and was bowled by Mitchell for 67. Jardine then threw Larwood and Allen the new ball for one last dip. Bradman employed his unorthodox methods to move to 50 in eighty-eight minutes. Again Larwood tired, but Allen had McCabe caught for 20. Australia went to stumps on three for 251 with Bradman 71 not out. All the batsmen had kept Larwood out on a wicket that was not dangerous.

But the next morning was an entirely different story as Bradman went on combating bodyline. He began by moving away from his leg stump as the ball was bowled. But the wicket was not letting the ball rise over hip-height. He let a short one go that nearly bowled him, and then backed away to the next in an attempt to lash it through the off-side. It crashed into the stumps and he was out bowled by Larwood for 76. As he hadn't been fending a dangerous ball away from his head, many observers, including Arthur Mailey, felt he had not needed to play Larwood the way he did on such a lifeless wicket.

He was, in effect, an indirect victim of bodyline. It was as if Bradman had programmed himself and couldn't adjust in the manner he had on the recent sticky in Sydney. Yet he had made a fair score — a good contribution in a 156-minute stay at the wicket.

Larwood summoned enough strength in the enervating conditions to get through Ponsford's defences and bowl him too, for 19, leaving Australia five for 267. Darling and Bromley made 17 and 26 respectively but couldn't halt the slump. Australia was out for 340.

Larwood took four for 101 off thirty-one overs, and was backed up by Allen, Hammond and Mitchell, who each took two.

England began at 2.55 p.m. with a sound but careful opening stand by Sutcliffe and Jardine which took them well into Monday morning, the third day. At 114, O'Reilly got through Jardine and had him caught for 46, ending the best opening partnership for England for the tour. The spinner also removed Sutcliffe LBW for 86 at 157, bringing the aggressive Allen to the crease. He started with a six off O'Reilly, but then went into his shell. Paynter, who was thought to be ill in hospital, came in and showed typical Lancastrian pluck as Hammond (20), Allen (13), Wyatt (12), Leyland (12), Ames (17) and Larwood (23) came and went in steady succession. England was eight for 271 at stumps.

On the fourth morning, Paynter hung in with fellow north-countryman Verity, until England had passed Australia. At 356, Ironmonger broke through and had Paynter caught for 83. On the same score, O'Reilly trapped Mitchell for 0 to end the innings. O'Reilly was the backbone of the attack, sending down 67.2 overs and taking four for 120. Ironmonger was tight with three for 69 from forty-two overs, while McCabe took two for 23.

Richardson came out determined, it seemed, to hit the England bowlers out of the game. He slammed Larwood for two fours in one over, and appeared to have succeeded when Allen was taken off. But his replacement, Mitchell, had him caught for 36. Woodfull was on 6 when Bradman came out set to take up where Richardson had left off.

Jardine kept Larwood on for a crack at the new man, but he gave Bradman no concern. Larwood retired to the deep. Bradman moved along quietly, picking up singles with Woodfull.

After twenty minutes, with Bradman on 12, Larwood was brought back. He switched to bodyline and Bradman, in ferocious mood, cut him three times to the fence to reach 24.

However, in the following over from Larwood, Bradman slashed and lobbed an easy catch into the covers. He seemed to have been more on top than in the first innings, but failed to go on with the innings. Larwood had thus bagged him twice for 100 in total, the second dismissal (with the score at 79) swinging the Test England's way. Australia lost Woodfull (19) caught off Mitchell, and Ponsford, caught off Allen for a duck, to be four for 108 at stumps.

On day five, 15 February, the slide continued, as the last six wickets fell for 67, for a total of 175. Only Darling, who was run out for 39, showed any resistance. Allen was the most consistent bowler, not for the first time in the series, taking three for 44. Larwood showed flashes of brilliance with three for 49, while Verity justified his selection with two for 30.

England had 160 to make to take the Ashes. It lost Sutcliffe for 2, caught off Wall, but after that left little to chance. At tea they were one for 45 in 100 minutes' batting. At 5.10 p.m. Jardine, who had batted two hours for 24, was LBW to Ironmonger. England was two for 78.

During the day, news came through from a Brisbane private hospital that Archie Jackson had died from tuberculosis, aged twenty-three. He had moved to Brisbane at the start of the 1932–33 season in the hope of improving his condition, which had been diagnosed in late 1931. The disease undoubtedly hampered Jackson in England in 1930, and cut short a great career.

England coasted to victory next morning. At 118, Ironmonger had Hammond caught for 14. Twenty runs later, Leyland was caught off O'Reilly for 86. Ames (14 not out) and Paynter (14 not out) saw the tourists through to four for 162, giving them a comfortable six-wicket win, and the Ashes.

England had deserved its triumph, with Larwood and Allen proving the best pacemen in the series. Larwood, however, was the real difference. He had worried all the Australian batsmen and while he didn't always take a bag of wickets, his dangerous speed and fine control allowed other bowlers to mop up after him. He had not dominated Bradman, but the methods he employed, particularly bodyline, had helped reduce the champion's effectiveness enough to give England the series.

The Australian team returned to Sydney by train with Jackson's body on board. Two days later, six Australian players — Woodfull, Richardson, Bradman, McCabe, Oldfield and Ponsford — were pall-bearers at his funeral.

DEAD-RUBBER BLUES

The series had produced ill-will all round and there was no frater-nising between the teams off the field, even at official functions. In the TV mini-series about the series, *Bodyline*, made a few years ago, Jessie Bradman was shown dancing with Jardine. 'I never spoke to the man,' she said. 'I had no time for him at all.'

Everyone on both sides, as well as officials and players' wives, wished the series was over. But there was still the Fifth Test to play at Sydney, with as much tension in the air as ever.

England swapped Mitchell for Voce. Australia brought in Old-field, P. K. Lee, Harry 'Bull' Alexander and O'Brien for Love, Wall, Bromley and the unfortunate Ponsford. Lee, an off-spinner, was meant to be a foil for the left-handers Paynter and Leyland, as he would be turning the ball away from them. Alexander was strong, fast and aggressive, and some saw him as an answer to bodyline.

Woodfull won the toss and batted again in weather-threatening conditions, only to see Richardson pat an easy catch to Jardine off the fifth ball from Larwood. Australia was one for 0, with the crowd not yet settled into their seats.

Bradman was greeted by relatively modest applause, mainly because there was little to cheer about in the 'dead rubber' match. It was the first time he had appeared in a Test in Sydney and he started confidently against Larwood, who left his off-side field intact for four overs of real speed in an attempt to remove his old adversary by normal means. It didn't work, so he resorted to one bumpy over of bodyline without success before being spelled.

Woodfull dug in for a long stay and Bradman kept the scoreboard ticking over without producing fireworks. Then Larwood came back for a pre-lunch burst and forced Woodfull (14) to play on. Australia was two for 59.

Larwood's next over to Bradman saw him cutting for four. The following ball was full on the leg-stump. Bradman moved to the off and tried to glance it but missed and was bowled for 48. It had been a fair innings by conventional standards, but nothing like what was expected of him. Bradman had been temporarily reduced to the level of only the world's best and Larwood had been responsible. The England star had claimed his wicket three times in a row, although only once had he got him cheaply. Arthur Mailey commented in his book, — *And Then Came Larwood*:

> *Bradman's innings was interesting from many points of view. [He had] tried almost every conceivable way to combat the Larwood menace. Early in the tour he played his natural game; then he tried defensive tactics, after which he threw discretion to the winds and slammed at everything. Now we found him just a little sub-dued but unorthodox.*

Australia was three for 67 at lunch and in trouble. After the break O'Brien and McCabe moved along nicely, O'Brien surprising by combining attack with his usual solid defence. Only Larwood was shown great respect as the score mounted. He had O'Brien dropped twice by Voce, but the tall left-armer made amends by having the batsman caught for 61. McCabe then joined with Darling, who was again shaping well at Test level, although he too was dropped twice. England's fielding seemed to have lost its edge, now that the pressure was off. However, there was no doubting Jardine's desire to make it a four-one thrashing. McCabe was out caught attempting to drive Verity for 73. He had gone missing since his magnificent First Test knock at Sydney and had come back into form far too late. Oldfield came in for nightwatch duties with Australia on five for 269.

He and Darling were able to see off Larwood and the other pacemen next morning and Oldfield in particular showed great courage after the crack on the skull he had taken from the speedster at Adelaide. Relieved to have got rid of Larwood, however, they relaxed against Verity. He promptly surprised Darling with a yorker and bowled him for 85. Australia was six for 328.

Lee came in for a heave-ho — 'strong arm with a little imagination' he called it — and hit up 42 in thirty-five minutes, which was a rate even Bradman would have been proud of. Australia went to lunch seven for 402, 133 runs having been scored in the ninety-minute session. Oldfield reached his fifty soon after, but then ran himself out trying to shield O'Reilly from Larwood. A bit of agricultural enterprise by O'Reilly at the finish lifted the tally to 435, and at last the home team had posted a respectable tally. Larwood again had the figures — four for 98 off 32.4 overs. Verity earned his keep with three for 62.

England began its innings just before 3 p.m. Jardine, one of the best players of pace in the world, had looked unusually unsettled against Alexander's speed. He was loudly cheered when he delivered one painful blow to the England captain's hip, demonstrating the ugly level to which the series had sunk. Alexander hit Jardine on the shoulder, and he was in trouble. Soon after this softening-up, O'Reilly beat the England skipper with flight and he was caught in slips by Richardson for 18. England was one for 31, and Hammond carried on with Sutcliffe to see the tourists one for 64 at tea. Late in the day, O'Reilly removed Sutcliffe (56), caught once more in slips by Richardson, at 153 and Larwood went in as nightwatchman.

Hammond and Larwood carried on next morning, with Hammond reaching 101 before Lee trapped him LBW. It was his sixth Test century in Australia, and while he was less than half as prolific as in 1928–29, he had still been a key batsman, along with the stubborn Sutcliffe. After lunch, when Larwood was still there with Leyland, Alexander tried bouncing him with four men on the leg-side, the nearest the Australians ever came to bodyline. It failed, and the 'Nottingham Express' showed how to hook and pull speed. With his adrenalin flowing, he then moved into Lee for 14 off one over before the spinner had him caught for 98.

Larwood had been under-rated as a batsman because he was usually reckless when coming in down the order, but his innings had been full of fine shots and he had scored faster than both Hammond and Leyland. His performance inspired the rest. Leyland (42 run out), Wyatt (51), and Allen (48) lifted England's score to 454 on the fourth morning, giving the tourists a lead of 19. They were determined to head their opponents, as they had done in all the Tests except the second at Melbourne, which they lost.

Lee bowled well and only lost control when Larwood briefly went after him, taking four for 111 from forty overs. O'Reilly suffered from poor fielding and dropped catches, but still took three for 100 off forty-five overs.

Australia batted again before lunch as a big crowd filled the ground for the final Larwood-Bradman clash of the summer. Larwood did his bit by bringing his opponent in after the second ball of the innings, when Allen, just five metres from the bat at short-forward square leg, jumped and pulled down a great catch from Richardson.

Bradman looked confident from the start. When Larwood switched to bodyline, Bradman several times stepped back and crashed him through the covers. Larwood took a player from the leg-trap and put him on the off, an acknowledgement that the batsman was mastering him.

At lunch the crowd was about 30,000, with Bradman looking good on 22 in twenty-five minutes at the crease. By the time he walked out with Woodfull again numbers had swollen to nearly 40,000 and the gates were shut for one of the greatest, most aggressive confrontations cricket had seen.

Larwood hit Woodfull on the back of the shoulder. The batsman took two minutes to recover. Bradman was struck a painful blow on the forearm, the only time he had been hit all season. Larwood was now bowling at his fastest for the entire series. Every time he was scored off, he would send down a vicious bouncer. Voce got into the act and hit Woodfull, again on the shoulder. However, the batsmen won through, and at 2.45 p.m. Larwood was taken off after two spells of the most express bowling yet seen at Sydney. The crowd clapped him — or was it the batsmen? — at the end of the stint. Bodyline had been conquered, but too late. Or had it? A second examination came with new bowlers. The batsmen were ready to take advantage of the joy of 'victory' over Larwood, and to a lesser extent Voce.

Bradman now went so hard at Allen that Jardine brought back Larwood, who was not happy about it at all. He had given Mr Jardine his heart and soul with bat and ball. His feet were injured, and he would have been quite happy not to have even played. But here the remorseless skipper was demanding more! Larwood, partly in protest, and partly because he was spent, bowled at medium-pace. Woodfull saw him out and the 100 partnership was reached.

Bradman smote Verity for a couple of fours. Larwood's feet were hurting so much that he asked Jardine if he could leave the field.

'Not as long as that little bastard is still in,' the skipper replied. At 115, Bradman (71) helped his rival out by playing over a surprise yorker from Verity and was bowled.

'You may go now, Harold,' Jardine called. A limping Larwood followed Bradman off the field and into the dressing-rooms. It was a fitting end for the series' chief antagonists. Neither would bat or bowl again in the 1932–33 Ashes.

Verity and Voce then ran through the Australians, who lost nine for 67. Woodfull (67) hung on with his usual courage, but ran out of partners and was eventually bowled by Allen attempting a quick run to keep the strike. The tally of 182 gave them a lead of only 163. Verity took five for 33 off nineteen overs, Voce two for 34, Allen two for 54, and Larwood one for 41.

The fine effort by Verity gave the Australians hope that Ironmonger and O'Reilly might bring off a great victory, but they were not as effective, or, to be fair, the English batsmen played with much more application than their Australian counterparts. The tourists achieved their target of 168 for the loss of just two wickets. Ironmonger removed Jardine for 24 and Leyland for a duck, but Wyatt (64) and Hammond (75) saw them through with ease. The latter hit the winning runs with a six off Lee.

The best Australian performer with the ball in the series was O'Reilly with twenty-seven wickets at an average of 26.81, from a total of 381 overs with an astonishing 143 maidens. Gubby Allen had another fine series (twenty-one wickets at 28.23 off 170 overs), and the oldest player in the series, Ironmonger, did creditably (with fifteen wickets at 27.00 off 245 overs), while Voce (fifteen at 27.13 off 133) and Wall (sixteen at 25.58 off 170) cancelled each other out.

However, the dominant player of the series was Larwood. He took thirty-three wickets at 19.51 off 218 overs with forty-one maidens. His strike-rate of a wicket every seven overs (56 balls), or roughly one per spell at the crease, was far superior to that of any other bowler.

Bradman's clash with Larwood was the key to the series. The bowler dismissed him four times, but Bradman still hit more runs — 151 — off him than any other batsman, including Woodfull, McCabe and Richardson, who all played one more Test than Bradman. Larwood sent down 115 balls to Bradman, whose strike-rate against the bowler was 76.16 runs per 100 balls, which is a faster rate than Australia's Dean Jones in modern one-day cricket. Bradman's strike-rate against the England bowlers overall was 74.85, which was way above that of Darling (60.90), McCabe (59.59), O'Brien (51.78), Richardson (46.73), Kippax (43.54), Bromley (40.24), Ponsford (39.60), Fingleton (32.96), and Woodfull (30.68). His rate in the 1930 series against England had been 61.64.

Importantly, Larwood did not dismiss Bradman once with a bodyline ball which he was forced to fend off. The batsman got himself out with his method of playing and attacking bodyline. Larwood appreciated that Bradman's evasive methods had not allowed him to soften him up, as he had all the other batsmen. Once hurt, bruised or worse, a player became unsure. His feet would not move as much or correctly. Larwood might not always take the wicket, but he was in part very often responsible for it.

When Warwick Armstrong wrote during the series that Bradman was 'scared of Larwood' and 'no more than a cocktail cricketer', for the way he played bodyline, Larwood himself refuted the accusations. In his book *Bodyline?*, published in 1933, a few months after the end of the series, he wrote:

> *Let me assure my readers that when bowling to [Bradman] my share of the battle was certainly not one of brute force and something ignorant. The bowler who is confronted by Bradman and*

doesn't think, doesn't bowl for long. Mere getting rid of the ball, leg-side bumpers for example, cuts very little ice when in opposition to such a cool and practised player as Don. That fellow is a very long way from being the 'cocktail cricketer' which Warwick Armstrong in a rather uncouth sneer styled him last season. Apart from his wonderful eye and wrists Don has a very quick thinking brain. To him, leg-side bumpers would be mere gifts for four as often as any bowler was fool enough, and incompetent enough, to serve them up.

Not for the first time, Armstrong's judgement was awry, and inept, especially for someone who had had such experience in Test-match cricket. Certainly the two main antagonists were much sharper, and yet more subtle, than the former Australian captain in their analysis of each other, which is understandable. Armstrong never bowled to Bradman or faced Larwood.

FACTS, DAMNED STATISTICS AND TRUTHS

England had won the series four-one thanks to Jardine's iron-rod captaincy and Larwood's great bowling, which included the use of the most destructive method against batsmen since the Ashes began more than fifty years earlier. Jardine's captaincy had been superior to Woodfull's in both strategy and tactics, but it remained to be seen if it would represent a continued winning style.

Jardine's dictatorial approach, outstanding strategic and tactical skill and obsessive 'hate' of Bradman had engineered an unimagined outcome for the visitors.

Bradman was certain he had employed the only possible tactics in terms of run-scoring against bodyline. His average for the series of 56.57 was better than any main batsman in eight innings or more on either side, and his aggregate of 396 was third only to Hammond and Sutcliffe, who each tallied 440 at an average of 55.00. Yet since they each played one more innings than Bradman, his aggregate per Test (99) was higher than both. Bradman was the only player to reach 50 in at least one innings of each Test he played. He also reached that score four times from eight knocks, as opposed to Hammond and Sutcliffe, each four times from nine. By any measure, he was the best and most consistent batsman of the bodyline series. Given his opponents, he was even more outstanding. No Australian got near him in playing Larwood, Allen, Verity and Voce. McCabe with 385 runs at 42.77 did respectably, but he was not consistent after his blazing start of 187 not out. Despite Woodfull's great courage and consistency, he scored only 305, averaging 33.88. Richardson, another player with intestinal fortitude, managed only 279 at 27.90. Ponsford's six innings yielded just 141 at 23.50, while Fingleton hit 150 at 25.00.

In the 1932–33 series Bradman's average still beat that of the complete Ashes careers of some of the finest batsmen ever on either side, including such England players as Percy Chapman (35.00); Denis Compton (42.83); Hammond (51.85); Hobbs (54.26); F. S. Jackson (48.79); Jardine (31.76); K. S. Ranjitsinhji (44.77); F. E. Woolley (33.28); and Bob Wyatt (33.31). For Australia, Warwick Armstrong ended with 35.03; Fairfax, 53.75; Fingleton, 31.95; Lindsay Hassett, 38.34; Clem Hill, 35.46; Kippax, 34.22; Charlie Macartney, 43.15; McCabe, 48.27; Arthur Morris, 50.73; Monty Noble, 30.72; Ponsford, 47.21; Jack Ryder, 44.16; and Woodfull, 44.07.

Nevertheless, Bradman's aggregate and average had been literally cut by half in 1932–33 by Larwood's bowling, and the effect of bodyline in particular. No batsman in history could have prevailed against Larwood employing those tactics. Perhaps the brilliant and hardheaded Viv Richards would have tried, but even he would have failed. If it is dubious to transport different players through eras, then one should perhaps try to imagine Richards facing Lillee and Thomson at their peak speeds with bodyline fields on fast Australian wickets. He failed in 1975–76 against orthodox bowling by these two, so his performance would most likely have been reduced further — that is, if they had been allowed to have five in the leg-trap and two in the deep while bowling their lethal deliveries into the ribcage and head.

Fred Trueman in the 1960s and Richard Hadlee in the 1980s,

because of their great pace, accuracy and control, also would have been impossible opponents with bodyline, not to mention Malcolm Marshall and Curtly Ambrose. Ask any batsman from Gower and Gooch to the Chappell brothers and Border how they felt about the West Indies of the 1970s and 1980s, without bodyline. Then ask them how they would have fared with those bowlers employing it. As it was, the West Indians went too far with short deliveries and the law was changed to restrict the number per over. The head-high bumper was prohibited altogether in one-day cricket.

Bradman's view of bodyline was the most perceptive. He warned that it would lead to each side stacking its team with speed merchants hell-bent on breaking ribs on a bad day and heads on a good one. While this brought spectators to the game for the 1932–33 bodyline series, in time attendances would have dwindled. Shot-making such as driving, cutting and glancing would have been out. Only the hook and pull to leg, unless a player had Bradman's eye, would be left. No amount of padding and head-covering would have avoided the pulverising of a batsman, let alone non-batsman.

Furthermore, bodyline was already being introduced and copied at lower levels of the game, with all the resultant injuries that might be expected from it. No other player at the Test level had Bradman's speed of reflexes to avoid being struck. This meant that batsmen at lower levels of the game were certain to be struck sooner or later by any halfway accurate or moderately quick bodyline practitioner, some seriously. Many felt it was a fluke that no-one had been killed in 1932–33. In the medium term, the great game of cricket would have been reduced to absurdity.

But in February 1933, the MCC naturally rejoiced in Jardine's and his team's great success. They had won under the rules as they stood and were heroes in the eyes of the British public. The larger question was, if bodyline continued, would cricket be the winner?

The celebrations turned sour even before Jardine and the team returned home, when F. R. Foster, one of several people consulted on 'fast-leg-theory' before the Australian tour, attacked the England captain.

'Douglas Jardine, I am ashamed of England's win,' Foster told the media. 'I will face you on your return with these words on my lips.'

Foster disassociated himself from bodyline and was incensed with being linked with it after his successful tour of Australia in 1911–12, when he did so well using physically unthreatening leg theory. He went further and called for the sacking of Jardine, suggesting Gubby Allen should captain England.

The greatest controversy and threat to the game was about to become a serious issue in the home of cricket.

27

AFTER THE ASHES, MORE DUST

In the face of it all he carried on and he triumphed.
— A. G. MOYES, COMMENTING ON BRADMAN IN THE BODYLINE SERIES

MALICE AN AFTERTHOUGHT

Bradman kept his employment options open during 1933 when approached by English professional teams such as Ramsbottom and Rochdale. He rejected the offers, but said he would be in a better position in early 1934, when his current work commitments would be over. If he were to play league cricket in England, it would clash with the scheduled 1934 Ashes tour, but with cables flying between the MCC and the Board of Control over bodyline, Bradman could not be sure there would be a series.

After the 1932–33 series, the Board of Control kept the pressure on the MCC in an attempt to have bodyline outlawed by giving umpires the power to take action against bowlers who resorted to it. The MCC was in a dilemma. They had appointed Jardine and had backed his methods to curb Bradman, which had succeeded to the extent of securing the Ashes. If they agreed with the Board of Control they would be betraying Jardine. The MCC procrastinated and suggested that the matter be deferred until after the Australians arrived in April 1934. The Board persisted through its vigorous representative in

311

London, Dr Robert Macdonald. The pressure mounted in June 1933, when the Governor of South Australia, Sir Alexander Hore-Ruthven, wrote to the British Secretary for the Dominions, James Thomas, putting the Australian side of the dispute and informing him of the depth of feeling about the issue in Australia.

'That feeling,' Hore-Ruthven wrote, 'rankles even to the extent of reluctance to buy English goods, which businessmen inform me is going on to a certain extent in this city [Adelaide] today.' Thomas showed the letter to his British Government cabinet colleague, Lord Hailsham, the MCC's president.

In his book, *Follow On*, the English cricket writer E. W. Swanton referred to a letter in which Lord Hawke, an MCC Board member, was quoted as saying that the real problem was how to prevent bodyline recurring 'without letting down Douglas Jardine too badly'.

The problem was exacerbated within days when the West Indies team touring the UK used bodyline tactics against Jardine's team. Two bowlers, Constantine and Griffith, who were not in Larwood's class, gave the England bats a pummelling in the Second Test at Manchester. Several players were bruised and Hammond had his chin split open. He was so upset that he said he would retire from first-class cricket if bodyline was not stopped. Jardine, however, batted gutsily for 127 against it and naturally, rather than complain, said 'leg theory' was a legitimate tactic. Nevertheless, he could not fight back hard with it. His main strike weapon, Larwood, was injured. He had not recovered from his breakdown in Australia, which had been caused by the extreme demands upon him.

The West Indies bowling caused Plum Warner to tell the UK *Daily Telegraph* that bodyline was creating 'anger, hatred and malice'.

HUMANITY UNLOCKED?

Bradman spent the Australian winter of 1933 attempting to keep fit, despite intermittent abdominal pains and 'dispiriting languor', which had dogged him since before the bodyline series. Doctors were mystified and could only prescribe relaxation. But he was just turning twenty-five with a solid year of cricket possibly in front of him.

In August, he taxed his mind rather than his body by sitting for and passing an examination on the laws of cricket set by the NSW Umpires' Association. His keenness on the laws and the betterment of the game, as already mentioned, had seen him earlier in the year — at the height of the bodyline crisis — write to the MCC humbly suggesting that batsmen using their pads against balls pitched outside the line of the off-stump should be judged LBW if, in the umpire's opinion, the delivery were going to hit the wicket. Such a law would not have been in the interests of batsmen, but made for better and brighter cricket as it would have forced bats to play the ball. It was several decades before his advice was belatedly heeded and such a rule was introduced.

Bradman himself needed no such encouragement to strike the leather as he began his seventh Shield season with a dazzling 200 in 184 minutes against Queensland at Brisbane. This innings made something of a prophet of Neville Cardus, who predicted Bradman would be an even better performer after the way he tackled bodyline. In an article entitled 'Bradman Becomes Human', he wrote:

> [Bradman] has at last escaped from bondage to his own tech-niques; he is now able to go beyond it, to send his spirits into the unknown. An artist should be free to transcend his skill, take brave chancy flights a little higher than he knows his wings will take him . . . Larwood has wakened up the spirit of Bradman, and transformed him from a worker by the book of arithmetic into a romantic lover of hazards . . .

In the midst of this thicket of mixed metaphors, Cardus had managed to hit upon one possible point. Bradman had come through the bodyline series with an even wider intelligence on the game.

Was his batting demonstrating that now? Certainly in that opening innings he had not hit 100 in about 130 minutes, which was his norm at a season's start, but instead had crashed his first century in ninety-two minutes. Bradman went on to smash twenty-four boundaries and it seemed a dramatic continuation of the unorthodoxy learned in the previous summer. He threw in a fair bit of cross-bat, and when a bowler tried 'off theory' Bradman gave him the reverse Larwood treatment, by pulling outside the off-stump and hoicking him into the vacant leg field.

However, Bradman would not always bat this way and at such a pace. He still batted with exceptional concentration and control, but now the excitement of the smashing six or loft into the deep, which had been largely buried since his Bowral days, or only unearthed in country exhibitions, was perhaps more of an option than before. Whether he would exploit this option would depend on his mood, the game he was in and the situation.

There was a negative side to this development. If he carried the 'gay cavalier' approach (as A. G. Moyes called it) into Tests beyond the bodyline series and into the 1934 Ashes Tests in England as Cardus was urging, it could prove his downfall and be disastrous for Australia. It would naturally please Cardus, who was not above the odd psychological ploy for his country. Most English journalists and the British public would be happy if Bradman went on scoring bright, brilliant 70s, and Australia kept losing.

Cardus and Bradman were friends and dined together on occasions. But Bradman was not impressed by this analysis. 'What about 1930?' he remarked, 'I scored 309 in a day in a Test. I couldn't have scored any quicker than that.'

Apparently Cardus had become a lover of some lusty lofting in the short, sharp knock. Too many of them would get any batsman, let alone Bradman, into trouble with selectors at Test level.

It was different in the Shield competition. Bradman's opening 200 in 1933–34, for instance, turned into an exhibition game against the mediocre Queenslanders. If he 'failed' there was always O'Reilly to reduce the opposition to losing scores. In that match the spinner took three for 92 and an incredible nine for 50, to give NSW a win by an innings and 171 runs.

Yet in the big games against a powerful England side, Bradman would need to make those gigantic scores as he had in 1930, if Australia were to have a chance. The 'gay cavalier' could easily become the 'buffoon dragoon' in the eyes of a fickle media and public if another Ashes series was lost.

In a Test trial match between V. Y. Richardson's XI and W. M. Woodfull's XI at Melbourne starting on 18 November, Bradman scored 55 and 101, but was strangely sedate in making the early part of his century. Both Woodfull and Fingleton got tons. In another trial game (NSW versus Rest of Australia) a few days later in Sydney, he was dismissed by leg-spinner Hughie Chilvers for 22. In the second innings, he had the unusual experience of faltering at 92 and dragged on a ball from Hans Ebeling, while McCabe and Woodfull scored centuries.

Meanwhile, cables were flashed across the world in an attempt to sort out the bodyline controversy. The tough Board of Control chairman, Dr Robertson, was adamant about securing assurances that bodyline would be outlawed in 1934. Otherwise, the tour would not go ahead. The MCC held its ground. It would not capitulate by making specific provisions to outlaw bodyline, but it assured the Board it agreed that bowling 'which is obviously a direct attack by the bowler upon the batsman would be an offence against the spirit of the game'.

Fortunately for the Ashes and the fifty-six years of contest that had gone before, Robertson retired as chairman in 1933 and was replaced by the conservative lawyer Aubrey Oxlade, who felt the tour had to go ahead, as long as the MCC came halfway, as it had. He engineered an agreement without either party giving ground, and without any specific commitments.

It was finally announced on 12 December, a few days before an MCC deadline, that the Australians would sail for the UK on 9 March. Before the season began the MCC would have to find a way of handling the 'Jardine' problem. In short, to ensure harmony, they would have to persuade him that it would be in the best interests of all concerned if he did not captain the side in 1934. Oxlade was awarded a CBE for his pains in the 1934 New Year's honours.

Bradman couldn't quite celebrate the news in Adelaide three days later when he was bowled for 1 by F. H. Collins in a Shield game against South Australia. However, he stayed around in the second effort long enough to challenge Grimmett, but the wily old leggie won the day by having him caught for 76 after a chancy knock. This enabled SA to win by ten wickets, with Grimmett taking five for 103 in NSW's second innings.

On 23 December, Bradman got back into stride with another sterling effort against Victoria at the MCG. His 187 not out in 295 minutes was a great innings of a different sort. In this game he received little support and had to mix attack with defence, while farming the strike as wickets tumbled to Fleetwood-Smith, who took seven for 148. Bradman hit 77 not out in his second dig in the drawn game.

Oxenham was the only Test bowler in the Queensland side in the return match with NSW over the New Year, and Bradman took unmerciful advantage of it with a crushing 253. His double century took 185 minutes — one more minute than he had taken in his previous 200 against the unfortunate northern State. He moved from 200 to 250 in a mere sixteen minutes, before being bowled by Brew. The 363 partnership (172 minutes) with Kippax (125) for the third wicket was the highest ever by Australians anywhere. Bradman again showed he was prepared to be audacious by slamming four sixes and twenty-nine fours. These performances were in keeping with his previous appearances against that State, with the addition of some lofting. Needless to say, NSW's six for 614 declared allowed it to win by an innings and 84 runs.

Bradman was periodically unwell through the season. It made his busy cricket schedule and three areas of work very demanding. Jessie eased the strain in her role as wife, nurse and assistant. He was fortunate to have such a strong and loving companion when their fourteen-year relationship as childhood friends, lovers and marriage partners entered such a testing time. Jessie even drafted his writing and broadcast material. 'I would take notes at the matches,' she recalled. 'That meant Don wouldn't have to worry about that while he was playing.'

They were both much relieved to see the contracts with 2UE, Associated Newspapers and Palmer's coming to an end in early 1934, when he would also be able to take a short break from cricket.

On the outside, Bradman was the nation's greatest legend. Most

Australians from prime ministers down had set 'The Don' on a pedestal. He was public property, whether he liked it or not, and he did not. Cardus didn't help in articles published in Australia and Britain after the bodyline series with comments such as:

> *The great point about it all is that Bradman, who once was scarcely human, is now definitely human, and therefore greater than ever. We have admired him in the past; now we shall begin to watch him with something warmer than admiration.*

Other observers had no doubts. Bradman was a god. Fallible yes, but a living idol. Such excessive adulation put extra strains on the private lives of two young people struggling to make their way in tough times. The public did not perceive that he and Jessie might have problems, worries, emotions and personal tensions. Some, for example, could not quite believe that Bradman was suffering an illness. Because it wasn't specified, it was not quite credible and it was viewed by many as an excuse, especially as every so often he would spend long periods in very physical batting performances. Those exertions might take up twenty-four publicised hours at the crease in half a year, and they gave a distorted view of the man.

It all meant that Sydney was stifling for the Bradmans, and they enjoyed escaping to see their families and friends at Bowral and elsewhere.

Bradman started the last game of the season against Victoria on 26 January 1934 with a severe recurrence of abdominal pain. This retarded his innings and made him go ultra-cautiously in reaching 10 in thirty-eight minutes. Once warmed up, he cut loose to add 40 in nineteen minutes to reach his fifty in fifty-seven minutes. After an hour he was in a ferocious hitting mood. His second fifty took seconds under half an hour giving him a century in eighty-seven minutes. He ended with 128 in only ninety-six minutes. Once he had overcome the illness, his extra dimension of big-hitting continued with four sixes, three of them in the last over from Fleetwood-Smith, who had him caught in the deep. It seemed as if he was giving his wicket to the

Victorian spinner. He kept heaving the ball high into the outfield as if giving catching practice.

Bradman had scored 645 in four successive innings — 187 not out, 77 not out, 253 and 128 — which passed his own State record. He headed the aggregates (1,192) and averages (132.44) for the first-class season. He, Woodfull and Kippax each scored four centuries. Kippax was making a bid to tour after a dip in his career over the past year.

FAREWELL TO SYDNEY

That blistering knock against Victoria was a fitting farewell to his great career with NSW. Once his job contract expired, Bradman was able to explore his options. He was set to tour England now that bodyline had been shoved under the carpet, which meant he could not play with a professional club. The Sydney *Sun* had offered him an attractive permanent contract, but this did not have maximum appeal. He would still be eating, playing, writing and sleeping cricket and he still dearly wanted somehow to separate his sport from work. He didn't mind his journalism, but as a player he was restricted and there were many experienced competitors. The radio broadcasts were an 'experience', and he coped, yet again he was restricted. People tuned in to hear 'The Don's' cogent remarks, but he wasn't a natural raconteur. His work in promotions at Palmer's was an up-market version of his operations at Mick Simmons, which had never suited his style and predilections.

A solution to his problems appeared when a member of the Board of Control, Harry Hodgetts, offered him a career in stockbroking. It gave Bradman the opportunity to test his skills in a field of facts and figures, which was something he had always been interested in. Hodgetts was a broker in Adelaide, which meant that the Bradmans would have to move to that city. On the one hand, this would take them far away from family and friends. On the other, it could allow the young married couple to avoid the glare of publicity that the home-State 'boy' was daily subjected to. They would be able to make a fresh start away from all that, even if they could never properly escape constant public scrutiny.

Don and Jessie decided to make the break. Bradman signed a six-year contract with Hodgetts. He could continue his cricket career from district level with Kensington Club in Adelaide right up to representing Australia. His salary would be £700 a year, reduced to £500 when he toured abroad. It was an exciting new challenge, and Bradman, at twenty-five years of age, looked forward to learning the business of stocks and shares, bears, bulls, puts and options.

Shortly after the negotiations were completed and the Bradmans moved to Adelaide, the Australian selectors announced their team for the 1934 tour of England. Those with Test experience were Woodfull, Ponsford, Bradman, McCabe, Kippax, Oldfield, Grimmett, O'Reilly, Wall, Bromley and Darling. The new faces were Ben Barnett (the second keeper), W. A. 'Bill' Brown, Arthur Chipperfield, Ebeling and Fleetwood-Smith.

Fingleton and Richardson were considered unlucky to miss out, but the selectors had one eye on the future and frowned on Richardson's thirty-nine years. Fingleton, on the other hand, blamed Bradman for not getting in the side. When I asked Bradman if there were any truth in this, he replied:

> *I wasn't a selector or captain then, but I always thought Billy Brown was a better opener than Fingleton and that he would do better on English soil. This proved correct in '34, '38 and '48. I may have expressed this to selectors at the time [1934].*

This partly explained Fingleton's instigation of what became a long-running feud with Bradman. He went to the trouble of writing a book on Victor Trumper pointing out why he was a better batsman than Bradman. This was some challenge. Trumper's average and aggregate in Tests were both about one-third of Bradman's. Fingleton suggested that Trumper didn't like big scores and that he wanted to get out at 50, although the journalist failed to explain how Trumper came to score a triple century against a county — something Bradman never managed.

Woodfull would captain again, but the mild surprise was

319

Bradman's selection as his deputy. Yet it was an intelligent choice given his relative youth. Kippax again was to have a role as the third selector, a tough situation seeing he would not be an automatic choice in the Test team.

Its possible composition did not look strong on paper. Bradman, Woodfull, Ponsford, Grimmett, O'Reilly and McCabe were proven class in the batting and bowling departments at the top level. But the rest were a gamble. It meant that pressure would be on the 'names' to perform at their top if Australia was to have even a fair chance of taking the series.

If Bradman had been fully fit the betting would have been more firmly on the tourists. But through all the preparation for change and touring, his nagging, debilitating sickness remained. A specialist recommended he not play any more cricket until he reached England in late April 1934.

28

IN SICKNESS AND IN HEALTH

*Set a field for Bradman? Twenty-two men would not have been
enough to plug all the holes he found in our run-saving
barbed-wire entanglements during his masterpiece.*
— MIDDLESEX CAPTAIN H. J. ENTHOVEN AFTER BRADMAN HAD HIT 100
IN 75 MINUTES IN 1934

JARDINE OF DISCONTENT

The Australians arrived in England to learn that Douglas Jardine
had announced from India that he did not wish to lead England
against Australia in the Ashes series. Rather than inform the MCC
first, he released a statement to the London *Evening Standard*: 'I have
neither the intention nor the desire to play cricket against Australia
this summer.'

It was curt, even churlish, but Jardine felt abandoned by the
MCC, whom he had served loyally by winning the Ashes, as desired.
He had been prompted to his decision by the change in the MCC's
policy on bodyline bowling, which he would have been prevented
from introducing in the series. Jardine had been left in an untenable
situation. He felt that his captaincy would be restricted. Worse than
that, the MCC's new position was tantamount to a condemnation of
his leadership in Australia. He felt betrayed. It upset him and then

angered him. Jardine, the man with 'iron in his soul', could not fully comprehend the criticism of his tactics.

What would have rankled most was not the press, or the Board of Control cables or even the implication that he had been unsports-manlike, but the fact that his main adversary, 'that little bugger' Bradman, had won the day. It was his vehement protest against body-line behind the scenes that had influenced the MCC more than any other single factor.

Jardine could not accept the Australian's view that the game would be destroyed by 'fast leg theory'. But the English experience of being on the receiving end of it in 1933 had persuaded many people that bodyline was a blot on cricket. Jardine's decision to opt out was the honourable thing to do, for to stay on and demand the captaincy would have split the MCC and enraged the tourists. If he were refused the leadership, it would be an insufferable humiliation.

His decision left Harold Larwood out on a limb. He would be fit enough to bowl in 1934, and the speedster wanted to get at the Australians again. But he would not play if disarmed. He had to have the option of using bodyline again. Otherwise, his honour too would be in question. Worse, he would be at the mercy of Bradman's bat as he was in 1930. English wickets were not as fast as Australian, and Larwood knew Bradman would be able to handle him with less diffi-culty in England, even with bodyline. Larwood made plain that he had no intention of being 'humiliated' again as he was at Leeds and The Oval.

'I didn't want to play against them if it meant I was going to be hit all over the field,' Larwood wrote. '. . . I had humbled them on their own pitches, and I didn't want them to humble me in England, especially as they said I was unfair.'

ON FIRE AT WORCESTERSHIRE

Woodfull sent Bradman out to bat in the opening tour game at Worcester against the player's wishes. He had left the *Orford*, on which the tourists had travelled over, looking tanned and apparently fit, but after a week in England his health had deteriorated to the point where he did not think he was well enough to play. The skipper, however, wanted his star weapon out there making runs in the first game and looking ready for action in the Ashes. It was important to send a message to the opposition: Bradman was fit and ready for the big contests.

The ploy was necessary because Bradman was beginning to look frail and a little emaciated, which was being picked up in photographs. It would be useful to Australia's cause if he could go to the crease and be . . . Bradman.

Worcester batted first and was dismissed long before tea for 112, Grimmett doing the damage with five for 53. The overcoated spectators stayed on in the cool afternoon in the hope they would see Bradman. Ponsford played his part by staying only half an hour before being caught for 13.

The contingent of media people — 109 journalists, fifty-seven photographers, and two film crews — were watching closely as he emerged from the pavilion with his hallmark swagger amid an air of excitement, which the New Road ground had not experienced since his last visit in 1930. Bradman's first tour innings in England was now a national event.

He began with a push to the on for a single. In the next over, he was lucky to avoid playing on, and then spent an uncomfortable twenty-two-minute period before tea. The consensus was that he began 'shakily', which seemed to confirm the rumours that he was unwell, and not capable of performing the feats of four years earlier. After tea, however, perhaps because of his favourite concoction, he looked like the twenty-one-year-old many at the ground under the Cathedral had seen thump, cut, drive, hook and glance his way to 236. His fifty came up in sixty-two minutes and critics noted three points. There was a fraction more urgency in his play; he was more inclined to hit over the top of the field; and if it were possible, he seemed even more self-assured, in keeping with his four years' extra maturity and experience.

The lofting was in keeping with a tendency first evidenced in the bodyline series, which had continued through 1933–34. Bradman was a young man in more of a hurry than ever. This attitude was partly engendered by personal worries about his stamina. He wanted big scores on the board before that puzzling fatigue and illness would set in. The century came and went in the course of a few glances at the scoreboard. It took him 104 minutes, a quarter of an hour quicker than in 1930.

At 102, the keeper fumbled a ball which spun past Bradman's bat, and may have been a chance, but that was the only near thing when he went to stumps on 112 not out. The morning papers speculated whether he would repeat his 1930 effort of a double hundred. Bradman himself was glad of the overnight rest and proceeded to steam into the bowling, lofting, late-cutting, driving and pulling his way to 200 in 198 minutes. He then jumped into every ball and threw his wicket away, bowled for 206 — something that would have been rare on the last tour. The malady that hung over him meant he had to conserve his strength. Yet no-one else, English or Australian, had ever opened two English seasons with double centuries. On top of that, his five first-class innings so far in the calendar year 1934 had realised 851 runs — 187 not out, 77 not out, 253, 128 and now 206 — the best run of his career to date.

The other batsmen — Woodfull (48), Ponsford (13), Kippax (0), McCabe (20) and Bromley (45) — did little to enthuse, although Oldfield performed well with 67. If first impressions were lasting, then Australia, despite Bradman, would be struggling, as many had predicted, to win the Ashes back. The bowling combination of O'Reilly (four for 25) and Grimmett (five for 27) in Worcester's second innings of 95 sent another signal to the opposition. Some of the batting might be suspect, but these magicians with the ball would have to be overcome if England were to retain that little urn locked away in a glass cabinet at Lord's.

REVERSALS OF FORTUNE

The next match at Leicester, which was drawn, saw O'Reilly take seven for 39, in dismissing the county for 152. He was loving the

English conditions. Then McCabe (108 not out) and Kippax (89) found form. Bradman maintained his touch with a fifty in little over an hour, but when he was on 65, George Geary, a prospect for a Test return, bowled him with a fast out-swinger.

In the third first-class game against Cambridge University, Bradman made headlines by scoring his first duck in England, bowled by J. G. W. Davies, a slow off-spinner, when Ponsford and Grimmett should have been making the big news for scoring 229 not out and taking nine for 74 respectively.

In the next match against the MCC at Lord's, the press sniffed something was wrong when Bradman managed only 5 before being caught and bowled by Freddie Brown. This time Ponsford (281 not out) and McCabe (192) swamped the headlines as Australia amassed five for 559 declared. The pair broke the world record partnership for the third wicket in making 389. Wyatt showed touch for the MCC in scoring 72 and 102 not out, while Patsy Hendren, at forty-five years of age, put up his hand for Test selection with 135.

Bradman's next knock of 37 against Oxford was an ordinary effort, but he came away with the satisfaction of winning his first match as captain by an innings and 33 runs. Ponsford (75) continued his return to form and Darling hit a 'don't forget me' 100. Grimmett reminded everyone that his form was holding by taking seven for 109.

Bradman's illness was hampering him, and when he scored a second duck for the season, this time against Hampshire at Southampton (caught off the very fast A. E. G. Baring), his tally was 313 from six innings at an average of 52.16. There was no chance now of the magic 1,000 by the end of May. It was disconcerting for him and the team as the First Test loomed on the horizon. McCabe showed his big leap forward from 1930, while Darling's 96 and Chipperfield's 116 not out were encouraging. But psychologically what the tourists needed now was not so much a solid double century from Ponsford or a gutsy ton from Woodfull as some great theatre from Bradman. The moment came when they met Middlesex at Lord's on 26 May.

Middlesex was all out for 258, with Hendren hitting 115 and booking his place in the England side. Grimmett likewise ensured his position in the Australian side with five for 27. The tourists batted against the giant (193 cm) Jim Smith, who beat Woodfull for pace with his second ball, getting him LBW. This brought Bradman onto the arena, much to the delight of the big crowd, who had stayed all day in the hope of glimpsing him. It was after five o'clock, yet people kept arriving at Lord's, once it was learned that Bradman was taking block.

Big Smith lumbered in and shaved his stumps with two swift deliveries. Bradman seemed sadly out of sorts. 'I had a duck in the last innings,' he recalled. 'Consequently, I wasn't confident.' But at least his sense of humour had not deserted him.

'What does a man do when he's out of luck, Patsy?' he asked Hendren in slips.

'Have a bash,' Hendren grinned, 'Have a go! You've nothing to lose.'

Bradman took the advice to heart. Smith trapped Ponsford, also for nought, whereupon Bradman retaliated by launching into both him and the young P. F. Judge, who was playing in his first match. The timing that had gone walkabout for weeks suddenly came back, and with it power, as he despatched balls through the covers, straight past the bowler, round to leg, down through the slips, and just for good measure, square past point and his trademark pull to mid-wicket. The opposition captain, H. J. Enthoven, juggled his field but he could not plug the gaps. 'The bowling was being scientifically liquidated,' Cardus wrote. 'Ball after ball crashed into the white fencing, by far the majority of them in an arc between cover-point and mid-off, the finest shot in cricket.'

Middlesex was paying for The Don's recent run of lowish scores. Ian Peebles came on bowling his leggies, and Bradman hooked three fours off him in five balls, racing through 50 in forty-nine minutes. The half-century seemed to be the signpost that urged him to put his foot down hard on the accelerator. Out went that left leg at full stretch down the pitch as Bradman drove on.

After an hour he was 74 not out. The crowd was enthralled. Could he get a century tonight? Bradman needed 25 runs in twelve minutes. Then it was just 19 with three overs to go before the umpires would flick off the bails. A run a ball. Bradman thumped Peebles square to the tavern for four. Two balls later, with the other batsman, Darling, now running singles to give his superior the strike, Bradman hammered a ball off the back foot through mid-on. Next ball he pulled one to square leg. His tally reached 94. Thirteen balls to go, and again in an atmosphere like a one-dayer. In the second-last over Bradman ran a single, but tight bowling stopped him from taking the strike. The clock ticked over to 6.29 p.m. One over to go and five to get.

Peebles was bowling. Bradman pushed back the first three balls. Were they that good? Or was 'The Don' just teasing the crowd? The next one, according to Cardus, gave him away, for Bradman nonchalantly stroked it past cover-point for four. 'The ball looked exactly the same as the other three,' Cardus noted.

He was on 99. Two balls to go and one run to get. Number five was on a good length. 'Bradman played it with exaggerated care, firm-footed and with a dead bat, disdaining to look for a run,' Cardus scribbled. 'The clock jerked to half past six.'

Peebles ambled in and speared in a faster one. Bradman pushed it just wide of mid-on and the batsmen scurried through. He had made it — a century on the last ball — including nineteen fours in just seventy-seven minutes. The crowd jumped the fence and mobbed him. He was grinning as he trotted off the field through a corridor of back-thumping hands.

The next day, his third-wicket stand of 132 with Darling (37) was soon broken, but a refreshed Bradman kept on for another forty-seven minutes, walloping another 60 runs. He was out smashing Peebles high to long-on, where a fieldsman (Hulme) took a sensational running catch near the boundary, rolling down the hill in front of the pavilion. Bradman's 160 had taken only 124 minutes. He hit a six, a five and twenty-seven fours — 119 in boundaries or 74 per cent of his total. So good was his placement that despite the occasional loft, he gave not even a hint of a chance.

Australia's 345 didn't seem enough to win in two days, but there was Grimmett. Whenever Bradman did great things with the bat, Grimmett would invariably match them with the ball. This time he took five for 27, and Middlesex was mown down for 114. Australia won by ten wickets.

Those who witnessed Bradman's innings had no doubts about the man's heightened powers even compared with 1930. No bowler in history, it was said, could have stopped him on that brilliant late-spring Saturday evening in North London. Whether he empowered himself depended largely on his mood at the time, which in turn was influenced by his physical condition.

Surrey was the next contestant at The Oval on 30 May, where one A. Sandham made a name for himself, hitting 219, with R. J. Gregory making 116, out of the county's seven for 475 declared. Australia replied and replied . . . scoring 629. McCabe was magnificent with 240, filling the breach left by Bradman in the big-scoring department, as was Ponsford, who made 125. Bradman, still off-colour, hit 77 of a 130-run partnership with McCabe, after the latter had opened up with Ponsford and they had chalked up 239. Bradman's fifty was the fastest of the match — in fifty minutes — and he had an untroubled time after the long wait in the pavilion. The game, purely practice with the First Test at Trent Bridge, Nottingham, one week away, was drawn.

LARWOOD'S TERMS OF ENDEARMENT

Larwood meanwhile had been struggling to get back fitness and pace after his long lay-off since breaking down in the last game of the bodyline series. He wanted to play in the First Test but decided to make himself unavailable, claiming lack of match fitness. His captain at Notts, Arthur Carr, had advised this, the strategy being that public demand would see him reinstated in the side for the Second Test, but on his terms, which meant he would be able to set his own fields, and therefore bowl bodyline.

To this point, Larwood understood the MCC's terms. A Notts

member, Sir Julien Cahn, had passed on to the paceman that if he wanted to be selected, he first would have to apologise to the MCC for bowling bodyline in Australia, and undertake not to employ it again. Larwood regarded this as treating him like a naughty school-boy, and he was not prepared to demean himself in such a manner. Better, he agreed with Carr, to sit out the First Test, and then to be invited to play again, without restrictions.

England chose Geary and Kenneth Farnes, making his first Test appearance, to lead the attack, with slow bowlers Verity and Mitchell. Ames was to keep, and the strong batting line-up comprised Cyril Walters, Sutcliffe, Hammond, Pataudi, Leyland and Hendren. Walters, the Worcestershire amateur, was to captain the side in place of Bob Wyatt, who had broken his thumb. It was Walters' first Test, and he had a tough task, especially as he would have felt inferior to old campaigners such as Sutcliffe, Hammond and Hendren.

Australia's batting order was Woodfull, Ponsford, Brown, Brad-man, McCabe, Darling, Chipperfield (making his debut), Oldfield, Grimmett, O'Reilly and Wall. The tourists appeared strong in bat-ting, but very limited in bowling. No-one doubted the great skills of Grimmett and O'Reilly, but after them it was extremely thin, espe-cially when McCabe would be asked to open the bowling with Wall.

Woodfull won the toss on 8 June and batted. He and Ponsford got off to a sound start with 77 before Farnes, a school-teacher, had the Australian skipper, also a man of the chalk, caught for 26. Fifteen minutes later the fast-medium bowler struck again and removed Ponsford, caught behind for 53. Farnes had not been billed as top speed, but he had found an extra yard for the big contest and was bowling with plenty of fire.

Bradman walked out to a respectful reception from the 15,000 present, which built to cheering as he reached the wicket. A handful in the crowd were hostile because they thought he was responsible for the omission of their home-town heroes Larwood and Voce from the England team. Bradman was receiving 'hate' mail. Some of the letters bore Nottingham postmarks.

However, any residual feeling soon subsided as the Notts crowd imbibed the world's batting champion, who scored 11 in the six minutes he was at the wicket prior to lunch. After the interval, his mind seemed to be back at Lord's against Middlesex delivering that blinding performance, for he continued to force the pace in a hectic manner. He hit six fours and raced to 29 in thirty-one balls and twenty-nine minutes. Then his innings ended just as spectacularly when he deflected a ball from Geary to Ames. It popped out of Ames' gloves and Hammond at slip grasped it.

Australia was three for 125. Lifted by taking the prize wicket, Geary bowled a beautiful in-swinger which caught Brown (22) dead in front and Australia was four for 146. Then Verity bowled Darling before he had settled and the tourists were in deep trouble at five for 153.

Arthur Chipperfield came out in the forty-five minutes before tea for his first-ever Test and played like a veteran with a real one in McCabe. They took Australia to five for 206 at tea. Rain ruined the rest of the day, leaving the visitors on five for 207 at stumps with McCabe 51 not out and Chipperfield 16.

Next morning, as Bradman was about to enter the ground, he caught the eye of a Nottingham miner. The man waved. Bradman stopped and asked if he were going in. The miner said he would dearly love to, but he didn't have any money.

'C'mon, I'll see you in,' Bradman told the man. He paid for his admission and a stand seat, and gave him a few shillings. The short conversation revealed that the miner — Herb Elliot, of Bradford — was unemployed and that he had a wife and eight kids. Bradman went on to the dressing-rooms and raised a subscription for the man. The gesture was leaked to the press, and it turned into a public relations exercise when photos of Elliot and his family were plastered across the news pages. It put a human face on the Australians and helped them with their mixed popularity in Sherwood Forest territory, where Larwood and Voce were Robin Hood and Little John, and the tourists the Sheriff's men.

Day two was memorable for Chipperfield, who played his natural attacking game as he moved steadily towards his hundred at lunch.

He had lost McCabe (65) to Farnes and Oldfield (20) to Mitchell, but Grimmett was showing once more he could bat a bit when required. Chipperfield was up the wrong end when the umpires signalled lunch, with his score on 99 in his first Test. First ball after the break he played tentatively and got an edge off Farnes to Ames and was on his way, one short of a dream debut. Australia struggled to 374 all out with Farnes taking five for 102 and Geary three for 101.

Walters, the England skipper, saw off Wall and McCabe, but soon found himself out of his depth with the wily O'Reilly and his spin-twin, Grimmett, who got him LBW for 17. Sutcliffe was joined by Hammond and they meandered to 102 before O'Reilly deceived Hammond and had him caught for 25.

England then went into a nose-dive, losing Pataudi (12) to Wall, and Leyland (6) and Sutcliffe (62) to Grimmett. O'Reilly was not to be ignored. Woodfull brought him back into the attack and he had Ames (7) caught going for his shots, leaving England on six for 165 — 209 behind.

England needed a stand, and Hendren, the oldest player on either side, performed superbly for the best innings of the match so far before O'Reilly bowled him for 79. He and Geary (53) had added 101 for the seventh wicket. At 266, England crumbled, losing three wickets to be all out for 268. Grimmett with five for 81 and O'Reilly with four for 75 gave Australia a great chance of victory, the lead being 106.

The tourists began mid-afternoon as if they didn't want to win when Farnes bowled Woodfull for 2, and Hammond did the same to Ponsford for 5. Quick runs were needed, but not quick wickets.

Bradman joined Brown at two for 32 and began where he had left off in the first innings. In half an hour at the wicket before tea he moved to 21. He lasted another sixteen minutes after the interval and was on his way for twenty-five caught behind attempting to drive Farnes. Australia was safe at three for 69 — 175 in front. McCabe and Brown then took the score to 181 on the fourth morning before Brown (73) was caught behind off Verity.

McCabe (88) had batted with the good touch he had shown

throughout the tour and was caught by Hammond in slips off Farnes trying to force the pace, as were Darling (10) and Chipperfield (4). Farnes ended with five for 77, giving him the remarkable first-up figures of ten wickets for 179. Woodfull declared after lunch with Australia eight for 273, which seemed too late to force victory in the four-day game. The lead was 379, and no batting combination in history was going to collect half that on the final day of the match facing the best spin combination yet seen.

Woodfull's judgement seemed awry when it took an hour to claim England's first wicket, Sutcliffe (24) caught off O'Reilly at 51. But soon his late declaration appeared more than perspicacious when wickets tumbled regularly for the next two hours.

With twenty minutes to the close, the Ashes defenders had lost their ninth wicket for 137. Verity and Mitchell defended grimly for ten minutes as the Australians went up for LBW decisions. Finally, with the score at 141 and just ten minutes remaining, umpire Dolphin had the unenviable duty of giving Mitchell out LBW for 0. Fittingly, the bowler was O'Reilly. He was superb, taking seven for 54 off 41.4 overs with twenty-four maidens. Grimmett backed him up with three for 39 off forty-seven overs, including twenty-eight maidens.

As the players raced off the ground to avoid the crush, Bradman caught his foot in the boundary rope and strained a thigh muscle, which was another disappointment on top of his other fitness problems. But for the moment, there was rejoicing in the tourist camp. Australia had won by 238 runs. Its tough task of retrieving the Ashes had taken an unexpected turn. Now England had to win to get back in the competition.

WAR OF THE THORNS

There was no rest for the successful, as the Australians met Northamptonshire the following day, 13 June, and Bradman batted number six with a runner. He made 65 in the first innings and was second top-score to Chipperfield, who hit 71 out of 284. The handicap slowed his scoring rate as well, his fifty taking 109 minutes. He batted 129 minutes in all, a time in which he would normally complete a century.

The county replied with 187, A. W. Snowden getting 105. Fleetwood-Smith grabbed one of his few tour chances and took five for 63. Australia's second effort was not impressive, with only Brown (113) in form. Bradman struggled for 25 out of 234. The tourists nearly snatched victory as Northampton collapsed to nine for 133 under pressure from Fleetwood-Smith's turn again. This time he had five for 29, giving him ten for 92 for the match, which was drawn. It was difficult to see him coming in to the Test side to make an extravagant spin trio, but Australia had to consider all options to strengthen its bowling.

While the tourists practised at Lord's in the week prior to the Second Test, Notts played Lancashire at Trent Bridge, in what was to be a trial game for Larwood and Voce, who were contenders for a Test spot. An England selector, T. A. Higson, was in attendance. Lancashire batted on a 'lively' wicket and the speed duo threw themselves into their task.

Neither set a full bodyline field, with just three men instead of four in the close leg-trap and one in the deep behind square, but their intent was clear as they repeatedly struck the Lancs line-up painful blows with deliveries that 'followed' the batsmen. Voce bowled an excessive number of bumpers, and Larwood made plenty rear into the ribcage. It was bodyline but for two leg-side fielders, and very effective, especially against county batsmen. Larwood took six wickets in twenty-nine balls and conceded a solitary run.

At the end of the innings the Lancashire management protested about the methods of the Notts bowlers, claiming that they had contravened the agreement reached by county captains after the 1933 season not to allow 'direct attack' bowling, which was a quaint euphemism for bodyline. Several of the injured batsmen, including George Duckworth, were photographed with extensive bruising. Duckworth went on record as now being very much against bodyline, although during the 1932–33 series he had seen 'nothing wrong with it'. Facing deliveries from bodyline's original great exponents changed attitudes.

The episode was an attempt to force the issue in front of a selector, which it did. The outcry from Lancashire and the press led Larwood to declare in the *Sunday Dispatch* on 17 June that he had 'definitely made up his mind not to play against Australia in this or any other Test'.

If he couldn't bowl the way he liked — that is, employ bodyline — he wouldn't play. The Notts captain, Carr, who had pushed the issue by encouraging the two pacemen to bowl 'at their best, unhindered', wrote a supporting article. Voce also spoke out in the *Sunday Express*.

The three Notts men and their press outlets thought they would force public opinion their way, especially since England had taken a drubbing in the First Test. But it was a significant miscalculation, which solved the MCC's problems over bodyline. All its key supporters and implementors were now finished at the international level.

29

THE LEVELLING

One of the things for which I shall hope is that we may get a
wicket early enough to force Bradman to face the new ball.
He is such a queer proposition as a batsman these days that one
never feels certain of the trends of events until he has been
disposed of.
— PERCY FENDER ON BRADMAN IN MID-1934

VERITABLE VERITY

England brought back Wyatt to captain the team and Bill Bowes to stiffen the bowling for the Lord's Test starting on 22 June. They left out Pataudi and Mitchell, while Australia dumped Ponsford for Bromley. Wyatt won the toss during the change to hot weather and went in on a batsman's wicket, which was fast and true. England seemed to have squandered the advantage when its fifth wicket fell by tea. Only Walters (82) had played strongly, whereas Sutcliffe (20), Hammond (2) and Hendren (13) had put up little resistance to Chipperfield's leg-spinners. He took his third wicket, Wyatt (33), and England was struggling at five for 182. However, Leyland and Ames steadied and took the home team into the second day in a 129-run partnership before Wall bowled Leyland for 100 with the new ball.

McCabe broke through again at 359 to have Ames caught behind for 120. The tail wagged England on to 440 by just before 3 p.m. Grimmett and O'Reilly were ineffective, but Wall was steady with

335

four for 108 off forty-nine overs. Chipperfield, in his first serious spell of leg-spinning at the top level, took three for 91 off thirty-four overs, but did not seem to solve Australia's bowling problems.

Australia started well enough until Bowes bowled Woodfull for 22 at 68. Bradman came to the wicket to an encouraging cheer and clearly had his last success at Lord's in mind again as he strode into the bowling. Cardus loved this one. 'We could feel that Bradman was the creative force of the day,' he wrote, 'and while he was at the wicket the hour was enchanted, that in the forge of his batsmanship molten history was being beaten into shape.'

Bradman, now the blacksmith, hit 14 off Farnes' first over to him. Geary replaced him, and was promptly off-driven for four. Wyatt switched point to the covers, and Bradman slashed the bowler through point. He was in that hectic mood again — a frame of mind that had seen him score in rapid succession against England 0, 103 not out, 8, 66, 76, 24, 48, 71, 29 and 25 in his last five Tests. Gone, it seemed, were the big hundreds, doubles and triples of 1928–29 and 1930. In their stead was machine-gun fire.

Wyatt was worried. He made another quick change of Verity to Geary's end. Bradman off-drove, cut and off-drove him again for three successive fours. Lord's was alive after two dull days. But it was too much for Woodfull in the dressing room. He became nervous. At the end of the over he sent a message out requesting Bradman to restrain himself.

'It put me in two minds,' Bradman recalled. 'Next ball from Verity I moved out to drive him, but bearing in mind instructions, I hesitated. Instead of driving the ball, I hit it back to Verity for a caught and bowled.'

Woodfull's orders not to play his natural game had the opposite effect to the one intended. The skipper's error had robbed the game of perhaps another century similar to the one against Middlesex, and instead Australia was two for 141. Bradman had batted forty-five minutes for his 36, which included seven spanking boundaries.

McCabe joined Brown and they took the score to two for 192 at stumps on Saturday night, 23 June. Sunday was very wet and

Australia recommenced on Monday on a very sticky wicket. Verity, the left-arm spinner, took full advantage with great bowling and ran through the tourists. Bowes had started the rot by having Brown caught at the wicket for 105 at 203, then Verity had McCabe (34) caught in slips by Hammond at 204. Moments after he had Darling (0) caught at 205. Chipperfield (37 not out) resisted but Verity went on to take seven for 61. Bowes gave support with three for 98. Australia's score of 284 was seven short of the follow-on.

Wyatt had no hesitation in enforcing it, and Woodfull contemplated how unfortunate his order to Bradman had been as he struggled to beat off Verity again. Bowes played his part by dismissing the first-innings century-maker Brown for 2 when the score was 10.

Bradman came in and, bearing in mind the wicket and his dismissal in the first innings, played cautiously. He was bogged down for just under half an hour for 13 runs. It was too much. Bradman showed his restlessness and jumped out to Verity, who had cunningly left no-one in the deep, thus inviting some hitting. Bradman obliged and promptly put the ball straight above the wicket. England had time to raffle it between the seven players who were in a position to catch it. Eventually Ames stepped forward with the gloves and it dropped neatly in.

Cardus caught the moment, noting that as the keeper moved into position, 'Bradman stood aside, exposed in a momentary embarrassment like a detected schoolboy.'

Australia was two for 43. Verity did the rest. He took six for 15 after tea, giving him eight for 43 for the innings, and the tourists were all out for 118. Victory was England's by an innings and 38 runs.

Verity had taken fifteen for 104. In perhaps the most devastating single day's bowling in a Test match he had taken fourteen wickets. This performance and the luck of the weather had seen the series squared.

MEDIOCRE AT MANCHESTER

The Australians entered the mid-season stretch of games against the counties before the Third Test still feeling confident they could take the series. Bradman's form continued to worry the tourists. Although McCabe, Brown and Darling were acquitting themselves well, the squad knew, even if it went unsaid, that he had to fire if the Ashes were to be won.

He continued his run of relative mediocrity with 17 in the next county game against Somerset at Taunton out of Australia's 309. Woodfull hit 84, Darling 79 and Ben Barnett, the substitute keeper, made a strong 51. Somerset had batted first for 116 and had been mesmerised by O'Reilly, who took nine for 38. He had emerged even above Grimmett as the pre-eminent bowler in England for the season. No opposition looked comfortable against his fast leg-breaks and variations. Somerset made 116 again in the second innings and this time Fleetwood-Smith demonstrated he was too good to be out of the Tests by taking six for 56.

The tourists played Surrey at The Oval and the county was beaten by six wickets, scoring 175 and 184. Grimmett took five for 33 in Surrey's second innings. Bradman, now Cardus's master of the short dig, hit 27 in thirty-two minutes. In the second, he gained a bit of confidence by scoring a fast 61 not out in seventy-six minutes to ensure that the tourists won comfortably. He hit the winning runs and it did him good.

This victory was offset when several of the tourists went down with a throat virus just before the start of the Third Test at Old Trafford, Manchester, on 6 July. Kippax had been ruled out of a place, but Bradman, Brown, Woodfull and Chipperfield were picked, despite having symptoms. At one point doctors feared the team may have been hit by diphtheria. Ponsford came back for Bromley in the line-up, and England dropped Farnes, Geary and Bowes for E. W. Clarke, J. L. Hopwood and Gubby Allen.

England won the toss and batted. It was sailing along nicely but slowly on the dead wicket in the extreme heat when O'Reilly struck. He had Walters (52) caught at short leg by Darling to make England one for 68. Next ball, he bowled Wyatt. Two for 68. Hammond came in. The Gloucester champion drove him for four, then next ball O'Reilly clean-bowled him too. England was three for 72, and the spinner had taken three wickets in four balls. It was one of the great overs in Test history. Hat-tricks would be taken, but against whom? O'Reilly had sent back three class cricketers not with luck but superb deliveries.

After that streak of brilliance there was a minor recovery as Sutcliffe and Hendren took the score on to 149 when O'Reilly broke through once more, having Sutcliffe caught for 63. However, thereafter it was a long time between wickets as Leyland and Hendren dug in and added another 191 runs. Mid-morning on day two O'Reilly struck again and caught and bowled Hendren for a patient 132 — a courageous performance for a man of his years in the summer heat.

England were on top with five for 340 when Leyland found a new partner in Ames for another crushing stand, taking the score on 142 to 482. O'Reilly collected his sixth successive victim when he had Leyland caught for a powerful 153. By this time Bradman and Chipperfield were confined to bed, and substitutes were fielding. If O'Reilly had gone down with the ailment — dubbed Wimbledon throat — England may well not have lost a wicket.

Grimmett finally broke the Tiger's run when he cajoled Ames into driving a catch straight to Ponsford. England ended with some big hitting by Allen (60) and Verity (61 not out) and was able to declare at the massive tally of nine for 627. O'Reilly finished with seven for 149 off fifty-nine overs.

Australia began the impossible chase knowing that Bradman and Chipperfield would be unlikely to do much. Brown and Woodfull were off-colour as well, but not as debilitated. But the team had to fight, for a capitulation to illness would see the Ashes lost. The task was to reach 487 and avoid the follow-on at all costs, which under the circumstances was a tall order. On the other hand, the pitch was offering the bowlers absolutely no assistance.

Woodfull sent Brown and Ponsford out to open. The latter was caught off Hammond for 12 in a poor start. McCabe came in as the tourists' form bat of the season and played with grace and power. He and Brown took the score to 230 before Clark had Brown (72) caught. McCabe went soon after caught off Hammond for a brilliant

137 and Australia was teetering at three for 242, still about halfway from avoiding the follow-on.

Bradman got out of his hotel sickbed at lunch-time and made his way down to the ground. He was listed to bat at the fall of the fourth wicket. Chipperfield, dropped to number eight in the batting order, was feeling even worse. He waited until the last minute possible to leave the hotel, in the hope that he would not have to bat until the fourth morning.

Woodfull and Darling carried the innings on until 3.35 p.m., when the score was 320. Then Verity came on and bowled Darling for 37. A reporter described Bradman's appearance as he made his way out to bat:

> It was unfortunately all too obvious that he is an ill man. His cheeks are very drawn and never before have I seen him look so thin. The smile that for so long has been planted on his face was completely absent.

There was no cheering, which surprised journalists, but Bradman looked so poorly that few may have recognised him as Woodfull juggled the order between the able-bodied and the infirm.

According to Cardus:

> He made one or two typical shots, but the one and only time when he showed us the real wonder-worker of the past was when he knocked a ball down and then cut it to the off before it could shoot on to his wicket.

Bradman still had something left, but it was an utter ordeal for him in the blazing heat. Yet he plucked up the last vestige of energy left in him and struggled through to tea on 25 not out in fifty minutes with Woodfull. Hammond was feeling it too and dropped a caught and bowled chance from Bradman when he was on 26.

Finally he fell, caught behind attempting to cut a wide ball from Hammond, having made 30 in sixty-six minutes and faced fifty-one balls. He and Woodfull had eased the score up to five for 378. Bradman went straight back to bed. Australia was exactly 100 short of batting again with four men and a crock left.

A quarter of an hour later, disaster struck with the score at 409. Woodfull tried for a quick run with Oldfield and was run out for 73. With the addition of only two more runs, the game swung further England's way when Verity had Oldfield caught for 13.

Chipperfield came to the wicket feeling anything but chipper. He dry-retched in the heat after taking his first runs and had to call for a drink. Verity took the home side a huge step closer to the Ashes by bowling Grimmett and Australia was eight for 419 and sinking.

However, O'Reilly provided a life-raft when he and Chipperfield struggled on to 454, before the latter also was on his way back to bed after being caught for 26 off Verity. That left O'Reilly with Wall. Somehow they clawed their way up to the 478 and beyond to 491, thus forcing England in again. Verity was once more the mainstay of the England bowling with four for 78 off fifty-three overs with twenty-four maidens. Hammond backed him up with three for 111.

The home side could have closed its innings after one ball at none for none, but instead waded on to none for 123 before declaring. Clearly Wyatt had decided that the wicket was too good to risk attempting such a bold win. Australia's second innings of none for 66 seemed to confirm his judgement, and the game fizzled out to a tame draw, with Patsy Hendren even having an over.

The Ashes equation now read this way. England only had to draw the next two or win one more to retain them. Australia could not afford to lose again, but had to win at least one and draw the other. The onus was thus firmly on the tourists to chase victory.

30

BACK AT THE BUSINESS END

The partnership of Ponsford and Bradman is surely the most dramatic and the most opportune that has ever happened in big cricket.
— ENGLISH NEWSPAPER REPORT ON THE FOURTH TEST AT LEEDS, 1934

RETURN AT THE LANE

Bradman had not fully recovered when he played against Derbyshire at Chesterfield on 11 July, the day after the Third Test. Yet he had to perform because so many of the squad were still feeling off-colour. Derbyshire batted first for 145, with Ebeling taking five for 28. Bradman went in with less than half an hour to play on the first day at one for 21. He decided to stand and deliver, scoring 49 not out. He completed his fifty off the first ball the next morning, stayed another twenty-two minutes and was then caught at the wicket for 71, the highest score of the match. Derbyshire fell apart again in the second innings and could only reach 139. Fleetwood-Smith once more showed he was unlucky not to be in the Test team with five for 38. Australia mopped up the required 31 runs on the third day, with Bradman 6 not out. The win by nine wickets was a little boost but a timely one.

The tourists had to play a strong Yorkshire side next morning,

14 July, at Sheffield, then the critical Fourth Test, which Australia had to win or draw. If it lost, they could kiss the Ashes goodbye.

Bradman turned out again. He had not scored a century for nearly two months, in the longest drought in his seven-year first-class career, which covered nine seasons. His 1934 effort in England now read 206, 65, 0, 5, 37, 0, 160, 77, 29, 25, 65, 25, 36, 13, 17, 27, 61 not out, 30, 71 and 6 not out.

His twenty innings had yet to see him reach 1,000. However, he had still managed 955 and an average of 53.05, which made his season only a failure by his own standards. Bradman was due statistically for a big score, but his performances were bound by his health, not the law of averages or the Bell Curve of career scores. He couldn't throw off the nagging illness, so his batting would depend on pure willpower. For that, he needed an inspiration and challenge.

It came in two measures. First, Jessie had been alarmed by the reports of her husband's ill-health. Only the captain had his wife on tour, and the rest of the players' close relatives and friends could not travel with them. It was particularly worrying and frustrating for Jessie. Each day she read a new 'inside' medical analysis about Don. The latest unofficial bulletin suggested he had serious heart trouble and was seeing a specialist. She sent an anxious telegram. Bradman reassured her and suggested that she 'wait until Leeds'. He was worried about his debilitating condition, but did not want Jessie to be concerned, especially when she was helpless to do anything.

The second boost to his spirits came from the strong Yorkshire team. The county scored 340 (A. B. Sellers 105), and in reply Australia was one for 16 midway through the second afternoon when Bradman came out to bat against the most powerful county attack in the land. It included Bowes, T. F. Smailes, G. G. Macaulay, C. Turner, Verity and Leyland, and was as good as any Test line-up.

Bradman began without fireworks at the Bramall Lane ground, as if he were tuning up, scoring 50 in seventy-four minutes. Then he hit out for his second fifty in twenty-six minutes, reaching his century in even time. His condition was still poor and he was scoring boundaries rather than going for runs. The last 40 of his innings was hit in twenty minutes, before he threw his wicket away lashing at every-thing. His 140 had taken exactly two hours, in which he hit 100 in boundaries — twenty-two fours and two sixes.

This innings was highly rated by all who saw it. *The Times* corre-spondent said it was 'one of the greatest exhibitions of his career. He employed every conceivable stroke, and it became impossible to set a field to him.' The *Daily Mail* suggested that Bradman's 'invincible wizardry menaces England's Test hopes'.

He partnered Woodfull in 189 for the second wicket, and the innings would have reminded the skipper what might have been at the Lord's Test if he had let Bradman loose against Verity. Woodfull himself managed 54 and Australia was dismissed for 348. The game petered out to a draw, but the tourists had held ground at a vital part of the tour when sides with lesser spirit would have conceded a game here or there.

A HEDONIST AT HEADINGLEY

Australia did not make changes for the Fourth Test at Headingley, beginning on 20 July, which was in itself a sign of confidence. The tourists had got this far on their leading personnel, and were still in the hunt for the Ashes. England replaced Allen, who had managed only one for 136 in the Third Test, with Mitchell, and lost the great Sutcliffe with a torn leg muscle. He was replaced by the Yorkshire opener, W. W. Keeton, who opened with Walters after Wyatt had won the toss.

The wicket was perfect and the weather fine. The new openers put on 43 before O'Reilly had Keeton (25) caught behind by Oldfield. From then on the bowlers seemed on top, backed up by superb keep-ing. Walters (43) was second to go at 83, caught and bowled by Chipperfield. Wall then did his team a great favour by bowling Hammond (37), who, like Bradman, was having a mediocre series. Chipperfield soon after bowled Hendren (29), and Grimmett, aided by the glovework of Oldfield and wiles of O'Reilly, did the rest. England was all out soon after tea for 200.

The Eyes Have It. Baby Bradman at seventeen months – a shot taken at Christmas, 1909.

Head Steady, Eyes Level. Bradman taking block at twelve, when he scored his first century, 115 not out, playing for Bowral School.

Relaxed and Ready. Bradman in February, 1929, aged twenty, demonstrates his comfortable, confident stance.

That's My Boy. Emily and Don greet each other after his triumphant 1930 tour of England. 'I know my Don would think too much about his mother to let success spoil him,' she said after he had made 334 at Leeds.

Wait and See. Don and Jessie in 1931. Bradman had proposed to her before the 1931 tour of England. Jessie had told him to wait until after the tour to see if they still felt the same. As this shot suggests, they did.

Fast Leg, Chest and Head Theory. Australian captain Bill Woodfull ducks under one from Larwood. The bodyline field is set for the hurried shot to leg.

Potting Pheasants. Larwood strikes Australian captain Bill Woodfull in the chest in the Third Test at Adelaide of the 1932-33 Bodyline series. The bowler likened attempting to strike batsmen to shooting wild birds.

Direct Hit. Larwood hits Bert Oldfield on the front of the skull when the player tries to hook him. The batsman was knocked out and received a fracture, but later blamed himself.

Gaunt Golf. A drawn-faced but still smiling Bradman in April, 1934, shows his golf form.

Sailing into Sporting Battle. Woodfull's 1934 touring team and the Davis Cup tennis squad on board *SS Orford* on the way to England.

304 Reasons to Smile. Bradman returns to the pavilion after his Test triple
century at Leeds in 1934. At that time he was suffering from a debilitating
mystery illness. A few weeks later he was near death from peritonitis.

Tea for Two. Don and Jessie during his recuperation, late 1934. Weeks earlier his badly infected appendix had been operated on in London.

Gone Dancing in Battersea. Jessie and a recovered Don on 5 January 1935, dancing at the Battersea Town Hall, London.

Two Heads are Better Than One. England skipper 'Gubby' Allen jokingly inspects Bradman's coin before the toss in the 1936 Sydney Test.

Not Too Close. Bradman and Jack Fingleton go out to bat in the Sydney Test of December 1936.

Youth and Maturity. Ross Gregory on debut and Bradman go out to face England in the 1937 Fourth Test at Adelaide. Gregory's great promise was cut short when he was killed in the RAAF while fighting for his country during World War Two.

The Pied Piper of Regent Street. Bradman and an amused Jack Fingleton are followed by a line of autograph-hunting young fans along Regent Street, London, in 1938.

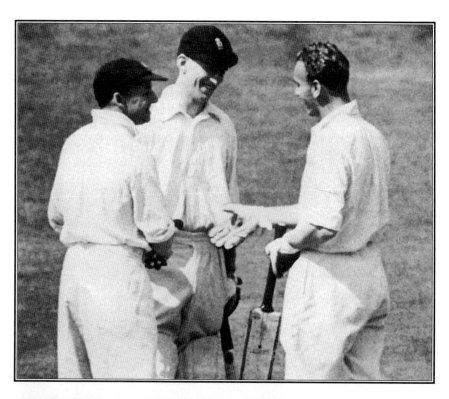

First Up. Bradman is first to congratulate Len Hutton at The Oval seconds after he had passed Bradman's 334 world record score. It was a bad Test for The Don. Apart from Hutton breaking his record, Bradman fractured his ankle while bowling and did not bat. Australia was thrashed.

Will He Smash a Third Triple? Bradman goes out to bat in the 1938 Leeds Test after scoring 334 in 1930 and 304 in 1934. This time he notched 103.

Eyes on the Ball. Bradman in the nets in 1940.

BOWLER	WKTS	RUNS
RANGNEKAR		
ADHIKARI		
KISHENCHAND		
GUL MAHOMED		
SARWATE		45
NAYUDU		19
HAZARE		
AMARNATH		23
MANKAD		43
SOHONI		56

INDIA 1ᵀ INNS	326
AUS.1ST INGS	
Nº OF OVERS	47
BATSMEN	
BRADMAN	99
MILLER	63
2 FOR	187

BATSMEN	OUT	FoF W
BROWN	8	11
ROGERS	16	31
WANTED AT MEMBs GATE		
SUNDRIES	1	

BAR

A Golden Single. Bradman drives to mid-on and takes the 100th run in his 100th first-class century against India in 1947-48.

(The Sydney Sun)

I Get Much More Turn This Way . . . In 1948 at Balmoral Castle, the Duke of Edinburgh appears to be getting a tip on his spinning action, to which Bradman had referred in a speech at the Cricket Writers' Club.
(The New York Times)

Defending the Bridge. Bradman and Bill Brown continuing a partnership at the Trent Bridge Test in 1948.
(The Age)

Beaten But Unbowed.
Bradman is bowled by
Pollard for 35 in the first
innings of the Fourth
Test at Leeds in 1948.
In the second innings he
hit 173 not out as part
of the biggest comeback
in cricket history,
which won the Ashes
and the series.
(S & G Press Agency)

No More Bowes' Bumpers. Bill Bowes greets his greatest foe at Tilbury in 1948
soon after the *RMS Strathaird* docked. The fine English bowler took
Bradman's wicket five times in Tests – for plenty.
(AAP Photo Library)

Home Forever. Jessie, John and Shirley greet Don after his triumphant return to Australia in October, 1948.
(The Advertiser, Adelaide)

Sweeping into History. Bradman sweeps a ball on his way to his last first-class century – at the MCG in his Testimonial in December, 1948.
(The Age)

A Cuppa with the Captain. Bradman chats with Australian skipper Richie Benaud during tea-break in the First Test against South Africa at Brisbane in 1963. Bradman's subtle influence over Australia's approach to the game was apparent until his retirement as a national selector in 1971.

(The Age)

The Leaning Tower of Power. In December 1965 Bradman gives Australian skipper Bob Simpson a pointer in the nets on footwork and balance.

(The Age)

Wisden Wisdom. Bradman refers to his most prized literary possession – a volume
of *Wisden.* He has just one of two complete private collections in the world.
(Dean Golja © 1995)

Cardus ridiculed the home team. 'They exhibited contemporary defensive technique at its comical worst . . . and turned their bats into crutches of senility,' he wrote. 'They pushed, groped, and stumbled with ludicrous feebleness.'

This was perhaps a little scathing and did not allow for the bowlers' outstanding effort. Grimmett had the figures with four for 57 from 30.4 overs, while O'Reilly still returned a more than creditable three for 46 off thirty-five. Chipperfield proved a useful alternative leggie with two for 35 off eighteen overs. Oldfield claimed four dismissals — two stumpings, one off each of the main spinners, and two catches — and did not let a single bye go through.

Ponsford and Brown began Australia's reply, and seemed in no trouble until Bowes bowled Brown for 15. Woodfull sent in Oldfield, but he was promptly caught behind off the same bowler at 0 with the score at 39. Woodfull now appeared, and Australia was in effect opening again with its old firm, but Bowes put paid to any thoughts of that developing by bowling the Australian skipper for a duck third ball. The tourists were three for 39 at stumps.

The next morning, Saturday, Ponsford (22 not out) and Bradman walked out in front of a packed house and under a sunny sky. The Yorkshire fans greeted them with a great roar. Many had vivid memories of 1930, when Bradman scored 309 not out in a day. While no-one was expecting anything like that because of his much-discussed ill-health and his fluctuating form, they were hoping for a great cameo — even perhaps a fast hundred like the one he had just belted at Sheffield.

Bowes had two balls left from his sensational over of the night before. The tall, bespectacled Yorkshireman strode in and thumped the delivery in short of a length. Bradman moved back and across, and drove the ball off the back foot between the bowler and mid-on to the boundary. Bowes swung his arms, indicating he had just bowled a 'loosener'. Then he turned, came in and pounded the last ball down on the same length but a bit wider out. Bradman moved his foot further back and across and crashed the ball through the same spot for a second four.

It was a beginning that had the crowd buzzing. Bradman was signalling that it was another day and he was another batsman altogether. His flag said attack and not defence or surrender. But this opening was symbolic rather than representative. The batsmen proceeded cautiously, though without being bogged down. Bradman was not in this morning for a brilliant interlude and run-a-minute scoring. He wished to summon something extra for himself and his country. Ponsford also seemed determined. He was on trial after mixed performances in the Tests of 53, 5, 12 and 30 not out. These scores, the batsman knew well, were not indicative of his season. He was having a big, typically heavy-scoring Ponsford tour and was leading the tourists' averages, being second only to McCabe in the aggregates.

At 29, Bradman was unaware that he had made 2,000 runs in Tests against England. At 50 in ninety-one minutes, he looked settled. He stepped up his scoring a fraction with Ponsford marginally slower. At 72, Bradman hooked Bowes hard to Hopwood's right hand at square leg and a very tough chance went down. That was enough of a warning for him to put his head down until lunch, when he was 76 not out. This was 29 less than in 1930 when he hit a pre-lunch century in record time on the first day, but Bradman was not even half as fit this time.

After the break Ponsford's wide bat and Bradman's deep courage began to overwhelm the attack as Wyatt tried every combination possible of Bowes, Hammond, Mitchell, Verity, Hopgood and Leyland. Bowes even tried bouncing them, but while he did hit Bradman and Ponsford twice each, he was definitely no Larwood.

After one series of bouncers, Bradman showed his disdain by going down the wicket between overs and patting down spots near the bowling crease, suggesting that that was where Bowes was pitching them.

Ponsford was enjoying his return. He appeared set against dismissal as Bradman began to pull out all his shots, except those that launched the ball to the heavens. He was not in the mood of the previous Monday at Sheffield, but he was vicious with anything loose, and his judgement of the ball's length was exceptional. Meanwhile, Ponsford used his bat like a broadsword to square-cut, and a wand for placement.

At 2.58 p.m. Bradman reached a hundred, and looked relieved. But there was no sign that he had had enough. He took his time taking block again, as if he was just in. A few in the crowd remarked on it, while others looked at the clock. He had taken 188 minutes to score his first hundred. At that rate, he might be looking for another by stumps.

The concentration of the two batsmen looked remorseless as Ponsford too reached his century. Bradman seemed more adventurous in the last hour before tea, and was playing with such force in the last few minutes that he was unlucky not to score a century in the session. His 93 took him to 169 not out, while Ponsford was 130 not out.

Bradman was near exhaustion point at tea. Muscles complained as he cooled down, but he was determined to drive home the advantage and crush the opposition. The tourists now realised that this Test could not be lost. The Ashes were not theirs yet, but they were far from England's.

At 189, Bradman took his aggregate in all Tests to 3,413, which exceeded Clem Hill's previous highest tally. Hill had done it in eighty-nine innings, while this was only Bradman's fortieth — exactly halfway to his career total of eighty Test innings. At 5.15 p.m. he reached 200. He acknowledged the applause with a wave and an even bigger grin than at 100. Among those clapping was a twelve-year-old boy named Jim Laker, who dreamed one day of playing against the Australian champion.

When the cheering had died, Bradman took block for the third time. Hendren made some passing comment, which made the batsman laugh. He had not had much to be joyous about for the season, but his 200 in 305 minutes was something to celebrate. It was his fourth double century in a day in a Test. No-one had ever achieved this at this level.

'Put on Dolphin,' a cynic in the crowd called out, referring to one of the umpires. Wyatt looked as if he might indeed throw the ball his way. But Bowes was battling hard, as was Verity, who sent down several maidens in succession at one point early in the afternoon.

England had the new ball and the field was rather forlorn. Bowes didn't even have a genuine slip to Bradman, although Hammond lurked somewhere around a close gully. Wyatt had arranged a run-saving field now as the batsmen began to open out. Ponsford turned aggressive and began to use his huge bat — it had been measured once in a Shield game because it appeared too wide — with even more vigour. Then, on 181, he pulled Verity for four but his foot just dislodged a bail. He was out at 5.57 p.m. and was clearly disappointed as he walked off, for he had looked as sound and dangerous as Bradman. A big double was in his sights, and Ponsford was as capable as Bradman of the massive innings, as his record of two 400s in first-class cricket proved.

The partnership had been worth 388 and was the highest-ever fourth-wicket stand in Tests. They had been the near-perfect pair. Bradman never liked to be outscored, and if McCabe had been with him there would have been some competition. But Ponsford liked to go at his own pace, and he preferred a partner *per se*, whether he was making more runs or not.

When McCabe did join Bradman, the latter seemed almost light-hearted in his approach as he went on the attack, lifting two terrific sixes that took him to 271 not out at stumps, with Australia on a commanding four for 494. He had hit 102 between tea and the close. His 380-minute innings had been a steady progression of combat, conquest and carnage.

Bradman hurried off the ground as the police cleared a path for him through the enthusiastic crowd who had rushed out to congratulate him. He slumped in the dressing-room surrounded by the rest of the team, who had already opened a bottle of champagne. Someone proposed a toast to him. Bradman refused to let them drink it.

'There's only one toast I'm listening to,' he said, raising a glass. 'To victory!' The dressing-room echoed his words.

He was so exhausted after his extraordinary feat he found it difficult to move at first. The other players had to help him undress and lift him onto the massage table, where his thin body (down to less than 64 kg) was given life by a trainer. He had given everything and had come through at the right moment. His 206 at Worcester was fine, and it would have been useful to achieve a big score earlier in the series. But now the fight for that little urn was at its height. And he had delivered his best.

In the streets of every British city posters acclaimed the day. The *Evening News* had close-of-play scores with a poster that read:

BRADMAN
BATS AND
BATS AND BATS

He was a walking headline and poster in England. His name had even sold papers in May when the posters said: BRADMAN 0. That didn't leave much to write about, but people paid their money to read the paragraph or two describing how Bradman had been dismissed for a duck. Now there was something substantial to muse over.

Tom Clarke of the *Daily Mail* caught up with him at the Prince of Wales Hotel in Harrogate that night. He asked Bradman if he was 'going after' his record of 334 on Monday. 'I am not out to make personal records,' he replied. 'My side required the runs.'

'But you're so close, there is plenty of time . . .' Clarke persisted.

'I am going out in the spirit that we Australians want to win this match,' Bradman told him.

He made a special effort to dine out with the tour squad and friends that Saturday night, even allowing himself a sip of champagne. Bradman, who still had the reputation of the loner of 1930 after hitting 309 in a day, was in convivial mood and fulfilling his responsibility now as the team's vice-captain.

He had Sunday to recover, but could hardly move during the day. However, he was buoyed by the papers that day, which gave him and Ponsford rave reviews for their performance, which had swung the series Australia's way. The *Yorkshire Post's* J. M. Kilburn described

Bradman as 'the champion of champions . . . He is a text book of bat-ting come to life with never a mis-print or erratum.' Wilfred Rhodes wrote:

> *The scoring machine — that is Bradman — got to work again today and our bowlers had to pay tribute as we all knew they would have to do, as soon as Bradman decided that the time had come for him to move seriously along the run-getting road . . . [He is] all the way round, the best scoring batsman I have seen.*

When he resumed on Monday, he was predictably not in synch. He was struggling to get his timing, but managed to reach 300 in 425 minutes. He was out soon after for 304, when Bowes removed his leg stump. Bradman's 430 minutes at the wicket was his longest Test and first-class innings, with two sixes and forty-three fours, which meant 184 in boundaries, each one saving him having to sprint up and down the wicket.

McCabe (27), Darling (12), Chipperfield (1), and Grimmett (15) lost their wickets going for quick runs. Australia added 90 while los-ing its last six wickets en route to 584, which gave it a lead of 384. Bowes took six for 142 and always bowled well, even when Bradman and Ponsford were in full stride, as did Verity, who finished with three for 113 off 46.5 overs.

England batted again, and the fall of wickets was steady. Keeton (12) was first to go at 28, bowled by Grimmett. Hammond was unfortunately run out for 20, then Walters was bowled by O'Reilly for 45, making England three for 87. Wyatt (44) was bowled by Grimmett at 152.

Rain overnight briefly delayed the fourth day's play and returned to interrupt proceedings again after four maidens were bowled in front of 5,000 loyal fans, most of whom had come to see England fight out a draw. Shortly after the second resumption, O'Reilly bowled a top-spinner which zipped straight through and trapped Hendren LBW for 42.

This brought keeper Ames to the wicket to join Leyland. The field crowded both men. Bradman, who had been active in the field despite his lengthy innings, gave chase to a ball, and stopped it with his foot. He turned sharply, tore a thigh muscle, and had to be helped off the ground. Moments later, Ames fell to Grimmett and England were five for 213. Leyland tried to manage the strike, and Hopwood seemed very fortunate to survive a bat-pad catch to Wall at silly mid-on off Grimmett.

Thunder overhead was a welcome sound for the beleaguered Englishmen. The ensuing storm washed out the rest of the game, thus robbing Australia of almost certain victory. Grimmett took three for 72 off 56.4 overs with twenty-four maidens, while O'Reilly took two for 88 from fifty-one overs, including twenty-five maidens.

Bradman could not play in the next few county games, and was fortunate to be taken under the wing of Sir Douglas Shields, an Australian surgeon based in London, who immobilised his injured leg in plaster for five days. Shields, one of several specialists to examine Bradman, was concerned about his general condition and invited him to be his guest at his spacious home set in two hectares of woodland at Slough, where he could convalesce.

Bradman's 'disappearance' fuelled more rumours about his condition, with journalists speculating that he would not play in the final Test. However, Bradman rested, read and listened to music. He also phoned Jessie again to reassure her that he would be part of Australia's 'Ashes victory'. To fulfil that prediction, the tourists had to win. A draw would leave the Ashes with England. Bradman was so determined to play, according to Bill O'Reilly, 'he would be batting in a wheelchair if necessary.'

31
PARTNERSHIP OF THE CENTURY

[Bradman's innings] was at least as good as any of his past prolific efforts with the bat, and that is saying a great deal.
— Douglas Jardine after Bradman's 244 in the Fifth Test at The Oval, 1934

A DOSE OF VOCE

Australia played Nottinghamshire in early August, in the second-last game before the Fifth Test without Bradman, who was making a good recovery. Larwood had not bowled in the last three county games because of recurring foot trouble, and was not available. Carr was also injured, but Voce played. Australia batted first and Voce bowled bodyline using a four-man leg-trap, with one and sometimes two in the deep. Five batsmen were caught in the trap as Australia struggled to 237. Woodfull showed typical guts with 81 and Chipperfield hit 57. Voce returned eight for 66.

Notts replied with 183 on the second day. Grimmett took four for 70 and McCabe three for 42. Australia began its second innings after tea. Voce sent down two overs of bodyline, including nine head-high bumpers, before poor light stopped play.

The Australian management complained to the MCC. Voce withdrew the next day, said to be suffering from 'shin soreness'. The tourists were abused by the crowd throughout the day before declaring at two for 230, with Brown on 100 not out and Kippax 75 not out.

Voce's performance was a protest against not being selected in the Test side, but it was an ill-timed, futile act similar to his and Larwood's efforts against Lancashire earlier in mid-June. However, he and Larwood were having trouble giving up the habit, despite the unpopularity of 'direct attack' bowling outside Nottingham. It took lots of wickets. Bodyline was having a slow, dangerous death.

HIGH NOON AT THE OVAL

Bradman missed six possible games before making a comeback in a game against the Army a few days before the Fifth Test. He scored a swift 79 and proved his fitness. Australia dropped Wall for Ebeling, and Darling for Kippax, who had scored consistently in the run-up to the Test. England left out Keeton, Hendren, Mitchell and Hopwood, and brought in Sutcliffe after injury, and the in-form veteran Yorkshireman, Frank Woolley, who was nearly forty-eight-years old. The inclusion of E. W. Clark and Allen was to bolster the speed attack on what was expected to be a fast track. 'Nobby' Clark was a left-hander similar to Bill Voce, but a shade faster. He also liked using bodyline.

The big game was to be timeless to decide the 1934 Ashes. The venue, like 1930, was under the gasometer at The Oval, London. It began on Saturday 18 August in front of a sell-out crowd. Woodfull won the toss and batted on a perfect wicket.

England started well when Clark bowled Brown (10) at 21 after half an hour. At exactly noon, all heads turned to the pavilion steps to see that now familiar swagger of the man who was Australia to most of the English population, or at least an idealised version of what it could produce. While millions appreciated his gifts, England's supporters were not going to let sentiment prevail over patriotic urges. They wanted a big, crushing win just as eagerly as their Australian counterparts.

When Bradman appeared, he was the great feared yet strangely loved enemy. The crowd hoped that the speed trio of Clark, Allen and Bowes could make him hop about enough for an indiscreet shot that would see the back of him. An English fan, Oscar Grant, who was at The Oval that day, told me:

> I was very young [nine], but remember the atmosphere because it was the first Test my father ever took me to. The word 'Bradman' was uttered with such reverence, such awe that I was curious. What was he like, this Australian? My father said we had to get him out early, or else. I asked, what else? He sighed and replied, 'or else you'll probably not see a better innings in your life'. I'm seventy and I haven't.

Bradman joined Ponsford, took block and special note of Clark's leg-side field of two close to the wicket and two out. He knew the bowler's penchant for bodyline, and this was getting close to it.

He saw out the over and weathered the next few from Clark and Bowes who both tested him with short ones. Bradman, however, like Ponsford, seemed at ease. There was no hurry, no need to break the speed barrier. They could bat into the English winter if they wished. Nevertheless, the score ticked over with pushes, glances, late cuts and drives from Bradman. Ponsford, as at Leeds, was placing the ball with perfection, and going for the occasional bludgeoning cut.

They liked batting with each other, these two. For Ponsford's part, Bradman meant disruption of the field and the bowler's line and length, which worked in his favour. For Bradman's part, Ponsford represented a dependable stayer, who would go the distance with him, which was vital. Nothing short of a massive total — 'approaching a thousand,' Woodfull half-jokingly said — would suffice.

At lunch they were both 43 and Australia was one for 100. It was a steady foundation. They both moved easily to 50 (Bradman in ninety-six minutes) after the long interval, and again it was the signpost which said 'Attack'. Wyatt presented his impressive speed bowling force, plus Hammond and Verity, but not even that fine spinner could halt the flow of runs, as both batsmen stepped up their rate.

Bradman swept to a hundred at 3.37 p.m. in 170 minutes, his second fifty in seventy-four minutes. His third half-century was a major moment in the Test, for he carved into the bowling at a run-a-minute to be 150 not out at tea, leaving Ponsford (120) behind, but, as ever, not in the shadow of his partner. It was a marriage of Ponsford's cut and Bradman's thrust.

Despite his condition, Bradman now looked the sprinter of yesteryear as he notched 107 in the session. After tea, the grin was back as he made yet another assault on a double hundred in a day in a Test. He was not so much merciless when the bowlers naturally tired, as the perfectionist in executing his game. He refused to attack the grey skies over the gasometer, no matter what Verity dished up. He was not even tempted when Wyatt and Leyland rolled their arms over. His timing, wrist-work and feet conspired to send the ball earthwards. Then when the score was one for 365, Clark came on with a new ball and pointedly set a bodyline field, as his skipper looked on.

Jardine and Larwood — watching the game in different parts of the ground — applauded this belated move as four men crouched close and low on the leg-side. Clark thumped down a head-high bouncer. Bradman swivelled, positioned and forgot himself. His vicious hook saw the dangerous ball sail over square leg and into the crowd for six. Nothing could stop him in this mood and at this stage. In the same over he pulled the bowler through mid-wicket for four. Sutcliffe went to collect the ball. He rested on the boundary rail as the ball was picked up, and grinned.

'Anyone got any suggestions?' he asked the spectators.

Bradman reached the 200 summit and planted the Australian flag on it at 5.50 p.m. The fourth fifty took him just an hour, and his second century had come up in 113 minutes. As he moved into his third hundred, he seemed to be planning shots even before the bowler released the ball. The spectators had long since resigned themselves to paying homage. They cheered, encouraged and applauded, their patriotism forgotten in the face of a performance that transcended all boundaries, national and fenced.

Bradman's last 44 took thirty-three minutes. At 244, he tried to hook a Bowes bumper, but the ball took the edge and Ames took the catch. It was 6.23 p.m. The innings had lasted 316 minutes. He faced 272 balls at a strike rate of 89.87 runs per 100 balls, and hit one six and thirty-two fours.

As he turned to head for the pavilion amid the applause of relief and appreciation, a photographer caught Bradman smiling broadly. There was much to laugh at, for Australia went to stumps a few minutes later with its score at two for 475. Ponsford was 205 not out. No team had been better placed on the first day of a Test match. The partnership of 451, of which Ponsford contributed 194, was a record for any wicket in all Tests, Ashes and others. This was the first time Bradman had scored successive double centuries in Tests, which equalled the feat previously performed by Hammond. It was the fifth time Bradman had scored 200 or more in a Test day.

CONSOLIDATION

Ponsford continued on Monday morning with typical concentration and was out, again hit wicket, for 266. It was the second-highest score ever in Tests by an Australian. When he left, Australia was four for 574, having earlier lost McCabe (10), bowled by Allen. If ever an opener had done his job it was Ponsford. Australia hammered on to 701, with other useful contributions from Woodfull (49) and Oldfield (42 not out). Bowes with four for 164 had the 'best' figures, while Allen took four for 170. After Clark broke through Brown for the first wicket, another 100 were hit off him before he bowled the last man, O'Reilly. He ended with two for 110.

England batted before tea and began as if it seriously planned to make 702. But at 104, Grimmett forced Sutcliffe into indecision and had him caught behind, which began a mini-collapse. O'Reilly had Woolley caught for four, and then snapped up Walters for 64. England was three for 115, and still 586 behind.

On Tuesday, day three, Leyland offered great resistance as Hammond (15) and Wyatt (17) were removed by Ebeling and Grimmett respectively. Ames (33) was forced out of the game with a back injury right in the middle of a vital partnership with Leyland. The latter ran out of partners and was bowled by Grimmett for 110, leaving England all out at tea for 321. Ebeling took three for 74, while Grimmett (three for 103) and O'Reilly (two for 93) toiled skilfully.

Woodfull did not enforce the follow-on, even with a lead of 380. At first impression this seemed a strange, ultra-conservative move, but the Australian skipper's thinking was influenced by the fact that there was no time limit to the game. His shallow bowling line-up was tired. Why not go back out and build a huge lead?

From a psychological point of view it was an intelligent move. The Australians only had to hit 20 to give them a lead of 400, a score which no Test team at that point had ever reached in the last innings. Every run after that would be a further blow to England, especially as the wicket would wear suitably for the tourists' outstanding spinners. Batting last in a timeless Test, no matter how perfect the wicket was on the first day, would be a difficult affair.

Frank Woolley had to keep in place of Ames. Australia's second effort began with Clark bowling bodyline. He had Brown (1) caught in the leg-trap by Allen with just 13 on the board. Bradman emerged from the pavilion to a roar that would have been appreciated by any English batsman. Often after a huge first innings a player would relax. Bradman did, but he still preserved his wicket as he patted himself in quietly. He had been at the wicket just twenty-three minutes for 9 runs with Clark bowling accurately and fast. Clark slipped him some deliveries aimed at the ribcage. The first bouncer was despatched square and high over two men in the deep for six onto the roof of a stand.

Clark had better luck with his considerable speed when Hammond caught Ponsford in the leg-trap. Bodyline was alive and effective.

McCabe was greeted by Bradman in the middle and they had a quick discussion. They decided to attempt to hit Clark to leg. Both batsmen employed the hook and pull and had the close field shielding their faces. After three very expensive overs, for 29 runs, Clark made his field more orthodox and gave up bodyline while these two were in.

McCabe partnered Bradman (76 not out) until stumps. The

tourists were two for 190. The next morning, day four, Bradman scored a single off Verity and faced Bowes. He shaped for the hook off the lanky Yorkshireman's second ball, misjudged the flight and was bowled for 77. Australia was three for 192. McCabe (70) became Clark's third victim at 213, and observers wondered when Woodfull would call a halt. The lead was 593. The betting was on 600, but the tourists fell steadily without a declaration until they were all out at 327, a score helped along by the sadly inept keeping of Woolley, who let go thirty-seven byes.

The lead was 707. Clark had justified his inclusion with five for 98 off twenty overs — figures that were increased in both columns by bodyline. Bowes used the bumper liberally but took his five for 55 with more conventional methods.

England batted again mid-afternoon but was no match for Grimmett and O'Reilly, who spun the home team out before stumps for 145. Grimmett was the destroyer with five for 64, while O'Reilly got two for 58, including Hammond caught and bowled for 15, one of two players who could have mounted a big response. The other was Sutcliffe (28), who was one of Grimmett's match-winning haul.

Australia had won by 562 runs, and the Ashes by two matches to one. It had been a triumph for Woodfull, who celebrated his thirty-seventh birthday on 22 August, the day the Ashes were won, and Ponsford, aged thirty-three, who were to retire from big cricket. If there had been a man of the match award it would have gone to Bradman, whose batting in effect had the game psychologically won by tea on the first day when he was 150 not out. He (758 runs at 94.75 for the series) and Ponsford (569 at 95.83) had lifted themselves to supreme heights when it counted.

A FINISH WITH RUNNING

The Tests were over, but there was still some serious first-class competition ahead. Bradman captained the Australians at Hove on 25 August and injured his thumb while fielding, which added to his many tour woes. Sussex declared at eight for 304, and the visitors answered with a withering 560. Kippax, who had not justified his inclusion in the Fifth Test, when he scored 28 and 8, cracked 250, while Darling, whom he had replaced, notched 117, and Brown 60. The injured acting-skipper dropped himself down to number seven and managed an uncomfortable 19 — on his twenty-sixth birthday. His token appearance ensured a profitable gate for the grateful Sussex management. Bradman was box-office wherever he went and was obliged to play whenever fit, just to please the local county. Fleetwood-Smith, who had taken five for 114 in Sussex's first dig, now took five for 87 in the second, to give his team a win by an innings and 35 runs.

The constant pressure was eased somewhat against Kent at Canterbury when the game was rained out. But Ponsford, 82 not out, and McCabe, 108, maintained their enthusiasm. It was back on again at Folkestone when the tourists played an England XI, who batted first and made 279, with Woolley (66) and Hammond (54) showing form that would have been more useful in the Test.

Bradman came to the wicket after lunch with the score at three for 131, and was in one of those exhibition moods. After being missed on one, he clobbered 50 in forty-eight minutes and reached a century in eighty-seven minutes. He then made the game a footnote to cricket history by dealing fearfully with the great leggie 'Tich' Freeman. In one memorable over of big-hitting, Bradman scored 30 — 4, 6, 6, 4, 6 and 4. He remained 149 not out, including four sixes and seventeen fours, in 104 minutes. It was the fiftieth century of his career in 175 innings. W. G. Grace, the previous best, took 282 innings — another 107 visits to the crease.

As Bradman was maintaining his great end-of-season form, Notts was playing its last county game of the year against Middlesex at Lord's. Voce employed bodyline, as he had in many games through 1934, and was devastating. He hit a lower-order Middlesex batsman, L. Muncer, in the head. The batsman crumpled to the ground and was unconscious as players crowded around him. He was carried off the field and did not recover for twenty minutes. Voce, unrepentant, kept on with bodyline and hit another player in the head and chest.

The Middlesex management reacted. It announced they would follow Lancashire's lead and not play Notts in 1935. The Australians had always said that once English players were on the receiving end, attitudes would change. Jack Hobbs then joined Walter Hammond in coming out against bodyline. A few brave souls commenting on the game were still bemoaning the fact that Larwood and Voce had not played in the Ashes series. But only one of them had ever faced 'direct attack' bowling, and not from the Notts pair. His name was Douglas Jardine. He would never, under any circumstances, say it was unfair. But his arguments were looking hollow.

THE EXHIBITIONIST

There was just one tour match left — versus Mr H. D. G. Leveson-Gower's XI, at Scarborough. The Australians had hoped for a truly festival match, but when they saw the line-up of quicks — Farnes, Bowes and M. S. Nichols — plus Verity, they knew it was going to be fast and competitive. The tourists won the toss, batted and Farnes bowled Brown for 3. Bradman was at the wicket and in a punchy, I'll-show-you frame of mind. He walloped 50 in forty minutes, and then raced to a century in eighty-two minutes. He added another 32 in just eight minutes, before being stumped by Duckworth off Verity for 132 — all before he hastened back to the pavilion for lunch.

Bradman had been at the crease for just an hour and a half, hitting a six and twenty-four fours, which amounted to 102 in boundaries. Clearly, he preferred standing and delivering to running in totting up the best score ever by any tourist of any nation before lunch. It put the Australians on an easy road to victory, especially when McCabe (124), Ponsford (92), and Chipperfield (53) built the score to 489. Leveson-Gower's mob could only manage 223 and 218 in reply, giving the tourists an innings win, and a satisfying end to the tour.

'Outside the Tests,' Bradman reflected, 'that Scarborough innings and the 160 against Middlesex were the two most satisfying innings I played in 1934, and probably the most exciting I ever played in England.'

He had ended the tour as he had begun it, with sensational batting and record-breaking. He had compiled 1,144 runs at 163 in his last eight innings, which enabled him to take the tour averages at 84.16 from an aggregate of 2,020, ahead of Ponsford (77.56 from 1,784), and McCabe, who topped the aggregates (2,078 at 69.26). O'Reilly (109 wickets at 17.04), Grimmett (109 at 19.80) and Fleetwood-Smith (106 at 19.20) were the key tour bowlers.

Bradman, Ponsford, Woodfull, O'Reilly, Grimmett and Oldfield had combined to make the tour and the Tests a triumphant achievement for Australia.

ON ETERNITY'S BRINK

Bradman was back in his London hotel on Saturday 22 September entertaining an old Bowral school friend, the singer Elsie Corry, at afternoon tea, when he felt abdominal pains. They became worse. He informed Woodfull and said he could not attend a dinner scheduled for that evening. The concerned skipper told J. R. Lee, a Harley Street physician, who happened to be at the dinner. Lee examined Bradman that night and again the next morning. The doctor, a brilliant diagnostician, was perplexed, but finally decided the symptoms indicated long-standing appendicitis. He sought a second opinion from the surgeon Douglas Shields, who agreed an operation was necessary. On Monday 24 September, Bradman was taken by ambulance to hospital. He was operated on by Shields.

The surgeon found that Lee had been correct. Bradman's appendix was badly infected and out of its normal position. The infection had reached the peritoneum, the membrane which lines the cavity of the abdomen. Shields accordingly removed the appendix and did what he could to cure the infection.

Bradman's illness, which had first affected him two years earlier, before the bodyline series, was a mystery no more. Yet it was no less malevolent for being identified. The pain continued after the operation and Bradman's temperature rose alarmingly. The doctors conferred. The patient now had peritonitis, an infection of the abdominal lining.

On the evening of Tuesday 25 September, the hospital released a bulletin on Bradman's condition. It was serious. Medicos reading between the lines expected him to die. There were no life-saving antibiotics available then to pump into him. Furthermore, he had lost much blood during the operation. It was thought he would need a blood transfusion, a drastic measure in 1934. But the idea was abandoned. The patient might not survive it. The doctors had to rely on Bradman's strength and will as he experienced three days of pain, nausea and high temperatures.

While this fight was under way, rumours abounded that he had died. Bradman's condition was front-page news in Britain and Australia. King George V reflected public feeling and asked to be 'kept advised' on Bradman's condition. Neville Cardus, on a sea voyage to recover from England's defeat, was cabled by his editor and told to write an obituary. In Australia, Jessie Bradman prepared to make the four-week sea trip to England. But it was feared that he would be dead long before she arrived. There was a quicker way, by air.

'Charles Kingsford Smith got in touch and kindly offered to fly me to London,' Jessie recalled. 'It would have taken a few days only. Charles was flying his new plane *Lady Southern Cross*, to England. He would be coming back in the London to Australia air race.'

However, aviation authorities would not allow him to take a passenger. Plane travel was in its infancy and it was a risky business. Kingsford Smith got to London and competed in the race. He and his plane were lost over the Bay of Bengal and never seen again.

On Thursday 26 September, when Bradman was at his lowest ebb, he received a cable from his wife: 'It's all right, Don, I'm coming.' Hardly able to speak, he smiled faintly when it was shown to him. Doctors Lee and Shields thereafter noticed an improvement in him. The message from Jessie gave him something to hang on for at this most critical time.

Jessie took the boat and was informed by cable during the trip that her husband had recovered and was off the immediate danger list. By the time she arrived on 27 October, Bradman was allowed to leave hospital. Douglas Shields told him he would need six months to recuperate. He was not allowed to touch a cricket bat for twelve months, which meant that he would miss the 1934–35 season in Australia and the tour of South Africa following that.

While Bradman was recovering in London, the MCC was attempting to bury bodyline by altering not the laws of the game, but its 'Instructions to Umpires'. They were directed to intervene in the case of 'systematic bowling of fast short pitched balls at the batsman standing clear of the wicket'. However mild the measure, in effect, bodyline was now outlawed.

Don and Jessie did not leave England until 18 December, and a big group of friends and media turned up to farewell them at Victoria station. By coincidence, Winston Churchill, then a backbench Conservative MP, was also at the train station seeing his wife off. Churchill saw a photo opportunity. He spoke to Tom Clarke, a journalist from the *Daily Mail*.

'Could you introduce us?' he asked.

Clarke spoke to Bradman. The cricketer was reluctant and coy. 'I wish I could go somewhere I wasn't recognised,' he said with a sigh.

Clarke cajoled Bradman further by saying that Churchill was a keen cricket fan. The Australian shrugged. 'I am only a cricketer,' Bradman protested, a little embarrassed. 'What are we going to talk about?'

Clarke assured him that Churchill just wanted to shake his hand, but made sure that a *Daily Mail* photographer was alerted. Bradman allowed himself to be coaxed across the platform to where Churchill was standing near the train. They were introduced. Churchill made polite small talk, congratulating Bradman on his form and Australia's win, and inquiring about his health. Photographers asked them to pose near the door to Churchill's carriage. They parted, one the most famous sportsmen in the Empire, the other soon to be the most important leader in the free world's fight against fascism.

PART FOUR

CAPTAIN
1935–1940

32

THE BROKER-CRICKETER

I had proved to my own satisfaction that it was too exacting for me to live cricket day and night, and I decided completely to divorce my business life from sport.
— BRADMAN ON HIS MOVE TO ADELAIDE AND START OF HIS LIFE AS A
BROKER

L-PLATES AT WORK AND PLAY

The Bradmans spent the remainder of the 1935 summer in Australia in Bowral and then on Anzac Day, 25 April, began their new life in Adelaide. They rented a villa in Kensington Park, a quiet suburb of the city (there are no loud ones), which was then halfway between a large country town and a major metropolis.

It suited Jessie and Don to settle down with Adelaide's 315,000 people scattered between the suburbs and the hills to the east. They bought a block of land in Holden Street, Kensington Park, and developed it. Bradman started work with Hodgetts' broking firm and began to learn the business. Initially his main job, as he described it himself, entailed 'meeting the clients and carrying through what they wished' in the way of investments. He had to study the public companies and distinguish between speculative scrip and solid stock, as well as learning the workings of the Stock Exchange itself, although

367

he did not operate there himself. Hodgetts' had its own full-time jobber on the floor.

He also had to learn the basic principles of accounting, which gave him the opportunity to develop his facility with figures, something he had always enjoyed. At twenty-six, Bradman felt he had at last found his niche in life away from cricket. But he was never out of the papers in any discussion of the game.

In May, the London *Daily Mail*, with which Bradman had a good association, published a series of articles on 'How to Play Cricket' complete with photos of him demonstrating every known stroke. It was so well received that the paper republished the series in booklet form under the same title.

His long break from the game enabled him to devote his energies to learning the stockbroking trade, and he applied himself to it with relish. Between times he played golf at the Mount Osmond Club, with its rolling hills and fine views over Adelaide, and won the club championship. However, as the winter months of 1935 rolled by, his thoughts turned again to cricket. It was more than a year since he had picked up a bat in anger.

Some jockeying behind the scenes by his boss, Harry Hodgetts, a man of some influence with the South Australian Cricket Association and the Board of Control, saw Bradman appointed as State captain and a selector. Hodgetts and others were moving quickly. They wanted Bradman to lead Australia the following year against England when it next toured Australia. It was all rushed, and he had no experience in Shield captaincy. However, he had been vice-captain of the tour side in England in 1934 and led it occasionally in county games. He at least knew there was a vast difference between taking directions on the field and giving them. The big thing in his favour was his intellect. He was simply sharper and brighter than the average first-class player. It showed in the way he analysed the game and wrote about it. Even the fact that he had written to the MCC about law changes and qualified as an umpire demonstrated he was using his keen brain to broaden his understanding of cricket's complexities and problems. This didn't mean he would make a good captain. Intelligence helped, but it did not necessarily equate to inspiring and assisting fellow players, providing adequate leadership or even making the quick, instinctively right decision in a crisis on or off the field.

He also had an innate desire to win, no matter what the occasion, situation or opposition. This set him apart from many of his peers. But again, it was not enough to make him a good tactician and strategist. He had to learn. Bradman was not a born leader. His independent nature meant that he preferred to go his own way, rather than be the team organiser. Yet it was inevitable that he would lead. It was not easy to conceive of Bradman going on into his thirties under the command of a much younger player who had a third of his experience, and a similar proportion of his aggregate and average.

His appointment as State captain was propitious. Vic Richardson, now forty-one, was away leading the Australian side in South Africa. It gave Bradman the perfect chance to take control, learn the skills and present Richardson with a *fait accompli* when he returned to contemplate his limited future.

Bradman, at twenty-seven, started his season with Kensington club with a series of second-grade and then first-grade innings in September and October of 27 not out, 46, 155, 81, 5, 112, 106, 60, showing he had lost none of the skill that made him the most outstanding batsman in the world. The quick brain, amazing feet, control, power, placement and range of shots were all evident. Most importantly for the public, he was still the entertainer.

He started the first-class season with 15 and 50 against a visiting Marylebone Cricket Club team which was on a brief tour of Australia and New Zealand. It included several top-line ex-Test players. His timing was predictably not quite as it should have been because of the long lay-off. He corrected this by the first Shield game on 18 December in Adelaide against NSW.

It was a strange moment for Bradman. Here he was playing against representatives of the State that had borne, nurtured and smothered him with pride. Now he was determined to crush them as he had every other rival.

Bradman won the toss, batted and waited until after lunch, with his side on one for 139, to walk to the wicket for the first time for South Australia and as captain at Shield level. He played himself in, then moved swiftly to 50 in sixty-seven minutes, and after that got his late cut working to perfection. He hit 100 in 131 minutes, before being caught and bowled going for his shots at 117. He had just seven fours, but was well satisfied with the effort, which was just one less than his first-ever century at Adelaide in 1927. The difference was that this time he did not have a bowler of Grimmett's stature to contend with him. The spinner was away with O'Reilly causing havoc in South Africa.

South Australia reached 575 and dismissed NSW for 351 and 219, thus giving Bradman an innings win in his first appearance as captain. It was a sour moment for his old State, but a glittering one for Hodgetts and Co, who had engineered the coup to secure Bradman for South Australia, which had experienced lean times, especially in the batting department.

A week later, on 24 December, the grins on the faces of its administrators and supporters became wider as they hosted Queensland. The lads from the sunshine State had suffered more than any team against Bradman, and now he was captain they did not know what to expect, except a thrashing. He won the toss, batted again and gave himself and his adopted State a Christmas present.

The Adelaide Oval was now bulging with fans as never before as he came in at one for 32 before lunch. He began correctly, his fifty taking sixty-seven minutes, then, as was his habit, he stepped up the rate to faster than a run a minute en route to another century. It took him 105 minutes. He maintained this rate through to 150, and then went into overdrive, moving to 200 in only another fourteen minutes. His double century had taken twelve minutes short of three hours at the wicket.

He scored 233 in 191 minutes with twenty-eight fours and one solitary six. The over-the-fence shot and late-innings loft were now a small feature of his batting. This was his third successive double century against Queensland. How its administrators would have wished for a Harry Hodgetts or some other entrepreneur to lure Australia's sporting Einstein to reside in sunnier climes. Not even Eddie Gilbert, the controversial Aboriginal speedster who was still suspected of throwing, could make any difference. He had got Bradman for a duck in their first encounter in November 1931, but this time the batsman won the argument.

Bradman declared at six for 642 and then his bowlers ran through a demoralised Queensland side for 127 and 289, giving the home team victory by an innings and 226. He won the toss again on New Year's Day 1936 against Victoria before a huge crowd in holiday mood on the MCG, which was being expanded to accommodate growing Australian Rules attendances. The extra capacity was needed as well in the summer when Bradman was in town. Sydney was still his favourite Australian arena, but he had a special rapport with the MCG spectators, for it was they who had inspired him to his first centuries in Ashes Tests. That Melbourne wicket, too, had a pinch more bounce than elsewhere, which suited Bradman's shots. He had never lost the reflex for the faster bouncing ball developed early on rural concrete.

That New Year's Day knock was one of responsibility. He was in at one for 8 and batted steadily through to a hundred in 152 minutes. The fans were more expectant than restless as he made much play of marking his crease for the next stanza of what was obviously going to be another big innings, featuring his full range of exhilarating strokes. Out came the flashing cut against the rising ball. Then he unveiled the hook and the pull with more gusto, and just for a tease, he went one-two-one down the wicket to the Victorian spinners for a hit over the infield. His second hundred took just 115 minutes and he went to stumps on 229 not out in five hours and ten minutes.

If anyone in Australia or England had any doubts about his return to fitness and maintenance of all his skills, they were now dispelled. Next morning Bradman gave an exhibition of more carefree batting in which he smashed another 128 in 114 minutes, taking him to 357 in 424 minutes with forty fours. He was throwing his bat at everything at the finish and donated his wicket with a skyer for the keeper.

It was the fifth triple century of his first-class career. While each one had overshadowed the couple of 300s he had belted for Bowral, it was those youthful country efforts which had given him a special taste for the huge score. When he approached that kind of tally he knew that exceptional feeling, which no-one else at any level of the game anywhere had ever sensed as much.

He left the centre of the MCG with South Australia's score on eight for 510 to a standing ovation. The game fizzled out to a draw, with Victoria making 313 and five for 250, but few cared. The crowd had seen Bradman at near his best, and certainly in his most prolific frame of mind, which was something for a true cricket fan to savour for life.

Not quite as savoury was the ongoing animus between Queensland and Bradman. The State's officials and players were tired of being humiliated by him in games which were reduced to embarrassingly one-sided affairs. They made sure there was a rock-hard pitch for the return bout between him and Eddie Gilbert at Brisbane. The Aborigine preserved his energy for his projectiles at Bradman and gave him an uncomfortable time before he had him caught for 31. This satisfied the foot-sore Queenslanders, who were spared having to endure another day of leather-chasing. Bradman had been brought back to the field, again, as with bodyline, by methods that were claimed by many to be unfair. Nevertheless, South Australia still won the game.

In the return match against NSW, local officials were relieved when he was out for a duck in a washed-out drawn game, while in the second game against Victoria, this time in Adelaide, Bradman was out for just one. But his twenty-one-year-old team-mate, Charlie Badcock, whom some had already given the unfortunate sobriquet 'the new Bradman', cracked a tremendous 325, which gave South Australia victory and the Sheffield Shield for the first time in nine years.

At the end of the following month, Bradman's team played a first-class game in Adelaide against Tasmania, which still had to wait another forty years to be admitted to the Sheffield Shield competition. He was in an exhibition mood from the very start against the decidedly weak opposition. He came in at one for 23 after Tasmania had been rolled for 158, and smashed his first 40 in fifteen minutes.

In the ninety-five minutes before stumps he rattled up 127 not out. The next morning he scored 135 before lunch, bringing him to 263 not out. His 200 came in 153 minutes. After the interval he slammed on to 300 in 213 minutes.

With the score at six for 552 when he was 369, he scooped a deliberate return catch to the bowler to end the batting banquet of forty-six fours and four sixes in 253 minutes. It was Bradman's sixth breaking of the 300 barrier and Adelaide had not seen anything like it since Clem Hill had hit 365 not out there in December 1900.

Hill sent him a telegram: 'Congratulations you little devil breaking my record.'

It was the last major tune-up before the winter lay-off and the return of the Englishmen. He had had nine first-class innings for an aggregate of 1,173 at an average of 130.3, which for anyone else would have been sensational. For Bradman, it was simply another rewarding and satisfactory season.

During the winter the Bradmans' two-storey home was finished, complete with a billiards room, which was Don's favourite, especially when he entertained friends. It was added to the house after he had been at Harry Hodgetts' home with Walter Lindrum one night when the king of the cue made a 'break' of 100, which Bradman could not match. It riled his competitive spirit. According to Bill Johnson, father of Ian Johnson, the Australian cricket captain of the 1950s, Bradman bought a billiards table and practised hard. By July of 1936 — a year later — he was able to make a break of 100.

Along with moving into their new home, Jessie and Don were also preparing for their first child, due later in the year. Bradman had another responsibility pushed his way when long-time Test selector Dr Dolling died and he was appointed to the panel in the latter's place. It was one he did not particularly care for at the time, but it was a pragmatic decision by the Board of Control. Its members had faced the reality that Bradman was the leading force in Australian cricket. He was the best player, he drew the crowds that made the game profitable, and he won the big games that gave the nation some much-needed prestige on the world stage.

33

WELCOME BELOVED ENEMY

O'Reilly was a marvellous bowler. Our battles were the most challenging, a real fight all the way.
— BRADMAN ON BILL O'REILLY

CLASH OF THE TITANS, ROUND TWO

England sailed across the world again in September 1936 with a strong contingent of players, eight of whom had toured in 1932–33. They were the captain, Gubby Allen, Verity, Voce, Ames, Hammond, Wyatt, Leyland and Duckworth. The new tourists were C. J. Barnett, A. Fagg, W. Copson, L. B. Fishlock, Kenneth Farnes, T. H. Wade, T. S. Worthington, J. Hardstaff, J. M. Sims and R. W. V. Robins.

Allen was appointed skipper because of his personality and good-will towards Australia after the bodyline tour. He was expected to heal the wounds created down-under with the uncompromising Jardine. Bill Voce, now twenty-seven, was the most interesting addition to the side, especially after his performance for Notts in August 1934 against Australia when he let go a barrage of bouncers and employed 'direct attack' methods.

Voce had to apologise in writing to the MCC for his bowling methods on the 1932–33 tour and undertake not to employ 'direct attack' — the English could not bring themselves to use the word 'bodyline' — tactics again. This seemed an unnecessary requirement. Voce was most unlikely to defy his strict captain, but Allen insisted that the Notts one-time miner put his name to the apology or he would not tour. The speedster swallowed his pride and did as he was told. He wanted to get at the Australians again, even if he couldn't set a hot leg-trap and bowl consistently at their ribs.

Larwood, his great partner in the bombardment, had got back to full fitness in 1936 and was bowling as fast as ever, heading the county bowling averages for the season. He may have considered touring if the MCC had invited him, but he would never apologise for the way he bowled. Nor would he be restricted in how he performed. Larwood was still concerned that he would be subject to a hammering from a rejuvenated Bradman, and McCabe, if he could not use tactics that might soften them up and then remove them. Consequently, England toured without the best fast bowler of the era.

Jardine could not resist entering the contest, at least on the psychological level. Writing in the London *Evening Standard*, he suggested that Bradman's run-scoring might be curbed if he was appointed captain of Australia. Jardine had questioned his appointment as vice-captain on the 1934 tour, saying that Kippax and Richardson would have been more suitable choices. Jardine was hoping to cause friction in the Australian camp, especially since Richardson had led a successful tour of South Africa.

Bradman had a chance to answer such insinuations by captaining the 'Rest of Australia' against the victorious 'Australia' led by Richardson in Sydney on 9 October. The game, a testimonial for Warren Bardsley and Jack Gregory, would sort out the national team and its leader for the First Test at Brisbane in early December. It also pitted Bradman against O'Reilly for the first time at this level, as well as Grimmett and the speedsters E. L. (Ernie) McCormick and Mick Sievers.

'Australia' batted first and piled up 363, with Brown (111), McCabe (76) and Oldfield (78) continuing their touring form, while Richardson could only manage 26. The South Australian slow bowler Frank Ward took seven for 127.

The 'Rest' batted twenty minutes into the second day with O'Brien and Badcock opening in front of nearly 20,000 spectators. They stayed together against the fierce McCormick and the tight O'Reilly until the score was 38, just under half an hour before lunch, when the spinner had Badcock (18) caught in his leg-trap by Fingleton. Bradman decided to preserve his wicket until after the break and sent in Ray Robinson. O'Reilly bowled him for 3. The skipper then sent in Tasmanian Ron Morrisby. O'Reilly counteracted by sending him back bowled for 4. The 'Rest' was three for 48 and there were fifteen minutes until lunch. Rather than be a possible fourth victim before the break, Bradman sent in the Queensland wicketkeeper-batsman Don Tallon. Sievers bowled him back to the pavilion for 3. At four for 51, and with ten minutes to go, the skipper finally appeared.

Bradman saw out Sievers with a single and faced O'Reilly. In the back of both their minds was that encounter at Bowral and Wingello eleven years earlier when the twenty-year-old student teacher and the seventeen-year-old real-estate agent faced each other for the first time. Bradman had in mind the 234 not out he belted at Bowral. O'Reilly preferred the memory of the following Saturday morning when the game continued at Wingello and he bowled the little dynamo first ball. But as he prepared to bowl now, he could not forget the pasting he had received and the many hammerings O'Reilly had seen Bradman dish out to others. He was determined to get him as early as possible.

The battle began with four men close in the leg-trap, all ready to snap a catch from a misjudgement of his biting spin. In those ten minutes, Bradman mistimed a few shots, but did not give a chance. After lunch, with O'Brien dropping anchor at one end, the big contest got properly under way. O'Reilly threw everything in his armoury at Bradman, but no matter what O'Reilly speared in, Bradman was ready. He seemed to know where the ball was going and what it was designed to do before it left the tall bowler's hand from O'Reilly's run-up and the angle of his chest, shoulder and arm. Bradman soon had the leg-trap turning away, arms protecting heads and bodies crouched in almost humiliating poses captured forever in photographs.

He pulverised his way to 50 in fifty-six minutes and saw off the world's greatest spin bowler, who grabbed his cap and muttered off into the field to see if Grimmett, formerly the number-one spinner, could do better. He too found Bradman impossible to bowl a good length to, as he danced down the wicket and shot ball after ball through the off- and on-sides.

Whomever Richardson used, Bradman delivered the same treatment without discrimination as he raced to 94 not out at tea. Long before then every player in the opposition knew he had them beaten. The thoroughness of his demolition was demoralising. All of them had seen it innumerable times before, but it was doubly dispiriting for a team that had just had a crushing victory in South Africa. That admirable effort had suddenly been put into brutal perspective as they disintegrated under the weight of Bradman's bat. The national side would surely have a new captain and composition in this new season.

At 200 O'Brien, who had done his job grandly, fell LBW to McCormick for 85. Soon after, Bradman reached 100 in 130 minutes. With five down, the bowlers concentrated on breaking through the rest of the line-up and to hell with Bradman, who could bat right through. But the batsman got more than his share of the strike in a stunning partnership with the in-form Alan McGilvray.

Bradman stepped up a gear. His square cut and delicate late cut were brought more into action, as was the pull off McCormick, who tried bouncing him. When the spinners came on, Bradman scattered O'Reilly's leg-trap for the second time in the day. When the players went deep and O'Reilly threw the ball up, the batsman again pierced the field, and went arrogantly over it. He left the fieldsmen flat-footed as they watched ball after ball speed past them. Bradman took only another thirty-eight minutes to reach 150.

In the next twenty-three minutes, Richardson brought on O'Reilly, Grimmett, Chipperfield, Sievers and McCabe. He then took them off and began again with McCormick and O'Reilly, but could do nothing to halt the torrent of runs as Bradman hoisted each of the spinners out of the ground, and skipped his way to 200. It had taken him 191 minutes. He had beaten the bowlers, the field and the clock. He was hitting high and hard and seemed to be trying to get out when he launched into Grimmett and was caught by O'Reilly in the deep. It was the second time that O'Reilly had been obliterated by Bradman, and the humiliation intensified the bowler's rivalry towards his 'pint-sized' opponent.

Bradman's 212 had taken 202 minutes. He had hit two sixes and twenty-six fours. His second hundred had taken an hour and the partnership with McGilvray was 177 in just seventy-eight minutes. McGilvray batted strongly for 42.

The 'Rest' ended with 385, then on day three, Richardson's team — no-one was referring to it as 'Australia' by then — was rolled for 180. Ward took another five for 100, to give him by far the best bowling figures of the match, in an effort that would later influence Bradman to select him for England in 1938. Bradman's side then wrapped up the game, scoring four for 161 to win comfortably by six wickets on 13 October, just as Allen's team docked at Fremantle.

As the team disembarked, a wharfie yelled: 'Hey, Gubby, did you hear Bradman's score in the trial game?'

'Yes,' Allen smiled. 'But who was he playing?' The friendly war for the Ashes, everyone hoped, had begun.

34

ANYONE FOR DOUBLES?

Don Bradman brought to his captaincy all the powers of concentration, the efficiency and command that made him the greatest compiler of runs the game of cricket has ever seen.
— NORMAN GILLER, WRITER

PERSONAL TRAGEDY

When the Bradmans had a son on 28 October the news was greeted in Australia almost like a royal birth. But doctors warned the couple privately that the child might not live. Good wishes poured in from all over the country, while the new father suffered in silence. Neville Cardus came to see him as planned that same night, and they discussed the forthcoming Ashes series. Bradman told the writer that he didn't intend to score any more double hundreds in Tests, which he knew would please Cardus, who had long since urged him in print and in private to give freer expression to his game, whatever that meant. Bradman said he would bat in the same style in the Tests as he had in 1934. In other words, he would go for his shots from the first over he faced. He also said he expected that O'Reilly would be able to control England's best bats, particularly Hammond and Leyland, using his leg-trap. The new Aussie skipper thought the series would be tight as usual, but that Australia would retain the Ashes.

379

He drove Cardus back to his city hotel and stopped off at the hospital to say goodnight to Jessie. She had been told that the baby would not live much longer.

'I'm afraid the little chap will not pull through,' he told Cardus.

The next day Bradman was again congratulated by the MCC team and had to put on a brave face once more. The child died on the morning of 29 October. Bradman pulled out of South Australia's game against the Englishmen that day to be with Jessie in their hour of tragedy. Flags were hung at half-mast at the Adelaide ground. Gubby Allen allowed South Australia to keep Bradman's place open until lunch-time in case he decided to play. But Jessie's need was far more important and greater than a game of cricket.

Bradman wrote in his autobiography:

In the lives of young parents there can scarcely be a sadder moment. The hopes and ambitions of a father for a son, fine and noble though they may be, are as nought alongside the natural love of the mother.

Bradman turned up at the Adelaide Oval on Saturday 30 October to pay his respects to the tourists. Hammond was running loose in the game, in which he hit a century in each innings. He had just completed two in Perth and was promising to be the handful for the home team that he was in 1928–29. Bradman's preoccupation with how to dismiss him, and his plans for O'Reilly as his destroyer, were well justified.

Bradman had a chance to maintain his own form at Melbourne in mid-November when South Australia played Victoria. He won the toss, put Victoria in and then withdrew from the action because of an attack of gastro-enteritis. Victoria racked up 401 with Keith Rigg in good form, making 97. Bradman batted despite not having fully recovered the following day, Saturday, in front of a crowd of 21,000. They had come to see Bradman bat, but also in combat with their 'quick', McCormick.

The bowler was in dangerous touch. He dismissed Badcock LBW

for 11, and A. J. Ryan the same way for 9, making South Australia two for 27, when a pale and drawn Bradman made his way out to face an assault intended to do more than tickle his ribs. McCormick knew it was another big chance to impress the likely Test skipper and selector. What better way than to whip a couple up around the heart or ear-lobes, and then york his middle-stump? The speedster would have settled for a catch or another LBW as he thundered in for several hostile overs. He had Bradman uncharacteristically hurrying his shots, and two found the edge along the ground and in the air through slips. But the sick man endured and saw McCormick off after a longer than normal spell. This allowed Bradman to play himself in further against less troublesome bowlers and he was soon going forward at his usual pace, moving from 30 to 50 and then to 90 in quick time. He stalled for a while in the 90s, but managed to make it to 100 in 134 minutes, which was just one boundary shot less than his effort in the testimonial match in Sydney a month earlier.

His last 90 had come in the tornado time of forty-six minutes and it seemed he was fulfilling his comment to Cardus that he was not going after double hundreds any more. Bradman hit high and hard after reaching 150, giving catching practice to the boundary riders and in general driving the fieldsmen frantic. Just before the close of play he was snaffled by O'Brien very deep in the country at long-on for 192. Despite his intention at times to smash the ball out of the huge arena, he didn't quite hit a six, but registered thirty-two fours in his exactly three-hour 'display'.

Bradman had again beaten the clock. The spectators had been kept in a state of high excitement all afternoon. Reporter E. H. M. Baillie noted that 'as he walked back to the pavilion they applauded tumultuously for one of the most remarkable batting displays ever seen on the ground. Bradman obviously was very tired and he limped slightly . . .'

People forgot that he was ill or that he might be still touched by events in his private life. They expected the Bradman show to go on. His artistic displays were now a key part of the nation's lifeblood. There was no athlete, sportsman, entertainer, politician or statesman who could come near him in terms of public respect, endearment and expectations. He was also a truly national figure. While Bradman quietly attached himself to South Australia and was keen for it to excel, he belonged to the whole country. In Sydney, they were sad he had gone, but he was still the Bowral Boy who had made it in their city, because that was where all the most important people came from. In Adelaide he was on a pedestal. He had honoured that province by deciding to reside there, and in so doing had raised its standing in its own eyes and those of the rest of the nation. In Melbourne, everyone was with him because of the way he set the MCG alight every time he walked out into it. In Brisbane there was a little resentment from officials and players as a result of the hidings he seemed to have reserved for Queensland, but the bulk of the public took it a different way. He, of course, wished to impress them. In Perth, Hobart and country centres his appearance had the same impact as a famous politician visiting a remote spot during an election campaign.

Yet Bradman was distinctly above politics despite overtures from both major parties to join them. Party officials dreamed of the vote-pulling power he would have, but did not realise that he stood and wanted to stand above the political fray. To join one side or the other would immediately alienate half the populace. He would be reduced from national idol to vulnerable human.

On the field, he was arousing such high expectations with every Australian crowd that they might not be satisfied with anything slower than his November-December efforts in Sydney and Melbourne. It was disconcerting for opposition bowlers and batsmen from either side. They could not provide these fabulous entertainment feasts regularly. Most batsmen, for instance, might give one sensational innings a summer. A player like McCabe would turn on two or three, whereas Bradman would produce six or eight monster exhibitions of power batting. Crowds reacted accordingly. While home-game gate receipts in Adelaide more than doubled with Bradman playing, takings in Sydney games without him were halved.

The build-up for the Tests was bigger than ever before and expectations of what 'The Don' would deliver were out of all proportion with reality. The public would not take into account the effects of his captaincy, the opposition or plain bad luck on his batting. Even though Bradman had become a brilliant performer on all tracks, including gluepots and stickies, there was always a chance that he, like anyone else, would be reduced by the conditions of the pitch. But Australians in the mid-1930s would not countenance failure from Bradman. As far as they were concerned, no-one could stop him.

35

A STICKY TIME
AS CAPTAIN

Tactically and technically, Bradman was a superb captain.
He could sum up the weaknesses and the strengths of players in
an instant.
— ALAN MCGILVRAY, NSW PLAYER AND RADIO COMMENTATOR

ALLEN'S OPENING SALVO

England had a new-look batting line-up for the First Test at Brisbane, with T. S. Worthington, C. J. Barnett and Arthur Fagg coming in before Hammond, Leyland, Ames and Hardstaff. The rest of the order was Robins, Allen, Verity and Voce. Australia had changes in both departments, and selected in batting order Fingleton, Badcock, Bradman, McCabe, R. H. Robinson, Chipperfield, Sievers, Oldfield, O'Reilly, Ward and McCormick. Grimmett was dropped from the Test side for the first time. The omission caused some controversy and much press comment. Bradman preferred Ward after his twelve wickets in the Test trial match in October. However, there were some tensions between Bradman and Grimmett. They didn't always see eye-to-eye and Bradman seemed to find the champion leggie difficult to captain.

Allen won the toss on 4 December and batted, only for the England openers to run into McCormick, whose first ball bumped shoulder-high to Worthington. The batsman took up the challenge and skied the ball. Oldfield caught it and the series had started with a sensation. McCormick then hit Fagg in the stomach. He recovered to feel a ball whistle past the back of his head. He was disconcerted by the two short legs, who though they formed only a third of a bodyline field were still part of what was definitely intimidatory bowling. However, after a few overs, one of these retired to slips, making it less dangerous to the batsman from the point of view of a dismissal, but just as worrying for his health. McCormick's speed caused Fagg to nick one to the keeper and England was two for 20. Hammond came in and McCormick had him caught by the one short leg for a duck.

At three for 20, the tourists needed a partnership and new man Barnett restored order with the reliable Leyland before he was fooled by O'Reilly into giving Oldfield another catch after a hard-hitting 69.

Leyland went on to a solid 126, while Ames (24), Hardstaff (43), Robins (38) and Allen (35) gave good support and showed England had real depth in reaching 358. O'Reilly took out the bottom half of the batting with five for 110 off 40.6 overs. McCormick, who broke down with a back injury, took three for 26 off eight overs.

Woodfull, now an interested spectator writing about the Tests, entered into the debate on whether Bradman's batting would be affected by the captaincy. There was a degree of generosity and also loyalty from The Rock in his comments:

Bradman impressed me in a very marked degree with his captaincy and field placing. Two English wickets fell as a direct result of his very clever leadership and O'Reilly's very skilful bowling. Both Hardstaff's and Verity's dismissals were most intelligent and well-planned moves.

I believe that when Bradman has had the necessary experience of two or three more Test matches as skipper he will prove himself to be one of the brainiest captains Australia has had for several seasons.

This was clearly a stiff riposte after Jardine's stirring of the pot. Woodfull cleverly waited until Bradman had made some telling moves as skipper. This way, his remarks held some weight and quashed Jardine's hasty interventions.

Australia began its reply after lunch and lost Badcock (8) bowled by Allen at 13. Bradman appeared and started with two thumping drives off Allen. It was a similar situation to the beginning of his 304 at Leeds in 1934 against Bowes. But this time he kept up the momentum in an hour of 'brilliant' batting until tea when he was 37 not out. At the break, the audience wondered if the comparison with Leeds was realistic. Cardus noted:

Bradman often begins against fast bowling as though some deep periodic law of fallibility works in him, making him one of the human family. His genius has its own logic and authority. Apparently he is free to play off any foot, and transform into greatness and grandeur what in other players would be errors fatal and unlovely. There is the gamin about him somehow.

Meanwhile, the player himself had the rest of the spectators wondering if this was going to be a cameo like those several innings in 1932–33 and 1934. The answer came ten minutes after tea. Voce had been tempting him outside the off-stump. He bowled a fast out-swinger, which Bradman tried to drive off the back foot. He was caught in the gully for 38, having faced fifty-six balls in seventy-one minutes at the crease. Woodfull said of his effort:

His interlude on Saturday proved the most exhilarating part of the Test match. Some of his strokes were positively cheeky, but still remained brilliant in a combination of amazing footwork and superb timing. But his style has altered since he made his double and treble centuries in England six years ago.

Then he was probably the most correct cricketer Australia had ever sent. He never lifted a ball off the ground and took no risks at all. Now he is ever seeking runs with uncanny strokes which are the delight of lovers of both orthodox and unorthodox cricket.

Again, the former skipper was heading off Jardine's initial predictions about Bradman's capacity to bat and lead. However, the verdict could not go either way until the series was either won or lost, presumably by the Fourth or Fifth Test.

McCabe came in to join the steady Fingleton and they made it to stumps with the score at one for 160. Early on Monday morning, day three, Voce tempted McCabe to hook. There was no better hooker in the game, but this time he hit it to a fieldsman and was on his way for 51, with Australia three for 166.

Fingleton was playing a sheet-anchor role, but the ship was sinking anyway under the pressure of Bill Voce, who was bowling fast and accurately. Fingleton (100) proved a second Woodfull with his patience and courage until Verity bowled him. After that, Australia tumbled to be all out for 234. Voce took six for 41 off 20.6 overs and probably felt better about his schoolboy note to Gubby Allen promising he wouldn't be naughty with lethal bowling. What put a grin on his rugged miner's visage was the dismissal of Bradman, which had turned the match for the tourists. Allen took three for 71 off sixteen overs, which reflected his belting from Bradman and McCabe.

England was helped by the absence of McCormick and even offerings from Fagg (26), Hammond (27), Leyland (33), Allen (68), Hardstaff (20) and Verity (19) on their way to 256, giving the tourists a lead of 380. Slow bowler Ward took the honours with six for 102 off forty-six overs, while Sievers helped his second Test chances with three for 29.

Australia had fifteen minutes on day four and a complete day five to reach that total plus one to win, which was expected to be a tough order. But while Bradman was fit, it was just feasible. However, the home side lost one for 3 in the few minutes at the wicket, which featured six heartfelt appeals against the fading light. Voce bowled Fingleton for a duck.

Rain catapulted down overnight and made the wicket both treacherous and dangerous. Allen showed just how much on only the second ball of the day when he had Badcock caught for 0. Australia was two for 3. Bradman sent in Oldfield in the hope that he could hold the fort long enough to allow the wicket to settle, so that he could then come in and make some sense of it. But the desperate tactic failed in the next over from Allen when Sievers, his nightwatch duties hardly done, injudiciously flicked at a kicker and was caught by a tumbling Voce in slips.

Bradman came in with the score three for 7 and the hopes of a nation on his shoulders. The tension was electric. Allen could afford to pack a close field and seemed prepared to let Bradman go for runs, if he could. The batsman played a straight one. Allen pitched up on the same good length, but the ball reared nastily, caught the shoulder of Bradman's bat and flew to Fagg at third slip who accepted the gift. The 'most incalculable' batsman in the world had been measured and done with, as were the home team's chances of even a draw.

Allen was thrilled as the players crowded around Fagg to shake the hand that had snaffled the bogey man. Captain to captain, Allen had had a telling victory bowling into the wind. Australia was four for 7. Oldfield (10) was bowled by Voce, and half the side was out for 16. Chipperfield chanced his arm for 26, but Australia was all out for 58. The innings had lasted just 12.3 overs, with Allen (five for 36), and Voce (four for 16) the only bowlers. It was the England skipper's Test. The tourists had been triumphant by 322 runs.

HARBOUR HORRORS

Mrs Worthington, alas, couldn't put her son on the stage at Sydney for the Second Test on 18 December. He was dropped to make way for the cockney leg-spin of Jim Sims (inevitably nicknamed 'Dim' in Australia), allowing England to gain an extra bowler while depleting the batting by an average of just four runs an innings, if the displaced person's First Test effort was any indication.

Australia didn't panic. O'Brien came in for Robinson, who similarly had managed only 5 in two knocks at Brisbane.

Bradman again lost the toss and led his team into the field. They were not fully fit. McCormick was still troubled by a back problem. Ward had had his nose broken in Brisbane and it was giving him breathing problems. However, McCormick had Fagg (11) caught by Sievers at 27. But that was the only early breakthrough. England settled in with Hammond looking determined and Barnett untroubled, apart from one difficult dropped catch in slips at 26.

At lunch, Australia lost Badcock with gastric trouble, and the home side's woes continued in the field until Ward bowled Barnett (57) at 118. Leyland joined Hammond, who was looking in commanding touch. Both batsmen seemed intent on preserving their wickets rather than pushing the advantage they had constructed. McCabe broke the dangerous 129-run stand by trapping Leyland (42) LBW at 247.

England went to stumps at three for 279 with Hammond 147 not out. He was back to the form that had crushed Australia in 1928–29. The next day he carried on with aplomb and with help from Ames (29), until the English keeper hit a very loose ball from Ward to Robinson, subbing for Badcock.

The score was four for 351. Allen (9) could not repeat his First Test form and was trapped LBW by O'Reilly at 368. Hardstaff came in for a grim time as Bradman crowded him. Then he trod on his wicket while belting one from O'Reilly straight to Robinson at square leg, who dropped it. All eyes followed this drama. Then McCabe noticed the broken stumps. He appealed, but the umpire said not out. He, being only human, had also followed the shot to Robinson.

England lost fifteen minutes' batting time due to rain between lunch and tea but only added 67, to be five for 418 at the break. Hammond gave one chance after scoring 200, but otherwise was batting at his cautious best and looking set to break a record or three. Hardstaff went on to 26 before McCormick bowled him at 424. Then the rain came and left England at six for 426 at the end of day two with Hammond 231 not out. The tourists had been batting for 489 minutes.

On the third day, Saturday, Allen thought it wise to declare at the overnight total, for he feared the weather might intervene again and rob him of victory. Also he wanted Australia in on the pernicious little sticky, which had been nicely prepared for England's bowlers by overnight rain. This tactical decision looked wise early as O'Brien played a hesitant glance at a ball from Voce that swung across him. The ball hit the leading edge of the bat and O'Brien was caught in slips for a duck.

With the score at one for 1, Bradman emerged to rapturous applause from his original home-town crowd, and all, it seems, was forgiven its prodigal son. Voce steamed in and bowled short of a length. It was a ball to play back to, but inattention or just early innings uncertainty caused Bradman to push forward. The ball came slowly off the pitch and the batsman popped it gently to a jubilant Allen at short leg.

Bradman had made his second 'golden [first-ball] duck'. The crowd was stunned. A few balls later McCabe played a terrible shot at a Voce delivery that lifted and was caught by Sims in slips. The Australian scorecard read three for 1 and it was heading for a sticky end. Chipperfield came in for a bit of arm-chancing again, when some sensible batting would have been more appropriate. He made a bright 13 before Allen had him caught in slips by Sims once more.

Australia was a miserable, unnecessary four for 26. Fingleton, doing his excellent impersonation of The Rock, was up the other end watching this ineptitude. Unfortunately for his country, he fell to the only truly difficult ball delivered in the innings and was caught by Verity off Voce at silly leg.

Wickets tumbled with embarrassing regularity and it seemed that the side would be lucky to reach 40, until O'Reilly came to the wicket at seven for 31. Knowing that he was incapable of 'sensible' batting, he could be excused for throwing his bat about for three sixes in 37. He lifted Australia's score to 80 all out just on lunch-time, which was pathetic, even given the state of the wicket.

Voce, with his leg-trap bowling, captured four for 10 off eight overs. The humiliation of his apology for bodyline was now very much worth the trouble. He was returning figures that surpassed his 1932–33 efforts. Even without bodyline, he was causing consternation among the Australian batsmen. Allen, who had forced Voce's backdown, was proving a shrewd operator with leadership and ball in hand. He wanted the tough Notts lad to put the wind up the Aussies merely by his presence, and had cajoled him into public repentance just so he could get him on the tour. This trick had worked. Voce's real and potential menace helped his fellow bowlers capitalise at the other end. Allen himself took three for 19 and Verity two for 17.

The England skipper enforced the follow-on after lunch. Australia faced a deficit of 348. O'Brien (17) played a shocking shot to be caught by Allen off Hammond with the score at 38. Bradman came in on a wicket that had improved, thanks to the sun and humidity. He was subdued early and crawled his way with the stubborn Fingleton to tea.

After the short interval, Bradman began to play a few strokes, but not many, as he struggled with timing and placement. At 24, he played a reckless cross-bat stroke to mid-wicket. Robins moved to the sharp chance but failed to hold it.

At 27, Bradman passed Clem Hill's record of 2,660 runs in Tests against England. Hill had taken seventy-six innings. This was Bradman's thirty-fourth. But the Australian leader would have traded a big double hundred now for that or any other record, for if he slipped Australia would surely fall. He reached 50 in 112 minutes, but the tardiness was necessary. There was no point in pleasing his friend Cardus or those with short attention spans with a 'marvellous' cameo in this knock. At stumps he was 57 not out, but Australia was still more than 200 behind.

The next morning he and Fingleton moved cautiously on until the latter was bowled for 73. They had added 124 in a good stand, but it was not nearly enough. Australia was two for 162 and 186 short of making England at least bat again. In came a more responsible-looking McCabe. He and Bradman represented a last chance for glory, for together they were capable of turning the game around, if in the right frame of mind. Bradman had looked 'moody' but not in the right one. It was not a great surprise to commentators such as Arthur Mailey, when he lifted his head in hooking at a slow long-hop from Verity. The ball clipped his pads and cannoned into the stumps.

He had scored 82 off 139 balls in 172 minutes of uncharacteristic batting. Perhaps salvaged from it was the fact that Bradman had a longish stay at the crease. However, it did not save Australia in the short term.

McCabe was 'graceful and artistic' according to Mailey, 'and seldom wasted energy on futile flourishing of the bat.' He moved to 93 and was unlucky to be given out LBW after hitting the ball, for Australia to be six for 318. It was a sign to run up the white flag and the side was all out for 324. This time it was Voce (three for 66) and Hammond (three for 29) who had combined to leave Australia an innings and 22 runs short.

England were two-nil up with three to play. They only had to win one of three to take the Ashes, whereas Australia had to win two now to retain them. However, the home team would have to show a complete reversal of form to have any chance. They had been caught on stickies at awkward times, but had been outplayed by a more accomplished England combination.

RECRIMINATION TIME

The knives were out for Bradman after Sydney. He was the natural scapegoat for the national 'disgrace' of being beaten by the 'Poms' again. Journalists began to speculate about his skills as leader, and there was talk of restoring Richardson to the captaincy. Some players were even reported to have suggested that Bradman should stand down in order to concentrate on his batting. But Richardson's form did not warrant a return and he was in his forties.

Pressure mounted when Arthur Mailey wrote:

Some members of the team have not been giving Bradman the co-operation that a captain is entitled to expect. There is definitely, and has been for some time, an important section of the team that has not seen eye to eye with Bradman, either on or off the field.

Woodfull, who had recommended him to the Board of Control for the captaincy, stayed clear of the controversy in print, but in private reportedly told some of his teaching colleagues at Melbourne High

School that 'O'Reilly and Fingleton want McCabe to be captain. With Australia 0:2 down they have decided that this is the moment to lobby against Bradman.'

Then another former player, Alan Fairfax, made some remarks to a reporter with the London *Daily Express*, which the cricketer later claimed were taken out of context and distorted. Allowing for usual journalistic 'licence' in order to get a headline out of a casual conversation, Fairfax seemingly suggested that perhaps the new skipper wasn't giving his time to the other players. 'He hasn't a chance to study their temperaments,' he was reported to have said.

> *You have to mother a cricket team, and Bradman is no mother. He is too brilliantly individual. Armstrong, Woodfull — they were the skippers to study the players' interests and get the best out of them. Don simply does not come up to that. He is a pleasant little chap, hard-headed, shrewd.*

What Fairfax appeared to be saying was that Bradman was not a leader by word, but a leader by deed and thought. He hadn't made time to take a player aside and inspire him to lift. Bradman would rather lead from the front and influence others by his own performances. He certainly didn't like to parent the lads. He took the attitude that if they needed fatherly advice or motherly comforting they were not temperamentally suited to the tough job of Test cricket.

McCabe came out and said Bradman had the full support of all the team. When everyone had had a say, the skipper himself got up and claimed there was no dissent. He defused the issue by saying:

> *More good would accrue if the Englishmen were given due credit for well-deserved victories and if the Australian team were accorded more sympathetic understanding from those people who really know nothing about the inner workings.*
>
> *I have never yet played in an Australian Eleven which was not 100 per cent loyal to its captain, and I know that I never will.*

This diplomatic statement endeared him to both the English for his sportsmanship in acknowledging their superiority in both Tests, and his own nation for his patriotic sentiments of loyalty and unity. He didn't add that he thought England had been fortunate with the weather and the wickets. It wasn't really necessary, for in his 'hard-headed, shrewd' way he knew the wheel of fortune would turn, probably within the series. He hadn't won the toss yet, and Australia's fickle atmospherics might interfere in all the remaining Tests. More importantly, Bradman himself had not hit real form. That would mean more than the weather, the opposition and any internal dissension combined.

36

LESS PAIN
IN THE RAIN

*His keen analytical brain has concentrated on his plans of
campaign long before the first shot was fired.*
— BILL O'REILLY ON BRADMAN'S SERIES PERSPECTIVE IN 1936–37

RABBITS AT THE FRONT

The country's dreadful summer continued when the two teams
confronted each other again in Melbourne on New Year's Day
1937. The weak batting at Brisbane and Sydney had seen O'Brien,
Badcock and Chipperfield axed for Keith Rigg from Victoria, Brown
and Darling. McCormick was unfit and his place was taken by
spinner Fleetwood-Smith, who had been in fine form for the season.
England put Worthington back into the spotlight, and played musical chairs with Fagg, who was put out.

The wicket was expected to present problems due to overnight
rain. Yet Bradman threw up his hands and smiled broadly when he
won the toss. He had no hesitation in batting. But Voce brought him
to the wicket early by having Brown caught behind for nought.

Bradman marched out in front of another bumper New Year Melbourne crowd of nearly 79,000, who gave him a dome-lifting reception
all the way to the centre. It was a hero's welcome as well as that of the
far and away sentimental favourite. He probed for twenty-two balls

395

and half an hour which produced 13 runs, yet there was real temper in a couple of pulls shots. He looked good, while Fingleton defended well. The wicket was difficult with an uneven bounce and was not conducive to a big score. With the tally at 33, he mistimed a pull off Verity and gave Robins at square leg an easy catch. A roar or rather a groan went up as Bradman tucked his bat under his arm, whipped off his gloves and hurried off. He was annoyed at his 'soft' dismissal at a time when he needed at least another three-hour stay at the wicket. Bradman had scored just 133 in his first five innings, exactly the same as in England in 1934.

Rigg battled in his first Ashes Test for 16 before Allen had him caught at 69. Fingleton defended his way to 38, before again falling to spin. This time Robins had him caught with the score at 79. McCabe once more restored some respectability with a responsible, but at times dashing 63, which saw Australia six for 181 at the rain-induced premature close. More wet came down overnight and stirred up a nice gluepot for the second day. Bradman let the team score drift to nine for 200 before he declared the innings over.

In came England to show how to play in such conditions, but it had forgotten that Hobbs and Sutcliffe had both retired. They had performed better than any pair in history on such wickets, but only Hammond and Leyland were anywhere near their class under these conditions.

The big Saturday crowd responded mightily when Worthington lobbed a straightforward catch to Bradman off McCabe, and exited, stage left. England was one for 0. Twenty minutes later Sievers had Barnett (11) caught at 14. The crowd went wild. They loved an underdog, especially if it were their own, and they sniffed a chance to run through England. Bradman crowded Leyland and Hammond, but they were brilliant in their stubbornness.

Bradman thought their efforts were 'beyond praise' on such an atrocious wicket, the worst he had ever seen. At 56, Leyland (17) pulled the ball hard to leg. Len Darling at mid-wicket dived full length to his left and held a 'miraculous' catch centimetres from the ground. Twelve runs later the same fieldsman took another great catch to dismiss Hammond off Sievers for 32 at 68. Superb fielding, and not the wicket, had directly removed the best English bats. From then on it was a quick collapse, too quick for Bradman. He sidled up to his bowlers with the score at seven for 76 and instructed them not to take the last wickets. He didn't want Australia to bat again that night.

The innings dragged with the bowlers heaving down lollipops, and the batsmen defending against balls that a schoolboy might have been able to play.

'Every moment I was afraid Allen would see through my tactics,' Bradman noted. The better part of half an hour slipped by with these secret tactics in play. Try as he may to not beat the bat, O'Reilly could not help bowling Hardstaff and causing Verity to be caught. At nine for 76, Allen finally woke up to Bradman's delaying ploy. He declared the England innings closed in order to bowl at the opposition.

The light was bad and rain again threatened. Bradman countered Allen by deciding to send in O'Reilly and Fleetwood-Smith. When the captain told him to pad up, Fleetwood-Smith's mouth opened in shock.

'Why do you want me to open up?' he asked.

'Chuck,' Bradman replied, 'the only way you can get out on this wicket is to hit the ball. You can't hit it on a good one, so you have no chance on this one.'

Fleetwood-Smith was not so dignified as to be deeply offended at the skipper's whimsical bluntness. Out he went with 'Tiger'. The Melbourne crowd understood Bradman's chess move but laughed at it. The tactic looked like backfiring when O'Reilly hit the first ball bowled straight back to Voce. Bradman then sent in Ward, who stayed a few minutes until a cloudburst ended play for the day.

The weather improved on Sunday and was fine on Monday as Ward and Fleetwood-Smith resumed, this time in front of nearly 88,000 fans, a record for a cricket match anywhere. True to Bradman's amusing strategy, Fleetwood-Smith went to the first ball that touched his bat. It came from Voce and ended with a catch to Verity. Australia was two for 3, but no-one cared, for they knew the wicket would improve.

397

Bradman sent in Rigg to accompany Ward, and the Victorian farmed the strike enough to see 38 on the board before Verity had Ward caught for 18. The bowler had done his job and vindicated Bradman's decision.

Bill Brown came in next, with the Australian skipper again showing his tactical skill. He was sending others in to make sure he, the only series-winner in the side, and McCabe, a match-winner, would bat on a strip that was improving all the time. But he wasn't sending in tail-enders. He had openers at his disposal.

At 74, Voce had Brown (20) caught. The crowd watched the pavilion and looked at the scoreboard. Its operators waited to slide a name into the large name-plate. A buzz went round the huge audience. It wasn't Bradman. Some wondered if he were ill. Fingleton marched out to belated, scattered applause from the restless outer.

At 2.49 p.m., Rigg (47) fell LBW to Sims at 97. The parochial crowd naturally clapped him for a good effort. Then the applause stopped and started again, to swell into a roar as a familiar figure came down the steps. The scoreboard began manhandling a name-plate. BRADMAN was slid into position, at last. Half the side was out, and the lead was 221.

In the captain's mind, the job was about one-third done. He looked a different player from the rest of the series right from the first ball, which he pushed for two. He batted positively without taking risks and was well supported by Fingleton, who now looked immovable while playing enough strokes to energise the score.

At 18, Bradman reached a personal milestone — 4,000 runs in all Tests. He passed fifty in eighty-five minutes, which included three stops and starts because of rain. However, the need to settle in each time was compensated by the slippery ball, which the bowlers had trouble gripping. Bradman was 56 not out at stumps with Fingleton also still there on 39, the tally of five for 194 giving Australia a more than useful lead of 318.

On the fifth day, Tuesday 5 January, 70,000 fans turned up hoping to see their hero go on to a century and a long-awaited 'kill'. It had been four years since England had gone down in Melbourne.

Allen now introduced a tactic to 'stop' Bradman, which consisted of putting the field out to force him to run singles, on the premise that the strike would be turned over, and that he would tire. Bradman took the 'bait', and racked up the runs.

He also hit twos, threes and fours in the pre-lunch session as he moved into the 90s, with Fingleton trailing not far behind and still looking sound. Just after the interval the skipper cut Voce for four to bring up his century. It had taken him 193 minutes, which was slow for him, but reasonable for anyone else. Considering the state of the pitch, the game and the series it was another match-winning performance, as was Fingleton's gritty, intelligent and patient effort.

The Melbourne crowd over-reacted, as was its wont with Bradman, and the players had to wait several minutes for the deafening noise to subside. He celebrated by waltzing his very quick one-two-one down the wicket to Sims and driving him for four. Then he pulled him with cruel vigour for another boundary. Sims answered with a ball that beat the bat — the first that had defeated him all day.

Bradman was in touch. He had given no chance in his innings to tea, when he was 164 not out as Australia's lead climbed over 400, with Fingleton also close to three figures. After tea, Bradman stepped up his rate, with only Verity able to put a significant brake on his progress.

Allen came on with the score at 323 and Bradman greeted him with a fierce off-drive for four off the back foot. It was a telling moment for two players with a healthy respect for each other as sportsmen and performers. Allen had won rounds one and two in Brisbane and Sydney, but now 'The Don' was getting something back. It was what all Englishmen feared. If he kept going on such a friendly wicket the entire complexion of the game and the series would move into undefined territory. In bookmaker parlance, all bets were off if Bradman held form and the wickets he encountered in the last two Tests were good. Allen had watched him win two series in 1930 and 1934 off his own blade at a time when England was thought to be clear favourite. Much to the England leader's chagrin, he was creating that possibility yet again.

While Bradman began his assault, Fingleton dug further in and kept his head down over the ball. He limited his backlift and forward thrust to a point where he was anonymous, while Bradman started firing. But Fingleton's signature was firmly on the claim to this game. His century was greeted with as much delight as Bradman's, such was the appreciation for his application. It was also recognition for his guts in Brisbane and Sydney in a losing side.

At 5.15 p.m. Bradman reached his double century, and created so much havoc that the England players took time out to sprawl out on the ground until the demonstration subsided. It was his first against England in Australia and had taken 304 minutes. Allen, the gentleman skipper and Ashes healer, shook his hand and even smiled, perhaps ruefully, for the Test was now out of his team's grasp.

Bradman took block again to more cheering and moved easily to 206. With the score at 443, Fingleton (136) was caught behind off Sims. The partnership of 346 — a world record for the sixth wicket — had taken 364 minutes, or a little over a day.

As almost ever, Bradman did not drop his guard with the loss of a big-innings partner. His appetite for a crushing score was not satisfied. So much for his comment to Cardus about forsaking double centuries. He had to make them now if Australia were to have any chance in the series. For the moment, the staging of the short, sharp, brilliant knock would have to be put aside until a festival match or a testimonial. Alternatively, he would wait until this stage on the way to a triple century, where he would cut loose, as he did for the last half-hour of the day.

The big crowd, intoxicated with Bradmania, cheered themselves hoarse as he unveiled every shot in his *How to Play Cricket*, plus a couple of his old baseball favourites through mid-wicket. He reached 248 not out at stumps in 399 minutes, having made 192 in a day. Even though he had missed out on his 200-plus in a day when he was into a big knock, his score during day four was still the best by Australia in an Ashes Test in his own country, surpassing Clem Hill's 182 in 1897–8.

Australia was six for 500 at stumps, with McCabe 14 not out —

a lovely symmetrical total, which was appealing to Bradman's flair for neat figures and no blotches on the scoresheet.

He suffered a bad cold overnight and started day five unwell. Consequently, he batted listlessly for just under an hour, adding 22 runs before he skied a shot to Allen at wide mid-on. His 270 was the highest by a captain in a Test match and the longest innings he had played. It was also the longest by an Australian in his own country. It had taken 458 minutes. Bradman hit twenty-two fours and faced 375 balls. He was ninth man out at 549, having received support from McCabe (22) and Sievers (25 not out).

In his book of the tour, *Australian Summer*, Cardus noted sadly and prophetically for England:

> *For weeks I had been saying that it was necessary for England to win the rubber before Bradman escaped from a vein of ill-luck; our bowlers had not been beating him technically; he had been getting out to unreal, inexplicable strokes. The big score cleared the air . . .*

Australia's final score of 564 put them 688 ahead and with a stranglehold on the game. Voce took three for 120, Allen two for 84 and Sims two for 109. But it was Verity who had the figures with three for 79 off 37.7 overs, which included the prize wicket of Bradman.

Australia started well when Ward had Worthington (16) caught at 29. After lunch, O'Reilly trapped Barnett (23) with what seemed to be a wrong'un at 65. Hammond, the danger man, settled in with typical head-down determination and strong strokes. He couldn't hope to win the game but he could still hold up events and perhaps even force a draw, if he could keep some partners.

At 117, however, Sievers bowled him for 51 and went a long way towards wrapping up the match. However, there was still the talented Leyland, but a steady loss of partners to Fleetwood-Smith (Ames 19, Hardstaff 17, and Allen 11) made it difficult for England at six for 195. Robins came to the wicket and he and Leyland added 40 in double-quick time, leaving England 453 behind at stumps with four wickets to fall.

They continued the next day in attacking mood. Robins reached 50 in forty-seven minutes with two off Sievers. He went on driving as Bradman took off McCabe and put on O'Reilly. Not even he could halt the flow. Leyland hit Fleetwood-Smith to the fence to make the partnership 100 in fifty-nine minutes. A short time later, England reached 300 in 252 minutes, and at least they were giving the big last-day crowd entertainment. Leyland moments later cover-drove Fleetwood-Smith for four to make him 103, including ten fours, in 168 minutes.

At 12.50 p.m. O'Reilly got his fast leg-break to spin sharply and he hit the top of Robins' off-stump. His delightful innings of 61 had taken just sixty-five minutes and he had hit seven fours in his 111-run partnership with Leyland. England was seven for 305, and was soon all out before lunch for 323, leaving Leyland 111 not out. Fleetwood-Smith removed five for 124 off 25.6 overs. He had been expensive but effective in his first Ashes Test, and a great partner for O'Reilly, who took three for 65.

Australia's 365-run win had reduced England's lead to two-one with two Tests to play at Adelaide and Melbourne. England had to win one or draw two to take the Ashes, whereas Australia had to win one to retain them. It meant that the Adelaide Test would be critical, with both sides going for a victory from the outset.

THE CARPETING

Straight after the Third Test, the Board of Control showed it was learning about timing when it summoned four of the Australian team — O'Reilly, Fleetwood-Smith, McCabe and O'Brien — before it to be admonished for allegedly not giving full support to Bradman, insubordination and their lack of physical fitness.

O'Reilly later blamed Bradman for the summons. But he denied it adamantly. At the time, Woodfull was also suggested as the one who informed the Board about the problems within the team. He also claimed it was untrue and remarked to friends: 'The dissent was well known in and outside the team. Board representatives in each State knew who the dissenters were.'

The 'carpeting' was done from a position of Board of Control strength. Australia was back on the winning trail, and calls for Bradman's replacement looked insubstantial after his sensational batting and brilliant tactical exercises during the Third Test. Bradman might not be 'parental' in his handling of the squad and its new boys. It was possible that the affable leader was sometimes distant to the team members. Maybe he wasn't a profane inspirer of men, or a big-drinker in the Aussie tradition. But regardless of opinions either way, there was no doubt now about his capacity to win the big chess matches with Allen or any other cerebral captain England might produce. His breaking of batting order rigidity; his avoidance of taking wickets, when time was more important on a sticky; his sending in of rabbits to open; his 'thinking' out of great opposing players like Hammond and Leyland through understanding their strengths and weaknesses — these moves were, in combination, unprecedented in Australian captaincy. Neither the Board of Control nor members of the team could have articulated what was happening before their eyes. But every one of them knew instinctively, whether they liked it or not, that Bradman was potentially going to be to captaincy what he was to batting: an unqualified cricketing genius.

In other words, Bill Woodfull's prophetic statement about his needing two or three Tests to show it was coming true on time. The Board of Control had not the slightest intention of thwarting or demoting him. Instead, they would back him with a rocket for the lads who were inclined to be open dissenters.

All players now realised that any member that did not support the skipper 'in every way, without dissent' would be in breach of contract. There was more at stake than grumbling, hurt feelings and critical opinions, for once the Ashes were lost they would be grains of sand on a beach of discontent. Bradman, given full support and a free rein, was the best bet for taking the series. In the end, nothing else mattered.

37

100 IN THE SHADE, BRADMAN 200 IN THE SUN

There is no argument about the name of the game's greatest match-winning stroke-player when Bradman is Bradman.
— CARDUS DURING BRADMAN'S INNINGS IN THE FOURTH ASHES TEST AT ADELAIDE, 1937

THE WORLD'S EIGHTH WONDER

Australia decided to strengthen its batting after being successful down to number eight in the match between an Australian XI and England at Sydney just before the Fourth Test. In that game Australia was at one stage six for 332, Bradman having notched 63, but ended up with eight for 544. Badcock, Chipperfield, Ross Gregory (making his debut) and McCormick, fit once more, came into the twelve, with Badcock carrying the drinks. Ward, Darling and Sievers were dropped. England left out Worthington and Sims in exchange for Farnes and Wyatt.

In the Fourth Test, Bradman won the toss and batted on Friday 30 January in typical Adelaide heat for that time of year. Brown was on edge and it showed in his uncertain running, which was causing the steadier Fingleton some alarms. The seemingly inevitable happened when the score was 26. Fingleton (10) backed up Brown, who called for a single and changed his mind when he saw Voce collect the ball on his follow-through. Fingleton scrambled to get back and was out by five or six centimetres from a good throw by Voce. It was a waste of a very good wicket. As the dejected Fingleton moved off the arena, the fans stirred in anticipation of Bradman appearing for the first time in a Test as a resident of Adelaide. But, he sent in Rigg who stayed with Brown until lunch. At the interval, Rigg was 20, Brown 42 and the score a satisfactory, if slow, 72. On the resumption, however, Brown turned a ball from Farnes to Allen fielding close at short leg.

Bradman emerged from the pavilion through a sea of supporters and cameramen, all intent on capturing a portrait of those steady eyes and that firm jaw. Everything was in place for a big effort, and the crowd at Adelaide's beautiful ground was in a loud, anticipatory mood. Many of them had vivid memories of that bitter game four years earlier which had nearly led to riots. This time there was a small contingent of police, who kept well out of sight.

The game was suddenly alive. Allen trotted up to his bowler and chatted to him, hands on hips, setting the field slowly and deliberately as if he had been up all night doing his homework. After all the preparation, Bradman simply pushed the first ball from Farnes to mid-wicket for an easy single. But then Rigg slashed an attempted square-cut and was caught behind by Ames. Australia was three for 73.

McCabe then joined Bradman for a cautious partnership which lifted the score to 136. Allen bowled a short ball to Bradman, who shaped to hook. But it came through lower than expected, took the edge of his bat and crashed into the stumps. Bradman went off to disappointed applause from the crowd after 26 in sixty-eight minutes with not a single boundary. They were clapping the memory of his past displays, for this one had been forgettable. New boy Gregory replaced him and stayed with McCabe until tea when the score was four for 163. They stepped up their rate after the interval until McCabe (88), who had batted superbly, went for a hook which once more led to his downfall when he mistimed it and lobbed it gently to Allen at wide mid-on.

Australia fell away steadily after that, with Gregory making 23 and Chipperfield playing his best Test innings in a fighting 57 not out. The final tally of 288 before lunch on Saturday morning was at least 200 below expectations under the ideal conditions. Farnes justified his return with three for 71 and was backed up by Hammond with two for 30 and Allen two for 60.

England surprised by opening with Verity and Barnett, who then surprised even more with a stand of 53 before Verity was dismissed for 19, caught by Bradman at square leg off O'Reilly when trying to pull. However, Australia's stocks rose when Hammond (20) was also caught off 'Tiger', who was in a fierce mood. England was two for 108. Leyland, the other big threat, was still there with the steady Barnett (92 not out) at stumps. England was two for 174, just 114 short with eight wickets in hand.

On Monday, Fleetwood-Smith broke through to find the edge of Leyland's bat when he was 45, for Chipperfield to take the catch at slip. England four for 190. A few minutes later, O'Reilly deceived Wyatt with a wrong'un and had him caught for 3. At 259, Fleetwood-Smith had Barnett LBW for an invaluable if sometimes lucky 129. Ames (52) helped England take the lead before he was bowled by the fiery McCormick. England then slid to be all out for 330, thanks to the spinners O'Reilly (four for 51) and Fleetwood-Smith (four for 120). McCormick extracted some unexpected life from the wicket to collect two for 81.

Australia batted a second time after tea, and Fingleton (12) was adjudged LBW to Hammond after two similar appeals had been turned down. Bradman then surprised the crowd by coming in first-drop an hour before the close.

His mind was set on a big innings, which was again needed for victory. He was tempted with short balls from Voce, Hammond and Allen but refused to use the hook shot, which had been his downfall in the first innings, to garner 26 not out at the close, with Brown 23 not out and the total one for 63, a lead of 21.

The biggest crowd of the Test packed the ground next day with the prospect of Bradman in full flight and Australia fighting for a win. He began cautiously, obviously intent on occupying the crease. At 88, Ames took a diving leg-side catch to dismiss the patient Brown, and McCabe now joined Bradman. These two normally fearless attackers inched the score along to lunch, when Bradman was 70 not out, having reached 50 in the fair time of 105 minutes.

After the break they began to force the pace a little until at 197 McCabe (55) belted a full-toss from Robins to leg and was caught on the boundary after a juggle by the sprinting Wyatt. Rigg came in for some nervous running between wickets before Farnes had him caught for 7 at 237. Gregory, who had more reason to be on edge, joined the skipper who eased the tension at 3 p.m. by pulling Robins for four to bring up his century.

It was becoming a masterly innings, though without his usual domination of the bowling. But he was giving no chances as he settled down to take his score to 136 at tea, with Australia some 250 clear of England with six wickets in hand.

In the final session Bradman was pinned down by some negative leg theory by Verity with a deep-set field, so that he added only 38 runs in 102 minutes to be 174 not out at stumps in the slowest big innings of his career so far. Gregory, with 36 not out, aided him in climbing to four for 341.

Gregory remained patient on the fifth morning until, with the score on 372, he was run out after nearly three hours for 50. He and Bradman had put on 135 for a lead of 337 with just half the side out.

With Chipperfield taking over Gregory's sheet-anchor role Bradman soldiered on to 199 and then turned Voce for three to the on to give him 202 in seven hours and two minutes at the crease. Nineteen minutes later, when on 212, Bradman hit a full-blooded drive on the full back to Hammond who somehow held it to make Australia six for 422. He had reached the boundary just fourteen times in his 437-minute stay, while Allen's tactics had forced him to take 110 singles.

Once again, Bradman had been the team's backbone when rigidity against defeat was needed. He had only once ever failed — in the

Adelaide Test in the bodyline series — when a rubber depended on him. In this 1937 performance he avoided adventure except when the England bowlers temporarily lost the plot. He never once yielded to the temptation to do something extravagant. Bradman had not batted for himself or the spectators, but for his country. More particularly he had batted with an eye for the history books, which could record a probable victory for Australia and a levelling of the series.

Hammond had Chipperfield caught for 31 to return the excellent figures of five for 57 and the rest of the home side collapsed to leave it on 433, a lead of 391. Hammond now again stood between Australia and victory when England batted a second time. Fleetwood-Smith took advantage of the crumbling wicket by bowling Verity (17) with his left-handed wrong'un and having Barnett (21) caught in the evening of the fifth day.

The next morning as the Australians were walking onto the field, Bradman came over to Fleetwood-Smith and handed the ball to this 'erratic genius'. 'The game is in your hands, Chuck,' Bradman said. 'You can win it for us.'

In the opening over, Fleetwood-Smith delivered a 'glorious sinuous ball', which drew Hammond (39) forward. It swerved away from him in the air, then spun back between bat and pad and bowled him. It was a very sweet wicket for Fleetwood-Smith, who had suffered at the bat of the great Englishman in 1932–33 in such a way as to delay his entry into the top level of cricket.

Shortly after this breakthrough, the spinner claimed Leyland, caught for 32, and Ames LBW in consecutive balls and England was six for 190. The pressure was kept up by O'Reilly, who, while not turning the ball nearly as much as the prodigious Fleetwood-Smith, was bowling on a good length. Bradman kept them on right through to lunch. After the resumption, McCabe had Wyatt (50) caught behind and, when Allen (9) fell caught to McCormick, England collapsed in the manner of the Australians' second innings to be all out for 243. Fleetwood-Smith took bowling honours with six for 110 off thirty overs, while McCormick managed two for 43.

Australia had won by 148 runs, and the series was square, thanks in the most part to Bradman's return to big-innings form. The next match and the Ashes series for the third time would hinge on his performance.

NASH'S LASH

In the run-up to the deciding Fifth Test, England experienced a hostile barrage of bumpers from Victoria's tough front-line bowlers, McCormick and Laurie Nash. The latter particularly unleashed several head- and rib-hunting deliveries an over in one burst, which upset captain Allen, Hammond, Barnett and all players who had to face him. Nash also brought a bit of the 'aggro' of a later age to his game. He and McCormick were Australia's version of Larwood and Voce, with all the venom but without the leg-trap.

In the tour game they showed in a thuggish way just what would have happened to cricket if bodyline had been left to go on. It totally vindicated Bradman's stand against bowling directed solely at maiming or intimidating the batsman into submission and/or losing his wicket. In the end, every Test team would be in search of brutes trained to break skulls with greater ferocity than the opposition.

When Nash was included in the thirteen-man Aussie squad for the final Test, Allen became understandably apprehensive. Would Australia be so underhand as to bombard his team with bumpers in an effort to knock England out of the final game? He spoke to a sympathetic Board of Control member, who in turn called for the squad to be reduced by one — namely, Nash. The selectors, including Bradman, stood firm in their role, which was supposed to be free from Board interference. The squad stayed at thirteen, Nash included.

Allen called for a pre-match meeting with Bradman. In an amicable luncheon rendezvous on Thursday 25 February, Bradman dissociated himself from what happened in Victoria. He hadn't been at the game. Nor would he have condoned what transpired. He assured Allen that there would be no excessive use of the bouncer in the Fifth Test. The Australian skipper reminded Allen that he 'refused to encourage bumpers as a matter of policy, even without a supporting field'.

Nevertheless, they both agreed the 'occasional' bumper was legitimate and a different matter altogether. Bradman, ever the sensible pragmatist, saw the situation as 'only a question of adhering to the spirit of cricket'. He told Allen that he would never instigate tactics that would harm the game or create ill-will between the teams. There were no official agreements because they weren't necessary. One or two bumpers in an eight-ball over would probably be considered reasonable, depending on who was receiving them and what harm they did. Three or four would be overstepping the line.

After this, Nash was a natural inclusion. His presence in the team would be a psychological threat to England whether he bowled bouncers or underarm grubbers. He came into the side with Badcock. They replaced Chipperfield and Brown. England brought back Worthington after another spell in provincial repertory and left out Robins, who had shoulder trouble.

THE DECIDER

The Victorian Governor, Lord Huntingfield, arrived at the MCG on Friday 26 February and the 50,000-plus crowd stood in bright sunshine to sing the national anthem, 'God Save the King', to mark the Diamond Jubilee of Test cricket between England and Australia. Minutes later, Bradman won the toss for the third time running and the home team batted.

Fingleton and Rigg started soundly but slowly and their tardiness began to annoy the crowd. Rigg (28) appeased them ten minutes before lunch by getting himself caught at the wicket off Farnes, who was getting some movement off the pitch. Australia was one for 42.

The crowd, more than half of whom it was estimated were women, waited. Some thought Bradman would hold himself back rather than risk losing his vital wicket in the couple of overs before the interval. A buzz went around the ground as his name appeared on the scoreboard and a moment later the vast stadium erupted as Bradman stepped onto the green. The clamour only abated when he was halfway out, then built again as he approached the wicket.

Farnes rolled his arms, made some tinkering changes in the field and consulted Allen. Then he ran in and bowled outside the off stump. Bradman tapped the ball down to third-man for a single. He was away . . .

Straight after lunch, Fingleton (17) and the crowd were put out of their misery when Farnes had him caught close to the wicket. 'Jack' had hit one four in a complete session and was unable to move the scoreboard or the crowd. It was a pity. Fingleton, behind Bradman and McCabe, had been the team's main hope with the bat, and he deserved more than the polite applause he received mainly from the Members as he left with the score at 54.

His replacement, the dashing McCabe, was just what the big crowd wanted. The skipper led the way, and McCabe followed. Bradman reached 50 in sixty-nine minutes and his partner passed that early milestone two overs later. The afternoon heat conspired to reduce the English bowlers' capacities as the pair hooked and pulled the short stuff with a glorious abandon. Allen made a strategic withdrawal mid-afternoon with very defensive field placings. First the slips disappeared. Then the leg-trap, except for Verity's bowling. But the run deluge could not be stopped. Bradman was 90 at tea with McCabe not far behind.

Refreshed after the twenty-minute break, the batsmen picked up where they had left off. Bradman climbed high into the 90s as did the temperature, and this combination caused the Englishmen to say that they felt worse than they had in the West Indies. At 4.33 p.m. he reached a chanceless century. It had taken just 125 minutes. Seventeen minutes later, the spectators had another opportunity for a sustained cheer as McCabe reached 100. He had lived a more charmed life, with a dropped catch and a near-miss, but he was still performing brilliantly.

At 303, Verity broke through to have McCabe caught for 112. The partnership of 249 in 163 minutes was the highest by Australia for the third wicket and their most important stand together since the equally vital Fifth Test at The Oval in 1930. Badcock joined Bradman and they took the score to three for 342 at stumps, with the

411

skipper on 165 not out. He had batted with precision and seemed always to be holding back from blazing too much or losing control.

The next day, Saturday, was another warm one and the anticipated 100,000 crowd for which the Melbourne Cricket Club had catered was nearer half that. Beach cricket, it seemed, beckoned more than the hothouse MCG. The final turn-out would depend on Bradman. If he got going again in the heat and approached 200, another 20,000 or 30,000 people would be seduced down to East Melbourne by train, tram, car and foot after play started.

Farnes graciously allowed them to decide on the seaside early enough not to ruin a full day by bowling Bradman for 169 with a very fast one in only the third over. The innings, one of his finest, had taken 223 minutes and included fifteen fours. A few thousand people set out for the trip to St Kilda or South Melbourne, or perhaps a sweltering drive down to Carrum.

In so doing they missed seeing the two tyros, Badcock and Gregory, build another fine partnership after a somewhat tentative start. Badcock, a short man, relied alternately on back cuts and jumping down the wicket, reminding many of a cross between Bradman and Charlie Macartney in this, his best innings for Australia. When crowded near a hundred, he danced at a ball from Verity and forced his first Test century. At 507, just before tea, Verity had him caught by Voce for 112. The 161-run stand had placed Australia in a strong position, Hammond and Leyland notwithstanding.

In the final session, Farnes finally removed Gregory for 80, after he had batted less spectacularly but with great promise. Then the tail fell steady until Australia was nine for 593. The crowd went on with their weekend content in the knowledge that victory for Australia was now likely.

The innings ended on Monday at 604, with Farnes taking six for 96 off 28.5 overs — a sterling performance considering his opponents, the wicket, the crowd and the weather. Voce took three for 123 and was not now as potent as earlier in the series.

England batted, and Barnett played as if it was a picnic game, scoring 18 runs in seventeen minutes before Nash had him caught behind swishing. Worthington (44) added to the drama at 96 when he hit his wicket while facing Fleetwood-Smith. Then O'Reilly swung the match further Australia's way by having Hammond (14) caught and bowling Leyland (7), to make England four for 140 by mid-afternoon.

Bradman's tactical skills became apparent with McCormick and O'Reilly bowling when he placed three men close to the bat on either side of the wicket. The idea was to make the batsmen think the wicket was playing tricks, when it wasn't.

Hardstaff then dug in with Wyatt until O'Reilly had him caught for 83 at deep mid-on at 202. Nash came on with the new ball and quickly wrapped up the tail by taking three wickets with the score on 236. He had great delight in beating Allen with sheer pace to have him caught behind for a duck. The aggressive paceman did not bowl one bumper in his fierce spell, which extracted more than even McCormick's speed from the wicket.

England was all out for 239. Nash was not tight, but he bowled well in his first Test despite the controversy surrounding his selection. He had played a lot more Aussie Rules football as a champion for the South Melbourne Club than cricket. His selection had caused a surprise, but his four for 70 justified the gamble. The England batsmen were never comfortable against his pace, especially his lifting ball. He was always dangerous, notably in tandem with McCormick. However, O'Reilly was the dominant bowler with five for 51 off twenty-three overs, and as usual was never mastered.

England was forced to follow on into the fifth day, 3 March, on a track that had been affected by rain overnight. McCormick broke through at 9 when he had Worthington (6) caught by Bradman. Hardstaff came in for a few balls before Nash bowled him for 1. O'Reilly trapped Barnett (41) LBW at 70. Hammond batted attractively for ninety-five minutes and collected 56, including nine powerfully struck fours. Then O'Reilly caused him to hit one straight to Bradman. The skipper's tactics and the highly tactical bowling, especially from O'Reilly, had allowed Hammond to take control only once in his nine innings of the series.

413

Fleetwood-Smith had Leyland (28) caught at 142 and six were out. The tail was quickly defeated and Nash in the outfield took a wonderful high catch from Farnes off Fleetwood-Smith to end the innings. England were all out for 165. McCormick took two for 33, O'Reilly three for 58 and Fleetwood-Smith three for 36. Nash only got one for 34, but kept the ball he had caught as a souvenir of his first Test match against England.

Australia won the game by an innings and 200 runs, and the series three-two. It had been a remarkable turnaround from two-nil down. Bradman's 270, 212 and 169 were behind the recovery. His 651 runs in those knocks came in fourteen hours and thirty-two minutes and included not one single chance apart from the deliveries that dismissed him. This almost supra-human display of concentration, discipline, technique and brilliance against a wide variety of top-quality bowling had for the third time won an Ashes series, and for the fifth time a competition against other countries. His Test aggregate this series was 810 and his average 90.00.

By the end of the 1936–37 season, Bradman stood head and shoulders above every other player of the era and in the history of the game. To cap his supreme position of Emperor of World cricket, the King of England sent him a telegram of congratulations, which noted that the 'five well-contested matches [were] played in the friendliest spirit in which Mr Bradman has once more given evidence of his pre-dominant skill as a batsman'. It was a sensible public relations gesture to show that the bodyline breach had been completely overcome.

Soon after the series, Bradman, in collaboration with the journalist William Pollock, began writing his life story, including aspects of his 1937–38 season. His form was steadily magnificent through the summer. In all first-class games he scored 1,437 runs at 89.8. He hit seven centuries with a highest score of 246, against long-suffering Queensland.

Meanwhile, plans were made by the London publishers Stanley Paul to bring out Bradman's book, entitled *My Cricketing Life,* in 1938 — just in time for the arrival of the new Australian touring side.

38

LAST SEASON OF PEACE

He is still the greatest batsman in the world, and goodwill tour or not, he remains the coolest and most ruthless strategist in cricket.
— CRAWFORD WHITE, WRITER

DIN OF OMISSION

Bradman's tour squad arrived in England in April 1938 to find an atmosphere akin to a lull before a storm. Hitler, the bully-boy Nazi leader, was throwing his weight around in Europe. He had illegally rearmed Germany and reoccupied the demilitarised Rhineland. He was beginning to rant about reuniting Germans 'beyond the Reich', which was fascist-speak for taking over Austria and Czechoslovakia. England was being run by the conservative 'National Government', led by Neville Chamberlain, a quiet diplomat of the old school who favoured appeasement with Germany and Italy. He was a decent, naive politician not strong enough for the hour, which called for a tougher leader like the more bellicose Winston Churchill, who had formed a parliamentary rump of disgruntled anti-appeasers.

The political situation in the UK and in troubled Europe dominated conversation as soon as Bradman and the team arrived, but apart from that he found little different in the England he loved. From

his sheltered, privileged perspective as the most fêted foreign sportsman ever to visit Britain, the place was wonderful. He was entertained
by the establishment, who embraced him as an individual with status
beyond that of a diplomat or even a national leader. With the busy
touring schedule he was exposed mainly to the townhouse, country
weekend, chauffeured Roll-Royce, dressing-for-dinner set. Occasionally, he noticed the opposite, unattractive side of British society where
down-and-outers sheltered at night by the Thames at Westminster, or
the unemployed congregated outside the grounds of working-class
towns, and it touched him enough to make the spontaneous anonymous gesture such as buying meals for beggars.

Bradman was back as leader for the first time, and that brought with
it responsibilities far beyond the playing arena. He had to make speech
after speech, which he loathed. His quirky, individual wit worked well
in his addresses and this endeared him to the British. They appreciated
foreigners who knew their history and could use their language with
individual style and humour. They demanded more from him, and
Bradman, who rarely refused a challenge of any kind in life, accepted
too much. He would always feel more comfortable going out to bat in
a packed arena than facing a sea of expectant faces, who wanted words
not scoring shots. But he did it all in the interests of Australia's image,
and however irritating these non-cricketing chores might be, his tough
inner-character could cope with them.

Bradman's cricket ambitions still took precedence, and the aim
was retention of the Ashes in Australia's control. This was always
going to be a very challenging task. The team he had was being called
the 'weakest' to tour this century. Its core of experience was made up
of Bradman, McCabe and O'Reilly, the great stars and proven match-
winners. Then there were Fleetwood-Smith, Ben Barnett, the keeper,
his understudy Charles 'Chilla' Walker, Brown and Chipperfield. The
new lads on tour were Badcock, Sid Barnes, Frank Ward, Lindsay
Hassett, Fingleton, McCormick (the only fast bowler) and the all-
rounders Edward White and Mervyn Waite.

Clarrie Grimmett was a controversial omission, but in the judgement of Bradman and his fellow selectors, the forty-six-year-old's best

days were behind him. He had not been selected against England in 1936–37. Bradman had observed the older player's reduction of the use of his leg-break in favour of his flipper since 1932–33, and had challenged him in 1937–38 during a Shield match by saying he didn't think Grimmett could still bowl a leg-break that would turn. Since Bradman had moved to Adelaide in 1935, they rarely came up against each other on the field, but they had one last battle early in 1937–38 during a testimonial match for Grimmett and Vic Richardson.

Grimmett bowled Bradman for 17 after half an hour's batting and was elated.

'That will teach him I can bowl a leg-break!' he told Richardson excitedly.

'You silly bloody bastard,' Richardson replied in his usual pithy manner. 'That will cost us a thousand quid each.' He was aware that a big innings by Bradman would have had the turnstiles clicking.

Bill O'Reilly claimed (in tapes left with the National Library of Australia's Oral History Archive made public after his death in 1992) that a dressing-room confrontation in 1937–38 between Grimmett and Bradman caused the spinner to miss the 1938 tour. I asked Bradman about the allegation.

'That's totally untrue,' he replied. 'It was just part of the long-running vendetta by O'Reilly and Fingleton.'

O'Reilly had long criticised Bradman to anyone who would listen, particularly fellow journalists. The ex-bowler was respected by his peers for his knowledge and opinions, but his remarks about his former captain could be petty, vindictive and insubstantial.

The selectors chose Fleetwood-Smith, who had taken thirty-two wickets at 25.84 in 1937–38, and Ward (twenty-five at 27.88) in front of Grimmett (thirty at 22.86). Fleetwood-Smith had earned his second spot after his effort in the 1936–37 series, which would have seen him selected in front of Grimmett. However, because of Australia's shortage of speed, the third spinner chosen for the tour was likely to get a run in the Tests. Ward was therefore lucky to get the nod in front of Grimmett based on his 'youth' — at twenty-nine he was seventeen years younger — and fielding skills.

It was a difficult decision to make. Bradman found choosing Chipperfield as an all-rounder above Ross Gregory even tougher, but it was felt that Gregory would have other chances to tour. (Sadly, he never did. He was killed in the RAAF during the Second World War.) Another player to miss out was keeper Bert Oldfield, who had first played for Australia in 1920–21. His age was also against him. His non-selection ended his Test career.

MORE SAUCE AT WORCESTER

A crowd of several thousand greeted the Australians on 29 April at Worcester station on a cold yet bright Saturday and another 11,000 were at the ground. The throng was too big for the venue which was more like a village green than a stadium and the number of people jammed round the oval spoiled the atmosphere under the Cathedral. The normally sedate ambience of a cricket game was usurped by a boisterous football-type crowd. A huge press and radio contingent was perched on scaffolding and a special stand flashing their cameras or giving ball-by-ball descriptions.

The main thought on everyone's mind was whether Bradman would start the season here with his third successive double century. Where even great players made few such scores in their whole careers, speculation centred on the likelihood of this man producing such a performance at will. Where most batsmen would be happy to start the season with a fifty in a couple of hours of tuning up, Bradman was immediately expected to exhibit somewhere near top form for four or five hours.

A conspiracy for such an outcome seemed under way when Lord Cobham's son, Charles Lyttelton, won the toss and decided to send the tourists in. With such a huge Saturday turn-out he had little choice, if he wanted to avoid a lynching. Then Brown played his part by going back in front of his stumps for a plumb LBW, so that as if on cue Bradman was able to make his appearance at 11.45 p.m. — just fifteen minutes into the match.

Bradman shed a couple of sweaters but left one on, picked up his bat and gloves and made his way out. For the next 105 minutes he toyed with the bowling almost contemptuously while strolling up and down the wicket for just 37 runs. Then came lunch. After that, Bradman cruised to 50 in 135 minutes, going constantly onto the back foot to stroke the ball hard through the field, never to it. He left some in the crowd gasping with the lateness of his cuts, glances and pushes. His second fifty was up so quickly that his 100 received a belated, surprised applause. His next took just thirty-five minutes, which meant he had conjured his way to the last hundred in a little over an hour. Only the scorers were aware of the trick. At 200, the few who were still sitting at Worcester stood and those standing struggled elbow to elbow to applaud loud and long. His performance had taken 244 minutes — four hours of entertainment for the connoisseurs not of batting, but Bradman, for he was unique in the way he built an innings. In all he plundered thirty-four fours in accumulating 258 in 293 minutes before being caught in slips having a mighty heave of a cut. He gave no chance and looked in total control of himself, the bowlers, the spectators and even the good Bishop who watched from the Cathedral belfry.

Unfortunately, the rest of the Australians seemed as if they had not acquired their land-legs after the long voyage. Only perhaps McCabe (34), who got his hook going, was comfortable, but his stay was too short. Even Badcock's 67 was a prodding, mistake-ridden disappointment for the crowd, who had read about not the new Bradman, but Bradman Mark 2. Once more the epithet could become an epitaph.

Australia's 541 allowed them to win by an innings and 77, but not before Lyttelton showed he was to the manor born with the bat, scoring a sound 50 in the first innings, while Cooper got 61 and Bull roared his way to 69 in the second Worcestershire effort.

McCormick found himself in a total mess over his twenty-eight step run-up and no-balled himself into oblivion. Fleetwood-Smith took eight for 98 in the first innings, then in the second he and O'Reilly took three wickets each to wrap up the game.

UNIVERSITY BLUES

The Australians caught the train to Oxford and made a mockery of the fixture against the students by hitting seven declared for 679 by lunch on the second day. Fingleton took his time scoring 124, McCabe got 110, and Hassett used the steady undergraduate medium-pacers to get his timing right in scoring a fluent 146. Bradman was at the wicket for less than an hour for 58. Oxford then crumbled to the spin of Fleetwood-Smith (nine for 59 in two innings) and Ward (five for 55) for 117 and 75.

On 7 May, Bradman stayed in London and went to Wembley to watch Salford beat Barrow 7–4 in the Rugby League Cup Final. He was invited to meet the players in a line-up before the game and present the winners' cup after it. It was an unusual honour for a foreigner. During the game he was kept informed of the progress of his team at Leicester, and was not pleased to hear that McCormick had still not got his run-up quite right. Nevertheless, he took three for 61 and three for 54 in backing up the in-form Ward who took five for 69 and four for 73 in dismissing the county either side of Australia's five for 590. Badcock found his bearings with one of his Bradmanesque performances and scored 198, while Hassett, 148 run out, continued his form, and Chipperfield with 104 not out found his. The tourists won by an innings and 163 runs.

Bradman left his royal-like duties to lead the side at Cambridge. This time O'Reilly (five for 55) in the students' first innings of 120 and Ward (five for 64) in their second knock of 163 were the destroyers, with Australia making a massive five declared for 708. Hassett continued his marvellous form with 220, as did Badcock with 186. Bradman, who had come in at one for 3, outscored Fingleton two-to-one en route to 137, while the opener continued his steady form with 111.

HORDES AT LORD'S

The side caught the train back to their Victoria Hotel in London for the start to the first big match of the tour against the MCC at Lord's on Saturday 14 May. Long queues formed outside the ground and 32,000 were squeezed in before the gates were closed. Perhaps half that many again were turned away, demonstrating not only that the tourists were a big attraction but that Lord's was too small for a major London venue, especially when Bradman was the drawcard.

He won the toss and, naturally, batted. The strong pace attack led by Farnes soon put back Brown for 5. He had that infamous awkward walk back through the Long Room, but fortunately for him, no-one noticed. All Members' eyes were on the figure that strolled confidently past him and out into the cool spring air. He managed to smile for photographers and then refocused on the job of keeping out Farnes, J. W. A. Stephens, big Jim Smith and Walter Robins, who was captaining the MCC.

Bradman started as he did half the time, with normal batting frailties, and while it was a cliché to say 'get him out early if you can', because it applied to all batsmen, he was likely to be more vulnerable early in his innings. He didn't really comprehend what 'lapse in concentration' meant after 50. Stephens' second ball softened him up with a 'sand-shoe crusher', which amused Jack Fingleton at the other end. He pointed to an overhead plane, which had a sheet advertisement flowing from it with the words: 'For sore feet, rub it in.'

Bradman obeyed, but in the next over was hit in the thigh by Farnes, which had him hobbling again. Yet the pain didn't stop him moving easily into the 20s. With memories of his magnificent century against Middlesex and Smith in 1934 still fresh to most of those present, Bradman cut the giant speedster for three fours in one over. He reached 50 in seventy-five minutes, and was 68 at lunch.

After the break he took control and went to his century with a mix of defence and brilliant attack. It took him 149 minutes. He arrived at 200 in 266 minutes and was 257 not out at the close with the team score at five for 428.

As usual when there was little to play for he was out early next day at 278. He sent a low, skimming catch to Robins off Smith after another innings in which he offered no chance and scarcely a false stroke. He hit thirty-five fours and one six in 349 minutes of compelling craftsmanship.

This was his eighth successive score over fifty, and fourteenth successive match in which he had hit a fifty at least in one innings or the other. The team scored 502, but only Fingleton (44) and Hassett (57) partnered him significantly in stands of 138 and 162 respectively. Smith took six for 139 off 42.5 overs.

Australia then dismissed the opposition for 214, with Fleetwood-Smith again doing well with four for 69. Only Bob Wyatt with 84 not out gave a class display. The MCC followed on with one for 87 before the weather and bad light robbed the game of a day and left it a lop-sided draw.

The juggernaut moved on to Northampton and Bradman (2) had his first failure of the tour when Australia scored six for 406. Brown made up for his poor start to the season by hitting 194 not out.

Early in the county's reply R. P. Nelson attacked hard and took the score to 78, when he belted a ball to Bradman, who dropped a hard catch. Nelson called for the run as the ball trickled away from the fielder. Bradman swooped on it and hurled it back to the keeper, who ran out the other batsman, H. W. Greenwood.

R. P. Nelson made 78 out of Northampton's first innings of 194, and in the follow-on the county totalled just 135. Ward took six for 75 in its first knock, while McCabe (four for 28) and Waite (three for 28) did the damage in the second.

On Saturday 21 May, the tourists batted against Surrey in front of 18,000 at The Oval and Bradman continued his regular weekend entertainment by hitting his first 50 in just sixty-nine minutes. His partner, Brown, congratulated him. 'Thanks, Billy,' Bradman said with a cheerful grin, 'it's nice to get a few now and again.'

Bradman then increased his rate to reach 100 in 135 minutes. But for some reason he slowed down and added only another 43 in the next hour ending with 143 in just under 200 minutes. It was the top score, but Brown (96) and Hassett (98) demonstrated England might have to contend with more than just Bradman and McCabe, as Australia reached 528.

Surrey replied with 271, and O'Reilly, with eight for 104 off thirty-six overs, showed that he was running into his best form at the right moment. The Australians had injuries to three of their bowlers, so Bradman did not enforce the follow-on and the tourists batted again, much to the irritation of the crowd.

Even though Bradman could have batted and pushed on towards the magic 1,000 in May, he let others — notably Badcock (95) and Barnett (120 not out) — get some form. He declared at 4 p.m. on the last day to let Surrey have a hit as the game fizzled towards a draw. Bradman was booed as he led the Australians out onto the field, which was a new experience for the twenty-nine-year-old.

'I'm sorry that it was an unpopular move,' he told journalists in explaining that he didn't want his injured men put under undue pressure, but made no apology for his decision. As captain he was responsible first to his team's interests. It was good public relations. He explained himself and left no questions open as to his motives, while not bowing to unreasonable media and spectator pressure.

THE RACE TO 1,000

The race for a thousand runs in May challenged Hitler for front-page treatment in many papers. His representative was having 'talks' about continued 'peace and co-operation' with the Czech Prime Minister. Observers wondered whether Hitler was a bellicose bluffer or really after another spelling of 'peace', namely a piece of Austria, Czecho-slovakia and any other country he fancied.

Meanwhile Bradman, Hammond and Bill Edrich of Middlesex continued their fight for a piece of sporting history. By Thursday 25 May, Bradman had 876, Hammond 781 and Edrich 981. But the weather was another factor and threatened to spoil the show, as it nearly had with Bradman in 1930. He put Hampshire in to bat at Southampton with 2,000 turning up to watch. Again, the skipper had put his personal ambitions second to that of his team. Instead of two chances before the end of May, Bradman would now probably have just one.

However, O'Reilly played his part in helping the leader by rolling the county with six for 65 in a score of 157. By mid-afternoon the ground was jam-packed with 10,000 fans wanting to see if Bradman could do it.

With rain forecast, he commenced a minute before tea at one for 78, and after the break had trouble with the county's spinners on the rain-affected wicket. He and Fingleton negotiated the problem and Bradman was 71 not out at stumps out of one for 204. Next morning, he defended his way on a further dampened wicket to be 100 in 152 minutes, still 24 short of his target.

Fingleton reached his century two overs after Bradman, but now the gods intervened. Rain stopped play at 12.55 p.m., with Bradman on 109 not out and still 15 short of those four figures.

Meanwhile, in the Worcester versus Middlesex game at Lord's, Worcester was bowled out by lunch for 83. Out marched Edrich on 981. He faced the big South African Test bowler R. J. Crisp, who was aptly named. Edrich received a juicy half-volley on the second ball of the innings and belted it back wide of and above the bowler. Crisp threw up a desperate left hand and the ball stuck. Edrich was out for 0 and stuck on 981. Hammond had the toughest task of the three, but was 79 not out overnight in his match for Gloucester against Surrey. The next morning he was bowled for 113, which left him on 894 and without another chance to notch the required runs.

Back at wet Southampton, the sun was shining and after thirty minutes, Bradman resumed with Fingleton and clobbered the necessary 15 runs. It was the second time he had achieved the May 1,000 in the bad weather at Southampton. At lunch Bradman declared the innings closed at one for 320, with himself on 145 and Fingleton 123.

Edrich's team played so well that they beat Worcester by an innings, thus depriving him of his 1,000 and leaving Bradman as the first player to make it in 1938. It had taken him just seven visits to the crease, which was several innings fewer than the other contenders, and he was then averaging 170.16. The feat was all the more meritorious for the fact that he had avoided contriving it by hogging the batting crease.

Journalists pressed for a conference or personal statement, but the team manager, W. H. Jeanes, told them: 'Bradman is very pleased but he does not talk about himself and has not said very much about it.'

His mind was far more concentrated on the forthcoming county match against a strong Middlesex at Lord's. Unfortunately, it was also rain-affected. Australia could only make 132, with Bradman (5) out for his second failure of the season. 'Dim' Sims the spinner did his Test chances some good by taking four for 25, while Robins secured two for 27 and W. Nevell, three for 38.

It was 28 May, and Edrich, who opened, still had a chance to capture 1,000 in time. However, he was bowled by O'Reilly for 9, and so hung precariously on 990 runs, and with very little prospect of achieving his goal. Middlesex's young Denis Compton scored a competent 65 before O'Reilly sent him back also bowled. Robins played well for 43 but was yorked by McCormick, who had been limiting his no-balls now to a couple a match. The county ended with 188 and McCormick took a season-best of six for 58, while O'Reilly shaped well for the bigger contests ahead with four for 56.

The rain had so interrupted play that Australia began its second innings at 2.45 p.m. on the last day, Tuesday 31 May. Edrich looked on in agony as Australia batted. Bradman was travelling well on 30 not out and McCabe 48 not out, with the score at two for 114 after the first seventy minutes.

Bradman told the Middlesex skipper, Robins, that he was declaring. The players began to walk off the field thinking Bradman had intended to finish the game early. It was due to end at 5.30 p.m. if the captains agreed there was no chance of a result, instead of the official closing time of 6 p.m. The crowd booed, and then looked rather stupid as Bradman led his men onto the field to bowl at least six overs before the close to the young Edrich. He would have easily enough time to score the precious 10 to reach 1,000 before May's close that fine spring night.

Edrich was amazed that 'a man such as Bradman' would allow a mere tyro like himself the opportunity to rank with such a great player in the very small 1938 'May 1,000 Club'. But Bradman judged from his performances that he deserved the chance.

425

'Good luck, Bill,' Bradman called from his position close to the wicket as McCabe prepared to bowl to him. 'We're not going to give them to you.'

Edrich scored a two and two fours and the coveted prize was his. He acknowledged the cheers from the big crowd that had stayed to perhaps see a Lord's cocktail hour cameo from Bradman. Instead, they applauded as he was first to shake Edrich's hand.

PAYNTER'S PICTURE, McCABE'S MASTERPIECE

In the game against Gloucestershire at Bristol starting on 1 June, O'Reilly (six for 32) and Fleetwood-Smith (three for 32) dismissed the county for 78. Australia replied with 164 on a slippery wicket and without Bradman, who had back problems. Only Badcock got going with 51. R. A. Sinfield, an off-spinner, held his hand high for Test selection with eight for 65, the best return against the tourists yet. The county's second effort of 107 was marginally better than its first with O'Reilly (five for 45) and Fleetwood-Smith (four for 39) again ruining the fun. Australia went on to win easily by ten wickets.

Meanwhile back at Lord's, a match between England and The Rest was sorting out the Test side. The Rest batted first and notched 278 of which Paynter's 79 was the only notable effort. Farnes (three for 51) and Verity (four for 71) appealed for places at Nottingham. England replied with 377. Pollard did best for The Rest with five for 57. Hammond, who turned himself from pro to amateur in order to captain England, hit 107, while Edrich (80) and another youngster named Len Hutton (40) helped their chances of a higher calling.

Edrich's performance and his great start to 1938 (at that point 1,058 runs at average 83.84) got him a berth with other Ashes newcomers in Hutton (773 at 77.30), Compton (758 at 58.15), off-spinner Sinfield and leg-spinner Doug Wright. The 'old' hands selected were Hammond — the skipper — Paynter, Ames, Verity and Charlie Barnett. Hammond had specifically asked for Paynter's inclusion. The left-hander was expected to counter O'Reilly and break up his line.

Australia, again minus Bradman with his back injury, had a final preparation against Essex and beat them by 97 runs. In a low-scoring game Ward took eleven for 77 for the match in a final bid to catch the tour selectors' eyes, but Fleetwood-Smith did nearly as well capturing seven for 45. It was enough for both of them and all-rounder Waite was made twelfth man. Australia's Test side in batting order was Fingleton, Brown, Bradman, McCabe, Hassett, Badcock, Ben Barnett, Ward, O'Reilly, McCormick and Fleetwood-Smith.

There was disagreement over Ward's selection. 'I didn't want him in,' Bradman remarked. 'It was embarrassing to me to have three spinners of the same type. How was I going to use them? I was over-ruled by the other selectors.'

On Friday 10 June, Hammond won the toss at Trent Bridge, which looked like a fairground with bunting and colourful flags bathed in cool sunshine. The new amateur captain acted most pro-fessionally and put his own side in to bat in front of a crowd that promised to approach 20,000. McCormick had Barnett dropped in his first over, and then Bradman threw O'Reilly the new ball at the other end. In McCormick's second over Hutton defended a short one and the ball rolled against his stumps. Umpire Chester inspected the bails, but they had not been dislodged. With these pieces of luck behind them the openers began to take toll of the Australian attack and Barnett crashed his way to 98 not out at lunch with England on 169 without loss. Barnett reached his century on the first ball after lunch and was finally bowled for 126 by McCormick, who had taken the new ball. England was one for 219.

Hutton reached his 100 with a drive off Fleetwood-Smith in his first Ashes innings, but was LBW next ball when trying to sweep the spinner.

Paynter was in good form as O'Reilly bowled Edrich for 5 and then Hammond for 26. The left-hander was given support by Comp-ton and they flayed the loose Australian bowling to leave England at four for 422 at stumps.

Next morning first Paynter reached his century, then Compton on debut got his with a cut off O'Reilly. Next over he swept Fleetwood-Smith and was caught on the square-leg boundary by Badcock for 102.

When a glowing Compton reached the dressing room, Hammond confronted him. 'You don't do that against Australia,' the skipper admonished. 'I thought I told you to get 200.'

Paynter obeyed the captain and went on to 216 not out in 319 minutes with one six, one five, and twenty-six fours. Hammond declared the innings closed at eight for 658 at 3.15 p.m. England had batted aggressively at 3.5 runs an over. The Australian Attorney-General and later Prime Minister, Robert Menzies, was in the pavilion as the tourists trudged off. 'Well-bowled, Bill,' he called to O'Reilly. 'But I always thought you were a spinner.'

O'Reilly scowled. 'Would have been OK,' he said, 'if it hadn't been for that bloody brothel of a wicket.'

He returned three for 164 off fifty-six overs, while Fleetwood-Smith took four for 153 from forty-nine. Ward's none for 142 off thirty overs were the worst figures anyone could recall first-up, and again observers wondered about the wisdom of leaving Grimmett to grow old and idle in Adelaide.

Australia began its reply. The gate was closed at lunch-time as the crowd peaked at just over 30,000 in preparation for Bradman batting. They soon got what they wanted when Wright caused Fingleton (9) to play on at 24 and The Don came out to tremendous applause to join Brown in the middle. They wondered if 658 would be enough after all, in view of his magnificent form during the tour.

Bradman soon had them gasping, not at his shots so much as his fallibility. Wright got a hand to a caught-and-bowled, but it was travelling too fast to stick. Bradman was streaky and uncomfortable against the tall leg-spinner, and the crowd soon grasped that he was this day a not-so-well-oiled machine. Missing perhaps was a cog of application or a rivet of concentration. For once, he was back in the ranks of the finest bats who ever stroked a ball. At tea, he had collected just 7.

After the break, Bradman continued to have problems with Wright who beat him four times with flight and spin. At 47, he slashed at Farnes and was dropped in the gully. Bradman moved to 51 in eighty-five minutes as the light closed in to make conditions gloomy.

He then received a sharp-turner from Sinfield outside the off, which he just touched with the thinnest of inside edges onto his right pad and through to Ames. The keeper whipped off the bails and appealed. All eyes swung to the square-leg umpire, who shook his head firmly. Ames then looked at umpire Chester at the bowler's end, who duly gave him out caught behind.

Bradman shouldered arms and marched off. He later congratulated Chester, whom he regarded as the greatest of umpires, on his perceptive decision. Australia then lost Brown (48) caught behind at 134 and Ward came in to join McCabe as nightwatchman, leaving Australia three for 138 at stumps.

Early on Monday morning, Farnes bowled Ward for 2. Wright had Hassett caught in Hammond's midriff for 1. Australia was five for 151 and heading for not just a poor first innings, but defeat. Badcock (9) played on to Wright in a similar manner to Fingleton and Australia was six for 194 and 464 runs behind, with the time at 12.40 p.m.

McCabe, who had held the innings together, decided enough was enough. It was too early to defend and he was a natural attacker anyway. He hooked Farnes for six to bring up 200 and raced to 105 not out at lunch with his team fumbling at seven for 261.

After the break McCabe took charge and moved into the bowling with hooks and drives in a partnership of 67 with Barnett who departed after making 22. After that it was all McCabe as he demolished the England attack, mixing upright grace and easy power. At one point he took four fours in one over from Wright.

Bradman was alone on the dressing-room balcony watching what he described as 'the best batting I ever saw or ever hope to see'. He put his head inside the room and called to his charges, who were variously engaged in other activities than watching Stan. 'Come and watch this,' Bradman ordered. 'You'll never see anything like it again.'

The team came out and watched enthralled as the mercurial McCabe reached 200 in 233 minutes. Fleetwood-Smith was kept away from the strike in a last-wicket stand that produced 77 runs in just half an hour as McCabe reduced England's bowlers to a rabble without cause, direction or length. At 3.34 p.m., his masterful display ended when he was caught at cover, just short of the clock. His final score of 232 had taken 235 minutes.

As McCabe entered the dressing-room Bradman shook his hand and told him: 'If I could play an innings like that I'd be a proud man.'

Australia was all out for 411. The good figures of Farnes and Wright had been ruined as they finished with four wickets each for 106 and 158 respectively. However, when the stardust of McCabe's brilliance had settled his team was still 247 in arrears. Despite the embarrassing hammering England had received, Hammond remained cool and sent the Australians back in. It was the sensible decision with a session and a day to play.

Fingleton and Brown contrasted sharply with what had gone before, but there was no point in them trying to emulate McCabe, especially with their team being so far behind. The crowd repeatedly booed the two Australians. Bradman, who had had enough of this kind of mob reaction, sent a message out to Fingleton to pull away from the crease if it continued. He obeyed as Verity came in to bowl.

'What's going on?' umpire Chester inquired.

'Don ordered me to,' Fingleton replied.

Hammond, at slip, agreed with the tactic. 'It's all right by me,' he called.

The noise grew. Fingleton sat down beside the pitch for a minute or so until the noise abated. Then he got up, took guard and batted on until Hammond brilliantly caught him left-handed off Edrich for 40. He had done the job his skipper asked of him.

Bradman came in to another hearty reception, despite the earlier booing and played out the last twenty minutes to be on 3 at the close with Brown 51 and Australia one for 102 and still 145 behind.

The odds favoured the home side into day four as 4,000 turned out to see a likely England win. Bradman continued with defence and scored just 16 in the first hour. The law of logic clearly said victory was impossible. The only outcomes were a big England win or a fighting Australian draw. There was no point in playing a glorious attacking hand to please the growing crowd. A swashbuckling 100 would lose much of its swash and all its buckle if Australia were beaten. Bradman was playing for an honourable draw, not a dishonourable defeat.

He made the point by crawling to 44 not out at lunch with Brown on a valiant 101 and Australia one for 199. This was a very different Bradman. For a decade at the first-class and Test level he had let others heave the anchor over the side while he cut attack after attack to pieces. Today he had taken on the sheet role himself in scoring 50 in 150 minutes, which was well below half his normal rate of scoring. The crowd had swollen to 11,000.

At 2.50 p.m. the method in his stodginess became apparent as Australia crept into the black, meaning England would have to bat again. Every run scored now would put the home team a further minute away from victory. The steady drip of attrition was stopped as Brown swept Verity and was easily caught at fine leg for 133, a fine knock for his country. Australia was two for 259, in reality two for 12 with 195 minutes to play.

McCabe was soon worried by Verity, who was getting more turn and overs as Hammond responded to press criticism that he had underused the spinner in the first innings. McCabe lifted the tempo and Bradman was also coaxed out of his shell for a 72-run stand in an hour. Then Verity made a point by getting McCabe (39) to nick to Hammond in slip at 331. There were still 135 minutes to play and Australia was only 84 ahead. If the tourists collapsed now, England could still take it.

Bradman's ruthless concentration and dour defence saw him reach 100 in 253 minutes as he was transformed from winner to saviour. However, he could not rest. Hassett came in and popped up a catch to a kicker from Verity and was on his way for 2. The countdown now read 125 minutes to play, a lead of 90 and six wickets to fall.

Badcock survived with his captain until tea, but soon after was bowled by a Wright wrong'un. In came the capable Barnett, who in the Oldfield tradition could bat more than a bit. Bradman took Verity. England's chances of pulling off a miraculous win faded, and the crowd grew frustrated. They booed and jeered.

Bradman asked Sinfield to stop scuffing up the pitch in line with the wicket when he bowled. The crowd, which had turned into a mob that would embarrass its Sydney Hill counterpart, howled even louder. Bradman stood away from the wicket to show who was in charge. The mob capitulated as mobs are wont to do, and Bradman batted on to be 144 not out in a match-saving effort that ranked in importance with some of his vigorous Test double hundreds. He batted 365 minutes and hit just five fours. It was his thirteenth century against England in forty-two innings — an average of a ton or more in every three visits to the crease.

Australia ended with six for 427, having actually declared at 6.15 p.m. The match was drawn. The tourists were left with some honour, especially as they were 180 ahead at the finish with four wickets still intact. Yet the reality was worrying. Its bowling was exposed as lacking pace and penetration. Bradman, Brown and McCabe excepted, the batting had not been strong enough.

The betting was definitely on England to win back the Ashes in the next four Tests.

39

LORD'S, TV AND THE NEW AGE GAME

I have always had the highest regard for Hammond's cricket, but can recall no instance when his superb artistry shone so brilliantly.
— BRADMAN ON HAMMOND'S DOUBLE CENTURY AT LORD'S IN 1938

TIME FOR THE GENTLEMEN

Familiarity between Hammond and Bradman was breeding admiration rather than contempt as both men tossed the coin again, this time at Lord's for the Gentlemen of England versus Australia game, just a day after the end of the Trent Bridge battle. Bradman won the toss, batted and top-scored with 104, the sort of tally which he was making commonplace on this tour. McCabe also kept his Test form and Chipperfield demanded attention with a hearty 51. Australia made 397. R. J. O. Meyer, a part-time Somerset all-rounder, took five for 66. The Gentlemen replied with a genteel 301. Mr Hammond made 7, while Mr Freddie Brown hit 88. Australia's ordinary Master Ward took five for 108, but he would have to do much more to impress his skipper after Trent Bridge.

Australia then belted a most ungracious four for 335 declared, with Fingleton (121) and Badcock (112) making the young and old Gentlemen dash up and down the Lord's 'slope' and round the boundary. After this, the suitably hyphenated Fleetwood-Smith, with his debonair good looks, took seven for 44, which wasn't so bad for the Gentlemen given his demeanour. They compiled an undignified 149 and were beaten. Hammond hit just 12, which was surely a ruse, given his fine form in other games.

Australia's next match was against Lancashire at Manchester. The tourists batted first and A. Nutter had an immediate impact by bowling Fingleton. Bradman only managed a round dozen, but Badcock (96) continued his fight for Second Test selection as did Hassett (118) until he too was bowled by the troublesome Nutter early on Monday morning.

Lancashire made it a contest by hitting 289. Brown and Fingleton annoyed those watching by holding on to their wickets, presumably to gain practice for the Lord's Test. The crowd voiced their disapproval in a manner that annoyed the players, but which was becoming common on this tour. The masses were finding their democratic voice in the TV age of 1938.

At lunch, Cardus complained about the slow scoring to Bradman, who agreed that his lads had been a trifle tardy.

'Something will be done about it,' the skipper assured him, which the writer assumed was because he had drawn Bradman's attention to it. The captain didn't exactly kick *derrière*, but asked them to move the score along. But that was just part of his response. Realising that he would have to do a bit more PR, Bradman came in at one for 153, after Nutter had done his intelligent best to remove Brown, bowled for 70. Bradman appeared at the wicket to a few cries of 'get on with it'. But it wasn't necessary. His mind was set on giving the impatient crowd something to talk about other than the snail-like performance from his openers as he hit a chanceless 101 not out in seventy-three minutes, including fifteen fours which encompassed pulls, cuts, glances and powerful driving off the back foot.

The crowd went away happy at having seen what happened to

have been the fastest century of the season so far. But time was not the issue. Bradman was letting all England know that he could return at will to the glory-day hitting of his impetuous youth of 1930.

After that Tuesday matinee he declared at two for 284 and the Lancastrians managed three for 80 before the end of the drawn game.

LESS GENTLEMEN, MORE LORD'S

England brought in Somerset's paceman Arthur Wellard for Sinfield at Lord's, which was to be the first televised Test match. Only about 5,000 of the rich and richer could afford a box with pictures, but nevertheless it was a start. Australia replaced Ward with Chipperfield. Again Bradman was apparently overruled at the selection table by vice-captain McCabe and third selector, Ben Barnett. He didn't want Fleetwood-Smith in because he was not fully fit after having an impacted wisdom tooth removed the day before. But Fleetwood-Smith was selected.

Hammond won the toss on Friday 24 June and batted in front of a crowd that was sitting with handkerchiefs on their heads, a sure indicator in London that it was hot. McCormick found some real devil in the pitch and Bradman put in two short legs. His astuteness paid off. Hutton (4) gave Brown a catch in that position. Edrich tried to move them by hooking but only succeeded in crashing the ball into his stumps for a duck. Hammond came to the wicket amidst cheering to join Barnett. The latter became McCormick's third victim, also caught by Brown in the leg-trap, making the score three for 31.

The bowler was on fire attempting to make up for the frustration of his season so far. He gave Paynter a rough time with bouncers, but the tough left-hander came through with Hammond, who drove O'Reilly and Fleetwood-Smith off their lengths. McCormick came back at 1 p.m. but too late. The two Englishmen were set. The lunch score was three for 134. Hammond was 70 not out.

The teams were presented to King George VI, who then sat back in a balcony box to watch Hammond play a regal innings with

435

Paynter, as they jointly demolished the thin attack. Just before 4 p.m. Paynter (99) was LBW playing back to O'Reilly. England was four for 253 and fully recovered after the bad start. Hammond was on 121 and taking his own advice of 'always hitting 200 against the Australians'. If anything, he had settled down for a slower period than his pre-lunch barrage.

Compton (6) was trapped LBW sweeping O'Reilly. The batsman had the ignominy of hearing umpire 'Tiger' Smith tell him he was 'a silly little chap' for getting out that way. Just before play, Tiger had warned Compton not to sweep O'Reilly. 'He'll get you leg-before,' he told him.

England went to tea at five for 283 with Hammond 139 not out. Not another wicket fell before stumps were drawn with England five for 409, and Hammond on 210. He had driven and pulled everything, including a leg muscle, but was still out there at the close in such a dictatorial mood that he made Hitler look democratic.

The 32,000 crowd, which had Lord's bursting, went away thrilled with the might of England. If the German Führer had plans to invade Britain that week, Nazi spies would have advised him to shelve them.

Queues began forming at 10 o'clock that evening for Saturday's play. The patrons were happy to sleep out on the warm night and touts were rumoured to be asking ten pounds a ticket and getting more than half that. The prospective feast was a cricket fan's perfect dream. Hammond could be going for a world record and Bradman to follow in an attempt to beat it.

McCormick ruined half the dream when he slammed a ball into the skipper's elbow and later bowled him with a great in-swinger for 240. Hammond had batted 367 minutes and hit thirty-two power-laden fours in what his great rival, Bradman, felt was the best performance he had seen from his opposite number. The King, 60,000 spectators over two days and another 5,000 with TVs had loved it. Hammond had been pure inspiration, as Bradman was to Australians.

Ames was caught in slips for 83 and England finished with 494. O'Reilly had the figures with four for 93, and McCormick was not far behind him with four for 101.

Australia made it to lunch intact at none for 26. At 2.51 p.m. Fingleton edged Wright to Hammond at slip and the tourists were one for 69. The packed crowd stood and craned their necks towards the pavilion as Bradman came out to thunderous applause. It wasn't quite a Nuremburg Rally response, but nor was it staged artifice. The little big man had more of a spring in his step with the sun on his baggy green. He seemed eager to get out there, perhaps over-eager. He had watched, chased and appreciated Hammond's big double. Now it was his turn.

The England skipper took off Wellard and put on Farnes for that much-needed extra pace in an attempt to snare this fearsome foe before he got two eyes in. Hammond often joked that 'Bradman was like Nelson. He always had at least one eye in from the first ball he faced.'

This seemed right as Farnes slipped his first ball at his leg-stump. Bradman waited longer on his back foot than any other batsman would dare, and glanced it to fine leg for four. Farnes dug one in. The ball rose sharply. Bradman swung into position and crashed it to the square-leg boundary. Hammond stroked his chin. This was encouraging. He put on Verity to cage him and hopefully force a rash stroke. The England captain suggested two slips, a ploy if ever there was one. Verity was turning his left-handed leggies, but not that much. Bradman belted him for four through mid-wicket and immediately went for a late, late cut, and chopped the ball into his stumps.

The crowd was stunned into silence. Then a belated roar went up as Verity threw his arms heavenward and yelped. He had Bradman for 18. The batsman's response was to throw his head back and laugh. It was his way of showing both embarrassment and resignation. *C'est la vie*. The beauty of the game was that it was unpredictable, and there was usually a second innings.

Spectators gave him a big send-off, as if he had hit a brilliant 81 not 18. It was a mixture of relief and disappointment, for some had travelled some distance and paid their last quid to see him answer Hammond.

Australia was two for 101. McCabe came in obviously thinking he could carry on as he had in the first innings at Trent Bridge.

However, he started with the wrong end of the knock, forgetting he had begun more sedately in that memorable performance. This time he crunched 38 in half an hour with one five and five fours, and then cut Farnes viciously to Verity. He couldn't get out of the way but was able to grip the ball into his stomach as he fell back from the impact.

Brown, playing the innings of his life, moved to 100 in 193 minutes in a partnership of 124 in 100 minutes with Hassett. Then Wellard came on from the Pavilion end and trapped Hassett LBW for 56. Two balls later he bowled Badcock with a straight half-volley for nought. Barnett came in and stayed with Brown (140 not out) until stumps with Australia on five for 299.

The crowd of 33,800 squeezed out of Lord's, not quite sated. Hammond had scored 30 in the morning and Bradman 18 in the afternoon. Yet it had been good, competitive cricket between two nations who never gave an inch while performing in the finest sporting spirit.

Monday started badly for the tourists when Barnett drove Verity as if he was still playing Sunday golf and Compton ran back in the covers to take the catch. Chipperfield, who had injured his finger trying to catch Hammond, was LBW for 1, and Australia at seven for 308, still 37 short of the follow-on.

O'Reilly came in and clubbed 42 in forty-four minutes before Farnes bowled him at 393, thus avoiding the follow-on. Then the speedster had McCormick caught at short leg first ball. Farnes was on a hat-trick. If he had been able to choose the third batsman to bowl to, he would have asked for Fleetwood-Smith, the rabbit's rabbit, who now took block. Farnes bowled up. Fleetwood-Smith pushed at it, got an edge and the ball sailed in and out of Compton's hands at slip. Then it rained on Farnes' parade and play was halted until 4.15 p.m.

After the break Brown reached 200 and went on to carry his bat with 206 not out, with Australia finishing on 422 — 72 in arrears. Farnes took three for 153, and Verity, the pick of the bowlers, four for 103.

The rain made batting tough for England in front of a crowd only half the size of the 30,000 at the start as McCormick had Barnett caught in the gully by McCabe. O'Reilly then had Hutton caught in the slips. England was two for 39 at the close, with Verity partnering Edrich.

On Tuesday morning, Edrich hooked McCormick early for four. The bowler gave him another, straighter short one and Edrich, his blood up, hooked again, but straight down McCabe's throat at square leg. England was three for 43. McCormick later removed Verity's off-stump to make the home team four for 64.

Hammond had a 'cork' thigh and needed a runner. On just 2, he scooped a ball from McCabe to Waite, who was subbing for Chipperfield, at square leg. England was five for 76. But the next little partnership of 54 between Paynter and Compton put England nicely clear at six for 128 when Paynter (43) was run out. The lead was 200, with 260 minutes left. England made it to lunch at six for 142. Compton's little gem of 72 not out and Wellard's blazing 38 allowed England to add another 100 to be all out for 242. The lead was 314. Australia had 160 minutes to go for them in about fifty overs. More than six an over — or one a ball — was a near-impossible ask in a Test where captains could place a field to restrict the flow from the first ball.

Ames had a fractured finger and Paynter had to keep. He went for a catch off Wellard and managed to deflect it to Hammond, thus removing Fingleton for four. The score was one for 8 and Bradman was in. Would he go into defence mode, or attack?

Farnes bowled him a fierce head-hunting bouncer, which he just managed to avoid. A few overs later he clouted three successive fours off Wellard and it seemed he might be thinking about chasing the runs. However, Brown had put up the shutters. The Australians were one for 59 at tea, with Bradman on 38 and Brown on 10 after eighteen overs. That left about thirty overs to make 256, or 8.53 an over. At 71, Brown was out for 10. Bradman on 49 not out was joined by McCabe. This combination was arguably the only one in history that could have tackled the nine runs an over required against such a good attack.

McCabe looked as if he were accepting the challenge as he

collected 21 from twenty-two balls in twenty-five minutes. The two added 40 in eight overs, with Bradman on 66 not out. Then Verity struck and had McCabe caught in slips by Hutton. Australia was three for 111, still 245 short with nineteen or twenty overs left. The task was now beyond even Bradman.

Hassett apparently had not been told it was an impossible challenge. He came in with his elfin grace and stroked his way to 42 in thirty-five minutes with one sweeping six off Wright, before the bowler got his revenge and disturbed his furniture. Bradman was 87 not out and the score four for 175. Badcock was caught at slip off Edrich for a first-ball duck to make it five for 180, with Bradman on 92.

As the setting sun shone on a fair summer's evening, most of the 20,000 crowd stayed to the close in the hope of seeing a sudden collapse and an England win. Instead they received a consolation as Bradman picked his way through the gaps to reach his fourteenth Test century against England in 142 minutes. He hit fifteen fours and gave no chances during his 102 not out in Australia's final score of six for 204. This left them 110 behind and it was an even bet who would have won given another hour and a half.

Two Tests had been played for two draws and the pressure was now on England. It had to win at least one of the remaining three to take the Ashes, while keeping Australia winless. With Bradman in the most consistent form of his entire career this seemed unlikely.

At the halfway mark of the 1938 season, he had hit 1,588 runs at 144.36 runs an innings. Hammond was second with 1,742 at 82.09, Brown third (1,304 at 81.50) and Hassett fourth (1,020 at 72.85). Yorkshire's Bill Bowes headed the bowling with forty-eight wickets at 11.91 apiece. Fleetwood-Smith (56 at 16.69) and O'Reilly (56 at 17.73) were the best of the Australians.

The tourists moved on to Chesterfield for a game against Derbyshire where the county scored 151 and 56 against Australia's four for 441 declared. Ward cleaned up with five for 45 and three for 8, with Waite in support taking three for 50 and five for 40. Billy Brown continued his team-boosting mid-season form with a powerful 265 not out.

Bradman came back for the game against Yorkshire at Bramall Lane on 2 July and scored 59 and 42 out of Australia's meagre efforts of 222 and 132 on a wet and difficult track. His performances were worth big hundreds under the conditions. Yorkshire's reply was 205, with Waite picking up the 'look-at-me' figures of seven for 101.

Yorkshire started the third day with 150 to make and all wickets intact. The county was three for 83 at lunch with Sutcliffe 36 not out and confident he could lead Yorkshire to the first victory against the tourists for the season. But rain returned and ruined their chances. When play was abandoned by agreement between captains Bradman and Sellers, the unhappy crowd threw cushions onto the ground. It still didn't make play recommence and Australia sneaked away with a draw, thus keeping their unbeaten record.

40

THE LONE DUELLIST

Bradman is in such form that he could have played by candlelight.
— SIR PELHAM WARNER ON BRADMAN IN THE DARK OF THE FOURTH TEST, 1938

LIVES WITHOUT WIVES

Bradman received a letter from the Board of Control on 5 July refusing permission for Jessie to join him at his expense at the end of the tour. The captain replied by writing a letter informing them that he was resigning immediately from Test cricket. The Board of Control had thus achieved what all England's bowlers could not, and the Ashes seemed likely to return to the UK. Roly Pope, the team doctor, had a chat with the skipper and persuaded him not to send the letter just yet.

On 6 July, Bradman told the press: 'I am very disappointed at the Australian Board of Control's decision but I cannot say at the moment whether I shall do anything further in the matter.'

Pope and manager Jeanes spoke to the rest of the team, now in their Manchester hotel preparing for the Third Test. The team decided to send a cable of protest to the Board in a show of solidarity with the skipper.

While they waited for the Board to reply, the entire Third Test was washed out without even the toss of the coin. The arithmetic for the Ashes became simpler. England had to win at least one Test and keep Australia down to no wins in order to take back the Ashes.

The team went on to Birmingham to play Warwickshire at Edgbaston. The county scored 179, with Ward taking four for 26 and O'Reilly three for 69. Australia replied with 390, with Bradman (135) and Brown (101) combining for a 206-run stand in 165 minutes. The county's second knock realised 118, with O'Reilly (four for 33) and Waite (three for 33) giving Australia an innings win and a rest day on Friday 15 July.

Players awoke to the news of a cable from the Board of Control, who had decided to allow not only Bradman but any member of the team to be joined by his wife. It was a sensible correction to a silly, authoritarian clause in the contract which was, in law, indefensible. The team could now get on with the business of defending the Ashes with its top player and leader.

GREAT DEEDS AT LEEDS

Australia batted first against Notts at Trent Bridge on 16 July, and had to face Voce. The 1934 dispute did not flare up again, however. The left-hander kept the ball on a reasonable length and delivered over the wicket to three short legs, not around it. Bradman hit 56 and Barnes 58 off 243. Notts were rolled by O'Reilly (five for 39) and Fleetwood-Smith (three for 35) for 147.

Australia batted a second time half an hour after lunch. Brown and Badcock opened with a stand of 121 before Bradman came to the wicket. He was joined by Hassett at 125 and they stayed together for another 216 in 140 minutes, with Hassett for a change dominating. He was out for 124, while Bradman went on to 144 before closing the innings at four for 453. Fleetwood-Smith continued his form against the counties and took five for 39 in Notts' dismissal for 137, giving Australia a 412-run win.

The Fourth Test began at Headingly, Leeds, on Friday 22 July with England replacing Hutton and Ames (both injured) and Wellard from the Second Test side — the Third not having been played — with W. F. Price, Bowes and Joe Hardstaff. Australia exchanged Chipperfield for Waite.

Hammond won the toss as usual and batted in the heavy grey atmosphere, which tempted him to send the opposition in to face Bowes' swingers. However, the England skipper feared facing the Aussie spinners on the last day.

England lost Edrich, bowled by O'Reilly for a duck, at 29. Fifteen minutes later, Barnett called Hardstaff for a run to mid-on, then sent him back when he saw that Hassett had trapped the ball. The throw back to O'Reilly saw Hardstaff run out. England was two for 34.

Hammond and Barnett became bogged in caution until lunch when the score was two for 62. At 88, Barnett (30) edged McCormick to the keeper and was on his way. Paynter and Hammond then made a promising stand of 54 before the England captain was bowled by an O'Reilly off-break for 70 with England four for 142. Paynter (28) then went stumped off Fleetwood-Smith and O'Reilly bowled Compton for a duck.

At tea, England had slipped to six for 171, and the slide to all out for 223 was completed at 5.35 p.m. O'Reilly toiled brilliantly for his five for 66, while Fleetwood-Smith kept pressure on at the other end with three for 73.

Australia lost Brown (22) bowled by Wright when he tried to hook a short one that kept low. At stumps the tourists were one for 31, with Barnett in as nightwatchman.

Next morning, the Saturday crowd was huge outside the ground as people fought for tickets from touts. After less then an hour, Fingleton (30) played a similar shot to Brown's the previous evening and was bowled by Verity at 87. The gates were shut and all waited for Bradman. The groundsman at Headingly, Dick Moulton, had come out with the bold prediction that he would not get a triple century in this match as he had done in 1930 (334) and 1934 (304). The pitch was 'too soft' because of rain and the outfield was slow. It was a bowler's wicket, Moulton warned.

Nevertheless, the crowd of more than 23,000 came expectant. Bradman always rose to the occasion at Headingly, and the Leeds spectators above all others in England appreciated his prowess. They gave him the most rousing reception of the tour so far. There was something very Yorkshire about his grit and determination that appealed to them, not to mention his sheer brilliance.

Bradman began watchfully and was 17 not out at lunch after thirty-six minutes. Barnett (57) was caught behind by Price off Farnes at 128 after a gallant 130 minutes. He was a nightwatchman for almost half the day.

After lunch McCabe (1) had his off-stump uprooted by Farnes and then Badcock was bowled for 4, leaving Australia struggling at five for 145 with Bradman solid on 29. The light was deteriorating so fast that Bradman removed his cap. He seemed relaxed and was enjoying the challenge. It was up to him to appeal against the light, but he refused to do so. If it rained, his team could be caught on a brutal sticky on Monday. It was better to bat on, which he did by defending and picking the right ball with which to keep the scoreboard ticking over.

He and Hassett (13) put on 50 before the latter was bowled by Wright. Bradman, on 63, was joined by Waite. Hammond forced Bradman's hand by taking the new ball. The Australian skipper appealed against the light and tea was taken three minutes early with the score at six for 205. Bradman was on 71 not out and farming the strike.

They resumed after twenty-two minutes. Bradman went on the attack cutting and driving Farnes for three fours. He edged Bowes through slips to give his team the lead. At 232, Waite, who had lasted forty-five minutes, was caught behind off Farnes. Bradman was on 97 not out. In the next over he pushed on to his twelfth century of the tour and so overtook Trumper who had scored eleven hundreds on tour in 1902. He was then bowled by Bowes for 103 when trying to cut him through slips. Just as the groundsman had foreseen, he didn't reach his triple century, but it had been one of his great Test hundreds. He hit nine fours in a chanceless 175 minutes at the wicket in possibly the worst Test match light ever played in.

The final Australian score of 242 gave it a negligible lead of 19. Farnes took four for 77, Bowes three for 79 and Wright two for 38. England reached none for 49 in fifty-five minutes off eighteen overs in variable light that in fact improved towards the close.

Sunday was a bleak, rainy day in Leeds, but the wicket remained relatively true. At 60, Barnett tried to hook McCormick, but skied a catch for his namesake, the Australian keeper, to take. At 73, Hardstaff got an unplayable leg-break from O'Reilly, after the volatile spinner had been riled by being no-balled and then swept for 4. The ball pitched outside leg-stump and nicked off bail. 'How do you play a ball like that?' a bewildered Hardstaff asked umpire Chester as he departed.

O'Reilly banked on next man in Hammond having seen the way that leg-break turned. The wily bowler gave him a wrong'un first up, which Hammond picked from his hand but still put it straight to Brown at short-forward square leg. England was three for 73, and reeling. Paynter (21) dropped anchor, but the rest of the side mainly fell to Fleetwood-Smith, who just missed a hat-trick, for 123. O'Reilly ended with five for 56, and Fleetwood-Smith four for 34.

Australia began batting after lunch and only had 105 to make. The crowd gave full throat in support of England now. At 17, Farnes got one to skid through and Brown (9) was caught in front LBW.

Bradman walked out to restrained applause and plenty of support for England's bowlers. Sentiment was thrown out the window, together with any desire to see even a bright 40 from The Don. A Test was now at stake. The wicket was poor and Bradman looked more serious than serene. The Ashes were in the balance. If Australia won, the Fifth Test would make no difference to who held them.

Farnes fired several good balls in. One hit him on the pads and earned an ambitious shout for LBW. Bradman then glanced the last ball of the over for four. If each Australian scored around 10, the game would be theirs. At 32, Fingleton (9) was LBW to Verity. Bradman was 10 not out. He moved to 14 and Wright came on again. He guided a ball through the gully for two. The next ball he edged to Verity.

Bradman didn't see the catch. He looked to confirmation from Frank Chester. 'Out, caught,' he said firmly and Bradman was on his

446

way to intense cheering with the score at 50. McCabe, who like Bradman could have settled the contest with a few well-chosen blows, hit a rank long-hop from Wright to Barnett and was out for 15 at 61.

Hassett decided there was no point waiting for rain. He thumped a good length ball from Wright for 3. Hammond rang the changes. Hassett struck out for fours off Bowes and Verity.

Inside the dressing-room the tension did odd things to different people. O'Reilly lived up to his nickname and paced the room in his pads. Bradman made himself his special cup of tea and found it hard to watch. Jeanes, the manager, had to leave the ground. In the street, he noted the low level of cheering and decided Australia was progressing. He returned inside in time to see Hassett slash at Wright for a catch in the covers. The smallest man on either side had made the biggest contribution in the critical moment with 33 in thirty minutes. Australia was five for 90 with fifteen to get and half the side intact. Barnett, a performer in the first innings, and Badcock, in the horrors, were batting.

At 96, rain interrupted play. The passing shower saw the players back on ten minutes later. England delayed as long as possible and asked for sawdust. Umpire Chester became testy and ordered Hammond to speed up proceedings. Farnes bowled two accurate maidens. Barnett took two singles off Bowes and Badcock 1.

At 4.15 p.m. Barnett cut Farnes square and then edged the next to the boundary. Australia was five for 107, and home — with the Ashes.

There was a scramble for stumps and a rush for the dressing-room. The crowd called for Bradman to appear. Both captains came out smiling together in their suits, posed for photos and shook hands. Then the last of the huge last-day crowd of 36,000 wandered away satisfied to have seen such a tight contest, which could have gone either way for most of the game.

ALL SQUARE AT THE OVAL

An invigorated Aussie squad went to Taunton, Somerset and ran through the county for 110. In a brisk, brutal reply Australia scored

447

six declared for 464, with Bradman turning on yet another of his big-innings displays. His first fifty took just seventy minutes and he moved easily on to 100 in 154 minutes — his thirteenth for the tour — including thirteen fours. He had not gone on to a double century since the MCC match, and it was a surprise to see him step up the pace and glide his way through that second hundred in just seventy minutes with nineteen fours, before throwing his wicket away at 202. Badcock scored 110, and looked more secure than in the Tests.

Fleetwood-Smith with five for 30 wrapped up an innings win by limiting the county to just 136 in its second effort. Then followed a washed-out drawn game against Glamorgan at Swansea, in which Bradman made 17 on a rain-affected wicket.

The travelling was incessant, with a second-class fixture in Scotland and another at Sunderland against Durham, which was delayed by . . . fog. They then had to come back to London on the evening of 8 August, for a game against Surrey at The Oval, and didn't get settled back into their hotel until after midnight. Consequently no-one shed a tear when the first day was washed out. The remaining two days ended in a predictable draw, with Australia making 297 and Surrey replying with seven for 105.

The peripatetic tourists then moved on to Canterbury to play Kent on 13 August. Everyone — except Brown (4) — got some batting practice, including Bradman (67), who had not visited the crease for nearly two weeks. Badcock (76), the consistent Barnes (94) and Barnett (54) looked in fine touch in Australia's 479, as did Waite with the ball, in taking four for 43 and five for 85 in Kent's 108 and 377. Australia was held up in Kent's second innings by 81 from the great old Frank Woolley, now fifty-one years old much as he denied it, and by Ames, who seemed over his finger injury with a fine 139, before winning by ten wickets.

After much discussion, England brought in Hutton, thirty-nine-year-old Yorkshireman Arthur Wood as keeper to replace the again-injured Ames, and Leyland. Out went Price, Wright and Barnett. The batting line-up was perhaps as strong as any England ever fielded, with the first seven made up of Hutton, Edrich, Leyland,

Hammond, Paynter, Compton and Hardstaff — all of them top-class bats.

Australia brought in Barnes for McCormick, who was suffering from shoulder trouble. Press reports and later post mortems claimed that he had declared himself fit. 'That wasn't correct,' Bradman said. 'McCormick said he *thought* he might be fit, which was a very different matter. It was a timeless Test. He had to be able to stand up. We decided against him.'

This meant the tourists were going to play without a recognised speedster, making the bowling line-up possibly the weakest ever to have represented the country. If the wicket was sound and the weather good, reliance on a two-pronged spin attack would be dangerous against the formidable England batting list.

If ever Bradman needed to call correctly it was at The Oval on Saturday 20 August. He even willed the coin to heads by going out to toss in his suit and hat, which was another way of saying he would have time to put on his whites and pad up while his openers got going. But not even he could make the coin end up heads. Hammond called correctly and batted.

'I want you there at tea,' he told Hutton and Edrich. 'Remember, this is a timeless Test.'

Edrich disobeyed orders and was out LBW to O'Reilly for 12. England one for 29 in forty-five minutes of a game that in theory could go on forever. Leyland came in and, along with Hutton, carried out Hammond's instructions to the letter. They were both still there at stumps with the score at one for 347. Hutton was 160 not out and Leyland 156 after facing 131 overs on a perfect wicket from a paper-thin attack that lacked penetration. Hutton was grateful to Leyland for taking most of the bowling from O'Reilly, who would have been the only threat to him.

Next morning, when both were on 187, Leyland was run out when Hutton foolishly called him through for a second run after Hassett fumbled the ball at mid-on, and was beaten by the return to the bowler's end. The partnership was worth 382 and England's total 411. The run-out looked the only way of gaining a breakthrough as the Australians watched Hammond coming to the wicket — an awesome prospect with such a score already on the board.

As Hammond warmed up, Fingleton tore a calf muscle badly and was finished for the day and possibly the match. Hammond played true to form, but fell LBW to Fleetwood-Smith for 59 at 546, with Hutton on 257. One run later O'Reilly put Paynter back in the pavilion LBW for 0. Then at 577, Compton was dismissed for 1 and at five for 555 Australia seemed to be breaking through at long last, but there was still Hardstaff to give Australia some solid stick.

At 6.17 p.m. Hutton late-cut O'Reilly for a single and brought up his 300 in 662 minutes. He had been in for 243.2 overs, which meant he was travelling at a little more than one run an over, thanks mainly to nudges, deflections, glances and the odd drive. He and Hardstaff (40 not out) appealed against the light and the second day was over.

On day three, Hutton set his sights on Bradman's 334 and reached it easily with a cut for four off Fleetwood-Smith. Bradman walked over and shook Hutton's hand with a broad grin. If it hurt to see his record go, he didn't show it in a photo for prosterity, which was symbolic of the excellent spirit in which these teams played in 1938.

Hutton went on to 364 before O'Reilly bowled him. He had outscored Hammond, who had hit 336 against New Zealand in a Test, setting a record that would surely last for some time, especially if timeless Tests were not often played. The 30,000 fans stood and cheered the marathon performance as he left the field. He batted for thirteen hours and seventeen minutes (or 797 minutes in all) and hit thirty-four fours. By comparison, Bradman in 1930 against an infinitely greater attack, including Larwood, Tate, Geary, Hammond and Tyldesley, made his 334 runs in 383 minutes — or half the time for approximately the same number of runs — and hit forty-six fours. The only other Ashes treble century until then had been Bradman's 304 also at Leeds in 1934. It took him 430 minutes and he hit two sixes and forty-three fours. Hutton's performance, however remarkable for its concentration and grit, would later be used as an argument against the timeless Test.

At 4.25 p.m. with the score seven for 887, Bradman was bowling when he went over on his weak ankle in a hole at the crease and fractured his tibia. White and Fleetwood-Smith helped him from the field. It was a tragedy for the game and Australia, for no-one would ever know how he would have responded on this perfect wicket to the challenge of the unprecedented score to which England was heading.

The home side plundered its way to seven for 903 before declaring, with Hardstaff on 169 not out. The bowling analyses were worth recording for their enormity. Waite sent down seventy-two overs for one for 150, O'Reilly took three for 178 off eighty-five overs, with twenty-six maidens, and poor Fleetwood-Smith returned one for 298 off eighty-seven overs. Of the others, Sid Barnes took one for 84 off thirty-eight overs. It had been slow, agonising torture rather than a quick slaughter.

With Bradman and Fingleton unable to bat, Australia went through the motions in two relatively inept batting displays to record 201 and 123. In the first innings, Brown hit a competent 69, while Hassett managed 42 and Barnes 41. Bowes was the destroyer with five for 49. In the second dig, Barnes completed a fair double with 33, while Barnett made a solid 46. Farnes was the star this time with four for 63 out of the eight wickets to fall.

Bradman's brilliant form in the season yielded thirteen centuries (three of them double hundreds), 2,429 runs and an average of 115.66. He had already hit a century in each Test. His scores in 1930 and 1934 at The Oval were 232, 244 and 77. Given this record, the perfect wicket, the indefinite duration and an England attack he had more than mastered, Bradman would almost certainly have scored a big innings in at least one of the two innings, possibly a double or even a triple century. The result of the game could have been markedly different.

Bradman's attitude to the rout was typically down-to-earth. 'We were all pretty tired and demoralised,' he said. 'We just didn't have the will when we were facing that sort of score.'

Speculation aside, the record rightly will always show that England walked away with the biggest Test win ever — by an innings and 579, thus drawing the rubber one-all. The Ashes remained with Australia to be contested again, with luck, at home in 1940–41. But with war clouds over Europe and Hitler on the march there was no saying when sporting hostilities would resume.

In the 1938 series, Bradman had six innings for 434 runs at an average of 108.50. He had been well-supported by Brown with 512 at 73.14. McCabe's sensational innings at Trent Bridge of 232 was the only time he produced his best in accumulating 362 at 45.25. More disappointing was Badcock who had eight innings and only scratched together 32 at an average of 4.57. He had hit 1,572 at 56 on the rest of the tour. It was puzzling for his skipper. Badcock had the right temperament for the big time, but had not been able to produce it in the Tests.

Hutton's one great innings of 364 brought his total to 473 from four innings at 118.25. Paynter also topped the century average with 101.75 from 407 runs in six innings, while Leyland had one knock for 187. In short, England's batting was far more productive through the series, mainly because the opposition provided only one effective bowler — O'Reilly — to challenge it. He took twenty-two wickets at 27.73, remarkable figures given the batting arraigned against him. McCormick was a disappointment with just ten wickets at 34.50, as was Fleetwood-Smith with fourteen at 51.93. Bowes (ten at 18.80), Verity (fourteen at 25.28), Farnes (seventeen at 34.17) and Wright (twelve at 35.50) toiled well for England.

A PLEASURE-FREE CONCLUSION

Australia went on more anti-climactically than in recent tours now that Bradman was out. It wasn't quite the same for England, the fans or indeed, the Australians. It irked Bradman greatly to have been beaten in the Fifth Test. It spoiled the team's unbeaten record. He had dearly wanted to go through undefeated and so outdo Warwick Armstrong's 1921 touring team.

A little more salt was rubbed into his aching ankle when Henry Leveson-Gower chose an XI to rival England's Fifth Test side. McCabe, the acting skipper, did not like such undue pressure at the very end of the tour, when a nice, friendly match would have been more acceptable.

An alleged remark about Australia's 'not wanting to lose' by Bob Wyatt angered McCabe and it seemed he might withdraw his team from the game until Wyatt spoke with him and denied the report. In the end the Invitation XI beat Australia by ten wickets, something that would be unconscionable under Bradman. It meant two losses for the season.

The skipper turned thirty while resting his injury at the Buckinghamshire home of his friend Walter Robins. 'Doing the Lambeth Walk,' which Bradman enjoyed, was out for some time. Even billiards were not allowed by his doctor. Each morning he answered about two hundred letters himself, belting out sixty words a minute on his own portable typewriter. After lunch, he took a nap and had treatment for his ankle.

Offers for jobs came in, which he considered. However, he was determined to return to Australia. There was speculation in the English press about whether he would ever come back to Britain as a cricketer. But, it was noted, he would still only be thirty-four in 1942 — the next scheduled visit.

Jessie arrived with the wives of McCabe, Jeanes and Fleetwood-Smith on 15 September and Bradman was able to greet her without a walking stick. They enjoyed their last few days in Buckinghamshire and London, a city still alive with theatre, cabarets and restaurants despite the threat of war. The Bradmans shopped and he went to Roote's to order a new Humber Snipe to be delivered to Adelaide.

On 19–20 September, the Czech government reluctantly accepted a joint Anglo-French plan to allow Germany to take control of German-speaking areas of Czechoslovakia, which was a sell-out to Hitler's territorial claims. Every day, the papers carried articles about war preparations in the UK. In London troops began digging trenches in the parks and depots opened for the fitting of gas masks.

The population was informed about air-raid shelters and the Underground in London was marked out by the authorities as a suitable place to take refuge. The British fleet was mobilised on 27 September.

Aware of the pressures, Bradman told a press conference before he and Jessie left England on 28 September: 'My greatest impression is of the magnificent calm and spirit of our British people during these last troublesome days. I know we all fervently pray for peace.'

The happily-united couple then travelled across France and Italy for two weeks before joining the *Orontes* at Naples. The Continent was a far different place from cheerful England, which was still hearing about appeasement from Chamberlain.

41

ONE MAN'S WAR — 1939–1945

We have got Ponsford out cheaply, but Bradman is still batting.
— A BRITISH MP AFTER MUSSOLINI HAD BEEN DEFEATED IN THE
SUMMER OF 1943

SHIELD DOMINATION — AS USUAL

Bradman, at thirty, batted at the beginning of the 1938–39 season at his peak or near to it. In six first-class innings in a row between 9 December and 25 January, he hit six centuries to equal the record set by England's C. B. Fry in 1901. They included 118 in an MCC Centenary Match in Melbourne (Bradman's XI v Rigg's XI), 143 for South Australia against NSW at Adelaide, 225 against Queensland at Adelaide, 107 against Victoria at Melbourne, 186 against Queensland at Brisbane and 135 against NSW at Sydney. This great run ended against Victoria in Adelaide when he made 5.

The consistency was a continuation of his formidable run in England where he scored thirteen centuries and five fifties in twenty-six innings. His 'year' (actually nine months) from May 1938 to late January 1939 saw him score nineteen centuries (including four 'doubles') and five fifties in thirty-three innings in two countries. His aggregate was 3,348 and his average exactly 124.

In the winter of 1939, Bradman was glad of the lay-off from

cricket after eighteen strenuous months. But his desk-bound work for Hodgetts as a broker caused him to play more golf and squash to keep fit. As ever, he thrived on competition and made it to the final of the South Australian squash championships, in which he encountered Davis Cup tennis player, Don Turnbull.

Bradman was beaten easily in the first set 0-9, and again in the second 4-9. His capacity to learn and improve under pressure showed in the third set when, down 1-5, he clawed his way back to win 10-8. He then quickly won the fourth set 9-3. He was again well down — 2-7 — in the deciding set but fought back to win 10-8.

It seemed that if Bradman was presented with a game with a smallish sphere, rules and an opponent, he would become more than competitive. He had to win. An adversary made him bristle with hidden reserves of energy. According to the Australian all-rounder Keith Miller, 'Bradman was a born competitor whether it be in the billiards room of his Adelaide home, on the golf course, the squash court or cricket field. He hated the idea of losing. It drove him to perform at his peak.'

On 10 July 1939, both the Bradmans had a new challenge of another kind when Jessie gave birth to a son, John Russell Bradman, who helped make up for the tragedy of their lost infant in 1936. Young John had been born into a most uncertain world. Two months later, Australian Prime Minister, R. G. Menzies (a relation of Jessie's) told the nation that because Germany had invaded Poland, 'Great Britain had declared war on her and that, as a result, Australia is also at war.'

Bradman thought his cricket career would be over, but the Government decreed that first-class games should go ahead in 1939–40 for the sake of national morale, together with Australian Rules and rugby fixtures in the following winter. Bradman took this to heart and managed to squeeze something extra out for the massive crowds that turned up at every venue he played.

Yet it wasn't just morale at stake. The grim news in Europe of German advances and talk of possible new threats closer to home led many men to attend these matches with the thought that they might never see Bradman perform, or even a Shield match played, again.

A big crowd turned out on 15 December 1939 to watch South Australia against NSW at Adelaide. Bradman came in forty minutes before the close at one for 17 after NSW had been dismissed for 336. He was 27 not out at stumps and went on the next day to a century in 149 minutes, just before lunch. He completed his 200 in 248 minutes before tea, and then lashed the bowling for a further 51 in twenty-three minutes. His 251 included two sixes and thirty-four fours — more in boundaries than even his 357 against Victoria in 1935–36. Bradman was batting with more precision and power than ever.

South Australia scored 430, and thanks to a still-performing Grimmett (six for 122), NSW's second effort was 248. South Australia was thus set 155 to win on the third afternoon. Bradman came in at one for 9 and spanked 90 not out in 100 minutes as South Australia cruised to victory. In just over six hours at the crease, he had hit 341 without giving a chance or being dismissed. It gave him a specific pleasure to tussle with and defeat O'Reilly, whom he now ranked above Grimmett as the greatest spinner he had ever faced.

Perhaps if Bradman had a 'height' to his powers, it was reached in that game against arguably the world's number one bowler. Bradman could do no more than score 300-plus at a very fast rate against such an opponent, and remain undefeated. A week later he went even faster and scored 138 in 115 minutes, setting up Badcock for his fine 236 and another innings victory for South Australia against Queensland. It was Bradman's fifth successive century against the long-suffering northern State — itself a record.

The mighty Bradman-led South Australian juggernaut continued on to Melbourne for the New Year game against Victoria, which began on 29 December. The MCG rocked with some power-hitting by new stars Keith Miller (108) and Percy Beames (101) in the first two days, as Victoria saw out 1939 with a tally of 475. Then on Saturday 30 December, Bradman was 52 not out in eighty minutes at the close.

The fans went home to celebrate uncertainly on New Year's Eve, then 30,000 turned up on New Year's Day to watch and cheer The Don. Many could recall his tyro efforts in the 1928–29 Ashes season, his gallantry against bodyline in 1932–33 and his sheer domination against Gubby Allen's 1936–37 outfit, not to mention his annual drubbing of Victoria but for a few rare occasions over twelve years.

Bradman moved steadily to 88 and then hit leg-spinner Doug Ring for three successive fours to reach 100 in 133 minutes. He went relentlessly on to 200 in 248 minutes and ended with 267 in 340 minutes. It was his thirty-fourth double century and overtook Hammond's thirty-three in about half as many innings. The knock also recorded his ninetieth first-class hundred.

The rest of January 1940 was uneventful by his standards, with scores of 0 and 97 against Queensland at Brisbane, and 39 and 40 against NSW in Sydney. O'Reilly got him LBW in the first innings on a turning wicket to gain a little revenge.

In February, perhaps sensing he might never play first-class cricket again, Bradman scored 42, 209 not out and 135 in two games in Perth against Western Australia. His 209 not out was the first sight of him for many people in the West, who had read and seen much on newsreels about him, but had never witnessed his skills. His thirty-fifth double century took the breathtaking time of 161 minutes and included one six and thirty fours. It was his fastest 200 thus far, indicating that he could still stretch the outer limits of not just big run-scoring, but the time taken to hit them. Then again, Bradman was just thirty-one years old. If he didn't get badly injured, sick or bored, there was no reason for not going on piling record upon record for the best part of another decade.

Outside his control was the all-engulfing prospect of world war, which in the middle of the twentieth century meant every human being's life and liberty were uncertain and at risk.

DARK DAYS OF WAR AND WOUNDS

France surrendered to Germany on 25 June 1940 rather than stand and fight. This meek capitulation to the Nazi military meant that the small island of Britain now stood alone against Hitler, who intended to control the whole of Europe, including Russia. Bradman was among tens of thousands of Australians who reacted by enlisting in the armed forces. He was passed fit for air crew duty in the RAAF and attended training courses.

The army and the other services thought of Bradman and other 'name' sportsmen as useful acquisitions for morale-boosting propaganda and publicity. He was offered a position as a divisional supervisor of physical training with Australian forces in the Middle East, which he accepted on 31 October.

Bradman managed just one game for Kensington against West Torrens at the start of the season and hit 212 out of 370 in 195 minutes. Then he was transferred to Frankston, Victoria, to commence the fitness programme and given the rank of lieutenant. He joined seventy-four others including Sergeant-Major Chuck Fleetwood-Smith, wrestlers Bonnie Muir and King Elliot, and international rugby player Max Carpenter.

The training was tough. It lasted from 9 a.m. to 4.30 p.m. daily and included all branches of athletics, physical jerks, wrestling and boxing as well as the treatment of injuries and organisation of sporting events. His competitive nature enabled him to reach the fitness level of the best in the school. But there was a downside to this exertion. It was rigorous and demanding and was too much for a man whose body had been weakened by prolonged bouts of illness.

In December 1940 a specialist examined Bradman's eyes and found the thirty-two-year-old's vision was surprisingly poor. It had deteriorated in recent years and it showed in two cricket matches that month and in January staged to raise funds for the armed forces. In the first, between South Australia and Victoria, he made nought and 6. In the second, Bradman's XI versus McCabe's XI, he scored 0 and 12. In both games he could not pick the flight of the ball. It was depressing for the man with the reputation of having the best 'eye' in the game's history. His great career seemed to be over.

Bradman spent two weeks in hospital for his eye ailment, which was attributed to his run-down condition. The rest improved his eyesight temporarily. In February, he went back to the Frankston training programme and led the Army fitness school in cricket matches against Frankston, the RAAF and the Fire Brigade, making

63, 35 and 112. There was just a touch of the old magic in these knocks but not enough to encourage him to think he would have a future in cricket. Late in the month he led a team to a win in an All-Australian All-Services athletic meeting.

His efforts aggravated the back problems which had kept him out of tour games in 1938 and had troubled him ever since. Fibrositis was diagnosed, but as with his mystery appendicitis, the illness was not well-defined or understood. He suffered persistent pain and was forced back to hospital in March, at an awkward time. Jessie gave birth to a daughter, Shirley Jane, on April 17.

In May, Bradman experienced excruciating back spasms. A month later he was in hospital again. The pain had spread to the muscles and nerves of his right arm. Jessie, along with looking after a baby and a two-year-old boy, was having to shave her husband.

In June, an Army medical board invalided him out of the armed services. The Bradman family retreated to the Mittagong farm of Jessie's parents for half a year of rest and rehabilitation. At the time of his thirty-third birthday, The Don had reached the lowest ebb of his life.

BACK TO BROKING

Bradman made a partial recovery thanks largely to the encouragement and nursing skills of his wife. Early in 1942, the family returned to Adelaide. Bradman again took up his work of handling clients at Harry Hodgetts' stockbroking business. Over the next year his health gradually improved, but not enough to play cricket, despite efforts by Kensington to cajole him to the crease. His back was improving marginally and he managed to play some gentle golf in the summer of 1942–43.

Bradman worked assiduously at Hodgetts' and was rewarded on 11 May 1943, when he was elected a member of the Adelaide Stock Exchange, despite only being an employee and not a partner in Hodgetts' firm. It meant Bradman could, if he wished, operate and trade on the Exchange in his own right.

Bradman did what he could for the war effort by becoming

honorary secretary and treasurer for South Australia of the Gowrie Scholarship Trust Fund, which raised £140,000 to provide school and university scholarships for members of the armed forces and their children.

Bradman played no cricket but his legendary status was not forgotten. On the downfall of Mussolini in the European summer of 1943, a British MP declared, 'We have got Ponsford out cheaply, but Bradman is still batting,' which seemed very flattering to Hitler.

In reality, The Don was not batting or intending to. The 1943–44 season came and went without the great name gracing a scoresheet anywhere. He was now thirty-five, and had had his biggest break from the game since 1925–26 when he first made the decision to play cricket. His back was still troubling him and he had no thought of playing again.

Meanwhile, the Allied forces everywhere were beginning to score victories against Hitler's war machine and the Japanese in the Pacific. On 14 March 1944, the long-awaited signal that was to initiate the assault on the Monte Cassino monastery in Italy read: 'Bradman will be batting tomorrow.'

It was a code that the British troops understood, but which befuddled the Germans. The Nazi Enigma coding machines, which passed messages within the Axis military, sent out pleas for an explanation. Who was this Bradman? What was this batting?

The following day they found out. The British mounted a massive assault on the opposition and took the monastery.

FALL AND RISE

On 30 April 1945, Hitler committed suicide in his Berlin bunker and a week later, on 7 May, the German military forces surrendered. The war in Europe was over. In the Pacific, Allied forces led by the US were preparing for a final assault on Japan.

Just when the future looked brighter, the Bradmans ran into a problem that shocked them with its suddenness. In July 1945 Harry Hodgetts' broking firm went bankrupt overnight. Bradman was out of a job. He had come to South Australia in 1934 to establish a career away from cricket which would offer him and his family security. Now, as he struggled to regain his health, that apparent security had evaporated.

Hodgetts had been unlucky. He had invested in a hotel complex in Darwin, which had been bombed by the Japanese. An agent of his in Broken Hill had misappropriated funds. Hodgetts had foolishly used investors' funds to cover his losses, but the broking business spiralled downwards and collapsed. An affidavit filed in the Adelaide Bankruptcy Court showed Hodgetts' deficiencies at £88,854. Some 238 unsecured creditors were named, with debts totalling £102,926. Bradman himself was owed £726.

In tiny Adelaide, the fall from grace for a pillar of the establishment was a tragedy of Mayor of Casterbridge proportions, especially as one of his now former employees was Bradman.

The police fraud squad investigated the collapse, resulting in criminal proceedings against Hodgetts, who was eventually found guilty of fraud and sentenced to five years in jail. Through no fault of his own, Bradman, as someone who handled Hodgetts' clients and whose name helped attract business, bore some of the stigma of the latter's defalcations in the ultra-conservative, parochial city.

However, the adversity created a new opportunity. Urged by friends and encouraged by Jessie, Bradman considered opening his own broking firm. It was a decision that had to be made quickly. Other offers, particularly to take up journalism with the now expected resumption of Test matches, were coming in. But at the back of Bradman's mind was the very slim chance that he would play cricket again. At thirty-six, he had not played for four years. His back problems had not been totally overcome, and he feared flare-ups which could quickly incapacitate him. Then again, he felt that little eel of hunger to don the pads again. If he accepted a writing contract, he would not be able to play the game. Bradman would be on the wrong side of the fence.

He decided to keep that slender playing option open, forget about journalism and set up the broking business. This meant long hours and little rest. But the indefatigable Jessie took a great deal of the workload and helped run the new firm, on top of bringing up John and Shirley. The little girl had been found to have cerebral palsy. While the disability did not affect her mental faculties and was not severe, it added to the Bradmans' caring responsibilities.

Gradually, Don Bradman & Co got under way. They opened a small suite of offices in Cowra Chambers at 23 Grenfell Street in the city. It reminded visitors of a tidy solicitor's office, and they thought Bradman looked the part from the beginning in his wood-panelled inner-sanctum. His desk was meticulously neat and reflected his logical and uncluttered mind. He soon acquired a reputation as an intelligent, trust-worthy broker who gave sound investment advice, despite the calamity of Hodgetts' disgrace.

Many of Hodgetts' old clients drifted back. Bradman's bankers offered financial support and the institutions from the weightier end of town, who were aware of the background to the fall of his former boss and Bradman's own brave rise, gave his business the appropriate nod.

Early in August 1945 the US abruptly ended the Pacific War by dropping two atomic bombs on Japan. Now there was nothing to stop life returning to normal. Among other things, cricket was back on the national agenda, and also on Bradman's mind. On 13 August, the South Australian Cricket Association (SACA) elected him as one of its three representatives on the Board of Control, ironically to fill the vacancy left by the unfortunate Harry Hodgetts.

There was a further irony in this development. He was now a member of the Board with which he had been in well-publicised con-flict on three occasions in his cricketing career. His seat had not been offered by his old adversaries, but given to him by the State he had made a Shield winner and to which he had given enormous service.

Four years after the onset of his back problems in 1941, the thirty-seven year-old Bradman had re-established himself, with Jessie's great assistance, to the stage where he could consider picking up a bat again. He was concerned that his abilities might have withered with time. The only way to test this was to take up the challenge of a first-class game and see if the old skills were still with him.

PART FIVE

INTO THE POSTWAR ERA 1946–1948

42

A MATTER OF
DESTINY

He seems likely to be his old dominating self by the end of
November when the first Test is due.
— JOURNALIST E. M. WELLINGS ON BRADMAN'S COMEBACK GAME
VERSUS MCC, OCTOBER 1946

TO PLAY OR NOT TO PLAY

Bradman's main international rival, Walter Hammond, led the England team to Australia at the beginning of the 1946–47 season, and promptly belted a double century in Perth, which put the two greats of the 1930s level in first-class 200s with thirty-six each. The England all-rounder, now forty-three, had thrown down the gauntlet to The Don.

Would he now make himself available for the Tests? It all depended on his form and fitness. The previous season — 1945–46 — he had two first-class games, one against Queensland, where he scored 68 and 52 not out, and the other against a Services team, in which he scored a run-a-minute 112. Observers had been quick to admire his form then, but Bradman himself was not convinced. He made himself unavailable for a tour of New Zealand. He had little confidence in his back, and would wait until he had tested himself against the tourists before deciding.

A year later, Bradman knew he could not be 100 per cent to play in Tests, and he had been offered a huge £10,000 to cover the series for a newspaper. He didn't like the idea of failure on the cricket arena, and there were always the 'possible adverse effects' on his business if he wasn't there to monitor and control it. There was also his age. He was thirty-eight. He had last played in a Test at the age of twenty-nine in 1938. For almost all sportsmen at the top of their field, from boxers to bikers, this would be considered too much of a gap.

On the other hand, there were public demands for him to play. Everyone from the PM to the Adelaide ground gate-keepers wished he would 'give it a go'. Even Jessie urged him to try. 'I wanted young John [then 7] to see Don play,' she said. 'What a pity for him to grow up without seeing his father in a Test.'

With pressures both ways, Bradman decided to play at least until November, which would encompass two games against the tourists and one against Victoria. He put in a long 'pre-season' of fitness, even travelling to see famed Melbourne masseur Ern Saunders for special treatment and an exercise routine that was meant to strengthen his back. Then he played for a South Australian team in second-class games against a visiting South Perth side and made 30 and 133. This was followed by a club game for Kensington in which he hit 117.

This all felt 'OK', but it was a long way from facing the might of England, all raring to knock him out of competitive cricket for good.

The tour party comprised Hammond, Hutton, Cyril Washbrook, Edrich, Compton, Hardstaff, Norman Yardley, Voce, Alec Bedser, Dick Pollard, Doug Wright, Jack Ikin, John Langridge, T. P. B. Smith, L. B. Fishlock, and wicketkeepers Godfrey Evans and Paul Gibb. On paper, it looked exceptionally strong in batting and balanced in bowling.

The home side would have a far greater difference in its composition with O'Reilly, Fingleton, Fleetwood-Smith, McCormick, McCabe and Grimmett all retired. Ross Gregory had been killed in action in the war. Many other players who had made their names in the 1930s were now too old or retired. Bradman's presence would be invaluable. Without his leadership and against such a powerful

England, Australia could be heading for a demoralising drubbing in line with the farce at The Oval in 1938.

THE COMEBACK

Bradman saddled up with 'considerable anxiety and diffidence' as South Australian captain against England and for two days he felt at times as if he were back in the nightmare of that 1938 Test. England scored more than 200 before it lost Washbrook (113). Then Hutton went for 136, while Edrich and Compton scored 71 apiece. Hammond failed with just 9, and declared the innings closed at five for 506.

Bradman felt that pre-innings tension before a big contest for the first time in years, and while he was his usual nerve-free self, he lacked confidence. But he didn't have time to dwell on it once the South Australian innings started. He came in before lunch of the third day in front of an expectant crowd who reflected the feelings of the nation and the cricketing world beyond. He couldn't possibly pick up from where he left off after half a decade. But how good would he be? Double hundreds would surely be beyond him, yet was he good for a first-class ton? There had been rumours of his strength and energy being drained by his back disorder during the war years, and that he was a feeble imitation of the great performer of yesteryear.

Bradman walked slowly out to the wicket. There was no cheeky grin or jaunty step now. He looked gaunt and thinner than his last Test appearance in 1938, and when he took off his cap, the hair was thinner, which added to his apparent frailty. That was the outer man who took block. What observers could not judge was the competitive grit of the inner being that had made him arguably the best performed sportsman of any type in the prewar period.

Alec Bedser and Doug Wright had been kept out of the game in order to give him new problems should he play in the Tests, but the attack was more than competent. Bradman looked tentative. He scratched his way to ten in half an hour. At 15, he was dropped by keeper Evans off Pollard, whose fast-medium pace and swing were troubling the batsman. His timing and coordination were missing. He was not as resilient as before. He didn't have quite the vitality or suppleness of the 1930s. This was a shell of the player who had cowed the best bowlers on the planet in the 1930s with skill, confidence, power and athleticism. Bradman's running between the wickets also seemed stiff-limbed and slow. He was not as alert or eager as in earlier days.

After lunch, though, gradually, the timing came back as brain, body and bat began to combine. There was something of the younger Bradman as his feet joined the growing rhythm in his shot-making against Pollard, Smith, Langridge, Edrich, Compton and even Hammond, who was still prepared to roll over the odd ball, despite the resistance from his shoulder and back. The length of time at the wicket warmed Bradman's muscles and a looseness of limb, even a suppleness, returned.

He reached 50 in ninety-seven minutes, a half-century that did not do much to persuade him that the risk of a return against the odds was worth it. He moved to 76 not out at tea, but was caught and bowled by the leg-spinner Peter Smith on the first ball after the break. He batted for 153 minutes and hit six fours. Bradman had top-scored for his State yet again.

'I was a shadow of myself, physically, mentally and in cricket form,' Bradman acknowledged but kept his judgement to himself, whatever the critics said. One writer commented that he had seen the ghost of a great cricketer and that 'ghosts seldom come back to life'. But the key thing was that while he felt he was a poor imitation of himself, he still thought he could summon the real Bradman.

Meanwhile South Australia, all out for 266 in its first innings, managed to struggle through with eight for 276 in its second and force a draw, thanks to opener R. J. Craig's 111 and tail-ender J. Mann's 62 not out. Bradman was out playing a wild shot and caught by Edrich off Pollard for 3, which demonstrated he perhaps had to regain a measure of concentration and discipline as well.

The reviews for his efforts in the game were mixed. Negative observers carped about his fielding, captaincy and his batting in the second knock. The more open-minded saw much to cheer about and suggested that he should play in the Tests. Johnnie Moyes, his former sports editor boss at the Sydney *Sun*, wrote him an inspiring letter, and he received a more than usual weekly ration of mail urging him to play for his country once more.

Bradman made himself available and helped select an Australian XI to play the tourists at Melbourne two weeks later. The selectors were looking for more pace with which to challenge England, especially after the near-fiasco of 1938, when McCormick missed his run-up at Worcester and never really got it right for the next twenty matches, and Australia opened at times with McCabe and O'Reilly. However, it was the leg-spin of Queensland's Colin McCool, who took seven for 106 in the tourists' 314, which caught the eye. Hutton (71), Washbrook (57) and Hammond (51) continued to show good pre-Test form.

Bradman came on to the MCG turf at one for 39 in front of a crowd of nearly 24,000, near the end of the second day of the damp, rain-affected game. He had just under an hour to bat and the crowd, which looked sparse in the now mighty MCG stadium, cheered him to the centre. They wanted their symbiosis with him to live again as it had in the glory days when it seemed that he delivered his best at Melbourne.

It was as if they knew that this innings was critical. If he failed or if he still judged himself a 'shadow', he could drop out, forever. Bradman responded by batting steadily and with a bit of the former command for 28 not out at the close. It was a notable step-up from his unsure start in Adelaide. His timing was there from the first few balls and he never let it go.

On the Monday he moved easily to 50 in ninety-two minutes, and then pulled a calf muscle. However, he was feeling in such touch that he carried on. Bradman and the big Monday crowd could feel a hundred coming on. A Reuter commentator, Norman Preston, who had seen him throughout the 1930s, saw no difference from his performances in the halcyon days. 'His sight remains acute and his brain and feet respond readily to deal with any type of delivery,' he noted, 'whether he decides to play forward or off the back foot.'

At 78, he stepped out of his crease to thump Compton, missed and was nearly stumped. It was his only chance. He proceeded into the 90s and dwelt there uncharacteristically for twenty-five minutes. It was still a very good sign. Bradman badly wanted a century, despite his injury. When he got it after 215 minutes, he flayed at everything, added six and threw away his wicket. Opener Arthur Morris with 118 booked his place in the Brisbane First Test as the Australian XI passed England with half its wickets intact.

Against Victoria, Bradman made 43 and a dashing 119 in just over three hours, which helped save his side from an innings defeat. The Vics had piled up 548, thanks to a cracking 188 from the flamboyant young all-rounder Keith Miller, a graceful 114 from Hassett, and a strong 87 from opener Ken Meuleman.

It was time for Bradman to make a decision. He was influenced by the retirement of O'Reilly, who had shown fine form postwar, but who feared his injured knee would not take another season on hard wickets. Bradman felt compelled to provide his experience on the field in order to restart Australian cricket in the postwar era.

Not surprisingly, Sid Barnes — who had played in just one Test — Bradman and Hassett were the only players with Ashes experience named in the Australian team, along with newcomers Morris, Miller, McCool, the off-spinner Ian Johnson, fast bowler Ray Lindwall, Meuleman (likely 12th man), keeper Don Tallon, left-arm medium pacer Ernie Toshack and left-hand googly spinner George Tribe in the twelve for Brisbane. Johnson and Lindwall were also more than useful batsmen, while McCool, like the fast-bowling Miller, was a genuine all-rounder.

CATCH OF FATE AT 28

Hutton, Edrich, Compton, Hammond, Wright and Voce were England's players with Ashes experience. The new men were Ikin, Gibb, Washbrook, Bedser and Yardley. On paper, England looked superior.

Bradman and Hammond walked out at the Gabba, Brisbane, on 29 November — a hot and humid day — to toss the coin. There was much tense but smiling banter for the cameras. Bradman called correctly for the first time against Hammond, and with some relief decided to bat. In England in 1938, the toss had prevented Australia from winning the rubber. Bradman and his fellow bats were invariably forced on the defensive chasing big scores, often on wet wickets. This success had given him a chance to redress the balance.

Arthur Morris (2) was caught by the brilliant Hammond in slips off Bedser at 9. The time was 12.15 p.m. Bradman strode out on the sparse, yellow ground in front of 12,000 fans. Characteristically, his collar was up to protect his neck against the heat and the shirt sleeves were rolled to just below the elbow. His cap was jammed down and the pads seemed big enough to protect his thigh tops. But apart from those things familiar to observant spectators, he looked drawn and old compared with the players around him — a performer out of place and time.

Bradman scratched out his block, examined the field and then poked and prodded his way to just 7 in the first forty minutes. Alec Bedser, the 6 ft 2 in (192 cm) medium-fast swing bowler, whom he had never faced before, had him in trouble. Seeing this, Sid Barnes, who was in fine form, began taking the strike. Perhaps, some thought, Bradman should have left cricket fans with a lasting memory of the world-beating legend of the prewar era. To expose himself to the bump of Voce and the guile of Bedser only seemed, on that discouraging morning, to dent the image. He crawled on, lacking confidence as Barnes, by contrast, played his strokes boldly until the score was 46 and Wright had him caught for 31.

With Hassett at the wicket, Bradman began to pick the gaps. In the next half-hour, he took his score to 28. He began using his famous late cut, which had brought him hundreds over the years. It was still there with all its grace and cheek. He still looked shaky, but his score was mounting and he was looking forward to the lunch-break a few minutes away.

Voce, Bradman's oldest adversary in the current team, was on and bowling tightly. He tried an away-swinging yorker and over-pitched it slightly and just outside off-stump. Bradman tried to chop down on the ball in order to guide it wide of the slips. The ball flew chest high to Ikin at second slip. The batsman thought it touched the bottom of the bat before hitting the ground, thus making it a 'bump-ball' and not a catch.

Bradman behaved as if it were just a bump-ball. He looked casually towards square leg, then down at the ground as he waited for the next ball, something observed of him throughout his career. There was no anxious look at slips and then the umpire.

The excited Englishmen, however, thought it was a real catch and reacted as if they expected Bradman to walk. When he did not, they appealed. Umpire Borwick shook his head.

'Not out,' he said without hesitation. Square-leg umpire Scott had a clear view of the action and agreed unequivocally with his colleague, who did not bother to consult him. The batsman was, under the rules of the game, always given the benefit of the doubt. But there was no doubt in the mind of either umpire. No benefit, in the adjudicators' judgement, was necessary.

Hammond at first slip was stunned. He had badly wanted to see The Don's back early. In his mind, this was the moment. At the end of the over the angry England captain walked past Bradman. 'A fine way to start a bloody series,' he said.

Bradman ignored the remark. Moments later, the players went to lunch. The break meant that everyone — players, umpires, officials, journalists and spectators — concentrated on reviewing the incident. There was no benefit of a video replay or any way to look at the incident from different angles, which may have determined if it was a bump-ball, or if it came off the outside edge of the bat as Ikin and Hammond contended. Opinion was divided and some journalists naturally seized on the incident, although it would have been impossible for anyone on the other side of the fence to judge. The reality was that Bradman and Hassett were the two batsmen who strode out after lunch.

The incident, and whatever Bradman had had to eat along with his unique tea, changed his demeanour at the wicket and his performance with the bat. Journalists in the press-box from O'Reilly and Fingleton to Cardus and Bruce Harris of the London *Evening*

Standard had the shadow, ghost and deceased Bradman rising for a 'Lazarus innings' (according to Cardus).

The alleged apparition added twenty-two in forty minutes to reach 50 in just under two hours and after that materialised as the postwar Bradman. He was slower between wickets and his run seemed a scamper more than a youthful charge, but that, plus a small diminution in power, were the only concessions to the eight years since he had played at the highest level. As the afternoon unfolded everything else of his genius rolled into play. The exceptional eye, the supple wrists, the lightning feet, the wide range of strokes, the uncanny placement and the exquisite timing were all on show for an audience, half of whom would only have heard about his capacities and not seen them.

Bradman thought he recognised himself in that session between lunch and tea when he collected 54 to be 82 not out. After the short interval, he was himself 'physically and mentally' as he reached a century after 194 minutes. Perhaps the most important feature of Bradman returned. As he held his bat high and removed his dark-green cap to acknowledge the cheering, he grinned.

Hammond, at slip, put his hands together as he simulated a brief clap, for he could not help but reflect on that decision just before lunch. Bradman seemed to notice. Behind the grin, he could have been thinking, 'Yes, indeed, a fine way to start a series . . .'

He ploughed on in the heat, moving as he did more than any other batsman, with concentrated intent towards his second hundred. He harvested runs at twice the pace he had reached before his century and seemed to have the attack at his mercy, with waspish Hassett, his loyal lieutenant, stroking along behind.

Just before stumps, Bradman, at 160, became the first player on either side to reach 4,000 runs in Ashes Tests. At the close of play he was 162 not out with the score at two for 292 and Hassett not out in the nervous 90s.

On Saturday 30 November, Bradman wanted his team to be still in by stumps. Memories of the disaster for him and his team at The Oval were vivid. He didn't necessarily want 900. But something in the order of 700 would make the skipper feel satisfied. Bradman wished to demoralise the Englishmen right at the start of the series and gain a big pyschological advantage.

There were 20,000 sitting in the hot sunshine as Bradman plundered 25 in the first half-hour. Edrich came on. His fourth ball was a fine in-swinger, which gained pace off the wicket and touched the pad on the way through to Bradman's off stump. He was out for 187 off 305 balls in a 318 minutes' stay in which he collected nineteen fours, and gave no actual chance. It was the highest Test score in an Ashes Test at Brisbane. His partnership with Hassett yielded 276 in 278 minutes.

Hassett (128) continued to play the anchor as Miller (79) got his shots going and paved the way for a fine knock by McCool (95). The innings finished on day three, Monday, with Johnson (47) playing steadily and Lindwall (31) having a dip. Australia tallied 645. Wright was the best of the bowlers with five for 167 off 43.6 overs.

Australia's new opening pair, Lindwall and Miller, had Hutton and Washbrook ducking and weaving — a far cry from the last attack England faced in 1938. Lindwall had a similar smooth run-up to Larwood's and seemed about as lethal as storm clouds gathered at lunch. After the break, storms held up play twice. In between, Miller had gone a long way towards winning the match. He took all four wickets to fall by the time the score was 56 — Hutton (7) bowled, Washbrook (6) and Edrich (16) caught, and Compton (17) LBW to a nasty shooter. Bad light ended play at 4.22 p.m. with England five for 117.

Overnight torrential rain flooded the pitch. It drained away by the start of play, leaving a sticky. Miller got some deliveries to kick and fly. He struck the batsmen and, with medium-pacer Toshack, hastened their departure for 141. Only Hammond (32) and Yardley (29) showed resistance to Miller, who took seven for 60. Toshack had three for 17.

England followed on, but struggled again on the drying gluepot to be dismissed for 172, with Toshack this time the destroyer with six for 82. Miller took two for 17 and Tribe two for 48.

Australia won by an innings and 332. It was sweet revenge for Bradman after nearly a decade to dwell on the last Ashes game at The Oval, which had seen a reverse dominance. He felt vindicated by his decision to come back and lead Australia into the postwar era.

43

DOUBLE AGAINST THE ODDS

I tore a leg muscle . . . followed by an attack of gastritis . . . my leg was heavily bandaged and the whole innings was played off the back foot.
— BRADMAN ON HIS INNINGS OF 234 IN THE SECOND TEST AT SYDNEY, DECEMBER 1946

THE WEEKEND FROM HELL

Bradman's name and fame got him into potential trouble with the Adelaide Stock Exchange at the end of the First Test at Brisbane. A photograph was flashed around the country showing a group of men outside his Grenfell Street office while he was making his 162 not out on the first day. It had a nice, symbolic touch. The name, DON BRADMAN & CO, Stock, Share and Investment Broker, was visible above an earnest-looking pipe-smoking army sergeant and a knot of suited, hatted gentlemen.

The cricketer himself was thousands of kilometres away in Brisbane, but the powers that were at the Exchange accused him of breaking the rules by advertising. He had to confront a committee.

'It happened because of the jealousies of one or two members,' Bradman said, 'and because of the way the business was progressing. I told them I could not control the press. Nor had I encouraged such publicity.'

Short of painting out his name, Bradman could do nothing about the increasing number of people who gathered outside his offices on Friday 13 December for the start of the Second Test at Sydney.

England replaced Gibb behind the stumps with Godfrey Evans, and Voce with Smith. Australia replaced Lindwall, who had chicken-pox, with the Victorian fast-medium man Fred Freer. Bradman went back to his toss-losing ways and England batted first. However, it proved a good day for the home side as England lost eight for 219. Ian Johnson at one point sent down eleven overs for one for 3. Only three of 88 balls from him were scored off, a great piece of control on a plumb wicket against top-class bats. His day's end figures were four for 31 from twenty-five overs. England was out on Saturday morning for 255, thanks mainly to Johnson's tidy, attacking off-spin. He finished with six for 42 off 30.1 overs.

McCool was more expensive, but still effective, taking three for 73 off twenty-three overs, getting Edrich (71) LBW and having Compton (5) and Hammond (1) caught behind by the aptly named Tallon.

Bradman, who had strained a thigh muscle late Friday when field-ing a ball with his foot, could not take the field on Saturday because of an attack of gastritis. Hassett captained the side in front of the crowd of close to 40,000. If ever the timing was right for injury and illness it was then.

The skipper received massage and heat treatment for his thigh, the traditional way until the 1970s to treat muscle injury (when ice packs replaced heat), as Barnes, under instructions, appealed several times against the light. The players went off at 12.55 p.m. Barnes was hooted roundly by the Hillites and members. The rain pelted down at 1.05 p.m. and delayed play until after 4 p.m. when Australia lost Morris (5), who played on to Edrich at 24. The skipper sent in Ian Johnson to 'day-watch' and pushed himself down the list to number six. Johnson, also acting on orders, appealed against the light and was successful. The batsmen were again booed by some of the 25,000 crowd left as they walked from the field at 4.54 p.m. with the score at one for 27.

Bradman, increasingly hampered by his injured leg and illness, went straight to bed and stayed there for most of the weekend. The weather improved by Monday 16 December, and Australia asked for the light roller to be used for seven minutes. The sun promised to dry out the wicket, although in the pre-lunch session it helped make Bedser, Edrich and Wright more hostile. The batsmen struggled. Johnson (7) was soon deceived by a slower ball from Edrich, which he pushed to Washbrook at cover-point. Australia was two for 37 and the crowd of 35,000 looked towards the pavilion. No Bradman. Hassett came out and was 30 not out at lunch with Barnes on 44. Australia was two for 88.

During the break, the big pre-Christmas Sydney crowd, starved of top-level cricket and Bradman for so long, squeezed up to 51,459 — the largest attendance ever at the SCG on a Monday. An estimated 20,000 were turned away. The turnstiles locked shut. The expectations and hopes were that the back-to-form NSW-born champion would at last score a century at Sydney, something which had eluded him since he began at the Test level eighteen years earlier.

At 96 after lunch, Hassett (34) was caught by Compton off Edrich and a roar went up as if an English wicket had gone down. The crowd anticipated the little super-star but was surprised to see the big, dark-haired and flamboyant Miller come out rolling his shoulders as he strode to the wicket.

Radio reports were talking about Bradman's illness and injury. There were rumours he had left the ground and was back at the hotel. Jessie, back in Adelaide doing the book-keeping at their broking firm, told a reporter that Don had been suffering from chronic gastritis — an inflammation of the stomach lining — for months. A whisper swept the ground saying that he would not bat. But those with binoculars focused on the dressing-room area and saw him there padded up.

Meanwhile, Miller, like a warm-up entertainer on a TV-game show, was exciting the audience by a combination of heaving drives and dead-bat shots. He gunned his way to 40 before being caught behind off Smith at 169. Barnes, tempering his penchant for fast-scoring after his bright 31 at Brisbane, had crawled to 71 not out. It was 3.50 p.m.

IN FOR A MIRACLE

All heads and binoculars turned to the Members' pavilion and a thunderous roar broke out as Bradman came down the steps. His tightly-strapped leg caused him to limp to the centre. After little food or sleep in three days, he was pale and drawn. His gastritis was giving him continuous pain.

Bradman had avoided appearing in the hope that he could at least gain another night's rest before batting, but to delay any further could engender a collapse that would hand England the match. As he approached the wicket he glanced at the scoreboard. Four for 169 meant England was on top. Two quick wickets now might mean Australia would be behind when the tourists began their second innings. After a few words to Barnes, he settled down over his bat. The excited crowd went quiet.

Smith bowled. Bradman went back and stayed back to block the ball. He had no choice. His pulled right leg thigh muscle prevented him from putting any weight forward. At tea, a few minutes later, he was 5 not out and the crowd demurred at Bradman's demure approach. The rumours were true. He was a crock, and he looked ill. But at least he was in.

After tea, however, some patrons contemplated the unthinkable — departing — as Bradman, with an excuse, and Barnes, on a big-scoring mission, proceeded like snails. In the next hour Bradman added 9 to be 14. Then at 20, he hit a bump-ball to Ikin at short leg off Bedser. The bowler turned to umpire Scott.

'That's not out, is it?' the bowler queried.

'Are you appealing?' Scott asked.

'Yes.'

'Not out,' said Scott.

No-one seriously considered it a catch, but the fact that it was Ikin who had taken the ball again gave some journalists a chance for a little beat-up. After this, Bradman opened out with some wonderful shots, all off the back foot. It was less difficult to strike on the off. The late cut, square-cut, cover drive and off-drives had the crowd cheering. Bradman, batting without a runner, struggled when going for a third run. The short, sharp singles were restricted.

He reached 50 (six fours) after 111 minutes, just four minutes before the close. At the other end, Barnes was plodding along against his better instincts. However, it was paying off for him and his team as he reached his first Ashes century after his promising consistency of 41 and 33 in 1938 and 31 in Brisbane.

Nearly 30,000 turned up on Tuesday to watch these two bat on in the morning unspectacularly. Barnes, 119 overnight, reached 166 at lunch, and Bradman added just 34 to be 86 not out at the break. Australia was 35 ahead still with six wickets in hand.

At 2.35 p.m. Bradman reached his first Test 100 at Sydney after 213 minutes at the wicket and a nearly two decades wait. It was his eighth century in successive Tests going back to 1937 and his twenty-third in all Tests. From then until tea he stepped back to the bowling with more gusto to be 151 not out.

After the short interval he improved his rating and scored at a run-a-minute to race Barnes — whom he had given more than four hours and 71 runs start — to 200 at 5.21 p.m. It had taken Bradman 371 minutes.

Then he cut loose, scoring 34 in twenty-two minutes, including his last 16 off one over from Compton. At 234, Bradman swung wildly at Yardley and was LBW. He had batted 393 minutes with twenty-four fours and no chance, which when added to his Brisbane effort meant he had batted twelve hours for 421 runs in two chance-less innings. No wonder he trotted off the ground to a standing ovation, his injury of little hindrance and the gastritis problems diminished. His 405-run partnership with Barnes was a fifth-wicket record and put Australia in an unassailable position at five for 514, 259 ahead.

The Sydney crowd began to leave the arena *en masse*. They had come to see Bradman. It seemed, unfairly, that the rest were incidental.

Next man in, Colin McCool, had trouble in forcing his way through the exodus of Members to get onto the field. 'I could have been wearing a false nose and moustache,' he remarked, 'and nobody would have noticed.'

Barnes apparently also thought it wasn't worth batting to an emptying house with seventeen minutes to the close. He was out soon after caught by Ikin off Bedser, also for 234. There were rumours that Barnes won a bet that he would get out at the same score as Bradman. 'I remember that story,' Bradman said, 'but I didn't believe it then or later. The fact that we were dismissed at the same score was coincidental.'

Australia went to stumps at six for 571. The next morning, Wednesday 18 December, McCool (12), Tallon (30), Freer (28 not out) and Tribe (25 not out) took the long handle to the England bowlers and crunched 88 in fifty minutes before Bradman closed the innings at eight for 659 — a thumping lead of 404. Edrich was the best of the bowlers with three for 79.

Hutton came out firing against a barrage of bumpers from Miller and hit a fast, powerful 37 in the twenty-five minutes until lunch before unfortunately treading on his wicket. Washbrook and Edrich dug in after lunch until they reached 118. Then McCool at silly-leg dived full-length close to the pitch to catch Washbrook (41) off Johnson. Edrich and Compton next turned on a fighting stand to bring England to three for 220. At that point, Compton (54) edged Freer to Bradman at slip. Hammond came in and was still with Edrich at the close with the score at three for 247.

There was a big chance on Thursday, the sixth and final day, that England could save the game. They were 157 in arrears but still with seven wickets to fall. Edrich, the talented fighter, reached his 100 with an on-drive off Johnson. Hammond engaged McCool in a powerful struggle in the morning until the score was 280. He lifted one straight drive too many and Toshack ran across twenty metres behind the bowler to take the catch. It was a telling moment in the match and the series. Hammond (37) was on his way with a rueful shake of the head. He had failed to build a big innings now in four successive appearances and it was disappointing considering his main rival's great form. Freer, using off-spin instead of swing, suddenly speared one in to bowl a surprised Ikin (17). England was five for 309. Then at 327, McCool deceived Edrich (119) with a low-trajectory, full-length ball, which rattled his stumps. England then gradually folded to be all out for 371, giving the home side victory by an innings and twenty-three runs. McCool had taken five for 109, and Freer two for 49.

Australia headed for Melbourne with a commanding lead of two-nil, and Bradman looking several years younger.

44

A GRIP
ON THE URN

If I were choosing a side out of all the cricketers who have ever lived, I would put Bradman's name down first. None of us had the measure of him and that's the plain fact.

— HAMMOND ON BRADMAN, NEAR THE END OF THEIR GREAT CAREER RIVALRIES

FLIRTING WITH THE MISTRESS

Before the Third Test at Melbourne, representatives of both sides of Australian politics approached Bradman about joining their parties. It was a tribute to the universal respect for him that both the left and right political interests in the country considered he was one of them. It was also a tribute to his skill in keeping part of his life private. Few really knew how he voted or thought about issues. The conservative side considered his stockbroking business, polished demeanour and love for England meant he would snap up their offer of a blue-ribbon seat. Labor looked at his background, heard his Aussie accent, noticed his mass appeal and felt he would sit very well with them. Both sides and their electorates were certain he was the greatest national symbol the country had had since Federation in 1901. His outstanding competitive spirit in winning for Australia was an emotive factor, which it was thought would make him an enormous vote-winner. Whenever he made speeches, they seemed to come from the lips of an experienced diplomat. He could be at once all things to all people with spirit, drive and high principles.

But Bradman never seriously saw himself as a politician, although he kept abreast of issues. He would later consider a diplomatic posting, but for the time being he was content with his lot in broking, although he and Jessie were finding it a strain running a business, a family and the most high-profile sporting team in the country.

His immediate concern was in wrapping up the Third Test at Melbourne, commencing Wednesday 1 January 1947. Australia left out Tribe for South Australian leg-spinner Bruce Dooland, and Lindwall came back in for Freer. England dropped Smith and brought back Voce. A big New Year crowd of 66,000 turned up mid-week and were pleased to see the Australian names being placed by the scoreboard in batting order. Bradman had won the toss.

Barnes and Morris took the score to 32 before Bedser had the latter LBW for 21. The crowd braced itself as Bradman came out to a typical MCG cheer. This was his eighth Test in Melbourne and he had scored at least a century in each of the other seven matches. Spectators were betting on him hitting another.

He started with such panache with 30 in thirty-eight minutes before lunch that all bets were off at the main break. The second session saw him reach 50 in seventy-nine minutes but then move sedately to 73 by tea, losing Barnes (45) also LBW to Bedser and Hassett (12) caught Hammond in slips off Wright. Australia was three for 143. England were doing well, considering that Voce and Edrich had leg injuries, which limited their performances.

Yardley took on the burden and had success after tea. Bradman (79) played too late at an off-break and dragged it into his stumps at 188. He had batted 169 minutes with just two fours. He walked off the field and was captured looking philosophical in a photograph taken just before the gate to the players' race. His 79 was a satisfactory effort, but it brought an end to his run of 100s at the biggest stadium in the country. The pragmatic expression reflected that he had come full circle from his first innings at Melbourne in the Third Test of the

1928–29 series when he made the same score, which took him 194 minutes off 203 balls. Then he had been the ambitious youth on the way up. He was hardly on the way down now, yet his great affair with the Melbourne public was nearing an end. If Sydney was the town that mothered and smothered him so much that he left home, then Adelaide was the wife and Melbourne was surely the exciting mistress, for whom he performed at his peak in fleeting visits.

Yardley, rather pleased with himself for snaring The Don twice in three innings, trapped Johnson next ball LBW for 0. McCool, who had batted so well in Brisbane, saved the hat-trick and the rest of the day, as well as the next, in a fine fighting knock of 104, partnered with Tallon (35) and Dooland (19). These late recoveries allowed Australia to reach an unconvincing but satisfactory 365. The English bowling spoils were evenly divided, with Edrich picking up three for 50 off 10.3 overs despite his injury, while Bedser took three for 99 off thirty-one.

England managed one for 147, losing only Hutton (2) to the speedy Lindwall by the close of 2 January. Day three featured steady contributions from most of the England bats, but was marred by controversial LBW decisions. Edrich (89) appeared to get an unlucky verdict when he was adjudged LBW to Lindwall after nicking the ball into his pad. However, Compton (11), who complained about a similar decision, appeared to everyone to be caught dead in front by a ball from Toshack. Even his batting partner Washbrook said he was definitely out. Compton, like one or two of the other England bats, was feeling the strain of failure as Australia squeezed the tourists. He had hit 17, 15, 5, 54 and now 11. It was well below the expectations of a great batsman who was feeling the pressure as the rubber and his form seemed to be slipping away.

Hammond, caught and bowled by Dooland for 9, was also having a poor run by his standards, but he was taking things with a resigned stoicism. He was forty-three years old, and nearing the end. Ikin (48) and Yardley (61) held up the home side further and managed to drag the tourists up to 351, just fourteen short of Australia. Dooland had the figures with four for 69 in his first Ashes effort.

Writing about Bradman's part in the next day's play, Arthur Mailey said in a typical piece of whimsy:

> *I think Bradman had planned a day of leisure in his bath on Saturday morning. He took a leisurely breakfast, then sat in the Windsor Hotel lounge reading letters until it was time to meander down to the ground, and after padding up, Barnes (caught Evans bowled Yardley, 32, with the score at 68) gave him sufficient time to yawn, stretch himself, and stroll out on the field.*
>
> *Bradman had a little time to play with, and there was no need to get hot and bothered about this business of winning Test matches.*

Certainly, The Don was hardly in a fluster as he eked out 3 in his first half-hour at the crease. He stroked edgily and was 19 at lunch. After the interval Mailey reassessed him: 'I had never seen Bradman look more comfortable and less likely to lose his wicket . . .'

Bradman promptly belied the words. He was missed behind off Bedser at 44. At 49 he gently patted a catch and bowl to Yardley, who was more stunned than anyone at his good fortune in taking the world's prize wicket for the third time. Bradman had lasted ninety-nine minutes. Australia, at two for 159, was in a reasonably sound position, provided there was no sudden collapse. At stumps on Saturday, it had avoided that to be four for 293. On Monday, Arthur Morris used this innings to show his true worth by completing a six-hour knock for 155 before Bedser bowled him. Miller slammed a useful 34 before Yardley induced a snick to Hammond, whose slipping and captaincy were making up to a degree for his lack of form with the blade. McCool gathered a hot 43, but it was Lindwall and Tallon who thrilled the 50,000 crowd as they hammered 154 runs in eighty-eight minutes.

Tallon crashed his way to 92 with ten fours in just 105 minutes and left the stadium with Australia's score on eight for 495, and out of England's reach. Lindwall was 81 when the last man, Toshack, came in. The crowd was amused by this rabbit's stiff-batted determination to help his fellow bowler to a ton. They cheered every shot by both men until Lindwall reached the magic — very special for a fast bowler — three figures. A hundred was exactly where his score was frozen nicely for posterity when he was caught by Washbrook off Bedser going for another six. Yardley took three for 67, Wright three for 131 and Bedser three for 176. A feature was Godfrey Evans' magnificent keeping. This was the third innings in succession he had not conceded a bye.

Australia was all out for 536, giving it a smoothly round lead of 550, which would have been soothing to the skipper's neat formulaic mind. It may have been the perfect mathematical equation, taking in the variables of time and runs ahead to ensure a win, had it not been for forty-seven minutes lost to rain on the last day. England ended with seven for 310 at stumps on day six.

The home side had been prevented from taking the rubber and the Ashes thanks mainly to Washbrook (112), who played a sound, patient and defiant role, Evans (53 not out), and Bedser (25) late in the innings. This defiance saw the crowd cheering wildly for England. Australians, particularly in Melbourne, traditionally favoured the underdog, as the old bulldogs had surely been so far. The spectators got their wish for a draw, presumably because this might keep the rubber alive until the Fifth Test at the MCG.

Miller had the best figures of two for 41 off eleven overs in an even performance by the Australian bowlers in England's second innings. The draw left England two-nil down with two to play. The Ashes were Australia's but England could still square the rubber with two wins.

THE BULLDOG BITES BACK

Bradman didn't play any cricket for three weeks before the Fourth Test at Adelaide, but returned to his office to work. Ideally, every cricketer needs to put in time in the middle consistently through a season, but Bradman had taken on perhaps too much. However, he was in confident, cheerful and determined mood when he lost the toss to Hammond on 31 January and led his team onto the field. The only change was Victorian opener Mervyn Harvey for the injured

Barnes. England had added Hardstaff to stiffen the batting at the expense of Voce, who had broken down.

It proved a good toss to win. The wicket was perfect for batting. Hutton started slowly and methodically as if he had a big score in mind. He and Washbrook were still there at tea, but soon the Australian bowlers effected a breakthrough, which saw England four for 220 before Compton and Hardstaff came together and steadied matters until stumps. Hutton (94), Washbrook (65), and Edrich (17) all fell to spin. Hammond (18), who had been in fine form in the run-up to the game, was bowled by Toshack, apparently deceived by the left-hander's sudden pace off the wicket.

Bradman had spin on to start the second day, Saturday, in front of 30,000, but at 245 was forced to take the new ball, which gave the overnight pair no trouble. They batted into the afternoon before Hardstaff hooked badly at a very short one from Miller and played it into his wicket. Compton at last found good form in a long stay that produced 147. Late in the innings, Lindwall took three wickets — all bowled — in four balls.

England amassed 460, its best effort so far, and left Australia with a nasty little session of forty minutes until the close. It lost one for 18 when first-gamer Harvey was bowled by Bedser for 12. The big crowd had turned up in the hope of seeing Bradman and now many wondered if he would appear with just eighteen minutes to go. He did.

The thunderous applause could have been valedictory, for the locals had remembered his recent cautious remarks about his future in cricket before the Test series began. Bradman played out Bedser and then faced him two overs later. He was swinging the ball and bowling well to a leg-side field. Bedser delivered one on off-stump, which swung late and hit the pitch on leg-stump. Bradman played inside the ball. It came back and hit middle and off.

The crowd groaned. Bradman moved off with 0 beside his name for the fifth time in Tests and thinking it was the best ball ever bowled to him.

Compton, no lover of Australian fans after his send-off in Melbourne when he disputed being given LBW, noted 'depression written on every face' in the crowd at Bradman's demise. 'You might have thought they'd lost their life-savings in a crash; apparently Bradman losing his wicket without scoring was almost as big a debacle.'

Not so for the Australian batting line-up. After starting Monday with two for 24, Morris (122) linked with Hassett (78) in a dreary but game-saving 189-run partnership to take the home team to four for 293 at stumps. Miller (33 not out overnight) led the way on the fourth day, and was well-supported by Johnson (52), Lindwall (20) and Dooland (29), who saw Australia to 487. Miller's big knock of 141 not out in 271 minutes ran hot and cold. At first he showed the dash which brought him to notice in the Australian Services side in England in 1945, then he was bottled up by tight bowling. His performance brought Australia back into the game, although a lead of twenty-eight was insufficient, especially as Hutton and Washbrook came out firing and put on 96 in eighty-eight minutes.

Early on day five, Washbrook (39) was caught behind off Lindwall at 100. Johnson beautifully bowled Hutton (76), but then Edrich began aggressively and stayed with the more sedate Hammond until lunch. After the break, Edrich (46) couldn't sustain his bid for glory and was caught by Bradman after a change of pace from Toshack's at times deceptive medium-pace bowling. The same trick worked against Hammond (22) who swept the ball fine to Lindwall to make England four for 188. Tight bowling by Toshack and Johnson, who was having a fine match, frustrated Hardstaff. Toshack bowled him for 9 and then trapped Ikin LBW for 1. Lindwall and Miller then chipped in for a new ball wicket each to make the score eight for 255.

Compton then farmed the strike and played for time rather than runs to be 52 not out at stumps with Evans, who had faced forty-four balls without scoring, not out 0. England were just 250 ahead, and the game was in the balance.

Compton continued the tactics throughout the next day's morning session. He refused to take singles. Bradman countered by putting fielders out to prevent fours. It took Evans ninety-five minutes to break his duck — a world record. He went on to 10 not out, with Compton 103 not out.

Hammond, inexplicably, waited until the first ball had been bowled after lunch before declaring at eight for 340, with Toshack taking four for 76 and Lindwall two for 60. The timing of the close deprived the spectators of ten minutes' play and left Australia with 314 to make in 195 minutes.

Bradman was open-minded about going for the runs, which would incur big risks. He waited until Morris and Harvey faced up to see what England's tactics would be. They were obvious from the first over. Bedser set a leg theory field with five on the on-side. If Hammond had opened with an attacking field and demonstrated he wanted to win, Bradman would have taken up the challenge. Instead he let his openers play at a pace which would diminish the chance of dismissal. The Australians were in a no-lose situation if they were not dismissed. A draw would give them the rubber.

The spectators voiced their disapproval of both sides' approach, but the Australian attitude appeared worse. The batsmen were not hitting out.

After tea, at 116, Yardley bowled Harvey for 31. Bradman came in with ninety minutes to play and 198 runs to score. He began as if he were after the runs and scored the fastest fifty of the match in sixty-eight minutes. But the game was over. Australia ended with one for 215, Bradman 56 not out and Morris 124 not out. Both Morris and Compton had the rare distinction of scoring a hundred in each innings of a Test.

Australia had retained the Ashes and won the rubber. But the public interest did not diminish in the Fifth Test in Sydney.

A FIGHT FOR PRESTIGE AT THE FIFTH

England dropped Hammond and Hardstaff and replaced them with Laurie Fishlock and Smith for the final encounter, beginning on 28 February. Hammond had been so disappointed with his form that he suggested, and the other tour selectors agreed, he should be left out. Officially, he was announced as 'ill' and vice-captain Norman Yardley took over the ship. Australia exchanged Johnson and Harvey for Ron Hamence of South Australia and Barnes.

Yardley won the toss and batted. Lindwall bowled Washbrook with a swinging yorker, but then Edrich and Hutton carried on for a partnership of 150 before Lindwall struck again. Edrich (60) tried to back cut a high-flying ball and was caught behind.

England was 188 when Fishlock (14), who had scratched for his runs, was bowled by McCool. Compton (17) was unfortunate to be out hit wicket when trying to force Lindwall off the back foot. Yardley (2) was beaten by a change of pace by the same bowler and caught by Miller, making England five for 225. Lindwall made it six by beating Ikin as he occasionally did all batsmen, with sheer pace. The ball removed middle stump.

The tourists were six for 237 at stumps, with Hutton playing a fine rear-guard knock at 122 not out. Saturday was washed out and when play resumed on Monday, Hutton had retired ill with severe tonsillitis, which helped Lindwall and Miller finish the tail with the score at 280. Lindwall bowled brilliantly throughout the innings to take seven for 63.

Australia's opening combination showed their strength and took the score to 126 before Bedser trapped Morris (57) LBW just after tea. The packed ground had once more come to see Bradman, especially after rumours that he would retire at the end of the series. These had been fuelled by the fact that he had played no cricket between the Fourth and Fifth Tests because of business commitments.

His innings reflected his lack of play in the month as he prodded uncertainly for twenty-seven minutes. On 12, he received a near full-toss from Wright, tried to hit it hard on the on, played across the ball, missed and was bowled off-stump. He walked from the wicket with a grin of embarrassment for having played such a shot. Australia was two for 146. Moments later, it was three-for, as Barnes (71) edged one to Evans off Bedser. Miller (23) pushed a leg-break from Wright to Ikin to make Australia four for 189 at stumps.

On day four, the Australians, in front of 20,000, collapsed to be all out for 253 with only Hamence (30 not out) in his first Test knock showing real fight. Wright had done the damage with seven for 105.

England, without the hospitalised Hutton, lost six for 144 by stumps, with only Compton holding up a real collapse brought on mainly by McCool on a wearing pitch. He spun the ball prodigiously at times and took four for 32 in the day, but Compton seemed to be untroubled.

On the fifth day, however, Toshack had Compton caught for 76. Evans put up a struggle until Miller bowled him for 20. Smith (24) also held up Australia until Lindwall had him caught behind and England were all out for 186, giving it a lead of 213. Australia had two days to get the runs, but the wearing wicket, not time, was to be the issue. Wright in particular was expected to get turn.

Australia began batting right on 1 p.m. and Yardley used Edrich to get the shine off the ball so he could bring Wright into the attack, which he did with the score at 6. Morris and Barnes took the score to 32 without loss at lunch. Then after the break, Morris (17) was run out. The score was one for 45. Bradman was in.

The big crowd on the Hill gave him a reception which lasted almost to the centre. He took block, and examined the wicket for several seconds while Yardley changed his field. Wright was bowling. Bradman surveyed the field, then settled over his bat. He played forward to two balls. The third was a big leg-break. Bradman cut and edged to Edrich at slip. He put down the sharp chance. Wright's hands went to his head in disappointment. It was the kind of miss that could lose or win a match.

Bradman settled quickly and began watchfully, but soon lost Barnes (30) caught behind off Bedser with the score at 51. The 214 required seemed some way off as Hassett joined his skipper and immediately settled into defence. Bradman was cautious but still playing his strokes to be twenty-two not out at tea. If Australia were to win, at least one player had to hit a strong half-century, which would take the pressure off the rest of the side. After the short interval Bradman struck out more, using his feet forward to Wright and his back foot to Bedser's variable bounce. The batsman's battle with spin was challenging and he moved his feet to kill or beat the turn in a classic performance. Bradman reached his 50 in ninety-seven minutes. It was a near match-winning effort and a cool captain's knock in a crisis.

After nearly two hours, Bradman (63) drove Bedser straight to Compton at mid-off and he took an easy catch. Bradman removed the gloves for the last time in an Ashes Test in Australia. He had hit seven fours in a 98-run partnership with Hassett which took the score to three for 149. Australia was just 65 from victory with Hassett looking comfortable as Miller joined him. They proceeded without hurry to 174 when Hassett (47) made a rare false push against Wright and was caught by Ikin. Once more, the brilliant diminutive deputy had helped win a game under pressure in the final innings.

Ten minutes later there was disquiet in the Australian dressing-room when Wright had Hamence (1) caught in slip by Edrich to make the home side five for 180. That left half the side to make 34.

The game was at its most critical point. Wright was bowling superbly. He bowled three successive big leg-breaks on the same spot. Each time the ball beat Miller's bat. Bradman, biting his nails in the dressing-room, sent a message out to Miller: attack.

When the leader gave an order, it was always obeyed. Miller lifted Bedser over mid-off for four. Next ball the batsman drove the ball back over Bedser's head for another boundary. The shackles had been broken. Miller (34 not out) took charge with the capable McCool (11 not out) to ease the score to five for 214 and victory by five wickets, thanks to Bradman's ability to sum up a situation, weigh the options and take the calculated risk. His skill as a strategist and tactician had proved decisive now over three Ashes series. As a batsman and thinking captain he had no peer. It is no disrespect to his fellow players to suggest that in 1936–37, 1938 and 1946–47, Australia could have fielded its second eleven and still done as well. Given an ordinary side like that of 1938, when the bowling options were more limited than ever in Australia's history, or a young, good team as in 1946–47, Bradman refused to cut the cloth accordingly. He always found creative ways to improve a side from ordinary to fair, or from good to very good.

Australia won the series with a three-nil whitewash. Bradman had triumphed and had been the most important player of either team.

He topped the Test aggregates with 680 at 97.14 and hit a fifty in at least one innings of every Test. Despite a limited Shield season he still reached 1,032 runs in first-class cricket.

Bradman would never silence his critics. There were just too many people commenting about him to please all of them all the time. But he certainly had the last smile after the remarks about his ghostly persona at the start of the season. He had also met the risky challenge of coming back, by succeeding with the bat and winning the series.

Bradman's prewar confidence had returned in force. He announced he would be available to play against the Indians next summer.

45

ONE MORE INDIAN SUMMER

If I were faced with a task on a materialistic plane, I would sooner have Bradman to work with than any other man I ever met.

— JOHN ARLOTT, ENGLISH CRICKET WRITER AND BROADCASTER

THE CONDITIONING

Bradman, now thirty-nine, had put in a solid winter of fitness and appeared in far better health when he stepped on to the field for his first encounter with the Indians led by Lala Amarnath on 24 October 1947. They had specifically requested he play against them, and again in the interests of the game he had returned.

Accordingly, he scored a brilliant century in ninety-eight minutes before stumps on the first day of the tourists' clash with South Australia, after coming in at one for 226 after tea. Many observers commented that this was the true reincarnation of the 1937–38 Bradman. More importantly, he had found a new enthusiasm for the game with his business life settled and his fitness better than it had been since 1940.

Bradman was going for his shots and the quick singles from the opening overs. The next morning he hit out with reckless abandon and scored another 54 in forty-four minutes, ending with 156 after being caught off a skyer at mid-on. He had been at the wicket just over two and a half hours for twenty-two fours. It was typical of the player to assert his dominance early over visiting teams. He started this in 1928–29 against the England side and did it again against the South Africans in 1931–32. This trend was similar in effect to his 'traditional' opening innings against Worcestershire on each tour of England. It stamped his authority on a season. Every opposition team was immediately conditioned to believing that Bradman and Australia were nigh-unbeatable. Each tour the visitors would lose one or two games out of more than thirty encounters, not necessarily because it was expected, but because Australia had terrific momentum from the first day of every tour.

The first game Bradman played against the Indians in 1947 was drawn, and while their attack seemed to vary between competent and mediocre, except for Vinoo Mankad, who was sometimes outstanding, their bats did well and promised competitiveness.

A few weeks later in his only Shield game of the season, Bradman hit exactly 100 in 162 minutes against a strong Victorian attack of Bill Johnston, Freer, Sam Loxton, Ian Johnson and Doug Ring. It was his ninety-ninth first-class hundred. Bradman was now conscious of a new pinnacle. He set his mind to reaching it in his very next first-class innings, which happened again to be against the Indians for an Australian XI, appropriately at Sydney, his favourite ground.

India batted first on Friday 14 November and scored 326. On Saturday, again appropriately, a capacity crowd rolled up to the SCG to see its twenty-year favourite Sydney son — despite his defection to Adelaide — hopefully create sporting history by scoring his 100th hundred. Billy Brown (8) obliged the masses before lunch by getting out and making way for Bradman.

He had eschewed public statements or predictions about his performances, but his demeanour with the bat in the first over showed he meant business, and his stock-in-trade was the century. He was aware that no player had ever got his 100th century at the first attempt — that is, the first innings after his ninety-ninth. Bradman played himself in carefully. Nevertheless the inevitable ticking-over of the scoreboard showed that he was challenged rather than constrained by his awesome aim.

His fifty came in the Bradman-respectable time of seventy-eight minutes. He needed a partner to create a big scoring momentum and Miller provided it. They crunched a hundred together in seventy-three minutes, Bradman on 66 and Miller 40.

The radio broadcast of the game ensured that the nation was tuned in. Sydneysiders began to hurry to the match. There was a chance that Bradman would create sporting history — again. At lunch the turnstiles clicked past 50,000 and officials began turning thousands away — something they had been doing on Saturday whenever Bradman was at the wicket since the late 1920s.

The crowd was strangely quiet as he struggled for a period and looked as if he might depart. The Indians, who had declared their respect for Bradman in elaborate terms, were now making him squeeze out every run on the road to a special record. Amarnath, Mankad and C. T. Sarwate tied up both batsmen for some time, forcing them to use all their professional skill to cope with a strong and accurate attack that had lifted to meet the occasion. Bradman reached 90 and then collected seven in an over to be three off the mark. Miller now gave him the strike against Sarwate. The batsman sneaked a single off the last ball of the over. Bradman took another run to make him 99. Amarnath put on Kishenchand for his first over of the tour, and the last before tea. It was not an act of generosity but an innings-breaking ploy. Bradman was curious. He had never seen this man bowl.

He pushed Kishenchand's first ball back along the wicket. The second was straight and bland. Bradman pushed to mid-on and was off like a hare for his 100th century in first-class cricket.

Bradman was thrilled at what he thought was his most 'exhilarating moment' in cricket as the huge crowd got to their feet in every section of the arena. He held his bat high, facing the Hill, then the Members. Miller (out later for 86) moved up the wicket and shook his hand. He had played his part by supporting Bradman and giving him the strike at a vital time so that he would not lose momentum.

Then some of the Indians shook his hand. They were proving a more clever and competitive group than they had let on in pronouncements early in the season, when some had spoken about 'hoping to see the great Donald Bradman score centuries' against them. They were getting their wish, but not without doing everything to prevent it coming true.

The hundredth hundred took him, despite the minor bogged-down moments, just 132 minutes. His first-ever century, against South Australia, had taken 161 minutes. The old Bradman was half an hour quicker in gaining his ton than the teenager.

He went to tea, relaxed and came out with Miller to give the spectators something extra to remember. The new ball had been taken. Bradman launched into it as if he were giving one of his festival performances. This was the way the fastest heavy-scoring cricketer in history really preferred batting — like a hurricane. In forty-five minutes, Bradman belted and placed another 71.

'I class that section of my innings as about the most satisfying of my career,' Bradman noted in his autobiography. He strained a leg muscle and threw his wicket away at 172 going for another big hit off Hazare. The ball was taken by Amarnath at deep mid-off. The batsman just failed to match the clock and was out after 177 minutes, eighteen fours, a six and no chance.

His 100th had taken him 295 innings, literally in hundreds of knocks less than those of his rivals Hobbs, Hendren, Hammond, Mead, Sutcliffe, Woolley, Grace, Sandham, Hayward and Tyldesley. The biggest scorer of all — Jack Hobbs — hit 197 centuries in 1,315 innings — a rate of one every six or seven innings compared to Bradman's century every three innings. Just as significant was the much faster rate at which he got them. In just six of those 100 century innings Bradman scored at less than 30 an hour. In all but two of that six, he was engaged in a fighting rear-guard performance to get his team out of trouble or avoid defeat.

In twenty-two cases he went faster than a run a minute, and had a 100 per cent strike-rate — 100 runs in 100 balls. In six instances he hit at 70 runs an hour and higher than 100 per cent. In another six knocks he reached 80 runs an hour and at a rate of greater than 125 per cent. His 1934 show against Lancashire had seen him reach 94 runs an hour — at a 150 per cent strike-rate. To put his 100 hundreds in the context of modern one-day cricket rates, every second time Bradman went to the wicket to score a century he was faster than Viv Richards at his one-day average pace.

Another distinguishing factor was Bradman's capacity to go on to a 'big' hundred. To that point he had hit thirty-six double centuries. Every third time he scored a century, he went on to a double. In about seventy per cent of his centuries he went well on to higher scores of 130, 150, 160, 170 and 180.

When he went out in the historic game against India, the bulk of the crowd, used to a diet of Bradman-scoring for a generation, cheered him to the gate, then got up and left.

On 18 November, they came back in their droves to see the Australian XI chase 251 to win in 150 minutes. Bradman came in at one for 60. He was determined to go for the runs, which he did but only collected 26 in thirty-two minutes before he was caught at forward short leg. Australia fell 47 short, thus giving India a great boost for the First Test at Brisbane ten days later.

RAIN BEATS THE TOURISTS

Bradman had tried hard to persuade India that wickets should be covered during the series, but Amarnath decided against it. The Australian skipper was thankful always to win the toss in Brisbane and bat. Better to get in before the torrential rain in Queensland. The Test team in batting order was Brown, Morris, Bradman, Hassett, Miller, McCool, Lindwall, Tallon, Ian Johnson, Toshack and Bill Johnston.

India's order was Mankad, Sarwate, Gul Mohomed, H. R. Adhikari, G. Kishenchand, V. S. Hazare, K. M. Rangnekar, S. W. Sohoni, Amarnath, C. S. Nayudu and the keeper, J. K. Irani.

Amarnath achieved the first breakthrough at 38 when he had Brown (11) caught behind. There were thirty-five minutes to lunch when Bradman took block. He was in fair form again as he moved easily to 21 at lunch. After the break he lost Morris, who was out hit-wicket for 47 at 97. His innings had been notable for his over-zealous backing-up. Mankad warned him that he could run him out while coming in to bowl. Morris took note. He didn't wish to go the way of Bill Brown in a previous match against the tourists.

Bradman cruised on to 50 in eighty-five minutes as the sky became dark. He was 86 at tea with Hassett looking comfortable.

Drizzle held up play for twenty minutes after the short break. Bradman was suddenly a man in a hurry. He brought up his 101st century, and third against India in three games, in 171 minutes. Then with the light very poor, he went into overdrive, scoring runs all round the wicket in a blistering forty-five minutes in which he added 60. Bradman could easily have appealed successfully against the light but declined. The Indians were very impressed with his skills and apparent dedication to playing the game. But they were not privy to local conditions. Bradman knew that the rain would bring a frightening sticky. It was better to get runs when you needed a miner's light to see the ball rather than play on a Brisbane gluepot.

Bradman was 160 not out and Australia three for 273 — Hassett having been caught off Mankad for 48 at 198 — when rain stopped play at 5.40 p.m. Saturday was nearly washed out, but at 5 p.m. disgruntled fans greeted the players with cheering and booing as they resumed. There had been demonstrations and requests for refunds.

Bradman added another 19 to be 179 not out under conditions made tricky by an unprepossessing sticky. He batted on again in impossible light but at 5.40 p.m. appealed and the second day was over.

Bradman began on Monday, day three, in a feverish chase for runs. He was hit by dangerous balls in the shoulder and groin. On 185 he cut at a low ball and hit his wicket. His innings took 288 minutes and included twenty fours. It was the thirteenth Test in a row in which he had scored at least one fifty. He declared the innings closed at eight for 382 after Miller hit a flurry of 6, 6, 4, 2 and 2, off successive balls to reach 52. Amarnath took four for 84, and Mankad three for 113.

The sticky was too much for the Indians, who were dismissed for 58, with Toshack taking a remarkable five wickets for 2 off 2.3 overs. Lindwall began the rout with two for 0 in his first over and finished with two for 11. Bill Johnston took two for 17. The tourists could only manage 98 in their second innings. Again, Toshack revelled in the dreadful batting conditions and snared six for 29, with Lindwall taking two for 19. Amarnath may have had a twinge of regret not taking Bradman's advice about the wickets, although he was gambling on being able to take advantage of the weather if the law of averages were to be upheld.

They were in the Second Test, which began in similar rainy conditions on 12 December at Sydney. India left out Rangnekar and Sohoni and brought in D. G. Phadkar and Amir Elahi. Australia replaced Toshack with Hamence. India won the toss, batted in rain-interrupted play and ran into hostile bowling from Miller and Lindwall on a lively wicket. The tourists were all out for 188 late in the second day with only Kishenchand (44) and Phadkar (51) able to contend with the conditions. Australia shared the wickets between Lindwall (one for 30), Johnston (two for 33), Johnson (two for 22), Miller (two for 25) and McCool (three for 71).

The innings got off to a sensational start when Mankad stopped while delivering the ball and whipped off the bails with Brown (18) out of his crease backing up too far — and consequently run out. From that moment the verb 'to Mankad' became part of cricket language. The bowler had actually done the same thing to Brown in a match against Queensland, but this was a Test and the cricket world took notice. The Australians, particularly Bradman, endorsed the legitimacy of a bowler's right to take a wicket this way. Otherwise, the batsman could cheat his runs. Mankad, more than fairly, had warned Brown first when under the rules he did not need to.

Bradman went in at one for 28 just before stumps after the Brown incident. He didn't have to face a ball until Wednesday 17 December due to the atrocious weather conditions. The wicket was almost unplayable, but Bradman lasted forty minutes for 13 before he was bowled. Australia scraped together 107 with only Hamence (25) scoring more than 20. Hazare (four for 29) and Phadkar (three for 14) did the damage.

The Indians had lost seven for 61 at close of play, with Johnston (three for 15) and Ian Johnson, again with two for 22, wreaking havoc among them. Their lead of 142 may have been enough on the last day, but rain washed out play once more leaving the sorry match a draw. Just ten hours' play had been possible. Amarnath, throwing the dice on the weather, had lost so far. But there were three Tests to play. Australia's summer continued to be wet.

MORE MELBOURNE MILESTONES

Australia replaced Brown with Barnes for the New Year Test at Melbourne. India brought in P. Sen as keeper, Rangnekar and Rai Singh for Irani, Amir Elahi and Kishenchand.

Bradman won the toss, batted and was at the wicket in the morning after Mankad had bowled Barnes (12) at 29. The big 1 January crowd were as pleased to see him as ever and gave him a great cheer all the way to the wicket. Bradman, however, was not in a mood for fireworks. He began cautiously before loosening up with late cuts, cover-drives and fine leg glances to reach 38 by lunch. His fifty came easily after eighty-four minutes and he moved along at about a fifty per cent strike-rate, or 30 runs an hour to be 99 at tea, having lost Morris (45) bowled by Amarnath. Australia was two for 204.

After the short break, Bradman brought up his fourth hundred in five games against the tourists, in 159 minutes. If at first they didn't quite understand why Bradman was revered worldwide, they certainly did now. He had returned to the confident, prolific scoring of the 1930s as if there had never been a break and he was ageless. His thirty-nine years showed a bit in the field, and he would never again be the sprinter between wickets, but for the rest, everything was as before.

At 132, he went down with cramp. He didn't wish to retire, so he got up to face the next ball from Phadkar. Bradman swung wildly, missed and was LBW. He hit eight fours and once more gave no chance. During the innings he passed 6,000 runs in Test cricket and was at 6,102 when dismissed.

Hassett (80) was the only other Australian to reach a half-century as the home team went on to 394 on the second day, Friday. Amarnath took four for 78 while Mankad had four for 135.

India replied with a good opening stand between Mankad and Sarwate before the latter was caught behind off Johnston for 36 at 114. Bradman then pulled a match-winning move by bringing on Sid Barnes to produce leg-spin. The opener hated bowling, even in the nets. He loathed the idea of ever being used as a stock-bowler or even a partnership-breaker. Hazare the dasher was in, and Mankad was on top playing a powerful, fast-scoring knock. Bradman felt he had to try something different to halt the flow of runs and prevent this link destroying his bowlers.

He threw the ball to a surprised Barnes, trotted over to him, and cajoled him to the bowling crease. In his second over, he deceived Hazare (17) into a nick to Tallon. In came Amarnath, one of the most successful Indian batsmen so far in the season. Barnes bowled a stock leg-break on leg stump and had him LBW for a duck. India was four for 188.

Mankad, hampered by a leg-strain and the need for a runner, went soon after for a striking 116, caught behind off Johnston. He had batted 139 minutes in one of the best innings of the summer. India were six for 262 at stumps.

Overnight rain and more in the morning caused the wet wicket to perform unevenly. Amarnath, tantalised by the prospect of putting the Australians in on a sticky, declared at nine for 291 after forty minutes. Bill Johnston took two for 33, Barnes — the bowling rabbit out of the hat — two for 25 and Ian Johnson four for 59.

Bradman countered Amarnath by opening the innings before lunch with tailenders Johnston and Dooland in the hope that they would make it to lunch, which would give the wicket a chance to dry out. They propped, scratched and dithered while Amarnath put seven men round the bat, and gave four chances between them before they were out for 3 and 6 respectively by the time the score reached

11. Johnson came in as a lunch watchman with Morris, but lost his wicket and Australia looked in a little trouble at three for 13. This brought Barnes in and he stayed with Morris until the break. The first part of the ploy had worked. Australia had not lost a frontline batsman in the difficult pre-lunch session. The Indians, however, were excited. They had removed three Australians in the session, including the capable Johnson, which was encouraging.

After lunch, Barnes (15) became the fourth wicket to fall — caught behind at 32. The large MCG crowd rose to Bradman as he stepped out in a precarious situation. The wicket was drying out as the day warmed up, and was playing fewer tricks than in the morning. Nevertheless, the pressure was on the home skipper.

Bradman started slowly as the wicket lost its venom, taking an hour over his first 23. He was 40 at tea and untroubled. After the break he looked noticeably more aggressive as he reached 50 in eighty-eight minutes. His next 50 to the century took just forty-two minutes and put him next to Warren Bardsley and his current partner Morris as the only Australians to collect a century in each innings of a Test.

The big Melbourne Saturday crowd who, like their counterparts in Sydney, had been cheering for Bradman over a generation, now delivered a special applause. There was a sense that this could be one of his last appearances in a Test in Melbourne. In nine unforgettable games, he had scored a century in eight since his first effort on 5 January 1929. This extra effort seemed to be making up for his double 'failure' — 79 and 48 — in Melbourne in the corresponding series against England a year earlier.

At the other end, Morris was steady as he reached 50 and then stepped up his own rate as Australia pushed well clear of danger and into a winning position.

Bradman kept up the pace as Morris approached his century, then gave the bowling over to him as stumps loomed. The opener reached his well-deserved reward with just two minutes to go. At the close Bradman was 127, Morris 100 and Australia four for 255. Amarnath, having a very good game with the ball, took three for 52.

Bradman kept his cards close until the next morning, when he surprised once more by declaring. The rain had machine-gunned on the Windsor Hotel overnight and persuaded him there was no point in going on. A soft, wet pitch would suit all his bowlers.

India duly crumbled to all out for 125 with Johnson (four for 35) and Johnston (four for 44) mopping up most of the wickets. Australia led two-nil with two to play. The Indian weather gods would have to be working overtime to square the series, especially with Bradman in form equal to the finest and most consistent of his twenty-year first-class career.

46

AT THE DOUBLE

I venture a guess that after his Majesty the King and Winston Churchill, Bradman is the best known man in the Empire.
— BILL O'REILLY AFTER HIS RETIREMENT FROM CRICKET IN THE MID-1940s

ONE LAST HURRAH FOR THE HOME CROWD

It was hot and sunny in Adelaide, presenting conditions that pleased the tourists, who left out Nayudu and Rai Singh for Kishenchand and Rangachari. Australia brought in Neil Harvey for his first Test and Toshack for Bill Johnston and Hamence. Harvey, a brilliant, nineteen-year-old left-hander, was being blooded with a view to the England tour later in the year.

Bradman won the toss on Friday 25 January and was in an hour before lunch at one for 20 when Morris was bowled by Phadkar. Rumours had been flying that Bradman would retire at the end of the season and his adopted home town turned out in force to see him.

He batted slowly but surely to be just 20 not out at the interval. Barnes, his partner, seemed more daring as he thrashed the ball after lunch, but the difference was that Bradman began to pierce the field. He moved to 50 in 101 minutes and this score acted as a green light. Bradman and Barnes seemed locked in a controlled race to a century. At 77, Bradman reached 1,000 for the season — the twelfth time he had done it. He nudged ahead of Barnes and was on 94 not out at tea, having given his hard-hitting partner half an hour's start.

After tea, Bradman reached 100 in 191 minutes — his third successive Test hundred and his fourth for the series. With the score at 256, he lost Barnes (112) LBW to Mankad. A nagging cramp was now affecting him as he began lofting the occasional shot and he was forced to play Phadkar and Rangachari off the back foot. Too much weight on the front foot caused the cramp to resurface. Hassett partnered Bradman as he punished the Indians mercilessly at a pace that approached his efforts during his 100th century knock. He reached 200 for the sixth time in a day in a Test, three times each in Australia and England. At the grand old age of thirty-nine years and 149 days, he became the oldest player to hit a double century in a Test. He was also the youngest when he made 254 at Lord's in 1930.

His last century came in seventy-nine minutes of power and placement, and was the sixth in one session in Tests. He now had double hundreds against the West Indies, South Africa, England and India. It also gave the competitive Bradman satisfaction to know he had hit his thirty-seventh double century — one ahead of his great, persistent rival Hammond.

At 201 he was bowled by Hazare going for another big smash. He was at the wicket 272 minutes and hit twenty-one fours and his now customary big-innings six. He left the field limping with Australia safe at three for 361. The applause was huge as he raised his bat. Many wondered if it would be the last time in front of an Adelaide crowd.

The next day, Hassett (198 not out) took the score forward with his own stylish method of dominance and was partnered by Miller (67) in a 142-run stand. Australia was dismissed for 674.

India had a short time to bat on Saturday evening and were two for 6 at stumps. Miller took the wickets of both Sarwate and the supposed nightwatchman Sen in two balls and was on a hat-trick on Monday morning. Amarnath came in, stopped the hat-trick with a glance for four and then proceeded to 46 before falling to Johnson, who induced a catch to Bradman at mid-on.

The tourists were three for 85 at lunch. It was more than 40°C in the shade mid-afternoon when the sound, correct Hazare got together with Phadkar for a 188-run stand, which took them into Tuesday in the continuing heat. Johnson eventually trapped Hazare (116) LBW at 321. Phadkar would not run singles as he approached his century. He preferred to go up and over to the sightscreen off Johnson.

Barnes was hit on the shoulder by a full-blooded Phadkar drive when fielding three metres from the bat. He laughed about it, but must have been in some pain as Bradman sent him into the country for a bit of relief. Lindwall came on, caused more controversy over whether he was dragging his back foot over the crease or not, and promptly bowled Kishenchand (10). Phadkar (123) was later LBW to Toshack and India was finally dismissed for 381. Johnson had the figures with four for 64, while Miller, devastating early, finished with two for 39.

Bradman was not tempted to bat again even though the heat was still fierce. India followed on. If it wasn't Miller, then it was Lindwall with an early breakthrough. He clean-bowled Mankad and Amarnath for ducks, while Toshack bowled Sarwate (11) to leave the visitors three for 33.

Hazare, whom Bradman considered a better opponent than the brilliant Amarnath, managed to complete a century in each innings before Lindwall took the new ball on the final day and bowled him for 145. After some middle-order resistance, India slipped to be all out for 277, thus giving the home side victory by an innings and 16 runs. Lindwall took seven for 38, magnificent figures considering India's score.

It inspired his skipper. He was now seriously considering leading the side to England for the Ashes tour in a few months' time. But it would not be similar to the one of 1938, which had one speedster, McCormick, who had failed to come up to standard. There was something more certain about the killer instinct in both Lindwall and Miller. They would be essential against England's great batting line-up, led by Hutton, Washbrook, Edrich and Compton. Without such fearsome speed and skill, there would be too much footslogging in the field, thus reducing the fitness of the tourists when it was their turn to bat. Beyond these two opening attack bowlers, he could possibly add McCool, Toshack, Johnson and Johnston for variety. Bradman could begin to dream of a grand strategy to defeat England.

However, the inspiration to tour had to be weighed against his business and his family concerns, his health and the chance of failure on tour. Bradman preferred to take responsibility for all major decisions, but if he toured England he would be away from his office for eight months, which would mean he would have to leave his operations in the hands of a deputy. Broking demanded financial decisions — such as when to buy or sell for a client at critical moments — that he alone wished to make. Leaving major management of his firm to another was a risk he didn't relish. Furthermore, he was leaving Jessie to look after their two children and the extra problems associated with Shirley's cerebral palsy.

On top of that was the gamble with his own health. His doctors had warned him that his chronic back problems could recur on such an arduous tour. He had no wish to return to the critical days of 1940 to 1945. Coupled with this was a natural concern that there was no better than a realistic fifty-fifty chance of success on the tour.

These factors made the decision to tour probably the most difficult of his sporting life. Many people in England were imploring him to come for the 'good of the game and the UK', which needed a brilliant distraction to help the battered nation over the horror and deprivation of war. Bradman on tour would mean the summer of 1948 would most likely be exciting and sensational.

After much agonising Bradman decided on what was best for Australian cricket and the game in general. He would tour.

With a sense of timing that was typical of his best batting, on 5 February 1948, he announced he would play his last first-class game in Australia in the Fifth Test against India, beginning the next day. He would, however, go with the Australian team to England to defend the Ashes. After that, he would retire completely from the game.

It was an inevitable decision, which the public had expected. Yet it still saddened every cricket fan in the country and many others who had only a vague notion of the game. Australian sport without the actuality or prospect of Bradman playing was not so much unthinkable as incomprehensible for a nation which had grown up with the legend.

Jealous rivals aside, perhaps only two people in Australia were really looking forward to his exit. They were Jessie and Don Bradman.

In the short term, he still had a job to do against India, and he set his mind on a farewell innings in Australia that would be remembered for a long time to come. Nothing less than a rattling great double hundred would be sufficient to do justice to himself and his support from all those fans who paid their money and sat through many a Bradman double matinee.

In a piece of pre-tour experimentation McCool, Ian Johnson and Toshack made way for fast-medium Queensland bowler Len Johnson, leg-spinner Doug Ring and pace bowling all-rounder Sam Loxton. Knowing that all the Australians were to a greater or less degree playing for tour spots, India braced itself and kept basically the same side except for swapping Rangnekar for Nayudu.

Bradman won the toss in fine Melbourne weather, batted and was walking down the steps at the MCG forty-five minutes before lunch with Australia one for 48 after Barnes had been run out for 33. He started in his usual fashion with a few streaky shots among an array of forceful drives, delicate late cuts and glances. With 35 on the board at lunch in quick time, he seemed set. After the break, he moved easily to 50 in seventy-three minutes. Then he felt a painful rip at the back of the ribcage while playing a drive. Bradman stopped, regained his breath and faced up again. The pain would not leave. He wondered if it were a return of the fibrositis which had crippled and plagued him from 1940 to 1945.

Bradman held his left side. He was in pain after every stroke. He refused a couple of singles that he would normally go for. Brown spoke to him. Bradman struggled on. Amarnath asked if he wanted to go off. Bradman shook his head and thanked him.

At 57 however, he signalled to Amarnath, Brown and the umpires that he would retire. It was a depressing moment and a reminder that he was in a vigorous sport at nearly forty years of age. He wondered if he had made the wrong decision about touring England. Maybe his ambitions had at last got ahead of his renowned good sense.

He trudged from the field. There would be no double hundred, not even three figures, just a paltry 57, a mere entrée on an average Bradman menu. The spectators clapped uncertainly, for they didn't know if his problem was temporary or permanent. If he could not bat again in an Australian Test cricket it was not a fitting departure.

Dr Keon-Cohen examined him in the dressing-room and diagnosed the injury as a torn cartilage under his left ribs. After getting over the disappointment of his innings being cut short, he enjoyed watching two Victorians — Neil Harvey (153) and Sam Loxton (80) — in a fine stand of 159 that would help their chances of tour selection. Harvey, in particular, impressed. The teenager had a touch of class reminiscent of the young Bradman and Archie Jackson. He feared nothing, used his feet to the spinners with a confidence touching arrogance and had all the shots. His performance was also a reminder to Bradman that it could be time to make way for younger players. But not yet. He had committed himself now to England in the northern spring and summer, and unless he broke down completely, he would be leading the tourists. Bradman was certain, as was just about every commentator in the land, that he was the best player to captain the side in the battle for the Ashes, 1948.

He declared the innings closed on Saturday at eight for 575.

On Monday 9 February, Bradman surprised by leading his team onto the field and hid himself in slips. Mankad made a courageous 111 before Loxton had him caught behind. Hazare (74) showed his ability once more before Lindwall trapped him LBW and Phadkar (56 not out) helped boost the tourists' total to 331 by the fourth day. Len Johnson took three for 66, Ring three for 103, Lindwall two for 66 and Loxton two for 61. Bradman, the unaccustomed slipper, took one catch to get rid of tailender Nayudu for 3.

Bradman enforced the follow-on and a demoralised Indian team collapsed on a perfectly dry, fine wicket for 67, giving Australia a four-nil win in the series. This time Len Johnson took three for 8, Bill Johnston two for 15 and Ring three for 15. The bowling had Bradman smiling. He now had an embarrassment of riches in each department of bowling from which to choose, and he was confident of real depth for the arduous UK trip.

He could also be satisfied with his own season. In the Tests he scored 715 runs at an average of 178.75. Against the Indians alone he hit 1,081 runs at 135.12. In all first-class matches he plundered 1,296 runs at 129.6.

Soon after the Indian series had finished, Bradman got together with the other selectors to choose the touring side. They took five hours agonising over whether to take Doug Ring or Bruce Dooland. In the end Ring got the nod. The others were Bradman, Hassett, 35, Brown, 35, Barnes, 29, Tallon, 32, Miller, 28, Lindwall, 26, Ian Johnson, 28, Bill Johnston, 26, McCool, 29, Loxton, 27, Morris, 26, Toshack, 31, Hamence, 32, Harvey, 19, Ring, 29, and R. A. Saggers (the second keeper), 31.

The average age was thirty-one. It was a balanced line-up that, given reasonable fitness, would at the very least put up a fight in an expected tight series.

47

THE LAST CAMPAIGN BEGINS

To say Don Bradman, even in 1948, was a phenomenon is merely to acknowledge the paucity of one's vocabulary.
— BRIAN SELLERS, FORMER YORKSHIRE CAPTAIN AND CRICKET WRITER

THE ON-AND-OFF FIELD MARSHAL

When George Orwell in 1948 was writing a fictional classic about a future society run by a brutal totalitarian regime, he decided on a title by juxtaposing the last two figures of the year and came up with 1984. Orwell's nightmare was inspired by the Communist regime in Russia, but his setting was England. The writer's overall vision was what the Australian tourists experienced briefly when they arrived in Britain in 1948 and took the quick train journey from Tilbury Docks to London through the grey, dreary, depressing inner-city. After the German bombing, it was in need of wholesale repair and restoration. Economic conditions were still poor and the team arrived with a mound of food parcels. It was also bitterly cold in late April.

Nevertheless the tanned, fit Australians were a cheerful, well-knit bunch. Their relaxed smiles brought some early sunshine to an England desperate for distractions. Their presence happily reminded Britain that a fine national tradition was back after the six-year intervention of a

514

mad foreign dictator. The tourists gave many people a symbolic sense that the Empire might not be lost and that Britain would be Great once more. It would help if England could win back the Ashes. What a boost that would be to morale and even the economy.

There was only one problem with that scenario: The Don. How, the British media wondered with open pessimism, could he and his 'terrible fellow Australian cricketers' be overcome? Hitler was relatively easy, one British journalist mused, compared with knocking off Bradman.

The man himself in those first ten days before the opening against Worcester was busy doing what touring captains had to do at lunches, dinners and receptions. He was harmless enough off the field, even charming and friendly. He put time into those excellent speeches, which he knew well the British liked to be amusing, especially at the Sportsman's Club and the Institute of Journalists. At the latter he made a plea for the press not to dwell on 'unfortunate incidents or sensations', which seemed on the surface to show a certain naivety towards what was a motivating force in the Fourth Estate.

Yet Bradman was hardly naive. His aim was to appeal to the more fair-minded editors on Fleet Street, who might present a balanced view of events. The other editors had to sell lots of newspapers. They would seize on any 'scoop' or headline that would boost circulation and/or give the home team an advantage. If they couldn't find one they would show that necessity was the mother of invention.

At the Cricket Writers' Club another guest was the young Duke of Edinburgh. Bradman mentioned that he had noticed his useful 'off-spin bowling action' (when waving to crowds). It was typical of his sharp, observant wit. The hosts and other guests enjoyed his humour and the fact that he didn't seem to take himself too seriously. He wasn't bombastic but modest, and the English loved suitably self-deprecatory jokes. Bradman could round off an address with some diplomatic remark which would always get extra applause. It had to be platitudinous, but it was always honest, heartfelt and apt.

In those demanding days Bradman appreciated a little ceremony like the Soccer Cup Tie final at Wembley. Nor was he opposed to a little pomp, such as the Silver Jubilee Service in St Paul's Cathedral to commemorate the wedding anniversary of King George VI and Queen Elizabeth. He was always as happy and relaxed as anyone could be with the royals in the rarefied atmosphere they generated, and they with him.

Bradman comprehended this and the never-ending mail (600 letters a day) as all part of the job, which he did unstintingly and often enjoyed. But he never lost focus on why he was in England again. He was determined to crush the opposition and win the rubber. More than that, he wanted to go right through the tour unbeaten. Not even Warwick Armstrong — a constant and at times fierce critic of Bradman — had achieved that.

He got down to business from the first net at Lord's in front of a small crowd of fascinated fans, all of whom had paid a shilling for the view, and a contingent of media personnel. Bradman stood at the front of the two net wickets and between the bowling run-ups. He occasionally made a remark to a bowler. Lindwall's run-up and drag were discussed. Miller was asked about his back, which played up when he bent it delivering a bumper.

The batsmen got more of his attention and they listened to him as they would a coach. He singled out McCool, who was having trouble judging the bounce on English turf. Bradman took him aside and, oblivious of onlookers, showed him how to play a stroke. McCool had scored 95 and 104 not out in the 1946–47 series, but the skipper was explaining something basic to him. He paid attention, nonetheless. But Bradman never talked down to his players. 'We were always pleased when he gave advice,' Ian Johnson said. 'You could not fault the way he handled the side at any level.'

Johnson recalled that Bradman didn't care what the players did in their spare time, as long as they turned up fit for play. It was an intelligent way to handle the men, for apart from Harvey, they were not boys. Several had seen war service and had matured faster because of it. Naturally, some liked a drink. They partied and enjoyed themselves, but none abused Bradman's guidelines. They were tougher men because of their experiences and it helped them play to win. They all respected and liked The Don.

Never had any skipper of any side had so much command of his troops. It was far better than 1936–37 and 1938 for Bradman when he had peers and fine performers like Bill O'Reilly who were liable to answer back or go their own way. Right or wrong, Bradman naturally preferred to have his way as captain, otherwise why lead? Now there was no rival voice of note, no-one to seriously question his leadership or judgement. The campaign for England in 1948 was his alone. His strategies would either succeed or fail. Field marshals Rommel and Montgomery had never quite had it so much their way in recent international conflicts of another kind.

A NOT QUITE TYPICAL OPENING

The Australians sent out what looked suspiciously like a full-strength team for the first game of the season against Worcester after the county won the toss and batted. The sun broke through the wet, freezing weather on 28 April and cheered the 15,000 well-rugged fans who packed the Cathedral ground to see the local side score a respectable 233 all out. It was led by Charlie Palmer (85), who threatened to get 100 before lunch until Toshack had him caught. Johnson was right onto a length from the first over and took the figures with three for 52 off twenty-three overs.

Australia proceeded next morning to one for 79, when left-arm slow bowler Howorth trapped the stroke-playing Barnes for 44. With flags flying across the city, the Cathedral chimes sounding, and the cheers of schoolchildren in the corner of a stand, Bradman stepped out to an expected double century to follow his other three such scores on previous tours — 236, 206 and 258.

He took a close look at Howorth for a while and then picked up the pace of the wicket with an acuteness of eye and speed of movement that made batting in England look easy to the players who would follow him. He proceeded to 50 in seventy-one minutes by skilfully steering the ball through the gaps. The only difference that observers could discern from the master craftsman of those three other massive innings was 'a certain stiffness' of the joints occasionally.

517

Otherwise he surprised no-one in arriving at 100 in 138 minutes. Then he stunned everyone by, on his own admission, throwing his wicket away. P. F. Jackson, an off-spinner, bowled him for 107 as he took a lusty swing. Bradman was worried that too much exertion could see a recurrence of the rib injury that had nagged him for the three months since the last Test against India.

He also wanted to give the new batsmen a chance, rather than monopolise the crease himself for four or five hours. Lindwall (30), Hassett (35), Brown (25) and Miller (50 not out) followed Morris (138), Bradman and Barnes in a useful beginning before the skipper declared at eight for 462.

Jackson took six for 135 off thirty-nine overs in a tidy display. Worcester scored 212 in its second dig. Johnson got some stick early but fought back for three for 75, while McCool took four for 29 in securing a win by an innings and 17 runs.

The next game against Leicestershire from 1 May promised to be Bradman's, looked like being Barnes' but was eventually Miller's. He came in at the fall of the first wicket. The crowd expected to see Bradman and fell silent at the confusing sight of the taller figure striding out. He bowed at the wicket in mock appreciation for his mute welcome.

Bradman came to the wicket later and belted 81 at a run a minute, as if trying to warm himself up on a freezing day. He seemed annoyed when he was out caught at the wicket. The crowd sighed, as if to suggest that they wished him a century or more. However, Miller proved no understudy as he harvested an unbeaten 202 against an attack which included the left-handed googly bowler Jack Walsh and off-spinner Jackson, two young Australians who had forsaken their homeland to ply their trade in England. Walsh bamboozled Harvey and Hamence, in an essentially all-Australian contest.

The tourists reached 448, with Jackson taking five for 91, and the county replied with 130. Ring got on a length and stayed there for five for 45. In the second effort, Leicester reached 147 and Johnson continued to impress with seven for 42.

On 5 May, Australia, minus Bradman, encountered its first sticky of the season at Bradford against Yorkshire. But it fooled the county more as it was rolled for 71, Bill Johnston taking four for 22, and Miller six for 42. Then Australia replied equally ineptly with 101. Only Miller, with 34, showed any skill on the mild gluepot, which advantaged the local spinner Tommy Smailes, who took six for 51. Bradman, back in London answering letters at the team hotel, became concerned with the scores and kept in touch with events by phone every half-hour.

Yorkshire could only reach 89 the second time around and Johnston (six for 18) and Miller (three for 49) again shared the wickets. Australia replied with six for 63 with Harvey 18 not out, and Tallon, 17 not out, saving the day to give the tourists a win by four wickets in just two days. Back in London Bradman was able to have a cuppa and relax.

FROM SURREY TO OXFORD

Bradman came back for a game against Surrey at The Oval on 8 May and was able to sit back with the pads on and enjoy Barnes and Morris as they opened with a stand of 136. It was not a pleasure that Bradman had experienced much in his long career at first-drop. It put him in a good frame of mind when he reached the wicket in front of 30,000 spectators just before lunch. The crowd response was different from what was usual in Australia where people were less restrained about voicing their opinion. In England, he was looked upon with awe, almost as a marvellous foreign freak who spoke the language but behaved a little strangely, albeit with a certain decorum, although he was outstandingly popular.

John Arlott, the gravel-throated *bon vivant*, writer and broadcaster, suggested that Bradman and the Australians differed from the English in their more tough-minded approach to the game, which they always played within the rules, but hard:

> There has long been a custom in English cricket for the batsman to 'give the bowler a chance' after he had scored a century. An Australian batsman merely takes guard afresh after the first

hundred; of Bradman's 108 scores of over one hundred, 37 have also been over two hundred.

In this game Bradman started confidently and kept it up throughout his stay. He and Barnes batted quickly without any audacious strokes or big-hitting as they put on 207 in just 138 minutes. Bradman produced 50 in seventy-seven minutes, and got to a hundred in 136 minutes, standard fare for him.

When he was on 146, the Surrey supporters took some cheer from seeing Alec Bedser bowl him. Barnes went on to 176. Hassett got 110, Ian Johnson 46 and Tallon 50 not out as Australia amassed 632. Bedser got four wickets, while the great off-spinner Jim Laker, in his first encounter with Bradman and the Australians, took just one, tailender Bill Johnston.

County treasurers across England were praying for the Australians in sunshine on the one hand and big gate receipts on the other, while the players themselves were becoming dispirited at the huge tallies the tourists were posting on good wickets.

Surrey responded with 141, with opener Laurie Fishlock carrying his bat untroubled for 81. Ian Johnson seemed to be sealing his First Test spot by continuing to take bags of wickets, this time five for 53. Surrey managed 195 in its second effort, giving the visitors a huge win by an innings and 296.

The slaughter continued against Cambridge University when Australia reached four for 414, thanks mainly to Brown, who struck real form with 200, and Hamence, 92. The students made 167 (Miller five for 46) and 196 (McCool seven for 78), of which a young Trevor Bailey contributed 66 not out to win a few important friends.

Bailey turned up next day — a Saturday — at Southend to play for Essex against the tourists in front of 16,000 holiday spectators, many of whom scheduled their vacations around the tourist fixture. The promising young all-rounder wished he hadn't been such a glutton for punishment. Australia batted first and got off to a thundering start losing its first wicket — Barnes (79) — at 145, twenty-two minutes before lunch. Bradman came in and continued the hot trend by belting 42 not out by lunch, including five fours in succession in one over from one F. H. Vigar. He went out in the same mood after lunch and streaked to 50 in thirty-four minutes, then raced to 100 in seventy-four minutes. Bradman was in bloodthirsty mood as he laid into Price and hit him too for five successive fours.

The captain was well-supported by first Brown (153), then Hamence (46), as he powered on to 187 in 124 minutes before being bowled by Peter Smith hitting across a straight ball in an attempt to reach the boundary for the thirty-third time. He scored at 90 runs an hour, the fastest rate of his entire first-class career. 'Never have I seen Bradman annihilate an attack in such convincing manner in such a short time,' Bill O'Reilly wrote back to Australia.

Sadly for Essex, the thrashing did not stop with The Don. Loxton, a heavy-hitter at any time if he had the mind, slammed 120, while Saggers, happy to have the chance for a smash, collected 104 not out. The Australian blitzkrieg continued for a record 721 in the day. No-one quite knew how such a figure was reached — at a rate of 90 an hour. The scoreboard didn't even have a '7' for the 'hundreds' column. It had never been necessary before. A commentary in Monday morning's *News Chronicle* by Crawford White said it all:

> *Bradman has not changed one whit. He is still the greatest batsman in the world, and good-will tour or not, he remains the coolest and most ruthless strategist in cricket.*
>
> *That mammoth 721 total against Essex on Saturday — the highest number of runs ever scored in one day — was far more than a holiday feast for the crowd. It was all part of his deliberate, merciless, efficient plan, brilliant in its execution, to build up the biggest possible psychological advantage for the Australians over English bowlers as a whole.*

Essex turned up on Monday, tired and defeated, to register 83. Toshack reaped the benefit of Saturday's carnage and took five for 31. Miller sped his way through three for 14. Bradman could hardly bat again after such a gigantic lead, so in went Essex for another turn.

This time they did better with 187. Pearce got 71 and Smith, who had returned four for 193 when Australia batted, hauled a few back and scored 54. Johnson got amongst the wickets again with six for 37, while Toshack took two for 50. In two days, Australia had won by an innings and 451.

At Oxford two days later, Australia rattled on 431, a tally notable for Brown's (108) third successive hundred. Loxton, ever the solid middle-order man, made 79 not out. The students could only muster 185, of which A. H. Kardar managed 54, and 156 to give the tourists another easy innings victory.

TENNYSON TENSIONS AT LORD'S

The pattern continued in the next game against the MCC at Lord's when Australia amassed 512. This time Miller, who missed out on the pillage at Essex when Bailey bowled him for a duck, jumped in for 163, while Bradman compiled 98. His run of scores so far in England was 107, 81, 146, 187 and 98. Since 1 January 1948, he could add 132, 127 not out, 201, 57 not out (all against India in Tests), and 115 for an Australian XI in Perth en route to England. Bradman's astonishing year had been without anything resembling a low score and very few chances. It demonstrated he was determined to make his last year in cricket a formidable one.

However, someone in the media had to find a way of spoiling the party. Clearly the British tabloids were sick of repetitive headlines, or 'Bradlines', as one editor called them. They wanted a bit of controversy, something to shock and perhaps tarnish the Australians' squeaky-clean image.

The opportunity arose when Lord Tennyson arrived at the Australian dressing-room at Lord's after Bradman was out and watching his team pile on the runs against the MCC. An attendant told him Tennyson was at the door and wished to see him. 'I wouldn't oblige him, if I were you, sir,' he added. Bradman asked why.

'He has been drinking, sir, rather heavily I would say,' the attendant replied. Bradman told him to say he was indisposed. Tennyson took it as a snub and rang some press contacts in London and Sydney, without saying that he had been inebriated at the time. Several stories appeared speaking of Bradman's 'needless brusqueness and lack of tact'. Bradman refused to comment.

Then, when the Australians were fielding in the same game, another incident was blown up about Barnes and his habit of standing so close to the batsman at silly leg. He was accused of putting a foot on the wicket itself. Barnes and Bradman were indulging in a bit of gamesmanship by putting pressure on inexperienced batsmen. But they were acting within the rules. No umpire intervened and no batsman complained. Bradman stood his ground as captain and Barnes did the same with his boots. The silence was deafening from the Australian camp. The skipper would not be drawn.

The honeymoon was over for the tourists. Despite Bradman's plea not to publish silly, provocative and needless articles that were only meant to stir the pot of controversy, it was now open season on the Australians, which meant Bradman as their natural figurehead.

Meanwhile Australia ran through the MCC for 189. Hutton stood up well with 52 while Toshack took six for 51. Then the MCC went in once more and performed poorly with 205, except again for Hutton, who made 64.

On 27 May, the tourists travelled to Manchester and drew with Lancashire, scoring 204 and four for 259. Young Harvey hit 76 not out in the second innings. Lancashire responded with 182, G. A. Edrich scoring 55, while Bill Johnston collected five for 49.

In the next game against Notts at Trent Bridge, Brown hit 122 and Bradman 86 out of 400 in reply to the county's 179, in which Lindwall built to real express speed for the first time on the tour and snared six for 14. There were cries of 'Larwood' and 'bodyline' as he bowled some very fast head-high bouncers. But the New South Welshman did not overdo it. Nor did he employ leg theory. Only Reg Simpson (74) stood up to him. In the second dig, Notts did better and staved off any chance of defeat with eight for 299, thanks to Hardstaff (107) and Simpson (70) again.

The day after this game, the tourists, *sans* Bradman, were at

Southampton to take on Hampshire on 2 June. The county began with 195 (Johnston, six for 74) and headed the Australians who were summarily removed on a sticky for just 117, with C. J. Knott taking five for 57. The tourists then crushed the county, dismissing them for 103. Miller (five for 25) bent his troublesome back and made the Hants bats pay, while Johnston swung the ball about to take five for 43.

Back in London the skipper began to sweat and sent an urgent wire to his deputy, Lindsay Hassett: 'Bradford was bad enough but this is unbearable, heads up and chins down.'

Hassett, the court jester, said later he was tempted to send back a reply: 'Your orders carried out, but many jaws and necks broken'.

Instead, he conveyed the Orwellian orders from Number One. The very in-form Brown hit 81 not out, while the promoted Johnson made a splendid 74, allowing Australia to score two for 182 and win by eight wickets.

Bradman, in the bunker at HQ, did a little jig when he received the news. It was time for the field marshal to visit the front, which he did near the beaches at Hove for a brief skirmish with the local county forces. Lindwall (six for 34) winkled them out with late swing and Sussex retreated with 86. Australia replied with five for 549 declared, with big guns Morris (184) and Bradman (109) firing, and Harvey (100 not out) brilliant in the unfamiliar terrain. The county bats came out for more punishment from Lindwall, who hit top form at the right time and took another five for 25, giving him the match figures of eleven for 59. They did not flatter the paceman's bowling as Australia won by an innings and 325.

Bradman then went back to HQ with his fellow selectors to choose the First Test team. McCool and Loxton were unfit, while Saggers was an automatic omission because of Tallon. That left fourteen. Hamence's form was not considered good enough, while all the selectors felt that Harvey was not quite ready. The twelfth man would be either Ring or Johnston. The latter was given the thumbs up because speed seemed a marginally better proposition than spin, and Johnston could revert to spin if required. The team in battle order was thus Morris, Barnes, Bradman, Miller, Brown, Hassett, Johnson, Tallon, Lindwall, Johnston and Toshack. On paper it was a very strong line-up.

England chose Hutton, Washbrook, Edrich, Compton, Hardstaff, Barnett, Yardley, Evans and Bedser, together with Laker and J. A. Young, who were both making their Ashes debuts. Again, on paper, England looked fractionally less strong in batting and more so in bowling. But Tests were never played on paper. There was no telling what conditions, luck, form, home ground and home support could do to a combination in a competitive situation. Given all these variables, the Test teams seemed very even. However, the one factor to upset the equation was Bradman.

48

ADVANTAGE AUSTRALIA

From late April until September 1948, in England, Donald George Bradman played cricket, captained a cricket team, made speeches, was polite to bores, ignored the spite of those who begrudged him what he had earned, kept his temper and consolidated a great public reputation.

— JOHN ARLOTT

PATIENCE AT THE BRIDGE

England captain Norman Yardley, who had taken over following Hammond's retirement, won the toss in the First Test at Trent Bridge, Nottingham, on Thursday 10 June in murky threatening conditions and elected to bat. The wicket was greasy but a good one and rain was in the air.

At 9, Hutton played outside the line of a faster ball from Miller and was bowled for 3. Rain intervened and England went to lunch at one for 13. After the break, Lindwall had Washbrook (6) dropped in slips, but soon after he was caught hooking to Brown at deep fine leg. It was a grim time for the home side until Toshack and Johnston relieved Miller and Lindwall. The tension eased, but at 46 Johnston broke through and bowled Edrich for 18. Two runs later the Victorian southpaw induced a nick from Hardstaff to Miller's toes at slip, and he showed that back or no back he could still stretch down for a fine catch.

Miller further showed he was a match-winner rather than just a good Test all-rounder by bowling Compton for 19. England slipped to eight for 74, thanks to the skill and enthusiasm of the bowlers. After tea, Bedser (22) and Laker (63) combined sensibly — better, in fact, than the specialist batsmen before them — for an 89-run stand which lifted England to a still ordinary 165, made in generally bad light. Johnston was steady and effective with five for 36, while Miller took three for 38. Lindwall's post-tea leg strain left him with one for 30.

The Australian openers saw out a tricky little pre-stumps period and went on to 73 the next morning before Morris was unlucky to play on to Laker.

'Bradman came in under a hail of cheering, such as would have disturbed most men,' John Arlott noted in his book on the series, *Gone to the Test Match*. 'At once he put everything aside but the problem of Laker, whom he inspected fastidiously.'

The Australian skipper went through his customary settling-in period, which may have been longer now than in his youth. But if he got through it, all those youthful traits returned to a point where he was mostly indistinguishable from the player of the 1930s.

At 121, Barnes (62) was out to an acrobatic catch from Evans, on which umpire Chester, stationed at point, had to adjudicate. Laker then had Miller caught for a duck. In came Brown before Hassett to take the new ball. Yardley countered by bringing himself on to trap Brown (17) LBW and Australia was four for 185 — in the black by 20, with six wickets to fall and Bradman still at the crease. He was through his scratchy session against Laker and Bedser, whom he regarded as the best medium-fast bowler he had faced. Bradman slowed his rate and was patient with Hassett as his partner. The skipper decided to build a big lead — slowly. He refused the temptation to punch holes in the leg field and played straight. Consequently, he reached 50 in 100 minutes and was 78 not out at tea.

He took eighty-six minutes more to reach his century, or 211 minutes in all. This rate was a response in large part to Yardley's very defensive field-placings. At the close Bradman was 130 not out, with Hassett, also capable of scruff-of-the neck batting, on 42 not out. Australia was four for 293 — 128 to the good — and on top.

Bradman had gained the physical and psychological advantage early in the first battle of the five-Test war, which was the aim ever since stepping off the *Strathaird* at Tilbury docks, over six weeks previously. Early in Bradman's Ashes career in 1928–29 and to 1936–37, his teams had got off to poor starts and had to fight back sometimes against nigh-impossible odds to win a series. Of late — namely 1938, 1946–47, 1947–48 (against India) and in this 1948 season — life had been made a great deal easier for himself and his side by starting well, and this was another factor behind his tactics of grinding out a lead, rather than a slash-and-burn approach.

That night, a wicketless Bedser met Bill O'Reilly at the Black Boy Hotel. The great Australian spinner discussed Bradman and suggested to Bedser that he should employ a backward short leg to him. Mentally, wily Bill was out there, wrestling with the Bowral Boy once more. Next morning Bedser put Hutton in the position from his first over. Bradman (138) had only been in a short time when he played an in-swinger around the corner and was caught by Hutton.

Bedser raised his arm in triumph to O'Reilly in the press-box, who himself felt more than a wriggle of excitement in the moment, at least enough to boast about it long afterwards and in print. The enjoyment of 'getting' Bradman overrode his guilt for helping the old enemy.

Thereafter, Hassett led the way for 137 before Bedser bowled him, and was backed up by Johnson (21), Lindwall (42), Toshack (19) and Johnston (17 not out) in reaching 509. Bedser ended with three for 113 off 44.2 overs, while Laker took four for 138 off fifty-five overs.

England began its second innings in sunnier conditions against an attack without the injured Lindwall. Miller rose to the occasion by tempting Washbrook to touch the ball down the leg-side for a Tallon catch to have England one for 5. Later, Bradman brought on Ian Johnson for Miller, and at 39 he had Edrich groping and nicking to the keeper.

This brought together England's two best bats, Hutton and Compton, who proceeded to show why by scoring at better than a run a minute. In response, Miller tried some short deliveries to induce a hook or unsettle Hutton, and was greeted by boos and cries of 'bodyline'. But the bowling was well within the rules, as there was not a leg-trap or even a deep fine leg for the hook. With every wave of abuse, Miller tossed back his hair and bowled another short one. Then he struck Hutton on the shoulder. The boos grew louder and at the close of play an angry mob pressed towards the pavilion. Unperturbed, Miller took his sweater from the umpire and strolled off last through them. The ugly moment died as the players disappeared, though it left a nasty reminder of unpleasant days long gone.

At stumps England was two for 121, with Hutton dangerous on 63 despite the bumper barrage, and Compton 36 not out. When play resumed on Monday the crowd was of a different mood, but the weather was gloomy again. Miller speared in a magnificent ball to bowl Hutton (74) and England was three for 150. Compton carried on with more than his share of luck, with three dropped chances behind the wicket, an LBW escape that the Australians thought was out, and a missed stumping. Between all this, he played grandly and was undefeated at stumps on 154, with Evans 10 not out and England on six for 345.

On Tuesday morning, after Compton had settled in well, Miller took the new ball and delivered a short one on leg-stump. Compton shaped to hook, but seeing the ball rising at him, changed his mind, ducked across his wicket — and fell on the stumps. This 'hit wicket' dismissal was comically tragic for the crowd, and an embarrassing end for the brilliant Compton (184). England's tail wagged and added 96 to finish at 441. Miller took four for 125 from forty-four overs and Johnston four for 147 from fifty-nine.

Australia had ample time to chase the 98 for victory, but first lost Morris for 9, bowled by Bedser at 38. Bradman came in with the pressure off and lasted only ten balls in thirteen minutes before Bedser caused him to play to Hutton in the leg-trap again for his first Test duck in England. In O'Reilly's mind, no doubt, he had dismissed

Bradman twice more. Australia was two for 48, but Barnes (64 not out) and Hassett (21 not out) polished off the remainder to give Australia an eight-wicket victory.

Bradman was pleased. He considered being one-up in England more important than in Australia, mainly because of the weather and the maintenance of touring momentum, hope and determination. Australia now had to lose two of four matches for England to win the rubber. Bradman, euphoria aside, did not think it was likely.

LORD'S FOR THE LAST TIME

The inspired tourists rolled on to Northampton to play Northants on 16 June. The county started with 119 and Australia replied with eight declared for 352, and acting-skipper Hassett led from the front with 127. He was proving a very good back-up for Bradman in every way. His relaxed, jovial spirit balanced the serious side of the captain, who was preoccupied with the heavy part of the tour. Underneath, little Lindsay was in his own way as steely as the skipper when it counted under pressure on the field. He was also batting at his top.

For Northants, A. Nutter returned after a decade to unbalance the visitors with five for 57, but the county's second effort of 169 was not enough to avoid a defeat by an innings and 64 runs.

On 19 June, Bradman took his place again for a return match against Yorkshire, this time at Sheffield, with very strong memories of a near-loss at Bramall Lane in 1938 and the near-debacle at Bradford in early May. The tourists had picked a powerful side as Bradman beat Yardley in the toss and batted in front of a big crowd with a note of tension in the air rivalling that of a Test.

A huge roar greeted Barnes' dismissal, yorked by Aspinal. Bradman walked out in what he considered the most 'electric' atmosphere he had ever experienced. He likened it to a bull-fighter entering the ring. A real scrap ensued and Bradman top-scored with 54 out of 249. Yorkshire replied with 206, Toshack taking seven for 81. Australia then made sure that it got right on top before declaring at five for 286, Brown hitting 113 and Bradman continuing his remarkable consistency by scoring 86. Yorkshire was four for 85 at the end of the drawn game and there were no arguments this time about who was superior. The Australian share of gate receipts and attendance figures also showed that they were four or five times greater whenever Bradman played.

The tourists took the train back to King's Cross and their London hotel to prepare for the Second Test at Lord's. Lindwall proved his fitness and was selected in the unchanged Australian side. England brought in batsman Tom Dollery, all-rounder Alex Coxon and leg-spinner Doug Wright, who had missed the First Test through injury, for Hardstaff (injured), Barnett and Young.

Bradman won the toss on Thursday 24 June and batted on a green wicket that had not fully dried out. Coxon soon had Barnes (0) caught by Hutton, in his now favourite spot of backward short leg. At one for 3, Bradman came out as so often before in his career as *de facto* opener for his farewell appearance at the home of cricket.

He began haltingly, as he defied the England attack's determined attempts to snuff him out. Bedser was a problem. He kept swinging the ball late across Bradman's legs and the batsman had difficulty in middling the ball and keeping it down and away from Hutton's paws at short backward-square.

He appeared to settle as lunch approached. At the break he was 35 not out in 108 frustrating minutes for him, the bowlers and the crowd. All wanted something else, but could not secure it. Bradman still had all his great technical skills but he was now slower to control the ball moving away from his bat, especially early in an innings, and had to rely more than ever before on his superb concentration. But the lunch-break broke it. Soon after he walked out with Morris for the second session, Bedser cajoled him at 38 into projecting the ball to the gleeful Hutton for the third time in successive innings. O'Reilly could not claim this one as his wicket, for it seemed that Bedser, Hutton and The Don were now locked in a game of catching practice.

Everyone was amazed, except for Bradman. Even though he had never been dismissed so quickly in the same way twice, let alone three times, he refused to let it worry him unduly. He could console himself with the thought that both dismissals at Trent Bridge were of little consequence. In the first, he had made a big score and was in control of a stroke that went straight to Hutton's chest. In the second, the game was as good as over when he left the scene. This Lord's effort was the first time it mattered, and even then his removal had not been quick. Bradman had batted nearly two hours, blunting England on an imperfect wicket.

Following Bradman's departure, Morris and Hassett took the score from two for 87 to three for 166 before the latter was bowled by Yardley for 47. Morris got a well-earned 105 in his best display yet, visibly transforming himself from a fine to a great bat in this one innings. However, it was England's day as Australia ended up seven for 258. On Friday morning, Tallon (53) led a spirited bit of tail-wriggling, supported by a rump of Johnston (29) and Toshack (20 not out). Together they brought Australia up to a respectable 350. Bedser's two for 67 did not state his excellence, while Coxon's two for 62 did well enough to encourage Yardley who, modestly as ever, himself took two for 35.

Miller's back put him out of action when Australia took the field, so it was Lindwall's turn to shoulder the bowling. With England on 17, he bowled a shortish ball which rose sharply for Washbrook to play at it when he knew he shouldn't, in a sort of nervous reflex, and Tallon did the rest.

At 32, Bradman brought on Johnson, who bowled Hutton (20) with a beautiful change of pace. With the score at two for 46, Lindwall came on for his sixth over. He had built up to top pace gradually, being careful not to strain his leg again, and clean-bowled Edrich with a beauty for five. Out came Dollery of Warwickshire for the toughest baptism imaginable at the highest level. He had been scoring well in the counties and on paper deserved a chance. But he had never faced anyone with Lindwall's speed. The second ball to him uprooted his stumps well before he had brought his bat down. It was a duck for any batsman to remember awake and asleep for the rest of his life.

England was four for 46 and in very much the same position as the first innings of the First Test, but with Compton in there was more hope. He handled Lindwall well and saw him off. Then he and Yardley provided some backbone for the innings and took the score to four for 133. By then Lindwall and Johnston were back with a new ball and they did all but settle the matter with a good combined spell. The latter had Compton (53) caught in slips by Miller and Lindwall crashed Yardley's off-stump back with the first ball of his second over. Laker (28) again showed fight until Johnson had him caught behind. England slid to nine for 207 at stumps, with Australia well on top.

Lindwall wrapped the innings early on Saturday at 215 and ended with five for 70 off twenty-seven overs in a grand exhibition of speed and control. Johnson was an effective slow foil, taking three for 72 off thirty-five, while Johnston took two for 43.

Barnes came out at the start of Australia's second innings looking very determined and was soon hitting the ball hard. He lost Morris after an excellent opening stand of 122. Bradman came to the wicket after lunch to a packed weekend London crowd obviously feeling more like batting than he had on Thursday. Still, he began hesitantly against some tight bowling by Laker and Bedser, the latter working hard to get him to play to Hutton again. If he could, the ploy might well become an obsession with Bradman, but it would have to come off early in his innings. It would be of little consequence if Bradman got a fifty first, let alone a hundred, for Australia was in a winning position with a lead of over 300 and plenty of batting to come.

Bradman countered the trap by eliminating his productive leg glance, and the bowler used his in-swinger less. He concentrated for a time on swinging it away and gave The Don something else to ponder. Meanwhile, Barnes was barnstorming along and building the lead. The game was slipping from England's grasp as he reached a century after tea. Bradman warmed up after reaching 50 in ninety-eight minutes to tea, and together they began to attack.

At 296, just when Bradman looked certain to score another hundred, Bedser got the edge with an out-swinger, which was caught by Edrich in slips. It was the fifth time in successive Tests that the bowler had got rid of Bradman, who for the first time in his career was being called somebody's 'rabbit'. But Bradman was still smiling. If he had been failing regularly in losing Australian sides, then being Bedser's bunny would have been no laughing matter. But he had scored 89 and Australia was well over 400 ahead with seven wickets in hand and likely to go two-nil up in the rubber. At stumps, the tourists were four for 343, Hassett having been bowled by Yardley for a duck. Miller was on 22 not out and Brown 7 not out, with Barnes having made a fine 141.

During the rest day, the tourists were the guests of Lord Gowrie, the former Governor-General of Australia, at Windsor Castle. They met Queen Mary at Frogmore, then later in the afternoon were taken to Eton College and shown its ancient buildings. After this sweeping tour of British privilege, the lads were refreshed and ready to dispense very few privileges to the national cricket team when play resumed for the fourth day on Monday.

The Australians were able to go on until Miller (74) fell to Laker and Brown (32) was caught behind off Coxon. Bradman then had the luxury of declaring at seven for 460, giving Australia a lead of 595, enough to demoralise any side's last-innings effort. England could not win and had to see out a day and a half of an excellent attack, even without Miller.

England started, stopped forty-five minutes for rain and began again until the score reached 42, when Lindwall caused Hutton (13) to drive at one and snick it to Johnson at slip. Bradman brought on Toshack. He was a relief to the Englishmen, none of whom relished facing Lindwall, but the spinner caused Edrich to jump out and edge one more to Ian Johnson at slip. England was two for 52.

It was very soon three for 65 as Washbrook also drove at Toshack and edged to Tallon. Compton and Dollery made it through to stumps at three for 106. Only rain or Compton, or a combination thereof, could still stop Australia winning.

On the fifth day, Tuesday 29 June, the weather looked like holding as Johnston conned Compton (29) — before he added to his overnight score — into going for an away-swinger which was juggled and held by Miller in slips. Yardley (9) was bowled by Toshack and seconds later Coxon was LBW for a duck to the same bowler.

Dollery, who had battled on for 37, was bowled again by the destructive Lindwall. England crumbled for 186 and was beaten by 405 runs. Toshack took five for 40, Lindwall three for 61 and Johnston two for 62.

Bradman liked the new equation much more than the last. England had to win all three remaining Tests to take the rubber. Australia only had to draw one to retain the Ashes, and win one to take the rubber. Yet he was not thinking negatively. The tourists were still unbeaten in all matches and he wanted to keep it that way. It crossed his mind too, that it was possible Australia could win all the Tests and beat Armstrong's tour effort in 1921 of a three-nil Ashes win.

49
MIDWAY AT MANCHESTER

> *In my knowledge, Bradman and Jardine stand out as the most learned on rules. Bradman can hardly be faulted. In fact, he knows more than some umpires about the game.*
> — JACK SCOTT, FORMER UMPIRE AND CRICKET WRITER

OLD WAYS AT OLD TRAFFORD

Australia moved across London on Wednesday 30 June to take on Surrey. Bradman won the toss and put the county in. He and the team wanted to take up an invitation to Wimbledon on Friday afternoon, where it seemed Australia's John Bromwich was likely to meet the American Robert Falkenburg, in the men's singles final. If they dismissed Surrey quickly, got ahead and removed them again, they could make it by 2 p.m.

Surrey made 221, with J. F. Parker showing impressive form scoring 76. Hamence was given a chance to open with Hassett against an average attack but was bowled for a duck, bringing Bradman to the wicket with an hour and a half till stumps. He went for strokes from the first over and was 50 in fifty-six minutes and 84 not out at the close. The next morning he was through a hundred in twenty more minutes. He then moved speedily to 128 before he made a wild heave and was caught at mid-on. Bradman hit fifteen fours and gave no chance in his sixth century of the tour. Hassett (139) later was out also having a bash. Australia reached 389. Surrey went in again and Fishlock (61), Parker (81) again and Errol Holmes (54) held up the tourists' tennis-watching plans. Surrey reached 289 leaving Australia 122 to make.

Bradman sent in Harvey and Loxton, who took the long handle route to the target in less than an hour making 73 and 47 respectively. The team was able to make Wimbledon and Bradman was seated in the Royal Box with the Duchess of Kent in front of him and Sir Norman Brookes behind. Bromwich lost despite at one moment in the fifth set holding three match points.

Bradman relaxed at the home of his friend Walter Robins, while his team went off to Bristol to play Gloucester on 3 July. The skipper was always concerned when not on the spot and he monitored the scores. At lunch Australia was approaching 200, with Morris already a century. Bradman relaxed with Robins, played some golf, dined and chatted in the knowledge that the Australians could not lose. On day two, they reached seven for 774. Morris slammed his way to 290, the highest score of the season, and confirmed his improvement to something approaching world class.

Loxton, 159 not out, and Harvey, 95, helped boost the oversized tally. The county responded with 279, the left-hander J. F. Crapp making 100 not out — one of just seven hundreds scored against the tourists for the entire season — and Ian Johnson taking six for 68. Gloucester followed on with 132. Ring (five for 47) and Johnson (five for 32) shared in the destruction, and gave the tourists another big win, by an innings and 363. Johnson's eleven for 100 for the match was the best performance by an Australian for the season, while his seven for 42 previously against Leicester was also the best individual innings effort of the tour.

The team then travelled across country to Manchester for the Third Test. Loxton's form earned him a berth at the expense of Brown. England rewarded Crapp with a place for his century against the tourists, brought in the Gloucester opener G. Emmett and the 1946–47 tourist Dick Pollard and restored J. A. Young for Hutton, Wright, Laker and Coxon.

Hutton's dumping was a shock. But he had been vulnerable to the concentrated bump and pace of Miller and Lindwall in the Tests, the MCC game and when they played Yorkshire. Bradman and his speed duo had planned this as sure as the work that went into D-Day. The skipper still had nightmares about The Oval in 1938 and he had been determined not to let it happen again while he was in charge.

Hutton's confidence had been shattered. It was better for England that this great player find it again in county games. He would be back, probably before the tour was out. But the selectors felt compelled to give others a chance.

Yardley won the toss at Old Trafford on Thursday 8 July and lost both his openers by 28. Washbrook (11) was bowled by a stunning Johnston yorker that 'floated' from leg-stump to off. Emmett was caught by Barnes on the bat at forward short leg from a fast Lindwall ball that jumped from just short of a length. Compton on 5 tried to hook Lindwall but edged the ball into his head and was helped from the field with blood coming from a cut above the eye.

Crapp replaced him and played calmly in the knowledge that he had seen this attack off before, albeit in a lesser game. He made it to lunch with Edrich with England on a slow two for 57.

Lindwall took the new ball and in his third over delivered an unplayable boomerang ball that curved back from outside the left-hander's off stump. Crapp (37) shouldered arms and felt the ball crash into his left foot dead in line, to leave England three for 96. Dollery (1) was then bowled by an in-swinger from Johnston. At 119 Lindwall had Edrich (32) caught behind.

Compton, his forehead plastered, joined Yardley who was soon dismissed caught by Toshack and England was six for 141. Evans (34) then came together with Compton in a happy run-a-minute partnership of 75 to reach seven for 231 at stumps. Compton, missed three times by Tallon, carried on with Bedser (37) for a strong stand the next day of 121 which took the score after lunch to 337, when they hesitated over a single due to some clever foxing by Bradman and Loxton, and Bedser was run out by Loxton by half the length of the wicket.

Pollard, the next man in, swung a half-volley from Johnson into Barnes' ribs some seven metres from the bat. He was carried off with a serious injury, which left him temporarily half-paralysed and oddly, with a somewhat longer legacy of a black eye. Compton curbed his natural exuberance to keep the innings together with a magnificent 145 not out, full of grace and power, as England carried on to a competitive 363. Lindwall (four for 99) and Johnston (three for 67) had the figures, while Toshack took two for 75. Again Miller was unable to bowl.

Barnes' misfortune forced Bradman to send Ian Johnson in to open the innings, but the improvisation didn't work. He was caught behind for 1, bringing Bradman to the wicket at 3 in front of a capacity audience of 30,000. He looked sounder than previously, but had only scored 7 when Pollard appealed for LBW after a fast delivery got through his defences. It seemed the entire crowd roared with Pollard as umpire Dai Davies responded to his raucous appeal with a raised finger. Pollard, a local Lancashire hero, had added to Bradman's woes at Old Trafford, where he had never succeeded in Tests.

Hassett joined Morris and restored some order until he hit out against Young's spin to be caught at cover by Washbrook for 38. Miller, 23 not out, and Morris, 48 not out, were there at the close with the score at 126 for three.

On the third day, Saturday, the new ball was taken. Morris (51) was caught off Bedser and Miller (31) was LBW to Pollard. Barnes gallantly insisted on batting but collapsed mid-pitch on 1 and was forced to retire. Loxton (36) and Lindwall (23) resisted, but Australia was all out for a poor 221.

England's response saw Washbrook hooking twice off Lindwall to Hassett who dropped the chance each time. The vice-captain borrowed a policeman's helmet but Washbrook declined to try any more hooks on his way to 85 not out. England reached three for 174, losing Emmett (0) caught behind off Lindwall, Edrich run out for 53, and Compton (0) caught in slips off Toshack, to be 316 runs ahead.

The fourth day, Monday, was washed out. On the last day, it rained again. Yardley declared. It stopped raining. Australia batted a second time on a soft but lifeless wicket and lost Johnson (6) early again. Bradman joined Morris just before 3 p.m. at one for 10 and they defended stoutly. Runs were unimportant, and they kept their wickets intact during the intermittent stints of play between rain. When stumps were finally drawn Australia was one for 92. Bradman batted 122 minutes in all for his 30 not out, while Morris (54 not out) completed a useful double.

The game ended in a tame and gloomy draw, but Bradman left the field satisfied. His team had retained the Ashes. With two games to go, he could still match Armstrong's three-nil result of 1921.

50

THE GREAT
ST MICHAEL'S
LANE SHOW

---

*I know I shall never cherish any memory more than the
reception at Leeds . . . Not only was it the greatest I ever
received in this country, but the greatest I have ever received
from any public anywhere in the world.*
— BRADMAN ON HIS LAST INNINGS AT LEEDS, 1948

EMPEROR WITH PADS

Australia had one game before the Fourth Test, back in London on 8 July at Lord's against Middlesex. The county managed 203, thanks to Denis Compton (62), who continued his fine form against the tourists. In reply Australia scored 317. Morris hit 109, and where Compton had emerged as England's best, the left-handed opener had surfaced through the tour as Australia's form player with the bat next to his skipper and Hassett. Loxton also resumed his good form with 123, while 'Dim' Sims, still toiling away for Middlesex at the age of forty-four, took six for 65. The county's second dig produced 135, and the game petered out to a draw.

The team then entrained to Leeds for the Test. Tallon was kept out by an injured finger and replaced by Saggers. Harvey got his first chance in England with Barnes not quite recovered from his blow. England dropped Young, Dollery and Emmett and brought back Hutton and Laker, together with Lancashire's Ken Cranston.

Bradman was disappointed to lose the toss on Thursday 22 July, given his past efforts at Leeds of 334, 304, 103 and 16. England batted and it took Lindwall to the second new ball to exact a breakthrough when he bowled Hutton (81) at 168. The innings restored Hutton in front of his home crowd.

Edrich continued with Washbrook with a stand of exactly 100 until in the last over of the day Washbrook (143) played a tired stroke to Lindwall at slip off Johnston. Bedser came in as nightwatchman to play out the last few balls and Edrich was 41 not out in England's slow but solid two for 268.

Next morning these two carried on in what looked like a possible match-winning 155-run partnership which took England to 423 when Johnson broke through and removed Bedser for 79. Three runs later, he got rid of Edrich for 111. Wickets tumbled after that, but England still finished with the hefty total of 496. Loxton was the tail-chopper with three for 55, while Johnson took two for 89 and Lindwall two for 79.

The big Yorkshire Friday crowd of more than 40,000, which would have doubled in number but for the lack of space, was in a good mood when Australia started its first innings. Hutton had been redeemed and England's tally was challenging, even for Bradman, the man who always won a warm response in Leeds. They all waited for him in the late afternoon sun.

Morris (6) unintentionally obliged them and was caught off Bedser fifty minutes before stumps. All heads turned towards the dressing-rooms at the St Michael's Lane end of the ground. A huge honour guard of fans stretching well onto the field clapped and cheered him as he was ushered through them on his way to the wicket by three policemen.

According to E. W. Swanton he was 'greeted like an emperor by the crowd'.

With everyone predicting at least a century from him, he rose to the occasion and lifted his form from the previous two Tests. Two marvellous hooks off Pollard and Bedser saw the ball sizzle across the turf to the ropes. Bradman reached 31 at stumps with Hassett on 13 and Australia at one for 63. Many left the ground speculating that if Bradman continued on in that form, England's lead of 433 might not be nearly enough for victory.

However, a little early morning rain stopped the guessing. It made the deck livelier — sharp enough for Bedser to get past Bradman's bat and into the flesh between hip and groin. He went down with the pain. At the other end, Pollard had Hassett (13) up on his pixie feet, fending off a ball, which carried to Crapp in slips.

Miller hit a three, and the Australian skipper had to face Pollard, who always seemed to go up another notch of enthusiasm with the challenge of Bradman. His fourth ball swung in late to beat the batsman's indecisive blade to flatten his off-stump. The roar from the crowd was a mix of delight, shock and dismay. Bradman's triple centuries of 1930 and 1934 were elevated to legendary status, for with only one chance left in the second innings almost certainly they would not now be accompanied by another. His 33 today seemed unnatural compared with those epic feats of the 1930s.

Harvey was now in with Miller, who proceeded to play one of those majestically powerful knocks of his which had first made people sit up in England during the war. The teenager with him was sheltered, not from the bowling but from seeing his partners under pressure. Instead, Miller inspired Harvey to let his youthful naivety run free while not losing his wicket. As John Arlott noted in his crusty Somerset wisdom: 'Here, before our very eyes, two of the greatest innings were being played. He would have been a poor cricketer who could allow partisan feeling to mar his delight in such greatness.'

Miller's knock was ended by Yardley, who had him caught in slip for 58 when Australia was 189 after a 121-run partnership in ninety-five minutes. But Harvey went on with Loxton for another 105 in ninety-six minutes. Eventually Laker bowled the little left-hander but not before he had collared and stroked fifteen glorious fours in his 112. No better first-up Ashes century had ever been played.

Loxton brought an added dimension of delight by hitting five superb sixes, one of which Bradman described as the 'most glorious' he had ever seen, on his way to 93 before he was bowled by Yardley. This unexpected big-hitting and fast scoring, more in keeping with a Festival game than a Test, brought Australia right back into the match with the chance of a surprise win rather than at best a tame draw.

Lindwall came in and kept up the pressure with a thumping 76 not out for Australia to be nine for 457 at stumps. The tourists had clouted 396 in a day that enthralled the crowd. Near the close, Johnston was out for 13 and stayed at the wicket to act as a runner for the injured Toshack. Johnston pretended to be refusing to leave and earned the abuse of gullible sections of the crowd. Then Toshack appeared and the joke was up.

The innings ended with the addition of only one run in the morning when Lindwall (77) edged Bedser to Crapp at second slip. Bedser finished with three for 92, Laker three for 113, Pollard two for 100 and Yardley two for 38.

Hutton and Washbrook began as if England were serious about winning with a strong partnership of 129. Then Harvey took a great running catch at long leg centimetres from the ground to remove Washbrook (65) off Johnston. Immediately afterwards, Hutton (57) mistimed a drive off Ian Johnson and was caught by Bradman at mid-off. Lindwall later had Edrich (54) LBW with the new ball, but not before the batsman had savaged Johnson with three fours and a six in four balls.

Lindwall forced Crapp (18) to play on. Then Johnston showed his versatility by bowling leg-breaks over the wicket. He dismissed Yardley (7), Cranston (first ball) and Compton (66) to leave England six for 278. The lead was 316 and with the wicket likely to turn on the last day, England were becoming the bookies' selection. Evans (47 not out) and Laker (15) took the score at stumps to eight for 362. Johnston took four for 95, and Lindwall collected two for 84.

Bradman wrote pessimistically in his diary that night: 'We are set 400 to win and I fear we may be defeated.' Next morning he told the team scorer, Bill Ferguson: 'I think we are going to lose this game. It's too many runs for any team to make in such a short time.' In Australia, the highest score to win a Test was 332. In England it was 263 — in 1902.

Next day, Yardley used the heavy roller in the hope of breaking the dry wicket, let Evans and Laker bat for two more overs and then declared at eight for 365. But like all such rollers, it had no effect on the wicket.

Australia had 404 to get in five and a half hours. England would normally send down about 100 to 120 overs in that time (that is, roughly twenty overs an hour), which meant Australia would have to score at four runs an over to win.

ONE FINAL MIGHTY CHALLENGE

Much that had gone before in this match had been brilliant. There had been performances with the bat and ball that would be remembered not just for their skill but their panache, free of inhibitions caused by thoughts of winning or losing. But the last day promised the sort of tensions that would separate out players who could perform at their best under pressure with flair and brilliance from those who couldn't. The batsmen in particular would be under enormous strain. There was no point in thinking about a bright 40, or maybe 70. That would only donate a wicket to England, or precipitate collapse.

Bradman would go for a win only if there was not an early collapse, if his top-order bats settled in and if Yardley did not set ultra-defensive fields. If England was too negative, Bradman could order the shutters to be shut and force a draw. That result would leave Australia with a two-nil lead, the rubber and the Ashes.

Despite the pessimism of his diary note and comment to Ferguson, he always considered a win was at least possible. Nor did he even contemplate playing for a draw unless it was absolutely necessary. Bradman the leader was ready to attack for a win and take risks if his quick, arithmetical brain told him runs, time and over calculations suggested a fair chance, given his considerable batting personnel. But a win for Australia on 27 July 1948 was very much against the odds, especially as no team in the history of Tests had ever hit anything like 400 in the last innings to win.

Hassett and Morris, however, began as if a draw were their aim, scoring six runs in six overs. But they must have only been trying to play themselves in, for when Laker was brought on to effect an early breakthrough they slammed 13 from his first over. Laker was getting turn but not quick turn. In the first hour, 44 runs were gorged out, leaving 360 to get in about ninety overs. The rate required was still around four an over.

Pollard and Bedser were keeping the batsmen quiet, but Yardley had to go for a win. He tried Compton, who bowled left-hand wrist-spin or 'Chinamen', like Fleetwood-Smith and Tribe. His first over cost 10 runs and the second was a near-wicket maiden, when Morris just survived a stumping. However, Compton then caught and bowled Hassett (13). It was clear now that England had erred by not including a leg-break bowler of consequence.

Bradman stood up in the dressing-room to cries of 'Good luck, Don' . . . 'Good luck, Braddles . . .' This was it. The last Leeds and Bradman show. A throng of people formed again near the gate to cheer him out. The big crowd gave him what O'Reilly called a 'magnificent ovation', something which may have touched him and turned his performance through emotion, if nothing had been at stake. But now everything was on the line. If England won it would be one-two down and with a chance to square the series at The Oval.

Bradman was more interested in the pavilion clock than the clamour as he slipped down between the lines of worshippers. Unusually, he had no plan locked into his tactical, calculating brain and was of two minds. He wanted to win. But he didn't want to lose. What should he do?

It was 1 p.m. Seventy-three minutes had gone and only 57 graced the scoreboard. The simple arithmetic said if there were 347 to get and 257 minutes to get them in, then Australia had to get well ahead of the clock at some stage to win. As he crossed the turf to the middle, he was now the lonely figure for the last time in his career who inspired the English commentator H. S. Altham to write:

> In the many pictures I have stored in my mind from the burnt-out Junes of forty years, there is none more dramatic or compelling than that of Bradman's small, serenely-moving figure in its big-peaked green cap coming out of the pavilion shadows into the sunshine, with the concentration, ardour and apprehension of surrounding thousands centred upon him, and the destiny of a Test match in his hands.

He scratched out his block. Yardley clapped his hands. Every player was on his toes, feeling the tension caused by the crowd's projection. Laker stood waiting for Bradman, who examined the field, particularly the posting of three very close short legs. He settled down over his bat.

Laker pitched on off-stump, well up, hoping that Bradman would play at the off-spin across his body and feed someone, anyone, in that leg-trap. The ball was halfway down the wicket in flight. The bat went back and up to stump height, earlier and quicker, it was claimed by every astute observer, than anyone else ever managed.

Then he made the little shuffle of his feet slightly to leg, positioning himself to drive not with the spin to mid-on, but against it. Bradman gave it the full flourish, and the ball shot through the vacant mid-off position straight to the ropes for four. The crowd roared as if a wicket had fallen. Laker frowned and bowled now on middle and off, right where he wished. Bradman made that slight sideways movement again, clearly protecting himself from playing it to the on. The ball was driven back to Laker. He was more pleased with that one. He speared the ball in further to leg. Bradman let it spin past. The over was over. The battle had begun.

Australia eased to one for 70 in eighty-two minutes. Morris and Bradman were making a gentle raid on the clock. Not enough to worry Yardley, but enough to stay in the region of the just-possible victory. Compton came on again and bowled a good over to Bradman, who nicked one wide of Crapp in slips. Yardley needed a real leg-break bowler to take advantage of the turn out of the rough, who could attack Bradman on his legs and that perceived weakness of popping the ball to the leg-trap, or turn one right across him for a catch in the slips.

The England captain threw the ball to Hutton. The Yorkshire crowd breathed his name in a murmur around the terraces. Len had bowled leg-breaks, and in a county game in 1947 had taken four for 44. But this was Test cricket. Morris was facing and batting like a true champion. Surely the Yorkshireman was being used so other bowlers could change ends . . .

He sent down three full-tosses in the last three balls of the over. Morris crashed them into the ropes either side of the wicket. The spectators clapped Morris's 50 perfunctorily and went coldly silent. Yardley was gambling. He had to.

Compton bowled another good over. Then on came Hutton for another. Bradman was facing. Hutton let go two more uncertain tweakers and it was Bradman's turn to despatch them for four each. Five fours off five balls in a row. The gamble had failed. The tempo of the game had changed. Bradman had hit 35 in thirty minutes. Now, he told himself, he knew what to do. Australia would go for a win.

Australia went to lunch at one for 121, having scored 95 runs in ninety minutes. It was ahead of the clock, but still with a monumental task of 284 runs in the final two sessions of 120 minutes each. About eighty overs would be sent down. The rate required was now down to 3.5 runs an over, which was still tough over such a long period. The middle session would tell the tale.

Most still favoured an England win. The wicket was worn badly. Laker was getting good turn, and more than once pitched outside Bradman's off-stump and made the ball pass outside leg.

'It looked certain that the Australians were due for a hard fight to stave off defeat,' O'Reilly observed in his book, *Cricket Conquest*.

'Compton, spinning the ball well, was likely to be the chief source of trouble.'

Morris set out in the first over after lunch to settle it with the Chinaman-bowler, Compton, one way or the other. He and Bradman took 15 off it. Cranston bowled and kept both men quiet. Yardley had a quick word to Compton, showing his confidence, and handed him the ball. He had to do that. He could not take him off after one bad over. Not since these two had belted Hutton away from the bowling crease. Compton looked jaunty — his affable self — as he turned and ran in to Morris. By the end of the six balls — each one pitched shorter and shorter — Australia had extracted another 15, making 30 in two overs. Yardley had to take him off now. At that rate Australia would wrap up the game by tea.

Bradman slowed a little but still had 50 in an hour. At 59, he cut Cranston hard in front of Yardley, who dived forward for the hardest kind of catch, but couldn't hold it. It was a chance, but it wasn't. Bradman was having trouble picking up the ball in the glare. There were no sightboards at Leeds. It was hot and sunny and men had removed their coats to leave a multi-coloured blur behind the bowler's arm. 'It was like looking at a draughts board,' he said.

He gave another hot chance in slips, which was grassed.

Australia reached 202 — halfway — with 165 minutes to get the next 202. Yardley took the new ball at one for 212. Bedser and Pollard quietened the batsmen. On 79, Bradman held his side as if he had strained it. His first thought was that it was a recurrence of his rib cartilage injury incurred against India at Melbourne in February. But instead it was an onset of fibrositis. Bradman told Morris to take most of the strike. Fortunately for Australia, the spasm passed. He celebrated by cutting Bedser for a perfectly timed square-cut to the boundary followed by a leg glance for another four. Bradman then drove through mid-wicket for two to take 10 off the over and reach 89. Australia was one for 243. In the ninety minutes after lunch these two had added 122 to swing the game the tourists' way.

Morris reached his century and the arithmetic looked better for Australia with every over as the left-hander took charge. At 4.10 p.m.

Bradman reached his century with his fifteenth four in 145 minutes. It was his twenty-ninth century in Tests. He smiled for the first time in the afternoon and raised his bat. The momentum was with Australia. A victory was possible. It seemed that luck was with both batsmen as England looked ragged in the field and Laker dropped an easy catch from Morris, on 136.

At 108, Bradman jumped down to drive Laker, who pushed it past him down the leg-side. Bradman swung and missed. Evans, unsighted, missed the chance of a stumping. It was a hard one, but such a great keeper would normally have got the wicket.

Bradman went to tea both relieved and determined with 108 not out. Morris was 150 and Australia was one for 288. They had added 167 in the two-hour session and needed 112 in the last. About forty overs would be bowled, which meant the Australians could now score at less than three an over, or one every two balls, to win. Nine wickets were still in hand.

After tea, both batsmen again hit powerfully. Morris on-drove Pollard for four and took the partnership to 300. Then with the score at 358, and the stand worth 301 in 217 minutes, Morris was caught by Pollard off Yardley for 182. Bradman was 143, and Australia was 46 short of victory.

Miller came to the wicket and took a back seat as Bradman took control of the bowling and played a series of shots which took his score to 169 and the total to 396. Miller (12) fell LBW to Cranston. Harvey hurried out at 6.11 p.m. but with eight runs to get and nineteen minutes to play, he could have strolled to the wicket. Bradman cut a four — his twenty-ninth — to bring up the 400 and take his score to 173 not out. He had batted 270 minutes and ranked this innings as one of his best.

At 6.16 p.m. Harvey formalised it with a four to bring up 404 and a truly great seven-wicket victory. The youngster grabbed a stump, as did Evans, while Bradman sprinted for the pavilion. Fans broke ranks near the boundary ropes and rushed towards the players.

Australia was three-nil up with one Test to play. Bradman the Great had won another Test and another series for his country.

51

CONQUEROR
TAKES ALL

A charming picture of a batsman returning to the pavilion.
This is the picture treasured by every member of the English
eleven. It is Mr Bradman.
— TOM WEBSTER'S CAPTION FOR A CARTOON OF A RETIRING CRICKETER

HOLLIES FROM HEAVEN

There was no time to celebrate one of the most important and great wins in the history of cricket. The team was bundled onto the night train for Derby and once at their hotel, Bradman had treatment for his side into the early hours. His back was playing up as it always did now during and after a long innings. The problem prevented him from going after a really big score, even though he was still quite capable of it, so that he would quite often throw his wicket away rather than run the risk of muscular breakdown. But, despite earning a much-needed rest, he was determined to play against Derbyshire the day after the Test, 28 July, to help maintain the team's unbeaten record, on which he was now concentrating.

He won the toss and batted. When it was his turn to go in he found his muscles had tightened up and he felt generally enervated. But he was somehow able to make the effort, and relying on his reflexes managed to get 62. Brown, who had not played at Leeds, came good with 140 and Australia compiled 456. Derbyshire replied with 240 and 182 (D. Smith 88) and McCool — also not in the Test side — took six for 77. Next was a rained-out game at Swansea against Glamorgan. The county hit 197, and Australia, minus its skipper, responded with three for 215. Miller maintained his form with 84, while Hassett had a stylish work-out for 71 not out.

Bradman came back to play against Warwickshire at Birmingham and scored 31 before being bowled by a topspinner from Eric Hollies, the leg-break and googly specialist, who collected the best haul against the tourists so far with eight for 107. This fine performance after the lack of such a bowler at Leeds made the England selectors take notice and he became a strong tip for a game at The Oval in a week's time. Hollies reduced the tourists to 254, but the county only managed 138 and 155 in reply. Australia made one for 41 (Bradman 13 not out) to win by nine wickets. Bradman went out to have another look at the spinner. Hollies wisely did not show him his googly. The bowler later claimed that he decided to deliver him one the second ball he bowled to him at The Oval, if he got the chance. He was the last of perhaps a thousand bowlers over two decades who had set his sights on bowling Bradman something special that could get him out.

After sunny Birmingham, it was back to Manchester for a re-match with Lancashire on 7 August, which was a benefit match for Cyril Washbrook. Bradman won the toss, something he had some success in doing outside the Tests, and batted. He seemed out of touch, started slowly and gave two chances from spinner W. B. Roberts before the latter had him caught for 28 in seventy-three minutes. It was clear he had not fully recovered from his effort at Leeds. However, Barnes showed he was ready for another Test with a strong 67 out of the team's 321. Lancashire could only garner 130.

Washbrook was pleased that Bradman did not enforce the follow-on, and even happier to see him 21 not out at the close of the second day. It meant a bumper gate the next morning, and Bradman responded with a century before lunch — the eighth time he had achieved this feat, and the fourth in England. This was a superb batting display against a strong attack comprising Pollard, Greenwood, Ikin, Roberts and Cranston. It gave Bradman confidence that he could lift himself for his last Test match at The Oval. Australia tallied three for 265 (Bradman 133, Barnes 90) declared. Lancashire was seven for 199 in reply, with Ikin making 99, when the game was drawn.

Lindwall bowled at incredible speed in this game, with Tallon and the slips standing a long way back. Bradman ranked it with the pace of Eddie Gilbert and Larwood in 1932. This all boded well for the Australians in the Fifth Test. Miller seemed well enough to bowl. Johnston was in good form still. Now Lindwall was hurling them down at a velocity equal to that of the fastest bowlers in history. This made Bradman quietly confident for The Oval. He had a big score to settle there after the 1938 drubbing. Nothing could erase the memory of that hideous seven for 903 scoreboard, but a big Australian victory would make it fade and recall the great triumphs of 1930 and 1934.

Bradman and several other members of the squad rested from a two-day drawn game against Durham in preparation for the final Test at The Oval, beginning Saturday 14 August.

LETHAL LINDWALL

Bradman lost the toss for the eighth time in nine tries calling heads, but it did not matter. Yardley batted. Bradman would have sent England in. He judged the wicket as adequate, despite the morning rain, but he was influenced by the slow, damp outfield, which would improve as the match progressed, if the weather held.

England was blooding new players now that the series had been lost. In came opening batsman J. G. Dewes of Cambridge and Middlesex, Glamorgan all-rounder Allan Watkins and Hollies, with left-hand orthodox spinner Jack Young being recalled. Washbrook was injured, while Pollard, Cranston and Laker were dropped. For the Australians Toshack had to be left out with knee trouble and Ian Johnson was made twelfth man, making way for Doug Ring and Barnes, with Tallon returning in place of Saggers.

Play was delayed for half an hour because of earlier rain and Miller began well by clean-bowling Dewes for 1 at 2. Edrich soon after hooked hard at Johnston and Hassett held a tough catch at square leg, without the help of a policeman's helmet, to make England two for 10.

A few minutes later Compton hooked at a short, rising ball from Lindwall, the force of which knocked the bat from his hands, while the ball flew safely along the grass to Hassett at long leg. Hutton came through for the run. Compton, flustered, started for the run, went back for his bat, and then started for the run again. Hassett picked up but did not throw, thus allowing Compton to scramble to the bowler's end.

It was a quirky act of sportsmanship, which not all players on both sides would have endorsed and O'Reilly in the press-box chastised Hassett for his charity. But it was not a costly gesture. Soon afterwards Lindwall bowled a fast short one at Compton, who hooked it beautifully and low but not past Morris at square leg, who held a brilliant catch. Compton was on his way for 4 and England was three for 17. Then Miller got the edge from Crapp's bat and Tallon did the rest to make it four for 23.

The imperturbable Hutton was not out at lunch with Yardley and England was a sorry four for 29. Not too long after the resumption, Lindwall bowled Yardley (7) with a very quick one that kept a smidgen low to leave England five for 35. Lindwall then softened up new man Watkins with a bouncer which hit him on the shoulder, for Johnston to trap him LBW at the other end for 0 and England was six for 42.

Lindwall was now revved up and unfairly fast for what remained. He didn't bother with bouncers at the rabbits — it wasn't done in 1948 anyway — and clean-bowled Evans (1) and Bedser (0). At eight for 45, Hutton hit Lindwall for the first four of the innings to ruin the bowler's figures at four for 18. Next ball he played a sound leg glance only for Tallon to move swiftly to his left to catch it centimetres from the grass, depriving Hutton of the chance of carrying his bat. Nevertheless, he had played a courageous hand of 30, which looked big out of nine for 47. Lindwall then crashed Young's castle and England were all out for 52, its lowest total ever against Australia.

Lindwall took six for 20, Miller two for 5 and Johnston two for 20.

Bradman could reflect that cricket was not just a 'funny' game, but a very odd and surprising one too. Ten years ago, he had suffered England going on forever to score nearly 1,000 runs. Now he was floating on a cloud with the old enemy barely scraping together a fifty.

Was there that much in the wicket? None of the Australian bowlers thought so. The openers Barnes and Morris backed them up by having little difficulty throughout a 117-run partnership before Barnes (61) was caught behind off a leg-break from Hollies.

OVAL AND OUT

The time was 5.50 p.m. The big crowd of 20,000, disappointed by England's awful flop, had stayed on to pay tribute to The Don. They cheered him wholeheartedly as he walked through the little wicket gate and onto a Test arena for perhaps his last-ever innings. It was both spontaneous and generous in its warmth and enthusiasm, for the England supporters had scarcely anything to cheer at all day. It was a splendid acclamation of the greatest batsman in the game's history.

Yardley called his men together in the middle to make himself heard above the din. 'We'll give him three cheers when he's at the wicket,' the England skipper said. Then he turned to Hollies and added: 'But that's all we'll give him. You bowl him out.'

Bradman was applauded all the way to the wicket. Before he took block, Yardley shook hands with him and called for three cheers. The crowd stood up and joined in as the England players clustered round the wicket, raised their caps and gave voice.

Memories of 1930 at The Oval came back to Bradman, when he had stood with the Australians around Jack Hobbs for his last Test. But while Bradman appreciated the crowd and Yardley's gesture he claimed he was definitely not emotionally moved. 'There were no tears in the eyes,' he said.

Bradman had a job to do and wanted a performance in line with his sequence of Test performances at this ground of 232, 244 and 77. In two innings there in 1948 against Surrey he had hit 148 and 128. He was keen to go out with a good score, unaware that if he hit just four more, he would have 7,000 runs in his Tests. As this was his eightieth innings with ten not-outs, those four runs would leave him with an average of exactly 100 runs every time he batted in a Test. This would have suited his mathematically attuned mind.

However, on the agenda first was nothing to do with averages or records, but getting set and capitalising on his team's wonderful position. The main thing on his mind was negotiating Eric Hollies, who was waiting to deliver his first ball to him. He was a long way from feeling as sentimental as the crowd, for this was the greatest enemy of bowlers since the game was invented.

It was now three minutes since the leggie had sent Barnes back to the pavilion. Bowling round the wicket, he came in and delivered a ripping leg-break. Bradman hurried back to play it defensively.

Hollies thought that the 'old boy' looked a little rushed. The bowler wasted no time in firing in the next one, a googly. It was on a tantalisingly good length. Bradman stretched for it and played outside it. The ball came back between bat and pad and nipped into the off stump. Bradman looked round incredulously at the broken wicket.

He didn't linger and was off before the crowd fully realised he was out, for a duck. He hurried off The Oval. The cheering began again. It built and followed him all the way back across the ground, through the gate and out of sight into the pavilion of rich memory and unprecedented performance.

MORRIS MAJOR

The Bradman era was not quite done yet. He had failed in that innings, which he did not expect necessarily would be his last, but there was still a Test match to command to victory. At the end of Saturday, Australia was two for 153, with Morris in charge on 77 not out, Hassett with him on 10 and the tourists 101 ahead.

Monday 16 August was Morris Day, for the star bat of the series went on until he was run out on 196 in Australia's score of 389. Hassett (37) and Tallon (31) gave him support, but it was a one-man battle between the left-hander and Hollies, who added Miller (stumped for 5), Harvey (caught for 17) and Tallon to Barnes and Bradman in his impressive bag of five for 131 off fifty-six overs.

England began again, 337 behind, only for Lindwall to break through at 20, when he beat Dewes (10) with swing to hit the wicket by way of bat and pad. The home team went to stumps one for 54.

Lindwall was brutally fresh on Tuesday morning and very keen to get at the Englishmen again. At 64, he delivered a near-unplayable ball which moved off the pitch and shattered Edrich's stumps. Most astute observers agreed it would have bowled any batsman.

Compton (39) stayed with the near-immovable Hutton until just after lunch, when he nicked a ball from Johnston to Lindwall at slip. England was three for 125. Miller had Hutton caught by Tallon for 64 at 153, in what may possibly have been a better innings than his record 364. The score may have been a sixth of his feat in 1938, but it needed ten times more talent and guts to hold out against these bowlers.

Miller was now backing up Lindwall with an unmatched variety of swing and spin. England stumbled to be seven for 174 at stumps. Wednesday was a formality and England was dismissed for 188. Johnston, the unsung hero, took four for 40, Lindwall three for 50, Miller two for 22 and Ring one for 44.

Australia won by an innings and 149 runs, and took the rubber four-nil. Morris topped Australia's batting average with 696 runs at an average of 87.00. Barnes made 329 at 82.25, while Bradman hit 508 at 72.57. Compton did best for England with 562 at 62.44, and Washbrook collected 356 at 50.85.

Lindwall (twenty-seven wickets at 19.62) and Johnston (twenty-seven at 23.33) were the destroyers for Australia. They were ably supported by Miller (fifteen at 23.15) when his back allowed. Bedser was England's best with eighteen wickets, but he was expensive at 38.22 runs per wicket. Yardley, in fact, topped his team's averages with nine at 22.66, highlighting England's lack of depth and penetration.

After that final game, about 5,000 people gathered in front of the pavilion to hear Bradman say some gracious things about Yardley and the England side. He thanked the crowd for their reception, and received another one. But it was his last-ever in a Test.

MOPPING UP

The Tests were over, but Bradman still kept the pressure on his troops. He wanted to go on winning in the next eight games for the season. First-up was Kent at Canterbury. Brown, still eager after missing out on the last three Tests, hit 106, while Bradman (65) and Harvey (60) contributed to the team's tally of 361. Kent could only muster 51 and 124, giving the tourists another big innings win. In a similar result against the Gentlemen of England at Lord's, Bradman fittingly scored a grand century and was in a happy, smiling mood. At 150, he donated his wicket to the Gents with a wafty loft to be caught in the deep, and seconds before it fell into safe hands, he was trotting off the ground. He had done enough, long ago having proved very many points. Everyone from the bleachers and the members to those in buildings outside and above the ground stood to him and applauded. As he approached the pavilion for the last time as a batsman, he took off his gloves, hung them around his bat handle, raised them high, removed his cap and bowed farewell, first to the crowd, then to the members in the pavilion. The applause increased and a cheer went up round Lord's at this last gesture of a player, who had undone even its greatest son, W. G. Grace.

This innings took his aggregate for the season past 2,000. Hassett hit a fine 200 not out and Brown 120 to assist the tourists to five for 610 declared. The Gents replied with 245 and 284 (Edrich 128), and Ring collected five for 70 in securing victory on 27 August, Bradman's fortieth birthday. His team gathered around at cricket HQ to sing 'happy birthday' to the skipper, who told them the best present they could give him would be to keep winning.

Bradman dropped out of a two-day match on 28 and 30 August versus Somerset at Taunton. The tourists did not dare let the resting captain down and hit five for 560 declared (Harvey 126, Hassett 103, and Ian Johnson 113 not out). Somerset responded with 115 and 71, Bill Johnston taking five for 34.

Bradman was finding that little extra for this last burst of his career, partly because he wanted to keep on winning and partly for the huge crowds who were still turning out after a bumper season of attendances. Bradman was loath to leave himself out of any match. If he did, game and club organisers might see it as a snub. He was still the drawcard. He ensured rich gate receipts.

The conquering captain returned for a game against the South of England at Hastings and did battle against a composite side that again was nowhere near a match for Bradman and his centurions. He got 143, Hassett 151, and Harvey 110. The South managed 298 in reply — Compton scoring 82 and Edrich 52 — to draw the match.

The final first-class game was the traditional one against Leveson-Gower's XI at the Yorkshire seaside resort of Scarborough. This match had been a controversial contest since 1934, mainly due to the insistence of the hyphenated patron, who kept selecting virtually an England Test team, while the Australians wanted to play a festival-type game on their last outing, especially after the extremely rigorous tour.

Bradman forgot about the fun approach and picked the fittest form side from the tourists. He knew the English attitude would be to attempt to ruin his clean slate and pinch a win in this unofficial 'Sixth Test'. Queues began forming at 5 o'clock on the first morning for Bradman's final match in England. Gower's XI — captained by Yardley — won the toss, and Lindwall bowled Hutton for a duck, a demoralising dismissal from which the home side did not recover. They were all out for 177 with Lindwall bowling again at his peak. No English side had an answer to him for the entire tour. His figures of six for 59 understated his performance by two or three wickets. He was well supported by Ian Johnson, who had been a strong contributor with the ball and useful with the bat right through the tour.

During the lunch interval on this first day, Yorkshire County Cricket Club announced that Bradman had been made a life member of the club, the highest honour a foreign player could be awarded at the first-class level. Manchester, Lancashire and Hampshire county clubs subsequently followed suit.

Australia replied to the invitation team's total with a reminder of why it had been superior since the Worcester game in April. Barnes and Morris got the side off to a strong start of 102 before Yardley bowled Morris for 62. Bradman came to the wicket in the rain-interrupted game thirty-six minutes before stumps. He was 30 at the close.

The next morning, some of the 17,000 people lined up right to the wicket to give him a typical Yorkshire welcome. Bradman negotiated the line, escorted by two burly policemen, determined not to let them down. He was pleased to find an easier wicket, and began slowly but soundly, reaching 50 in ninety-one minutes. That signpost — as it so often had been in his career — marked the moment in which he let Bradman be Bradman for the last time in a first-class game in England. His next 50 came at a run-a-minute. His century was his eleventh for the tour. The skipper raised his bat high without any extravagant gesture, but with just the hint of a grin of satisfaction. He had put the issue of an unbeaten tour beyond doubt. It gave Bradman much private pleasure to know that he had done better than Armstrong's tourists of twenty-seven years ago, who had lost the last two games of the tour.

Mission accomplished, he stepped into the bowling after lunch to add 44 in thirty-eight minutes. He went after Bedser but paid the bowler the compliment of his wicket as soon as he moved through 150 to 153 by skying the ball to Hutton in the covers. Again Bradman was hurrying off the ground as the catch was taken. He disappeared from view, Jack Fingleton noted, 'before this huge Yorkshire crowd at the Scarborough festival had time to warm its hands in appreciation to him. Bradman was lost to view for ever as a first-class batsman on an English ground.'

Bradman batted faultlessly for 194 minutes in collecting two sixes and nineteen fours. This had been his third successive hundred. It was the second time he had done it in England and the tenth time in all he had scored three centuries or more in a row.

Barnes (151) also helped put the issue of the tourists' superiority beyond doubt as the team posted 489. The Gower XI limped to two for 75 at the close, with Johnson getting Hutton for 27 and Fishlock for 26. Bradman bowled his one and only over of 1948 — the last of the match — and was given a great ovation as he led his team off the field. The game was drawn with Australia's tour record ending at twenty-three wins and nine draws. Fifteen of those victories were by an innings. The closest win was by four wickets. At no stage of the tour in either a Test or otherwise was an Australian eleven in grave danger of defeat. In the drawn matches, Australia was on top but for the Third Test at Manchester. Even then, the tourists' score of one for 98 in the last innings, with Bradman in and looking sound, meant that the opposition was a long way from a victory.

After the moral victory at Scarborough, Australia had two second-class matches against Scotland to finish the tour, at Edinburgh and Aberdeen. The Scots may not have provided great opposition but they made up for it with brilliant hospitality, which the visitors loved at the end of the arduous thirty-two-match to date first-class tour. The first-class games, jammed into each other with the team scrambling by train, bus and car from one venue to another, became one long blur of determined, relentless, but usually exhilarating and rarely dry, cricket.

However, even at Edinburgh, the team did not let up, beating the Scots by an innings and 40 runs. At Aberdeen, Bradman turned out to please the locals and ensured that even if the hosts' hospitality became too much, their cricket would not. Ten thousand turned out to see Scotland hit 178 and Bradman smash a whirlwind 123 not out — two sixes and seventeen fours — in eighty-seven minutes, supported by McCool with 108 and Johnson with 95, in the tourists' tally of six for 407 declared. The home side was then rolled for 142, giving Australia a win by an innings and 87 runs to go through a thirty-four-game tour undefeated.

The averages told the story of the team's mainstays. Bradman not only led the team with strategic and tactical adroitness never equalled by any other tour skipper, but topped the batting figures with the highest aggregate of 2,428 runs at the best average of 89.92, hitting eleven centuries and a further eight fifties.

Next best was Hassett with 1,563 at 74.42, followed by Morris with 1,922 at 71.18 and Brown 1,448 at 57.92. The depth was notable. Sam Loxton, who only fought his way into the Test side by the third match, hit 973 at 57.23. Harvey, who joined it in the Fourth Test, collected 1,129 at 53.76. A player of Miller's calibre found himself ranking a humble seventh with 1,088 at 47.30.

The bowling figures were also instructive. Lindwall was the outstanding performer with eighty-six wickets at 15.86. Second was Bill Johnston, with 102 at 16.42. Not far behind were Miller (fifty-six at 17.58), McCool (fifty-seven at 17.82) and Ian Johnson (eighty-five at 18.37). Others to reach the half-century were Toshack (fifty at 21.12) and Ring (sixty at 21.81). Tallon (thirty catches and thirteen stumpings) and Saggers (twenty-three and twenty) were consistently first-rate behind the stumps throughout the tour.

Finally, The Don's record at the end of 1948 showed his power and consistency as the longest reigning champion the game had yet produced. Over two decades he had 334 innings with forty-three not outs and a grand total of 27,851 runs at an average of 95.7. Given that he often threw his wicket away when in total command of a bowling side in a conservative estimate of fifty of these innings, the average is an understatement of his domination of the world cricket arena throughout his career.

Bradman was a relaxed man at the end of the tour as he and his team were entertained by the King and Queen at Balmoral. The off-field grand finale was a luncheon at the Savoy Hotel in London in The Don's honour which was arranged by *The People* newspaper and attended by a host of dignitaries and players of note who had competed against him. He was presented with a replica of the historic 2,000-year-old Warwick Vase found near Rome in 1770 by Sir William Hamilton. The cost of the gift was raised by an appeal organised by *The People*. There was a considerable amount over. The paper wanted to give Bradman a cheque, but he wouldn't accept it. Instead he requested that the money should be used to lay concrete pitches in parks in England for the benefit of young cricketers.

Whether Douglas Jardine was invited or not to the Savoy is unknown, but Harold Larwood, by then a non-smoking Blackpool tobacconist and a future migrant to Australia, was present. He and The Don were pictured shaking hands fifteen long years after the greatest controversy in cricket, which nearly finished the Ashes as a competition.

By the end of the 1948 season in England, the game and Bradman had endured triumphantly.

PART SIX

LIFE AFTER
CRICKET
1949–

52

THE POWER AND THE INFLUENCE

It was once said that 'nothing in this world is precious until we know that it will soon be gone', but that was never true of the batting and fielding of Mr Bradman.
— SIR WILLIAM NORMAN BIRKETT

KNIGHT OF THE LONG BLADE

On the boat trip home Bradman was approached by a representative of Payne's Sweets, who wanted him and some other players to appear in Australian newspaper advertisements. The Payne's rep was surprised that Bradman did not negotiate a bigger deal for himself. But he refused to take more than his team-mates, even though he was the leader and arranged the agreements.

A few weeks later when they arrived home, the Payne's man flew to Adelaide to sign the contract and give Bradman his payment. Bradman said he could not go on with it, but did not give a reason. The Payne's man had drawn the cheque and urged him to take it, but he refused.

'Give it to the Spastics Society,' Bradman told him, which was where the money went.

'I think he knew he was about to be knighted,' said Ian Johnson, who appeared in the advertisement. 'He could hardly appear in a newspaper ad selling sweets.'

Bradman's cricket career was not quite over when he returned home. In December 1948, he played in his own testimonial match at the MCG and scored 123 in front of 53,000 people. In February 1949, he played in a testimonial for Alan Kippax and Bert Oldfield in Sydney and hit a fast 53 in front of 41,575. Finally, in March 1949 it was Adelaide's turn to see Bradman in a State game, for South Australia against Victoria, which was a testimonial for Arthur Richardson. He made a top score of 30 in South Australia's first innings but injured his ankle while fielding and could not bat in the second.

Bradman, as generous as ever to his former team-mates and the cricketing fraternity, had played on in these games. It was as if no-one in the game or the public wanted to let him go. But enough was enough. Apart from the odd social game over the next twenty years, those unequalled skills would never be seen again.

His career was now finished, and as if to mark the delineation between his playing days and what would follow, he was sworn in as a Knight Bachelor in recognition of his services to cricket and to Commonwealth sporting links.

The title 'Sir' separated Bradman further from the sportsmen of the era, and added to the mystique of his performance and standing. It enhanced the legend, but also distanced him from the circumstances of it. He was an ordinary man who had emerged from a humble country background to become the finest performer and most astute leader Australia had produced. From another perspective it suited Bradman. By 1949, he had had enough of public acclamation, hero worship and the 'Bradmania' that dogged him. 'Sir' meant he had retired from all that.

In April 1949 he looked forward to a life without playing the game, which initially meant stockbroking six days a week as he worked assiduously to build his business. Golf became his leisure sport. He loved it and began to reduce his handicap. However, he was still the most powerful non-playing influence in cricket. Bradman was still a Test selector, a South Australian State selector and a member of the Board of Control.

Bradman was a friend of Robert Menzies, who became Prime Minister again in 1949. Menzies felt Bradman would make an excellent ambassador and asked him if he would be interested in the position of Australian High Commissioner in London. Bradman would have liked that position. He had been a *de facto* ambassador on four tours of Britain, especially in 1948 when he was the most high-profile individual in the country. His appointment would have been an astute move. Menzies sounded out the possibility among his colleagues but received a negative response from within the Liberal Party. The High Commissioner's job was seen as the plum diplomatic post. In addition, Menzies would have lost a possible prize perk which he could use either to reward a fellow politician or remove him from the local scene. Bradman was informed that he would not be offered the job. There was also a chance at one stage that he would become secretary of the Melbourne Cricket Club, but that did not eventuate. He had been asked to nominate for the job by a committee man and assured he would get the job. In the end, the chairman had the casting vote and used it in favour of the other candidate, Vernon Ransford.

While making the transition from cricket life to challenges after it, he used the first winter months of retirement to work on his autobiography, *Farewell to Cricket*, for the British publishers Hodder & Stoughton, which appeared in June 1950 and was serialised in *The People* in London. The book covered his career, but modestly skimmed over his major performances. Bradman took time to answer his critics and defend his actions and decisions, as well as putting his case on major issues such as bodyline. It sold well but naturally received mixed reviews. Some critics were irritated by the fact that the writer had a rational argument for everything he did. But this was Bradman.

On the playing field as captain, if he wanted a bowler to move a fieldsman he would explain exactly why each time. If a bowler wanted a move made, he would have to make sense of it to The Don. Bradman might disagree, but he would let the bowler try it if he wished. He never acted on the field or off on whim. He showed a similar approach in his book and in particular his analysis of bodyline was forceful and level-headed. Not surprisingly, it did not please Douglas Jardine, a commentator on the game since his retirement from the Test scene after 1933, who eagerly criticised his old adversary: 'A good deal of its interest lies in what the writer might have said and did not say, but it gives a picture of a rather lonely traveller.'

Above and beyond the attacks, however, *Farewell to Cricket* remained a cogent account of a life that dominated a sport like no other. No cricket library was complete without it. Over the years it became a classic of the sport.

INTERLUDE OF ANXIETY

In 1951, poliomyelitis struck South Australia, and among the victims was the athletically gifted twelve-year-old John Bradman. Jessie looked after him and Don was forced to give up many of the duties that took him interstate, such as those of national selector. 'John spent a year in a steel frame in this room,' Jessie said in their living room. 'We both bathed him and gave him therapy every day.'

At the end of this period of anxiety John recovered. He went on to be an outstanding 120-yard hurdler, setting a State record for the event. The experience of the illness was a further reminder of the gulf between the reality of life and the artifice of legend. While the image of Bradman seemed to have increased in stature rather than diminished like that of most sports people once they are off the public stage, he and Jessie in private were having more than the usual number of family tragedies and vital challenges. Again, Jessie was the family's rock in another personal crisis.

'I don't think Don would have got through many things [in the 1930s and 40s] like his own illnesses and the pressures on him,' a close friend told me, 'without Jessie. She is a magnificent person.'

It is a common thought about Jessie, whose strength through all their problems was also Don's strength. He had acknowledged this often in referring to their marriage as 'the greatest partnership of his life'. It transcended cricket, broking and every other endeavour he undertook.

They hated being apart from each other for long periods. But those days were over with his retirement. Now when he travelled to England for more than a fortnight, she accompanied him. For instance, in 1953 they went to London for the Test Series (won by England), which he covered for the *Daily Mail*. Bradman found himself sitting in the press-box next to Jardine, who was also writing for a paper. I asked him if they chatted to each other.

'Not really,' Bradman said with the hint of a wry smile. 'We occasionally disagreed about what was happening on the field.'

England's captain Len Hutton claimed that Bradman's incisive observations, especially about individual members of Lindsay Hassett's team, gave him an advantage on the field in the Tests. During the Second Test at Lord's, Hutton took Bradman aside and thanked him for the daily advice and tactical wisdom in the *Mail*.

BROKING AWAY

Bradman's own health, associated with his back and fibrositis problems, suffered so much under the strain of his broking and investment business that in June 1954 he retired from it at the age of forty-five. Len Bullock, the employee who had run it so competently in Bradman's absences, took it over. Bradman remained a consultant, but was able to take up a number of directorships with companies, which together brought him a similar income to his broking operations, but with far less stress. Over the next twenty-five years these included Endeavour Ltd; Centurion Ltd; Tecalemit Aust Pty Ltd; Kelvinator Aust Ltd; Argo Investments Ltd; Bounty Investments Ltd; Leo Investments Ltd; F. H. Faulding & Co Ltd. He was also an alternate director of Uniroyal Holdings Ltd, chairman of Wakefield Investments, and on the local advisory board of Mutual Acceptance Ltd. His move also allowed him more time for the occasional journalism and he again covered the 1956 series in England, which Australia again lost.

Bradman described his financial circumstances as 'comfortable' since that period, to which his ten-roomed home in Kensington Park was testimony, although he was irritated by false rumours that he had become a millionaire.

His next book for Hodder & Stoughton, *The Art of Cricket*, an illustrated manual on cricket technique, was published, again successfully, in 1958, the same year that his old nemesis Jardine died of lung cancer.

THROW-AWAY OBSERVATIONS

At the end of the 1958–59 season Richie Benaud's team at last restored Australia to superiority in the Ashes over England, but it had taken a decade since Bradman's retirement to achieve it. In that series, which Australia won four-nil, complaints were voiced about bowlers alleged to be 'chuckers'. The spotlight fell on the fast Victorian left-hander Ian Meckiff, who had been effective in the Tests taking seventeen wickets at 17.1 runs per wicket, but not the best bowler. Davidson (twenty-four at 19) and Benaud (thirty-one at 18.8) had more impact on the series. In England's second innings of the Second Test, Meckiff was devastating, taking six for 38 off 15.2 overs. I myself saw every ball delivered on that day and it would have been very difficult to tell with the naked eye whether he contravened the rules. Meckiff, lanky and long-armed, let the ball go with an unusual whip of his left wrist and an open-chested delivery. For the most part his action seemed legitimate. However, every now and then he let go a very quick one, which was regarded as dubious. In fairness to Meckiff, only analysis from slow-motion film could tell.

Bradman became chairman of a select committee on throwing in 1959, and in 1960 he and Board of Control chairman Bill Dowling travelled to London for a meeting of the International Cricket Conference (ICC), which was to discuss the issue on the agenda. Delegates watched films of bowlers' actions. A new definition of throwing was included in the laws of the game, but the matter was left in the hands of umpires, who had to adjudicate on deliveries. The issue was not yet resolved.

Not long after the London trip, Bradman was elected chairman of the Board of Control, the first former Test player to hold the position. He was also the unofficial chairman of selectors. Twelve years after his retirement from competition he had become the nation's cricket supremo.

DO AS I SAY AND USED TO PLAY

Bradman was respected by all the captains who came after him, including Richie Benaud. They got on well, especially after Australia's winning back of the Ashes in 1958–59 after a lean decade. However, the cricket had not enthused big crowds. Both the Australians and Peter May's England team had played a defensive series. Despite Australia's success, people stayed away in droves. The cricket, except for real enthusiasts, was boring. Then in 1960–61 the famous West Indies team led by Frank Worrell toured the country.

The night before the Brisbane Test against the West Indies, Bradman asked to address the players. He said the selectors would be predisposed towards individuals who played attractive, winning cricket — those who pulled in the crowds. Bradman was not bombastic, overbearing or insistent. He simply stated what was in the best interests of the game. Another dull five Tests following 1958–59 would be bad for the sport. Although there was little competition from other spectator sports in the summer of the 1960s, people had more disposable income than before the war, which meant they had a greater range of pleasure pursuits. Cricket was just one of many pastimes from boating to motoring and board-riding. It would die a slow death if it was not attractive.

Bradman's statement was timely. He had been behind the West Indies' last visit in 1951–52. They were a team of brilliant 'goers', who would have to be met with fight and aggression, or the series would be lost.

During the first 'Gabba' Test, the West Indies hit 453, Australia replied with 505, and then the West Indies compiled 284, setting Australia 233 to win in 314 minutes on the last day. On paper that looked a fairly feasible task. But an early batting collapse saw the home team staggering at six for 92, thanks mainly to the speed and fire of Wesley Hall. Australia was six for 110 at tea and in trouble with Benaud and Davidson the not-out batsmen. They had 123 to get to win in two hours' play. There was not a set number of overs to be bowled in the last hour, which meant that Benaud and Davidson, if still in, would have to contend with Worrell being able to slow the game right down if there was a chance the West Indies would lose.

The onus was very much on the Australians. Both Benaud and Davidson by nature were strong hitters. They either had to score fast while preserving their wickets, or defend. The latter was the less difficult option by far.

Bradman was among the 4,100 spectators at the game. He came into the dressing room at the short break, poured himself some tea and sat next to Benaud on the bench outside the room. According to Benaud, in a foreword to the book *Images of Bradman*, he was asked: 'What are the tactics?'

'We're going for a win,' Benaud replied. This meant some brave batting on the skipper's behalf. Yet it was a policy right in line with Bradman's advocacy on the eve of the Test. Benaud may have been inclined to play safe, but the advice had left him with a subtle pressure.

'Pleased to hear it,' was Bradman's laconic response, looking straight ahead.

Benaud (52) and Davidson (80) went for victory in a grand 134-run partnership and the policy paid off. The game ended with the teams tied in the most exciting finish ever to a Test. After that, crowds came back to the Tests in their tens of thousands. In the next Test match at Melbourne a world-record 90,800 people came through the gates on the Saturday. The series, which the home team won, was probably the most sensational ever played in Australia.

The Don's influence was still there, in his selections, advice and approach.

Significantly, Meckiff was not selected for the 1961 England Ashes tour. He had modified his action against the West Indies, but had been less effective. He had been injured in the Third Test and missed the fourth and fifth matches. His selection for England would have been a close call. But even Meckiff himself, though disappointed, accepted his form had not necessarily warranted selection in the seventeen-man tour squad.

When he did work his way back into the Australian Test team in 1963–64 against South Africa in Australia, he was called for throwing in the First Test in Brisbane. It forced him to retire from cricket. The problem was over.

INNOVATOR, FIRER, RELUCTANT POLITICIAN

In his role as a selector and chairman of the Board of Control, Bradman found that making decisions was invigorating and enjoyable, while at times also tough and onerous.

'I never criticise a selector after having been one,' he said with a rueful grin. 'It is the most difficult job.' He thinks a great selector's skill is being able to project a player's temperament into the first-class arena. Richie Benaud considers Bradman himself was the game's most outstanding selector.

One poignant selection or non-selection among many in his time as hirer and firer of the national side occurred in the 1965–66 Ashes series when Victorian left-hander Bob Cowper was made twelfth man for the Fourth Test at Adelaide. Cowper had played fairly well in the first three Tests, scoring 22, 99, 5, 60 and 0. But he was dropped because Bradman and his fellow selectors felt he had not been aggressive enough. In the previous Test in Sydney he had top-scored with 60 but it had taken over four hours. The Test side already had openers Lawry and Simpson who were sound rather than dashing players. Cowper, batting at first-wicket down, made a third. In came Keith Stackpole, Ian Chappell and Tom Veivers.

Cowper was naturally unhappy about his dumping, especially as he had not been a failure in the series. He was selected again for the Fifth Test at Melbourne and came back determined to make a point. He batted in his usual style and compiled 307, which was the only triple century ever made in a Test in Australia and beat Bradman's record of 299 not out against South Africa.

In the 1970–71 Ashes series in Australia, Bradman had more demanding problems as both chairman of the Board and a selector. A freak weather break during the first four days of the 1971 New Year Test at Melbourne caused the game to be washed out. It was a troubling time for the Board, which lost enormous revenue from the biggest crowd-pulling venue in the country. The spectators were also frustrated with no play. At very short notice, Bradman organised a one-day game between England and Australia which attracted 46,000 people. The home team won an exciting match. Bradman and the rest of the Board concluded it was a commercial winner. By chance, the international one-day game was born, eight years after England's internal one-day Gillette Cup began in 1963.

Bradman enjoys one-day cricket and regards it as a development in line with society's needs for fast entertainment. 'It's popular and we must provide entertaining cricket to help the game survive,' he said. 'It also helps subsidise the Test and Shield competitions.'

Bradman saw some artificialities in the shorter game, such as the disproportionate number of overs played by the opening batsmen. But on balance he supports it. He was a natural 'one-day' type himself. Depending on circumstances, he always played to hit the biggest number of runs in time to win a match. Putting an over-limit on his performances would have accentuated his approach and style. Bradman's leadership of the powerful 1948 side reflected a fast-scoring, big-hitting attitude, even at critical times in the Tests.

A less palatable event in the 1970–71 Test series was the unceremonious sacking of Australian skipper Bill Lawry after the Fourth Test in Adelaide. He learnt of his demise via a radio report on his way to the airport the morning after the Test. Australia had lost the series against a battling, relatively untalented England side led by the grittily determined Ray Illingworth. Lawry had followed on from the winning Benaud and Simpson leadership periods, but had run into defeats against South Africa and England. It was time for a change. Young South Australian Ian Chappell was appointed captain and the move ushered in a new and successful era in Australian cricket. It was Bradman's last important act as an Australian selector — a job he had held continuously from 1936 to 1971, except for the 1952–53 South African tour of Australia because of his son John's illness.

The Board of Control issued an invitation to South Africa to tour Australia in 1971–72, which was controversial in itself. The English

Cricket Council had been asked by the British Home Secretary to cancel a tour by the South Africans in 1970.

Bradman and the Board wanted the Springboks. They were the best team in the world at the time and would have created big gates, attacking cricket and powerful competition. A genuine political minority in Australia had awakened consciousness about the problems of apartheid.

Some politicians, trade unionists, church representatives, academics and other concerned citizens appealed to Bradman to stop the visit, while newspaper polls were registering that between sixty-five and seventy-five per cent of Australians were 'for' the visit.

Bradman did his homework and understood the issue beyond his apolitical invitation. On the one hand, he owed the visit to an eager cricket public. On the other were the broader moral issue and the confrontations the proposed tour might bring, with the resultant bad image for the country.

Bradman made a point of attending a Rugby Test with the South African Ambassador in 1970 and it had a profound effect on him. 'The ground was protected by barbed-wire barricades,' he said, 'and the police were ready for things such as smoke bombs and flares. But the barricades didn't stop the protesters. They invaded the arena.' He went away convinced that it would be impossible to police a cricket match. There would be violence. Any game would be ruined and cricket would be the worse for it.

This experience swayed him more than any other that any attempt to stage a tour would be dangerous and embarrassing to the nation. The Board met on 9 September 1971 and decided to cancel the tour. Bradman informed the press. It was difficult for him. He disliked being dragged into politics.

The cancellation left a void in 1971–72, but Bradman and the Board were quick to fill it by inviting a squad of great internationals to play for the Rest of the World (ROW) against Australia. It was a fine series, and included great players such as Gary Sobers, Rohan Kanhai and Clive Lloyd (West Indies); Intikhab Alam, Zaheer Abbas and Asif Masood (Pakistan); Sunil Gavaskar, 'Rooky' Engineer and Bishen Singh Bedi (India); Richard Hutton and Bob Taylor (England); Hilton Ackerman, Graeme Pollock and Tony Greig (South Africa); and Bob Cunis (NZ).

The tour was a success. The ROW won two, Australia one and two were drawn. Bradman thought Sobers' 254 in an innings at the MCG was the best performance he had seen in Australia. At the end of the tour the ROW team held a farewell dinner and invited only one guest, Bradman. The international players appreciated his efforts and skills in making the series work.

After the 1971–72 ROW tour, his second and final three-year term as Chairman of the Board was up. His services to the game had gone far beyond the call of duty, but he stayed on as a Board representative for South Australia. The exposure from the South African cancellation and the ROW maintained Bradman's profile in 1970 and 1971 and generated publicity, which he did not seek or care for.

In 1972, it became too much for Bradman's son, John. Jessie described his reaction:

> He was a tutor in law [later lecturer] at Adelaide University, and a legal VIP from the UK was visiting. Some in the faculty were introduced to him. When he met John, the person doing the introductions said 'And this is the son of Sir Donald Bradman.' That was the last straw for John. He went out and changed his name by deed-poll to Bradsen.

John is reported in Irvin Rosenwater's book, *Sir Donald Bradman*, to have said:

> I was popped in a metaphorical glass cage to be peered at or discussed. I am no longer prepared to accept being seriously introduced as simply someone's son. I am an individual not a social souvenir.

According to Jessie, 'we were fully in support' of John's decision. Bradman himself agreed. It was an unfortunate by-product of the legend, which never sat well with them.

By 1974, both were not in the best of health. Don was ill on a trip to London for an annual dinner of the Lord's Taverners, a charity fund-raising body, where he delivered the annual address. At sixty-five he was advised to restrict his activities and travel. He would undertake very few more public engagements and avoid work projects such as further book assignments. Jessie had heart trouble and contemplated open-heart surgery, then still in its early days. In 1978, she had an operation, which was successful and she regained good health.

WORLD WAR THREE

By 1975, Australia had regained pre-eminence in cricket thanks largely to the Chappell brothers, Ian and Greg, Dennis Lillee, Jeff Thomson and Rod Marsh. However, disgruntlement with 1975 Test match payments of just $400 a game, when gate receipts were exceptionally high, coincided with the desire of media proprietor Kerry Packer to buy the rights to televise Test cricket for his network Channel 9.

When the Australian Cricket Board (ACB) — as the Board of Control had been renamed in September 1973 — gave the rights to the ABC Government network, Packer, several entrepreneurs and cricketers combined to take over the game. Packer and his team saw the way in which Bradman had secured performances from internationals in 1971–72 in the ROW matches. They had taken note of the great success of the international one-day game in Melbourne. In what was commonly known as 'World War Three' in cricket circles, conflict between Packer and the cricket establishment broke out. Packer had the money and the TV network to buy players and stage games. The ACB had control of the game as it was traditionally known. Packer contracted enough players to stage matches but the ACB, with its influence right down to club level, forbade him and his outfit the use of grounds and even practice wickets.

By the time Bradman made a very rare public appearance and spoke at a dinner to mark the Centenary Test between England and Australia in March 1977, the Packer operation, known as World Series Cricket (WSC), was ready to begin. Packer tried to negotiate with the controllers of cricket worldwide — the ICC — to effect a compromise between his efforts and the established world of the sport, but talks broke down.

Bradman, while not in the front-line for the ACB, was very much against the outside intrusion and the wholesale buying of players. I asked him if, because of his own disputes with the Board of Control in the early 1930s, he had any sympathy with the players. He replied that there was no parallel with his case in 1932 (in agreeing to play cricket for Australia and write, coincidentally, for the papers of Kerry Packer's grandfather Robert Clyde Packer) and the players in 1977. But as regards the need for him in 1932, and the players of 1977, to make a living he acknowledged that times had changed since his day:

I had avoided being a professional. I would get to the office at 7 a.m. and then walk to the ground to play at 11 a.m. It wasn't unusual for me to arrive at the match, walk on the field in my suit and toss the coin. Straight after the game I would return to the office and work for several more hours. That could not happen today. There are so many additional tours — to the West Indies, Sri Lanka, Pakistan and India. Cricketers must be professional.

Packer went on with WSC in the season of 1977–78. His teams particularly depleted the Australian Test XI, which began to lose series. The result was costly for Packer and costly for the ACB. By some behind-the-scenes negotiations between Packer and NSW Labor leader Neville Wran, WSC was able in 1979 to get the lights on at the SCG for the staging of nationally televised night cricket, which was a big success. WSC began gaining revenue.

Eventually Packer and the ACB compromised. He secured the rights to televise Tests and the ACB regained control of the game and players, who were given watertight contracts, which allowed for greater remuneration in line with other sports.

The split in the camp left bitterness on both sides. But time heals, and cricket survived, more or less intact, with a highly popular one-day cricket programme thrown in.

53

TRUST
AND LEGACY

Sir Donald and the Foundation want the Museum to be a complete cricket centre, not just a place where one man is put on a pedestal.

— RICHARD MULVANEY, THE DIRECTOR OF THE BRADMAN MUSEUM

A VISION SPLENDID

In the early 1980s, Bowral lawyer Garry Barnsley thought the town would benefit from something special — perhaps a museum — to mark where Don Bradman grew up and began his cricket career. Tourist attractions alone would bring gains to the already affluent NSW landmark, which was known worldwide for just one reason. For decades people from around Australia and many other nations had drifted into the town in search of the legend. Where did he live? Where was the water tank? Where's the school he went to? Is that the oval where he made 234 against O'Reilly?

Barnsley was on to something. In the early 1980s, Sir Donald Bradman, AC (1979), happened to be on a golfing holiday in Bowral. The lawyer heard about the visit and approached him. Bradman was initially lukewarm to the museum concept — mainly because he was concerned that it could lead to further hero worship. Yet still Bradman was helpful. He would be more interested in a

cricket centre as such, rather than a musty memorial. Barnsley persevered and worked on more local community support for the idea.
The Bradman home in Glebe Street was at first identified as a likely
part of any museum. Then, in 1985, the NSW Government gave a
grant of $100,000 to start the project. The Wingecarribee Shire
Council formed a committee which was chaired by Barnsley. The
concept grew in scope from the Glebe Street home to a new museum
building on the Bradman Oval (so named in 1947) across the road
where the young Don began it all in 1925.

A notable early member of the committee was Bruce Collins, a
Sydney barrister with a home in Bowral. He energetically worked on
the project and attracted corporate sponsors, including the New
Zealand businessman and cricket lover Sir Ronald Brierley.

A Trust Foundation was formed and Sydney architects Devine,
Erby, Mazlin were contracted to build a two-stage, two-building
museum project. The first part was an attractive pavilion in the old
style with a gabled slate roof. Don and Jessie were now more enthusiastic with the concept's wider perspective. He donated documents
and equipment, such as cricket gear and bats. The Trust bought the
Glebe Street house.

In 1989, the Foundation hired Richard Mulvaney, then thirty-
one, to be the museum's director and curator. Mulvaney, a BA in Pre-
history from the ANU Canberra, who had followed up with a
Diploma of Museum Studies from Victoria College, Melbourne,
brought a professionalism to the project that has ensured it will meet
the standards of excellence Bradman brought to the game itself. An
archaeologist turned social historian, he worked at the Australian
War Memorial and the Australian Institute of Aboriginal Studies
before becoming the curator for three years of the Sovereign Hill historical complex in Ballarat, Victoria, which is a museum centre for
the old gold-mining district. It too became a big focus for tourists
wishing to comprehend an important historical part of Australia.
Now, Bradman's past is Bowral's gold.

Mulvaney took up residence in the old Bradman home in Glebe
Street, which will also later be a public attraction. Also in 1989, stage

one of the project — the pavilion — was opened. Don (then eighty-one) and Jessie (eighty) refused all offers of travel and motored from Adelaide to Bowral to attend. The Foundation had been helped by corporate sponsorship, but funding slowed in the recession. By the early 1990s, work was commenced on the second stage of the museum, a stunning, exquisitely designed two-storey building behind the pavilion. It is particularly sensitive to the Bradman Oval's park setting, which reminds visitors of the village green with an Australian flavour, determined by gum trees and a bush mountain backdrop rather than an English cathedral. The Museum aims to explain, explore and celebrate the history of Australian cricket, which is where Bradman, with his unparalleled comprehension and knowledge of the game and its background, has been a vital guiding force. Mulvaney's skills have been applied to direct the museum's activities and attractions to show cricket's place in the nation's culture. It is all meeting a grand vision and has the feel of a sophisticated, state-of-the-art dynamic exhibition.

The second building has four galleries. One is a changing exhibition space examining a topical issue in modern cricket. It might be the art of leg-spinning on one occasion, or the development of the game's laws on another.

'We'll consider everything,' Mulvaney remarked. 'Perhaps we will do something on advertising in cricket or even sledging.'

Other galleries will pay tribute to many great Australian cricketers.

There is also an eighty-seat theatrette to show films from what is expected to be an extensive film library. There will be a book collection for public research, and a collection of cricket photographs. Computer-driven interactive displays will allow visitors to sit down in front of a screen and test their eye-hand coordination as if they were facing Lindwall, Lillee or Larwood. They might then bowl to a computerised Bradman and feel the humiliation and frustration of being walloped or stroked for four through cover-point or mid-on.

Mulvaney, a curator with a modern approach, wants to avoid the image of a 'museum' in the stuffy sense of the past, and make it live. 'Visitors will experience the 1930s, for instance, in a lounge, where they will sit and listen to an original Test match broadcast,' he said.

He also wants to set up a water tank — a replica of the one where Bradman idled his way into cricket folklore and sporting history.

'People will be able to test their skills against Bradman's by hitting a golf ball with a cricket stump against the tank's eighteen-inch-high circular brick stand,' Mulvaney said. 'They will then comprehend how hard it is, but how a master of this simple activity would develop amazing skills.'

The Foundation's vision goes beyond that of the conventional museum and will encompass extra attractions. The oval itself is a sought-after venue for visiting teams and is ideal for touring sides. The Foundation runs coaching clinics, some for children from outside the area who live-in at a nearby college. A scholarship scheme has been set up for awards to young cricketers, who will attend Australian universities as well as Oxford, which has strong cricket traditions and is amenable to the concept.

'Women cricketers will be eligible in this and all other activities,' Mulvaney pointed out. 'One student a year will go to Oxford. She or he will have to be at first-class [cricket] level and have an honours degree from an Australian university. The individual will also have to be community-spirited.'

Each year the best young cricketer in the country receives the Sir Donald Bradman Award of Excellence as well as one of the 100 Gray-Nicholls bats signed by him. Winners include Darren Lehmann, Michael Bevan, Damien Martyn, Michael Slater and Matthew Hayden.

The Foundation has product and publishing arms. An example is a video of a coaching film Bradman made in the 1930s in England. People with cricketing backgrounds and connections are sending material such as diaries, which could be put into book form. The outstanding book, *Images of Bradman*, edited by Peter Allen and James Kemsley, was published by the Museum in 1994 and included more than 400 photographs, including rare archival prints.

The Foundation is also able to market and merchandise products using Bradman's name exclusively — which he signed over to the Foundation in 1992 — in order to provide further finance for the museum, its work and expansion.

'It means we can license his name and products around the world, in perpetuity,' Mulvaney commented, expressing the enormity of Bradman's generosity. Bradman himself will not receive a cent from the Foundation or any of its projects. Other Museum funds have come from private and corporate sponsors, and government sectors.

THE PACKER RAPPROCHEMENT

In March 1996, the Museum approached Australia's richest man, Kerry Packer, in the hope of securing funds to complete its second and most important building. Would Packer consider a telethon on his Nine Network to raise the necessary money to ensure completion? In exchange it was suggested that Bradman might just be persuaded to do an interview for the network's exclusive use. This was a considerable offer. Bradman had said *nyet* to every commercial television approach since the medium began in Australia in 1956.

Mulvaney had floated the idea of a TV interview with Bradman.

'To my surprise Sir Donald didn't reject the idea,' Mulvaney said. In the past, network offers from the UK and Australia had been knocked back. Kerry Packer's Nine Network was the most persistent.

In recent years (former Australian Prime Minister) Bob Hawke was rejected when he asked Bradman to be top of his 'wish-list' of famous people for interviews on *60 Minutes*. Hawke offered Bradman a six figure sum over lunch at the Bradman home. Bradman said 'No'. According to sources at *60 Minutes*, Hawke then told him:

'I'll even throw in $50,000 of my own money.'

Bradman responded with another unequivocal negative. Then Ray Martin, via his producers at his *Midday Show*, made another big offer. The Don again was not interested. But Bradman sent him a letter saying that if he ever did do a TV interview, it would be with Martin.

Later Mike Munro, host of Nine's *This Is Your Life*, wanted Bradman for his first star name of the series, but soon joined the long list of TV personalities who could not persuade him to face the all-intrusive tube.

Meanwhile, British TV host and sports journalist Michael Parkinson was trying everything to get Bradman to appear on the BBC. But he had pushed too hard with articles that wavered between pleas and frivolity, which didn't please his prospective target.

'The nearest I got to Sir Donald was at Adelaide (during the Ashes Test of 1994–95) a few days ago when I sat in the same row but fifteen people away,' Parkinson wrote in a UK *Daily Telegraph* article. He later joked that he held the tea cup that Bradman had used that day.

Bradman was amused by that but not Parkinson's habit of not letting the facts get in the way of a good story. He reported Harold Larwood as saying he had Bradman caught at the wicket before he had scored in the Leeds Ashes Test of 1930. It just didn't happen. The journalist also wrote a story concerning Bradman's first encounter with champion leg-spin bowler Bill O'Reilly in 1925 when Bowral played Wingello. Parkinson slipped in an apocryphal remark about the Wingello captain, Selby Jeffrey, lighting his pipe in slips and so missing a Bradman nick.

Five characteristics that stand out in Bradman are his concentration, determination, directness, sharp wit and, the one he prides the most, his integrity — which is linked to a near obsession about factual detail.

Parkinson received a letter of complaint from the Don, which expressed concern that he had cast doubts on Bradman's sportsmanship. Consequently, the Yorkshireman was off the Don's list of favourite journalists.

Kerry Packer, too, had not been high on Bradman's list of friends from the Fourth Estate ever since the mid-1970s when Packer tried to take over cricket with his World Series.

'Kerry saw the chance to bury the hatchet with Sir Donald,' a Channel Nine producer observed. Bradman invited Packer to lunch at his home at a date timed for Lady Bradman's return from hospital after successful chemotherapy treatment for her chronic leucaemia. The Bradmans were both suffering ill-health at the time but Packer would not have been aware of it had he not been forewarned. Lady Bradman turned on her legendary hospitality, including a three-course lunch.

The talk in the living room under the gaze of a large Bradman portrait centred on, not surprisingly, cricket. Packer and Bradman got on well. They are both direct of manner and, in their own style, accustomed to getting their own way. Kerry Packer's famous power of persuasion was in evidence as Bradman was talked around. Packer pointed out how important to the nation a visual document would be.

The deal was a telethon on Nine to raise the money to complete the Museum (which Packer would guarantee up to a million dollars). In exchange Nine would make a documentary based on interviews with a Nine journalist. It was an enormous coup for Packer and his network.

'Who would you like to do the interviewing?' Packer, the experienced salesman, asked Bradman. 'You can have anyone you like.'

'Ray Martin,' Bradman replied without equivocation, remembering his written commitment.

The Museum may become a shrine of sorts to Bradman, but he and the Foundation do not want this. They aim to make the structure a complete cricket centre, not just a place for worship of him and his career. Bradman wants to leave a great and lasting legacy to cricket and its impact on Australian culture, not a monument. This way the attraction of his name, the genius of his performances and the humanity of the individual will live on, and produce great things for the game.

THE REPUBLICAN MONARCHIST

The Museum's development is but one of many interests for Bradman in his retirement years, more than a decade after he relinquished links with the ACB in 1981. He plays eighteen holes of golf at least twice a week and with his handicap of 15 can beat his age. He is an avid sports watcher. Before one of our interviews early in 1995 he had been up all night watching Australia on TV beat the West Indies in the Fourth and deciding Test, and then the golf that followed. He likes Aussie Rules on TV and regards it as 'the best of all football codes'. Bradman still enjoys his billiards. He and Jessie play regular games of bridge with a group, and in a sense are enjoying life more than in the early days. They have more time together in their eighties and can enjoy the normal pleasures of everything from good wine and entertaining at home to a motoring holiday, such as the one they made for the opening of the Museum. As long as the media do not find out, they can check into a hotel en route in the country and possibly not even be recognised.

As ever, he wants his private life kept private. He reads widely and beyond cricket, although this is still his main interest. Bradman has two cricket libraries at his home, one in the billiards room and another in the upstairs study, where he has a complete set of *Wisden* year books. When we were checking some detail in the manuscript, Bradman often demonstrated his prodigious long-term memory by reaching for, say, *Wisden* in 1926, to recall a player's performance in a county game. Not only was it valuable having access to the subject of the biography, but it was invaluable being able to refer to his mental memory bank, which like his performances on the field would be difficult to match. Like all buffs, he is obsessed with the figures.

Bradman must surely be the buff's buff. He enjoys having access to all the numbers of all the first-class games ever played. While checking countless references over several months, I don't recall him being incorrect on any occasion. Yet he appreciates the descriptive word on the game as much. When I said how much I liked reading Cardus, he said 'Yes, but have you read Thompson?' I had not. He gave me a reference to a book dealer in London. He also subscribes to *Wisden*'s monthly magazine.

Bradman's pet hate then as now was not people wanting autographs, but those wanting his scrawl on the spot without supplying pen or paper. 'On one occasion a woman wheeling a pram asked me to sign an autograph because he would like it when he grew up,' he recalled. He wasn't interested. 'She had neither pencil nor paper.' At the age of eighty-seven, he was still plagued by this in quiet, leafy Kensington Park, Adelaide, almost half a century after he last played, he said ruefully:

I can't get to the corner without someone approaching me. Only last week when I was walking in the street, a chap pulled up in a car and asked, 'Are you Don Bradman?' There wasn't any point in saying 'no', so I said 'Yes, I'm Don Bradman'. He said he wanted my autograph. I asked if he had a pen and paper. The chap asked me to 'wait', pulled his car over, and entered a shop to get a pen and paper. Meanwhile, I had to just stand there . . .

I asked if he ever wished he didn't have fame and instant recognition. 'Yes, often,' he replied. 'I wish I never had it.' He went on to say that if he had another life he certainly would not want fame. He had never sought or chased it. He had little time for 'celebrities' or those who were 'famous for being famous'.

Something in Bradman's appeal has lingered over the generations and is worldwide. He even receives mail from nations he has never visited.

'Apart from the tour of England in 1948,' he said, 'when I got 600 letters a day, I'm getting more mail now than I did at the peak of my career.'

He makes a point each day of answering the sensible letters. People send him clippings of interest and he is in regular correspondence with old friends, especially in Britain. Bradman still types his cogent responses, punctuating them wherever possible with his sometimes gentle, sometimes wry wit.

Bradman stays abreast of modern politics and takes an interest in current issues such as the question of republicanism. I asked him about his feeling on the subject and it was the one issue on which he would not be drawn. Every indication would suggest he would naturally be a monarchist. It would be odd with his background and experiences if he were not. He was born only a few years after this country was federated, and developed an affection and affinity with the royals from 1930. Bradman is knighted and was a Freemason. He admires the stable institutions of parliament, democracy and the law, which have been inherited from Britain.

The contradiction in all this is the fact that Bradman did a great deal, arguably more than any other individual Australian in the twentieth century, to define a character that was distinctly, culturally Australian. He did not mimic the accents or demeanours of those from the Mother Country. Bradman used his skills to destroy and humiliate the representatives of England at every opportunity. He was always sporting and within the rules, but there are no beg-pardons in Test series, only winners and losers. He played it hard but fair, and while involving himself in the social niceties of the British tour, he made it plain by his performances and strategies that he wanted to conquer the English on the national sporting field, which was a substitute for war. The pitch was the place where the differences between nations were drawn out under specific rules of mostly peaceful combat. When Bradman, the Australian, looked like dominating cricket and embarrassing the seat of the Empire for decades, the British fought back, legally, in an attempt to ruin him with bodyline. More than any other person, he drew out the patriotism of Australians and to a marginally less extent the British, and created the feelings of 'them' and 'us'.

He gave a fledgling nation a sense of self and identity more than anyone else, clearly a motivating force in creating a republic. Unwittingly, he was an early, powerful republican.

A newspaper informed him in 1995 that he had been suggested as a possible first president of the Republic of Australia.

'I think I might be getting a bit old for it,' the eighty-seven-year-old Bradman said, dryly.

ONE IN TEN BILLION

Biochemist Charles Davies recently argued, scientifically at least, that Bradman was the greatest sportsman, not just cricketer, of all time. Davies looked at the best cricketers and found that his Test average of 99.94 runs every time he batted was more than fifty per cent higher than that of the next best players — Herbert Sutcliffe, George Hedley, Graeme Pollock and Sid Barnes — who all fell in the range of 60.73 to 60.97. Davies' analysis did not include the speed at which the runs were scored, the opposition or the situation of the game and series when they were made. On all counts, Bradman's performances would again be rated much higher than the others. For instance, Bradman often scored his runs under pressure when Australia was well-down in the series and great performances were required. This occurred in Ashes contests in 1928–29, 1930, 1932–33, 1934 and 1936–37. In the second half of his Test career, he also had the enormous added responsibility of captaincy.

If these factors were weighted and added, Davies' case would be even stronger. Yet it's convincing as it is. Using the so-called Bell statistical curve on a graph, he shows that Bradman's average is so far from the norm that we would have to wait for another million Test players before someone approaching it would emerge. The waiting, Davies reckons, would go on for 100,000 years. Making the conservative assumption that one in every 10,000 people (who at some time play the game) actually go on to Test level, the world would be searching for that one player in *ten billion*.

Davies says the Bell curve could be applied to all sports — even football, high-jumping, tennis, swimming and running, provided there was a defined and agreed yardstick. If a standard could be set with goals scored, times raced, metres reached, sets won and so on, Davies says he would be 'amazed if any other sportsman proved to be as far ahead of the pack as Bradman'.

That conclusion puts him ahead of Bjorn Borg, Mark Spitz, Rod Laver, Ron Barassi, Herb Elliott, Dawn Fraser, Greg Norman, Carl Lewis, Ayrton Senna, Jack Nicklaus — the lot. But beyond the stats, one thing is certain. There will never be another like *The Don*.

54

INTO THE
NINETIES AGAINST
THE ODDS

L ady Bradman died in October 1997, aged 88, leaving Don to
carry on alone, without the love, strength and support of his
'greatest partner', who sustained him through 65 years of marriage.
He feels the loss enormously; yet with close friends and family near,
he battles on. And as his 90th birthday approaches, he can look back
on a life blessed with true greatness, experienced by few, and
longevity against all odds. For him, every year has been a bonus since
the age of 25 when he was operated on for peritonitis, which was
expected to finish him. The life of this hard-headed pessimist and
survivor has spanned most of the 20th century, and Australia as a
nation.

Reading a book recently on his home town of Bowral, Bradman
recalled hopping on a horse used by the town's gas-lamp lighter and
helping the man with his task in the main street as early as 1918.

Ten years later, he burst onto the sporting scene, never to leave it
while cricket is played or sporting achievements are debated. In
1938, he captained Australia in England and in 1948, after the ravages of World War II, he led his country's finest ever side there for the
most successful tour ever.

In 1958 — forty years ago — his main sporting enemy, Douglas
Jardine, the charming Scottish-born lawyer with the iron will and
brutal bowling tactics aimed at destroying Bradman for the sake of

the British Empire, died of lung cancer. Another decade on Bradman was Australia's cricket supremo, presiding over the nation's dominance of the game.

By 1978, at 70, he was long-retired from administration and angry about the efforts of Kerry Packer to take control of the game. Away from that central plank of his public life, he was enjoying himself more than ever with his wife Jessie, secure after his successful career as a stockbroker and professional company director, and searching for the privacy he never attained.

By 1988, moves were afoot for building the Bradman Museum. In April 1998, while avoiding all public appearances in his quest for 'rest and privacy', Bradman did attend an Adelaide function for his 1948 Test team of 'invincibles' to celebrate the 50th anniversary of their unbeaten tour of England. He was in good form, described by Sam Loxton as 'chipper'. Reflecting on his four score and ten, could he be judged — as every Prime Minister since the 1930s has — to have stood above such exalted individuals in Australia's short history as John Monash, Weary Dunlop, Mark Oliphant and Arthur Boyd? It is impossible to measure, but two things are certain: he is the greatest Australian sportsman ever and the leading popular figure in our nation's history, at home and internationally, notwithstanding Ned Kelly.

In common with those other high achievers in war, art and science, he is immune to praise about his skills and is concerned only with his own measure of achievement in his main craft: cricket. During the interview for *The Don*, we discussed what was his best innings ever. I suggested it was his 334 at Leeds in 1930, when he hit 309 not out in a day — still arguably the top batting feat in two hundred years of the game. Bradman plumbed for his 254 at Lord's earlier in the 1930 Test Series.

'It was the best I played in a technical sense,' Don said. 'Every ball went where it was intended, even the one that got me out.'

Bradman, the perfectionist, concentrated on limiting the number of false strokes he would make in a day's dashing batting. If he made one it was too many. Bradman cared little for what others thought of his performances. He marched to his own inner drum that told him how well he was travelling.

Apart from the amazing sporting achievements that set him apart, what was the real Bradman character like? Before I started this biography, I had heard intimidating rumors: he could be blunt; he didn't suffer intelligent people gladly, let alone fools. I was warned that he wouldn't cooperate with Dean Golya — the photographer who accompanied me — for more than five minutes on the first day of interviews at Bradman's Adelaide home. I didn't know if any of these stories were accurate or just the usual myths about a famous individual. We arranged the interviews through mail, and had yet to meet.

I hired a car, so if Dean were 'dismissed' after a few minutes at Bradman's house, he could explore Adelaide while the interview went on. On that hot February day in 1995, Lady Jessie Bradman, 85, radiant and courteous, greeted us at the front door with the disconcerting news that Don had a toothache. Dean glanced at me. Would this mean he would make it even tougher for him to steal a few shots? Lady Bradman showed us into the famous living-room with its emphasis on floral furniture and decorations. Seconds later, Bradman appeared in casual attire.

His physique was taut, with sinewy, strong forearms — the limbs that had thumped a cricket ball more often per innings and with more timing and power, pound for pound, than any other cricketer.

'What do you want?' he said in that familiar nasal voice as he opened his hands to us, indicating that he was at our disposal. I would ask questions while Dean took spontaneous shots.

'Fine,' said the Don, settling himself on a sofa. Dean proceeded to take around 400 photographs from many angles over the next six hours of interview. So much for the warnings about photographers. The Don was oblivious of the ubiquitous camera, capturing him in the longest portrait session he has ever given. Dean secured what was required. I did not want an old man in repose, as interesting as such impressions can be. The aim was to portray him as he approached 90 — intellectually vigorous, humorous, pensive, thoughtful and with powers of concentration that would put any monk to shame. Add a refreshing directness and integrity and you have much of the Bradman character and demeanor. The Don said that he wanted to be remembered above all for integrity. He should have no fear. It was writer Raymond Chandler who said *honesty is an art.* The Don has it down to a fine art.

It is worth quoting English cricket writer Sir Neville Cardus, who once described a Bradman innings thus: 'It was never uninteresting; he simply abstained from vanity and rhetoric.' Such were his responses to hundreds of questions I put to him on that first day and over the ensuing five months. His answers were button-down, logical and without a misplaced syllable. Allied to his succinct use of the language was an obsession with accuracy, which bordered on eccentricity. Australian Cricket Board staff would often send him written information for comment or approval. The Don would send some letters back. The request would be ignored; instead, there would be grammatical corrections scribbled in the margins.

I was thankful for his humour. For a few seconds here and there his impassive, impenetrable visage would transform into George Burns, *sans* cigar:

Q: *How would you go against the recent crop of great West Indian fast bowlers? What would your average be?*
A: About 50.
Q: *50? Why 50? That's half your actual average . . .*
A: Well, I will be 88 next birthday.
Q: *How did you keep fit as a youngster?*
A: I chopped a lot of wood.
Q: *Modern top cricketers do a lot of training to keep fit: weights, sprints, distance running, callisthenics, diet and so on. How did you keep fit as a first-class cricketer?*
A: I did a lot of running between the wickets.

The first interview session went an hour over the allotted time. I decided The Don had been too generous and called a halt.

'I enjoyed that,' he said with a grin as he bounced off the sofa. 'Dean, would you like more shots?'

We moved to the front garden for more photos. Dean tried to get him to smile. He wouldn't. Dean appealed silently to me. I stood behind The Don and tried a joke.

'Just think, Sir Don, you'll be able to tell your grandchildren you were photographed with one of Australia's great writers.' The Don laughed and loosened up enough for Dean to capture him smiling.

Lady Bradman joined us on the porch for the best photos taken of her in her twilight years. They caught her mature beauty and grace.

I completed the biography over the next five months, with countless other interviews, usually over the phone. The Don would send me helpful items — even some of the more bizarre letters he received from around the world, names and addresses withheld.

At the end of the project he asked if he could read the book, which was not part of our original arrangement. We had agreed that it was to be 'unauthorised'; no-one would interfere with the editorial.

'I only want to check the manuscript for factual errors,' The Don explained. I agreed, having come to know him as vanity-free and not precious about fair criticism. I sent the book overnight to him in Adelaide. A day later, I received a phone call. He had read it — all 250,000 words. What's more, he had typed notes — four pages of them — of comments and mistakes. I was stunned. In my experience, no editor had ever read through a sizeable manuscript so fast and efficiently. Of course, he knew the terrain; it was *his* life. Yet his attention to information he had never seen before was remarkable. Could I make another trip to Adelaide to discuss it? I arrived a few days later. Anticipating Lady Bradman's hospitality, I brought flowers. Don greeted me at the door at 9.30 a.m.

'Oh, thanks a lot,' he said, reaching for the flowers.

'They're for Jessie.'

'Oh,' he said. 'Why doesn't anyone ever bring me flowers? They're always for Jessie.'

The Don led me upstairs, passed his favourite action portrait of himself executing a cover drive, and into the inner sanctum — the Bradman study. It was small and dominated by a cricket library featuring a complete set of Wisden year books, one of only two private sets in the world. We sat opposite each other at a card table, each with a copy of the manuscript, and began sifting through his eighty points. I was relieved to find he had mainly picked up literals and typing errors. He made no reference — as anticipated — to the 'editorial' that considered his character and style.

'. . . Now, point 14, you have me going out to bat at Leeds, flanked by two *bury* policemen,' he said, looking over his glasses at me like a benign schoolmaster. 'You mean *burly*, don't you?'

The Don loved a malaprop: 'Point 24. You've got here that I "did it for prosperity". You mean posterity, don't you?'

We began slicing through the manuscript, stopping for coffee mid-morning and a drink in the living-room at noon. By now, The Don's amazing recall was coming into play. He was certain, for instance, that he had hit his first run ever in his maiden innings at Lord's, in 1930, to mid-off. I had it rolling to mid-on. He asked for my sources. I produced three. He squinted into the distance of 65 years and, with the unbombastic certitude of his peculiar brilliance, described the shot and who ran across from where to field it.

'I remember it particularly,' he said. 'It was my first Test run at Lord's.' There could be no argument.

Bradman's Test average of 99.94 or rounded off, a century every time he went out to bat, was well known. *Un*known was his average from the time he first played competitively at eleven years until his first full season of cricket at sixteen years. I checked several sources and came up with 166, an indication for those who had cared to check his efforts by 1923, that the 'Boy from Bowral' might just be extraordinary. The Don, point 35, questioned this.

'I think you've given me one too many innings,' he said, indicating a particular match for Bowral when he was fourteen. Again, the question: 'What are your sources?'

The Don listened. Unconvinced, he stood up, wandered over to his library and pulled out a tiny 1922–23 scorebook. He was correct, once more. We made our re-calculations and arrived at the same figure (which will one day make a trivial pursuit question) — 187. A more testing question for sporting buffs would be the boy Bradman's school-boy average. The answer? He didn't have one. It stood at infinity — he was never dismissed in a school match. (A fact that caused other schools to avoid playing Bowral High if Bradman were selected to play against them. He was just too good and made any contest one-sided.)

The Don also queried the position of one hit made in his record as the fastest century-maker in any game of cricket anywhere in the world. Bradman had moved from 54 to 154 in just 12 minutes in a 1931 match between a combined Blue Mountains team and the Lithgow Pottery Cricket Club. He noticed that in the three (then eight-ball) overs he took to score the runs, I had one scoring shot in incorrect sequence. The list of shots was 6, 6, 4, 2, 4, 4, 6, 1 (first over, 33 runs), 6, 4, 4, 6, 6, 4, 6, 4 (second over, 40 runs) and 6, 6, 1, 4, 4, 6 (third over, 27 runs).

There was method in his exceptional attention to detail. The Don was a perfectionist in everything he did. Cricket just happened to be his first choice of sport. He sat an umpire's exam at 24 years and qualified to stand in first-class matches. Forty years later, Colin (now Lord) Cowdrey invited him to play Royal Tennis in London. The Don asked for the thick rule book and studied it overnight before he played.

'Don knew the rules better than me and I'd been playing the game for years,' Cowdrey told me.

Coupled with this absorption of such knowledge was his attitude to technical development in any sport. He took the cliche 'practice makes perfect' to another dimension. A case in point was his application to billiards. As mentioned earlier, he played world champion Walter Lindrum one Adelaide night in 1935. Lindrum asked him to 'break' first. The Don reached 57. Lindrum, the king of the cue, then made a break of 100. This riled The Don's competitive spirit. He had a billiards room built into his new home in Kensington Park. According to Lady Bradman, he practised almost every day for a year before inviting Lindrum to play him again. This time, Bradman matched Lindrum in a break of 100 plus.

At age forty, when he retired from cricket, he turned his formidable mind to golf. Within weeks he had ironed out the cricket movements that had produced the greatest shot range the game had seen, but which made it difficult to hit low golf scores. The result was the rhythm of a professional golfer, breaking par at every course he played.

Bradman's approach was always to apply his mind to any sport's history, then its rules and parameters and, finally, use his physical agility and talent to play as well as he could. It's not surprising that his book, *The Art of Cricket*, first published in 1957, is still the finest instructional work on the game. Having studied the game as if he were taking a Masters degree, The Don then reduced it to its basics in demonstrating how it should be performed.

This total command of his chosen sport has given him outstanding vision. He showed this early in his career, when comparing baseball with cricket in a discussion with American star baseballer, Babe Ruth, in 1931. Ruth wanted to know what impressed The Don about the American game. The reply surprised him. The Don thought the skill levels were comparable. It was the professional presentation of baseball that attracted him. He predicted cricket might one day have to be better marketed to survive.

In 1939, he pleaded in Wisden for cricket to adapt to the quickening tempo of modern life, and for administrators to consider ways of speeding up the game. He urged that cricket should be seen as public entertainment and called for more modern scoreboards, especially in England. The Don suggested the game's planners should keep up with financial problems.

Twenty-one years on, it was The Don who introduced one-day cricket to Australia when a Melbourne Test match against England was washed out during the 1970–71 Ashes series. The concept alarmed purists, but not him; he saw it as a necessary accessory to keep the game popular and financial.

In 1986, he again demonstrated prescience when he suggested that instant TV replays should be used for run-outs, stumpings and disputed catches. By the mid-1990s only disputed catches had yet to be decided with the aid of technology.

As ever, Lady Bradman's great hospitality was evident at lunch on that final day of reviewing *The Don*. She brought in help to prepare a three-course meal, complete with excellent wines. During the break, we relaxed and discussed issues other than cricket. The Bradmans proved to be a well-informed couple on everything from politics to the republican debate. Bradman and I coasted through the remaining points in the manuscript in the afternoon, and discussed many things, including Lady Bradman's health. She had suffered for years from chronic leukemia. The Don's deep love and respect for her courage and character came up, as it had in several previous discussions.

'She'll be telling people how well she feels on the day she dies,' he said. There is no doubt that her strength sustained him through thick and thin, and the Bradmans' long relationship saw plenty of the latter, especially in health matters concerning them and their children.

We discussed 'fame' and how it had destroyed others, from sportspeople to entertainers such as Elvis Presley. The Don had held onto his small-town, family values no matter with whom he mixed, which strengthened, rather than diminished, his character and being. He felt for Boris Becker, who would not be able to visit any country without being recognised. Tennis stars — more than cricketers — could hide nowhere.

I asked him, if he had his time over again, would he want fame.

'No,' he said emphatically. 'I hate it.'

Despite The Don's heartfelt disdain for the limelight, he could never escape it. Something in the Bradman mystique has lingered over the most of the twentieth century.

Those letters keep pouring in from all over the world, long after he retired from circket in 1948. He has replied to about a million of them in that polite and tight style. Each recipient would probably place the response among his or her most treasured documents, creating a strong enough Bradman constituency in itself.

Add to that perhaps another 20 million items, from bats and balls to books and portraits, that he signed over seventy years — all held dear by their owners and passed on through generations — and there is a mighty Bradman supporter base that will linger for centuries yet. It helps explain why The Don maintained his fame and affection *out there*, rather than avoided it. His legendary status had been secured during the Depression years when he performed at his peak as a batsman. Whether in school, country, club, state or Test innings, he entertained over three decades with an astonishing consistency unmatched in sporting history. Whenever The Don batted, the full-house sign went up and spectators were treated to his flashing blade. Like the mighty horse, Phar Lap, The Don was a sure thing, scoring long, big and fast, and lifting the spirits of all who watched. Bradman was to Test and state cricket then what the one-day version of the game is to the survival of cricket today — a huge crowd-puller.

That memorable day with the Bradmans ended with coffee in the evening followed by another three-course meal. A taxi arrived. The Don thumped the car's bonnet in a last gesture of farewell. As we drove away, the driver asked: 'Was that who I thought it was?'

I only needed to say 'yes'.

Discussions over the book didn't end there. I had shown The Don my choice of the front cover photograph. Lady Bradman liked it. He was more circumspect, but didn't object. I had chosen a non-cliched shot of him, waiting to bat at age twenty in a Shield game for NSW, in which he scored a triple century. His casual cross-legged stance and enigmatic gaze spelt both cool determination and pensiveness. It was a look that meant despair and disaster for a thousand bowlers. Out of 1500 photos I judged it to be the most telling portrait of Bradman, the great competitor.

The Don had other ideas. When the book's editor at Pan Macmillan, Amanda Hemmings, sent him a copy of the cover, he wrote to her complaining that his cricket attire needed a clean-up. He was wearing a NSW jacket and he appeared glum. I rang Don and explained my choice, adding that his pads could be air-brushed. Further, the fact that he was wearing a NSW blazer was irrelevant. Everyone who knew his name associated it first with representing Australia. I argued that, rather than glum, he looked determined. Having had many discussions with him up to this point, I realised when he remained unconvinced.

'What's more, the editor [Amanda Hemmings] said you look sexy,' I said as a last resort.

'She's fifty years too late,' he quipped. It was the argument-breaker. The photo was in. That wry wit, which I suspect has kept him sane through an eternity of adulation and attacks, is always lurking. Given his batting average, the symmetry of the obvious head-line cliche prevalent as he reaches the milestone of ninety years, 'Bradman into the 90s,' will please his numerate brain, despite his observation that 'old-age is no fun.'

MILLENNIUM MAN

As the Millennium grew closer, Bradman gave 'audiences' to fewer people, although top cricketers with a little persuasion from inter-mediaries could gain face to face meetings. On his ninetieth birthday Bradman had tea with India's Sachin Tendulkar and Shane Warne, two of his favourite cricketers. They discussed bowlers such as Bill O'Reilly, whom Bradman bracketed with Clarrie Grimmett and Warne as the best leg-spinners ever. Tendulkar, who Bradman regarded as the world's best contemporary bat, queried the Don about his stance and backlift.

Bradman had met Warne and liked him. He was very impressed with Tendulkar as a cricketer and character, who he expected to go on to bigger things in an already outstanding career. He hoped Warne would come back (he was overcoming shoulder surgery at the time) and acknowledged him as Australia's biggest 'entertainer' in several decades — an individual drawcard who was terrific for the game.

After Mark Taylor equalled his Australian world Test record with a score of 334 not out in Pakistan, Bradman wrote to him on 16 November 1998:

Might I take the opportunity of congratulating you on your wonderful batting performance overseas during which you equalled my 334. It was extremely generous of you to declare when our scores were level — a most sportsmanlike act — when you could have so easily gone on to take the record for yourself. Your recognition of the interests of the team will never be forgotten. May I wish you personally and team the best of luck in the forthcoming Tests.

The South Australian Cricket Association arranged for Taylor to meet Bradman at his home on 9 December 1998, two days before the Adelaide Test (always a time when the pressure was on Bradman to see visitors), the third of the 1998–99 Ashes series. Taylor expected it to be tough going and he wondered what he would say for two hours. He was surprised (as have been many contemporary cricketers) at how well informed his host was and how interested he was in current events in the game. Bradman wanted to get Taylor's version of the bribery affair, and the involvement of Mark Waugh and Shane Warne. He asked about all the Pakistani players, including Salim Malik, who had tried and failed to bribe Warne, Tim May and Mark Waugh. Taylor did manage to ask Bradman some questions. One was about Archie Jackson.

Taylor's 334 innings made him comprehend better the pressures on Bradman. Now the ordinary things in life, Taylor noted in his book, *Time to Declare,* such as a restaurant meal, were more difficult to do with friends and family without interruption from mostly well-meaning fans, who nevertheless invaded his privacy. He appreciated Bradman had experienced this kind of attention for seven decades.

Early in August 1999, Steve Waugh was granted a meeting. Waugh was torn between being part-journalist and part fellow captain exchanging intelligence. Waugh wanted to know how Bradman would combat Tendulkar in three Tests against India that were about to be played. The Don let that one go through to the keeper, preferring to not give advice beyond what he had already said about the champion Indian. (In 1996, he noted that Tendulkar used a heavy bat, which he hinted could be his undoing on Australia's bouncier wickets, provided bowlers were equipped to deliver top class deliveries moving away outside the off stump.)

The last months of 1999 brought Bradman, then 91, more than ever into the spotlight that he abhorred. Media around the world began rating their top sportsman and people for the century and Bradman figured prominently, even occasionally in the US, that has yet to be rated above Holland as a cricket nation. Bradman took all the sports awards in Australia as the country's greatest sportsperson. In England, London's *Daily Telegraph* named him second only to Muhammad Ali as the top sports performer.

Twenty world experts also chose Bradman as captain of Australia's Team of the twentieth century. He would rather not have the attention but felt obligated when asked to respond to awards. Bradman either made media statements or sent his son John as his emissary. An instance of this was a reply at a televised ABC top sportsperson award.

The one that meant most to him was being named one of *Wisden's* Five Cricketers of the twentieth century. One hundred cricket experts and commentators were asked for their best five. Every one of them chose Bradman. Ninety chose Gary Sobers, followed by Jack Hobbs (30), Viv Richards (25) and Shane Warne (27).

ORATION FOR A NATION

On 17 August 2000, ten days before Bradman's ninety-second birthday, the Australian Cricket Board held its inaugural Sir Donald Bradman Oration at the Australian Club in Melbourne. The event was the brainchild of its chief executive, Malcolm Speed. The first ever speech was delivered by Prime Minister John Howard. It didn't have quite the verve of an extemporaneous address he gave at the opening of the Museum at Bowral in August 1996. Then Howard was like an old style politician on the hustings speaking about something that genuinely moved him. His oratory was outstanding. When I mentioned this to him on the Oration night, he said he was compelled to read his speech this time. He wanted it to be accurate for the distinguished audience of mainly cricket aficionados.

It was an excellent and fitting beginning to an event sure to become a tradition. Howard's words were from the heart. Bradman was his hero. Like every national leader before him stretching back to Billy Hughes in 1930, Howard through his love of the game had helped lift the cricketer to 'greatest living Australian' status, a most demanding, daunting epithet, even for Bradman.

Now the Prime Minister examined why Bradman had been 'elevated to the honoured status that he now occupies in the nation's psyche.'

'It could be said that his place was assured by his unparalleled record at the crease and certainly no exponent of the game has neared his achievement,' he said. During the Depression, 'Australia was in desperate need of a hero and his cricket helped lift the spirit of the nation. It held us together when the squalid sentence of mass un-employment risked splitting apart the social fabric of the nation. His message of hope carried through the country by the new medium of radio, which could not only reach but also inspire vast numbers of the population.

'He reminded Australians that they were capable of great things in their own right, that at a time when confidence ebbed away from their collective soul, they were competitive, resourceful and talented people.'

'They were well and truly separated from England, comprised a sovereign nation and displayed an egalitarian individualism that was uniquely Australian.'

John Bradman, displaying a quiet dignity and eloquence on a night attended also by his children Tom, Greta and Nicholas, responded well and paid tribute to his father, describing him as his 'warm and close friend.'

'He really has been very touched by the honour of this occasion . . . it is very true that he remains unimpressed by himself.'

Before the speeches, a film was shown of some highlights of Bradman's career. Commenting on this, John said:

I have a complex tangle of emotions seeing those films of my father. One of my favourite images is of my father after the duck (in his last Test innings) . . . tossing his head and wandering off . . . no fuss! . . . that's the man he is.

John added:

What does he stand for? I hope we can go beyond hero worship and try and understand what figures like him mean to the community. One letter he received was from two young brothers. 'Dear Don Bradman. We are having an argument about whether you are alive or dead. Please reply and let us know which one of us is right.'

The proverbial pin could not be heard crashing to the floor as John then read his father's address to the dinner:

Little did my parents dream that on 27 August 1908 their new-born son would have an oration named after him and delivered by the Prime Minister. On their behalf I thank the Australian Cricket Board for the idea and our most distinguished citizen for so generously giving his time to deliver the Address.

There was no radio or TV in my days as a toddler but somehow I developed a love of cricket which has stayed with me for nearly 90 years.

My father never made a century in his life but always wore with pride a gold medal on his watch chain for some bowling feat.

Whilst my mother prepared the evening meal I persuaded him to bowl to me in the back yard. In those humble days I was taught the rudiments of the game which consumed so much of my later life.

As my days on earth so rapidly draw to a close, I am proud to have set an example of all that is best in our noble game.

My father took me to a Test match in Sydney in 1921 and I was so impressed that I told him I would never be happy until I played there.

Today the Bradman Museum stands where I played in my youth and I hope it will forever stand as a monument to our game. Despite recent sad developments, cricket will survive and remain our most noble game and I shall always remain proud of the part I played in its history and development.

These words had all the humility, simplicity, poignancy and integrity that so distinguished the man over most of the last century.

THE NOT SO GOOD BRADMAN DRIVE

The year 2000 brought a problem that Bradman didn't need as he turned 92. In 1999 he sanctioned the renaming of west Adelaide's Burbridge Road to Sir Donald Bradman Drive. Signs of trouble first emerged when a café owner on the road moved to change her business's name to *Bradman Café Restaurant*. The Bradman Foundation threatened legal action.

But it could not stop businesses on the road clamouring to change their titles to include the new name. Even a sex shop moved to call itself *Erotica on Bradman*. It upset him and his family.

Bradman wanted the renaming scrapped. But West Torrens City Council, demonstrating bureaucratic and insensitive rigidity, said it was too late. The renaming had been gazetted on 3 August 2000. Road signs had been completed. About 2000 businesses and residents had been informed the changes would take effect on 1 January 2001. But prime minister John Howard came to the rescue of his friend by changing the law to protect Bradman's name. From 13 October 2000, a 'Bradman clause' was made part of the corporations law regulations to stop commercial exploitation of the Don's name.

There was more trouble in November 2000 with allegations that a publisher had tried to sell some personal letters from Bradman. The media outcry that followed caused denials from the publisher and selling agents. The letters were not sold.

More pleasant was a visit to Sydney just prior to the Sydney Olympic Games by freedom fighter Nelson Mandela. The great man had wanted to meet the Don at a summit on 'What Makes a Champion', but Bradman had long ago withdrawn from all public engagements. Instead he forwarded an autographed picture and message that was read to Mandela by actor Jack Thompson.

It said:

> *I wish to convey a very warm welcome and my very best wishes to Mr Mandela. I revere Mr Mandela for his courage under adversity, his integrity on the world stage as a statesman and his compassion for mankind. I acknowledge Mr Mandela as a champion of humanity.*

Mandela had long regarded Bradman as a hero. On 12 March 1986, when visited in prison in South Africa by a group of seven 'eminent persons', including Australia's former Prime Minister, Malcolm Fraser, one of the first questions he asked them was: 'is Don Bradman still alive?'

It seemed to have been a question that exercised the great and not so great, reflecting the fact that Bradman had become, while he was alive, larger than life. His feats and reputation had long passed into legend.

Postscript

Sir Donald Bradman died peacefully in his sleep with his family around him at his Adelaide home early on the morning of Sunday 25 February 2001. He had finally succumbed to pneumonia, after a ten-week illness. He was 92.

He leaves a great legacy as a cricketer, and a man of high principles and integrity. Don Bradman had many gifts, but his gift of inspiration to sport is perhaps the most important.

SAINT DON: THE SYMBOL OF TWENTIETH CENTURY AUSTRALIA

Freedom fighter Nelson Mandela said on his visit to Australia in 2000 that Don Bradman was 'one of the divinity.' Mandela, a keen Australia-watcher and sports lover all his life, would know, wouldn't he? The question is why? Why would this *cricketer* and son of a country carpenter be so regarded by the most humane human being of the twentieth century and the bulk of Australia and the cricketing world?

The complete answer could not be his ranking as second only to Muhammad Ali by many international expert analysts as the greatest sportsperson of the last one hundred years. It certainly is a factor, but not *the* factor in bestowing a kind of Sainthood on Bradman. But just because his two-decade record at the top of his chosen sport placed him statistically at least 40 per cent better than the rest of the best, it does not translate to deification, hero-worship or immortality. It's not enough. Nor is the fact that he was around for most of the century.

Legends and Saints are more often than not created from those who die young. Consider Jesus Christ, Julius Caesar, Phar Lap or even Diana, Princess of Wales. Bradman lived two to ten times longer than them and proved an amazingly durable, positive and awe-inspiring identity. Instead of dropping off as a hero after he retired from cricket at 40, his status grew and grew and never stopped. It wasn't for want of trying *not* to be hero-worshipped. There are plenty of media people since his retirement that have experienced the wrath of Bradman for an indiscretion, a rudeness, an invasion of his precious privacy, or simply because they wished to produce the ten millionth piece of media coverage of him. Instead of ingratiating himself with members of the Fourth Estate he treated them with at times thinly veiled contempt and eschewed them. This is not in the rulebook of those who seek fame. Pandering to media requests or grovelling to it at every opportunity is among the top dictates for achieving conventional recognition and status. Yet it is the media that has mostly pandered to him. For more than seventy years, the Bradman 'mystique' developed around his inaccessibility. His name and anything vaguely associated with it was cause for a news item with a photo and footage. A sportsman like Tiger Woods? Write a piece or make a documentary about excellence in sport and make sure there is reference to, and 'visual' of the Don. A brilliant new Indian cricketer? Prepare a radio broadcast or an Internet item and be sure to include comparative figures for when they were both 12 years old, with photos. A popularity contest? Put Bradman in it to spice it up. A new sporting stadium? Include a Bradman room and send out a mass media release with his name in the first paragraph to grab attention. Want a group of 'leading Australians' for a poll to see who would be the peoples' choice for the first President of the Republic? Pop in his name. Top of the list for opening the Olympics in Sydney or the Commonwealth Games in Melbourne? Suggest Don.

So is there a clue to his 'divinity' or ever-lasting fame here? Become famous at something — anything — and then shut yourself off from the world for the rest of your life so that the mystery about you grows? We saw it happen with former British Foreign office spy and espionage fiction writer, John Le Carré. He finally cracked after 20 years as a ghost walking around Cornwall and Hampstead Heath and became a media 'personality' and 'raconteur'. Trouble is, his outstanding writing seemed to lack a certain verve after his coming out of the reclusive closet. He was human after all and enjoyed fame as much as anyone else. But not Bradman. It took him forty years to appear on commercial television in 1996. He only did it then because Kerry Packer gave $1.2 million to complete the building of the Bradman Museum at Bowral. Bradman, as was his want, did not receive a cent of that donation. And he hated the whole ordeal of exposure, made worse for him by a stroke at 87. In one way he was closer to 1930s screen actress Greta Garbo, who unwillingly created an enigma by 'retiring' youngish as a filmstar and stating 'she wanted to be alone.' Yet Bradman did not actually retire from cricket. He was a key administrator (as a state and national selector and member of Boards) until he was well into his seventies in the early 1980s. He could hardly be alone and without influence. But he still preferred the backroom to the media room. It wasn't that he couldn't handle the media. Nobody did it better when it came to a succinct thought, direct statement, or good photo opportunity if it had to be had. It was just that he thought the media limelight was mostly superfluous, to be used as a vehicle for a message, not for vanity or ego boosting.

Even if he were a young man today, you couldn't imagine Bradman becoming a media star — an ex-captain pontificating on television, although in his early days he had a radio spot and at times wrote for newspapers on Test cricket. As it was, he chose, or more accurately, circumstances chose, stockbroking as his profession. Bradman at 26, disappeared (when he wasn't playing cricket) into the confidential world of stocks and shares. With the exception of Rene Rivkin, it is essentially a world of grey people in suits. If you wished to avoid media attention it was as good as the morgue, and nearly as unpublic as the upper echelons of banking.

This attempt to become grey and anonymous failed to give him privacy but instead enhanced his aura until long ago his image made him seem to many commentators to be akin to an Australian version of royalty. There were differences. The British Royals were more or less born to it. Bradman's elevation was due to substance. He earned it. The royals had to exude that doubtful trait of 'charm.' Bradman's charm was that apart from exhibiting all the normal niceties at public events, he was always transparently *him*. He seemed incapable of small talk — another reason for avoiding, if he could, functions, where small-talking champions aired their skills. Perhaps the only Royals he was really like were the Duke of Edinburgh and his daughter, and particularly the latter. Bradman, like Princess Anne, was capable of telling media people to 'naf off.' This endeared him (and her) to the media more. In a manner, this attitude embodied what intrinsic royal 'power' was about. The media were there to serve as a vehicle, and as servants, were not to be pandered to. As long as this power was not abused, at least not in public, it would be maintained. A key divergence here is that Bradman never needed the media, it needed him. Without media support, or without a continual presence through the media, the British Royals would have been reduced to riding bikes and smaller habitation, like their counterparts in Holland.

Bradman avoided politics. Both major parties wanted him. Labour party officials listened to his accent, took into account his roots and thought he was ideal for them. The conservatives looked at his job, noticed how all 'classes' of Australian society admired him, and claimed him as one of them. Bradman gave a decided *nyat* to becoming a politician, although he did flirt with being a diplomat — as Australia's high commissioner to the UK. By not becoming a political partisan Bradman enhanced or at least maintained his image as the 'greatest Australian ever born', or 'greatest living Australian', or even the 'most significant Australian (in terms of image) of the twentieth century.' Where say half the population might admire a Gough Whitlam, the other half for reasons of political sympathy would not. Thus Bradman by the end of the twentieth century was far more universally popular — polls suggest at least twice as popular — as any politician from Billy Hughes to Bob Hawke.

The substance beneath the mythology was created by the perfect coincidence between Bradman's incredible feats with the bat and

Australia's decline into a miserable economic depression that lasted from the late 1920s to the mid-1930s, a seven-year period.

In 1927 Prime Minister Bruce opened the new Federal Parliament in Canberra, moved his office there and announced that Australia 'was on the threshold of achievement.' This remark was a good argument for those critics who suggested politicians based in Canberra would be isolated from the real world. Yet when it was uttered the world looked, not rosy, but not ugly to the average Australian, who was unaware of the impact of over-borrowing in London by Australia and especially New South Wales. Bradman at this moment of false national optimism was unknown outside those following Grade cricket in Sydney. At 18, he had made his debut at the St George Club with a run-a-minute innings of 110 before being run out. Yet his first season (an aggregate of 289 runs at 48.16 in six completed innings) was not world shattering. The fact that he made 320 not out for his country team Bowral in April 1927 was simply not newsworthy even in Sydney.

In late October 1928, the price of wheat and wool (both then essential to Australia's prosperity) fell through the floor. Bruce's 'threshold of achievement' was suddenly, shockingly, the edge of an abyss. Right on cue, young Don, now 20, crashed a compelling double for NSW versus Queensland at Brisbane's Exhibition Ground, scoring 133 and 131 not out. In a flash the unknown was being talked about as a prospect to make the Test team to play against Percy Chapman's English tourists. He made it and scored a century in his second Test.

A few months later in January 1929, a loan issue for the Commonwealth of Australia collapsed with 84 per cent of it not taken up and left in the hands of underwriters. Precisely at the moment Bradman cracked a formidable 340 not out for NSW versus Victoria at Sydney, a feat that was reported on the front page of every Australian paper right up against items about the ramifications of the loan collapse.

In the Test arena, England, mainly due to Hammond with the bat (a massive 905 runs in the 1928–29 Tests at an average of 113.33

from nine innings) was giving a weak Australian attack a walloping. The only consistent hope in the wake of this onslaught was the form of Bradman. Spectators jammed all the grounds to see him and will him on against the English. He and Australia were at once the underdog. Yet there was another dimension to the feeling among fans. English financiers were dictating to Australia how to manage its economy. This amounted to deflationary measures and an increase in the cost of borrowing — a squeeze that was putting, and would continue to put, enormous numbers of Australians out of work. The England players, then, were symbolic of the patronising pressure being put on the 'colonials.' They were heckled. Douglas Jardine, then a most accomplished bat, was a target. His harlequin cap and neck choker seemed to the fans to represent the arrogant, insensitive image of the British establishment that was seen to be creating tough times.

At the time of his 340 — a score that signalled this gifted newcomer would challenge Hammond as world champion run-plunderer — the economic crisis became personal for Bradman. He lost his job at Deer Westbrook's Sydney real-estate office. It had been set up to sell housing estates, but this type of operation went flat in the sudden 'recession'. (It was yet to be labelled a depression.) Bradman, who had left school at 14 and had no qualification apart from his real-estate work, felt the humiliating experience of being, not a creator of magic statistics, but an unprepossessing one himself. Unemployment in the first quarter of 1929 rose from 9.3 per cent to an alarming 12.1 per cent. Wherever Bradman went around Sydney he saw what the *Labour Daily* called 'ill-dressed, sad-eyed and gaunt-faced men' gathering outside government Labour Bureaux to collect their meagre food rations. These could be exchanged for meat, groceries and other items and then redeemed from the government in cash by the shopkeeper.

It worried Bradman. But he didn't need to join the dole queues. Mick Simmons' sports store employed him. He hated the job but was grateful for work. It took the pressure off and he celebrated by being the match-winner against England with 123 and 37 not out in the Fifth Test at Melbourne. The crowd was near hysterical at this result.

For a few precious days the nation could submerge the mental anguish over the bleak immediate future and celebrate. England had been defeated. Bradman was proving the champion the fans had predicted (and prayed) he would be. By the end of the series only Hammond had performed better.

Through 1929, the recession deteriorated into the Great Depression, triggered by the Crash on Wall Street. Wool and wheat prices fell to rock bottom. Overseas loans from England, the monetary lifeblood of an over-extended nation, evaporated. A countrywide drought added an uncontrollable physical element to the deplorable conditions in the country.

At the beginning of the 1929–30 season, Australia's export revenues were plummeting. Half of it (heading for under 100 million pounds) would be used to service foreign debt, which meant that much less was available for loans. The banks restricted the amount of money on offer and interest rates climbed. Taxes went on non-essential items like cricket bats and tennis rackets. The squeeze threatened Mick Simmons. Bradman wondered if he would be out of work again.

Instead of panicking he went out and made runs. Fans flocked even to second grade games in the bush to see him. Saturday afternoons at St George were a lockout. So were Shield games. He cranked up for first-class matches, including 157 against a touring MCC side. Then he smashed a breath-taking double hundred *and* a century in the trial game to decide the team for the 1930 Ashes tour of England. It was exhilarating. The fans — the masses of people from every walk of life who filled the arenas around the country — felt somehow symbiotically linked to this unassuming youthful new champion. They had cheered for him before he had been proven at the highest level, screamed when he was dropped from the Test side for one game, applauded as he caught up with their dreams. Everyone from battlers to bankers felt a part of his rise and rise. They looked in the mirror and saw a bit of hope, a reflection of Bradman in all of them. They had willed him on, prayed for him and gloated with bravado about what he would do to the Poms in England. Figures and averages began to spill onto the sports pages in the country, in Sydney and across the nation. In five categories of the game in 1929–30 from second grade to first class, Bradman was averaging more than a hundred every time he batted. No one had done anything like this, not even the great Victor Trumper and certainly not the English champion W.G. Grace. In a desperate, dispiriting summer, here was someone to take the collective mind occasionally off the continual bad news as businesses crashed, farmers committed suicide and dole lines stretched around the blocks in every city.

And finally in early January 1930, just as everyone dreaded entering another fearful year of economic malaise, he performed in such a way that put him in a dimension all his own. The location was Sydney; the opponents Queensland. Bradman smashed and accumulated 452 not out in 415 minutes. It was an act of sporting obliteration at once both brutal and poetic. It was the highest score by anyone anywhere in first class cricket. This innings was beyond any dream by anyone except the performer himself. More importantly it was a show that inspired and made everyone who saw it, read or heard about it, proud that one of their own, a humble country kid at that, could reach such perfection. He didn't give a chance, not one in just under seven hours of precision carving up of the opposition. What's more, he wanted to go on to 600. He was more than a little miffed that his skipper, Kippax, declared when he was setting himself to do it. Bradman's hunger was mindboggling, his powers of concentration super-human and his stamina formidable.

Australians began to speculate seriously now that he might just challenge the might of England in their own backyard. And while this was being discussed in innumerable pubs, churches, businesses, homes and schools, the economic disaster subsuming the country was momentarily, here and there, forgotten. Bradman, at the lowest point in a fledgling nation's short history was one ray of hope. There was nothing else, certainly not on a national, unifying level, that could deliver.

When Bradman reached England for the first time those moments of distraction fused into a long running drama for Australia as millions followed the fortunes of Bill Woodfull's team. They read with anger that despite Bradman opening the tour under the cathedral at Worcester with a big double hundred, English critics were applying psychological warfare tactics by suggesting their hero was flawed. Australian indignation was reserved more for this than the squalor of the now well-set Depression. Bradman, aware, but unaffected by praise or attacks, launched on and on. At the Oval against Surrey, he silenced one of his biggest critics, the county's captain, Percy Fender, by making 252 not out in a dazzling 290 minutes. Only the rain stopped Bradman going on to 400. It was a portent of things to come. And they came in a torrent of run-making that may never be bettered in Test cricket. He scored 974 runs from seven innings at an average of 139.14. It was a performance that more or less matched say, the combined Test averages of Ian Chappell, Neil Harvey and Stan McCabe, or in another instance, Arthur Morris, Lindsay Hassett and Bill Ponsford. Instead of his career superiority of being nearly twice as good statistically as the rest of the greats of the game, he was, in that one glorious English summer, worth three top batsmen from any era.

In that huge aggregate, he hit four different kinds of innings that could truly be called unsurpassable exhibitions of each batting 'genre.' In the first Test at Trent Bridge he hit a fighting 131 in 260 minutes, which was hailed as one of the finest ever rear-guard performances in the final, uphill innings of a Test (lost by Australia). In the Second Test, he hit 254 in 320 minutes. Bradman himself claimed it as technically the best innings he ever played. In the Fourth Test at Leeds, he scored 334 — 309 of them in a day, a feat yet to be equalled in Test history. Its supremacy was in the speed of accumulation — the fastest first day pre-lunch century ever, and 220 by tea. At the Oval he hit a series winning 232 — a pressure knock on a difficult wicket against a strong attack that included a hostile Harold Larwood.

At the precise moment in July 1930 that he was reaching the heights with that mighty triple hundred, Sir Otto Niemeyer, a director of the Bank of England, was in Australia advising its leaders to 'balance its budgets,' stop raising loans and cut back on expenditure on public works. This was accepted in a supine way by the Australian establishment, including James Scullin's ruling Labour Government. It led to a further spiral into the Depression's void.

Bradman's batting appeared a symbolic whack back at Otto and his peers. Those Australians who comprehended the ramifications of what the English bankers were advising cheered him on with extra venom.

Bradman came home the conquering hero. He had, in the modern, crude Aussie vernacular, 'stuck it up the Poms.' This in itself gave the local collective psyche an immeasurable boost, especially as Otto and his English bankers and financiers mates were increasingly blamed (over the next few years) for the nation's plight.

Right at the depth of the Depression, Bradman had dispensed hope, pride and inspiration. He had also humiliated the rulers of the British Empire, something that no other foreigner, in peace or wartime, had been able to do in several hundred years. The Empire reacted. It felt compelled to attempt to put 'that little bastard' as England's new captain, Douglas Jardine, called Bradman, in his place. The tiny (in population) Dominion backwater in the 'far, Far East' had to be pushed back into line.

Jardine, one of the Empire's establishment sons (born in Scotland, brought up in India, educated at Westminster and Oxford, a lawyer) was just the disciplinarian to do it. He symbolised all that was detested in the image of *Great Britain* by the Australians across the board from the strong Labour voting Irish Catholic population to those even with conservative British heritage. His haughty manner, dress, and real hate for Australians (ever since Warwick Armstrong had denied him a century for Oxford against his all conquering tourists in 1921) was familiar to crowds. Jardine didn't smile on the field; he didn't have the will, wit or humour to respond in a placatory way to the crass catcalls and banal chants such as 'Jardine, sardine.' Even a bow may have saved the day. Yet on second thought, even if that had worked in 1928–29, it would never have done in 1932–33 while his pacemen — Larwood, Bill Voce — two toughies from down coal-mines in Nottingham — and Bill Bowes, hurled down 'bodyline.' This was the infamous method of bowling designed to maim and intimidate batsmen. Any 'fingers up' from Jardine would have created a riot.

He resented the abuse he received in 1928–29 with a passion that added to his desire to bring Bradman down in front of his adoring fans. Jardine didn't quite succeed. Bradman was too clever to be brutalised as he set about devising a daring method to counter-act Bodyline. But Jardine did reduce him to half his effectiveness (an average of 56 resulted, which was still better than anyone else on either side) in previous Test series encounters against England, the West Indies and South Africa. It was enough to send the Ashes back to England.

The whole Bodyline affair served to elevate Bradman to martyrdom. He was now not just the great sporting hero. He was the target for foul-play by the former Colonial masters, who had been seen to show their true colours. There were serious mutterings about Australia withdrawing from the Commonwealth and becoming a Republic. Then in 1934, Bradman returned to England to conquer it again with further masterful innings at critical times (304 at Leeds and 244 at the Oval). These critical performances were made while suffering from a deadly illness to which he all but succumbed after making a supreme effort for his country. Heroism, martyrdom, and the impression that he was even prepared to die for his country on the playing field, cemented his image beyond the stuff of legend and myth. And Bradman was still only 26 years.

These phenomenal developments on the cricket field go some way to explaining why his image was so outstanding over the last seven decades of the twentieth century. But there were other traits and issues at play that would sustain it.

Bradman was diplomatic in public. There may not be a public record of his criticism of any other person. Even in private he rarely directly expressed ill feeling towards anyone, although it's safe to say he must have had his dislikes. You don't become the tallest of tall poppies in Australia without creating enemies. He was aware of which members of the media or the cricket fraternity were against him. When Bill O'Reilly and Jack Fingelton tried to get rid of him as captain of Australia in 1936–37, Bradman went public and called for unity in the fight against the common foe — England. This diffused the issue and Australia united to defeat England 3:2 (thanks mainly to Bradman's great batting again, this time with scores of 270, 212 and 169) after losing the first two Tests. Yet under-currents flowed for decades afterwards.

Fingelton blamed Bradman for his non-selection of the 1934 Ashes tour of England (Bradman, when asked, advised selectors that Bill Brown was a better bat on English soil) and was viewed as 'the ring-leader' of a minority cabal against the captain in 1936–37. Fingelton was supported by O'Reilly. Their dislike for the Don was precipitated by cricket events but deepened by the sectarianism of the time, which had two extremes. On one side were the Irish Roman Catholics who voted Labour and resented the monarchy and British Empire — the inspiration for the modern-day Republican move-ment. On the other side were those who were Empire-supporting English by origin and Protestants who voted conservative and resented Papal connections. Among the second group were Free-masons, who formed a secret society and pledged their allegiances to 'King and Empire.' Bradman, at the direction of his skipper, Alan Kippax, at the Sydney St George cricket Club in 1930, had become a Freemason. But he was never a very active member. When he moved to less sectarian-split Adelaide in 1935 he let his Freemason-connections lapse. Yet Fingelton and O'Reilly noted the link. O'Reilly had never come to terms with the thrashings he had taken from Bradman at the wicket, beginning in a country match when they both still youths. His disgruntlement was exacerbated by Brad-man's early wowserism. After belting O'Reilly around the park, or when dismissed on occasions by the 'best bowler' he ever faced, he didn't wish to 'mix with the boys' and have a drink after stumps were drawn. You got the impression from O'Reilly that if Bradman had been a mixer, the leg-spinner may have been better disposed towards him. But his aloofness at first bothered and later rankled him.

O'Reilly and Fingelton implied that Bradman's lack of post-match socialising was connected to his being a Freemason. It was a useful excuse in their minds for bringing Bradman down. It led to baseless rumours about him being anti-Catholic. It stuck for decades with a small number of the Church's hierarchy and conspiracy theorists including a few journalists who wished to stir the pot. Yet it was far from the truth. He fought for the selection of talented players with Irish background. Like him, they played it hard but fair. They put serious passion into playing against England yet enjoyed their cricket.

In 1936–37 Bradman was a selector, who backed seven Test players of Irish descent — the most in cricket history. In the case of rugged Victorian speedster Laurie Nash, he argued strongly at the selection table and won. Nash's biographer, E.A. Wallish, claimed that Bradman threatened to resign as a player and selector if Nash was not picked. Bradman denied this in a letter to me late in 2000. He wrote:

> . . . *there was never the slightest suggestion that the selection committee might resign if he was not approved. There were rumblings from the English captain (Gubby Allen) but that amounted to nothing.*

Rumours abounded at the time that the Board was against Nash's selection (which Bradman also denied). But if some of its members were not happy with him, Bradman's argument for him won them over. Having experienced Bodyline, he wanted to make sure he had the aggressive, in-form paceman in the team for the Fifth and deciding Test of the 1936–37 Ashes. Besides this Bradman was fond of Nash because of his character and courage.

'He wanted to perform even when fatigued,' he told me. 'He carried injuries from his (Aussie Rules) football but never complained.'

Skipper Bill Woodfull refused to consider Nash in 1932–33 because it would have started a tit-for-tat Bodyline war. But Bradman wanted him in as both an insurance policy against Bodyliner Voce being tempted to use it again against Australian batsmen, and an intimidatory weapon. Bradman played psychological warfare games with the English over whether he would select Nash for the final Test on the MCG. They only learned on the day of the match that he was playing. They were beaten before the contest began.

The accusations against Bradman did not wash with the other Catholics in the side — Leo O'Brien, Chuck Fleetwood-Smith, Ernie McCormick, (who all liked and respected Bradman) and Stan McCabe, who regarded Bradman as a 'mate.'

Fingelton seemed ambivalent. He wrote a book that suggested Victor Trumper was a better batsman than Bradman. Yet he also produced a compelling tome, *Brightly Fades the Don*, on Bradman's triumphant all conquering tour of England in 1948. O'Reilly was open about his dislike for Bradman, although he was always quick to say Bradman was the greatest bat who ever lived. As the decades rolled on the bad blood created by him and Fingelton surfaced and was carried to their graves. In O'Reilly's case it went beyond it.

In the mid-1990s information in tapes made by O'Reilly that were critical of Bradman was released posthumously by a journalist in a pre-arranged spurious beat up. The tapes were long on hyperbole and devoid of specifics but received wide publicity. Justifying his bizarre act, O'Reilly said he didn't criticise Bradman in public while he (O'Reilly) was alive because he 'didn't want to piss on a national monument.'

When I asked Bradman for a reaction, he replied, 'In principal, I agree with Bill that you shouldn't desecrate a national monument.' He paused and a characteristic half-grin formed before he added, 'And if there were a national monument to Bill, and even if it was on fire, I would never desecrate it.'

He appeared the statesman, while his detractors were reduced to seeming like miserable hatchet men. When questioned (over five years) about certain individuals he only once replied with open criticism of a cricketer.

'Oh, him,' he said, 'he's hopeless, always has been.'

The rest of the time he made his point by a subtle remark, a look or a non-comment, or he rationalised why someone was against him.

What did he think of Douglas Jardine?

'He was a very good bat,' he said, deadpan.

Bradman let his guard down once on Clarrie Grimmett, the great leg-spinner, who wasn't selected for the 1938 Ashes tour of England.

'He was difficult to captain,' he remarked, intimating that he wanted loyalty on the tour and that Grimmett would give him trouble.

Bradman saw his former NSW skipper Alan Kippax as 'jealous', which may well have been true. The Bowral Boy came along in the late 1920s and over-shadowed his record (and everyone else's) to such an extent that Kippax, who had a fair Test record (34 innings at an average of 36.12), felt he didn't receive the accolades he thought were due to him. His sports store in Sydney also struggled against that of Mick Simmons, who employed Bradman as a front-of-store glad-hander.

You couldn't say Bradman loved to hate like say, writer Patrick White or NSW premier Jack Lang, men who bore grudges and continually honed them. But he certainly privately wished to find ways to take on attackers, and seemed to relish such challenges. Before he stopped playing he said nothing and let his blade and leadership do the talking, which made fools of critics for two decades. On retirement, he received a criticism — some of it malicious, most of it empty. But as he said, he had to 'take it on the chin'. If he judged it fair and factual, he didn't let it bother him.

The Bradman legend began in the depression, was enhanced by near-martyrdom during Bodyline and remained untouched by the behind-the-scenes battles over his style and early captaincy. His ruth-less application of cricketing genius allowed him and Australia to rule world cricket from 1930 to 1948 except for the 1932–33 blip of Bodyline. This strengthened his image ever further until he retired in 1949 and was knighted. That accounts for his unshakeable hold on the title of 'Greatest Australian ever born' for half of the last century. But what of the other half?

His faults centred on a tendency to be unpalatably direct, especially for the pompous, those impressed by their own importance, wasters of his precious time and the hundreds of users and hangers on over the decades who wanted a piece of him — from journalists to business-men. Yet over-riding this was a person of exceptional integrity and character: humble, vanity free and quick to make a generous comment about another, if merited. In private he was humorous with a sharp wit and interested in others' views. These features came through over the decades coupled with other important factors that extended, maintained and built the legend of Australian twentieth century legends from 1950 to 2000 and beyond.

First, no one came remotely near Bradman's batting record. His average and big innings grew in proportion as the decades rolled by. Second, he became the most prolific and expert letter writer of the era, sending out an estimated 1.3 million letters in response to the five or six million he received over his lifetime. It was the only way Bradman could reach out personally to his correspondents. Written responses became a habit — a self-imposed obligation to his count-less fans worldwide. This developed into an obsession, even an addiction. Most recipients of any reply from him placed it among their most prized possessions. The result was a huge constituency of supporters, from the world's movers and shakers to the most humble. Bradman's clear, concise prose, often with a witty or penetrating line reflected his outstanding mind, and made you comprehend in a small way what bowlers, or opponents in any competitive environment, faced. Third, he did endless work for charity, mostly in private and without help, which he couldn't really afford. Apart from sitting down at his battered portable in his modest upstairs study every day for at least four hours, most days of every week would see him sign-ing or writing something for worthy causes, or just fans. If that seems unimpressive on the surface, think of anyone devoting everything to others half a day of every day for seven decades, even well into their nineties. How Bradman stayed sane and on top of this output is remarkable, especially when there was mail overload on his birthday and at Christmas. Then a truck was needed to deliver it all to him personally. At times he wrote to me that the mail was 'driving him insane' as he tried to keep on top of it.

On his 90th birthday he told me:

'I've a pile of mail you couldn't jump over.'

After that, it overwhelmed and depressed him, and he needed secretarial help provided by the Bradman Museum.

Apart from all this, Australia never had a 'hero of the people' who quite matched Bradman, even in the second half of the century, with the exception of champion swimmer Dawn Fraser, who collected gold at three different Olympics from 1956 to 1960. Bob Menzies was a towering figure for two decades, but never had support from Labor voters — about half the constituency needed to challenge the Don. Bob Hawke's star flashed across the sky of popularity for a while in the 1980s, but he diminished his public image to a degree by a grab for post prime ministerial money (you had to pay him for an interview) from his many business contacts from China to Canberra. Malcolm Fraser did better by doing endless 'good works' for a foreign care agency and signing up for worthy causes at home, such as Aborigine rights and the Republic. But it didn't bring him hero worship. His aloofness, patrician bearing and lack of charisma would never qualify him as a 'man of the people.' Barry Jones was a hugely popular figure, and a rare bird in Australia — an admired intellectual — after his gallant performances in Bob Dyer's pick-a-box TV quiz show. But when he disappeared from our screens about 1960 he didn't bob up again until he joined the Labour Party, which turned off half his 'fame' constituency.

Bradman was named by *Time* magazine alongside Rupert Murdoch as an Australian among the first 100 most influential figures of the twentieth century. Think of it. 'Our Don Bradman' mixing it with Mandela, Ghandi and Churchill. On one level, he did. Ghandi expressed a fervent hope to meet him, but was assassinated before he could. Bradman did mix it with Britain's mighty war-time leader. He was leaving Victoria station London in 1934 when Churchill used journalist connections to arrange a meeting and a photo opportunity. Winston needed Don, but Don would have avoided the meeting if he could. Mandela regarded him as a hero and was keen to meet him on two visits to Australia. Bradman, an admirer of the freedom fighter, was too ill each time.

Murdoch, a high achiever by any measure, never excited the masses, and harmed his limited popularity by becoming an American citizen. Swimmer Kieren Perkin, a wonderful modern 'role model,' stopped the nation and caused the heart to beat faster during the 1996 Atlanta Olympics, as did Kathy Freeman at Sydney in 2000. Aviators Bert Hinkler and Charles Kingsford Smith soared for a short period and caused hats to be thrown in the air. Scientists such as pathologist Howard Florey and nuclear physicist Mark Oliphant had their moments, but their fine work with experimentation did not draw regular enthusiastic applause. Poring over penicillin dishes and magnetrons were not spectator sports. This did not invalidate them as 'greater' Australians than the Don. They were. Florey had an enormous impact on medicine. Oliphant changed the course of World War Two with his work on the atomic bomb and radar. But these high achievers were much less known.

Perhaps only Phar Lap, the fabulous stayer with the big heart, challenged Bradman as Australia's number one icon. Yet he would be disqualified, not because he wasn't human. His winning record made him the punters' favourite for a few years, but his early death limited his claim.

If you were looking for one image, one face, one performer, one communicator that most represented Australia in the twentieth century, it had to be Donald George Bradman.

THE DON
STATISTICAL
RECORD

* Not out
+ Retired hurt

FIRST-CLASS CAREER

Debut: 1927/28 New South Wales v South Australia, Adelaide

Season	Country	M	Inn	NO	Runs	HS	0s	50	100	Avrge	Ct	St	Runs	Wkts	Avrge	Best
1927/28		5	10	1	416	134*	1	1	2	46.22	1	-	66	2	33.00	2/41
1928/29		13	24	6	1690	340*	-	5	7	93.89	3	-	139	3	46.33	1/26
1929/30		11	16	2	1586	452*	-	4	5	113.29	4	-	300	4	75.00	2/93
1930	England	27	36	6	2960	334	-	5	10	98.67	12	-	301	12	25.08	3/35
1930/31		12	18	-	1422	258	1	4	5	79.00	7	-	184	4	46.00	3/54
1931/32		10	13	1	1403	299*	2	-	7	116.92	5	-	54	1	54.00	1/4
1932/33		11	21	2	1171	238	1	7	3	61.63	6	-	230	6	38.33	2/106
1933/34		7	11	2	1192	253	-	4	5	132.44	4	-	69	1	69.00	1/30
1934	England	22	27	3	2020	304	2	6	7	84.17	9	-	0	-	-	-
1935/36		8	9	-	1173	369	1	1	4	130.33	7	-	0	-	-	-
1936/37		12	19	1	1552	270	2	2	6	86.22	10	-	-	-	-	-
1937/38		12	18	2	1437	246	-	5	7	89.81	13	1	-	-	-	-
1938	England	20	26	5	2429	278	-	5	13	115.67	8	-	6	-	-	-
1938/39		7	7	1	919	225	-	-	6	153.17	3	-	0	1	0.00	1/0
1939/40		9	15	3	1475	267	1	4	5	122.92	11	-	-	-	-	-
1940/41		2	4	-	18	12	2	-	-	4.50	-	-	-	-	-	-
1945/46		2	3	1	232	112	-	2	1	116.00	1	-	-	-	-	-
1946/47		9	14	1	1032	234	1	4	4	79.38	4	-	-	-	-	-
1947/48		9	12	2	1296	201	-	1	8	129.60	9	-	4	-	-	-
1948	England	23	31	4	2428	187	2	8	11	89.93	11	-	2	-	-	2/12
1948/49		3	4	-	216	123	-	1	1	54.00	3	-	12	2	6.00	2/12
Total		234	338	43	28067	452*	16	69	117	95.14	131	1	1367	36	37.97	3/35

	M	Inn	NO	Runs	HS	0s	50	100	Avrge	Ct	St	Runs	Wkts	Avrge	Best
Test Cricket	52	80	10	6996	334	7	13	29	99.94	32	-	72	2	36.00	1/8
Sheffield Shield	62	96	15	8926	452*	5	20	36	110.20	38	1	444	12	37.00	3/54
Opponents															
AL Hassett's XI	2	3	-	186	123	-	1	1	62.00	1	-	12	2	6.00	2/12
Australian Services	1	1	-	112	112	-	-	1	112.00	-	-	-	-	-	-
Australian XI	1	2	-	19	14	-	-	-	9.50	-	-	36	1	36.00	1/36
Cambridge University	3	3	-	169	137	1	-	1	56.33	1	-	103	6	17.17	3/35
Derbyshire	3	4	1	183	71	-	2	-	61.00	2	-	24	1	24.00	1/24
England XI	5	5	1	546	149*	-	2	3	136.50	1	-	59	3	19.67	3/52
ENGLAND	37	63	7	5028	334	6	12	19	89.79	20	-	51	1	51.00	1/23
Essex	1	1	-	187	187	-	-	1	187.00	-	-	-	-	-	-
Gentlemen of England	2	2	-	254	150	-	-	2	127.00	2	-	-	-	-	-
Glamorgan	2	3	1	94	58	-	1	-	47.00	2	-	-	-	-	-
Hampshire	3	3	1	336	191	1	-	2	168.00	4	-	-	-	-	-
HDG Leveson-Gower's XI	1	1	-	153	153	-	1	1	153.00	-	-	2	-	-	-
INDIA	5	6	2	715	201	-	1	4	178.75	6	-	4	-	-	-
Indians	2	4	-	366	172	-	-	2	91.50	1	-	-	-	-	-
J Ryder's XI	1	2	-	349	225	-	-	2	174.50	1	-	56	1	56.00	1/56
KE Rigg's XI	1	1	-	118	118	-	-	1	118.00	-	-	0	1	0.00	1/0
Kent	4	4	1	355	205*	-	2	1	118.33	2	-	-	-	-	-
Lancashire	5	10	4	446	133*	-	-	2	74.33	4	-	29	-	-	-
Leicestershire	3	3	1	331	185*	-	2	2	165.50	2	-	-	-	-	-
M.C.C.	17	26	2	1343	278	-	8	3	55.96	9	-	302	4	75.50	2/106
Middlesex	4	6	1	254	160	-	-	1	50.80	-	-	-	-	-	-
New South Wales	9	14	3	864	143	1	2	4	78.55	10	1	-	-	-	-
New Zealanders	1	1	-	11	11	-	-	-	11.00	1	-	-	-	-	-

Team	M	I	NO	Runs	HS	100	50	Avg	Ct	Runs	Wkts	Avg	Best
Northamptonshire	3	5	-	149	65	-	1	29.80	-	31	-	-	-
Nottinghamshire	2	3	-	286	144	1	2	95.33	1	19	2	9.50	2/19
Oxford	3	3	-	127	58	-	1	42.33	-	62	2	31.00	2/41
Queensland	18	26	4	3085	452*	3	4	140.23	14	-	-	-	-
Scotland	1	-	-	-	-	-	-	-	-	4	-	-	-
SJ McCabe's XI	1	2	-	12	12	1	-	6.00	1	-	-	-	-
Somerset	3	3	-	336	202	1	2	112.00	2	-	-	-	-
South Africans	2	3	-	384	219	1	2	128.00	2	42	-	-	-
South of England XI	1	1	-	143	143	1	1	143.00	1	-	-	-	-
South Australia	11	20	-	1269	258	4	6	63.45	4	295	8	36.88	3/54
SOUTH AFRICA	5	5	1	806	299*	4	-	201.50	4	2	-	-	-
Surrey	7	8	2	839	252*	2	2	139.83	4	31	-	-	-
Sussex	3	4	-	184	109	1	-	46.00	1	-	-	-	-
Tasmania	5	5	-	751	369	3	1	150.20	3	21	-	-	-
The Rest	2	4	-	216	92	-	2	54.00	-	57	1	57.00	1/30
Victoria	27	42	9	3861	357	13	10	117.00	14	87	2	43.50	1/4
VY Richardson's XI	2	3	-	242	212	1	-	80.67	1	-	-	-	-
Warwickshire	2	3	1	179	135	1	-	89.50	1	-	-	-	-
West Indians	2	4	-	178	73	-	2	44.50	-	-	-	-	-
WEST INDIES	5	6	-	447	223	2	-	74.50	2	15	1	15.00	1/8
Western Australia	6	7	1	731	209*	3	-	121.83	5	5	-	-	-
WM Woodfull's XI	1	2	-	156	101	1	1	78.00	1	18	-	-	-
Worcestershire	4	4	-	807	258	2	-	201.75	4	-	-	-	-
Yorkshire	5	7	-	460	140	1	4	65.71	-	-	-	-	-

	M	Inn	NO	Runs	HS	0s	50	100	Avrge	Ct	St	Runs	Wkts	Avrge	Best
First Innings		106	4	9014	357	6	24	35	88.37	26	1	389	7	55.57	2/19
Second Innings		124	7	11389	369	6	17	53	97.34	37	-	381	9	42.33	3/35
Third Innings		65	15	5715	452*	-	15	24	114.30	18	-	233	4	58.25	1/4
Fourth Innings		43	17	1949	173*	4	13	5	74.96	50	-	364	16	22.75	3/52
Venues in Australia															
Adelaide	40	60	6	4840	369	2	15	18	89.63	29	-	219	7	31.29	3/54
Brisbane (Gabba)	12	16	-	1593	226	3	2	8	99.56	9	-	17	-	-	-
Brisbane (Exhib)	4	7	1	620	223	-	1	3	103.33	2	-	-	-	-	-
Hobart (TCA)	2	2	-	283	144	-	-	2	141.50	2	-	21	-	-	-
Launceston	2	2	-	99	79	-	1	-	49.50	-	-	-	-	-	-
Melbourne	30	47	8	4024	357	2	9	19	103.18	16	-	103	4	25.75	2/12
Perth	6	8	1	643	209*	-	-	4	91.86	2	-	111	2	55.50	2/106
Sydney	46	76	9	6128	452*	5	17	22	91.46	31	1	587	11	53.36	2/41
Total in Australia	142	218	25	18230	452*	12	45	76	94.46	91	1	1058	24	44.08	3/54
Venues in England															
Birmingham	2	3	1	179	135	-	-	1	89.50	2	-	-	-	-	-
Bradford	1	1	-	1	1	-	-	-	1.00	2	-	-	-	-	-
Bristol	1	2	-	56	42	-	-	-	28.00	-	-	-	-	-	-
Cambridge	3	3	-	169	137	1	-	1	56.33	1	-	103	6	17.17	3/35
Canterbury	4	4	1	355	205*	-	2	1	118.33	2	-	-	-	-	-
Chesterfield	2	3	1	121	71	-	1	-	60.50	1	-	24	1	24.00	1/24
Derby	1	1	-	62	62	-	1	-	62.00	1	-	-	-	-	-
Edinburgh	1	-	-	-	-	-	-	-	-	-	-	4	-	-	-

Venue	M	Inn	NO	Runs	HS	0s	50	100	Avrge	Ct		Wkts		
Folkestone	2	2	1	212	149*	-	1	1	212.00	-	7	-	-	-
Hastings	1	1	-	143	143	-	-	1	143.00	-	-	-	-	-
Hove	2	2	-	128	109	-	-	1	64.00	2	-	-	-	-
Leeds	4	6	1	963	334	-	-	4	192.60	1	-	-	-	-
Leicester	3	3	1	331	185*	-	2	1	165.50	2	5	-	-	-
Liverpool	1	2	1	57	48*	-	-	-	57.00	1	5	-	-	-
Lord's	14	21	2	1510	278	-	3	6	79.47	4	1	-	-	-
Manchester	7	12	4	470	133*	-	-	2	58.75	5	24	-	-	-
Northampton	3	5	-	149	65	-	1	-	29.80	2	31	-	-	-
Nottingham	6	11	1	812	144*	1	3	4	81.20	2	-	-	-	-
Oxford	3	3	-	127	58	-	1	-	42.33	-	19	2	9.50	2/19
Scarborough	3	3	-	381	153	-	1	2	127.00	1	54	3	18.00	3/52
Sheffield	4	6	-	459	140	-	4	1	76.50	1	-	-	-	-
Southampton	3	3	1	336	191	1	-	2	168.00	4	-	-	-	-
Southend	1	1	-	187	187	-	-	1	187.00	-	-	-	-	-
Swansea	2	3	1	94	58	-	1	-	47.00	2	-	-	-	-
Taunton	3	3	-	336	202	-	-	2	112.00	1	-	-	-	-
The Oval	11	12	2	1392	252*	1	3	6	139.20	3	37	-	-	-
Worcester	4	4	-	807	258	-	-	4	201.75	-	-	-	-	-
Total in England	92	120	18	9837	334	4	24	41	96.44	40	309	12	25.75	3/35

Batting Position	Inn	NO	Runs	HS	0s	50	100	Avrge
1/2	11	1	1071	225	-	2	5	107.10
3	240	32	21463	452*	13	51	89	103.19
4	40	4	2224	192	1	9	8	61.78
5	17	3	1319	304	1	3	6	94.21

	M	Inn	NO	Runs	HS	0s	50	100	Avrge
6		23	2	1515	234	-	4	7	72.14
7		5	1	462	270	-	-	2	115.50
8		2	-	13	13	1	-	-	6.50

Teams	M	Inn	NO	Runs	HS	0s	50	100	Avrge	Ct	St	Runs	Wkts	Avrge	Best
AR Morris's XI	1	1	-	53	53	-	1	-	53.00	-	-	72	2	36.00	1/8
AUSTRALIA	52	80	10	6996	334	7	13	29	99.94	32	-	461	14	32.93	3/35
Australian XI	87	109	15	8396	278	2	25	36	89.32	41	-	12	3	4.00	2/12
DG Bradman's XI	5	8	-	505	212	1	-	3	63.13	3	-	712	15	47.47	3/54
New South Wales	41	69	10	5813	452*	3	17	21	98.53	17	1	36	1	36.00	1/36
The Rest	2	4	-	46	25	-	-	-	11.50	1	-	0	-	-	-
South Australia	44	63	8	5753	369	3	12	25	104.60	36	1	18	-	-	-
VY Richardson's XI	1	2	-	156	101	-	1	1	78.00	-	-	-	-	-	-
WM Woodfull's XI	1	2	-	349	225	-	-	2	174.50	1	-	56	1	56.00	1/56

Innings	NO	Bwd	Cgt	LBW	Stp	RO	HW	HB Wickets	Bwd	Cgt	C&B	LBW	Stp	HW
338	43	78	174	27	11	4	1	34	9	14	1	5	5	-

Highest Score: 452* New South Wales v Queensland, Sydney, 1929/30

100s	Team	Opponent	Venue	Season
118*	New South Wales	South Australia	Adelaide	1927/28
134*	New South Wales	Victoria	Sydney	1927/28
131	New South Wales	Queensland	Brisbane (Exhib)	1928/29
133*	New South Wales	Queensland	Brisbane (Exhib)	1928/29
132*	New South Wales	M.C.C.	Sydney	1928/29
112	AUSTRALIA	ENGLAND	Melbourne	1928/29
340*	New South Wales	Victoria	Sydney	1928/29

175	New South Wales	South Australia	Sydney	1928/29
123	AUSTRALIA	ENGLAND	Melbourne	1928/29
157	New South Wales	M.C.C.	Sydney	1929/30
124	WM Woodfull's XI	J Ryder's XI	Sydney	1929/30
225	WM Woodfull's XI	J Ryder's XI	Sydney	1929/30
452*	New South Wales	Queensland	Sydney	1929/30
139	Australian XI	Tasmania	Hobart (TCA)	1929/30
236	Australian XI	Worcestershire	Worcester	1930
185*	Australian XI	Leicestershire	Leicester	1930
252*	Australian XI	Surrey	The Oval	1930
191	Australian XI	Hampshire	Southampton	1930
131	AUSTRALIA	ENGLAND	Nottingham	1930
254	AUSTRALIA	ENGLAND	Lord's	1930
334	AUSTRALIA	ENGLAND	Leeds	1930
117	Australian XI	Somerset	Taunton	1930
232	AUSTRALIA	ENGLAND	The Oval	1930
205*	Australian XI	Kent	Canterbury	1930
121	New South Wales	South Australia	Sydney	1930/31
258	New South Wales	South Australia	Adelaide	1930/31
223	AUSTRALIA	WEST INDIES	Brisbane (Exhib)	1930/31
220	New South Wales	Victoria	Sydney	1930/31
152	AUSTRALIA	WEST INDIES	Melbourne	1930/31
135	New South Wales	South Africans	Sydney	1931/32
226	AUSTRALIA	SOUTH AFRICA	Brisbane (Gabba)	1931/32
219	New South Wales	South Africans	Sydney	1931/32
112	AUSTRALIA	SOUTH AFRICA	Sydney	1931/32
167	AUSTRALIA	SOUTH AFRICA	Melbourne	1931/32

167	New South Wales	Victoria	Sydney	1931/32
299*	AUSTRALIA	SOUTH AFRICA	Adelaide	1931/32
238	New South Wales	Victoria	Sydney	1932/33
157	New South Wales	Victoria	Melbourne	1932/33
103*	AUSTRALIA	ENGLAND	Melbourne	1932/33
200	New South Wales	Queensland	Brisbane (Gabba)	1933/34
101	VY Richardson's XI	WM Woodfull's XI	Melbourne	1933/34
187*	New South Wales	Victoria	Melbourne	1933/34
253	New South Wales	Queensland	Sydney	1933/34
128	New South Wales	Victoria	Sydney	1933/34
206	Australian XI	Worcestershire	Worcester	1934
160	Australian XI	Middlesex	Lord's	1934
140	Australian XI	Yorkshire	Sheffield	1934
304	AUSTRALIA	ENGLAND	Leeds	1934
244	AUSTRALIA	ENGLAND	The Oval	1934
149*	Australian XI	England XI	Folkestone	1934
132	Australian XI	England XI	Scarborough	1934
117	South Australia	New South Wales	Adelaide	1935/36
233	South Australia	Queensland	Adelaide	1935/36
357	South Australia	Victoria	Melbourne	1935/36
369	South Australia	Tasmania	Adelaide	1935/36
212	**DG Bradman's XI**	VY Richardson's XI	Sydney	1936/37
192	South Australia	Victoria	Melbourne	1936/37
270	AUSTRALIA	ENGLAND	Melbourne	1936/37
212	AUSTRALIA	ENGLAND	Adelaide	1936/37
123	South Australia	Queensland	Brisbane (Gabba)	1936/37
169	AUSTRALIA	ENGLAND	Melbourne	1936/37
101	South Australia	Western Australia	Adelaide	1937/38

246	South Australia	Queensland	Adelaide	1937/38
107	South Australia	Queensland	Brisbane (Gabba)	1937/38
113	South Australia	Queensland	Brisbane (Gabba)	1937/38
104*	South Australia	New South Wales	Sydney	1937/38
144	Australian XI	Tasmania	Hobart (TCA)	1937/38
102	Australian XI	Western Australia	Perth	1937/38
258	Australian XI	Worcestershire	Worcester	1938
137	Australian XI	Cambridge University	Cambridge	1938
278	Australian XI	M.C.C.	Lord's	1938
143	Australian XI	Surrey	The Oval	1938
145*	Australian XI	Hampshire	Southampton	1938
144*	AUSTRALIA	ENGLAND	Nottingham	1938
104	Australian XI	Gentlemen of England	Lord's	1938
101*	Australian XI	Lancashire	Manchester	1938
102*	AUSTRALIA	ENGLAND	Lord's	1938
135	Australian XI	Warwickshire	Birmingham	1938
144	Australian XI	Nottinghamshire	Nottingham	1938
103	AUSTRALIA	ENGLAND	Leeds	1938
202	Australian XI	Somerset	Taunton	1938
118	**DG Bradman's XI**	KE Rigg's XI	Melbourne	1938/39
143	South Australia	New South Wales	Adelaide	1938/39
225	South Australia	Queensland	Adelaide	1938/39
107	South Australia	Victoria	Melbourne	1938/39
186	South Australia	Queensland	Brisbane (Gabba)	1938/39
135*	South Australia	New South Wales	Sydney	1938/39
251*	South Australia	New South Wales	Adelaide	1939/40
138	South Australia	Queensland	Adelaide	1939/40
267	South Australia	Victoria	Melbourne	1939/40

Score	Team	Opponent	Venue	Season
209*	South Australia	Western Australia	Perth	1939/40
135	South Australia	Western Australia	Perth	1939/40
112	South Australia	Australian Services	Adelaide	1945/46
106	Australian XI	M.C.C.	Melbourne	1946/47
119	South Australia	Victoria	Adelaide	1946/47
187	AUSTRALIA	ENGLAND	Brisbane (Gabba)	1946/47
234	AUSTRALIA	ENGLAND	Sydney	1946/47
156	South Australia	Indians	Adelaide	1947/48
100	South Australia	Victoria	Adelaide	1947/48
172	Australian XI	Indians	Sydney	1947/48
185	AUSTRALIA	INDIA	Brisbane (Gabba)	1947/48
132	AUSTRALIA	INDIA	Melbourne	1947/48
127*	AUSTRALIA	INDIA	Melbourne	1947/48
201	AUSTRALIA	INDIA	Adelaide	1947/48
115	Australian XI	Western Australia	Perth	1947/48
107	Australian XI	Worcestershire	Worcester	1948
146	Australian XI	Surrey	The Oval	1948
187	Australian XI	Essex	Southend	1948
109	Australian XI	Sussex	Hove	1948
138	AUSTRALIA	ENGLAND	Nottingham	1948
128	Australian XI	Surrey	The Oval	1948
173*	AUSTRALIA	ENGLAND	Leeds	1948
133*	Australian XI	Lancashire	Manchester	1948
150	Australian XI	Gentlemen of England	Lord's	1948
143	Australian XI	South of England XI	Hastings	1948
153	Australian XI	HDG Leveson-Gower's XI	Scarborough	1948
123	**DG Bradman's XI**	AL Hassett's XI	Melbourne	1948/49

Best Bowling: 3/35 Australian XI v Cambridge University, Cambridge, 1930

Batting — Innings by Innings

Team	Opponent	Venue	HO	Fielder	Bowler	Score	Runs	Avrge
		1927/28 in Australia						
New South Wales	South Australia	Adelaide	ct	NL Williams	JD Scott	118	118	118.00
	Victoria	Melbourne	bwd		CV Grimmett	33	151	75.50
			lbw		AEV Hartkopf	31	182	60.67
New South Wales	Queensland	Sydney	bwd		DD Blackie	5	187	46.75
			bwd		FJ Gough	0	187	37.40
New South Wales	South Australia	Sydney	ct	LPD O'Connor	OE Nothling	13	200	33.33
			c&b	DG McKay	DG McKay	2	202	28.86
New South Wales	Victoria	Sydney	st	AT Hack	CV Grimmett	73	275	34.38
			st	JL Ellis	CV Grimmett	7	282	31.33
			no		DD Blackie	134*	416	46.22
		1928/29 in Australia						
The Rest	Australian XI	Melbourne	ct	WAS Oldfield	CV Grimmett	14	430	43.00
			bwd		RK Oxenham	5	435	39.55
New South Wales	Queensland	Brisbane (Exhib)	ct	LPD O'Connor	HM Thurlow	131	566	47.17
			no			133*	699	58.25
New South Wales	M.C.C.	Sydney	bwd		AP Freeman	87	786	60.46
			no			132*	918	70.62
Australian XI	M.C.C.	Sydney	no			58*	976	75.08
			lbw		MW Tate	18	994	71.00
AUSTRALIA	ENGLAND	Brisbane (Exhib)	lbw		MW Tate	18	1012	67.47
			ct	APF Chapman	JC White	1	1013	63.31

Team	Opponent	Venue		Caught/Dismissed by	Bowler	Score	Aggregate	Average
New South Wales	Victoria	Melbourne	bwd		HSTL Hendry	1	1014	59.65
AUSTRALIA	ENGLAND	Melbourne	no			71*	1085	63.82
New South Wales	South Australia	Adelaide	ct	G Duckworth	WR Hammond	79	1164	64.67
			ct	CV Grimmett	G Geary	112	1276	67.16
New South Wales	Victoria	Sydney	ct		TW Wall	5	1281	64.05
			bwd		TW Wall	2	1283	61.10
AUSTRALIA	ENGLAND	Adelaide	no	H Larwood	MW Tate	340*	1623	77.29
			ct			40	1663	75.59
New South Wales	M.C.C.	Sydney	ro	GE Tyldesley	JC White	58	1721	74.83
New South Wales	South Australia	Sydney	ct	CW Walker	CV Grimmett	15	1736	72.33
			ct	CW Walker	TA Carlton	35	1771	70.84
AUSTRALIA	ENGLAND	Melbourne	ct	MW Tate	G Geary	175	1946	74.85
			ct			123	2069	76.63
			no			37*	2106	78.00

1929/30 in Australia

Team	Opponent	Venue		Caught/Dismissed by	Bowler	Score	Aggregate	Average
New South Wales	Queensland	Brisbane (Exhib)	ro	(Oxenham/Brew)		48	2154	76.93
			ct	LPD O'Connor	FM Brew	66	2220	76.55
New South Wales	M.C.C.	Sydney	bwd		TS Worthington	157	2377	79.23
WM Woodfull's XI	J Ryder's XI	Sydney	ct	A Jackson	RK Oxenham	124	2501	80.68
			lbw		CV Grimmett	225	2726	85.19
New South Wales	South Australia	Adelaide	ro	(Lonergan/Walker)		2	2728	82.67
			lbw		CV Grimmett	84	2812	82.71
New South Wales	Victoria	Melbourne	bwd		HH Alexander	89	2901	82.89
			no			26*	2927	83.63
New South Wales	Queensland	Sydney	ct	HF Leeson	A Hurwood	3	2930	81.39
			no			452*	3382	93.94

Team	Opponent	Venue	Fielder	Bowler		Runs	Agg	Avge
New South Wales	South Australia	Sydney	VY Richardson	HE Whitfield	ct	47	3429	92.68
New South Wales	Victoria	Sydney	RN Ellis	H Ironmonger	ct	77	3506	92.26
Australian XI	Tasmania	Launceston		LJ Nash	lbw	20	3526	90.41
Australian XI	Tasmania	Hobart (TCA)	AW Rushforth	GTH James	ct	139	3665	91.63
Australian XI	Western Australia	Perth	RJ Bryant	WA Evans	ct	27	3692	90.05

1930 in England

Team	Opponent	Venue	Fielder	Bowler		Runs	Agg	Avge
Australian XI	Worcestershire	Worcester	CF Walters	GW Brook	ct	236	3928	93.52
Australian XI	Leicestershire	Leicester			no	185*	4113	97.93
Australian XI	Yorkshire	Sheffield	GG Macaulay	GG Macaulay	c&b	78	4191	97.47
Australian XI	Lancashire	Liverpool		EA McDonald	bwd	9	4200	95.45
					no	48*	4248	96.55
Australian XI	M.C.C.	Lord's		MJC Allom	bwd	66	4314	95.87
				GTS Stevens	lbw	4	4318	93.87
Australian XI	Derbyshire	Chesterfield	H Elliott	TS Worthington	ct	44	4362	92.81
Australian XI	Surrey	The Oval			no	252*	4614	98.17
Australian XI	Oxford	Oxford		HM Garland-Wells	bwd	32	4646	96.79
Australian XI	Hampshire	Southampton	CP Mead	GS Boyes	ct	191	4837	98.71
Australian XI	Middlesex	Lord's		JW Hearne	bwd	35	4872	97.44
				GTS Stevens	bwd	18	4890	95.88
Australian XI	Cambridge University	Cambridge	TWT Baines	RHC Human	ct	32	4922	94.65
AUSTRALIA	ENGLAND	Nottingham		MW Tate	bwd	8	4930	93.02
				RWV Robins	bwd	131	5061	93.72
Australian XI	Surrey	The Oval	MJC Allom	T Shepherd	ct	5	5066	92.11
Australian XI	Lancashire	Manchester	G Duckworth	FM Sibbles	ct	38	5104	91.14
					no	23*	5127	91.55
AUSTRALIA	ENGLAND	Lord's	APF Chapman	JC White	ct	254	5381	94.40
			APF Chapman	MW Tate	ct	1	5382	92.79

Team	Opposition	Venue	How out	Fielder	Bowler	Score	Runs	Avge
Australian XI	Yorkshire	Bradford	lbw		E Robinson	1	5383	91.24
AUSTRALIA	ENGLAND	Leeds	ct	G Duckworth	MW Tate	334	5717	95.28
Australian XI	Scotland	Edinburgh	dnb			-	5717	95.28
AUSTRALIA	ENGLAND	Manchester	ct	KS Duleepsinhji	IAR Peebles	14	5731	93.95
Australian XI	Somerset	Taunton	c&b		A Young	117	5848	94.32
Australian XI	Glamorgan	Swansea	bwd		FP Ryan	58	5906	93.75
			no			19*	5925	94.05
Australian XI	Northamptonshire	Northampton	ct	APR Hawtin	VWC Jupp	22	5947	92.92
			bwd		AL Cox	35	5982	92.03
AUSTRALIA	ENGLAND	The Oval	ct	G Duckworth	H Larwood	232	6214	94.15
Australian XI	Gloucestershire	Bristol	ct	FJ Seabrook	CWL Parker	42	6256	93.37
			bwd		CWL Parker	14	6270	92.21
Australian XI	Kent	Canterbury	lbw		AP Freeman	18	6288	91.13
			no			205*	6493	94.10
Australian XI	England XI	Folkestone	lbw		MJC Allom	63	6556	93.66
Australian XI	England XI	Scarborough	bwd		CWL Parker	96	6652	93.69
			dnb			-	6652	93.69
1930/31 in Australia								
New South Wales	South Australia	Sydney	ct	DE Pritchard	CS Deverson	61	6713	93.24
			ct	MG Waite	CS Deverson	121	6834	93.62
Australian XI	The Rest	Melbourne	bwd		AA Mailey	73	6907	93.34
			c&b	AA Mailey	AA Mailey	29	6936	92.48
New South Wales	West Indians	Sydney	ct	I Barrow	GN Francis	73	7009	92.22
AUSTRALIA	WEST INDIES	Adelaide	ct	GA Headley	FR Martin	22	7031	91.31
			ct	GC Grant	HC Griffith	4	7035	90.19
New South Wales	South Australia	Adelaide	bwd		VY Richardson	258	7293	92.32

Team	Opponent	Venue				Score		
New South Wales	Victoria	Melbourne	ct	HSTL Hendry	EL a'Beckett	2	7295	91.19
AUSTRALIA	WEST INDIES	Sydney	ct	I Barrow	GN Francis	25	7320	90.37
AUSTRALIA	WEST INDIES	Brisbane (Exhib)	ct	GC Grant	LN Constantine	223	7543	91.99
New South Wales	Victoria	Sydney	ct	BA Barnett	HH Alexander	33	7576	91.28
			ct	KE Rigg	H Ironmonger	220	7796	92.81
AUSTRALIA	WEST INDIES	Melbourne	ct	CA Roach	FR Martin	152	7948	93.51
New South Wales	West Indians	Sydney	bwd		LN Constantine	10	7958	92.53
			lbw		HC Griffith	73	8031	92.31
AUSTRALIA	WEST INDIES	Sydney	ct	GN Francis	FR Martin	43	8074	91.75
			bwd		HC Griffith	0	8074	90.72

1931/32 in Australia

Team	Opponent	Venue				Score		
New South Wales	Queensland	Brisbane (Gabba)	ct	LW Waterman	E Gilbert	0	8074	89.71
New South Wales	South Africans	Sydney	c&b	Q McMillan	Q McMillan	30	8104	89.05
			ct	AJ Bell	DPB Morkel	135	8239	89.55
AUSTRALIA	SOUTH AFRICA	Brisbane (Gabba)	lbw		CL Vincent	226	8465	91.02
New South Wales	South Africans	Sydney	ct	SH Curnow	Q McMillan	219	8684	92.38
AUSTRALIA	SOUTH AFRICA	Sydney	ct	KG Viljoen	DPB Morkel	112	8796	92.59
AUSTRALIA	SOUTH AFRICA	Melbourne	ct	HB Cameron	NA Quinn	2	8798	91.65
			lbw		CL Vincent	167	8965	92.42
New South Wales	Victoria	Sydney	ct	SAJ Smith	H Ironmonger	23	8988	91.71
			bwd		LE Nagel	167	9155	92.47
AUSTRALIA	SOUTH AFRICA	Adelaide	no			299*	9454	95.49
AUSTRALIA	SOUTH AFRICA	Melbourne	dnb			-	9454	95.49
New South Wales	South Australia	Sydney	bwd		TA Carlton	23	9477	94.77
			bwd		TW Wall	0	9477	93.83

1932/33 in Australia

Team	Opponent	Venue	How out	Fielder	Bowler	Score	Runs	Avg
Australian XI	M.C.C.	Perth	ct	WR Hammond	H Verity	3	9480	92.94
New South Wales	Victoria	Sydney	ct	sr Nawab of Pataudi	GOB Allen	10	9490	92.14
			ct	LPJ O'Brien	LO Fleetwood-Smith	238	9728	93.54
Australian XI	M.C.C.	Melbourne	no			52*	9780	94.04
			lbw		H Larwood	36	9816	93.49
New South Wales	M.C.C.	Sydney	bwd		H Larwood	13	9829	92.73
			lbw		MW Tate	18	9847	92.03
New South Wales	Victoria	Melbourne	bwd		W Voce	23	9870	91.39
			ct	EH Bromley	H Ironmonger	157	10027	91.99
AUSTRALIA	ENGLAND	Melbourne	bwd		WE Bowes	0	10027	91.15
			no			103*	10130	92.09
AUSTRALIA	ENGLAND	Adelaide	ct	GOB Allen	H Larwood	8	10138	91.33
			c&b		H Verity	66	10204	91.11
New South Wales	M.C.C.	Sydney	bwd		TB Mitchell	1	10205	90.31
			ct	LEG Ames	WR Hammond	71	10276	90.14
New South Wales	South Australia	Sydney	ct	AJ Ryan	TW Wall	56	10332	89.84
			bwd		PK Lee	97	10429	89.91
AUSTRALIA	ENGLAND	Brisbane (Gabba)	bwd		H Larwood	76	10505	89.79
			ct	TB Mitchell	H Larwood	24	10529	89.23
AUSTRALIA	ENGLAND	Sydney	bwd		H Larwood	48	10577	88.88
			bwd		H Verity	71	10648	88.73

1933/34 in Australia

Team	Opponent	Venue	How out	Fielder	Bowler	Score	Runs	Avg
New South Wales	Queensland	Brisbane (Gabba)	ct	WC Andrews	RM Levy	200	10848	89.65
VY Richardson's XI	WM Woodfull's XI	Melbourne	ct	WM Woodfull	TW Wall	55	10903	89.37
			ct	LS Darling	DD Blackie	101	11004	89.46

New South Wales	The Rest	Sydney	ct	CW Walker	HC Chilvers	22	11026	88.92
			bwd		HI Ebeling	92	11118	88.94
New South Wales	South Australia	Adelaide	bwd		FHK Collins	1	11119	88.25
			ct	TW Wall	CV Grimmett	76	11195	88.15
New South Wales	Victoria	Melbourne	no			187*	11382	89.62
			no			77*	11459	90.23
New South Wales	Queensland	Sydney	bwd		FM Brew	253	11712	91.50
New South Wales	Victoria	Sydney	ct	LS Darling	LO Fleetwood-Smith	128	11840	91.78

1934 in England

Australian XI	Worcestershire	Worcester	bwd		R Howorth	206	12046	92.66
Australian XI	Leicestershire	Leicester	bwd		G Geary	65	12111	92.45
Australian XI	Cambridge University	Cambridge	bwd		JGW Davies	0	12111	91.75
Australian XI	M.C.C.	Lord's	c&b	FR Brown	FR Brown	5	12116	91.10
Australian XI	Oxford	Oxford	lbw		JH Dyson	37	12153	90.69
Australian XI	Hampshire	Southampton	ct	CP Mead	AEG Baring	0	12153	90.02
Australian XI	Middlesex	Lord's	ct	JHA Hulme	IAR Peebles	160	12313	90.54
Australian XI	Surrey	The Oval	ct	HS Squires	AR Gover	77	12390	90.44
AUSTRALIA	ENGLAND	Nottingham	ct	WR Hammond	G Geary	29	12419	89.99
			ct	LEG Ames	K Farnes	25	12444	89.53
Australian XI	Northamptonshire	Northampton	ct	AH Bakewell	AD Matthews	65	12509	89.35
			bwd		AD Matthews	25	12534	88.89
AUSTRALIA	ENGLAND	Lord's	c&b	H Verity	H Verity	36	12570	88.52
			ct	LEG Ames	H Verity	13	12583	87.99
Australian XI	Somerset	Taunton	ct	WT Luckes	JC White	17	12600	87.50
Australian XI	Surrey	The Oval	ct	EW Brookes	ERT Holmes	27	12627	87.08
			no			61*	12688	87.50

Team	Opposition	Venue						
AUSTRALIA	ENGLAND	Manchester	ct	LEG Ames	WR Hammond	30	12718	87.11
Australian XI	Derbyshire	Chesterfield	ct	H Elliott	LF Townsend	71	12789	87.00
			no			6*	12795	87.04
Australian XI	Yorkshire	Sheffield	bwd		M Leyland	140	12935	87.40
AUSTRALIA	ENGLAND	Leeds	bwd		WE Bowes	304	13239	88.85
AUSTRALIA	ENGLAND	The Oval	ct	LEG Ames	WE Bowes	244	13483	89.89
Australian XI	Sussex	Hove	bwd		WE Bowes	77	13560	89.80
Australian XI	Kent	Canterbury	bwd		G Pearce	19	13579	89.34
Australian XI	England XI	Folkestone	dnb			-	13579	89.34
Australian XI	England XI	Scarborough	no			149*	13728	90.32
			st	G Duckworth	K Farnes	132	13860	90.59

1935/36 in Australia

Team	Opposition	Venue						
South Australia	M.C.C.	Adelaide	lbw		JM Sims	15	13875	90.10
			lbw		JH Parks	50	13925	89.84
South Australia	New South Wales	Adelaide	c&b	RH Robinson	RH Robinson	117	14042	90.01
South Australia	Queensland	Adelaide	ct	D Tallon	RM Levy	233	14275	90.92
South Australia	Victoria	Melbourne	ct	SO Quin	EH Bromley	357	14632	92.61
South Australia	Queensland	Brisbane (Gabba)	ct	ER Wyeth	E Gilbert	31	14663	92.22
South Australia	New South Wales	Sydney	ct	RCJ Little	LC Hynes	0	14663	91.64
South Australia	Victoria	Adelaide	ct	JA Ledward	HI Ebeling	1	14664	91.08
South Australia	Tasmania	Adelaide	c&b	RC Townley	RC Townley	369	15033	92.80

1936/37 in Australia

Team	Opposition	Venue						
DG Bradman's XI	VY Richardson's XI	Sydney	ct	WJ O'Reilly	CV Grimmett	212	15245	93.53
			ct	JHW Fingleton	CV Grimmett	13	15258	93.04
South Australia	Victoria	Melbourne	ct	LPJ O'Brien	RG Gregory	192	15450	93.64

Team	Opposition	Venue		Fielder	Bowler	Score	Agg	Avge
Australian XI	M.C.C.	Sydney	bwd		TS Worthington	63	15513	93.45
AUSTRALIA	ENGLAND	Brisbane (Gabba)	ct	TS Worthington	W Voce	38	15551	93.12
			ct	AE Fagg	GOB Allen	0	15551	92.57
AUSTRALIA	ENGLAND	Sydney	bwd		W Voce	0	15551	92.02
South Australia	M.C.C.	Adelaide	ct	GOB Allen	H Verity	82	15633	91.96
AUSTRALIA	ENGLAND	Melbourne	ct	RWV Robins	H Verity	13	15646	91.50
			ct	GOB Allen	H Verity	270	15916	92.53
South Australia	M.C.C.	Adelaide	ct	LEG Ames	CJ Barnett	38	15954	92.22
AUSTRALIA	ENGLAND	Adelaide	bwd		GOB Allen	26	15980	91.84
			c&b	WR Hammond	WR Hammond	212	16192	92.53
South Australia	Queensland	Brisbane (Gabba)	st	D Tallon	ER Wyeth	123	16315	92.70
South Australia	New South Wales	Sydney	lbw		WJ O'Reilly	24	16339	92.31
			no			38*	16377	92.53
AUSTRALIA	ENGLAND	Melbourne	bwd		K Farnes	169	16546	92.96
South Australia	Victoria	Adelaide	ct	HI Ebeling	LO Fleetwood-Smith	31	16577	92.61
			ct	AL Hassett	EL McCormick	8	16585	92.14

1937/38 in Australia

Team	Opposition	Venue		Fielder	Bowler	Score	Agg	Avge
South Australia	New Zealanders	Adelaide	ct	EWT Trindill	J Cowie	11	16596	91.69
DG Bradman's XI	VY Richardson's XI	Adelaide	bwd		CV Grimmett	17	16613	91.28
South Australia	Western Australia	Adelaide	ct	RJ Wilberforce	G Eyres	101	16714	91.33
South Australia	New South Wales	Adelaide	ct	LJ O'Brien	WJ O'Reilly	91	16805	91.33
			ct	AG Chipperfield	WJ O'Reilly	62	16867	91.17
South Australia	Queensland	Adelaide	ct	GW Baker	PL Dixon	246	17113	92.01
			no			39*	17152	92.22
South Australia	Victoria	Melbourne	ct	MW Sievers	RG Gregory	54	17206	92.01
			ct	MW Sievers	RG Gregory	35	17241	91.71

Team	Opponent	Venue		Fielder	Bowler	Score	Agg.	Avge
South Australia	Queensland	Brisbane (Gabba)	ct	D Tallon	PL Dixon	107	17348	91.79
South Australia	New South Wales	Sydney	ct	JV Hackett	T Allen	113	17461	91.90
			ct	SJ McCabe	LJ O'Brien	44	17505	91.65
South Australia	Victoria	Adelaide	no			104*	17609	92.19
			bwd		EL McCormick	3	17612	91.73
Australian XI	Tasmania	Launceston	ct	JA Ledward	FLO Thorn	85	17697	91.69
Australian XI	Tasmania	Hobart (TCA)	ct	CJ Sankey	RV Thomas	79	17776	91.63
			bwd		CL Jeffery	144	17920	91.90
Australian XI	Western Australia	Perth	st	OI Lovelock	AG Zimbulis	102	18022	91.95

1938 in England

Team	Opponent	Venue		Fielder	Bowler	Score	Agg.	Avge
Australian XI	Worcestershire	Worcester	ct	SH Martin	R Howorth	258	18280	92.79
Australian XI	Oxford	Oxford University	lbw		G Evans	58	18338	92.62
Australian XI	Cambridge	Cambridge University	ct	FG Mann	JV Wild	137	18475	92.84
Australian XI	Lord's	M.C.C.	ct	RWV Robins	J Smith	278	18753	93.77
Australian XI	Northampton	Northamptonshire	ct	KC James	RJ Partridge	2	18755	93.31
Australian XI	The Oval	Surrey	ct	EW Brookes	EA Watts	143	18898	93.55
Australian XI	Southampton	Hampshire	no			145*	19043	94.27
Australian XI	Lord's	Middlesex	ct	DCS Compton	W Nevell	5	19048	93.83
			no			30*	19078	93.98
AUSTRALIA	Nottingham	ENGLAND	ct	LEG Ames	RA Sinfield	51	19129	93.77
			no			144*	19273	94.48
Australian XI	Lord's	Gentlemen of England	ct	BH Valentine	RJO Meyer	104	19377	94.52
Australian XI	Manchester	Lancashire	ct	R Pollard	WE Phillipson	12	19389	94.12
			no			101*	19490	94.61
AUSTRALIA	Lord's	ENGLAND	bwd		H Verity	18	19508	94.24
			no			102*	19610	94.73

Australian XI	Yorkshire	Sheffield	st	A Wood	TF Smailes	59	19669	94.56
			ct	W Barber	TF Smailes	42	19711	94.31
Australian XI	Warwickshire	Birmingham	ct	K Wilmot	JH Mayer	135	19846	94.50
Australian XI	Nottinghamshire	Nottingham	lbw		A Jepson	56	19902	94.32
			ct	A Jepson	EA Marshall	144	20046	94.56
AUSTRALIA	ENGLAND	Leeds	bwd		WE Bowes	103	20149	94.60
			ct	H Verity	DVP Wright	16	20165	94.23
Australian XI	Somerset	Taunton	bwd		WHR Andrews	202	20367	94.73
Australian XI	Glamorgan	Swansea	st	HG Davies	JC Clay	17	20384	94.37
Australian XI	Kent	Canterbury	ct	LJ Todd	AE Watt	67	20451	94.24
AUSTRALIA	ENGLAND	The Oval	dnb			-	20451	94.24

1938/39 in Australia

DG Bradman's XI	KE Rigg's XI	Melbourne	bwd		LE Nagel	118	20569	94.35
South Australia	New South Wales	Adelaide	bwd		JJ Murphy	143	20712	94.58
South Australia	Queensland	Adelaide	ct	GW Baker	CP Christ	225	20937	95.17
South Australia	Victoria	Melbourne	ct	AL Hassett	MW Sievers	107	21044	95.22
South Australia	Queensland	Brisbane (Gabba)	ct	CP Christ	LWT Tallown	186	21230	95.63
South Australia	New South Wales	Sydney	no			135*	21365	96.24
Victoria	South Australia	Adelaide	ct	LO Fleetwood-Smith	FLO Thorn	5	21370	95.83

1939/40 in Australia

South Australia	Victoria	Adelaide	ro	(Miller/Sievers)		76	21446	95.74
			lbw		DT Ring	64	21510	95.60
South Australia	New South Wales	Adelaide	no			251*	21761	96.72
			no			90*	21851	97.12

Team	Opposition	Venue		Fielder	Bowler	Score	Agg	Avg
South Australia	Queensland	Adelaide	ct	CD Hansen	JA Ellis	138	21989	97.30
South Australia	Victoria	Melbourne	ct	IW Johnson	LO Fleetwood-Smith	267	22256	98.04
South Australia	Queensland	Brisbane (Gabba)	ct	PL Dixon	J Stackpole	0	22256	97.61
			ct	D Tallon	GG Cook	97	22353	97.61
South Australia	New South Wales	Sydney	lbw		WJ O'Reilly	39	22392	97.36
South Australia	Western Australia	Perth	ct	DK (S)Carmody	CG Pepper	40	22432	97.11
			ct	OI Lovelock	CWT MacGill	42	22474	96.87
South Australia	Western Australia	Perth	no			209*	22683	97.77
			ct	AG Zimbulis	G Eyres	135	22818	97.93
The Rest	New South Wales	Sydney	ct	RA Saggers	WJ O'Reilly	25	22843	97.62
			ct	CL McCool	AG Cheetham	2	22845	97.21

1940/41 in Australia

Team	Opposition	Venue		Fielder	Bowler	Score	Agg	Avg
South Australia	Victoria	Adelaide	ct	MW Sievers	WJ Dudley	0	22845	96.80
			bwd		MW Sievers	6	22851	96.42
DG Bradman's XI	SJ McCabe's XI	Melbourne	ct	GE (C)Tamblyn	JA Ellis	0	22851	96.01
			bwd		WJ O'Reilly	12	22863	95.66

1945/46 in Australia

Team	Opposition	Venue		Fielder	Bowler	Score	Agg	Avg
South Australia	Queensland	Adelaide	ct	D Tallon	CL McCool	68	22931	95.55
South Australia	Australian Services	Adelaide	no			52*	22983	95.76
			ct	DK Carmody	RG Williams	112	23095	95.83

1946/47 in Australia

Team	Opposition	Venue		Fielder	Bowler	Score	Agg	Avg
South Australia	M.C.C.	Adelaide	c&b	TPB Smith	TPB Smith	76	23171	95.75
Australian XI	M.C.C.	Melbourne	ct	WJ Edrich	R Pollard	3	23174	95.37
			ct	R Pollard	DCS Compton	106	23280	95.41

South Australia	Victoria	Adelaide	st	EA Baker	IW Johnson	43	23323	95.20
			st	EA Baker	GE Tribe	119	23442	95.29
AUSTRALIA	ENGLAND	Brisbane (Gabba)	bwd		WJ Edrich	187	23629	95.66
AUSTRALIA	ENGLAND	Sydney	lbw		NWD Yardley	234	23863	96.22
AUSTRALIA	ENGLAND	Melbourne	bwd		NWD Yardley	79	23942	96.15
			c&b	NWD Yardley	NWD Yardley	49	23991	95.96
South Australia	M.C.C.	Adelaide	ct	J Langridge	DVP Wright	5	23996	95.60
AUSTRALIA	ENGLAND	Adelaide	bwd		AV Bedser	0	23996	95.22
			no			56*	24052	95.44
AUSTRALIA	ENGLAND	Sydney	bwd		DVP Wright	12	24064	95.11
			ct	DCS Compton	AV Bedser	63	24127	94.99

1947/48 in Australia

South Australia	Indians	Adelaide	ct	CT Sarwate	V Mankad	156	24283	95.23
			st	PK Sen	V Mankad	12	24295	94.90
South Australia	Victoria	Adelaide	lbw		IW Johnson	100	24395	94.92
Australian XI	Indians	Sydney	ct	L Amarnath	VS Hazare	172	24567	95.22
			ct	CT Sarwate	V Mankad	26	24593	94.95
AUSTRALIA	INDIA	Brisbane (Gabba)	hwk		L Amarnath	185	24778	95.30
AUSTRALIA	INDIA	Sydney	bwd		VS Hazare	13	24791	94.98
AUSTRALIA	INDIA	Melbourne	lbw		DG Phadkar	132	24923	95.13
			no			127*	25050	95.61
AUSTRALIA	INDIA	Adelaide	bwd		VS Hazare	201	25251	96.01
AUSTRALIA	INDIA	Melbourne	R/H			57+	25308	96.23
Australian XI	Western Australia	Perth	ct	TM Outridge	TE O'Dwyer	115	25423	96.30

Team	Opponent	Venue				Score		Avg
Australian XI	Worcestershire	Worcester	bwd		PF Jackson	107	25530	96.34
Australian XI	Leicestershire	Leicester	ct	P Corrall	MW Etherington	81	25611	96.28
Australian XI	Surrey	The Oval	bwd		AV Bedser	146	25757	96.47
Australian XI	Essex	Southend	bwd		TPB Smith	187	25944	96.81
Australian XI	M.C.C.	Lord's	ct	WJ Edrich	JHG Deighton	98	26042	96.81
Australian XI	Lancashire	Manchester	bwd		MJ Hilton	11	26053	96.49
			st	EH Edrich	MJ Hilton	43	26096	96.30
Australian XI	Nottinghamshire	Nottingham	bwd		F Woodhead	86	26182	96.26
Australian XI	Sussex	Hove	bwd		J Cornford	109	26291	96.30
AUSTRALIA	ENGLAND	Nottingham	ct	L Hutton	AV Bedser	138	26429	96.46
			ct	L Hutton	AV Bedser	0	26429	96.11
Australian XI	Yorkshire	Sheffield	ct	NWD Yardley	JH Wardle	54	26483	95.95
			ct	L Hutton	R Aspinall	86	26569	95.92
AUSTRALIA	ENGLAND	Lord's	ct	L Hutton	AV Bedser	38	26607	95.71
			ct	WJ Edrich	AV Bedser	89	26696	95.68
Australian XI	Surrey	The Oval	ct	MR Barton	HS Squires	128	26824	95.80
AUSTRALIA	ENGLAND	Manchester	lbw		R Pollard	7	26831	95.48
			no			30*	26861	95.59
Australian XI	Middlesex	Lord's	ct	DCS Compton	PA Whitcombe	6	26867	95.27
AUSTRALIA	ENGLAND	Leeds	bwd		R Pollard	33	26900	95.05
			no			173*	27073	95.66
Australian XI	Derbyshire	Derby	bwd		EJ Gothard	62	27135	95.55
Australian XI	Warwickshire	Birmingham	bwd		WE Hollies	31	27166	95.32
			no			13*	27179	95.36
Australian XI	Lancashire	Manchester	ct	A Wilson	WB Roberts	28	27207	95.13
			no			133*	27340	95.59

						Score	Runs	Avrge
AUSTRALIA	ENGLAND	The Oval	bwd		WE Hollies	0	27340	95.26
Australian XI	Kent	Canterbury	ct	BH Valentine	E Crush	65	27405	95.16
Australian XI	Gentlemen of England	Lord's	ct	MP Donnelly	FR Brown	150	27555	95.35
Australian XI	South of England XI	Hastings	ct	FG Mann	TE Bailey	143	27698	95.51
Australian XI	HDG Leveson-Gower's XI	Scarborough	ct	L Hutton	AV Bedser	153	27851	95.71

1948/49 in Australia

						Score	Runs	Avrge
DG Bradman's XI	AL Hassett's XI	Melbourne	ct	RN Harvey	B Dooland	123	27974	95.80
			ct	RA Saggers	WA Johnston	10	27984	95.51
AR Morris's XI	AL Hassett's XI	Sydney	ct	KD Meuleman	KR Miller	53	28037	95.36
South Australia	Victoria	Adelaide	bwd		WA Johnston	30	28067	95.14

Leading Australian Run-Scorers

Batsman	First-class Career	M	Inn	NO	Runs	HS	50	100	Avrge
DG Bradman	1927/28 - 1948/49	234	338	43	28067	452*	69	117	95.14
AR Border	1976/77 - 1994/95	374	608	96	26462	205	137	70	51.68
GS Chappell	1966/67 - 1983/84	322	542	72	24535	247*	111	74	52.20
KJ Greives	1945/46 - 1964	490	746	79	22454	224	136	29	33.66
KD Wessels	1973/74 - 1994/95	280	480	43	21826	251	114	58	49.94
RN Harvey	1946/47 - 1962/63	306	461	35	21699	231*	94	67	50.93
RB Simpson	1952/53 - 1977/78	257	436	62	21029	359	100	60	56.22
IM Chappell	1961/62 - 1979/80	263	448	41	19680	209	96	59	48.35
WE Alley	1945/46 - 1968	400	682	67	19612	221*	92	31	31.88
WM Lawry	1955/56 - 1971/72	250	417	49	18734	266	100	50	50.90
FA Tarrant	1898/99 - 1936/37	329	541	48	17952	250*	93	33	36.41

DC Boon	1978/79 - 1994/95	250	421	40	17547	227	77	55	46.06
C Hill	1892/93 - 1924/25	252	416	21	17213	365*	82	45	43.57
W Bardsley	1903/04 - 1926/27	250	376	35	17025	264	74	53	49.92
WL Murdoch	1875/76 - 1904	391	679	48	16953	321	85	19	26.86
VT Trumper	1894/95 - 1913/14	255	401	21	16939	300*	87	42	44.57
AL Hassett	1932/33 - 1953/54	216	322	32	16890	232	76	59	58.24
KD Walters	1962/63 - 1980/81	259	426	57	16180	253	81	45	43.84
WW Armstrong	1898/99 - 1921/22	269	406	61	16158	303*	57	45	46.83
ME Waugh	1985/86 - 1994/95	208	327	44	15868	229*	76	52	56.07
VE Jackson	1936/37 - 1958	354	605	53	15698	170	72	21	28.43
SMJ Woods	1886 - 1910	401	690	35	15345	215	62	19	23.42
L Livingston	1941/42 - 1964	236	384	45	15269	210	78	34	45.04
SE Gregory	1889/90 - 1912	368	587	55	15192	201	65	25	28.55
CG Macartney	1905/06 - 1935/36	249	360	32	15019	345	53	49	45.78

Highest Individual Scores for Australian Teams

Runs	Batsman	Team	Opponent	Venue	Season
452*	DG Bradman	New South Wales	Queensland	Sydney	1929/30
437	WH Ponsford	Victoria	Queensland	Melbourne	1927/28
429	WH Ponsford	Victoria	Tasmania	Melbourne	1922/23
383	CW Gregory	New South Wales	Queensland	Brisbane	1906/07
369	DG Bradman	South Australia	Tasmania	Adelaide	1935/36
365*	C Hill	South Australia	New South Wales	Adelaide	1900/01
359	RB Simpson	New South Wales	Queensland	Brisbane	1963/64
357	DG Bradman	South Australia	Victoria	Melbourne	1935/36

356	BA Richards	South Australia	Western Australia	Perth	1970/71
355*	GR Marsh	Western Australia	South Australia	Perth	1989/90
352	WH Ponsford	Victoria	New South Wales	Melbourne	1926/27
345	CG Macartney	Australians	Nottinghamshire	Nottingham	1921
340*	DG Bradman	New South Wales	Victoria	Sydney	1928/29
336	WH Ponsford	Victoria	South Australia	Melbourne	1927/28
334	DG Bradman	AUSTRALIA	ENGLAND	Leeds	1930
325*	HSTL Hendry	Victoria	New Zealanders	Melbourne	1925/26
325	CL Badcock	South Australia	Victoria	Adelaide	1935/36
324*	DM Jones	Victoria	South Australia	Melbourne	1994/95
321	WL Murdoch	New South Wales	Victoria	Sydney	1881/82
315*	AF Kippax	New South Wales	Queensland	Sydney	1927/28
311	RB Simpson	AUSTRALIA	ENGLAND	Manchester	1964
307	RM Cowper	AUSTRALIA	ENGLAND	Melbourne	1965/66
306*	DW Hookes	South Australia	Tasmania	Adelaide	1986/87
304	DG Bradman	AUSTRALIA	ENGLAND	Leeds	1934
303*	WW Armstrong	Australians	Somerset	Bath	1905
300*	VT Trumper	Australians	Sussex	Hove	1899

Highest Wicket Partnerships for Australian Teams

Runs	Wkt	Batsmen	Team	Opponent	Venue	Season
464*	5th	ME Waugh & SR Waugh	New South Wales	Western Australia	Perth	1990/91
462*	4th	DW Hookes & WB Phillips	South Australia	Tasmania	Adelaide	1986/87
456	1st	WH Ponsford & ER Mayne	Victoria	Queensland	Melbourne	1923/24
451	2nd	WH Ponsford & DG Bradman	AUSTRALIA	ENGLAND	The Oval	1934

Score	Wkt	Batsmen	Team	Opponent	Venue	Season
433	8th	A Sims & VT Trumper	Australians	Canterbury	Christchurch	1913/14
431	1st	MRJ Veletta & GR Marsh	Western Australia	South Australia	Perth	1989/90
428	6th	MA Noble & WW Armstrong	Australians	Sussex	Hove	1902
424	4th	IS Lee & SO Quin	Victoria	Tasmania	Melbourne	1933/34
405	5th	SG Barnes & **DG Bradman**	AUSTRALIA	ENGLAND	Sydney	1946/47
397	5th	W Bardsley & C Kelleway	New South Wales	South Australia	Sydney	1920/21
390*	3rd	JM Wiener & JK Moss	Victoria	Western Australia	St Kilda	1981/82
389	3rd	WH Ponsford & SJ McCabe	Australians	MCC	Lord's	1934
388	4th	WH Ponsford & **DG Bradman**	AUSTRALIA	ENGLAND	Leeds	1934
388	1st	KC Wessels & RB Kerr	Queensland	Victoria	Melbourne	1982/83
382	1st	WM Lawry & RB Simpson	AUSTRALIA	WEST INDIES	Bridgetown	1964/65
378	2nd	LA Marks & KD Walters	New South Wales	South Australia	Adelaide	1964/65
377	4th	KR Miller & JH de Courcy	Australians	Combined Services	Kingston	1953
375	1st	WM Woodfull & WH Ponsford	Victoria	New South Wales	Melbourne	1926/27
374	1st	GR Marsh & MRJ Veletta	Western Australia	Tamil Nadu	Perth	1988/89
374	2nd	RB Simpson & RM Cowper	Australians	NE Transvaal	Pretoria	1966/67
363	3rd	**DG Bradman** & AF Kippax	New South Wales	Queensland	Sydney	1933/34
362	3rd	W Bardsley & CG Macartney	Australians	Essex	Leyton	1912
358	2nd	C McKenzie & HHL Kortlang	Victoria	Western Australia	Perth	1909/10
356	3rd	**DG Bradman** & RA Hamence	South Australia	Tasmania	Adelaide	1935/36
355	3rd	W Bardsley & VS Ransford	Australians	Essex	Leyton	1909

TEST CAREER

Debut: 1928/29 AUSTRALIA v ENGLAND, Brisbane (Exhib)

Season	Opponent	Venue	M	Inn	NO	Runs	HS	0s	50	100	Avrge	Ct	St	Runs	Wkts	Avrge	Best
1928/29	ENGLAND	Australia	4	8	1	468	123	-	2	2	66.86	2	-	-	-	-	-
1930	ENGLAND	England	5	7	-	974	334	-	-	4	139.14	2	-	1	-	-	-
1930/31	WEST INDIES	Australia	5	6	-	447	223	1	-	2	74.50	4	-	15	1	15.00	1/8
1931/32	SOUTH AFRICA	Australia	5	5	1	806	299*	-	-	4	201.50	2	-	2	-	-	-
1932/33	ENGLAND	Australia	4	8	1	396	103*	1	3	1	56.57	3	-	44	1	44.00	1/23
1934	ENGLAND	England	5	8	-	758	304	-	1	2	94.75	1	-	-	-	-	-
1936/37	ENGLAND	Australia	5	9	-	810	270	2	1	3	90.00	7	-	-	-	-	-
1938	ENGLAND	England	4	6	2	434	144*	-	1	3	108.50	-	-	6	-	-	-
1946/47	ENGLAND	Australia	5	8	1	680	234	1	3	2	97.14	3	-	-	-	-	-
1947/48	INDIA	Australia	5	6	2	715	201	-	1	4	178.75	6	-	4	-	-	-
1948	ENGLAND	England	5	9	2	508	173*	2	1	2	72.57	2	-	-	-	-	-
Total			52	80	10	6996	334	7	13	29	99.94	32	-	72	2	36.00	1/8

Opponents	M	Inn	NO	Runs	HS	0s	50	100	Avrge	Ct	St	Runs	Wkts	Avrge	Best
ENGLAND	37	63	7	5028	334	6	12	19	89.79	20	-	51	1	51.00	1/23
INDIA	5	6	2	715	201	-	1	4	178.75	6	-	4	-	-	-
SOUTH AFRICA	5	5	1	806	299*	-	-	4	201.50	2	-	2	-	-	-
WEST INDIES	5	6	-	447	223	1	-	2	74.50	4	-	15	1	15.00	1/8

	Inn	NO	Runs	HS	0s	50	100	Avrge	Ct	St	Runs	Wkts	Avrge	Best
First Innings	22	1	2387	334	1	4	9	113.67	10	-	-	-	-	-
Second Innings	28	1	2310	304	3	1	10	85.56	3	-	-	-	-	-
Third Innings	15	3	1565	270	-	4	7	130.42	5	-	-	-	-	-
Fourth Innings	15	5	734	173*	3	4	3	73.40	14	-	32	2	16.00	1/8

Venues in Australia	M	Inn	NO	Runs	HS	0s	50	100	Avrge	Ct	St	Runs	Wkts	Avrge	Best
Adelaide	7	11	2	970	299*	1	3	3	107.78	6	-	42	2	21.00	1/8
Brisbane (Gabba)	5	7	-	736	226	1	1	3	105.14	4	-	17	-	-	-
Brisbane (Exhib)	2	3	-	242	223	-	-	1	80.67	2	-	-	-	-	-
Melbourne	11	17	4	1671	270	1	3	9	128.54	9	-	2	-	-	-
Sydney	8	12	-	703	234	2	3	2	58.58	6	-	4	-	-	-
Total	33	50	6	4322	299*	5	10	18	98.23	27	-	65	2	32.50	1/8

Venues in England	M	Inn	NO	Runs	HS	0s	50	100	Avrge	Ct	St	Runs	Wkts	Avrge	Best
Leeds	4	6	1	963	334	-	-	4	192.60	1	-	-	-	-	-
Lord's	4	8	1	551	254	-	1	2	78.71	1	-	1	-	-	-
Manchester	3	4	1	81	30*	-	-	-	27.00	2	-	-	-	-	-
Nottingham	4	8	1	526	144*	1	1	3	75.14	-	-	-	-	-	-
The Oval	4	4	-	553	244	1	1	2	138.25	1	-	6	-	-	-
Total	19	30	4	2674	334	2	3	11	102.85	5	-	7	-	-	-

Batting Position

Batting Position	Inn	NO	Runs	HS	0s	50	100	Avrge
3	56	7	5078	334	5	10	20	103.63
4	10	1	485	112	1	1	3	53.89
5	3	-	427	304	1	-	2	142.33
6	8	1	681	234	-	2	3	97.29
7	3	1	325	270	-	-	1	162.50

Innings	NO	Bwd	Cgt	LBW	Stp	RO	HW	HB
80	10	23	39	6	-	1	1	-

Wickets	Bwd	Cgt	C&B	LBW	Stp	HW
2	1	-	-	1	-	-

Highest Score: 334 AUSTRALIA v ENGLAND, Leeds, 1930

100s	Team	Opponent	Venue	Season
112	AUSTRALIA	ENGLAND	Melbourne	1928/29
123	AUSTRALIA	ENGLAND	Melbourne	1928/29
131	AUSTRALIA	ENGLAND	Nottingham	1930
254	AUSTRALIA	ENGLAND	Lord's	1930
334	AUSTRALIA	ENGLAND	Leeds	1930
232	AUSTRALIA	ENGLAND	The Oval	1930
223	AUSTRALIA	WEST INDIES	Brisbane (Exhib)	1930/31
152	AUSTRALIA	WEST INDIES	Melbourne	1930/31
226	AUSTRALIA	SOUTH AFRICA	Brisbane (Gabba)	1931/32
112	AUSTRALIA	SOUTH AFRICA	Sydney	1931/32
167	AUSTRALIA	SOUTH AFRICA	Melbourne	1931/32
299*	AUSTRALIA	SOUTH AFRICA	Adelaide	1931/32
103*	AUSTRALIA	ENGLAND	Melbourne	1932/33

Score	Team	Opponent	Venue	Year
304	AUSTRALIA	ENGLAND	Leeds	1934
244	AUSTRALIA	ENGLAND	The Oval	1934
270	AUSTRALIA	ENGLAND	Melbourne	1936/37
212	AUSTRALIA	ENGLAND	Adelaide	1936/37
169	AUSTRALIA	ENGLAND	Melbourne	1936/37
144*	AUSTRALIA	ENGLAND	Nottingham	1938
102*	AUSTRALIA	ENGLAND	Lord's	1938
103	AUSTRALIA	ENGLAND	Leeds	1938
187	AUSTRALIA	ENGLAND	Brisbane (Gabba)	1946/47
234	AUSTRALIA	ENGLAND	Sydney	1946/47
185	AUSTRALIA	INDIA	Brisbane (Gabba)	1947/48
132	AUSTRALIA	INDIA	Melbourne	1947/48
127*	AUSTRALIA	INDIA	Melbourne	1947/48
201	AUSTRALIA	INDIA	Adelaide	1947/48
138	AUSTRALIA	ENGLAND	Nottingham	1948
173*	AUSTRALIA	ENGLAND	Leeds	1948

Best Bowling: 1/8 AUSTRALIA v WEST INDIES, Adelaide, 1930/31

Batting — Innings by Innings

Team	Opponent	Venue	HO	Fielder	Bowler	Score	Runs	Avrge
		1928/29 in Australia						
AUSTRALIA	ENGLAND	Brisbane (Exhib)	lbw		MW Tate	18	18	18.00
			ct	APF Chapman	JC White	1	19	9.50
AUSTRALIA	ENGLAND	Melbourne	bwd		WR Hammond	79	98	32.67
			ct	G Duckworth	G Geary	112	210	52.50

AUSTRALIA	ENGLAND	Adelaide	ct	H Larwood	MW Tate	40	250	50.00
AUSTRALIA	ENGLAND	Melbourne	ro	MW Tate	G Geary	58	308	51.33
						123	431	61.57
			no			37*	468	66.86

1930 in England

AUSTRALIA	ENGLAND	Nottingham	bwd		MW Tate	8	476	59.50
			bwd		RWV Robins	131	607	67.44
AUSTRALIA	ENGLAND	Lord's	ct	APF Chapman	JC White	254	861	86.10
			ct	APF Chapman	MW Tate	1	862	78.36
AUSTRALIA	ENGLAND	Leeds	ct	G Duckworth	MW Tate	334	1196	99.67
AUSTRALIA	ENGLAND	Manchester	ct	KS Duleepsinhji	IAR Peebles	14	1210	93.08
AUSTRALIA	ENGLAND	The Oval	ct	G Duckworth	H Larwood	232	1442	103.00

1930/31 in Australia

AUSTRALIA	WEST INDIES	Adelaide	ct	GC Grant	HC Griffith	4	1446	96.40
AUSTRALIA	WEST INDIES	Sydney	ct	I Barrow	GN Francis	25	1471	91.94
AUSTRALIA	WEST INDIES	Brisbane (Exhib)	ct	GC Grant	LN Constantine	223	1694	99.65
AUSTRALIA	WEST INDIES	Melbourne	ct	CA Roach	FR Martin	152	1846	102.56
AUSTRALIA	WEST INDIES	Sydney	ct	GN Francis	FR Martin	43	1889	99.42
			bwd		HC Griffith	0	1889	94.45

1931/32 in Australia

AUSTRALIA	SOUTH AFRICA	Brisbane (Gabba)	lbw		CL Vincent	226	2115	100.71
AUSTRALIA	SOUTH AFRICA	Sydney	ct	KG Viljoen	DPB Morkel	112	2227	101.23
AUSTRALIA	SOUTH AFRICA	Melbourne	ct	HB Cameron	NA Quinn	2	2229	96.91
			lbw		CL Vincent	167	2396	99.83

AUSTRALIA	SOUTH AFRICA	Adelaide	no			299*	2695	112.29
AUSTRALIA	SOUTH AFRICA	Melbourne	dnb			-	2695	112.29

1932/33 in Australia

AUSTRALIA	ENGLAND	Melbourne	bwd		WE Bowes	0	2695	107.80
AUSTRALIA	ENGLAND		no			103*	2798	111.92
AUSTRALIA	ENGLAND	Adelaide	ct	GOB Allen	H Larwood	8	2806	107.92
AUSTRALIA	ENGLAND		c&b	H Verity	H Verity	66	2872	106.37
AUSTRALIA	ENGLAND	Brisbane (Gabba)	ct	TB Mitchell	H Larwood	76	2948	105.29
AUSTRALIA	ENGLAND		bwd		H Larwood	24	2972	102.48
AUSTRALIA	ENGLAND	Sydney	bwd		H Larwood	48	3020	100.67
AUSTRALIA	ENGLAND		bwd		H Verity	71	3091	99.71

1934 in England

AUSTRALIA	ENGLAND	Nottingham	ct	WR Hammond	G Geary	29	3120	97.50
AUSTRALIA	ENGLAND		ct	LEG Ames	K Farnes	25	3145	95.30
AUSTRALIA	ENGLAND	Lord's	c&b	H Verity	H Verity	36	3181	93.56
AUSTRALIA	ENGLAND		ct	LEG Ames	H Verity	13	3194	91.26
AUSTRALIA	ENGLAND	Manchester	ct	LEG Ames	WR Hammond	30	3224	89.56
AUSTRALIA	ENGLAND	Leeds	bwd		WE Bowes	304	3528	95.35
AUSTRALIA	ENGLAND	The Oval	ct	LEG Ames	WE Bowes	244	3772	99.26
AUSTRALIA	ENGLAND		bwd		WE Bowes	77	3849	98.69

1936/37 in Australia

AUSTRALIA	ENGLAND	Brisbane (Gabba)	ct	TS Worthington	W Voce	38	3887	97.18
AUSTRALIA	ENGLAND		ct	AE Fagg	GOB Allen	0	3887	94.80

		Venue		Fielder	Bowler	Score	Runs	Avge
AUSTRALIA	ENGLAND	Sydney	ct	GOB Allen	W Voce	0	3887	92.55
AUSTRALIA	ENGLAND	Melbourne	bwd		H Verity	82	3969	92.30
AUSTRALIA	ENGLAND	Adelaide	ct	RWV Robins	H Verity	13	3982	90.50
AUSTRALIA	ENGLAND	Melbourne	ct	GOB Allen	H Verity	270	4252	94.49
AUSTRALIA	ENGLAND		bwd		GOB Allen	26	4278	93.00
AUSTRALIA	ENGLAND		c&b	WR Hammond	WR Hammond	212	4490	95.53
AUSTRALIA	ENGLAND		bwd		K Farnes	169	4659	97.06

1938 in England

		Venue		Fielder	Bowler	Score	Runs	Avge
AUSTRALIA	ENGLAND	Nottingham	ct	LEG Ames	RA Sinfield	51	4710	96.12
AUSTRALIA	ENGLAND		no			144*	4854	99.06
AUSTRALIA	ENGLAND	Lord's	bwd		H Verity	18	4872	97.44
AUSTRALIA	ENGLAND		no			102*	4974	99.48
AUSTRALIA	ENGLAND	Leeds	bwd		WE Bowes	103	5077	99.55
AUSTRALIA	ENGLAND		ct	H Verity	DVP Wright	16	5093	97.94
AUSTRALIA	ENGLAND	The Oval	dnb			-	5093	97.94

1946/47 in Australia

		Venue		Fielder	Bowler	Score	Runs	Avge
AUSTRALIA	ENGLAND	Brisbane (Gabba)	bwd		WJ Edrich	187	5280	99.62
AUSTRALIA	ENGLAND	Sydney	lbw		NWD Yardley	234	5514	102.11
AUSTRALIA	ENGLAND	Melbourne	bwd		NWD Yardley	79	5593	101.69
AUSTRALIA	ENGLAND		c&b	NWD Yardley	NWD Yardley	49	5642	100.75
AUSTRALIA	ENGLAND	Adelaide	bwd		AV Bedser	0	5642	98.98
AUSTRALIA	ENGLAND		no			56*	5698	99.96
AUSTRALIA	ENGLAND	Sydney	bwd		DVP Wright	12	5710	98.45
AUSTRALIA	ENGLAND		ct	DCS Compton	AV Bedser	63	5773	97.85

1947/48 in Australia

		Venue			Score	Agg	Avrge
AUSTRALIA	INDIA	Brisbane (Gabba)	hwk	L Amarnath	185	5958	99.30
AUSTRALIA	INDIA	Sydney	bwd	VS Hazare	13	5971	97.89
AUSTRALIA	INDIA	Melbourne	lbw	DG Phadkar	132	6103	98.44
AUSTRALIA	INDIA	Adelaide	no		127*	6230	100.48
AUSTRALIA	INDIA	Melbourne	bwd	VS Hazare	201	6431	102.08
			R/H		57+	6488	102.98

1948 in England

		Venue				Score	Agg	Avrge
AUSTRALIA	ENGLAND	Nottingham	ct	L Hutton	AV Bedser	138	6626	103.53
AUSTRALIA	ENGLAND		ct	L Hutton	AV Bedser	0	6626	101.94
AUSTRALIA	ENGLAND	Lord's	ct	L Hutton	AV Bedser	38	6664	100.97
AUSTRALIA	ENGLAND		ct	WJ Edrich	AV Bedser	89	6753	100.79
AUSTRALIA	ENGLAND	Manchester	lbw		R Pollard	7	6760	99.41
AUSTRALIA	ENGLAND		no			30*	6790	99.85
AUSTRALIA	ENGLAND	Leeds	bwd		R Pollard	33	6823	98.88
AUSTRALIA	ENGLAND		no			173*	6996	101.39
AUSTRALIA	ENGLAND	The Oval	bwd		WE Hollies	0	6996	99.94

Leading Australian Run-Scorers

Batsman	Test Career	M	Inn	NO	Runs	HS	50	100	Avrge
AR Border	1978/79 - 1993/94	156	265	44	11174	205	63	27	50.56
DC Boon	1984/85 - 1994/95	101	181	20	7111	200	31	20	44.17
GS Chappell	1970/71 - 1983/84	88	151	18	7110	247*	31	24	53.46
DG Bradman	1928/29 - 1948	52	80	10	6996	334	13	29	99.94
RN Harvey	1947/48 - 1962/63	79	137	10	6149	205	24	21	48.42

KD Walters	1965/66 - 1980/81	75	125	14	5357	250	33	15	48.26
IM Chappell	1964/65 - 1979/80	76	136	10	5345	196	26	14	42.42
WM Lawry	1961- 1970/71	68	123	12	5234	210	27	13	47.15
MA Taylor	1988/89 - 1994/95	66	119	8	5005	219	30	13	45.09
RB Simpson	1957/58 - 1977/78	62	111	7	4869	311	27	10	46.82
IR Redpath	1963/64 - 1975/76	67	120	11	4737	171	31	8	43.46
SR Waugh	1985/86 - 1994/95	76	117	23	4440	200	27	8	47.23
KJ Hughes	1977- 1984/85	70	124	6	4415	213	22	9	37.42
RW Marsh	1970/71 - 1983/84	97	150	13	3633	132	16	3	26.52
DM Jones	1983/84 - 1992/93	52	89	11	3631	216	14	11	46.55
AR Morris	1947/47 - 1954/55	46	79	3	3533	206	12	12	46.49
C Hill	1896- 1911/12	49	89	2	3412	191	19	7	39.22
GM Wood	1977/78 - 1988/89	60	113	6	3374	172	13	9	31.53
VT Trumper	1899- 1911/12	48	89	8	3163	214*	13	8	39.05
CC McDonald	1951/52 - 1961	47	83	4	3107	170	17	5	39.33
AL Hassett	1938 - 1953	43	69	3	3073	198*	11	10	46.56
ME Waugh	1990/91 - 1994/95	48	77	4	3072	140	18	8	42.08

Highest Individual Scores for Australia

Runs	Batsman	Opponent	Venue	Season
334	DG Bradman	England	Leeds	1930
311	RB Simpson	England	Manchester	1964
307	RM Cowper	England	Melbourne	1965/66
304	DG Bradman	England	Leeds	1934
299*	DG Bradman	South Africa	Adelaide	1931/32
270	DG Bradman	England	Melbourne	1936/37

Highest Wicket Partnerships for Australia

Ttl	Wkt	Batsmen	Opponent	Venue	Series
451	2nd	WH Ponsford & DG Bradman	England	The Oval	1934
405	5th	SG Barnes & DG Bradman	England	Sydney	1946/47
388	4th	WH Ponsford & DG Bradman	England	Leeds	1934
382	1st	WM Lawry & RB Simpson	West Indies	Bridgetown	1964/65
346	6th	JHW Fingleton & DG Bradman	England	Melbourne	1936/37
336	4th	WM Lawry & KD Walters	West Indies	Sydney	1968/69
332*	5th	AR Border & SR Waugh	England	Leeds	1993
329	1st	GR Marsh & MA Taylor	England	Nottingham	1989
301	2nd	AR Morris & DG Bradman	England	Leeds	1948
298	2nd	WM Lawry & IM Chappell	West Indies	Melbourne	1968/69
295	3rd	CC McDonald & RN Harvey	West Indies	Kingston	1954/55
277	2nd	RB McCosker & IM Chappell	England	The Oval	1975
276	3rd	DG Bradman & AL Hassett	England	Brisbane	1946/47
275	2nd	CC McDonald & AL Hassett	South Africa	Adelaide	1952/53
274	2nd	WM Woodfull & DG Bradman	South Africa	Melbourne	1931/32
264	3rd	IM Chappell & GS Chappell	New Zealand	Wellington	1973/74
260*	6th	DM Jones & SR Waugh	Sri Lanka	Hobart	1989/90
260	1st	MA Taylor & MJ Slater	England	Lord's	1993
259	2nd	WB Phillips & GN Yallop	Pakistan	Perth	1983/84
251	4th	GM Wood & CS Serjeant	West Indies	Georgetown	1977/78

Leading Run-Scorers in Test Cricket

Batsman	Country	M	Inn	NO	Runs	HS	50	100	Avrge
AR Border	Australia	156	265	44	11174	205	63	27	50.56
SM Gavaskar	India	125	214	16	10122	236*	45	34	51.12
GA Gooch	England	118	215	6	8900	333	46	20	42.58
Javed Miandad	Pakistan	124	189	21	8832	280*	43	23	52.57
IVA Richards	West Indies	121	182	12	8540	291	45	24	50.24
DI Gower	England	117	204	18	8231	215	39	18	44.25
G Boycott	England	109	193	23	8114	246*	42	22	47.73
GS Sobers	West Indies	93	160	21	8032	365*	30	26	57.78
MC Cowdrey	England	115	188	15	7624	182	38	22	44.07
CG Greenidge	West Indies	108	185	16	7558	226	34	19	44.72
CH Lloyd	West Indies	110	175	14	7515	242*	39	19	46.68
DL Haynes	West Indies	116	202	25	7487	184	39	18	42.30
WR Hammond	England	85	140	16	7249	336*	24	22	58.46
DC Boon	Australia	101	181	20	7111	200	31	20	44.17
GS Chappell	Australia	88	151	19	7110	247*	31	24	53.86
DG Bradman	Australia	52	80	10	6996	334	13	29	99.94
L Hutton	England	79	138	15	6971	364	33	19	56.67
DB Vengsarkar	India	116	185	22	6868	166	35	17	42.13
KF Barrington	England	82	131	15	6806	256	35	20	58.67
RB Kanhai	West Indies	79	137	6	6227	256	28	15	47.53
RN Harvey	Australia	79	137	10	6149	205	24	21	48.42
GR Viswanath	India	91	155	10	6080	222	35	14	41.93

Highest Test Averages
(Qualification: 20 innings)

Batsman	Country	M	Inn	NO	Runs	HS	50	100	Avrge
DG Bradman	Australia	52	80	10	6996	334	13	29	99.94
JC Adams	West Indies	21	32	8	1591	174*	8	4	66.29
RG Pollock	South Africa	23	41	4	2256	274	11	7	60.97
GA Headley	West Indies	22	40	4	2190	270*	5	10	60.83
H Sutcliffe	England	54	84	9	4555	194	23	16	60.73
E Paynter	England	20	31	5	1540	243	7	4	59.23
KF Barrington	England	82	131	15	6806	256	35	20	58.67
EC Weekes	West Indies	48	81	5	4455	207	19	15	58.62
WR Hammond	England	85	140	16	7249	336*	24	22	58.46
GS Sobers	West Indies	93	160	21	8032	365*	30	26	57.78

Highest Test Averages for Australia
(Qualification: 20 innings)

Batsman	M	Inn	NO	Runs	HS	50	100	Avrge
DG Bradman	52	80	10	6996	334	13	29	99.94
GS Chappell	88	151	18	7110	247*	31	24	53.46
J Ryder	20	32	5	1394	201*	9	3	51.63
AR Border	156	265	44	11174	205	63	27	50.56
RN Harvey	79	137	10	6149	205	24	21	48.42
KD Walters	75	125	14	5357	250	33	15	48.26
WH Ponsford	29	48	4	2122	266	6	7	48.23
SJ McCabe	39	62	13	2748	232	13	6	48.21
MJ Slater	27	47	2	2163	176	8	6	48.07
SR Waugh	76	117	23	4440	200	27	8	47.23

SHEFFIELD SHIELD CAREER

Debut: 1927/28 New South Wales v South Australia, Adelaide

Season	State	M	Inn	NO	Runs	HS	0s	50	100	Avrge	Ct	St	Runs	Wkts	Avrge	Best
1927/28	New South Wales	5	10	1	416	134*	1	1	2	46.22	1	-	66	2	33.00	2/41
1928/29	New South Wales	5	9	3	893	340*	-	1	4	148.83	-	-	48	1	48.00	1/26
1929/30	New South Wales	6	10	2	894	452*	-	4	1	111.75	2	-	101	2	50.50	2/93
1930/31	New South Wales	4	6	-	695	258	-	1	3	115.83	-	-	142	3	47.33	3/54
1931/32	New South Wales	3	5	-	213	167	2	-	1	42.60	3	-	10	1	10.00	1/4
1932/33	New South Wales	3	5	1	600	238	-	3	2	150.00	1	-	56	3	18.67	1/4
1933/34	New South Wales	5	7	2	922	253	-	2	4	184.40	3	-	21	-	-	-
1935/36	South Australia	6	6	-	739	357	1	-	3	123.17	6	-	0	-	-	-
1936/37	South Australia	4	6	1	416	192	-	2	2	83.20	-	-	-	-	-	-
1937/38	South Australia	6	12	2	983	246	-	4	4	98.30	6	1	-	-	-	-
1938/39	South Australia	6	6	1	801	225	-	-	5	160.20	3	-	-	-	-	-
1939/40	South Australia	6	10	2	1062	267	1	4	3	132.75	9	-	-	-	-	-
1946/47	South Australia	1	2	-	162	119	-	-	1	81.00	-	-	-	-	-	-
1947/48	South Australia	1	1	-	100	100	-	-	1	100.00	2	-	-	-	-	-
1948/49	South Australia	1	1	-	30	30	-	-	-	30.00	2	-	-	-	-	-
For New South Wales		31	52	9	4633	452*	3	12	17	107.74	10	-	444	12	37.00	3/54
For South Australia		31	44	6	4293	357	2	8	19	112.97	28	1	0	-	-	-
Total		62	96	15	8926	452*	5	20	36	110.20	38	1	444	12	37.00	3/54

Opponents	M	Inn	NO	Runs	HS	0s	50	100	Avrge	Ct	St	Runs	Wkts	Avrge	Best
New South Wales	8	12	3	837	143	1	2	4	93.00	9	1	-	-	-	-
Queensland	17	24	3	2965	452*	3	2	14	141.19	11	-	62	2	31.00	2/41
South Australia	11	20	-	1269	258	1	6	4	63.45	1	-	295	8	36.88	3/54
Victoria	26	40	9	3855	357	-	10	14	124.35	17	-	87	2	43.50	1/4

Venues	M	Inn	NO	Runs	HS	0s	50	100	Avrge	Ct	St	Runs	Wkts	Avrge	Best
Adelaide	21	32	3	2779	258	-	8	11	95.83	15	-	177	5	35.40	3/54
Brisbane (Gabba)	7	9	-	857	200	2	1	5	95.22	5	-	-	-	-	-
Brisbane (Exhib)	2	4	1	378	133*	-	1	2	126.00	-	-	-	-	-	-
Melbourne	11	16	4	1658	357	-	4	6	138.17	5	-	8	-	-	-
Sydney	21	35	7	3254	452*	3	6	12	116.21	13	1	259	7	37.00	2/41

Leading Run-Scorers

Batsman	State	M	Inn	NO	Runs	HS	50	100	Avrge
DW Hookes	SA	120	205	9	9364	306*	44	26	47.78
RJ Inverarity	WA/SA	159	275	32	9341	187	45	22	38.44
DG Bradman	NSW/SA	62	96	15	8926	452*	20	36	110.19
GS Chappell	SA/Qld	101	173	20	8762	194	42	27	57.27
SC Trimble	Qld	123	230	13	8647	252*	40	22	39.85
LE Favell	SA	121	220	4	8269	164	43	20	38.28
AR Border	NSW/Qld	98	166	18	7907	200	42	19	53.43
JD Siddons	Vic/SA	104	179	17	7867	245	36	24	48.56
IM Chappell	SA	89	157	13	7665	205*	45	22	53.22
AMJ Hilditch	NSW/SA	109	192	11	7613	230	32	18	42.06

DM Jones	Vic	84	146	13	7453	324*	28	24	56.04
MRJ Veletta	WA	114	198	20	7306	262	40	18	41.04
PJP Burge	Qld	83	138	12	7084	283	30	22	56.22
GR Marsh	WA	100	175	12	7009	355*	28	21	43.00
GM Wood	WA	109	174	25	6904	186*	32	20	46.34
DM Wellham	NSW/Tas/Qld	110	182	23	6739	167	46	12	42.38
HN Dansie	SA	107	196	6	6692	185	32	17	35.22
WM Lawry	Vic	85	139	14	6615	266	38	17	52.92
RB Simpson	NSW/WA	78	133	21	6471	359	28	17	57.78
KD Mackay	Qld	100	162	22	6341	223	31	14	45.29
C Hill	SA	68	126	6	6274	365*	27	18	52.28
TM Moody	WA	89	154	9	6175	272	32	13	42.59
PR Sleep	SA	127	211	37	6106	146*	29	12	35.09
AF Kippax	NSW	61	95	8	6096	315*	14	23	70.07
GM Ritchie	Qld	94	154	14	6096	213*	34	14	43.54
VY Richardson	SA	77	146	7	6014	203	27	18	43.27

Highest Individual Innings

Total	Batsman	Team	Opponent	Venue	Season
452*	DG Bradman	New South Wales	Queensland	Sydney	1929/30
437	WH Ponsford	Victoria	Queensland	Melbourne	1927/28
365*	C Hill	South Australia	New South Wales	Adelaide	1900/01
359	RB Simpson	New South Wales	Queensland	Brisbane	1963/64
357	DG Bradman	South Australia	Victoria	Melbourne	1935/36
356	BA Richards	South Australia	Western Australia	Perth	1970/71

355*	GR Marsh	Western Australia	South Australia	Perth	1989/90
352	WH Ponsford	Victoria	New South Wales	Melbourne	1926/27
342*	DM Jones	Victoria	South Australia	Melbourne	1994/95
340*	DG Bradman	New South Wales	Victoria	Sydney	1928/29
336	WH Ponsford	Victoria	South Australia	Melbourne	1927/28
325	CL Badcock	South Australia	Victoria	Adelaide	1935/36
315*	AF Kippax	New South Wales	Queensland	Sydney	1927/28
306*	DW Hookes	South Australia	Tasmania	Adelaide	1986/87

Highest Wicket Partnerships

Wkt	Ttl	Batsmen		Venue	Season
5th	464*	ME Waugh & SR Waugh	NSW v WA	Perth	1990/91
4th	462*	DW Hookes & WB Phillips	SA v Tas	Adelaide	1986/87
1st	431	MRJ Veletta & GR Marsh	WA v SA	Perth	1989/90
5th	397	W Bardsley & C Kelleway	NSW v SA	Sydney	1920/21
3rd	390*	JM Wiener & JK Moss	Vic v WA	St Kilda	1981/82
1st	388	KC Wessels & RB Kerr	Qld v Vic	St Kilda	1982/83
2nd	378	LA Marks & KD Walters	NSW v SA	Adelaide	1964/65
1st	375	WM Woodfull & WH Ponsford	Vic v NSW	Melbourne	1926/27
3rd	363	DG Bradman & AF Kippax	NSW v Qld	Sydney	1933/34
3rd	345	W Bardsley & JM Taylor	NSW v SA	Adelaide	1920/21
1st	337	CC McDonald & KD Meuleman	Vic v SA	Adelaide	1949/50
7th	335	CW Andrews & EC Bensted	Qld v NSW	Sydney	1934/35
2nd	334	A Jackson & DG Bradman	NSW v SA	Adelaide	1930/31
6th	332	G Thomas & NG Marks	NSW v SA	Sydney	1958/59

1st	331	BA Courtice & RB Kerr	Qld v Tas	Brisbane	1984/85
3rd	330	GM Wood & GR Marsh	WA v NSW	Sydney	1983/84
1st	328	C Milburn & D Chadwick	WA v Qld	Brisbane	1968/69
3rd	326	ML Love & SG Law	Qld v Tas	Brisbane	1994/95
5th	325	NC O'Neill & BC Booth	NSW v Vic	Sydney	1957/58
2nd	323	ID Craig & RN Harvey	NSW v Qld	Sydney	1960/61
1st	319	RB McCosker & J Dyson	NSW v WA	Sydney	1980/81
5th	319	RT Ponting & RJ Tucker	Tas v WA	Hobart (Bel)	1994/95
5th	315	MA Noble & SE Gregory	NSW v Vic	Sydney	1907/08
2nd	314	WH Ponsford & HSTL Hendry	Vic v Qld	Melbourne	1927/28
1st	310	GR Marsh & MRJ Veletta	WA v Tas	Hobart (Bel)	1988/89
2nd	308	BA Richards & IM Chappell	SA v WA	Perth	1970/71
1st	308	RB Simpson & G Thomas	NSW v WA	Sydney	1963/64
10th	307	AF Kippax & JEH Hooker	NSW v Vic	Melbourne	1928/29
3rd	304	KC Wessels & GM Ritchie	Qld v Tas	Devonport	1981/82
2nd	304	W Bardsley & MA Noble	NSW v Vic	Sydney	1908/09
2nd	302	WN Phillips & DM Jones	Vic v SA	Melbourne	1991/92
4th	301	LPJ O'Brien & LS Darling	Vic v Qld	Brisbane	1932/33
5th	301*	RB Simpson & KD Meuleman	WA v NSW	Perth	1959/60

BIBLIOGRAPHY

Allen, Peter & Kemsley, James, *Images of Bradman*, The Bradman Museum, Bowral, 1994

Arlott, John, *Gone to the Test Match*, Longmans, Green and Co, London, 1949

Barker, Ralph, *Ten Great Innings*, Chatto & Windus, London, 1964

Beecher, Eric, *The Cricket Revolution*, Newspress, Melbourne, 1978

Bowes, Bill, *Aussies and Ashes*, Stanley Paul, London, 1961

Bradman, Sir Donald, *The Bradman Albums*, Rigby Publishers, Adelaide, 1987

Bradman, Sir Donald, *Farewell to Cricket*, Hodder & Stoughton, London, 1950

Cardus, Neville, *Australian Summer*, Souvenir Press, London, 1987

Derriman, Philip, *Bodyline*, Fontana, Melbourne, 1984

Davis, Anthony, *Sir Donald Bradman*, Cassell, London, 1960

Docker, Edward Wybergh, *Bradman and the Bodyline Series*, Angus & Robertson, Sydney, 1978

Fingleton, J H, *Brightly Fades the Don*, Collins, London, 1949

Fingleton, J H, *Cricket Crisis*, The Pavilion Library, London, 1986

Fingleton, J H, *Four Chukkas to Australia*, William Heinemann, London, 1959

Flanagan, Andy, *On Tour With Bradman*, Halstead Press, Sydney, 1950

Larwood, Harold, *Bodyline?*, Elkin Mathews & Marrot, London, 1933

Larwood, Harold and Perkins, Kevin, *The Larwood Story*, Bonpara, Sydney, 1982

Le Quesne, Laurence, *The Bodyline Controversy*, Secker & Warburg, London, 1983

Lindsay, Philip, *Don Bradman*, Phoenix House, London, 1951

Mailey, Arthur, *–And Then Came Larwood*, The Sportsman's Book Club, London, 1933

Mason, Ronald, *Ashes in the Mouth*, Penguin, London, 1984

Meckiff, Ian and McDonald, Ian, *Thrown Out*, Stanley Paul, London, 1961

Morris, Barry, *Bradman, What They Said About Him*, ABC Books, Sydney, 1994

Moyes, A G, *Bradman*, Angus and Robertson, Sydney, 1948

O'Reilly, W J, *Cricket Conquest*, Werner Laurie, London, 1949

Page, Michael, *Bradman, The Illustrated Biography*, Sun Books/Macmillan, Melbourne, 1983

Peebles, Ian, *Straight from the Shoulder*, Hutchinson, London, 1968

Rosenwater, Irving, *Sir Donald Bradman*, Batsford, London, 1978

Tebbutt, Geoffrey, *With the 1930 Australians*, Hodder and Stoughton, London, 1930

Valentine, Barry, *Cricket's Dawn That Died*, Breedom Books, London, 1991

Wakley, B J, *Bradman The Great*, Nicholas Kaye, London, 1959

INDEX

A

a'Beckett, Ted
 (1928-29) 97, 98, 99,
  100, 101, 112,
  118, 123;
 (1930) 165, 184, 191,
  205-6, 207
Adelaide Tests
 (1928-29) 112-19;
 (1932-33 bodyline)
  287-95;
 (1936-37) 404-9;
 (1946-47) 488-91;
 v India (1947) 507-9;
 v West Indies (1930-31)
  230-1
Allen, G.O. 'Gubby' 170,
 171, 192;
 (1932-33) 300, 305;
 (1936-37) 374, 375,
  380, 384, 388,
  391, 399;
 and bodyline bowling
  264, 279, 288-9,
  374, 375
Allom, Maurice 144, 170,
 173
Allsop, Arthur 145, 154
Ames, Leslie 67, 264, 374,
 384
Andrews, Tommy 41, 92
Armstrong, Warwick 24,
 75, 116, 179, 516;
 on bodyline 95;
 on Bradman 98, 119-
  20, 306-7
Australia v England
 (1928-29) 83-90, 92-
  6, 98-108, 112-19,
  123-38;
 (1932-33 bodyline)
  271-3, 278-84,
  287-95, 297-300,
  301-6;
 (1936-37) 384-8, 388-

92, 395-402, 404-
 9, 410-14;
 (1946-47) 472-6, 478-
  83, 485-95
Australia v India 500-9,
 511-13
Australia v South Africa
 242-53
Australia v West Indies
 (1930-31) 229-36;
 (1960-61) 571-2

B

Badcock, Charlie 372,
 376, 384, 412, 416,
 419, 452
Bailey, Trevor 520
Bannerman, Charles 154
Bardsley, Warren 72, 92,
 375
Barnes, Sid 416, 472, 473,
 482, 507, 509, 523,
 533, 539, 560
Barnett, Ben 416
Barnett, C.J. 374, 384
Barrett, Fred 144
batting partnerships
 Jackson and Bradman
  114-15, 210;
 Kippax and Bradman
  8, 49-50, 52-3, 54,
  70, 76-7, 78, 250;
 Ponsford and Bradman
  156-7, 346-8
batting performances
 county matches (1930)
  164-82, 224-6;
 county matches (1934)
  322-8, 343-4, 358-
  9, 360-1;
 county matches (1938)
  418-19, 421-2,
  423-4, 425, 434,
  448;
 county matches (1948)

517-18, 519-21,
 536-7, 560;
ducks 28, 325, 390,
 555-6;
India Tests 496-504,
 505, 507-8, 511,
 513;
loss of form (1934)
 338, 343;
NSWCA country tour
 141-2, 143;
run rate 111, 499-50,
 414;
Shield 37-8, 48, 49-57,
 70, 71, 143-4, 231-
 2, 240-1, 249-50,
 313-14, 315-16,
 317-18, 380-1,
 456-8, 497, 566;
South Africa Tests
 243-5, 246-7, 248,
 250-1, 252;
Tests (1928-29) 82-90,
 91, 92, 94, 97-8,
 99-100, 102-6,
 114-15, 117-19,
 125-30, 130-2,
 136-9, 485-6;
Tests (1930) 3-12, 184-
 5, 187-90, 195-7,
 203-5, 208-9, 215-
 22, 226, 263;
Tests (1931-2) 280,
 281-4, 298, 299-
 300, 301-2;
Tests (1934) 329-30,
 331, 336, 337, 339,
 340-1, 345-50;
Tests (1936-37) 386,
 388, 391-2, 395-6,
 398, 405, 406-7,
 410-12;
Tests (1938) 428-9,
 430-2, 437, 439-
 40, 444-5, 446,
 452;